Wolfgang Faber · Martin Gebser ·
Yanhong Annie Liu
Editors

Logic Programming and Nonmonotonic Reasoning

18th International Conference, LPNMR 2026 Klagenfurt, Austria, September 7–11, 2026 Proceedings

Springer

Editors
Wolfgang Faber
University of Klagenfurt
Klagenfurt, Austria

Martin Gebser
University of Klagenfurt
Klagenfurt, Austria

Yanhong Annie Liu
Stony Brook University
Brooklyn, NY, USA

ISSN 0302-9743 ISSN 1611-3349 (electronic)
Lecture Notes in Artificial Intelligence
ISBN 978-3-032-38319-8 ISBN 978-3-032-38320-4 (eBook)
https://doi.org/10.1007/978-3-032-38320-4

LNCS Sublibrary: SL7 – Artificial Intelligence

This Springer imprint is published by the registered company Springer Nature Switzerland AG
The registered company address is: Gewerbestrasse 11, 6330 Cham, Switzerland

Preface

This volume contains the papers presented at the 18th International Conference on Logic Programming and Non-monotonic Reasoning (LPNMR 2026), held during September 7–11, 2026, in Klagenfurt, Austria. LPNMR is a forum for exchanging ideas on declarative logic programming, non-monotonic reasoning, and knowledge representation. The aim of the conference is to facilitate interactions between researchers and practitioners interested in the design and implementation of logic-based programming languages and database systems, and those working in knowledge representation and non-monotonic reasoning. LPNMR strives to encompass theoretical and experimental studies that have led or will lead to advances in declarative programming and knowledge representation, as well as their use in practical applications. The past editions of LPNMR were held in Washington, D.C., USA (1991), Lisbon, Portugal (1993), Lexington, Kentucky, USA (1995), Dagstuhl, Germany (1997), El Paso, Texas, USA (1999), Vienna, Austria (2001), Fort Lauderdale, Florida, USA (2004), Diamante, Italy (2005), Tempe, Arizona, USA (2007), Potsdam, Germany (2009), Vancouver, Canada (2011), Coruña, Spain (2013), Lexington, Kentucky, USA (2015), Espoo, Finland (2017), Philadelphia, USA (2019), Genoa, Italy (2022), and Dallas, Texas, USA (2024).

LPNMR 2026 received 46 submissions. Every submission was single-blindly reviewed by three Program Committee members. In total, 28 papers were accepted as regular long papers, and 4 as short papers. Thus, 32 of the 46 papers were accepted. The scientific program also included a Recently Published Research (RPR) submission as well as three invited talks given by Chitta Baral, Arizona State University, USA, Elena Bellodi, University of Ferrara, Italy, and Thomas Eiter, Vienna University of Technology (TU Wien), Austria.

The 6th International Workshop on the Resurgence of Datalog in Academia and Industry (DATALOG 2.0) and the 5th International Workshop on HYbrid Models for Coupling Deductive and Inductive ReAsoning (HYDRA) were co-located with LPNMR 2026. A Doctoral Consortium (DC) was also part of the program. We would like to express our warmest thanks and acknowledgments to those who played an important role in the organization of LPNMR 2026: the Program Committee and additional reviewers for their fair and thorough evaluations of submitted papers, Joaquín Arias and Jorge Fandinno for coordinating the workshops, Giuseppe Mazzotta and Isabelle Kuhlmann for organizing the DC, Đorđe Marković and Antonio Ielo for advertising the conference and its workshops through a number of channels, and the local organization committee and other volunteer members for working hard towards the success of the event. Finally, we are also grateful to the University of Klagenfurt on whose campus the conference was organized. The following organizations within the university provided direct financial support: the University of Klagenfurt's Research Council and the Technical Sciences Promotion Association.

LPNMR 2026 received support from several organizations. We gratefully acknowledge the Artificial Intelligence Journal (AIJ), the Association for Logic Programming

(ALP), DLVSystem, the Journal of Artificial Intelligence Research (JAIR), Potassco Solutions, Springer Nature and the U.S. National Science Foundation (NSF). Finally, the conference was managed with the help of EasyChair.

July 2026

Wolfgang Faber
Martin Gebser
Yanhong Annie Liu

Lecture Notes in Computer Science

Lecture Notes in Artificial Intelligence 16952

Founding Editor

Jörg Siekmann

The series Lecture Notes in Computer Science (LNCS), including its subseries Lecture Notes in Artificial Intelligence (LNAI) and Lecture Notes in Bioinformatics (LNBI), has established itself as a medium for the publication of new developments in computer science and information technology research, teaching, and education.

LNCS enjoys close cooperation with the computer science R & D community, the series counts many renowned academics among its volume editors and paper authors, and collaborates with prestigious societies. Its mission is to serve this international community by providing an invaluable service, mainly focused on the publication of conference and workshop proceedings and postproceedings. LNCS commenced publication in 1973.

Organization

General Chair

Wolfgang Faber	University of Klagenfurt, Austria

Program Chairs

Martin Gebser	University of Klagenfurt, Austria
Yanhong Annie Liu	Stony Brook University, USA

Workshop Chairs

Joaquín Arias	Universidad Rey Juan Carlos, Spain
Jorge Fandinno	University of Nebraska at Omaha, USA

Doctoral Consortium Chairs

Giuseppe Mazzotta	University of Calabria, Italy
Isabelle Kuhlmann	FernUniversität in Hagen, Germany

Publicity Chairs

Đorđe Marković	University of Klagenfurt, Austria
Antonio Ielo	University of Calabria, Italy

Program Committee

Mario Alviano	University of Calabria, Italy
Joaquín Arias	Universidad Rey Juan Carlos, Spain
Mutsunori Banbara	Nagoya University, Japan
Chitta Baral	Arizona State University, USA
Bart Bogaerts	KU Leuven, Belgium
Pierangela Bruno	University of Calabria, Italy

Pedro Cabalar	University of Corunna, Spain
Francesco Calimeri	University of Calabria, Italy
Stefania Costantini	University of L'Aquila, Italy
Alessandro Dal Palù	University of Parma, Italy
Carmine Dodaro	University of Calabria, Italy
Esra Erdem	Sabanci University, Turkey
Jorge Fandinno	University of Nebraska at Omaha, USA
Johannes K. Fichte	Linköping University, Sweden
Andrea Formisano	University of Udine, Italy
Gerhard Friedrich	University of Klagenfurt, Austria
Marco Gavanelli	University of Ferrara, Italy
Gopal Gupta	University of Texas at Dallas, USA
Markus Hecher	CNRS, Artois University (CRIL), France
Jesse Heyninck	Open Universiteit, Netherlands
Antonio Ielo	University of Calabria, Italy
Daniela Inclezan	Miami University, USA
Tomi Janhunen	Tampere University, Finland
Matthias Knorr	NOVA University Lisbon, Portugal
Isabelle Kuhlmann	FernUniversität in Hagen, Germany
Joao Leite	NOVA University Lisbon, Portugal
Yuliya Lierler	University of Nebraska at Omaha, USA
Vladimir Lifschitz	University of Texas at Austin, USA
Marco Maratea	University of Calabria, Italy
Giuseppe Mazzotta	University of Calabria, Italy
Thomas Meyer	University of Cape Town, South Africa
Michael Morak	University of Klagenfurt, Austria
Enrico Pontelli	New Mexico State University, USA
Francesco Ricca	University of Calabria, Italy
Fabrizio Riguzzi	University of Ferrara, Italy
Patrick Rodler	University of Klagenfurt, Austria
Orkunt Sabuncu	Potassco Solutions, Turkey
Chiaki Sakama	Wakayama University, Japan
Zeynep G. Saribatur	TU Wien, Austria
Torsten Schaub	University of Potsdam, Germany
Guillermo R. Simari	Universidad Nacional del Sur, Argentina
Theresa Swift	Johns Hopkins Applied Physics Lab, USA
Alice Tarzariol	University of Klagenfurt, Austria
Daniele Theseider Dupre	University of Eastern Piedmont, Italy
Matthias Thimm	FernUniversität in Hagen, Germany
Hans Tompits	TU Wien, Austria
Van-Giang Trinh	Ho Chi Minh City University of Technology, Vietnam

Mirek Truszczynski	University of Kentucky, USA
Joost Vennekens	Vrije Universiteit Brussel, Belgium
Johannes P. Wallner	TU Graz, Austria
Kewen Wang	Griffith University, Australia
Stefan Woltran	TU Wien, Austria
Jia-Huai You	University of Alberta, Canada

Additional Reviewers

Arvid Becker
Alessandro Bertagnon
Andrea Cuteri
Sopam Dasgupta
Federica Di Stefano
Salvatore Fiorentino
Maximilian Moeller
Lucrezia Mosconi
Hidetomo Nabeshima
Abhiramon Rajasekharan
Luis Angel Rodriguez Reiners
Nicolas Rühling
Veronika Semmelrock
Takehide Soh
Dieter Vandesande

Abstracts of Invited Talks

LPNMR in the Age of LLMs: Verification, Policy, and Trustworthy Agency

Chitta Baral

School of Computing and AI, Arizona State University, USA
chitta@asu.edu
http://chitta.orissalinks.com/

Abstract. Large language models have dramatically expanded the apparent reach of AI systems, enabling fluent interaction, flexible task execution, and increasingly sophisticated agentic behavior. Yet their impressive performance also exposes a fundamental limitation: generated outputs are not, by themselves, justified conclusions. LLMs may hallucinate facts, overlook constraints, fail to respect preferences, or produce reasoning that is persuasive but invalid. This is especially problematic when LLM-based agents are used in settings where correctness, compliance, explainability, and safety matter. In this talk, I will argue that traditional research in logic programming, non-monotonic reasoning, and knowledge representation is not merely relevant to the current wave of AI systems; it is likely to be essential for building reliable ones. Logic programming provides declarative ways to specify rules, constraints, policies, defaults, exceptions, and goals. Non-monotonic reasoning provides principled mechanisms for reasoning with incomplete information, revising conclusions in light of new evidence, handling defaults and exceptions, and representing competing preferences. These are precisely the kinds of reasoning challenges that arise in LLM-based agents. I will discuss two complementary roles for logic programming and non-monotonic reasoning in future AI architectures. First, they can help train, evaluate, and structure models so that they acquire more disciplined forms of reasoning. Second, and perhaps more importantly for safety-critical applications, they can serve as external verification and control layers: checking LLM-generated plans, explanations, tool calls, policy decisions, and intermediate conclusions before these are shown to users or passed to subsequent stages of an agent pipeline. The talk will highlight scenarios in which such techniques are particularly valuable, including agents that must satisfy policy constraints, respect policy preferences, reason under incomplete information, justify their conclusions, and avoid unsafe or non-compliant actions. I will suggest that the future of high-quality AI agents is not a choice between neural and symbolic methods, but a careful integration of generative capabilities with declarative specifications, non-monotonic reasoning, and formal verification. For the logic programming and non-monotonic reasoning community, this moment presents both a challenge and an opportunity: to bring decades of work on formal reasoning into the design of trustworthy AI systems.

Probabilistic Logics for Declarative Process Mining

Elena Bellodi

University of Ferrara, Italy
elena.bellodi@unife.it
https://ai.unife.it/team/prof-elena-bellodi/

Abstract. Business processes underpin many real-world domains, from healthcare and manufacturing to e-commerce, by defining how activities are coordinated to achieve organizational goals. Process Mining (PM) aims at discovering, analyzing and monitoring business processes from event logs. While classical approaches assume complete observations in logs and deterministic process models, real-world applications are inherently affected by uncertainty. Event logs may contain missing or ambiguous events, while process models may need to distinguish between mandatory requirements and soft recommendations rather than strict Boolean constraints. This talk introduces the foundations of "Declarative" Process Mining based on the DECLARE language and reviews the current state of the art on uncertainty management in this field. It then shows how probabilistic logics, and in particular Probabilistic Logic Programming (PLP), provide a natural semantic framework for modeling uncertainty in both process models and log activities. By transferring the Distribution Semantics from PLP to Declarative PM, probabilities can be associated with process models' constraints and uncertain events, yielding a unified framework for the main tasks in PM: (probabilistic) conformance checking and (probabilistic) process discovery. Recent developments on efficient conformance checking algorithms and PLP-based discovery are also presented. The talk concludes by discussing current research directions, including scalable inference, causal process discovery, and richer forms of uncertainty over event data.

Answer Set Programming for Reinforcement Learning

Thomas Eiter

TU Wien, Austria
thomas.eiter@tuwien.ac.at
http://www.kr.tuwien.ac.at/staff/eiter

Abstract. Reinforcement Learning (RL) is a highly successful branch of machine learning for training an agent to maximize rewards in a given environment. RL comes in different incarnations and flavors, and is actively advanced. In the recent years, there has been increasing interest in using symbolic AI approaches, including Answer Set Programming (ASP), for improving the expected behaviour of RL-trained agents, especially with regard to trustworthiness and guarantees. In this talk, we review different usages of ASP for RL, where we put a focus on enforcing ethical behavior or norms based on deontic constraints that the agent should adhere to. Notably, such constraints can emerge after the training and require instant action, such as fixing the agent's policy for staying operational, and retraining the agent, possibly on the fly. Real-time requirements and large state spaces make this a challenging application domain for ASP, which needs to be addressed with further advancing ASP technology.

Contents

Regular Papers

Regular Papers

Emergency Planning for Norm Violations via ASP-Based Stream Reasoning

Sebastian Adam[1](✉), Francesco Calimeri[2,3], Thomas Eiter[1], Luca Laboccetta[2,3], Simona Perri[2], and Giorgio Terracina[2]

[1] Vienna University of Technology, Favoritenstraße 9-11, 1040 Vienna, Austria
{sebastian.adam,thomas.eiter}@tuwien.ac.at

[2] AI Lab DeMaCS, University of Calabria, Via P. Bucci, 87036 Rende, CS, Italy
{francesco.calimeri,luca.laboccetta,simona.perri, giorgio.terracina}@unical.it

[3] DLVSystem Srl, Viale della Resistenza 19/C, 87036 Rende, Italy

Abstract. Reinforcement learning (RL) is widely used to train decision-making agents in domains such as autonomous driving, healthcare, and game playing. However, RL agents typically optimize numerical rewards without explicitly accounting for ethical, social, or legal norms, which is problematic in safety-critical and dynamic settings. Policy fixing addresses this issue by augmenting RL agents with symbolic reasoning for detecting or anticipating norm violations and applying emergency plans minimally altering the learned policy. Answer Set Programming (ASP) enables fixes that balance reward optimization with norm satisfaction. Existing approaches, however, rely on batch reasoning, solving each step from scratch and struggling with temporal norms requiring information over time. In this paper, we propose an ASP-based Stream Reasoning extension supporting incremental, stateful processing of observations. The approach improves efficiency and naturally supports dynamic, time-bound normative obligations. Experimental results show improved scalability in demanding scenarios and effective temporal norm management.

1 Introduction

Reinforcement learning (RL) and other machine learning approaches play a central role in modern artificial intelligence (AI), with applications ranging from healthcare [26] to autonomous driving [13] and to game playing [22], to mention a few; notably, RL has recently been fruitfully employed in the training process of large language models [11]. These applications are enabled, or at least strongly supported, by the performance and scalability of RL methods. At the same time, the black-box, data-driven nature of RL and related machine learning approaches raises well-known challenges, especially when agents are expected to comply with ethical, social, or legal norms that are not naturally captured by a numerical reward function. A standard RL agent is trained to optimize a reward signal, not to reason explicitly about norm compliance. In safety-critical

W. Faber et al. (Eds.): LPNMR 2026, LNAI 16952, pp. 3–18, 2027.
https://doi.org/10.1007/978-3-032-38320-4_1

settings, requirements are often represented as hard constraints, and techniques such as shielding [14] can prevent an agent from executing unsafe actions.

However, ethical and social norms are not always well represented as hard constraints. They may admit exceptions, interact with other norms, or specify what should be done after a violation. For this reason, integrating normative reasoning into RL remains a challenge, attracting attention in multi-objective RL [16,19] and in approaches combining RL with Deontic Logic (DL) [15,21].

A major issue arises when a trained policy violates norms that were unforeseen or underspecified during training. For instance, an autonomous vehicle might strictly follow traffic laws but repeatedly overtake cyclists at the minimum legal distance—a behavior that is legally admissible yet socially undesirable. Retraining the policy to fix this is often costly and time-consuming, particularly for computationally expensive models.

Policy fixing [1] addresses this issue by avoiding immediate retraining. Instead, an additional logic-based component, encoded in Answer Set Programming (ASP), monitors the behavior of the agent and repairs norm violations by generating emergency plans. This allows the original RL policy to remain in use while a symbolic layer intervenes when norm compliance is at risk. The approach is also attractive from the perspective of transparency, since the reasons for an intervention can be traced through the logic program. This is in line with a broader body of work that couples sub-symbolic learning with sound logic-based reasoning, invoked when the learned component is uncertain or potentially unsafe; for instance, automated commonsense reasoning has been used to correct low-confidence object-detection misclassifications in autonomous driving [12].

Limitations. However, the policy-fixing framework of [1] exhibits important limitations. It depends on an external procedural engine (e.g., Python) to orchestrate sequential ASP calls and maintain temporal continuity by carrying time-based information across successive executions. Moreover, whenever the emergency-planning component is activated, evaluating the ASP program is treated as a fresh problem. In particular, each observation may lead to re-grounding and solving from scratch, increasing the computational overhead of the agent. This stateless interaction with ASP is especially problematic when norms have an explicit temporal nature, since temporal compliance requires maintaining and updating information across time.

Contributions. We revisit the policy-fixing setting of [1] and propose an alternative formulation based on ASP-based Stream Reasoning (SR). The key idea is to move from a purely batch-oriented paradigm to a stateful, incremental reasoning process that continuously incorporates new observations. SR looks like a natural candidate, as it supports evolving observations and maintains knowledge over time; however, it is worth noting that applying SR to policy fixing is far from immediate: while SR naturally supports reasoning over past and current observations, emergency planning also requires reasoning about possible future actions and states. Thus, integrating SR into policy fixing requires a specific modelling strategy, rather than a direct replacement of a batch ASP solver. We provide an SR-based formulation in which the repeated external orchestration of fresh ASP instances is avoided. We introduce a hybrid implicit/explicit time-management strategy: past and current information are handled through the stream, while future planning steps are explicitly represented with respect to the current time point. We also show how this formulation supports dynamic policy switching during emergency planning. To illustrate the benefits of our approach, we consider the Gardener domain of [1] (Fig. 1) and extend it with temporal norms, showing that the proposed approach can handle normative scenarios involving exceptional conditions and multi-objective trade-offs. Experimental results show that the incremental nature of the proposed solution not only improves computational performance and scalability, but also enhances the quality of norm compliance, particularly in demanding settings where traditional batch-oriented approaches struggle.

Organization. The rest of this paper is organized as follows. Section 2 introduces preliminaries, while Sect. 3 outlines the reference policy-fixing framework and the Gardener problem. Section 4 describes our SR-based solution and extensions. Section 5 reports experimental results. Finally, Sect. 6 concludes and outlines future work.

2 Preliminaries

Reinforcement learning (RL) [24] is a machine learning paradigm in which agents learn to act in an interactive environment while optimizing decisions based on rewards. At each step, the agent observes the current state, selects and executes an action, and receives feedback. Over time, it learns a policy that maps states or observations to actions that maximize expected reward. While this optimization-based approach is effective in domains where behavior can be evaluated numerically, requirements not captured by the reward function may be ignored. In particular, standard RL agents do not explicitly reason about logical constraints, obligations, permissions, or prohibitions. When safety constraints must be enforced, shielding techniques [14] can be used to prevent unsafe actions.

However, ethical or social norms are rarely represented as strict hard constraints, requiring more advanced approaches such as Deontic Logic (DL) [8] or multi-objective decision-making techniques [20]. Integrating normative behavior into RL policies therefore remains a complex challenge and has attracted significant attention in multi-objective RL [16,19] and RL-DL integration [15,21].

Norms are ethical, social, or legal rules that agents must follow. Unlike hard constraints, norms generally allow some form of violation, either explicitly through exceptions or implicitly, since violating a norm does not usually make the system infeasible. To formally capture this defeasibility and reason about normative systems (i.e., sets of norms), we use DL. Typically, a DL extends classical logic with the deontic operators for obligation $\mathbf{O}(p)$, permission $\mathbf{P}(p)$ and prohibition $\mathbf{F}(p)$, which can intuitively be read as: p is obligatory, p is permitted and p is forbidden, respectively. In many DLs, like the standard deontic logic *KD* [25], $\mathbf{O}$ is taken as the primitive operator that defines the others through negation. Specifically, permission is defined as $\mathbf{P}(p) := \neg\mathbf{O}(\neg p)$ and prohibition as $\mathbf{F}(p) := \mathbf{O}(\neg p)$.

To address different expressiveness needs, several DLs have been developed. For example, while KD cannot handle *contrary-to-duty* (CTD) norms, which specify obligations after primary violations, Defeasible Deontic Logic (DDL) [17] handles CTDs via prioritized defeasible rules. In temporal domains, deontic modalities can be combined with temporal logics, e.g., Linear Temporal Logic (LTL) [18], enabling temporal norms expressing time-dependent obligations. The simplest temporal norms are *maintenance norms*, fulfilled by compliance at every step [10]. More complex forms include *deadline norms*, requiring compliance before a specific time, and *achievement norms*, requiring eventual achievement of a desired state.

Reasoning about compliance in temporal normative systems requires handling both defeasibility and time. ASP is well-suited for this because its non-monotonic nature naturally captures defeasible norms. Several ASP-based approaches encode normative systems, including *DELX* (Deontic Equilibrium Logic with eXplicit Negation) [5], which provides a direct reduction from normative systems to ASP. Its temporal extension, DeoTel [23], preserves this reducibility. Additionally, other frameworks combine temporal deontic logic with ASP to verify norm compliance via bounded model checking [9]. For smaller normative systems, direct manual ASP encodings may also suffice [1].
Stream reasoning (SR) concerns reasoning over continuously evolving data streams. A stream can be viewed as a sequence of time-indexed event sets, where each time point contains the information observed at that moment. Unlike one-shot reasoning, where all facts are available at once, SR systems continuously update conclusions as new observations arrive, possibly considering recent or past events. This makes SR well-suited for dynamic domains where decisions depend on temporal evolution, such as monitoring, IoT, healthcare, and other real-time environments. Crucially, SR in our setting is inherently *non-monotonic*: as new events arrive, previously derived conclusions may have to be retracted. A plan deemed safe at one time point can become unsafe once a frog enters the perception window; an active obligation must be withdrawn as soon as it is discharged; and an obstacle (e.g., a killed plant) ceases to constrain future moves. Such defeasible, observation-dependent revision of conclusions, together with the defeasible nature of norms (which admit exceptions), is exactly what non-monotonic formalisms like ASP capture naturally, whereas a purely monotonic stream-query language would not. A prominent logic-based SR formalism is LARS (Logic for Analytic Reasoning over Streams) [3], which extends ASP-style reasoning with temporal modalities and window operators. The full LARS language is very expressive, but intractable in the general case. Systems such as Laser [2], Ticker [4], and Distributed-SR [7] support key fragments of the LARS language.

***DP*-sr**. In this work, we build on *DP*-sr [6], a declarative ASP-based framework for stream reasoning. *DP*-sr represents observations as time-associated events and supports reasoning through SR-oriented constructs, which we briefly summarize here, as the framework is not yet widely known. A *DP*-sr program is a set of ASP rules evaluated incrementally at each incoming time point. Every atom carries an (often implicit) temporal markup recording the time points at which it holds, and the special term **@now** denotes the current time point. The key SR-specific constructs are: *(i) streaming literals with window operators*, written `L in [w]` and `L in {w}`, which restrict the evaluation of literal `L` over the stream relative to the current time point. The two differ in the set of time points they consider: `[w]` denotes the *whole window* of the `w` most recent time points, i.e., all offsets $\{0, 1, \ldots, \mathtt{w}\}$ (e.g., `[3]` covers $\{0, 1, 2, 3\}$), whereas `{w}` denotes the *single* time point at offset `w` only. Hence `L in [1]` holds if `L` holds at the current point or one step away, while `L in {1}` holds only if `L` holds exactly at the time point one step away; *(ii) temporary rules*, deriving auxiliary information needed only at the current step without permanently adding it to the stream; *(iii) inertial event generators* (`#generate`), producing events that persist over future time points until an expiration or a deactivation event; and *(iv) external atoms* (`&...`), interfacing the reasoner with external procedures (e.g., an RL policy). These constructs let ASP encodings naturally reference current, past, and transient information. A key feature of *DP*-sr is its support for modelling event patterns and temporal consequences while maintaining declarative reasoning. Its architecture separates the stream-oriented language layer from the ASP back-end, enabling different ASP solvers to be used depending on the application. This makes *DP*-sr well suited for policy fixing, which can then be formulated as an evolving reasoning process over observations and time-dependent conditions rather than as independent batch ASP calls. We rely on an ASP-based SR formalism (rather than, e.g., Prolog or s(CASP), where streams could be handled as lists) because policy fixing is naturally cast as an *optimization* problem: weak constraints let us declaratively balance RL action preferences against norm-violation penalties, and the existing Baseline [1] is itself ASP-based, enabling a fair comparison.

3 Policy Fixing and the Gardener Problem

The policy-fixing framework introduced in [1] (the *Baseline* from now on), considers an RL agent that is already trained and operational, but whose learned policy is later found to violate some norm. The RL component provides the agent's standard behavior: given the current state or observation, the learned policy selects the action expected to maximize the original reward objective. Norm compliance, however, introduces additional ethical, social, or legal requirements. A violation occurs when the agent reaches a forbidden state, performs a prohibited action, or causes an undesirable effect. The problem is therefore not that the policy fails at reward optimization, but that it may not satisfy requirements that emerge only after training and were not encoded in the reward function. Since retraining can be expensive and time-consuming, policy fixing provides an intermediate repair mechanism.

Emergency Plans. The core idea is to augment the RL agent with a symbolic reasoning component that monitors behavior and intervenes when norm compliance is at risk. Rather than replacing the learned policy, the framework computes alternative action sequences, called *emergency plans*, that prevent or reduce future violations over a bounded horizon while remaining as close as possible to the original policy. Policy fixing therefore enables the agent to remain operational and norm-aware while a fully compliant policy is trained.

ASP Planning. In [1], policy fixing is encoded as an ASP planning problem. The ASP component receives the current environment state, a domain model, the relevant norms, and information about the preferred behavior of the learned policy, then computes an emergency plan over a finite horizon H. The bounded horizon is important: longer horizons improve anticipation of future violations but increase reasoning cost. Repairs can also be recomputed during execution as new observations arrive. Norm compliance may be enforced strictly or in a utility-based way. In the strict setting, plans leading to violations are excluded. In the utility-based setting, violations receive penalties, allowing optimization of the trade-off between following the learned policy and minimizing normative cost. This is useful when full compliance is impossible within the selected horizon or would require excessive deviation from the original policy.

Environment Types. A further feature of the approach [1] is its applicability to both deterministic and nondeterministic environments. In deterministic settings, actions lead to a unique follow-up state. In nondeterministic settings, the environment may evolve independently of the agent, and the same action may result in different future states. Policy fixing must therefore reason about both the agent's planned actions and possible environment evolutions.

3.1 The Gardener Problem

The running example in [1] is the two-dimensional board game *Gardener*. This is simple enough to inspect agent and reasoning behavior, yet expressive enough to highlight the tension between reward-oriented and norm-aware actions.

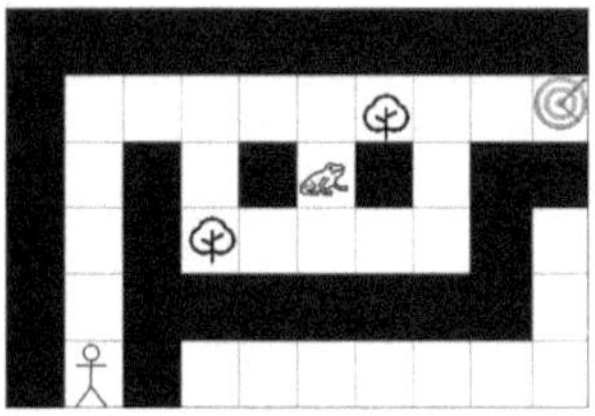

Fig. 1. A Gardener instance

Instances. Each instance consists of a grid containing an agent, a target cell, walls and further plants and frogs. The agent's goal is to reach the target as quickly as possible using actions $\mathcal{A}$ = {north, east, south, west}; naturally, walls are not traversable. Plants remain static while frogs move randomly at each step using the same action set as the agent. Thus Gardener features both deterministic instance (no frogs) and nondeterministic instances (some frogs), as frog movements create multiple possible future states.

Maintenance Norm. The domain includes a maintenance norm in form of the *prohibition* **F**(*kill*), obliging the agent at every step to not kill living beings. Moving onto a cell occupied by a plant or frog kills it and constitutes a norm violation. The agent must therefore balance efficient navigation with avoiding harmful paths. In nondeterministic instances, a path that is safe in one evolution may become unsafe in another, illustrating the need for policy fixing to anticipate future violations.

RL-Baseline. In the baseline setting [1], the RL policy is trained only to reach the target quickly. If the norm is introduced after training, the policy may still choose paths that kill plants or ignore possible frog movements. Policy fixing repairs this by computing emergency plans that deviate from the preferred policy when necessary, for example by selecting longer but safer routes.

ASP Solving. The repair mechanism in [1] repeatedly invokes a batch-oriented ASP solver. At each step, the current observation is encoded into a new ASP problem, an emergency plan is computed, and the selected action is executed. While effective, this makes every reasoning step a fresh computation. Moreover, reasoning over the entire board becomes infeasible even for medium-sized instances. The proposed solution uses a moving window of radius `R` centered on the agent, but requires recomputing relative positions of plants, frogs, and walls at every step, which is computationally expensive.

The present work starts from the same policy-fixing setting and Gardener domain, but investigates an ASP-based SR formulation in which observations and temporal information are managed as part of an evolving reasoning process.

4 ASP-Based Stream Reasoning for Emergency Planning

In this section, we present our *DP*-sr [6] based approach for handling emergency planning for norm violations. We first consider the Gardener problem definition as presented in [1]. Next we extend the problem with temporal (deadline and achievement) norms, to show the flexibility and potentialities of our solution. Following the Baseline [1], we encode these norms *directly* as ASP rules and weak constraints rather than through a deontic front-end. This is a deliberate modelling choice and not a limitation of the architecture.

Streaming Grid State. In the baseline formulation, the environment was simulated through repeated calls to a batch-oriented ASP solver. In our approach, the grid state is continuously received from the stream, where frog positions and environmental properties are incrementally updated. *DP*-sr processes agent positions through a continuous reasoning loop, enabling true temporal awareness and allowing the agent to react to dynamic obstacles and obligations. The approach also avoids recomputing relative positions of plants, frogs, and walls, while maintaining a perception window of radius R centered on the agent, restricting reasoning to a small portion of the grid.

Incremental Stream Reasoning. Furthermore, in the baseline approach, planning is repeatedly invoked from the current environment state with a finite planning horizon; this entails repeatedly rebuilding and solving new ASP instances. Our approach instead exploits incremental stream reasoning to continuously monitor the grid and to trigger re-planning only when relevant environmental changes occur. In the following, we present our solution with code excerpts.[1]

4.1 Tackling the Gardener Problem via ASP-Based SR

In *DP*-sr, time is implicitly managed by the chronological order of stream events. While this naturally enables reasoning about the past, projecting future events, such as during planning tasks, requires explicit timestamp handling. To bridge this gap, we adopt a hybrid approach. Specifically, we introduce a dynamic temporal model that reasons about past events using the native *DP*-sr framework, while handling future events as explicit time points determined around the *DP*-sr `@now` operator.

Assume now that the position of the agent in the grid is handled by the predicate `p(R,C)`. We can easily reconstruct the agent's past movements by simply looking at past time points ("native" stream reasoning features). To plan a new agent position `p(R1,C1)` in a future time point `T1>@now`, instead, we must explicitly associate `p(R1,C1)` to `T1` as `p(R1,C1,T1)`. Now, at each time point, the current position of the agent is `p(R,C,T)` with `T=@now`.

[1] The interested reader can find the complete code on https://github.com/lucalabo/emergency_planning_stream.

Agent Parameters. The solution to the problem is based on two parameters: a **perception radius** (`R`) and a **planning horizon** (`H`). The radius `R` defines the agent's sensing range for danger; the horizon `H` represents the number of future time steps considered by the reasoning engine when generating an emergency plan. They define the depth of the "moving window" used to evaluate future possibilities relative to the current time point, represented by the `@now` operator. Together, these parameters balance the trade-off between computational efficiency and the agent's ability to proactively avoid norm violations.

Specifically, at each time step two options are available: (i) plan new moves of the agent up to the current time horizon, (ii) propagate previously planned moves. Option (i) is activated when either no more moves are available in the plan or a dangerous situation is detected requiring to re-plan; otherwise option (ii) is activated. In this setting, the agent only engages in complex ASP reasoning when it detects a potential conflict or a mobile danger (e.g., a frog) in its immediate vicinity. In stable states, the agent remains reactive, minimizing computational overhead.

We outline the main portions of the corresponding code in the sequel.

1) Reasoning Scheme. The following reasoning scheme is evaluated at each time step in the stream:

```
    % Planning Activation logic
r1: has_future_moves  :- p(_,_,T) in {1}, T > @now.
r2: activate_planning :- not has_future_moves.
r3: activate_planning :- active_frog(_).

    % One move per step when planning
r4: n(T) | s(T) | e(T) | w(T) :- plan_step(T), activate_planning, not reached.

    % Apply moves: move at time T produces position at time T+1
r5: p(R-1,C,T+1) :- p(R,C,T), n(T), activate_planning.
    ...similar rules for s(T), e(T), w(T)

    % Inertial propagation of planned movements
r6: p(R,C,T) :- p(R,C,T) in [1], T > @now, not activate_planning.

    % --- Map Constraints ---
r7: :- p(_,C,_), C < 0.
r8: :- p(_,C,_), C > S, size(S).
    ...
r9: :- p(R,C,_), wall(C,R).
```

Rules r_1 and r_2 check whether future moves are available from a previous plan. Rule r_3 detects a potential danger in the planned path; in particular, `active_frog` detects the frogs that step into the window of perception (details are omitted to keep code presentation short). Planning (r_4) is actually computed only if `activate_planning` is true. Subsequently, r_5 projects choices over the next time points. The number of future time points is handled by the parametric horizon `H`, and addressed by `plan_step` in r_4 which identifies the time points within the current horizon; again, related details are not shown for simplicity. In time steps when re-planning is not necessary, rule r_5 propagates positions that were planned at some previous time step onto the stream. Constraints expressed by rules r_7–r_9 ensure that planned movements are valid.

2) Planning Step. For each planning step, the action moving the agent is chosen with the support of the currently active policy. *DP*-sr allows to easily link an external evaluation of movement preference based on RL with external atoms;

```
r10: action(A,S,COL,ROW) :- p(R,C,@now), action_radius(Rad),
                  &generate_nearby_actions(C,R,Rad;A,S,COL,ROW), activate_planning.
```

Here, if planning is active, all possible moves from the current agent position are scored according to the current policy preferences. The score is encoded by `S`, returned by `&generate_nearby_actions` for each available `action` from `ROW,COL`; `S` $\in \{0..3\}$; higher scores denote preferred actions.

As clarified below, this strategy enables dynamic switching among policies based on the agent's state.

3) Move Choice. The actual choice of the best move is handled with the support of weak constraints similarly as in [1]. The following code portion considers action scores and temporal distance. In fact, penalties potentially occurring in the near future are more probable and predictable than penalties that may occur closer to the temporal horizon; hence the former are weighed more than the latter.

```
r11: action_taken(0, T, C, R) :- p(R,C,T), p(R+1,C,T+1).
     ...
r12: penalty_action(S1, T) :-  action_taken(A,T,C,R), action(A,B,C,R), my_horizon(H),
               RankDiff = (3 - B), T1 = T - @now, S = (H - T1), S1 = S * RankDiff.
r13: :~ penalty_action(S,T). [S@1,T]
```

4) Penalisation. Penalties associated with the risk of stepping onto a frog or onto a plant are handled similarly. An example for plants is given next:

```
r14:  on_plant(C,R):- plant(C,R), p(R,C,@now).
r15:  #generate(plantKilled(C,R);on_plant(C,R)).
r16:  bad_plant(T, C, R) :- p(R,C,T), plant(C,R), not plantKilled(C,R) in {1}.
r17:  penalty_plant(W,T,C,R) :- bad_plant(T, C, R), my_horizon(H), T1 = T-@now,
              W = (H-T1)*10.
r18:  :~ penalty_plant(W,T,C,R). [W@1,T,C,R]
```

Penalties relative to frogs are handled similarly, taking into account that frog positions are nondeterministic. Here, rule r_{14} detects whether the agent steps onto a plant. If this happens, the plant is killed and must not be considered in future steps; this is managed by the inertial event generator `#generate` in rule r_{15}. In *DP*-sr, an inertial event is a complex event with stream-controlled lifespan; it remains true for all future time points until an expiration time is reached or a deactivation event is detected. In our context, once a plant is killed it remains killed for all future time points. Thus, a plant is "bad", i.e., it introduces a penalty, if it has not been already killed and the agent steps on it at a certain time point `T` (rule r_{16}). Penalty computation is handled by rule r_{17}.

Observe that weak constraints in r_{13} and in r_{18} allow the system to "select" the plan (i.e., the best answer set) that combines moves preferred by the learner with those that reduce the risk of violating some norms.

Time-Quality Tradeoff. We stress the relevance of the time horizon parameter. A short horizon reduces reasoning time, as the number of steps to plan is low. However, moves are then chosen almost in a greedy manner and, consequently, the risk of violating norms can increase. Conversely, a long temporal horizon allows to explore more alternatives and to provide a better plan, at least in principle. However, the nondeterministic nature of frog moves can easily make risk prediction of stepping onto a frog unreliable.

Thus finding a value of `H` that provides a good tradeoff between time and quality is crucial.

4.2 Extending Gardener with Temporal Norms

Key strengths of the proposed stream reasoning framework are (1) its flexibility in integrating multi-objective agent behavior and (2) its ability to track the temporal validity of exceptional conditions.

Dynamic Policy Switch. We previously exploited the **`activate_planning`** predicate to switch between two different behaviors (propagate or re-plan moves). The same strategy can be applied also to switch between different policies responding to a dynamically changing environment. A clear example of dynamic policy adaptation is provided by temporal norms: dynamic obligations or constraints that are activated and deactivated in real-time based on the agent's actions and interactions with the context. Unlike static environment rules, these norms have a finite temporal window and often mandate a specific corrective action. We have considered two main examples of temporal norms in our reference Gardener problem: the *Mud-Water* norm and the *Oil-Fire* norm.

The Mud-Water Washing Norm. The *Mud-Water* norm introduces a temporal obligation triggered by environmental contamination. When the agent steps onto a cell containing mud, it enters a **`dirty`** state. In this state an obligation is active, requiring the agent to reach a water cell in order to "wash" within a given deadline of `K` steps. Hence, the *Mud-Water* norm $dirty \rightarrow \mathbf{O}_{\leq K}(reach\_water)$ acts as a *deadline/achievement* norm. The logic program tracks the persistence of the **`dirty`** state using the stream's temporal operators:

```
     % Activation: stepping on mud
r19: dirty(T) :- T=@now, p(R,C,T), mud(C,R).
r20: activate_planning :- T=@now, p(R,C,T), mud(C,R).
     % Persistence: stays dirty for K steps unless water is reached
r21: dirty(T) :- dirty(T) in {1}, T1=@now, steps_mud(K), T1-T <= K, not on_water(T1).
r22: is_dirty :- dirty(_).
     % Policy Switching: use water-seeking policy when dirty
r23: action(A,S,COL,ROW) :- p(R,C,@now), action_radius(Rad),
                 &generate_water_actions(C,R,Rad;A,S,COL,ROW), is_dirty.

r24: mud_violation(T) :- dirty(T) in {1}, T1=@now, steps_mud(K), T1-T = K,
                 not on_water(T1).
r25: :~ mud_violation(T). [10@1, T]
```

When the **`is_dirty`** atom is true, the system dynamically switches from the standard navigation policy to a specialized Water Policy which prefers moves getting the agent to the nearest water pots. If the agent fails to reach a water cell within the `K`-step limit, a high-priority penalty is triggered that incentivizes compliant behavior in real-time.

It is worth noting that the change is localized to the policy-computation part of the program. The same **`action`** predicate is still used to represent candidate moves, so the rest of the encoding, including action generation and action selection through weak constraints, remains unchanged. The only required modification is to prevent the standard policy from being activated when the agent enters in the **`dirty`** state (**`not is_dirty`** must be added to rule r_{10})

The Oil-Fire Norm. The *Oil-Fire* norm imposes a temporal safety constraint. By stepping onto an oil cell the agent enters an `inflammable` state, representing temporary flammability that lasts for `K` steps. During this period, entering a cell containing fire is treated as a severe norm violation and is penalized accordingly. If the agent violates this constraint while in the inflammable state, the system activates a severe penalty. In terms of DL, the *Oil-Fire* norm *inflammable* $\rightarrow$ $\mathbf{F}(enter\_fire)$ is a conditional, time-bounded *prohibition.*

```
     % Activation: stepping on oil lasts for k steps
r26: inflammable(T) :- T=@now, p(R,C,T), oil(C,R).
r27: inflammable(T) :- inflammable(T) in {1}, T1=@now,steps_inflammable(K), T1-T <= K.
r28: activate_planning :- T=@now, p(R,C,T), oil(C,R).

     % Safety Constraint: avoid fire while inflammable
r29: penalty_fire(T) :- inflammable(T), p(R,C,T), fire(C,R).
r30: :~penalty_fire(T). [10@1,T]
```

Again, this mechanism highlights the ability to swap policies or enforce temporary safety rules without rebuilding the core logic. In this case, the norm affects only penalties to potential moves; as a consequence, there is no need to change the agent objective and policy. This makes the proposed architecture highly adaptable to evolving emergency planning scenarios.

5 Experiments

The setting for our experiments has been designed in order to properly assess both performance and adaptability of the proposed framework in varying environmental conditions. The experiments fall into two main categories:
Baseline Comparison: Performance comparison against the baseline Gardener problem configuration. We want to evaluate the efficiency of the SR approach in terms of navigation quality and computation time against the batch-oriented solution in [1] as the baseline.
Normative Adaptation: Evaluation of the agent's behavior within the extension to the Gardener problem featuring temporal norms. We want to assess the agent's ability to dynamically switch between navigation policies and satisfy mandatory obligations.
In order to get a clear picture, we considered several metrics: *(i) Norm Compliance*: the number of norms violated during execution. *(ii) Mission Efficiency*: the total number of steps required to reach the target destination. *(iii) System Performance*: average time per step, to verify real-time responsiveness. Note that we did not consider total running time because this metric would not allow comparing the batch-oriented approach with the SR one. Moreover, measuring both the number of steps and the average time per step allows us to keep the focus on both real-time responsiveness and time-to-target effectiveness.
Reproducibility. All tests were conducted on a Lenovo ThinkPad T460s workstation equipped with an Intel(R) Core(TM) i5-6300U CPU running at 2.40 GHz (with a maximum frequency of 3.0 GHz), 8 GB of system memory, and a 64-bit architecture. All data and material for reproducing experiments can be downloaded at https://github.com/lucalabo/emergency_planning_stream.

5.1 Comparing the SR Solution Against the Baseline

Instances. To ensure a fair and comprehensive assessment, experiments have been conducted using four different configurations for the grid: 50×50, 100×100, 150×150, and 200×200 cells, all featuring walls, plants, and frogs. Walls account for approximately 10% of grid cells; as for plants and frogs, frequency varies. In smaller grids (i.e., 50×50 and 100×100), they account for 2.5% of the cells, each: 62 plants + 63 frogs in the 50×50 grids, 250 plants + 250 frogs in the 100×100 grids. In larger scenarios (i.e., 150×150 and 200×200), the density of plants and frogs is increased to 5%, in order to test the systems in a "crowded" scenario; this results in 1,125 plants and 1,125 frogs in the 150×150 grid, and 2,000 frogs and 2,000 plants in the 200×200 grid.
Agent Parameters. As previously pointed out, two primary parameters govern the agent's behavior: the perception radius (`R`) and the planning horizon (`H`) (see Sect. 4.1). We considered several combinations of `R` and `H`; due to space constraints, we present here only some of the relevant combinations, with `R` in the interval {3,5} and `H` in the interval {4,8}.
Results. Table 1 summarizes the experimental results, which we discuss along the three metrics introduced above. As for *Norm Compliance*, the two approaches are almost equivalent, with some improvement of *DP*-sr for the most complex configurations. *Mission Efficiency* is also comparable between the two solutions; no clear winner emerges across configurations. This is likely due to the nondeterministic nature of frog moves and random positioning of plants. These two results provide evidence of the effectiveness of the proposed solution on the quality side. The real shift comes with *System Performance*: while the Baseline is competitive, even better, than *DP*-sr for small-sized problems, as soon as the size and complexity of the problem increases on each of the three parameters (size, radius, and horizon) *DP*-sr significantly outperforms the Baseline on average time per step. As an example, in the `150x150, R=5, H=8` configuration, *DP*-sr reduces the average time per step by about 96% (from 49.3 s for the Baseline down to 2.2 s). Similarly, in the `200x200, R=5, H=8` configuration, *DP*-sr reduces the average time per step by about 92% (from 56.3 s down to 4.3 s). Furthermore, it is important to point out that increasing `R` and `H` in *DP*-sr corresponds to a reduction in plants/frogs killed on all the grids, with only a marginal increase of the time per step.
Summary. The results clearly show that, while the Baseline remains competitive in simpler configurations, *DP*-sr scales significantly better on large grids and supports larger values of both `R` and `H`, making it possible to explore better trade-offs while keeping response times acceptable.

5.2 Analysis of Temporal Norms Management

We next analyze the agent's behavior under the influence of the temporal norms introduced in Sect. 4.2. The experimental environment was configured with interacting elements distributed as follows: 10% water, 5% mud, 5% oil, and 5% fire. These are additional to walls, plants and frogs of the corresponding configurations introduced above. This setting ensures a regular presence of norm triggers, forcing the agent to frequently deviate from the path initially preferred by the RL policy. Table 2 summarizes the results, including the penalties associated with norm violations: *fire_penalties*, measuring contacts with fire while the agent is in a flammable state, and *mud_penalties*, measuring failures to reach water within the deadline after contact with mud.

The *Mud-Water* norm requires the agent to reach a water cell within 10 steps after becoming "dirty". The data show that, in larger map sizes (100×100 and 150×150), the

Table 1. Comparison between the **Baseline** and ***DP*-sr** (averages over 10 runs).

Grid Size	Config.	System	Steps	Time/Step (ms)	Plants Killed	Frogs Killed
50 × 50	R = 3, H = 4	Baseline	81.6	216.7	0.3	0.4
		DP-sr	66.8	742.9	0.1	0.1
	R = 5, H = 4	Baseline	84.0	505.7	0.2	0.9
		DP-sr	58.0	750.5	0.0	0.2
	R = 5, H = 6	Baseline	98.2	2649.0	0.4	0.7
		DP-sr	66.0	771.0	0.0	0.1
100 × 100	R = 3, H = 4	Baseline	111.8	447.9	1.9	1.4
		DP-sr	115.0	1069.9	1.5	1.6
	R = 5, H = 4	Baseline	112.8	1319.5	1.5	1.6
		DP-sr	120.0	1155.0	1.6	1.0
	R = 5, H = 6	Baseline	142.8	8554.5	2.4	2.4
		DP-sr	175.0	1176.3	1.7	0.9
150 × 150	R = 3, H = 4	Baseline	141.8	1113.6	1.7	0.9
		DP-sr	162.8	2013.8	1.7	1.6
	R = 5, H = 4	Baseline	148.0	2342.3	1.3	1.0
		DP-sr	178.0	2100.9	1.9	1.9
	R = 5, H = 6	Baseline	168.2	10663.3	2.3	2.0
		DP-sr	191.2	2151.3	1.9	1.9
	R = 5, H = 8	Baseline	200.6	49299.6	2.9	1.5
		DP-sr	186.8	2211.3	1.6	1.6
200 × 200	R = 3, H = 4	Baseline	224.2	2424.1	2.3	3.2
		DP-sr	206.6	4014.1	1.8	3.7
	R = 5, H = 6	Baseline	270.4	12735.8	2.9	5.1
		DP-sr	284.6	4291.0	2.4	3.0
	R = 5, H = 8	Baseline	312.4	56318.1	2.6	4.7
		DP-sr	262.0	4298.4	2.0	2.3

Table 2. Experimental results with temporal norms activated (averages over 10 runs).

Grid Size	Config.	Steps	Time/Step (ms)	Mud Pen.	Fire Pen.	Plants/Frogs Killed
50 × 50	R = 3, H = 4	113.4	814.5	0.8	0.2	0.2/0.6
	R = 5, H = 4	111.0	829.6	1.1	0.0	0.2/0.3
	R = 5, H = 6	103.6	875.4	1.3	0.0	0.1/0.1
100 × 100	R = 3, H = 4	182.0	1349.7	0.0	2.1	1.5/1.0
	R = 5, H = 4	238.2	1421.0	0.0	1.8	2.0/1.6
	R = 5, H = 6	204.1	1429.1	0.0	2.8	1.4/1.0
150 × 150	R = 3, H = 4	190.2	2470.9	0.0	1.7	2.3/1.7
	R = 5, H = 4	193.2	2630.1	0.1	2.0	2.1/2.3
	R = 5, H = 6	217.6	2671.9	0.0	2.4	2.3/1.7

agent successfully satisfies this obligation almost every time, with penalty averaging near zero across most configurations. In more confined environments, like the 50×50 map, the agent has less room to maneuver and deviate toward water before the deadline expires.

The *Oil-Fire* norm presents distinct challenges, since it acts as a temporary safety constraint lasting 5 steps. Avoiding fire-related penalties becomes harder in densely populated environments, with fire cells accounting for 5% of the grid. In such scenarios, the agent may have to balance several competing objectives: following the navigation policy, satisfying other active norms, avoiding mobile obstacles. This can make it more likely to enter hazardous zones while the flammability state is still active.

Summary. Overall, the system shows stable behavior in terms of both *Norm Compliance* and *Mission Efficiency*: compared with the corresponding configurations in Table 1, only a limited increase in the number of steps needed to reach the target is observed. As for *System Performance*, the introduction of the new norms causes only a moderate increase in the average time per step, mainly due to a higher probability of re-planning. This proves the effectiveness of the proposed solution, suggesting that it can accommodate additional temporal norms without substantially affecting responsiveness.

6 Conclusion

We have presented an ASP-based SR solution for online policy fixing in dynamic environments based on *DP*-sr. The transition from a batch-oriented ASP encoding assisted by an external procedural engine, as in [1], to a purely SR approach proved to be a decisive factor for scalability: experiments show that, thanks to the incremental nature of *DP*-sr, the processing latency remains manageable as the environment's complexity (in terms of possible evolutions) increases.

A major advantage of this approach is its capacity to naturally handle complex, time-bound normative obligations without an external procedural engine. The successful management of the *Mud-Water* and *Oil-Fire* norms demonstrates that the agent seamlessly pivots between general-purpose RL navigation and specialized safety behaviors. The **@now** operator and external atom mechanism (e.g., `&generate_actions`) enable a modular, "plug-and-play" integration of precomputed logics, paving the way for sophisticated *Multi-Policy Arbitration.*

Beyond policy fixing, this work shows how ASP-based SR can support online planning in dynamic domains, by combining declarative plan generation with the incremental monitoring of events and time-dependent conditions.

Outlook. We plan to extend the proposed approach to deal with weighing rankings from multiple external policies simultaneously, resolving conflicts between competing norms (e.g., deciding whether to prioritize fire safety over a washing deadline) based on higher-level ethical priorities. In particular, the proposed framework can be naturally evolved to robotic applications.

Acknowledgments. This research was funded in whole or in part by the Vienna Science and Technology Fund (WWTF) project ICT22-023 and the Austrian Science Fund (FWF) 10.55776/COE12; project ASVIN - Assistente Virtuale Intelligente di Negozio, CUP B29J24000200005; project "Fa.Per.M.E. - Caratterizzazione dei fattori di rischio [...]", CUP H53C22000640006. Francesco Calimeri is member of the Gruppo Nazionale Calcolo Scientifico-Istituto Nazionale di Alta Matematica (GNCS-INdAM).

Disclosure of Interests. The authors have no competing interests to declare that are relevant to the content of this article.

References

1. Adam, S., Eiter, T.: ASP-driven emergency planning for norm violations in reinforcement learning. In: AAAI, pp. 14772–14780. AAAI Press (2025)
2. Bazoobandi, H.R., Beck, H., Urbani, J.: Expressive stream reasoning with laser. In: d'Amato, C., et al. (eds.) ISWC 2017. LNCS, vol. 10587, pp. 87–103. Springer, Cham (2017). https://doi.org/10.1007/978-3-319-68288-4_6
3. Beck, H., Dao-Tran, M., Eiter, T.: LARS: a logic-based framework for analytic reasoning over streams. Artif. Intell. **261**, 16–70 (2018)
4. Beck, H., Eiter, T., Folie, C.: Ticker: a system for incremental ASP-based stream reasoning. Theory Pract. Log. Program. **17**(5–6), 744–763 (2017)
5. Cabalar, P., Ciabattoni, A., van der Torre, L.: Deontic equilibrium logic with explicit negation. In: Gaggl, S., Martinez, M.V., Ortiz, M. (eds.) JELIA 2023. LNCS, vol. 14281, pp. 498–514. Springer, Cham (2023). https://doi.org/10.1007/978-3-031-43619-2_34
6. DP-sr: Official Website (2026). http://ares.mat.unical.it:20140/it/home
7. Eiter, T., Ogris, P., Schekotihin, K.: A distributed approach to LARS stream reasoning (system paper). Theory Pract. Log. Program. **19**(5–6), 974–989 (2019)
8. Gabbay, D.M., Horty, J., Parent, X.: Handbook of Deontic Logic and Normative Systems. College Publications (2013)
9. Giordano, L., Martelli, A., Dupré, D.T.: Temporal deontic action logic for the verification of compliance to norms in ASP. In: ICAIL, pp. 53–62. ACM (2013)
10. Governatori, G., Hulstijn, J., Riveret, R., Rotolo, A.: Characterising deadlines in temporal modal defeasible logic. In: Orgun, M.A., Thornton, J. (eds.) AI 2007. LNCS (LNAI), vol. 4830, pp. 486–496. Springer, Heidelberg (2007). https://doi.org/10.1007/978-3-540-76928-6_50
11. Ji, K., He, J., Gu, Q.: Reinforcement learning from human feedback with active queries. Trans. Mach. Learn. Res. 2025 (2025)
12. Kimbrell, K., Wang, T., Chen, F., Gupta, G.: Correcting autonomous driving object detection misclassifications with automated commonsense reasoning. In: Technical Communications of the 41st International Conference on Logic Programming (ICLP), pp. 128–142. EPTCS (2025)
13. Kiran, B.R., et al.: Deep reinforcement learning for autonomous driving: a survey. IEEE Trans. Intell. Transp. Syst. **23**(6), 4909–4926 (2022)
14. Könighofer, B., Bloem, R., Jansen, N., Junges, S., Pranger, S.: Shields for safe reinforcement learning. Commun. ACM **68**(11), 80–90 (2025)
15. Neufeld, E.A., Bartocci, E., Ciabattoni, A., Governatori, G.: Enforcing ethical goals over reinforcement-learning policies. Ethics Inf. Technol. **24**(4), 43 (2022)
16. Noothigattu, R., et al.: Interpretable multi-objective reinforcement learning through policy orchestration. CoRR abs/1809.08343 (2018)
17. Nute, D.: Defeasible Deontic Logic, vol. 263. Springer, Dordrecht (1997). https://doi.org/10.1007/978-94-015-8851-5
18. Pnueli, A.: The temporal logic of programs. In: FOCS, pp. 46–57. IEEE Computer Society (1977)
19. Rodriguez-Soto, M., López-Sánchez, M., Rodríguez-Aguilar, J.A.: Multi-objective reinforcement learning for designing ethical multi-agent environments. Neural Comput. Appl. **37**(31), 25619–25644 (2025)

20. Roijers, D.M., Vamplew, P., Whiteson, S., Dazeley, R.: A survey of multi-objective sequential decision-making. J. Artif. Intell. Res. **48**, 67–113 (2013)
21. Shea-Blymyer, C., Abbas, H.: Formal ethical obligations in reinforcement learning agents: verification and policy updates. In: AIES (1), pp. 1368–1378. AAAI Press (2024)
22. Silver, D., et al.: Mastering the game of Go with deep neural networks and tree search. Nature **529**(7587), 484–489 (2016)
23. Soldà, D., Cabalar, P., Ciabattoni, A., Neufeld, E.A.: Tackling temporal deontic challenges with equilibrium logic. In: AAMAS. International Foundation for Autonomous Agents and Multiagent Systems / ACM, pp. 1950–1958 (2025)
24. Sutton, R.S., Barto, A.G.: Reinforcement Learning - An Introduction, Adaptive Computation and Machine Learning. MIT Press (1998)
25. Von Wright, G.H.: Deontic logic. Mind **60**(237), 1–15 (1951)
26. Yu, C., Liu, J., Nemati, S., Yin, G.: Reinforcement learning in healthcare: a survey. ACM Comput. Surv. **55**(2), 5:1-5:36 (2023)

ASP Sous-Chef

Mario Alviano, Pietro Macrì, Luis Angel Rodriguez Reiners(✉), and Pierpaolo Sestito

DEMACS, University of Calabria, Via Bucci 30/B, 87036 Rende, CS, Italy
{mario.alviano,pietro.macri,luis.reiners,pierpaolo.sestito}@unical.it

Abstract. ASP Chef is a web platform in which Answer Set Programming (ASP) pipelines are composed by chaining ingredients, each encapsulating a distinct operation. Despite this pipeline paradigm, effective utilization still demands familiarity with both ASP and the available ingredient library. This paper presents two complementary extensions leveraging large language models to lower this barrier. The first extension is an advisory assistant that provides guidance in real time during recipe authoring. It employs a retrieval protocol to fetch ingredient documentation on demand, ensuring that the model remains contextually relevant while operating within tight token limits. This assistant is offered in two configurations: a local version leveraging WebGPU and the MLC framework for private inference directly on the device, and a remote version that connects to external providers such as Ollama or Groq for high performance reasoning. The second extension is an agentic interface via the Model Context Protocol (MCP), which exposes ASP Chef as a structured tool environment for external language model agents such as Claude and Copilot. A dedicated Python bridge maintains a live mirror of the active recipe, provides tools to inspect and manipulate the pipeline, and propagates all changes to the browser in real time via server sent events. Together, these two integrations successfully span interactive assistance during user authoring and fully automated pipeline construction and refinement driven by autonomous agents.

Keywords: Answer Set Programming · ASP Chef · Model Context Protocol · Large Language Models · WebGPU · Neuro-Symbolic Integration · AI Agents

1 Introduction

ASP Chef [1] is a web-based platform for building possibly long pipelines through a *recipe* metaphor, in which Answer Set Programming (ASP) is often used as a core engine to address several computational tasks. Users compose a recipe by chaining *ingredients*, each encapsulating an operation such as encoding a problem instance, filtering answer sets, or rendering outputs as tables and graphs. While this pipeline paradigm facilitates the assembly and reuse of workflows, effective use of the platform still demands familiarity with both ASP [14] and the available ingredient library. An initial step toward AI-assisted development

W. Faber et al. (Eds.): LPNMR 2026, LNAI 16952, pp. 19–34, 2027.
https://doi.org/10.1007/978-3-032-38320-4_2

within ASP Chef was established by Alviano et al. (2025) [3], who introduced dedicated ingredients for interacting with remote Large Language Model (LLM) APIs directly within a recipe. While that work demonstrated the value of combining symbolic reasoning with LLMs for tasks such as data extraction and result interpretation, the language model was placed strictly within the execution flow of the pipeline. In this capacity, it acted as a data-processing node with no role in how the recipe itself was composed or adjusted.

Extending model integration into the pipeline authoring process introduces a fundamental question regarding the exact role that the artificial intelligence should occupy relative to the system. Literature generally bifurcates this involvement into advisory and agentic paradigms [19]. In an advisory setting, the model delivers textual support to aid human comprehension, while the user executes all modifications to the environment [15,18]. Conversely, in an agentic setting, the model couples with external tools to execute structured operations, enabling it to inspect system states and iterate autonomously [13,16].

The ASP Chef ecosystem integrates both modalities to address these distinct operational needs. When a user requires assistance to comprehend the internal mechanics of an ingredient or trace data flow, the platform leverages the advisory configuration to provide interactive support in real time. However, when the objective shifts to the autonomous construction or programmatic restructuring of a pipeline, such as injecting new ingredients, tuning parameters, or reordering operations, the system provides the agentic interface. Under this paradigm, the model moves beyond unstructured textual dialogue, directly treating the recipe as a structured and mutable object to be manipulated via discrete tool execution.

Example 1. Consider a recipe in which a graph is represented by predicates `node/1` and `link/2`, and two nodes are marked as `start/1` and `target/1`. In an advisory interaction, the user may ask:

> *"I have predicates `node/1`, `link/2`, `start/1` and `target/1`. Which ASP Chef ingredient should I add to compute a Hamiltonian path?"*

The LLM could answer by identifying an ASP Chef ingredient, such as *Search Models*, and providing a snippet of code for the required ASP rules. However, the recipe remains unchanged until the user manually implements the suggestion. In an agentic interaction, instead, the user may ask:

> *"Complete the recipe by computing a Hamiltonian path for `node/1`, `link/2`, `start/1` and `target/1`, and show the result graphically."*

In this case, an agent is expected to inspect the current recipe, select suitable operations, set the input, add or configure ingredients, and verify the resulting pipeline through structured tool calls.

To ensure reliability and functional validity within the ecosystem, both configurations remain strictly anchored to the live execution environment. The advisory assistant (Sect. 3) achieves this alignment by scoping the focus of the model to the active recipe and dynamically retrieving documentation for available ingredients, thereby preventing hallucinations and ensuring that suggestions correspond strictly to valid syntax. Operating directly within the browser, this interactive advisor is offered in both local and remote configurations to balance user privacy with processing performance. Conversely, the agentic interface (Sect. 4) enforces operational consistency through a formal toolset that exposes the live recipe state. Instead of relying on ambiguous textual descriptions that risk generating syntactically invalid operations, external agents manipulate pipelines through structured tool executions, which a dedicated Python bridge synchronizes with the browser user interface in real time. Crucially, across both modalities, the LLM neither replaces the ASP solver nor alters the underlying semantics of the ingredients. The scope of the model remains strictly confined to the orchestration layer, where it facilitates the construction, configuration, and refinement of recipes. Consequently, formal reasoning remains entirely delegated to the robust ASP systems that the pipeline invokes during execution.

2 Background

Answer Set Programming. A program is a set of rules defining conditions (conjunctive bodies) under which atoms must be derived (atomic heads) or guessed (choices). Programs are associated with zero or more answer sets, i.e., interpretations satisfying all rules and a stability condition [11]. Programs are extended with `#show` directives of the form

`#show` $p(\overline{t})$ `:` *conjunctive_query*`.`

where p is an optional predicate, $\overline{t}$ is a possibly empty sequence of terms, and *conjunctive_query* is a conjunction. Answer sets of the program are projected according to the `#show` directives. We refer the ASP-Core-2 format for details [9].

ASP Chef. An *operation* O is a function receiving as input a sequence of interpretations and producing as output a sequence of interpretations. Operations may produce side outputs (e.g., a graph visualization) and accept parameters to influence their behavior. An *ingredient* is an instantiation of a parameterized operation with side output. A *recipe* is a tuple of the form (*encode*, *Ingredients*, *decode*), where *Ingredients* is a (finite) sequence $O_1\langle P_1\rangle, \ldots, O_n\langle P_n\rangle$ of ingredients, and *encode* and *decode* are Boolean values. If *encode* is true, the input of the recipe is mapped to [[`__base64__("`s`")`]], where $s = \mathit{Base64}(s_{in})$ (i.e., the Base64-encoding of the input string s_{in}). After that, the ingredients are applied one after another. Finally, if *decode* is true, every occurrence of `__base64__(`s`)` is replaced with (the ASCII string associated with) $\mathit{Base64}^{-1}(s)$. Among the operations supported by ASP Chef there are $\mathit{Encode}\langle p, s\rangle$ to extend every interpretation in input with the atom `p("t")`, where $t = \mathit{Base64}(s)$; $\mathit{Search\ Models}\langle \Pi, n\rangle$ to replace every interpretation I in input with up to n answer sets of $\Pi \cup \{p(\overline{t}).\mid p(\overline{t}) \in I\}$; $\mathit{Parse\ CSV}\langle \Pi, \mathit{decode\_predicate}, \mathit{output\_predicate}\rangle$ to replace every atom $\mathit{decode\_predicate}(c)$, representing a CSV content $\mathit{Base64}^{-1}(c)$, with facts of the form $\mathit{output\_predicate}(\mathit{row}, \mathit{col}, \mathit{value})$.

Logic-Driven Templates. To bridge the gap between logical interpretations and structured user-facing output (e.g., JSON, HTML, or natural language), ASP Chef employs a custom template system based on Mustache queries. A Mustache query `{{` Π `}}` contains an ASP program Π. When applied to an interpretation I, it evaluates $\Pi \cup I$ and renders the projected answer set. The system introduces logic-driven formatting directives, supports f-strings (e.g., `{{f"id: ${X}"}}`) and multi-stage expansion to enable complex loops and conditionals. The Mustache template system serves as the primary interface for data transformation within ASP Chef. Many core ingredients rely on it to map symbolic interpretations to external formats or services. For instance, the *@vis.js/Network* ingredient uses Mustache to generate the JSON configuration required to render interactive graphs. Similarly, the *@LLMs/Chat Completion* ingredient employs templates to dynamically construct prompts by interpolating ASP facts into natural language queries before they are sent to an LLM provider. We refer [3,4] for details.

Example 2. We are designing a package delivery route for a small courier company. A delivery driver starts at a given point and needs to reach another point, making sure to visit every location exactly once. Connections are also given.

```
Starts at Point A and reach Point G.
A is connected to B and C.          B is connected to A, C and D.
C is connected to A and D.          D is connected to B, C, and E.
E is connected to D, F and H.       F is connected to E and G.
G is connected to F and H.          H is connected to F.
```

For this to work, the *encode* flag must be enabled within the recipe. A CSV representation of the input can then be obtained by *@LLMs/Chat Completion* using the following Mustache template:

```
{{ #show base64(X) : __base64__(X).
Give me the start point in the first line, and the reach point in the
second line. After that, list all directed connections, one per line,
separated by space.
```

After that, *Parse CSV* and *Search Models* can obtain a relational representation in predicates `start/1`, `target/1`, `node/1` and `link/2`, as well as a Hamiltonian path (if any). Full recipe at https://tinyurl.com/aspchf/LPNMR2026/ex-2.

Browser-side and High-Performance LLM Inference. The deployment of Large Language Models (LLMs) has traditionally relied on centralized cloud providers. However, recent advancements in hardware acceleration and model optimization have enabled a shift toward local and specialized inference architectures. WebGPU is a modern web standard that provides low-level, hardware-accelerated access to the GPU directly within the browser [12]. Unlike its predecessors, it is designed for general-purpose GPU computation (GPGPU), making it a viable target for neural network inference. *MLC LLM* is a universal compilation stack that optimizes models for various backends, while *WebLLM* serves as its JavaScript-based runtime. Together, they allow LLMs to execute entirely on the client side, ensuring that data processing remains local to the browser. Alternatively, specialized hardware and lightweight serving frameworks have optimized LLM performance for diverse environments. *Groq* utilizes a *Language Processing Unit* (LPU) architecture, a deterministic networking and memory-first approach designed to minimize the latency of auto-regressive inference. In parallel, frameworks like *Ollama* have popularized the use of local inference servers, allowing users to run and manage models via standardized APIs over local networks. These technologies provide high-throughput alternatives to browser-side execution while maintaining varying degrees of data sovereignty.

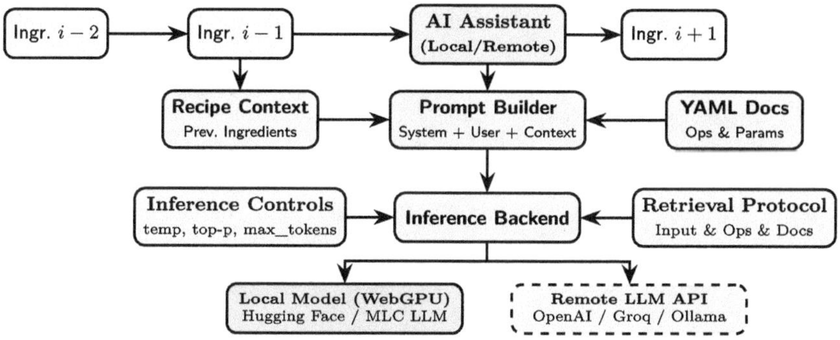

Fig. 1. Architecture of the AI Assistant: a unified prompt pipeline with interchangeable local (WebGPU) and remote inference backends.

3 The Advisory Assistant

To lower the barrier to entry for (possibly complex) pipeline construction, we introduce an *advisory layer* in ASP Chef through two specialized ingredients that embed a conversational "Sous-Chef" directly into the recipe, providing real-time guidance on ingredient behavior, data-flow debugging, and pipeline expansion:

- The *@LLMs/Local AI Assistant* ingredient is designed for local inference directly within the browser to preserve user privacy. This component leverages WebGPU alongside the MLC framework. Because the generation processes occur entirely on the local hardware of the user, the interface exposes granular controls over the inference process, including temperature, top p, and repetition penalty. This variant is optimal for scenarios involving sensitive data where transmitting information to external endpoints is prohibited.
- The *@LLMs/Remote AI Assistant* ingredient functions as a gateway to high performance external inference engines. This component allows the environment to establish connections with local network servers running Ollama or cloud infrastructure managed by providers such as Groq via application programming interfaces (APIs) compatible with OpenAI. By migrating the computational workload away from the browser, this ingredient can leverage

larger language models that possess superior reasoning capabilities. The configuration panel for this variant is simplified to focus entirely on parameters independent of the provider.

Both ingredients share a common architecture (Fig. 1) designed to overcome the context limitations and hallucination risks of standard LLMs. The assistants operate on a *bounded view* of the pipeline. Instead of ingesting the entire environment, they receive a configurable number of preceding ingredients (via the `Context Ingredients` parameter). This allows the assistant to recognize specific predicates, such as `node/1` or `path/2`, and identify potential schema mismatches between adjacent operations. To ensure that advices remain anchored to the actual capabilities of the platform, the assistants utilize a structured retrieval protocol. The system prompt mitigates the risk of the LLM proposing non-existent ingredients by defining specific tokens for tool execution: `@@ASP_CHEF_TOOL OPERATIONS: LIST` to see the available catalogue; `@@ASP_CHEF_TOOL DOC:` $O_1, \ldots, O_n$ to retrieve the documentation for a specific ingredient. When these tokens are produced, the ASP Chef host intercepts the call, injects the requested specifications into the context, and resumes the generation process.

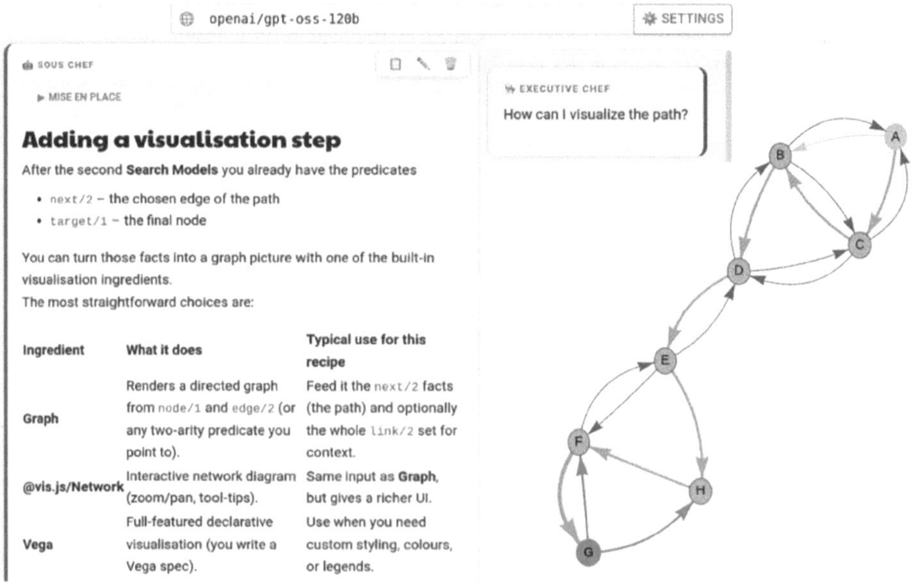

Fig. 2. Remote AI Assistant (*openai/gpt-oss-120b*) suggesting how to visualize the Hamiltonian path for Example 3: the assistant identifies the relevant predicates from the bounded recipe context and recommends visualization ingredients (result shown on the right).

Example 3. Continuing Example 2, a user may insert the *@LLMs/Remote AI Assistant* at the end of the recipe. Upon asking *"How can I visualize the path?"* (see Fig. 2), the assistant recognizes the Hamiltonian predicates from the bounded context. It then uses the `DOC` command to fetch the documentation for *@vis.js/Network*, ultimately suggesting the Mustache configuration to the user.

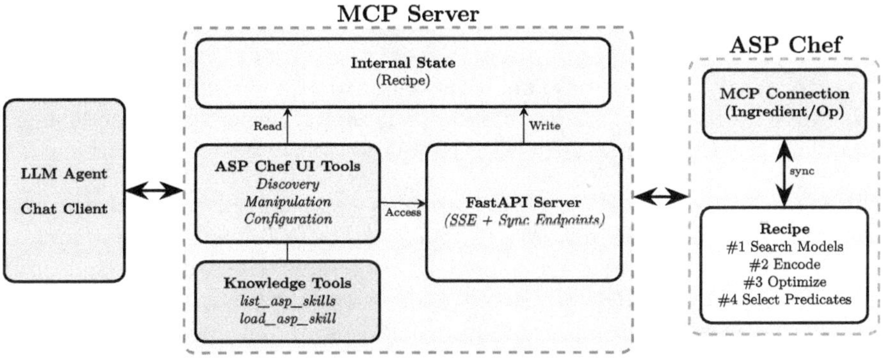

Fig. 3. Architecture of the agentic interface. Tool calls are forwarded to the browser via SSE; manual browser edits are propagated back via `POST /sync`.

4 Agentic Recipe Manipulation via MCP

The Model Context Protocol (MCP) [5] enables an autonomous interaction mode in ASP Chef, allowing an LLM-based agent to inspect and manipulate recipes programmatically. Unlike the advisory mode, where the AI provides textual guidance to a human, the agentic mode allows the AI to act as a direct operator. The agent queries the current pipeline state, browses the ingredient library, and issues structured commands to build or refine the recipe without manual intervention.

The architecture (Fig. 3) consists of a three-way synchronization loop between the LLM Agent, a Python-based MCP Server, and the ASP Chef browser environment. The Python MCP Server acts as a bridge, utilizing *FastMCP* for the JSON-RPC channel with the agent and *FastAPI* for the browser connection. It maintains an internal `RecipeState` object as a live mirror of the recipe. Communication with the browser is handled via two endpoints: `/events` (a Server-Sent Events stream to push commands) and `/sync` (a POST endpoint where the browser reports the updated state). In the browser, a dedicated *@LLMs/MCP AI Assistant* ingredient listens to the SSE stream. When a command arrives, it is applied to the current recipe. The ingredient then immediately posts the updated state back to the server, ensuring the agent maintains a consistent view of the recipe. To prevent accidental disconnections, the ingredient rejects any agent commands targeting itself.

The MCP server exposes tools that mirror the manual operations available in the ASP Chef UI, organized into three functional categories:

- *Discovery tools* (`get_recipe`, `get_operation_docs`, `search_operations`, `get_operation_catalogue`) allow the agent to inspect the current pipeline and browse the ingredient library before acting.
- *Manipulation tools* (`add_operation`, `edit_operation`, `remove_operation`, `swap_operations`, `duplicate_operation`) give the agent full structural control over the recipe.
- *Configuration tools* (`set_input`, `set_global_option`, `toggle_apply`, `toggle_stop`, `toggle_show`) allow the agent to provide input data and adjust pipeline-level settings. In particular, `set_input` accepts an `encode` flag to handle input that is not valid ASP syntax.

Additionally, the MCP server provides specialized *Knowledge tools* (`list_asp_skills`, `load_asp_skill`) inspired by established agent architectures [6]. These components implement a progressive disclosure mechanism for specific domain knowledge. To avoid exhausting the token context limits of the language model, logic programming theory is organized into focused modules such as scheduling, aggregates, or graph reachability. The agent utilizes `list_asp_skills` to browse compact metadata descriptions and subsequently invokes `load_asp_skill` to retrieve the full text of a module only when the information is relevant to the active assignment.

To ensure reliable agent behavior, the system prompt enforces two critical invariants, namely *index safety* and *state safety*. Regarding index safety, since structural changes shift the indices of subsequent ingredients, the agent must call `get_recipe` before any tool requiring an `at_index` argument and never reuse an index from a previous turn. As for state safety, `edit_operation` is designed to replace the entire options object, therefore the agent first retrieves the current options object and performs a local merge before sending the updated object, avoiding the accidental erasure of existing options.

Example 4. Continuing Example 2, The *@LLMs/MCP AI Assistant* can independently construct and subsequently extend the recipe to deliver visual insights. The agent begins by calling `get_recipe` and `search_operations` to locate and configure the *Search Models* ingredient with the Hamiltonian path logic. Once the symbolic pipeline is established, the agent calls `get_recipe` again to inspect the output schema. Upon seeing that the ASP encoding relies on predicates `node/1`, `link/2`, `start/1`, `target/1` and `next/2`, it searches for visualization tools and identifies *@vis.js/Network*. To extend the recipe, the agent calls `get_operation_docs` for the visualizer to understand its Mustache template requirements. It then issues an `add_operation` command to append the network graph at the end of the pipeline. Crucially, the agent configures the ingredient to highlight the path by mapping the `next/2` predicates to explicit color and width attributes within the edge configuration.

5 Evaluation

We conducted a two-fold evaluation: a quantitative survey with colleagues for baseline usability, and a series of expert case studies to test the agentic interface on complex puzzles.

5.1 User Study: Accessibility and Perceived Efficacy

We conducted a study with users ($N = 7$) of varying familiarity with ASP (from no knowledge to researchers). Participants were first tasked with solving fundamental reachability and integrity constraint exercises manually to familiarize themselves with the ASP Chef environment and the advisory AI assistant. Following this baseline, participants utilized the agentic interface to solve a Job Shop Scheduling problem. The objective was to obtain an optimal schedule and generate a functional timeline visualization using the `@vis.js/Timeline` library. Exercise skeletons are available at https://asp-chef.alviano.net/s/mcp-acceptance-grade#pit0500/asp-chef-short-links.

Table 1. User Survey Summary ($N = 7$). Mean scores (μ) are reported on a 5-point Likert scale (5: Highest/Easiest).

Dimension	Key Metric	Mean (μ)
Debugging	Ease of Fixing AI Errors (5: Easy)	3.71
Education	Pattern Awareness (5: Improved)	3.71
Shift	Logical Clarification (5: High)	4.28
Reliability	Solution Confidence (5: Confident)	4.14

The survey results summarized in Table 1 indicate that the integration of the MCP agent significantly lowered the barrier to complex modeling. While the agent produced a correct solution on the first or second attempt in only 42.9% of cases for the scheduling problem, 100% of participants successfully reached a valid solution through iterative dialogue. Most notably, despite the need for corrective loops, 100% of users reported a preference for solving similar logic problems with the MCP agent over manual authoring in the future.

The study revealed a significant shift in user mental models: 57.1% of participants reported that the agent fundamentally changed their approach to constraint writing, allowing them to focus on high-level dependency definitions rather than syntactic debugging. The visualization layer proved to be the most highly-rated component ($\mu = 4.57$); 100% of users found the timeline representation clearer than raw ASP output, noting that logical errors (such as task overlaps) became visually obvious. Finally, the study validated the platform's design as a collaborative *Sous-Chef* rather than a black box: while confidence in the results was high ($\mu = 4.14$), 85.7% of participants emphasized that they always verify AI-generated code manually. This confirms that the AI assistants effectively supports human-in-the-loop verification without sacrificing user agency.

5.2 Expert Case Studies: Fortress and Aquarium

To assess the capacity of the system for complex modeling, the authors utilized the *@LLMs/MCP AI Assistant* (via Co pilot CLI powered by GPT-5.4) to solve the Fortress and Aquarium puzzles (Fig. 4). The full agentic trajectories for both sessions, including intermediate recipes and tool-call logs, are available at https://asp-chef.alviano.net/s/LPNMR26/mcp-expert-session.

The Fortress task served as a stress test for the *human-in-the-loop* debugging capabilities of the platform, specifically targeting the common hurdle of transforming raw data into symbolic facts. The agent managed this "symbolic plumbing" by first automating the data ingestion process, which involved configuring a parsing pipeline to accommodate a space-delimited format and mapping raw indices to a structured vocabulary (`poi/3`, `rows/1`, and `cols/1`). Beyond mere data mapping, the agent engaged in active logical probing during the modeling phase; it proactively identified a constraint ambiguity regarding the fortress geometry, prompting the user to clarify whether the interior could be disjoint or required a single connected region. This interaction highlights the agent's transition from a passive tool to a partner that identifies missing domain knowledge before it leads to logical failure. As illustrated in Fig. 5, the development was driven by four corrective loops fueled by visual feedback:

(a) Fortress tutorial solution

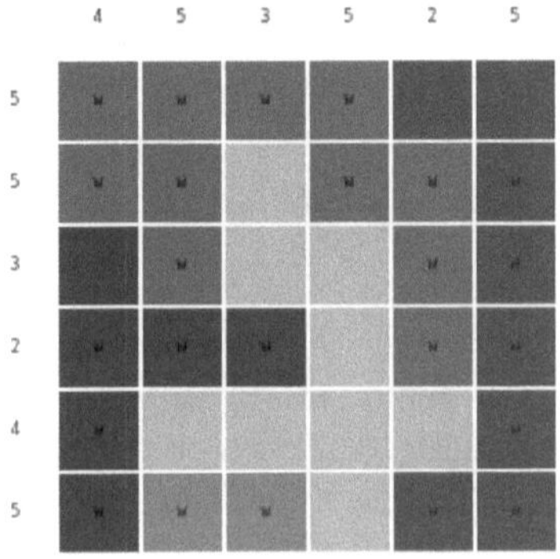

(b) Aquarium tutorial solution

Fig. 4. Tutorial examples for Fortress and Aquarium (https://asp-chef.alviano.net/s/).

- *Data Typing:* The agent refactored the parsing pipeline after initially quoting numeric values. Further inspection revealed a mistake in the documentation, which was subsequently corrected.
- *Visualization Iteration:* The agent utilized the `edit_operation` tool to resolve rendering issues where Points of Interest (POIs) were initially missing from the Fabric.js template.

- *Visual Error Detection:* Tasking the agent to render "must-be-free" safety zones visually exposed an off-by-one error in the Manhattan distance calculation that was otherwise obscured in the logic.
- *Sub-symbolic Logic Repair:* Upon the user clarifying that the path length must include the POI cell, the agent refined the ASP rules to produce the final validated 23×23 solver.

The Aquarium puzzle evaluation (Fig. 6) focused on the agent's ability to address missing logic in a skeleton recipe. This session demonstrated a full recovery trajectory from a logically unsound model to a visually high-fidelity solution:

- *Naive Gravity Constraints:* The agent initially implemented a grid-wide gravity rule, `:- fill(R,C), size(S), R < S, not fill(R+1,C)`, which failed to account for the irregular boundaries of the defined aquarium blocks. While this resulted in a "No Stable Models" report during the session, we subsequently visualized this specific logical failure for this paper (Fig. 6a) by temporarily relaxing the hint constraints into weak constraints.
- *Self-Correction:* Upon being reported the lack of stable models (and no additional information), the agent identified the wrong constraint and explained the issue to the user. After that, it performed a self-correction of the ASP rules, redefining vertical filling to respect block-level invariants.
- *Visual Alignment:* The agent initially produced a visualization with misaligned block boundaries and water levels. Guided by user feedback on these visual artifacts, the agent utilized the `edit_operation` tool to refine the Fabric.js template, ensuring graphical coordinates perfectly mapped to the underlying symbolic grid.

6 Related Work

The integration of LLMs with symbolic reasoning has attracted considerable attention, with ASP frequently serving as the formal reasoning layer. In [LLM]+ASP [20], LLMs act as semantic parsers mapping natural language to ASP representations. Similar motivations drive question-answering systems based on goal-directed ASP [7] and commonsense reasoning agents combining LLMs with s(CASP) [21]. Complementing these approaches, a related thread explores structured intermediate representations to bridge neural and symbolic components. Notably, the LLMASP framework maps complex natural-language knowledge into well-defined, structured schemas that mediate between the LLM and the symbolic solver [2]. Grounding LLM behavior in these explicit, typed descriptions reduces reliance on unpredictable free-form prompting while making the neuro-symbolic boundary inherently more controllable.

ASP Chef has itself been extended with LLM-oriented ingredients [3], allowing recipes to invoke remote LLM APIs for information extraction, prototyping, and result interpretation, with the model acting as one pipeline step whose output feeds downstream ingredients. A complementary MCP-based approach is

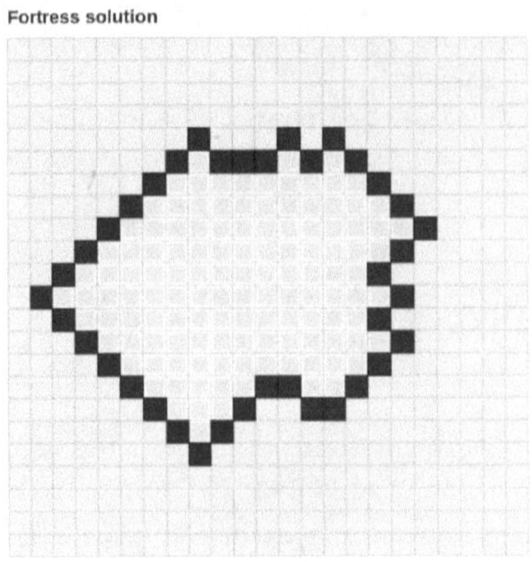

(a) Initial parsing and cell-based layout (after resolving numeric quoting and connectivity ambiguity).

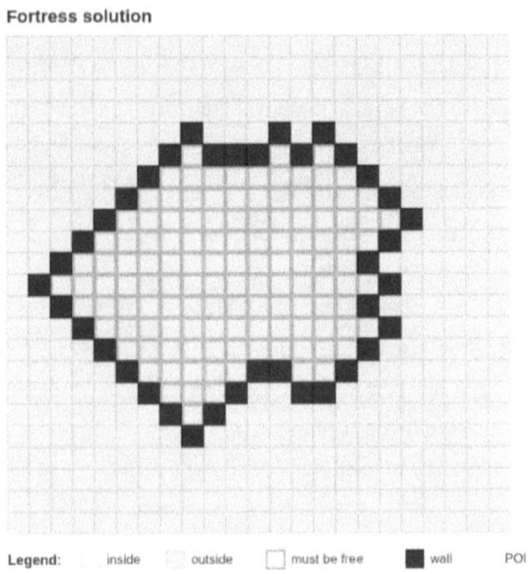

(b) Diagnostic rendering of *must-be-free* safety zones to verify reachability logic.

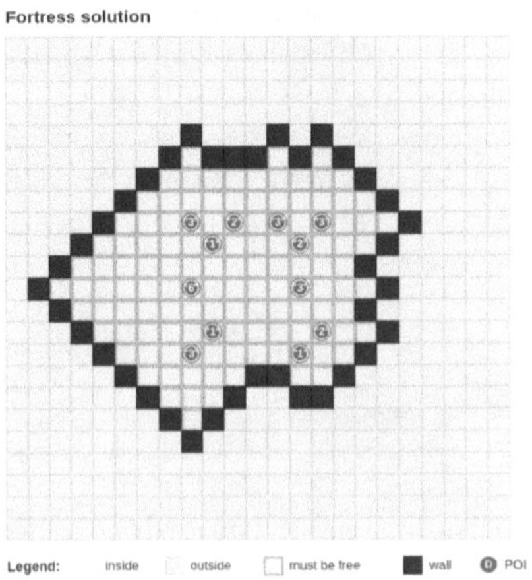

(c) Integrated POI overlay revealing an off-by-one error in Manhattan distance calculation.

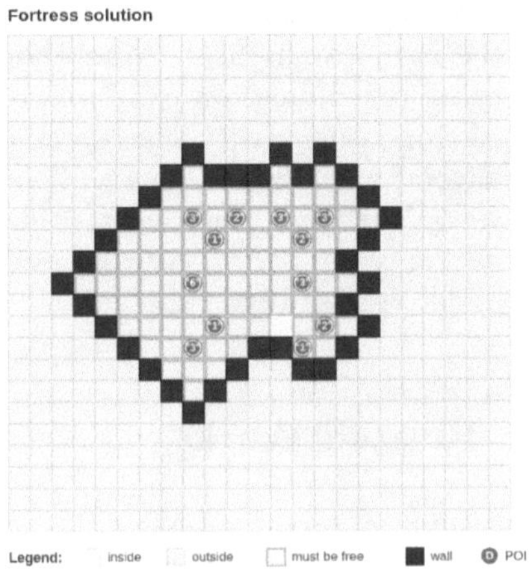

(d) Final validated solution for the 23×23 grid following logic repair. One inner cell is not a "must-be-free" cell.

Fig. 5. Expert Case Study: Iterative development of a Fortress solver using the Agentic Interface. The sequence illustrates the detection of sub-symbolic distance errors via visual feedback and the resolution of spatial modeling ambiguities.

presented in [17], which bridges LLMs and symbolic solvers (constraint programming, SAT, MaxSAT, SMT, and ASP) through a standardized interface, demonstrating MCP as a general mechanism for exposing formal reasoning tools to language models. LLM-assisted debugging and repair of ASP programs is explored in [8], where neural models are paired with structured error informa-

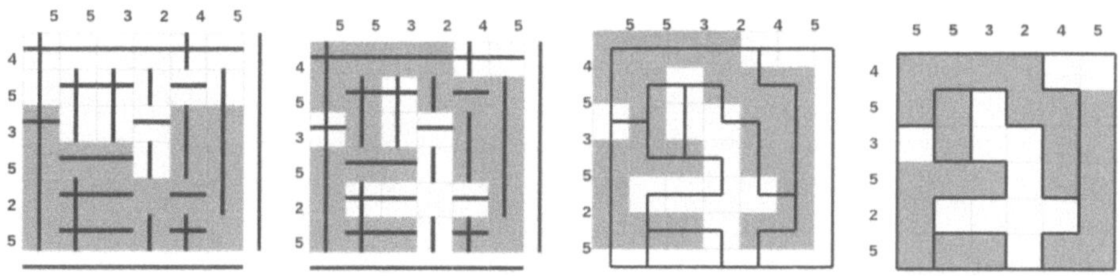

(a) Blocks ignored (b) Broken blocks (c) Misaligned water (d) Final solution

Fig. 6. Expert Case Study: Iterative repair of an Aquarium solver. The sequence (a–d) highlights the agent's transition from a naive gravity model to a block-aware implementation, alongside the incremental refinement of the graphical template.

tion to identify and correct faults in logic encodings. The suitability of ASP for agent architectures, knowledge representation, action reasoning, and deliberative behavior is surveyed in [10].

The present work builds on these threads while addressing a distinct concern: supporting the meta-authoring and manipulation of the ASP Chef pipelines themselves. While [3] treats the LLM as an internal ingredient and [8] targets specific program repair, the Advisory Assistant positions the LLM as an orchestrator operating on the recipe as a whole. The structural conditioning principles of [2] are applied at the environment level: the Local AI Assistant retrieves YAML ingredient documentation on demand, and the MCP server exposes the entire recipe workspace through typed tool schemas. In both integrations, formal reasoning remains delegated to the underlying ASP solvers; the LLM focuses on the construction, configuration, and refinement of the surrounding pipeline.

7 Conclusions and Future Work

This paper has explored the integration of LLMs within the recipe based symbolic ecosystem of ASP Chef, establishing a collaborative framework that enhances the interaction between human programmers and declarative environments. By implementing both advisory and agentic interfaces, the system successfully bridges the divide between unstructured linguistic reasoning and rigorous deductive paradigms, acting as an intellectual accelerator for formal modeling. The advisory assistant demonstrates that client side model execution can successfully preserve data privacy without sacrificing contextual awareness. Simultaneously, the remote configuration complements this local capability by providing high performance inference through external providers, ensuring that users can opt for superior reasoning capacity when local hardware resources are limited. By utilizing a shared retrieval protocol, both advisory variants anchor generative responses within the active recipe state, mitigating hallucinations and ensuring syntax compliance.

Conversely, the agentic interface transforms the development environment into a structured tool ecosystem via the Model Context Protocol. Rather than aiming for fully isolated execution, this interface establishes a mixed initiative workflow where the language model serves as an intelligent companion to the programmer. The synchronization loop managed by the Python bridge, alongside progressive disclosure mechanisms and structural safety invariants, allows the agent to handle mechanical boilerplate, manage schema mappings, and automate pipeline configurations. By offloading these low level administrative tasks to the agent, the human developer can focus entirely on high level conceptual modeling. Throughout this integration, formal reasoning remains entirely delegated to the robust ASP solvers, preserving the absolute semantic rigor of the platform. Notably, the aesthetic and structural quality of the resulting visualizations demonstrates the pragmatic value of this division of labor. When comparing these outputs directly to standard tutorial configurations, the generated layouts exhibit superior clarity, optimal node distribution, and precise thematic highlighting. This synthesis preserves the absolute semantic rigor of ASP while simultaneously democratizing access to declarative modeling techniques for a wider audience of users.

Future research will focus on two primary objectives. First, we intend to expand the context awareness of the companion agent by exposing the runtime state and the intermediate data outputs generated by each individual ingredient in the recipe. Providing the agent with access to these intermediate transformations will allow it to assist the programmer in tracing data flow anomalies and validating pipeline logic step by step. Second, we aim to integrate an automated feedback loop that ingests compiler errors and solver diagnostics reports directly into the tool context. This integration will empower the companion agent to analyze execution failures in real time, enabling it to suggest precise structural corrections and help the programmer troubleshoot complex logic programs during development.

Acknowledgments. This work was supported by the Italian Ministry of Health (MSAL) under POS projects CAL.HUB.RIA (CUP H53C22000800006) and RADIOAMICA (CUP H53C22000650006); by the Italian Ministry of Enterprises and Made in Italy under project STROKE 5.0 (CUP B29J23000430005); under PN RIC project ASVIN "Assistente Virtuale Intelligente di Negozio" (CUP B29J24000200005); by Regione Calabria under project NextGenGuides "Innovazione Tecnologica per le Guide Turistiche del Futuro tramite l'ausilio di tecnologie innovative AI e sistemi di geolocalizzazione avanzata" (CUP J39I24002040005); under project MOZART "Modelli e tecniche di mOdernizzazione di applicaZioni e data silos a supporto di clienti esterni, field force e impiegati di backoffice basati su AI GeneRativa e apprendimento auTomatico" (CUP J49I24001740005); by the LAIA lab (part of the SILA labs). Mario Alviano is a member of Gruppo Nazionale Calcolo Scientifico-Istituto Nazionale di Alta Matematica (GNCS-INdAM).

References

1. Alviano, M., Cirimele, D., Rodriguez Reiners, L.A.: Introducing ASP recipes and ASP chef. In: Arias, J., et al. (eds.) Proceedings of the International Conference on Logic Programming 2023 Workshops co-located with the 39th International Conference on Logic Programming (ICLP 2023), London, United Kingdom, July 9th and 10th, 2023. CEUR Workshop Proceedings, vol. 3437. CEUR-WS.org (2023). https://ceur-ws.org/Vol-3437/paper4ASPOCP.pdf
2. Alviano, M., Grillo, L., Scudo, F.L., Rodriguez Reiners, L.A.: Integrating answer set programming and large language models for enhanced structured representation of complex knowledge in natural language. In: IJCAI, pp. 4330–4338. ijcai.org (2025)
3. Alviano, M., Macrì, P., Rodriguez Reiners, L.A.: ASP chef chats with large language models. In: Proceedings of the Thirty-Fourth International Joint Conference on Artificial Intelligence, IJCAI 2025, Montreal, Canada, 16–22 August, 2025, pp. 10989–10993. ijcai.org (2025). https://doi.org/10.24963/IJCAI.2025/1247
4. Alviano, M., Rodriguez Reiners, L.A., Faber, W.: ASP chef grows mustache to look better. Theory Pract. Log. Program. **25**(4), 417–436 (2025). https://doi.org/10.1017/S1471068425100094
5. Anthropic: Model context protocol: A standard for AI system integration (2024). https://modelcontextprotocol.io. Accessed 28 Oct 2025
6. Anthropic: Equipping agents for the real world with agent skills (2025). https://www.anthropic.com/engineering/equipping-agents-for-the-real-world-with-agent-skills. anthropic Engineering Blog
7. Basu, K., Gupta, G.: Natural language question answering with goal-directed answer set programming. In: ICLP Workshops. CEUR Workshop Proceedings, CEUR-WS.org (2021)
8. Brancas, R., Manquinho, V., Martins, R.: Combining logic and large language models for assisted debugging and repair of ASP programs. In: ICST, pp. 646–657. IEEE (2025)
9. Calimeri, F., et al.: ASP-Core-2 input language format. Theory Pract. Log. Program. **20**(2), 294–309 (2020). https://doi.org/10.1017/S1471068419000450
10. Dyoub, A., Costantini, S., Gasperis, G.D.: Answer set programming and agents. Knowl. Eng. Rev. **33**, e19 (2018)
11. Gelfond, M., Lifschitz, V.: Logic programs with classical negation. In: Warren, D., Szeredi, P. (eds.) Logic Programming: Proceedings of the Seventh International Conference, pp. 579–597 (1990)
12. Han, Y., Bi, W., An, R., Tian, D., Yang, Q., Ma, Y.: Gl2gpu: accelerating webGL applications via dynamic API translation to WebGPU. In: Proceedings of the ACM on Web Conference 2025, pp. 751–762 (2025)
13. He, J., et al.: Frontiers of large language model-based agentic systems - construction, efficacy and safety. In: CIKM, pp. 5526–5529. ACM (2024)
14. Lifschitz, V.: Answer Set Programming. Springer, Cham (2019). doi: https://doi.org/10.1007/978-3-030-24658-7
15. Mei, K.Q., Chen, Y.J., Liu, S.T.: Navigating "limerence": Designing a customized chatgpt-based assistant system. In: Stephanidis, C., Antona, M., Ntoa, S., Salvendy, G. (eds.) HCII 2025. CCIS, vol. 2526, pp. 162–172. Springer, Cham (2025). https://doi.org/10.1007/978-3-031-94162-7_16
16. Singh, A., Ehtesham, A., Kumar, S., Khoei, T.T.: Enhancing AI systems with agentic workflows patterns in large language model. In: AIIoT, pp. 527–532. IEEE (2024)

17. Szeider, S.: Bridging language models and symbolic solvers via the model context protocol. In: SAT. pp. 30:1–30:12. LIPIcs, Schloss Dagstuhl - Leibniz-Zentrum für Informatik (2025)
18. Thompson, A.: ChatGPT for conversational AI and chatbots: Learn how to automate conversations with the latest large language model technologies, Packt Publishing Ltd. (2024)
19. Xi, Z., et al..: The rise and potential of large language model based agents: a survey. Sci. China Inf. Sci. **68**(2) (2025). https://doi.org/10.1007/S11432-024-4222-0
20. Yang, Z., Ishay, A., Lee, J.: Coupling large language models with logic programming for robust and general reasoning from text. In: Findings of ACL, pp. 5186–5219. Association for Computational Linguistics (2023) ACL (Findings) (2023)
21. Zeng, Y., Rajasekharan, A., Basu, K., Wang, H., Arias, J., Gupta, G.: A reliable common-sense reasoning socialbot built using LLMs and goal-directed ASP. Theory Pract. Log. Program. **24**(4), 606–627 (2024)

From Pixels to Predicates: A Robust Perception Front-End for ASP-Based Game Reasoning

Denise Angilica(✉), Tayyab Ateeq, Pierangela Bruno, Emanuele Galardo, and Giovambattista Ianni

University of Calabria, Rende, Italy
{denise.angilica,tayyab.ateeq,pierangela.bruno,emanuele.galardo, giovambattista.ianni}@unical.it

Abstract. Bridging the gap between raw visual perception and symbolic reasoning remains a central challenge for general-purpose AI agents. While deep learning models excel at object recognition, they often require task-specific training data and lack the structural guarantees needed by downstream logical solvers. We present an agnostic grid reconstruction framework that transforms 2D images of structured environments, specifically game boards, into logical assertions without pre-trained models or manual labeling. We propose two complementary methods: Grid-First Detection (GFD), based on classical image processing and genetic auto-tuning, and Object-First Detection (OFD), based on zero-shot segmentation for repeated-object discovery. Both produce a lightweight symbolic abstraction of the board that can be directly consumed by Answer Set Programming (ASP) encodings. We further embed this abstraction in a closed-loop *sense–abstract–reason–act–verify* architecture for dynamic visual environments. After an action is selected and executed, the system monitors the environment until the symbolic state stabilizes, avoiding decisions based on transient visual effects such as animations, cascades, or delayed updates. This supports robust replanning even when exact post-action prediction is unavailable. Overall, the approach enables rapid deployment of symbolic reasoning agents in visually rich, dynamic environments where data-driven training is impractical.

Keywords: Answer Set Programming · Agnostic Grid Reconstruction · Knowledge Extraction from Images · Zero-shot Perception · Symbolic Abstraction · Genetic Auto-tuning · State Representation

1 Introduction

Knowledge Representation and Reasoning (KRR) methods enable agents to make decisions based on explicit symbolic models, constraints, and strategies. However, in many interactive contexts the state of the environment is not available in terms of structured symbols and it must be inferred from raw sensory

W. Faber et al. (Eds.): LPNMR 2026, LNAI 16952, pp. 35–51, 2027.
https://doi.org/10.1007/978-3-032-38320-4_3

inputs such as images. This perception-to-symbol gap remains a major obstacle to reusing KRR decision-making processes across visually diverse tasks.

Grid-based games are an attractive domain for studying this integration. Their mechanics are naturally defined over discrete structures such as cells, adjacency, and object types, making them well suited to declarative formalisms like Answer Set Programming (ASP) [9]. At the same time, the same abstract rules recur across visually different implementations of the same game family, with varying board geometry, sprites, backgrounds, and interface elements. Thus, a reusable KRR-based game agent requires a perception front-end robust to visual diversity and able to produce a consistent symbolic abstraction.

A second, often overlooked, challenge arises once an agent physically *acts* in a visual environment, for instance through a touchscreen interface. Actions may have delayed effects (e.g., animations), execution noise (e.g., imprecise swipes), or non-deterministic consequences. In such settings, it is not enough to plan from a single snapshot: the agent must close the loop, verify whether the intended outcome occurred, and replan when necessary.

This paper addresses the following question: *Can we build a domain-agnostic pipeline that abstracts grid-game states, taken from game board images, into logical predicates for KRR, while remaining robust under real interactive dynamics?* This paper does not aim to propose new game-solving techniques or new computer vision algorithms. Instead, it addresses a recurring practical limitation of ASP-based agents: symbolic reasoning often assumes that facts are already available, whereas real environments expose only raw sensory data. Our goal is therefore to provide a reusable symbolic perception front-end and a robust interaction architecture that enable declarative reasoning systems to operate directly on visual environments without requiring task-specific training data or access to an internal state representation.

The main contributions of this paper are: (i) an *Agnostic Grid Reconstruction* (AGR) formulation for extracting grid structure and repeated object types from screenshots of unknown grid-based games; (ii) two complementary AGR methods, Grid-First Detection (GFD) and Object-First Detection (OFD), based on geometric-first and object-first reconstruction; (iii) a lightweight "pixels-to-facts" abstraction layer that exposes visual observations as logical facts suitable for ASP and other KRR systems; (iv) a closed-loop monitoring mechanism combining post-action stabilization and symbolic validation for robust reasoning in dynamic visual environments; and (v) an end-to-end deployment on a touchscreen robot demonstrating the practical integration of perception and ASP reasoning.

As a concrete running test case throughout the paper, we instantiate the framework on match-3 games, which combine grid-structured reasoning with dynamic and partially unpredictable visual evolution. In match-3 games, swapping adjacent objects to create alignments may trigger animations, cascades, and further automatic matches, making the post-action state temporarily unstable.

The perception and reasoning layers have intentionally different scopes of generality. While reasoning modules naturally remain domain-specific and encode the rules of a particular game family, many visually different environments share common structural properties, such as grids and repeated objects. By decoupling symbolic perception from reasoning, a single perception front-end can support multiple reasoning modules and substantially reduce the engineering effort required to deploy ASP agents on new visual domains.

The proposed pipeline has been integrated into BrainyBot [2], extending its earlier template-based perception module and adding closed-loop action monitoring; the corresponding codebase and experimental materials are available [8].

The paper is organized as follows. Section 2 illustrates the pipeline. Section 3 formalizes AGR. Section 4 describes GFD and OFD. Section 5 details the pixels-to-facts mapping. Section 6 presents action-success monitoring. Section 7 sketches an agnostic ASP match-3 player as a downstream application. Section 8 describes the robotic deployment. Evaluation and related work follow.

2 Pipeline Overview

Our approach can be described as an agent following an end-to-end *sense–abstract–reason–act–verify* loop. More in detail, in the *sense* phase, the agent acquires an observation of the current environment state (for instance, a screenshot of what appears on some target device's display). The observation is processed by a perception module that extracts relevant elements and raw quantitative attributes, e.g., pixel coordinates, color, shape, or segmentation masks.

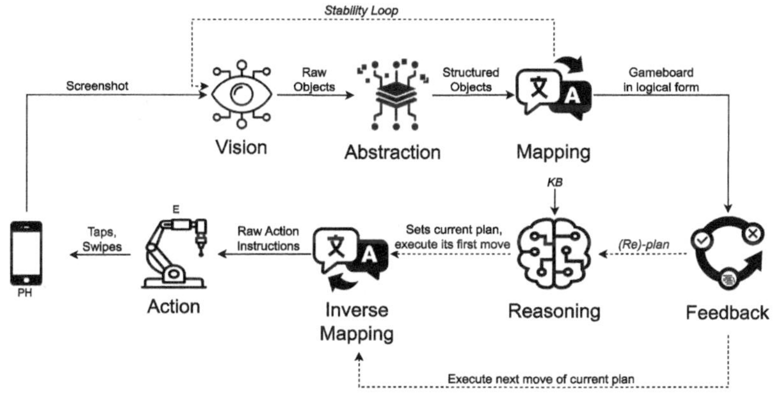

Fig. 1. Overview of the closed-loop pipeline from pixels to predicates to KRR decision-making, including action-success monitoring.

In the *abstract* phase, these detections are converted into a discrete symbolic state representation for KRR. This step exploits lightweight assumptions about the domain structure (e.g., a nearly rectangular lattice of cells) to infer higher-level entities and relations, such as cell coordinates, and mitigate perception noise by filtering duplicates and removing spurious detections.

In the *reason* phase, the abstract state is translated into logical facts and combined with a declarative encoding of domain rules and agent strategy. A KRR engine, here an ASP solver, computes one or more solutions, typically selecting an action or action sequence that optimizes the encoding objective. Depending on the chosen modality, the execution loop can be reactive, recomputing one action after each observation, or partially planned, executing multiple precomputed actions while monitoring consistency with the expected plan evolution.

In the *act* phase, the chosen abstract action is grounded into a concrete command in the environment. For touchscreen games, this may correspond to a tap at screen coordinates (x, y) or a swipe along a segment (x_0, y_0, x_1, y_1); more generally, grounding maps symbolic action parameters to the actuator interface of the underlying platform, e.g., software events, API calls, or physical motion commands. After execution, a feedback loop waits for stabilization and checks whether the observed predicates satisfy the expected outcomes of the last actions; otherwise, replanning is triggered. Figure 1 summarizes the modules.

3 Problem Statement: Agnostic Grid Reconstruction

We define *Agnostic Grid Reconstruction* (AGR) as the task of extracting a symbolic grid model from an image under minimal assumptions on visual style.
Problem Input. An input instance is an image I with height h and width w pixels.
Problem Output. We assume I contains occurrences of unknown repeating shapes arranged in a (possibly partial) rectangular grid. The output is a pair $\langle S, G\rangle$ where $S = \{S_1, \ldots, S_p\}$ is a set of shape types and $G = \langle n, m, g\rangle$ is a grid of size $n \times m$ where each cell content is $g(i, j) \in S \cup \{empty, nil\}$. Here *nil* denotes an *invalid* cell not belonging to the logical grid (e.g., missing corners), while *empty* denotes a valid cell containing no object.

As an intermediate byproduct, we also compute a matrix b where $b(i, j) = (x, y)$ is the pixel position of the center of the bounding box corresponding to cell (i, j), when available. This latter matrix plays a crucial role when symbolic decisions must be translated back to concrete touch actions.

AGR is intended as a symbolic interface between perception and reasoning. From $\langle S, G\rangle$ (and optionally b), we generate a set of ground predicates describing the grid domain (indices and valid cells), observed content (shape type or empty), and optional cell-to-pixel coordinates.

4 Agnostic Grid Reconstruction from Screenshots

AGR can be approached from two complementary directions: detecting the grid first and then classifying cell contents, or detecting objects first and then inducing the grid. We thus propose two strategies: Grid-First Detection (GFD) and Object-First Detection (OFD).

We assume that target object types are rendered as pixel-identical sprites, as in many mobile grid games. We do *not* assume prior knowledge of object classes or labeled data. Game screens may also contain decorative elements, status boards, and other content outside the main grid. Concerning gameplay, moves, i.e., actions that trigger transitions between grid states, may be animated and take an unknown time to stabilize. Future board states may be fully or partially deterministic, depending on the game.

Both GFD and OFD begin by transforming the input screenshot I into a refined image I^f emphasizing the Region of Interest (ROI) likely containing the board. All pixels outside the ROI are masked to black.

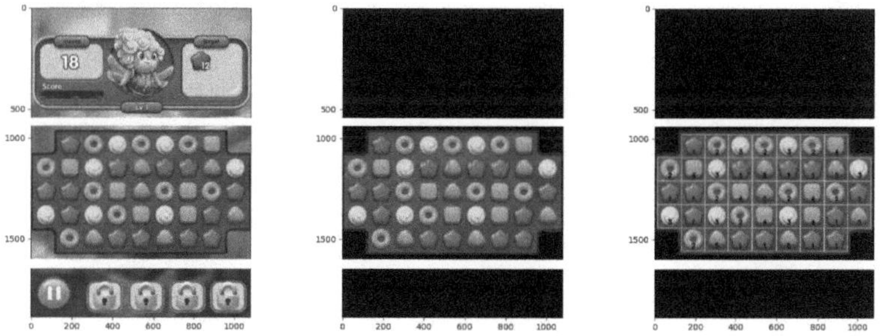

Fig. 2. Example evolution of screenshot I into refined image I^f, then candidate cell boxes and object labels. White gaps indicate omitted parts for space.

4.1 Grid-First Detection (GFD)

In GFD, the pipeline first reconstructs the grid geometry and then extracts cell patches for classification. The method combines classical edge detection and line detection [20], and geometric reasoning to infer a set of candidate horizontal and vertical lines (H and V). Intersections of consecutive pairs of lines define candidate rectangular cells.

Since line detection is sensitive to visual characteristics and resolution, GFD includes an automatic hyperparameter tuning mechanism based on evolutionary optimization (Sect. 4.4).

4.2 Object-First Detection (OFD)

In OFD, the pipeline first detects candidate object instances, then groups them into rows and columns to induce a grid. We run a zero-shot segmentation model (Segment Anything Model, SAM [14]) on I^f to obtain masks corresponding to object candidates. After filtering candidates, we cluster them based on spatial alignment to estimate the number of rows R and columns C. This yields candidate line sets H and V used to define grid cells, similarly to GFD.

4.3 Object Classification via Seed-Based Template Matching

From candidate grid lines H and V obtained by either GFD or OFD, we generate a set of rectangular boxes $B = \{b_1, \ldots, b_N\}$, each representing a potential cell. For each $b \in B$, we extract the corresponding patch (i.e. its subimage) from I^f. Invalid cells (outside the logical board) and empty cells are filtered out.

Visually identical patches are then identified using a fast seed-based template matching strategy: we select an unassigned patch as a *seed* template and match it against remaining patches; all matches are assigned the same object type identifier. The process repeats until all valid cells are assigned a type. This yields the set of discovered shape types S and the grid labeling function $g(i, j)$.

Figure 2 illustrates the progression from the input screenshot I to the refined image I^f, candidate cell boxes, and assigned object labels.

4.4 Automatic Parameter Autotuning for GFD

GFD relies on several hyperparameters controlling grid reconstruction. Since fixed values often fail to generalize across games and resolutions, we introduce a genetic-algorithm procedure that calibrates GFD from a single reference image. Genetic algorithms are population-based optimization methods that evolve candidate solutions according to a fitness function measuring their quality [4].

Given I^f, the goal is to identify a parameter vector θ that yields a stable and geometrically consistent reconstruction. The search space is defined by intervals derived from empirical operator ranges. Algorithm 1 summarizes the approach.

Algorithm 1: Genetic Autotuning for GFD

```
Input: Preprocessed image I^f, parameter bounds Θ
Output: Optimized parameter set θ*
Initialize population P_0 ⊂ Θ randomly;
for g = 1 to G_max do
    foreach individual θ ∈ P_{g-1} do
        Run GFD on I^f using parameters θ;
        Compute fitness F(θ);
    Form new population P_g via selection, crossover and mutation;
    if no improvement for G_stall generations then
        break;
return θ* = arg max_θ F(θ)
```

Fitness. Each candidate θ is evaluated by a composite fitness score capturing: (i) the ratio $\mathcal{R}$ between number of detected objects and number of unique object types (encouraging repetition, typical in grid games); (ii) regularity of cell dimensions (low standard deviation of widths/heights); (iii) coverage ratio of the reconstructed grid over the ROI. A Pareto-like dominance criterion is used, prioritizing (i).

Reuse and Faster Reconstruction. The optimal θ^* is stored and reused for subsequent screenshots of the same game at the same resolution. The tuning phase also yields estimates of mean cell width and height. These priors can speed up reconstruction by generating regularly spaced grid coordinates within the bounding extent of non-black pixels in I^f, then filtering and classifying candidate cells.

5 From Pixels to Symbolic Grid Facts

AGR outputs low-level detections in the image space, each consisting of an object label and an approximate center (x, y). The abstraction phase converts these detections into a symbolic grid representation by grouping aligned centers into rows and columns and mapping each detection to a grid position (I, J). If multiple detections map to the same grid position, only the most reliable one is retained. The resulting board is encoded as a set of ground facts of the form `cell(ID,I,J,L)`, where `ID` is a unique cell identifier, `I` and `J` denote row and column indices, and `L` is the symbolic label associated with that cell. The label domain is numeric: `-1` denotes an empty cell, while positive integers from `1` to `N` identify the different object types detected in the image, where `N` is the number of distinct visual elements discovered in the current board. Thus, the perception module transforms a screenshot into a discrete symbolic board representation that can be directly consumed by the reasoning module.

This abstraction is intentionally lightweight. Rather than relying on game-specific symbols or semantic class names, it represents the board as a labeled grid whose labels are inferred from visual similarity. The resulting facts provide a compact interface between perception and ASP-based reasoning, while remaining agnostic to the visual appearance and semantics of the underlying game.

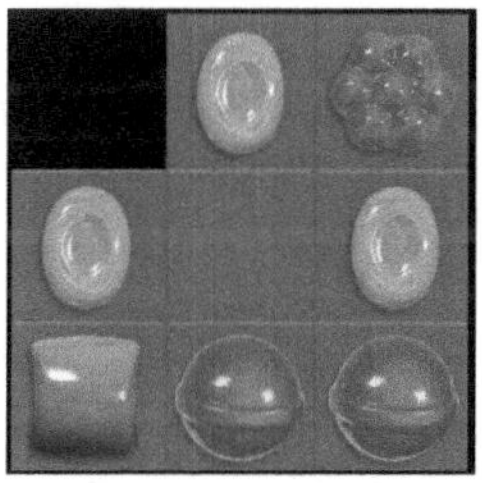

(a) Cropped screen extracted from the Candy Crush Saga game.

```
                 cell(0,0,0,1).  cell(1,0,1,2).
cell(2,1,0,1).  cell(3,1,1,-1).  cell(4,1,2,1).
cell(5,2,0,3).  cell(6,2,1,4).   cell(7,2,2,4).
```

(b) Example symbolic abstraction generated from the image.

Fig. 3. Mapping of a screenshot region to symbolic grid facts.

Figure 3 illustrates the symbolic abstraction of a portion of a screenshot. The example also shows how the representation method preserves the spatial arrangement of cells even when the logical board shape is not fully rectangular.

6 Closed-Loop Action-Success Monitoring in Dynamic Visual Environments

In interactive visual environments, the effect of an action is often not immediately observable. Animations and stochastic game events may prevent the agent from reliably interpreting the first post-action frame. For this reason, our architecture includes a monitoring stage that waits for a stable post-action state and, whenever possible, checks whether the expected outcome in terms of the expected future configuration of the game board has occurred.

The monitoring stage is organized around two components: *stabilization* and *validation and continuation*. Stabilization ensures that the evaluation loop is resumed only from a sufficiently stable post-action observation. Validation and continuation determine, once stabilization has been reached, whether execution can proceed as intended or whether reasoning must restart from a newly observed state, e.g., in the case an action didn't change the environment as predicted.

These components are general, but their role varies depending on the degree of determinism of the target game family. In highly dynamic games such as match-3, stabilization is essential while validation may be weak or absent due to the stochastic nature of the domain. In contrast, in more deterministic board games, such as checkers-like domains, both components can be exploited more directly because the symbolic successor state is more predictable and fully observable.

Stabilization. After executing an action, the system acquires a sequence of observations and repeatedly applies the perception-and-abstraction pipeline, obtaining abstractions $A_1, A_2, \ldots$. Rather than reasoning on raw images, it monitors convergence at the symbolic level: when $A_t = A_{t+1}$ for some t, the abstraction is considered stabilized and denoted by A'.

This step is especially important in game families where the visual state evolves through intermediate animations. For example, in match-3 games, a single swap move may be followed by cascades and refilling. A screenshot captured too early may therefore represent only a transient configuration that should not be given to the reasoner. By waiting for abstraction-level convergence, the agent avoids making decisions from unstable perceptual evidence.

In slower and more deterministic board games such as checkers or similar turn-based domains, stabilization is often simpler. A move typically changes only a small number of cells and does not trigger long visual cascades. Nevertheless, stabilization remains useful even there, because it guards against capture animations or delayed rendering. Thus, stabilization is the common prerequisite for robust monitoring across both deterministic and stochastic target domains.

Validation and Continuation. Once a stabilized abstraction A' has been obtained, the system determines how execution should proceed. Operationally, the reasoner may provide a set F of auxiliary atoms of the form `feedback(X)` representing symbolic properties that should hold after successful execution. Validation succeeds whenever $F \subseteq A'$, i.e., whenever all expected feedback atoms are found in the observed post-action abstraction. In this way, monitoring does not require predicting the entire successor state, but only those symbolic conditions that are relevant for validating the action outcome.

In deterministic board games, validation can be performed using explicit content-level feedback atoms. For instance, in a checkers-like domain, if the agent decides to move a piece from cell `(i1,j1)` to cell `(i2,j2)`, the expected feedback set may include atoms such as `feedback(cell(id1,i1,j1,empty))` and `feedback(cell(id2,i2,j2,man_black))`. After stabilization, the content of the `feedback/1` atoms is checked to be a subset of A'. If the test fails, then either the action was not executed correctly or the environment evolved unexpectedly.

In contrast, in non-deterministic domains, such as match-3, exact post-action content prediction is generally impractical, since the resulting board may depend on stochastic addition of game objects. In such cases, the expected feedback set may be empty. Accordingly, once stabilization is reached, the newly observed abstraction A' is directly adopted as the current state for subsequent reasoning. Thus, monitoring is still essential, but its role shifts from successor-state verification to ensuring that replanning starts from a stable symbolic state.

This difference also affects the execution mode. In deterministic domains, actions can be executed as part of a previously computed multi-step plan, and validation makes it possible to monitor whether the observed state remains consistent with the expected plan evolution after each step. If validation fails, the remaining plan can be aborted and the sense–abstract–reason loop restarted from the newly observed state. In contrast, in non-deterministic domains such as match-3, execution is naturally reactive, with one action recomputed after each stabilized observation. For this reason, the absence of non-empty feedback conditions is less problematic, since no long-horizon plan needs to be preserved across uncertain state transitions.

More generally, the framework supports a spectrum ranging from strong successor-state checks in predictable, planned domains to weak or empty feedback conditions in reactive, non-deterministic ones.

7 Agnostic ASP Decision-Making for Match-3

To demonstrate that the symbolic abstraction produced by AGR can directly support game-independent reasoning, we implemented an ASP encoding for move selection in match-3 games. The encoding operates on the board representation generated by the perception front-end and searches for a swap between two adjacent cells that yields at least one match.

Input Representation. The encoding receives facts of the form `cell(ID,I,J,V)`, as described in Sect. 5. The encoding is therefore agnostic to the semantics of object types: it only reasons over equality and inequality of symbolic labels. Consequently, the same encoding can be applied to visually different match-3 games without any modification to the logical model or to the perception front-end, provided that the extracted abstraction preserves the board structure.

Move Generation. A legal move is modeled as a swap between two adjacent cells. The predicate `can_swap/2` identifies pairs of horizontally or vertically adjacent cells with different non-empty labels.

The choice rule `{swap(C1,C2):can_swap(C1,C2)}=1` enforces the selection of exactly one swap candidate. Auxiliary predicates then derive the symmetric view of the swap and identify the cells whose content is affected by the action. *Board Transformation.* The encoding defines a derived representation of the successor board through the predicate `new_cell/4`. Cells not involved in the swap preserve their original content, while swapped cells inherit the label of their exchange partner. In this way, the ASP program reasons on the hypothetical board obtained by applying the chosen move, without modifying the original input facts. To illustrate the flavor of the encoding, Listing 1.1 reports a small excerpt. The first rule identifies intervals that cannot form a match between two equal-valued cells because an intervening cell has a different value. The second rule derives horizontal matches on the transformed board by selecting equal-valued cells not separated by such interruptions. The last two rules define the transformed board after a swap: unchanged cells retain their value, while swapped cells inherit the value of their exchange partner. The final integrity constraint requires that at least one match exists.

Listing 1.1. Excerpt of the ASP encoding for move selection in match-3.

```
not_a_match_from_to(ID,ID1):- new_cell(ID,I,J,V), new_cell(ID1,I,J1,V),
    V!="", new_cell(ID2,I,J2,V1), V1!=V, J2>J, J2<J1.
match(I,J1,I,J2,J2-J1+1) :- V!="",new_cell(ID,I,J1,V),
    new_cell(ID1,I,J2,V), not not_a_match_from_to(ID,ID1), J2-J1>1.
new_cell(ID,I,J,V) :- cell(ID,I,J,V), not swapped(ID).
new_cell(ID,I,J,V1) :- cell(ID1,I,J,V), cell(ID,_,_,V1), swapped(ID,ID1).
:- not match.
```

Match Detection. Matches are detected on the transformed board by searching for maximal horizontal or vertical runs of equal labels. The encoding derives facts of the form `match(I1,J1,I2,J2,N)`, representing a contiguous segment of length `N`. Auxiliary predicates exclude non-maximal or interrupted runs, so that only valid match segments are retained. A constraint requires the existence of at least one match, thereby discarding swaps that do not produce an immediate alignment. Among the admissible swaps, the optimization component favors solutions that maximize the number of cells participating in some match. This criterion reflects the practical objective of selecting swaps that produce an immediate useful effect while preserving agnosticism with respect to game-specific sprite semantics. *Output.* The encoding returns the selected action through facts of the form `swap(C1,C2)`, which identify the two cells to be exchanged. These symbolic actions are then grounded to concrete touchscreen gestures by mapping the selected grid cells to image-space coordinates computed by the perception module. Overall, this encoding shows that a lightweight, automatically extracted symbolic abstraction is sufficient to support declarative move selection in visually diverse match-3 games, without relying on game-specific object names or manually engineered templates.

8 Implementation: Robotic Touchscreen Deployment

To validate the proposed pipeline in a realistic embodied setting, we instantiated the sense–abstract–reason–act–verify loop on an existing robotic system interacting with a mobile match-3 game on a touchscreen device [2]. This implementation also addresses two limitations of the original robot: template-based grid reconstruction and the lack of any mechanism to verify whether an executed action succeeded. The purpose is not to introduce additional domain knowledge, but to assess whether AGR and the monitoring mechanism remain effective under practical sensing and actuation noise. Deploying the pipeline on a physical robot introduces several practical sources of uncertainty beyond those already present in the game itself, including swipe imprecision, calibration drift, variable action duration, and partial observability during visual transitions. The robotic implementation therefore provides a realistic stress test for the proposed approach.

8.1 System Components and Data Flow

The deployed system follows the same architecture described in Sect. 2. In the *sense* phase, the current game state is acquired as a screenshot of the target device. In the *abstract* phase, the screenshot is processed by the AGR front-end, using either GFD or OFD, followed by object classification. The result is translated into a set of symbolic facts of the form `cell(ID,I,J,L)`, which provide the input to the ASP reasoner.

In the *reason* phase, the symbolic board is combined with the match-3 encoding described in Sect. 7 and submitted to the ASP solver through EmbASP [6]. The solver returns one selected action, represented as a fact `swap(C1,C2)`, identifying the two cells to be exchanged. In the *act* phase, this symbolic action is converted into a concrete touchscreen gesture and executed by the robot. Finally, in the *verify* phase, the system acquires new observations until the symbolic abstraction stabilizes, and then restarts reasoning from the newly observed board.

8.2 Grounding Symbolic Actions to Touchscreen Gestures

The ASP encoding selects actions at the symbolic level, namely swaps between adjacent grid cells. To execute such actions physically, the system uses the geometric byproduct of AGR, namely the estimated center position associated with each reconstructed cell. Given a selected action `swap(C1,C2)`, the implementation retrieves the corresponding image-space coordinates of the two involved cells and converts them into a swipe trajectory from the first center to the second.

Screen-to-Robot Calibration. To execute gestures reliably, screen coordinates must be mapped to robot coordinates. We perform a one-time calibration procedure by associating a set of reference points on the touchscreen with corresponding robot end-effector targets. From these correspondences, we estimate a geometric mapping that allows the robot to transform any screen point into a target position in its own workspace. This mapping is then reused to execute taps and swipes during gameplay.

8.3 Closed-Loop Execution in Practice

In a real touchscreen environment, the result of a swipe is rarely observable immediately. Animations, delayed visual effects, and cascades may produce transient intermediate states before the board settles into a new stable configuration. For this reason, after each action the robot does not immediately invoke the ASP solver again. Instead, it repeatedly acquires screenshots and reruns the abstraction pipeline until two consecutive symbolic states coincide.

In the present match-3 instantiation, the monitoring stage is used primarily for stabilization and replanning rather than for checking exact expected successor contents. Indeed, because swaps may trigger cascades and stochastic refill, the post-action board cannot in general be predicted reliably at the content level. Thus, once stabilization is reached, the newly observed abstraction is accepted as the current state and fed to the reasoner for the next decision step.

9 Evaluation

9.1 Dataset and Evaluation Protocol

We evaluated the proposed AGR pipelines, namely GFD and OFD, on a dataset of 544 screenshots collected from five popular match-3 mobile games: *Candy Crush Saga*, *Candy Charming*, *Sweets Match*, *Candy Fever*, and *Fruits Mania*. The dataset covers 8–10 levels per game and includes screenshots captured at five different screen resolutions. Each screenshot was manually annotated by marking the center coordinates of all valid grid cells and by assigning the same class identifier to visually identical objects within that image. To assess the agnostic nature of the proposed abstraction method, class identifiers are assigned independently in each screenshot. In a deployed agent operating on a fixed game, however, identifier persistence can be enabled so that visually identical object types retain the same class identifier across successive observations.

For GFD, parameter autotuning was evaluated using a leave-one-out protocol within each game–resolution pair: one image was used for autotuning, and the resulting parameter configuration was validated on all remaining images from the same game and resolution. Since OFD does not require parameter tuning, it was evaluated directly on all images.

9.2 Evaluation Metrics

Performance was assessed at two complementary levels. *Grid-level metrics* evaluate the correctness of grid reconstruction and cell localization, while *global-level metrics* evaluate the correctness of both cell localization and label assignment.

Detected cells were matched to ground-truth cells using the Hungarian algorithm [15], based on spatial proximity and class consistency. Precision, recall, and F_1 score were computed for both evaluation levels. At the global level, a detected cell is counted as a true positive only if both its position and its assigned label match the ground truth. A misclassified cell, therefore, contributes simultaneously to a false positive, due to the incorrectly assigned label, and to a false negative, due to the missed correct one, as standard in multi-class matching. Cells detected outside the ground-truth grid contribute to false positives, whereas missed annotated cells contribute to false negatives. True negatives are not defined, since most image regions do not correspond to valid grid cells.

For GFD, we also report the *Catastrophic Autotuning Failure Rate* (*CAF_rate*), defined as the fraction of validation folds whose global F_1 score falls below 10%. This metric captures rare cases in which the autotuning process converges to a clearly unsuitable parameter configuration, resulting in near-zero performance.

For all metrics, we report the mean, standard deviation, and 10%-trimmed mean, expressed as percentages.

9.3 Quantitative Results

Table 1. Summary of grid-level and global-level performance for GFD and OFD.

Metric	GFD			OFD		
	AVG (%)	Std (%)	Trim. AVG (%)	AVG (%)	Std (%)	Trim. AVG (%)
Grid Precision	96.14	14.44	100.0	94.7	13.1	98.1
Grid Recall	96.75	13.09	100.0	96.2	11.7	99.6
Grid F_1	96.18	13.50	99.78	95.3	12.3	98.7
Global Precision	86.45	27.52	93.86	82.2	31.6	88.9
Global Recall	86.65	26.96	93.90	82.7	30.8	89.2
Global F_1	86.46	27.30	93.78	82.4	31.3	89.0
CAF_rate	4.31	20.31	0.0	–	–	–

Table 1 summarizes the performance of both GFD and OFD. Overall, both methods achieve high grid-level accuracy across games and resolutions, confirming that AGR can reconstruct board geometry reliably under diverse visual styles and display settings. GFD achieves slightly stronger and more stable performance, with mean grid-level F_1 above 96% and mean global-level F_1 above 86%. This gap between grid-level and global-level results indicates that recovering board geometry is generally easier than assigning consistent symbolic labels to visually similar but potentially ambiguous objects.

For GFD, a small fraction of runs exhibits catastrophic autotuning failures, as reflected by a *CAF_rate* of 4.31%. In these cases, the genetic search converges to poor parameter configurations, yielding near-zero performance. However, the 10%-trimmed mean is substantially higher than the plain average at the global level, indicating that performance is stable in the large majority of conditions and that failures are rare but severe outliers.

OFD achieves competitive grid-level performance, with mean F_1 around 95.3%, confirming that object-driven induction can also recover board geometry effectively. However, its global-level results show larger variability than GFD.

This is mainly due to the domain-dependent segmentation quality of SAM, whose output is not equally reliable across all game styles. In particular, some game families yield near-perfect results, whereas *Fruits Mania* produces substantially lower scores because some objects are systematically split into multiple segments by SAM. This effect propagates to the reconstructed labeled grid and causes a marked drop in global-level performance.

Overall, the evaluation highlights a trade-off between the two proposed strategies. GFD provides more stable behavior through geometry-driven reconstruction, while OFD offers a more flexible object-centered alternative whose performance depends more strongly on the quality of zero-shot segmentation.

10 Related Work

Our contribution lies at the intersection of (i) recovering structured game state from pixels by exploiting repeated grid-like patterns, and (ii) using ASP/KRR for decision-making in a closed-loop acting system.

Match-3 and Sorting Puzzles. Match-3 games exhibit nontrivial combinatorial structure and have been shown NP-hard [12]; further analyses of their properties appear in [13]. Most algorithmic treatments assume direct access to an abstract state, whereas our focus is on reliably *deriving* such a state from visual observations and enabling KRR decision-making across visually different implementations.

Vision for Game-State Recognition and Repeated Patterns. When commercial games do not expose an internal state, vision becomes necessary for credible agents; for instance, the Angry Birds competition provides participants with a vision module that encodes the scene [17]. In physical board games, a large body of work targets chess and Go recognition from camera images [18,21], typically combining grid detection with piece/stone recognition. More broadly, detecting repeated visual patterns in semi-regular layouts is a classic vision problem with applications beyond games [16]. Prior pipelines for puzzle games often rely on template matching [2], which can be effective but typically requires per-game engineering. Recent foundation models such as SAM [14] enable general-purpose segmentation, and extensions such as T-SAM [7] further target efficient segmentation of repeated similar elements. Our work combines classical grid cues (GFD) with zero-shot segmentation (OFD) to produce an explicit symbolic interface.

ASP in Acting Systems and Game Modelling. ASP has a long tradition in modelling games and combinatorial problems (e.g., as reflected in the ASP Competitions) [10,11] and has been applied in game AI contexts [3,5,19]. For end-to-end integration, [1] connects ASP with ROS-enabled robots, and EmbASP provides a practical interfacing layer [6]. Complementarily, our contribution emphasizes the *pixels-to-predicates* front-end and action-success monitoring needed when the state must be inferred from dynamic visual observations rather than accessed from an internal game API.

It is worth noting that, in contrast to learning-based approaches, our objective is to support immediate deployment in unseen visual environments without requiring training data or access to internal game APIs. Accordingly, we favor explicit symbolic abstractions over end-to-end learning.

11 Conclusion

We presented a domain-agnostic pipeline for reconstructing grid-game state from screenshots and exposing it as a lightweight symbolic abstraction suitable for ASP-based reasoning. The proposed pipeline bridges perception and symbolic decision-making by converting visual observations into grid facts of the form `cell(ID,I,J,L)`, which can be consumed directly by declarative encodings without relying on supervised training or game-specific semantic labels.

To instantiate this idea, we introduced two complementary reconstruction strategies. GFD exploits geometric regularities through classical image processing and genetic autotuning, whereas OFD follows an object-driven approach based on zero-shot segmentation and spatial clustering. The experimental evaluation on screenshots from five match-3 games and multiple resolutions shows that both pipelines achieve high grid-level accuracy, confirming that board geometry can be recovered robustly across visually diverse environments. The results also show that symbolic label assignment is the more challenging stage, and highlight a trade-off between the stability of geometry-driven reconstruction and the flexibility of object-first induction.

The current work also has several limitations. AGR assumes environments exhibiting approximately grid-structured layouts and repeated visual elements, and the paper demonstrates generality mainly on the perception side, using a single reasoning module as a running example. Furthermore, unlike recent neurosymbolic approaches, the framework does not attempt to automatically infer game rules or learn latent symbolic representations. Extending the approach toward broader classes of visual environments and integrating automated rule acquisition constitute promising directions for future work.

Beyond one-shot perception, we embedded the abstraction layer into a closed-loop *sense–abstract–reason–act–verify* architecture. Here, monitoring stabilizes post-action observations and supports replanning from the new symbolic state, especially in non-deterministic domains such as match-3 games. A robotic touch-screen deployment further demonstrates that the proposed pipeline remains applicable under realistic sensing and actuation noise. The development code for the proposed architecture, detailed experimental information, together with the implementation for several videogames, is available at [8].

More broadly, we view the proposed pixels-to-predicates abstraction as a step toward declarative agents that can operate directly on visual environments without relying on manually engineered interfaces or internal APIs. We believe that bridging raw perception and symbolic reasoning remains a fundamental challenge for declarative AI systems, and extending the proposed ideas to richer environments and tighter integrations with learning-based methods represents a promising direction for future research.

Acknowledgments. This work was partially supported by the AI4Nature and SINTESI projects, funded under the PNRIC 2021–2027 program (DM n. 307/2025) and by the Italian MUR and MIMIT under the PN RIC project ASVIN.

References

1. Andres, B., Rajaratnam, D., Sabuncu, O., Schaub, T.: Integrating ASP into ROS for reasoning in robots. In: Calimeri, F., Ianni, G., Truszczynski, M. (eds.) LPNMR 2015. LNCS (LNAI), vol. 9345, pp. 69–82. Springer, Cham (2015). https://doi.org/10.1007/978-3-319-23264-5_7
2. Angilica, D., Avolio, M., Beraldi, G., Ianni, G., Pacenza, F.: From vision to execution: Enabling knowledge representation and reasoning in hybrid intelligent robots playing mobile games, pp. 45–55. KR (2023)
3. Angilica, D., Ianni, G., Pacenza, F.: Declarative AI design in unity using answer set programming. In: CoG, pp. 417–424. IEEE (2022)
4. Bäck, T.: Evolutionary algorithms in theory and practice - evolution strategies, evolutionary programming, genetic algorithms. Oxford University Press (1996)
5. Calimeri, F., et al.: Angry-hex: an artificial player for angry birds based on declarative knowledge bases. IEEE Trans. Comput. Intell. AI Games **8**(2), 128–139 (2016)
6. Calimeri, F., Fuscà, D., Germano, S., Perri, S., Zangari, J.: Fostering the use of declarative formalisms for real-world applications: The EmbASP framework. New Gener. Comput. **37**(1), 29–65 (2019)
7. Daroya, R., Chandran, D., Maji, S., Fanelli, A.: T-SAM: transductive learning for segment anything model. In: CVPR, pp. 6419–6428 (2025)
8. DeMaCS-UNICAL: Brainybot. https://github.com/DeMaCS-UNICAL/BrainyBot
9. Erdem, E., Gelfond, M., Leone, N.: Applications of answer set programming. AI Mag. **37**(3), 53–68 (2016)
10. Gebser, M., Liu, L., Namasivayam, G., Neumann, A., Schaub, T., Truszczyński, M.: The first answer set programming system competition. In: Baral, C., Brewka, G., Schlipf, J. (eds.) LPNMR 2007. LNCS (LNAI), vol. 4483, pp. 3–17. Springer, Heidelberg (2007). https://doi.org/10.1007/978-3-540-72200-7_3
11. Gebser, M., Maratea, M., Ricca, F.: The seventh answer set programming competition: design and results. Theory Pract. Log. Program. **20**(2), 176–204 (2020)
12. Gualà, L., Leucci, S., Natale, E.: Bejeweled, candy crush and other match-three games are (NP-)hard. In: CIG, pp. 1–8. IEEE (2014)
13. Hamilton, A., Nguyen, G.T., Roughan, M.: Counting candy crush configurations. Discret. Appl. Math. **295**, 47–56 (2021)
14. Kirillov, A., et al.: Segment anything. In: ICCV, pp. 3992–4003 (2023)
15. Kuhn, H.W.: The Hungarian method for the assignment problem. Naval Res. Logistics Quarterly **2**(1–2), 83–97 (1955)
16. Qu, H., Zhou, Y., Mok, P., Flatz, G., Li, L.: Efficient and effective detection of repeated pattern from fronto-parallel images with unknown visual contents. Signals **6**(1), 4 (2025)
17. Renz, J., Ge, X., Gould, S., Zhang, P.: The angry birds AI competition. AI Mag. **36**(2), 85–87 (2015)
18. Song, J., Li, S.: A robust algorithm for Go image recognition in Go game. In: IEEE ICCC, pp. 1397–1401 (2018)

19. Stanescu, M., Certický, M.: Predicting opponent's production in real-time strategy games with answer set programming. IEEE Trans. Comput. Intell. AI Games **8**(1), 89–94 (2016)
20. Szeliski, R.: Computer Vision - Algorithms and Applications, 2nd edn. Texts in Computer Science. Springer, Cham (2022). https://doi.org/10.1007/978-3-030-34372-9
21. Wölflein, G., Arandjelovic, O.: Determining chess game state from an image. J. Imaging **7**(6), 94 (2021)

Abduction in the Landscape of Probabilistic Logic Programming

Damiano Azzolini[1(✉)] and Markus Hecher[2,3]

[1] University of Ferrara, Ferrara, Italy
damiano.azzolini@unife.it
[2] University of Potsdam, Potsdam, Germany
hecher@cril.fr
[3] Université Artois, CNRS, UMR 8188, Centre de Recherche en Informatique de Lens (CRIL), Lens, France

Abstract. Abductive reasoning is a central task in artificial intelligence, which has been given semantics in the context of Probabilistic Logic Programming with the introduction of the class of probabilistic abductive logic programs (PALPs). In a nutshell, a PALP is a probabilistic logic program extended with a set of abducible facts. The goal is to find the optimal set of sets (possibly only one) of abducibles, called abductive explanation, such that the probability of a query is maximized. In this paper, we investigate the relation with Maximum-a-Posteriori detailing similarities and differences and provide a complexity study. Overall, this work provides a comprehensive characterization of abduction in Probabilistic Logic Programming.

Keywords: Abduction · Probabilistic Logic Programming · Statistical Relational Artificial Intelligence

1 Introduction

Abductive reasoning requires the ability to handle situations where data is missing, finding applications in many real-world scenarios [18,27,34] and playing a crucial role for the explainability of modern AI systems [16,17]. Although abduction has a long tradition in Logic Programming [12], only recently [2] it has been integrated with *Probabilistic Logic Programming (PLP)* [25]. Following the initial proposal of [2], a probabilistic abductive logic program (PALP) is a logic program extended with probabilistic facts, i.e., facts associated with a probability, and *abducible facts* (abducibles, for short). The goal is to find the smallest set, according to set-inclusion, of abducibles such that the probability of a given query is maximized.

Maximum-a-posteriori (MAP) [5] is a crucial task in AI. In a nutshell, given a conjunction of ground atoms q, it requires finding the most probable state for a set of variables V, called MAP variables, such that $\mathrm{P}(V \mid q)$ is maximized. This requires considering a set of variables subject to *maximization* and another set of variables subject to *marginalization*. This has some similarities with abduction [22], although a comparison in the context of PLP has been missing. Furthermore, in the literature [5,19,22] (but

W. Faber et al. (Eds.): LPNMR 2026, LNAI 16952, pp. 52–66, 2027.
https://doi.org/10.1007/978-3-032-38320-4_4

also in practical solvers), only one state has been considered for MAP in PLP. However, when multiple states yield the same optimal probability, there is an ambiguity about which state to select. Thus, here we discuss MAP when *multiple* states are considered and propose two encodings to model MAP as abduction and abduction as MAP. To better position abduction in the PLP atlas, we also provide a computational complexity study, showing that it reaches beyond the third level of the polynomial hierarchy.

To summarize, we provide the following contributions: i) we consider MAP as discussed by [5] and argue that when multiple states are associated with the same optimal probability, all these states should be considered; ii) we study the relationship with PALP (as proposed in the literature, e.g., [2]) and show that probabilistic abduction can be framed as MAP plus an additional minimality check (and in the other direction, so MAP as abduction); and iii) we perform a complexity study of PALP, where it turns out that under reasonable assumptions in computational complexity, one can reach beyond the third level of the polynomial hierarchy. This shows that PALP is indeed harder than MAP, basically due to the optimality criterion imposed on the set of computed solutions.

Overall, our paper closely investigates PALP and precisely positions it in the probabilistic logic programming landscape. The paper is structured as follows. Section 2 introduces background, together with the probabilistic abductive logic framework, Sect. 3 proposes an encoding to cast MAP as abduction and an encoding to cast, in a special case, abduction as MAP. Section 4 provides the complexity study, Sect. 5 surveys related works, and Sect. 6 concludes the paper.

2 Background

Logic Programming. A *normal rule* is of the form $h :- b_i, \ldots, b_m$ where h is an *atom* called *head* and each b_i is a *literal*, i.e., an atom or its negation (which we denote by prepending not). The conjunction of the b_is literals is called *body*. A normal logic program $\mathcal{P}$ is composed of a set of normal rules. In the following, every time we write logic program, we consider a normal logic program. Given a program $\mathcal{P}$, we define the Herbrand universe as the set of constants that appear in it. The Herbrand base $B_{\mathcal{P}}$ of a program $\mathcal{P}$ is the set of possible ground atoms that can be obtained from the predicates in $\mathcal{P}$ and constants from the Herbrand universe. A rule is *ground* if it does not contain variables. The process that consists of replacing variables with constants in all possible ways is called *grounding*. An interpretation I is such that $I \subseteq B_{\mathcal{P}}$. A ground atom a is true in an interpretation I (denoted with $I \models a$) if $a \in I$. A ground literal $not\ a$ is true in an interpretation I if $a \notin I$. A normal rule is true in an interpretation I if all literals in the body are true in I and its head is also true in I. The Well-founded semantics [31] assigns a three-valued interpretation to a logic program. A three-valued interpretation [24] I is a tuple $I = \langle T, F \rangle$ where T and F represent the set of true and false atoms in I, respectively, and is called consistent if $T \cap F = \emptyset$. An atom is undefined w.r.t. an interpretation I if it does not belong to T or F. If, for an interpretation $I = \langle T, F \rangle$, $B_P = T \cup F$, then I is called *two-valued*. A consistent three-valued interpretation I is a model of a program $\mathcal{P}$ if every rule in $\mathcal{P}$ is true in I. Following the proposal of [24], we define two operators, $\mathcal{T}(T)$ and $\mathcal{F}(F)$ which, given a program $\mathcal{P}$ and an interpretation $I = \langle T, F \rangle$, compute the true and false atoms, respectively, that can be derived from $\mathcal{P}$ knowing I. Both are monotonic [24]. The operator $\mathcal{I}(I) = I \cup \langle T, F\rangle$ is also monotonic [24] and its least fix point is considered as the well-founded model of $\mathcal{P}$, $WFM(\mathcal{P})$.

Abductive Logic Programming. An *integrity constraint* is of the form $:- \ b_1, \ldots, b_m$ where each b_i is a literal. An abductive logic program is a tuple $(\mathcal{P}, \mathcal{C}, \mathcal{A})$ where $\mathcal{P}$ is a normal logic program, $\mathcal{C}$ is a set of integrity constraints, and A is a set of ground atoms (called *abducibles*) that do not appear in the head of rules of $\mathcal{P}$. Given an abductive logic program $(\mathcal{P}, \mathcal{C}, \mathcal{A})$ and a query q (i.e., a conjunction of ground atoms) a subset $\Delta \subseteq \mathcal{A}$ is called *abductive explanation* if $\mathcal{P} \cup \Delta \models q$ and, $\forall c \in \mathcal{C}, \mathcal{P} \cup \Delta \not\models c$. Moreover, for each $\Delta \subseteq \mathcal{A}$, we require $\mathcal{P} \cup \Delta$ to have a two-valued well-founded model [31]. An abductive logic program may have more than one abductive explanation. In this case, different criteria impose a preference [12]. Among them, we find subset minimality, cardinality minimality, and penalization minimality (assuming that each abducible is associated with a cost).

Probabilistic Logic Programming. Uncertain data can be handled with Probabilistic Logic Programming [25]. A probabilistic fact [10] is of the form $\pi :: p$ where $\pi \in [0, 1]$ and p is an atom. A probabilistic logic program is a tuple $(\mathcal{P}, \mathcal{F})$ where $\mathcal{P}$ is a normal logic program and $\mathcal{F}$ is a set of probabilistic facts. We consider here the Distribution Semantics (DS) [26]. We use the acronym PLP to denote both Probabilistic Logic Programming under the Distribution Semantics and a program is such a language. The context will clarify the meaning. A selection is a subset of atoms of probabilistic facts and induces a *world*, i.e., a normal logic program obtained by including in $\mathcal{P}$ each atom p_i of the corresponding selection. Each world is required to have a two-valued well-founded model. A world w is associated with a probability $\mathrm{P}(w)$ computed as

$$\mathrm{P}(w) = \prod_{p_i \in w} \pi_i \prod_{p_i \notin w} (1 - \pi_i) \tag{1}$$

since probabilistic facts are considered independent. The probability of a ground atom q called the *query* is computed as

$$\mathrm{P}(q) = \sum_{w_i \models q} \mathrm{P}(w_i). \tag{2}$$

That is, a world contributes to the probability of the query if the query is true in it. The probabilities of all worlds sum up to 1. To clarify, consider the following example.

Example 1. This program has 3 probabilistic facts.

```
0.1::a.
0.3::b.
0.4::c.
q :- a.
q :- b,c.
```

Suppose that we are interested in computing the probability of q. We have $2^3 = 8$ worlds to consider. For example, the world where a is included and b and c are not included has probability $0.1 \cdot (1 - 0.3) \cdot (1 - 0.4) = 0.042$. Overall, we obtain $\mathrm{P}(q) = 0.208$.

The Maximum-a-Posteriori (MAP) task [5,28] in PLP is defined as follows: a MAP program is a tuple $(\mathcal{P}, \mathcal{F}, \mathcal{V})$ where $\mathcal{P}$ is a normal logic program, $\mathcal{F}$ is a set of probabilistic facts, and $\mathcal{V}$ is a set of query random variables (which we also call MAP facts), each associated with a probability. Practically, these have the same syntax as probabilistic facts (i.e., $\pi :: p$). Given a query q (which is often called evidence), the goal is to solve

$$\mathrm{MAP}(\mathcal{V} \mid q) = \arg\max_{X \subseteq \mathcal{V}} \mathrm{P}(X \mid q). \tag{3}$$

The result Eq. 3 is called the MAP state and we denote the probability of q in such a state with $\mathrm{P}^{\mathrm{MAP}}(q)$. If $\mathrm{P}(q) = 0$, we assume that $\mathrm{MAP}(\mathcal{V} \mid q) = \emptyset$ and $\mathrm{P}^{\mathrm{MAP}}(q) = 0$.

Example 2. Let us extend Example 1, where the functor *map* denotes MAP facts.

```
map 0.2::d.
0.1::a.
0.3::b.
0.4::c.
q:- a,d.
q:- b,c,d.
```

Here, $\mathcal{V} = \{d\}$ (Eq. (3)). For the query q, we have $\mathrm{MAP}(\mathcal{V} \mid q) = \{\{d\}\}$ and $\mathrm{P}^{\mathrm{MAP}}(q) = 0.0416$.

Computational Complexity. In this paper, we consider standard complexity classes [1] such as NP, #P, and PP [15], i.e., the class of decision problems that can be solved with a probabilistic Turing machine. We use the polynomial hierarchy [33], where $\Pi_0^{\mathsf{P}} = \Sigma_0^{\mathsf{P}} = \mathsf{P}$, $\Sigma_{i+1}^{\mathsf{P}} = \mathsf{NP}^{\Sigma_i^P}$, $\Pi_{i+1}^{\mathsf{P}} = \mathsf{coNP}^{\Pi_i^P}$, with $i > 0$, such that D^{O} is the class D of decision problems, solvable with an oracle of an O-complete problem.

2.1 Probabilistic Abductive Logic Programs

The authors of [2] introduced the class of *probabilistic abductive logic programs* (PALPs). In brief, a PALP is a PLP extended with a set of *abducible* facts, denoted with the functor *abducible*, and a (possibly empty) set of *probabilistic* integrity constraints. A probabilistic integrity constraint is an integrity constraint associated with a probability having the form $\pi :- b_1, \ldots, b_n$, where the probability can be considered as the strength of the constraint. Note that a probabilistic integrity constraint $\pi :- ic$ can be rewritten as a (deterministic) integrity constraint by adding an additional fresh probabilistic fact p_i not appearing elsewhere in the program in the body. That is, $\pi :- ic$ can be rewritten as $:- ic, p_i$ with $\pi :: p_i$. So, in the following definitions, we only consider deterministic integrity constraints.

Definition 1. *A* probabilistic abductive logic program (PALP) *is a tuple* $(\mathcal{P}, \mathcal{F}, \mathcal{C}, \mathcal{A})$ *where* $\mathcal{P}$ *is a normal logic program,* $\mathcal{F}$ *is a set of probabilistic facts (the tuple* $(\mathcal{P}, \mathcal{F})$ *is a PLP),* $\mathcal{A}$ *is a set of abducibles that do not appear in the head of rules, and* $\mathcal{C}$ *is a possibly empty set of integrity constraints.*

Consider a PALP $(\mathcal{P}, \mathcal{F}, \mathcal{C}, \mathcal{A})$ and a query q. The joint probability of the query and the constraints given a set of atoms $\Delta \subseteq \mathcal{A}$, $\mathrm{P}(q, \mathcal{C} \mid \Delta)$, is the sum of the probabilities of the worlds where all constraints are satisfied and Δ is an abductive explanation for q. Starting from a probabilistic abductive logic program, if we fix the truth value of the probabilistic facts, we obtain an abductive logic program (since the abducibles are still to be decided). Then, if we also decide the values for the abducibles, we obtain a logic program. If we denote with $\mathcal{P}_w^{\Delta}$ the logic program obtained fixing in $\mathcal{P}$ the atoms of the probabilistic facts considered in a world w and including the abducibles in Δ and with $\mathcal{C}_w$ the set of integrity constraints considered in w, we have

$$\mathrm{P}(q, \mathcal{C} \mid \Delta) = \sum_{w \mid \mathcal{P}_w^{\Delta} \models q \wedge \mathcal{P}_w^{\Delta} \not\models \mathcal{C}_w} \mathrm{P}(w). \tag{4}$$

Note that integrity constraints do not eliminate worlds but only make the query false in them.

We can also remove the dependency on the integrity constraints from Eq. (4), in this way. For each integrity constraint c_i of the form $:-\ b_{i1}, \ldots, b_{im}$ we add a rule $ev_i :-\ b_{i1}, \ldots, b_{im}$. Then, for a query q, we add a rule $q^c :-\ q \wedge \bigwedge_i not\ ev_i$, and consider q^c as the query. That is,

$$\mathrm{P}(q, \mathcal{C} \mid \Delta) = \mathrm{P}(q^c \mid \Delta).$$

From now on, we consider q^c as target query and remove the superscript c, to lighten the notation.

Let us define the optimal set of explanations Δ^* as the set of set of abducibles producing the highest probability for the query, i.e.,

$$\Delta^*(q) = \operatorname*{arg\,max}_{\Delta \subseteq \mathcal{A}} \mathrm{P}(q \mid \Delta). \tag{5}$$

That is, each $\Delta \in \Delta^*(q)$ gives the highest possible probability for the query (recall that arg max returns a set of sets).

Definition 2. *Given a PALP* $(\mathcal{P}, \mathcal{F}, \mathcal{C}, \mathcal{A})$ *and a query* q*, the probabilistic abductive logic problem (PABD) requires finding the minimal set of abducibles according to the criterion* c*, called* probabilistic abductive explanation *such that the probability of* q *is maximized. We denote this as*

$$PABD_c(q) = \phi_c(\Delta^*(q)) \tag{6}$$

where ϕ_c *returns the minimal set of explanations according to the optimality criterion* c*. We use* $\mathrm{P}^{abd_c}(q)$ *to denote the probability of the query when considering the abductive explanation under the optimality criterion* c*.*

That is, Eq. (5) represents the sets of explanations associated with the highest probability of the query and Eq. (6) computes the *abductive* explanations, i.e., those that are minimal according to the selected criterion. In other words, *first*, we need to find the explanations that result in the highest probability of the query. Then, if there are many of such sets, ties are broken, and only the minimal ones are considered, representing the probabilistic abductive explanation. As for MAP, in the corner case of $\mathrm{P}^{abd_c}(q) = 0$, we assume that $\Delta^*(q) = \emptyset$.

The authors of [2] only considered minimality in terms of set inclusion, but other criteria exist in the literature, as proposed by [12]:

- $\phi_{\subseteq}(\Delta^*(q)) = \{\Delta \in \Delta^*(q) \mid \nexists \Delta' \in \Delta^*(q), \Delta' \subset \Delta\}$, i.e., subset minimality;
- $\phi_{\leq}(\Delta^*(q)) = \{\Delta \in \Delta^*(q) \mid \nexists \Delta' \in \Delta^*(q), |\Delta'| < |\Delta|\}$, i.e., cardinality minimality;
- $\phi_{\sqsubseteq}(\Delta^*(q)) = \{\Delta \in \Delta^*(q) \mid \nexists \Delta' \in \Delta^*(q), cost(\Delta') < cost(\Delta)\}$, i.e., penalization minimality, where $cost$ is a function returning the cost of a set of abducibles.

In the case of $\phi_{\sqsubseteq}(\Delta^*(q))$, we consider, for example, that each abducible a_i is associated with a cost c_i and as a cost of a set of abducibles the sum of the costs of the selected abducibles. This can also be combined with subset minimality or cardinality minimality to further break ties, but we do not consider it here. Let us now show how these three criteria differ with a small propositional example.

Example 3. Consider the following PALP.

```
abducible aa.
abducible bb.
abducible cc.
0.12::a. 0.3::b. 0.4::c.
q:- a, aa.
q:- b, bb, c, cc.
:- aa, bb, cc.
```

The integrity constraint $:-\ aa, bb, cc$ can be replaced by a rule $ev :-\ aa, bb, cc$, add a rule $qr :-\ q, not\ ev$, and we can ask for the probabilistic abductive explanation for qr. We have $2^3 = 8$ possible sets of abducibles, $\{\{\}, \{aa\}, \{aa, bb\}, \{aa, cc\}, \{bb\}, \{bb, cc\}, \{cc\}, \{aa, bb, cc\}\}$, each identifying a PLP that has 8 worlds, listed in Table 1. From Eq. (5), $\Delta^*(q) = \{\{aa\}, \{aa, bb\}, \{aa, cc\}, \{bb, cc\}\}$, since for all sets $\Delta \in \Delta^*(q)$, $\mathrm{P}(q \mid \Delta) = 0.12$. If we consider cardinality as the minimality criterion, we have $\phi_{\leq}(\Delta^*(q)) = \{\{aa\}\}$. However, $\phi_{\subseteq}(\Delta^*(q)) = \{\{aa\}, \{bb, cc\}\}$. If the abducibles are associated with a cost, say $cost(aa) = 1$, $cost(bb) = 2$, and $cost(cc) = 1$, and $cost(\Delta) = \sum_{a \in \Delta} cost(a)$, $\phi_{\sqsubseteq}(\Delta^*(q)) = \{\{aa\}\}$ with a cost of 1.

Example 4. Consider a medical domain where some symptoms are related to some diseases with a certain probability. Suppose a patient wants to know the most likely disease given that they observe some symptoms. The following PALP models the described scenario.

Table 1. Worlds and probabilities for Example 3.

w_{id}	a	b	c	$P(w)$
0	F	F	F	$(1-0.12)\cdot(1-0.3)\cdot(1-0.4)=0.3696$
1	F	F	T	$(1-0.12)\cdot(1-0.3)\cdot 0.4=0.2464$
2	F	T	F	$(1-0.12)\cdot 0.3\cdot(1-0.4)=0.1584$
3	F	T	T	$(1-0.12)\cdot 0.3\cdot 0.4=0.1056$
4	T	F	F	$0.12\cdot(1-0.3)\cdot(1-0.4)=0.0504$
5	T	F	T	$0.12\cdot(1-0.3)\cdot 0.4=0.0336$
6	T	T	F	$0.12\cdot 0.3\cdot(1-0.4)=0.0216$
7	T	T	T	$0.12\cdot 0.3\cdot 0.4=0.0144$

```
abducible disease(sore_throat).
abducible disease(swollen_lymph_nodes).
abducible disease(lack_of_sleep).
0.75::causes(sore_throat,cough).
0.35::causes(sore_throat,fever).
0.85::causes(swollen_lymph_nodes,cough).
0.40::causes(swollen_lymph_nodes,fever).
0.20::causes(lack_of_sleep,cough).
0.80::causes(lack_of_sleep,fever).
0.1:- disease(sore_throat), disease(swollen_lymph_nodes).
0.4:- disease(sore_throat), disease(lack_of_sleep).
0.4:- disease(swollen_lymph_nodes), disease(lack_of_sleep).
symptom(X):- causes(M,X), disease(M).
```

The probabilistic facts $causes(D, S)$ state that the disease D is related with S with a certain probability. For example, the first probabilistic fact states that a sore throat ($sore\_throat$) is related to cough ($cough$) with probability 0.75. Then, three probabilistic integrity constraints state that some combinations are unlikely to be observed together, while other combinations are more common. Lastly, the rule states that a symptom X is present if there is a disease M that causes it. If we ask for the probabilistic abductive explanations (considering the set inclusion as minimality criterion) for $symptom(fever)$, we get $disease(lack\_of\_sleep)$ with probability 0.80. However, if we ask for $symptom(fever)$ and $symptom(cough)$, we get $disease(sore\_throat)$ and $disease(swollen\_lymph\_nodes)$ with probability 0.5284125.

If $\Delta^*(q)$ computed with Eq. (5) has cardinality 1, the three minimality criteria return the same solution (recall again that the first goal is to obtain the *highest* possible value for the probability of the query, the optimality criterion imposes preferences on the set of atoms).

3 Relating MAP and Probabilistic Abduction

The definition of abduction of Eq. (6) and the definition of the MAP task of Eq. (3) are similar, as both involve $\arg\max$. However, there are some differences: MAP facts are associated with a probability, while in abduction, abducibles do not have a probability value attached, and the set obtained with $\arg\max$ in MAP is not subject to further minimality checks, as happens for abduction. We also note that the definitions appearing in the literature of MAP for PLP [5, 19, 22] consider only *one* state, ignoring the possibility of having multiple states. Thus, they consider $\arg\max$ as returning only one set. This, however, leaves ambiguity on how such a state should be selected in case there are multiple ones, and it is also reflected on practical solvers.

Observation 1 *Existing MAP solvers treat* $\arg\max$ *as returning only one element, which leaves ambiguity.*

Justification 1 *To confirm Observation 1, we tested the program* $\mathcal{T} = \{map\ 0.5 :: m0., map\ 0.5 :: m1., 0.2 :: a.\ q :- a, m0, not\ m1.,\ q :- a, not\ m0, m1.\}$ *on two existing solvers: aspmc*[1] *(commit* `4482d67`*) [19] and cplint*[2] *(commit* `80448e1`*) [5]. According to Eq. 3, two sets give the highest probability (0.05):* $S_0 = \{m0\}$ *and* $S_1 = \{m1\}$*. Both solvers return only* S_1*. However, if we rewrite the first rule with* q *in the head as* $q :- a, not\ m1, m0$ *(so swapping the order of the last two literals in the body), both return* S_0*. We also tested ProbLog*[3] *(version 2.2.9 commit* `d5cece5`*) but we obtained a wrong result where none of the MAP facts is selected (but still only one state is considered).*

Thus, considering only one solution is not ideal as the result may depend on the order of literals and rules. So, in the following, we assume, if not explicitly stated, that MAP returns *all* the sets of MAP fact associated to the highest probability. In light of this, it is natural to investigate the relationship between MAP and abduction and check whether one task can be related to the other. Here, we provide two encodings showing that MAP programs and PALPs are equivalent for the computation of the probability of the query. This leads to the conclusion that the probabilistic abductive logic problem is equivalent to the MAP problem plus a minimality check.

Theorem 1. *Let* $(\mathcal{P}, \mathcal{F}, \mathcal{V})$ *be a MAP program and* q *be a query. Then, it is possible to construct a PALP* $(\mathcal{P}, \mathcal{F}', \mathcal{C}, \mathcal{A})$ *such that* $\mathrm{P}^{abd_c}(q) = \mathrm{P}^{\mathrm{MAP}}(q)$*, for every minimality criterion* c*.*

Proof. Build the set of abducibles as $\mathcal{A} = \{m_i \mid \pi_i :: m_i \in \mathcal{V}\}$. Build the set of probabilistic facts as $\mathcal{F}' = \mathcal{F} \cup \{\pi_i :: f_{m_i} \mid \pi_i :: m_i \in \mathcal{V}\}$. Build the set integrity constraints as $\mathcal{C} = \{ :- m_i, not\ f_{mi}.,\ :- not\ m_i, f_{mi}. \mid \pi_i :: m_i \in \mathcal{V}\}$. Each abducible duplicates the number of worlds (i.e., those with the abducible true and those with the abducible false). To correctly simulate a MAP fact $\pi_i :: m_i$, the integrity constraints ensure that the abducible m_i and its corresponding probabilistic fact f_{mi} have the same

[1] https://github.com/raki123/aspmc.

[2] https://github.com/friguzzi/cplint.

[3] https://github.com/ML-KULeuven/problog.

sign (both true of both false). In this way, we are left with the same worlds as the initial MAP program. The proof is completed by noting that $\arg\max_{X\subseteq\mathcal{V}} \mathrm{P}(X \mid q) = \arg\max_{X\subseteq\mathcal{V}} \mathrm{P}(X, q)$ and $\arg\max_{\Delta\subseteq\mathcal{A}} P(q \mid \Delta) = \arg\max_{\Delta\subseteq\mathcal{A}} \mathrm{P}(q, \Delta)$.

```
map 0.2::d.
0.1::a. 0.3::b.
0.4::c.
q:-a,d.
q:-b,c,d.
```

```
abducible d.
0.2::fd.
q:-a,d.
q:-b,c,d.
:- d, not fd.
:- not d, fd.
```

Fig. 1. MAP program (left) and its corresponding PALP version (right). Highlighted elements on the right represent the results of transforming the MAP fact of the left listing.

Example 5. The program of Example 2 (Fig. 1 left), is converted into the PALP of Fig. 1 right. Here, $\mathrm{P}^{abd_c}(q1) = 0.0416$, which is the same results obtained in Example 2.

Theorem 2. *Let $(\mathcal{P}, \mathcal{F}, \mathcal{C}, \mathcal{A})$ be a PALP and q be a query. Then, it is possible to construct a MAP program $(\mathcal{P}, \mathcal{F}, \mathcal{V})$ such that $\mathrm{P}^{\mathrm{MAP}}(q')/0.5^{|\mathcal{A}|} = \mathrm{P}^{abd_c}(q)$, for every minimality criterion c.*

Proof. Construct a MAP program comprising of all the rules of the abductive program, all the probabilistic facts, and a MAP fact $0.5 :: a_i$ for each abducible a_i. Since the probability of a_i of being true or false is the same (0.5), we can rewrite the probability of a world w as $\mathrm{P}(w) = 0.5^n \cdot \prod_{p_i\in w} \pi_i \cdot \prod_{p_i\notin w}(1-\pi_i)$, where the products range over the probabilistic facts and $n = |\mathcal{A}|$. Thus, $\mathrm{P}(X, q) = 0.5^n \cdot \sum_{w\models X,q} \mathrm{P}(w)$, which, divided by 0.5^n, coincides with $\mathrm{P}(q, \Delta)$ where $\Delta = X$. So, the probability of the query associated with the probabilistic abductive explanation can be computed from the probability of the MAP state.

Example 6. Consider the following PALP

```
abducible a.
abducible b.
0.2::fa.
0.3::fb.
q :- a, fa.
q :- b, fb.
```

We have $\mathrm{P}^{abd_c}(q) = 0.44$. If we apply the conversion of Theorem 2, we obtain

```
map 0.5::a.
map 0.5::b.
0.2::fa.
0.3::fb.
q :- a, fa.
q :- b, fb.
```

$\mathrm{P}^{\mathrm{MAP}}(q) = 0.11$. $\mathrm{P}^{\mathrm{MAP}}(q)/0.5^2 = 0.44 = \mathrm{P}^{abd_c}(q)$.

Theorem 1 and 2 only relate the probability of the query in the two tasks and do not consider the atoms appearing in the MAP and in the probabilistic abductive explanation. If there is only one such a set of atoms (either for MAP or abduction), then the conversions also preserve these (modulo renaming). If we consider abduction and then generate a MAP program by applying Theorem 2, if there are multiple sets of abducibles in the probabilistic abductive explanation, the MAP state will be a superset of it, as no minimality is imposed. Conversely, if we apply Theorem 1, we obtain a subset. Note that the two sets may coincide, depending on the optimality criterion selected. For instance, if cost minimality is selected (with no further minimality criteria) and all abducibles have cost 0, the two coincide.

Example 7. Consider the MAP program

```
map 0.5::m0.
map 0.5::m1.
0.2::a.
q :- m0, m1, a.
q :- m0, a.
```

There are two possible MAP states: $M_0 = \{m0\}$ and $M_1 = \{m0, m1\}$. If we convert the program into a PALP, we get

```
abducible m0.
abducible m1.
0.5::fa0.
0.5::fa1.
0.2::a.
:- m0, not fa0.
:- not m0, fa0.
:- m1, not fa1.
:- not m1, fa1.
q :- m0, m1, a.
q :- m0, a.
```

$PABD_{\subseteq}(q) = \{M_0\} \subset MAP(\mathcal{V} \mid q)$ and $PABD_{\leq}(q) = \{M0\} \subset MAP(\mathcal{V} \mid q)$. Lastly, if $cost(m0) \geq 0$ and $cost(m1) = 0$ then $PABD_{\sqsubseteq}(q) = \{M_0, M_1\}$, otherwise $PABD_{\sqsubseteq}(q) = \{M_0\}$.

4 The Complexity of PLP Abduction

To study the complexity of abduction in PLP, we consider a couple of decision problems. One source of complexity is the non-deterministic guess required for verifying abductive explanations. A second source is required to compute the probabilities.

Theorem 3 (Explanation Verification is Hard). *Given a rational γ, checking whether a given abduction candidate Δ is indeed an abductive explanation where a given query q holds with probability $< \gamma$, is $\mathsf{coNP}^{\mathsf{PP}}$-complete for minimality criterion $c \in \{\leq, \subseteq\}$.*

Proof. Membership: First, we compute $\gamma' = \Sigma_{w|w\models q} \mathrm{P}(w \mid \Delta)$ and verify whether $\gamma' < \gamma$, which works in $\#\mathsf{P}$ and therefore in P^{PP}, as $\#\mathsf{P} \subseteq \mathsf{P}^{\#\mathsf{P}} = \mathsf{P}^{\mathsf{PP}}$ [1]. To verify whether Δ is indeed an abductive explanation, we guess any candidate set $\Delta' \neq \Delta$ (in NP) and then check that $\Sigma_{w|w\models q} \mathrm{P}(w \mid \Delta) > \gamma'$ (in PP). If we cannot find such a Δ', we return a positive answer (and reject otherwise). Therefore, this procedure works in $\mathsf{coNP}^{\mathsf{PP}}$. For verifying c-minimality, we can afford to guess any c-smaller candidate Δ' (in NP) such that $\Sigma_{w|w\models q} \mathrm{P}(w \mid \Delta') < \gamma'$ (in PP). So, we obtain an algorithm contained in $\mathsf{coNP}^{\mathsf{PP}}$.

Hardness: We reduce from $\forall X.\exists_{\geq p} Y.\varphi(X,Y)$ in 3CNF with $p > 0$, $n = |X|$, $n' = |Y|$, $m = |\varphi|$, and abductive explanations will be assignments over X. Since $\mathsf{PP} = \mathsf{coPP}$, we actually reduce from $\forall X.\exists_{<2^{n'}-p} Y.not\ \varphi(X,Y)$. We also add a special abducible s, which will be used to switch off satisfiability check if X is the explanation:

```
abducible x₁. ... abducible xₙ. abducible s.
```

We add probabilistic facts for variables in Y, as well as a special y variable for s, which will be above the possible minimum of $\frac{2^{n'}-p}{2^{n'}}$, so we take some $0 < \epsilon < 1$ and define:

```
0.5::y₁. ... 0.5::yₙ'.    (2^n' - p - ε)/2^n' ::y.
```

For every 3CNF term t of the form $\circ_1 x_{i_1} \vee \circ_2 x_{i_2} \vee \circ_3 x_{i_3}$ with sign $\circ_j$ of x_{i_j} and every $z \in X$, we construct:

```
sat_t :- ∘₁x_i₁.   sat_t :- ∘₂x_i₂.   sat_t :- ∘₃x_i₃.
usat :- not sat_t₁, ..., not sat_tm.
```

We obtain $usat$ also if we pick the special abducible s.

```
usat :- s. :- s, not x₁. ... :- s, not xₙ.
:- s, not y. :- not s, y.
```

The set $X \cup \{s\}$ of abducibles is c-minimal if we do not find a smaller candidate that has at most $2^{n'} - p - 1$ dissatisfying assignments. Consequently, $\Delta = \{x_1, \ldots, x_n, s\}$ is the c-smallest abducible explanation such that $P(q \mid \Delta) < \gamma$ with $\gamma = \frac{2^{n'}-p}{2^{n'}}$ and $q{=}usat$ iff $\forall X.\exists_{<2^{n'}-p} Y.\varphi(X,Y)$.

Guessing a candidate results in an additional source, which then results in reaching beyond the third level of the polynomial hierarchy. Note, however, that for this increased complexity we need to ask some property of the smallest abductive explanation Δ. For hardness, we ask whether some abducible s is contained in Δ, as abductive explanation existence immediately implies that there exists a smallest one.

Theorem 4 (Finding Smallest Explanations Is Harder). *Existence of a c-smallest abductive explanation Δ containing an abducible s such that $\mathrm{P}(q \mid \Delta) < \gamma$ for some query q and rational γ is $\Sigma_2^{\mathsf{P}^{\mathsf{PP}}}$-complete.*

Proof. Membership: First, we guess a set Δ of explanations with $a \in \Delta$, which works in NP. Then, we verify Δ, which is in coNP^{PP} by Theorem 3. Thus, the complexity lies in $\Sigma_2^{\text{P}^{\text{PP}}}$.

Hardness: We can adapt the hardness proof of Theorem 3, where below we just describe the additional rules we add. We reduce from $\exists Z.\forall X.\exists_{\geq p} Y.\varphi(Z, X, Y)$ with φ being in 3CNF and $n = |X|$, $n' = |Y|$, $n'' = |Z|$, $m = |\varphi|$ where we add abducibles over Z:

```
abducible z_1. ... abducible z_n''.
```

To ensure we do not minimize over Z, we also place copies of variables in Z as abducibles that correspond to false states.

```
abducible \overline{z_1}. ... abducible \overline{z_n''}.
```

We require for every z_i that either it is set to true or to false:

```
:- \overline{z_i}, z_i.        :- not \overline{z_i}, not z_i.
```

The remaining rules are exactly as in Theorem 3. Thus, there is a c-smallest abducible explanation Δ with $\mathrm{P}(usat \mid \Delta) < \frac{2^{n'} - p}{2^{n'}}$ such that Δ contains s iff $\exists Z.\forall X.\exists_{\geq p} Y.\varphi(Z.X, Y)$ holds. Note that for a set Δ to witness a positive instance, it is required that $\Delta \supseteq Y \cup \{s\}$.

Our complexity study proves that PALP is harder than MAP (which is NP^{PP} [22]), mainly due to the optimality criterion imposed.

5 Related Work

Our study is based on the definition of abduction in Probabilistic Logic Programming of [2], where the authors introduced the task and proposed a practical algorithm to solve it. Our work is complementary, since we better inspect the similarities with the MAP task and also provide computational complexity results. MAP was recently studied in the context of Logical Credal Networks by [21]. They call MAP an abductive task. Differently from them, we consider MAP and abduction as two different tasks, even if they are tightly related. Furthermore, credal networks are a different type of formalism from the one we adopted in this paper. The authors of [30] proposed a probabilistic logic programming framework based on prior distributions on variables, together with practical algorithms to solve the task. The abductive framework considered here is different. In addition, the work described in [12] investigated the complexity of abduction in (deterministic) Logic Programming, thus not considering probabilities.

There are several probabilistic logic languages under the DS, such as ProbLog [10], LPAD [32], and PRISM [26], which are all equivalent in terms of expressivity [25]. In particular, the ProbLog framework [11] considers MAP but does not account for abduction. The same applies to the other two. Probabilistic Answer Set Programming under the Credal Semantics (PASP) [9] is a formalism related to PLP and extends it by considering the stable model semantics [14], thus allowing multiple stable models per world.

The complexity of many tasks in PLP and PASP is well known [22] but the complexity of abduction, as we consider in this paper, has never been studied. Abduction is also related to decision theory [7].

The authors of [6] introduced the IFF^{prob} semantics, which extends the IFF operational semantics [13] to abductive logic programs extended with probabilistic integrity constraints. Differently from this paper, they do not discuss the computational complexity of the task or the similarities with MAP. The proposal of [23] integrates the abduction task within Bayesian networks, considering a restricted type of integrity constraints, but no discussion of the complexity of the task is given. Similar differences, in addition to targeting different semantics, also apply to [8] and [29].

6 Conclusions

In this paper, we start from the proposal discussed in [2], where the authors introduced the probabilistic abductive logic framework (PALP), and compare it against MAP as defined in [5]. Here, i) we discuss that when multiple states are associated with the optimal probability for MAP, all these should be considered; ii) we show that PALP and MAP are tightly connected, by proposing encodings to convert one task into the other; and iii) we provide a complexity study of PALP. Overall, this work provides a clear overview of PALP and precisely positions it in the Statistical Relational Artificial Intelligence (StarAI) landscape.

There are many directions for future work. A natural extension is to propose an algebraic model counting [20] representation for abduction, as this already exist for many other tasks in StarAI [3,4,19]. Then, given the high computation complexity of the task, developing approximate algorithms is of interest. However, here there are different options consisting in approximating the probability, the optimality of the states, or both. Another work consists in investigating the relationship between abduction and MAP under different semantics, and under different languages, such as Probabilistic Answer Set Programming [9].

Acknowledgments. Markus Hecher has been supported by the French National Research Agency (ANR), grant ANR-25-CE23-7647-01, and the Austrian Science Fund (FWF), grant 10.55776/J4656. Damiano Azzolini is a member of the Gruppo Nazionale Calcolo Scientifico – Istituto Nazionale di Alta Matematica (GNCS-INdAM).

Disclosure of Interests. The authors have no competing interests to declare that are relevant to the content of this article.

References

1. Arora, S., Barak, B.: Computational Complexity: A Modern Approach. Cambridge University Press, Cambridge (2009)
2. Azzolini, D., Bellodi, E., Ferilli, S., Riguzzi, F., Zese, R.: Abduction with probabilistic logic programming under the distribution semantics. Int. J. Approximate Reasoning **142**, 41–63 (2022). https://doi.org/10.1016/j.ijar.2021.11.003

3. Azzolini, D., Bellodi, E., Kiesel, R., Riguzzi, F.: Solving decision theory problems with probabilistic answer set programming. Theory Pract. Logic Program. **25**(1), 33–63 (2025). https://doi.org/10.1017/S1471068424000474
4. Azzolini, D., Riguzzi, F.: Inference in probabilistic answer set programs with imprecise probabilities via optimization. In: Kiyavash, N., Mooij, J.M. (eds.) Proceedings of the Fortieth Conference on Uncertainty in Artificial Intelligence. Proceedings of Machine Learning Research, vol. 244, pp. 225–234. PMLR (2024)
5. Bellodi, E., Alberti, M., Riguzzi, F., Zese, R.: MAP inference for probabilistic logic programming. Theory Pract. Logic Program. **20**(5), 641–655 (2020). https://doi.org/10.1017/S1471068420000174
6. Bellodi, E., Gavanelli, M., Zese, R., Lamma, E., Riguzzi, F.: Nonground abductive logic programming with probabilistic integrity constraints. Theory Pract. Logic Program. **21**(5), 557–574 (2021). https://doi.org/10.1017/S1471068421000417
7. Van den Broeck, G., Thon, I., van Otterlo, M., De Raedt, L.: DTPROBLOG: a decision-theoretic probabilistic Prolog. In: Fox, M., Poole, D. (eds.) AAAI 2010 (2010)
8. Christiansen, H.: Implementing probabilistic abductive logic programming with constraint handling rules. In: Schrijvers, T., Frühwirth, T. (eds.) Constraint Handling Rules. LNCS (LNAI), vol. 5388, pp. 85–118. Springer, Heidelberg (2008). https://doi.org/10.1007/978-3-540-92243-8_5
9. Cozman, F.G., Mauá, D.D.: The joy of probabilistic answer set programming: semantics, complexity, expressivity, inference. Int. J. Approximate Reasoning **125**, 218–239 (2020). https://doi.org/10.1016/j.ijar.2020.07.004
10. De Raedt, L., Kimmig, A., Toivonen, H.: ProbLog: a probabilistic Prolog and its application in link discovery. In: Veloso, M.M. (ed.) IJCAI 2007 (2007)
11. Dries, A., et al.: ProbLog2: probabilistic logic programming. In: Bifet, A., et al. (eds.) ECML PKDD 2015. LNCS (LNAI), vol. 9286, pp. 312–315. Springer, Cham (2015). https://doi.org/10.1007/978-3-319-23461-8_37
12. Eiter, T., Gottlob, G.: The complexity of logic-based abduction. J. ACM **42**(1), 3–42 (1995). https://doi.org/10.1145/200836.200838
13. Fung, T.H., Kowalski, R.: The IFF proof procedure for abductive logic programming. J. Logic Program. **33**(2), 151–165 (1997). https://doi.org/10.1016/S0743-1066(97)00026-5
14. Gelfond, M., Lifschitz, V.: The stable model semantics for logic programming. In: ICLP/SLP 1988, vol. 88, pp. 1070–1080. MIT Press (1988)
15. Gill, I., J.T.: Computational complexity of probabilistic turing machines. In: Proceedings of the Sixth Annual ACM Symposium on Theory of Computing, pp. 91–95 (1974)
16. Hu, W.C., Dai, W.Z., Jiang, Y., Zhou, Z.H.: Efficient rectification of neuro-symbolic reasoning inconsistencies by abductive reflection. In: AAAI (2025)
17. Ignatiev, A., Narodytska, N., Marques-Silva, J.: Abduction-based explanations for machine learning models. In: AAAI 2019, vol. 33, pp. 1511–1519 (2019)
18. Karlsen, B., Hillestad, T.M., Dysvik, E.: Abductive reasoning in nursing: challenges and possibilities. Nurs. Inq. **28**(1) (2021)
19. Kiesel, R., Totis, P., Kimmig, A.: Efficient knowledge compilation beyond weighted model counting. Theory Pract. Logic Program. **22**(4), 505–522 (2022). https://doi.org/10.1017/S147106842200014X
20. Kimmig, A., Van den Broeck, G., De Raedt, L.: Algebraic model counting. J. Appl. Log. **22**(C), 46–62 (2017). https://doi.org/10.1016/j.jal.2016.11.031
21. Marinescu, R., Lee, J., Bhattacharjya, D., Cozman, F., Gray, A.: Abductive reasoning in logical credal networks. NeurIPS **37**, 67968–67986 (2024)
22. Mauá, D.D., Cozman, F.G.: Complexity results for probabilistic answer set programming. Int. J. Approximate Reasoning **118**, 133–154 (2020). https://doi.org/10.1016/j.ijar.2019.12.003

23. Poole, D.: Probabilistic horn abduction and Bayesian networks. Artif. Intell. **64**(1), 81–129 (1993). https://doi.org/10.1016/0004-3702(93)90061-F
24. Przymusinski, T.C.: Every logic program has a natural stratification and an iterated least fixed point model. In: PODS 1989, pp. 11–21. ACM Press (1989). https://doi.org/10.1145/73721.73723
25. Riguzzi, F.: Foundations of Probabilistic Logic Programming Languages, Semantics, Inference and Learning, 2nd edn. River Publishers, Gistrup, Denmark (2022)
26. Sato, T.: A statistical learning method for logic programs with distribution semantics. In: Sterling, L. (ed.) ICLP, pp. 715–729. MIT Press (1995). https://doi.org/10.7551/mitpress/4298.003.0069
27. Shi, X., et al.: Language models can improve event prediction by few-shot abductive reasoning. In: NeurIPS (2023)
28. Shterionov, D.S., Renkens, J., Vlasselaer, J., Kimmig, A., Meert, W., Janssens, G.: The most probable explanation for probabilistic logic programs with annotated disjunctions. In: ILP, pp. 139–153 (2015)
29. Simari, G., Subrahmanian, V.: Abductive inference in probabilistic logic programs. In: ICLP TC, pp. 192–201 (2010)
30. Turliuc, C., Dickens, L., Russo, A., Broda, K.: Probabilistic abductive logic programming using Dirichlet priors. Int. J. Approximate Reasoning **78**, 223–240 (2016). https://doi.org/10.1016/j.ijar.2016.07.001
31. Van Gelder, A., Ross, K.A., Schlipf, J.S.: The Well-founded semantics for general logic programs. J. ACM **38**(3), 620–650 (1991)
32. Vennekens, J., Verbaeten, S., Bruynooghe, M.: Logic programs with annotated disjunctions. In: ICLP (2004)
33. Wagner, K.W.: The complexity of combinatorial problems with succinct input representation. Acta Informatica **23**, 325–356 (1986)
34. Zhang, P., Liu, Z., Zhou, N., Liu, H.: Fault diagnosis for smart grids over knowledge graph and abductive reasoning. In: PSGEC (2024)

On the Complexity of Model Checking for Temporal Equilibrium Logic

Oscar Barreca[1(✉)], Thomas Eiter[2], and Davide Soldà[2]

[1] Center for Scalable Data Analytics and AI (ScaDS.AI) Dresden/Leipizig, Technische Universität Dresden, Dresden, Germany
oscar.barreca@tu-dresden.de

[2] Technische Universität Wien, Vienna, Austria
{thomas.eiter, davide.solda}@tuwien.ac.at

Abstract. Given an interpretation I and a formula φ written in a logic L, the problem of *model checking* (MC) for L is the problem of determining whether I is a model of φ. In this work, the computational complexity of MC for *temporal equilibrium logic* (TEL), a temporal extension of ASP, is investigated. The complexity of the *universal* and the *existential variant* of MC for TEL over Kripke structures, and of MC over linear traces, is determined. The complexity of these problems when the set of temporal operators, the *temporal height* or the *implication height* of the input formula is restricted is also determined.

Keywords: Model checking · Temporal logics · Nonmonotonic logics · Complexity analysis

1 Introduction

Given a formula φ written in a logic L and an interpretation I for φ, the problem of *model checking* (MC) for L is the problem of deciding whether I is a model of φ. The MC problem is studied in the context of temporal logics, like *linear temporal logic* (LTL) [27] or *computation tree logic* (CTL) [14], where the interpretation I is taken to be a Kripke structure, but also for other logics and formalisms, like *circumscription* [13], *answer set programming* (ASP) [16], *default logic* [23] and *SAT* [7].

Motivated by the growing interest in temporal reasoning and planning, and by the emergence of practical tools [9, 11], the present work is dedicated to the study of the computational complexity of the MC problem for *temporal equilibrium logic* (TEL) [12], a temporal and nonmonotonic logic extending the nonmonotonic, but atemporal, *equilibrium logic* (EL) [24, 25] to the temporal setting. Given that EL extends the syntax of ASP to allow the free intermixing of logical operators while preserving the *stable model semantics* [18], TEL can ultimately be seen as a temporal extension of ASP.

Contributions. This work studies the complexity of deciding the TELKS problem, the MC problem for TEL over Kripke structures. The obtained complexity results justify the division of this problem into two variants, TELKS∀, the universal variant of TELKS,

W. Faber et al. (Eds.): LPNMR 2026, LNAI 16952, pp. 67–82, 2027.
https://doi.org/10.1007/978-3-032-38320-4_5

and TELKS∃, the existential one. A restriction of TELKS over traces, TELT, is also studied.

Fragments of the TELKS∃, TELKS∀ and TELT problems are also studied by restricting the set of allowed temporal operators, the *temporal height* (the number of nested temporal operators) and the *implication height* of a formula (the number of nested $\rightarrow$ operators). For $P \in \{\text{TELKS}\exists, \text{TELKS}\forall, \text{TELT}\}$, $P^k_m(O_1, \dots, O_r)$ denotes the MC problem P where the set of allowed temporal operators is $\{O_1, \dots, O_r\}$ and where the formulas have a temporal height of value at most m and an implication height of value at most k.

A summary of the results is given by Table 1. Similarly to LTL [27], deciding TELKS∀ is PSPACE–complete. However, unlike LTL its restriction TELT over linear traces remains PSPACE–complete, instead of becoming polynomial-time tractable [15], and it remains so even under the $\text{TELT}^1_2(\bigcirc, \mathbb{R})$ fragment. On the other hand, TELKS∃ displays a strong similarity to the satisfiability problem for TEL [4], both on a complexity level, given that both problems are EXPSPACE–complete, and on a conceptual one, given that both problems ask about the existence of a model under the TEL semantics.

A detailed exposition of the same results under a slightly different notation can be found in [2].

Table 1. Contributions of the work.

Problem	Complexity
TELKS∀	PSPACE–complete (Theorem 1)
TELKS∃	EXPSPACE–complete (Theorem 4)
TELKS∀($\mathbb{R}$), TELKS∀($\bigcirc, \mathbb{R}$), TELKS∀($\mathbb{U}, \mathbb{R}$)	PSPACE–complete (Theorem 7)
TELKS∃($\mathbb{R}$), TELKS∃($\bigcirc, \mathbb{R}$), TELKS∃($\mathbb{U}, \mathbb{R}$)	EXPSPACE–complete (Theorem 9)
TELT, TELT^1_2	PSPACE–complete (Theorem 11, Corollary 2)
TELT($\bigcirc, \mathbb{R}$), $\text{TELT}^1_2(\bigcirc, \mathbb{R})$	PSPACE–complete (Theorem 13, Corollary 3)

Related Work. The complexity of the satisfiability problem for TEL has been studied by [4], while expressivity results by [5]; in particular, these two results provide a connection between TEL and ∃∀LTL [28]. Closely related to the present work, [10] discusses the complexity of satisfiability for a variant of TEL producing shorter traces by adopting a stronger notion of minimization, whereas [22] investigates MC for *quantified LTL* (QLTL). A different temporal extension of ASP, based on a notion of reduct rather than on EL, along with an analysis of its computational properties is given by [19]. Different reduct-based metric temporal extensions of ASP, including LARS [3], its weighted variant [17], and DatalogMTL [6] have been also studied.

2 Background

In this section, general notions of complexity theory and TEL are introduced. Knowledge of the *here-and-there* (HT) logic [20], of EL [24,25] and of the Kripke semantics for intuitionistic logic [21,29] is essential to understand TEL in detail, but for reasons of space no explanation of these topics is included here.

Complexity Theory. Given a language L, understood as a set of words of finite length, a *decision problem* is a subset P of L. Elements of P are called *positive instances*, whereas elements of its complement $\overline{P} \stackrel{\text{def}}{=} L \setminus P$ *negative instances*. If not specified beforehand, the *host language* L of P, consisting of both the positive and negative instances, is denoted by Σ_P.

Given two decision problems P_1 and P_2, a *Karp reduction* is a function $f : \Sigma_{P_1} \to \Sigma_{P_2}$ such that $x \in P_1$ iff $f(x) \in P_2$ and such that $f(x)$ can be computed in polynomial time with respect to the size $|x|$ of x.

TEL. On an abstract level, TEL can be seen as the union of EL and LTL. On a more concrete level, however, TEL is the union of *temporal here-and-there* (THT), a temporal extension of HT, with EL, a nonmonotonic extension of HT.

TEL shares the same syntax of THT, which in turn shares the same syntax of LTL:

Definition 1 (THT syntax). *Given a set A of atomic symbols, a formula φ is a THT formula if described by the $\varphi \stackrel{\text{def}}{=} \bot \mid p \mid \varphi \vee \varphi \mid \varphi \wedge \varphi \mid \varphi \to \varphi \mid \bigcirc\varphi \mid \varphi \mathbb{U} \varphi \mid \varphi \mathbb{R} \varphi$ grammar, where $p \in A$.*

In Definition 1, $\bigcirc$ is referred to as the *next* operator, $\mathbb{U}$ as the *until* and $\mathbb{R}$ as the *release* one. On the basis of these basic operators, a few derived ones can be also introduced: $\neg\varphi \stackrel{\text{def}}{=} \varphi \to \bot$, $\top \stackrel{\text{def}}{=} \neg\bot$, $\varphi_1 \leftrightarrow \varphi_2 \stackrel{\text{def}}{=} (\varphi_1 \to \varphi_2) \wedge (\varphi_2 \to \varphi_1)$, $\Box\varphi \stackrel{\text{def}}{=} \bot\mathbb{R}\varphi$, and $\Diamond\varphi \stackrel{\text{def}}{=} \top\mathbb{U}\varphi$. $\neg$ is the *default negation* operator, whereas $\Box$ and $\Diamond$ are the *always* and the *eventually* operators.

An interpretation for the LTL logic is a *trace* consisting of a finite or infinite sequence of atomic propositions from a countable set A. The length, or number of states, of an LTL trace T is denoted by $|T|$. If T is infinite, the length of T is denoted by ω. Given two traces T and U of equal length, $T \leq U$ if, for all i, $T_i \subseteq U_i$, and $T < U$ if $T \leq U$ and some i exists for which $T_i \subset U_i$.

Differently than for LTL, an interpretation for the THT logic is not just a single LTL trace, but a pair $M \stackrel{\text{def}}{=} (H,T)$ of LTL traces of finite or infinite length subject to the condition that $|H| = |T|$ and $H \leq T$. M is said to be a *total* THT interpretation if $H = T$, in which case M can be expressed as a single LTL trace T. The length of a THT trace M is defined as that of its constituting traces, in symbols $|M| \stackrel{\text{def}}{=} |H| = |T|$. By M_i, the pair (H_i,T_i) is meant.

Definition 2 (THT semantics). *A THT interpretation $M = (H,T)$ satisfies a THT formula φ at step i, written $M,i \models \varphi$, if it satisfies the following conditions:*

1. *$M,i \not\models \bot$;*
2. *$M,i \models a$ if $a \in H_i$;*
3. *$M,i \models \varphi_1 \vee \varphi_2$ if $M,i \models \varphi_1$ or $M,i \models \varphi_2$;*
4. *$M,i \models \varphi_1 \wedge \varphi_2$ if $M,i \models \varphi_1$ and $M,i \models \varphi_2$;*
5. *$M,i \models \varphi_1 \to \varphi_2$ if:*

   (a) $(H,T),i \models \varphi_1$ *implies* $(H,T),i \models \varphi_2$, *and*
   (b) $(T,T),i \models \varphi_1$ *implies* $(T,T),i \models \varphi_2$;
6. $M,i \models \bigcirc\varphi$ *if* $i+1 < |M|$ *and* $M,i+1 \models \varphi$;
7. $M,i \models \varphi_1 \mathbb{U} \varphi_2$ *if* $\exists j \in [i..|M|)$ *such that* $M,j \models \varphi_2$, *and* $\forall j' \in [i..j), M,j' \models \varphi_1$;
8. $M,i \models \varphi_1 \mathbb{R} \varphi_2$ *if* $\forall j \geq i, M,j \models \varphi_2$, *or* $\exists k \in [i..|M|)$ *such that* $M,k \models \varphi_1$ *and* $\forall k' \in [i..k], M,k' \models \varphi_2$.

For an LTL trace T and a THT formula φ, $T \models \varphi$ is written in place of $T,0 \models \varphi$. (Similarly for a THT trace (H,T).) Additionally, $T,i \models_{\text{LTL}} \varphi$ is written in place of $T,i \models \varphi$ to make the LTL semantics explicit. (Similarly for THT.)

The semantics of THT from Definition 2 coincides with the one of LTL, but differs from it in the interpretation of the $\to$ operator, requiring a formula of the form $\varphi_1 \to \varphi_2$ to follow the same behavior of the HT logic. Under total traces the semantics of THT and LTL do however coincide:

Proposition 1 ([1]). *Given an LTL trace T of length λ, a THT formula φ and a time point $k \in [0..\lambda)$, $T,k \models_{LTL} \varphi$ iff $(T,T),k \models_{THT} \varphi$.*

The semantics of TEL is defined on top of the one of THT by adding a minimization process, analogous to the one that EL adds to HT but extended to the temporal case:

Definition 3. *A THT interpretation M is a temporal equilibrium model (TEM) of a THT formula φ if $M = (T,T)$ is total, $M \models_{THT} \varphi$ and $\nexists H < T$ for which $(H,T) \models_{THT} \varphi$.*

Since TEMs are, by definition, required to be total traces, they are typically expressed as a single LTL trace.

TEL and MC. Although typically interpreted over linear traces, in a MC context it is appropriate to interpret TEL over Kripke structures in about the same way as it is done for LTL [27].

Definition 4. *A Kripke structure is a tuple $K = (Q, q_0, \to, A, L)$, where Q is a finite set of states, $q_0 \in Q$ is the initial state, $\to \ \subseteq Q \times Q$ is a total transition relation between states, A is a set of propositional atoms, and $L : Q \to 2^A$ is a labeling function between states and sets of propositions.*

A relation $R \subseteq S \times S$ is said to be *total* if, for every $s \in S$, $\exists s' \in S$ such that $(s,s') \in R$. As an alternative notation, $q \to q'$ is written in place of $(q,q') \in \ \to$ to mean that state q has state q' as one of its successors in the relation $\to$.

Given a Kripke structure K, a *path* π within K is either a finite sequence $\pi \stackrel{\text{def}}{=} q_0 q_1 \cdots q_n$ of states from Q such that for all $i \in [0..n)$, $q_i \to q_{i+1}$; or an infinite sequence $\pi \stackrel{\text{def}}{=} q_0 q_1 q_2 \cdots$ of states from Q such that for all $i \geq 0$, $q_i \to q_{i+1}$. A *trace* within K is a sequence T of sets of atomic propositions obtained by a path from K. In other words, if $\pi = q_0 q_1 q_2 \cdots$ is an infinite path from K, then the infinite trace T obtained from π is $T \stackrel{\text{def}}{=} L(q_0) \cdot L(q_1) \cdot L(q_2) \cdot \cdots$. (Similarly for the case of a finite path.)

The complexity results from the upcoming sections justify the introduction of two different, albeit related, semantics for the interpretation of a TEL formula over a Kripke structure. A Kripke structure K is said to be a TEM of a THT formula φ under the *universal semantics* if for all traces T in K, T is a TEM of φ. Similarly, K is said to be a TEM of φ under the *existential semantics* if there exists a trace T in K which is a TEM of φ.

3 The TELKS Problem

Given a Kripke structure K and a THT formula φ, the problem of MC for TEL, denoted TELKS, is the problem of determining whether K is a TEM of φ. As already anticipated, two distinct semantics exist for how to interpret whether K is a TEM of φ, giving rise to two distinct variants of the TELKS problem:

Definition 5 (TELKS∀). *The* universal variant *of the MC problem for TEL over Kripke structures is the language* TELKS∀ $\stackrel{\text{def}}{=} \{(K,\varphi)\}$, *where K is a Kripke structure and φ a THT formula such that all traces in K are a TEM of φ.*

Definition 6 (TELKS∃). *The* existential variant *of the MC problem for TEL over Kripke structures is the language* TELKS∃ $\stackrel{\text{def}}{=} \{(K,\varphi)\}$, *where K is a Kripke structure and φ a THT formula such that a trace in K exists which is a TEM of φ.*

No TELKS problem without the specification of the concrete variant properly exists, and the use of this term is meant only as an abbreviation or a generalization in contexts where it is not relevant to specify the concrete variant.

The TELKS∀ Problem. TELKS∀ is the first variant of the TELKS problem to be studied. For this problem, the following holds:

Theorem 1. *Deciding* TELKS∀ *is* PSPACE*–complete.*

The way the PSPACE–hardness of the TELKS∀ problem can be shown is by a Karp reduction from the corresponding LTL problem, asking whether, for a given Kripke structure K and an LTL formula φ, φ holds on all traces obtained from K. More formally, the LTLKS∀ and the LTLKS∃ problems are introduced in about the same style as the TELKS∀ and the TELKS∃ ones from Definition 5 and Definition 6, adapting the previously given definitions to the LTL semantics.

The PSPACE–hardness of the LTLKS∀ problem [27] and the fact that this problem can be reduced to the TELKS∀ one allow deducing the PSPACE–hardness of the TELKS∀ problem. The way the reduction from the LTLKS∀ problem to TELKS∀ can be obtained is by means of the following formula:

Definition 7 (Excluded middle axiom for TEL). *Given a finite alphabet A, the* excluded middle axiom *for TEL is the formula* $\varphi_{\text{EM}}(A) \stackrel{\text{def}}{=} \bigwedge_{p\in A} \Box(p \vee \neg p)$.

Proposition 2 ([8, **Proposition 1**]). *Given a THT formula φ defined over the alphabet A and a THT interpretation (H,T), $(H,T) \models_{THT} \varphi \wedge \varphi_{\text{EM}}(A)$ iff $H = T$ and $T \models_{LTL} \varphi$.*

The idea of the reduction from LTLKS∀ to TELKS∀ consists of using the $\varphi_{\text{EM}}(A)$ formula to disable the minimization process in the semantics of TEL. In particular, given an instance (K,φ) of the LTLKS∀ problem, an instance (K,φ') of the TELKS∀ problem is obtained such that $(K,\varphi) \in$ LTLKS∀ iff $(K,\varphi') \in$ TELKS∀.

Theorem 2. *Deciding* TELKS∀ *is* PSPACE*–hard.*

Before continuing to discuss the complexity of TELKS∀ and show its PSPACE membership, a number of techniques is introduced. The first of these techniques is the *star translation* [8], a transformation that allows a THT interpretation to be encoded into an LTL one. THT interpretations are represented by a pair (H,T) of LTL traces, and this translation allows to merge (H,T) into a single LTL trace M:

Definition 8. *Given a THT trace (H,T) with atoms drawn from a set $A = \{a_1, \ldots, a_n\}$, the* star translation *$(H,T)^*$ of (H,T) is the LTL trace M such that for all i, $M_i \stackrel{\text{def}}{=} \{a' \mid a \in H_i\} \cup \{a \mid a \in T_i\}$.*

Setting $X' \stackrel{\text{def}}{=} \{x' \mid x \in X\}$, M can therefore be said to be defined over the alphabet $A^* \stackrel{\text{def}}{=} A \cup A'$, in such a way that if $a' \in H_i$, then $a \in T_i$. Equivalently, M can also be said to satisfy the formula $\varphi_{\leq}(A) \stackrel{\text{def}}{=} \bigwedge_{a \in A} \Box(a' \rightarrow a)$, corresponding to the requirement that $H_i \subseteq T_i$ for a THT interpretation (H,T). Conversely, for any LTL trace M defined over a set $A \cup A'$ of symbols such that $M \models_{\text{LTL}} \varphi_{\leq}(A)$, a THT trace (H,T) can be found such that $(H,T)^* = M$. More precisely, the following holds:

Lemma 1 **([8, Lemma 1]).** *Given an LTL trace M constructed over a set of atoms $A \cup A'$ such that $M \models_{LTL} \varphi_{\leq}(A)$, a* unique *THT trace (H,T) over A exists such that $H \leq T$ and $(H,T)^* = M$.*

Other than for THT traces, the star translation is also defined for THT formulas:

Definition 9. *The* star translation *for THT formulas is a function $(\cdot)^*$ from THT formulas to THT formulas, defined by structural recursion as:*

$$\bot^* \stackrel{\text{def}}{=} \bot, \quad p^* \stackrel{\text{def}}{=} p', \quad (\varphi_1 \vee \varphi_2)^* \stackrel{\text{def}}{=} \varphi_1^* \vee \varphi_2^*, \quad (\varphi_1 \wedge \varphi_2)^* \stackrel{\text{def}}{=} \varphi_1^* \wedge \varphi_2^*,$$
$$(\varphi_1 \rightarrow \varphi_2)^* \stackrel{\text{def}}{=} (\varphi_1^* \rightarrow \varphi_2^*) \wedge (\varphi_1 \rightarrow \varphi_2), \quad (\bigcirc \varphi)^* \stackrel{\text{def}}{=} \bigcirc \varphi^*,$$
$$(\varphi_1 \mathbb{U} \varphi_2)^* \stackrel{\text{def}}{=} \varphi_1^* \mathbb{U} \varphi_2^*, \quad (\varphi_1 \mathbb{R} \varphi_2)^* \stackrel{\text{def}}{=} \varphi_1^* \mathbb{R} \varphi_2^*.$$

As an example, $(\Box(a \rightarrow b) \wedge \Diamond(\neg b))^* = \Box(a' \rightarrow b' \wedge a \rightarrow b) \wedge \Diamond(\neg b' \wedge \neg b)$.

Defining the star translation over THT traces and THT formulas allows turning THT satisfiability into LTL satisfiability:

Lemma 2 **([1, Theorem 4]).** *Let φ be a THT formula and (H,T) a THT interpretation. Then $(H,T), k \models_{THT} \varphi$ iff $(H,T)^*, k \models_{LTL} \varphi^* \wedge \varphi_{\leq}(A)$.*

This equivalence between THT and LTL traces can be brought one step further by introducing the $\varphi_{<}(A) \stackrel{\text{def}}{=} \bigvee_{a \in A} \Diamond(\neg a' \wedge a)$ formula, requiring a THT interpretation to be non total. For this formula, the following holds:

Lemma 3 **([8, Lemma 4]).** *For any LTL trace M constructed over a set of atoms $A \cup A'$ such that $M \models_{LTL} \varphi_{\leq}(A) \wedge \varphi_{<}(A)$, there exists a* unique *THT trace (H,T) over A such that $H < T$ and $(H,T)^* = M$.*

As a consequence, a restriction of Lemma 2 to non-total traces also holds:

Lemma 4. *Let (H,T) be a THT interpretation for which $H < T$. Then $(H,T),k \models_{THT} \varphi$ iff $(H,T)^*,k \models_{LTL} \varphi^* \wedge \varphi_{\leq}(A) \wedge \varphi_{<}(A)$.*

Before proving the PSPACE–membership of TELKS∀, another technique is introduced which, given a Kripke structure K, obtains an LTL formula encoding the behavior of K. More specifically, this formula encodes the states of K, constrains the way each state can be reached by the others, and enforces the set of literals holding at a state of K (and only that set of literals) to be satisfied. This technique, already described by [26, p. 13] under a different formulation, is termed *K-embedding* and is defined as follows:

Definition 10 (K-embedding). *Given a Kripke structure $K = (Q, q_0, \rightarrow, A, L)$, the* K-embedding *of K is the THT formula*

$$\varphi_K \stackrel{\text{def}}{=} q_0 \wedge \bigwedge_{q \in Q} \Box\left(q \rightarrow \bigcirc \bigvee_{q \rightarrow q'} q'\right) \wedge \bigwedge_{q \in Q} \Box\left(q \rightarrow \bigwedge_{a \in A \cap L \nabla q \partial} a \wedge \bigwedge_{a \in A \setminus L \nabla q \partial} \neg a\right)$$
$$\wedge \bigwedge_{q \in Q} \Box\left(q \rightarrow \bigwedge_{q' \in Q \setminus \{q\}} \neg q'\right).$$

Proposition 3 (Characterization of K-embeddings). *Given an LTL formula φ constructed over an alphabet A and a Kripke structure $K = (Q, q_0, \rightarrow, A, L)$, an LTL trace T within K exists such that $T \models_{LTL} \varphi$ iff $\varphi \wedge \varphi_K$ is LTL-satisfiable.*

Lemma 5. *Let φ be an LTL formula constructed over an alphabet A and $K = (Q, q_0, \rightarrow, A, L)$ a Kripke structure. Then an LTL trace T within K exists such that $(H,T) \models_{THT} \varphi$ for some $H < T$ iff $\varphi^* \wedge \varphi_{\leq}(A) \wedge \varphi_{<}(A) \wedge \varphi_K$ is LTL-satisfiable.*

Proof. If an LTL trace $T = T_0 T_1 T_2 \cdots$ within K exists such that $(H,T) \models_{\text{THT}} \varphi$ for some $H < T$, then by Lemma 4 the star-translation $M = (H,T)^*$ of (H,T) LTL-satisfies $\varphi^* \wedge \varphi_{\leq}(A) \wedge \varphi_{<}(A)$. Given that T is from K, each state of T draws its atoms from a single state of K. This makes it possible to label each state of T with an atom $r_i \in Q$, indicating which state from K a single state of T_i obtains its atoms from; however, rather than perform this labeling to T, it is performed to M, so that a new trace $M' \stackrel{\text{def}}{=} (M_0 \cup \{q_0\}) \cdot (M_1 \cup \{r_1\}) \cdot (M_2 \cup \{r_2\}) \cdots$ is obtained. M' continues to satisfy $\varphi^* \wedge \varphi_{\leq}(A) \wedge \varphi_{<}(A)$ and, additionally, also satisfies φ_K, because all of the subformulas of φ_K are satisfied. Hence $\varphi^* \wedge \varphi_{\leq}(A) \wedge \varphi_{<}(A) \wedge \varphi_K$ is LTL-satisfiable.

Conversely, if $\varphi^* \wedge \varphi_{\leq}(A) \wedge \varphi_{<}(A) \wedge \varphi_K$ is LTL-satisfiable, then an LTL trace M over the alphabet $A \cup A' \cup Q$ exists which satisfies it. Since $\varphi^* \wedge \varphi_{\leq}(A) \wedge \varphi_{<}(A)$ is defined only over the $A \cup A'$ alphabet, it continues to be satisfied by the projection M' of M over the $A \cup A'$ alphabet, defined as $M'_i \stackrel{\text{def}}{=} M_i \cap (A \cup A')$. In particular, given that M' satisfies $\varphi_{\leq}(A) \wedge \varphi_{<}(A)$, by Lemma 3 a unique THT trace (H,T) over the A alphabet exists such that $H < T$ and $(H,T)^* = M'$. Additionally, since $M', 0 \models_{\text{LTL}} \varphi^* \wedge \varphi_{\leq}(A) \wedge \varphi_{<}(A)$, by Lemma 4 $(H,T), 0 \models_{\text{THT}} \varphi$. Finally, since M satisfies φ_K, the projection M'' of M' over the A alphabet, $M''_i \stackrel{\text{def}}{=} M'_i \cap A$, is a trace from K. But M'' is T itself. Hence an LTL trace T within K such that $(H,T) \models_{\text{THT}} \varphi$ for some $H < T$ exists. □

Thanks to Lemma 5, the last major result of this section can be derived:

Theorem 3. TELKS$\forall \in$ PSPACE.

Proof. Given that PSPACE = coPSPACE, to prove TELKS$\forall \in$ PSPACE, $\overline{\text{TELKS}\forall} \in$ PSPACE is shown.

To prove whether a given $(K,\varphi) \in \Sigma_{\overline{\text{TELKS}\forall}}$ belongs to $\overline{\text{TELKS}\forall}$, an LTL trace T within K needs to be found which is not a TEM of φ. By Definition 3, an LTL trace T within K is not a TEM of φ if either (a) (T,T) is not a total THT trace; or (b) $(T,T) \not\models_{\text{THT}} \varphi$; or (c) $\exists H < T$ for which $(H,T) \models_{\text{THT}} \varphi$.

As condition (a) never holds, only condition (b) and condition (c) need to be verified.

To verify whether a trace T exists such that $(T,T) \not\models_{\text{THT}} \varphi$, a trace T such that $T \not\models_{\text{LTL}} \varphi$ is looked for. The problem of looking for such a trace can be reduced to the validity problem of a formula over a Kripke structure, that is to the problem of verifying whether $T \models_{\text{LTL}} \varphi$ for all traces T in K. If $T \not\models_{\text{LTL}} \varphi$ for some trace T in K, then (K,φ) is declared to belong to $\overline{\text{TELKS}\forall}$; conversely, if $T \models_{\text{LTL}} \varphi$ for all traces T in K, the next condition is examined. Since checking the validity of an LTL formula over a Kripke structure is in PSPACE, this type of check is also in PSPACE.

To verify whether an LTL trace T within K such that $(H,T) \models_{\text{THT}} \varphi$ for some $H < T$ exists, the formula $\psi \stackrel{\text{def}}{=} \varphi^* \wedge \varphi_{\leq}(A) \wedge \varphi_{<}(A) \wedge \varphi_K$ is constructed and checked for satisfiability. By Lemma 5, if ψ is satisfiable, then an LTL trace T in K such that $(H,T) \models_{\text{THT}} \varphi$ for some $H < T$ exists, in which case (K,φ) is declared to belong to $\overline{\text{TELKS}\forall}$. If, instead, ψ is unsatisfiable, then by contraposition of Lemma 5 no LTL trace T from K such that $(H,T) \models_{\text{THT}} \varphi$ for some $H < T$ exists, in which case (K,φ) is declared not to belong to $\overline{\text{TELKS}\forall}$. Since by [27] deciding whether an LTL formula is satisfiable is in PSPACE, this third check is also in PSPACE. □

The TELKS$\exists$ Problem. The TELKS$\exists$ problem is the second variant of the TELKS problem to be considered. Contrasting with TELKS$\forall$, the following holds for TELKS$\exists$:

Theorem 4. *Deciding* TELKS$\exists$ *is* EXPSPACE*–complete.*

The way the EXPSPACE–hardness of TELKS$\exists$ can be shown is by a reduction from the satisfiability problem TEL, already shown to be EXPSPACE–hard [4]. Specifically, given a formula $\varphi \in \Sigma_{\text{TEL}}$, a pair $(K(\varphi),\varphi')$, composed of a Kripke structure $K(\varphi)$ and a THT formula φ' is associated to it, such that φ admits a TEM iff a trace T exists in $K(\varphi)$ which is a TEM of φ'. The Kripke structure associated to φ is defined as follows:

Definition 11 (Associated Kripke structure). *Given a THT formula φ defined over an ordered alphabet $A \stackrel{\text{def}}{=} \{p_1,\ldots,p_n\}$, the* associated Kripke structure *of φ*[1] *is the Kripke structure $K(\varphi) \stackrel{\text{def}}{=} (Q,\{\alpha\},\rightarrow,A \cup \{\alpha,\beta\},L)$, where $Q \stackrel{\text{def}}{=} \{\alpha,\beta\} \cup \{p_1,\overline{p_1},\ldots,p_n,\overline{p_n}\}$ and $\rightarrow$ and L are obtained by generalizing the example of Fig. 1.*

The formula φ' associated to the initial THT formula φ is, instead, based on the following transformation:

---

[1] Although the associated Kripke structure $K(\varphi)$ of a THT formula φ is said to depend on φ, it actually only depends on the alphabet A on which φ is defined.

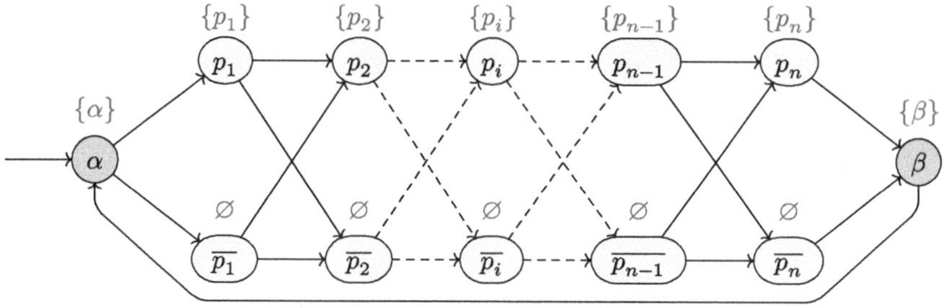

Fig. 1. The associated Kripke structure K_φ for a THT formula φ defined over an alphabet $A = \{p_1, \ldots, p_n\}$.

Definition 12 (L-transformation). *The* L-transformation *is a function from THT formulas to THT formulas, defined by structural recursion as:*

$$\bot^L \stackrel{\text{def}}{=} \bot; \quad p_i^L \stackrel{\text{def}}{=} \bigcirc^i p_i; \quad (\varphi_1 \odot \varphi_2)^L \stackrel{\text{def}}{=} \varphi_1^L \odot \varphi_2^L,\ \odot \in \{\vee, \wedge, \rightarrow\};$$
$$(\bigcirc\varphi)^L \stackrel{\text{def}}{=} \bigcirc^{n+2}\varphi^L; \quad (\varphi_1 \mathbb{U} \varphi_2)^L \stackrel{\text{def}}{=} \neg\alpha \vee \varphi_1^L \mathbb{U} \alpha \wedge \varphi_2^L; \quad (\varphi_1 \mathbb{R} \varphi_2)^L \stackrel{\text{def}}{=} \alpha \wedge \varphi_1^L \mathbb{R} \neg\alpha \vee \varphi_2^L.$$

Given a THT formula φ over an alphabet $A \stackrel{\text{def}}{=} \{p_1, \ldots, p_n\}$, its associated Kripke structure $K(\varphi)$ and an infinite LTL trace T, an LTL trace $T_{K(\varphi)}$, referred to as the *unfolding of T over $K(\varphi)$*, can be associated to T where the set of literals of each state T_i of T is spread over a sequence of $n+2$ states. For instance, if $T \stackrel{\text{def}}{=} \{a,b,c\} \cdot \{a,c,d\} \cdot \{a\}^\omega$, then $T_{K(\varphi)} = \underbrace{\{\alpha\}\cdot\{a\}\cdot\{b\}\cdot\{c\}\cdot\emptyset\cdot\{\beta\}}_{\{a,b,c\}} \cdot \underbrace{\{\alpha\}\cdot\{a\}\cdot\emptyset\cdot\{c\}\cdot\{d\}\cdot\{\beta\}}_{\{a,c,d\}} \cdot \underbrace{\left(\{\alpha\}\cdot\{a\}\cdot\emptyset\cdot\emptyset\cdot\emptyset\cdot\{\beta\}\right)^\omega}_{\{a\}^\omega}$.

With these notions at hand, the following can be stated:

Lemma 6. *Let φ be a THT formula defined over the finite alphabet A and $K(\varphi)$ its associated Kripke structure. Then for any THT trace (H,T) over 2^A and any $k \geq 0$, $(H,T), k \models_{THT} \varphi$ iff $(H_{K(\varphi)}, T_{K(\varphi)}), (n+2)k \models_{THT} \varphi^L$.*

One final lemma useful to show the EXPSPACE–hardness of TELKS∃ is the following, showing a correspondence between the TEMs of a given formula φ and the TEMs found within its associated Kripke structure:

Lemma 7. *Let φ be a THT formula and T an LTL trace. Then T is a TEM of φ iff $T_{K(\varphi)}$ is a TEM of $\varphi' \stackrel{\text{def}}{=} \varphi^L \wedge \varphi_\alpha \wedge \varphi_\beta$, where $\varphi_\alpha \stackrel{\text{def}}{=} \square(\alpha \vee \neg\alpha)$ and $\varphi_\beta \stackrel{\text{def}}{=} \square(\beta \vee \neg\beta)$.*

Theorem 5. *Deciding* TELKS∃ *is* EXPSPACE*–hard.*

Proof. To show the EXPSPACE–hardness of deciding TELKS∃, a Karp reduction $f : \Sigma_{\text{TEL}} \rightarrow \Sigma_{\text{TELKS}\exists}$ is defined such that $\varphi \in$ TEL iff $f(\varphi) \in$ TELKS∃. Since by [4] deciding TEL is EXPSPACE–hard, deciding TELKS∃ turns out to be also EXPSPACE–hard.

The reduction f is defined as $f(\varphi) \stackrel{\text{def}}{=} (K(\varphi), \varphi')$, where $K(\varphi)$ is the associated Kripke structure of φ and $\varphi' \stackrel{\text{def}}{=} \varphi^L \wedge \varphi_\alpha \wedge \varphi_\beta$. What needs to be shown is that f is a function from Σ_{TEL} to $\Sigma_{\text{TELKS}\exists}$, that $\varphi \in$ TEL iff $f(\varphi) \in$ TELKS∃, and that f is computable in polynomial time.

The first and third points can be easily argued. To show the second point, $\varphi \in \text{TEL}$ is supposed. If $\varphi \in \text{TEL}$, an LTL trace T exists which is a TEM of φ, and by Lemma 7 the unfolding $T_{K(\varphi)}$ of T over $K(\varphi)$ is a TEM of φ'. Therefore a trace from $K(\varphi)$ which is a TEM of φ' exists, and $(K(\varphi),\varphi') \in \text{TELKS}\exists$. Conversely, if $\varphi \in \Sigma_{\text{TEL}}$ is such that $(K(\varphi),\varphi') = f(\varphi)$ belongs to TELKS∃, then an LTL trace $T_{K(\varphi)}$ in $K(\varphi)$ exists which is a TEM of φ'. Further, an LTL trace T such that $T_{K(\varphi)}$ is the unfolding of T over $K(\varphi)$ also exists, and by Lemma 7 T is a TEM of φ. Therefore $\varphi \in \text{TEL}$. □

What remains to be done for the TELKS∃ problem is show its membership to EXPSPACE. To that end, the K-embedding technique, previously introduced to show the PSPACE–membership of TELKS∀, is modified to obtain what could be thought of as a weakened version of it:

Definition 13 (K-quasiembedding). *Given a Kripke structure $K = (Q, q_0, \rightarrow, A, L)$, the* K-quasiembedding *of K is the THT formula*

$$\psi_K \stackrel{\text{def}}{=} q_0 \wedge \bigwedge_{q \in Q} \Box\left(q \rightarrow \bigcirc \bigvee_{q \rightarrow q'} q'\right) \wedge \bigwedge_{q \in Q} \Box\left(q \rightarrow \bigwedge_{a \in A \cap L \nabla q \partial} \neg\neg a \wedge \bigwedge_{a \in A \setminus L \nabla q \partial} \neg a\right)$$
$$\wedge \bigwedge_{q \in Q} \Box\left(q \rightarrow \bigwedge_{q' \in Q \setminus \{q\}} \neg q'\right).$$

K-quasiembeddings are defined almost exactly as K-embeddings, with the only difference that each atom a in the state of a Kripke structure K is required to be *not false*, expressed as $\neg\neg a$, rather than true, expressed as a. As HT (and, by extension, THT) is a three-valued logic, $\neg\neg a$ does not automatically imply a, as $\neg\neg a$ is satisfied by the $(\{a\},\{a\})$ interpretation, corresponding to assigning the "true" truth value to a, or by the $(\emptyset,\{a\})$ one, corresponding to assigning the "unknown" or "assumed" truth value to a.

The purpose of K-quasiembeddings remains however equivalent to those of K-embeddings: K-quasiembeddings allow turning a MC problem into a satisfiability one:

Lemma 8. *Let φ be a THT formula constructed over the alphabet A and $K = (Q, q_0, \rightarrow, A, L)$ a Kripke structure. Then an LTL trace T in K exists which is a TEM of φ iff $\varphi \wedge \psi_K$ admits a TEM.*

Proof (abridged). If an LTL trace $T = T_0 T_1 T_2 \cdots$ in K exists which is a TEM of φ, then the LTL trace $T' \stackrel{\text{def}}{=} (T_0 \cup \{\rho_0\}) \cdot (T_1 \cup \{\rho_1\}) \cdot (T_2 \cup \{\rho_2\}) \cdot \cdots$ can be also defined which marks every state T_i of T with an atom $\rho_i \in Q$, indicating which state of K T_i obtains its atoms from. Since $(T,T) \models_{\text{THT}} \varphi$, $(T',T') \models_{\text{THT}} \varphi$ continues to hold. Additionally, it can be shown that $(T',T') \models_{\text{THT}} \psi_K$ also holds, meaning that $(T',T') \models_{\text{THT}} \varphi \wedge \psi_K$. What then needs to be shown is that $\nexists H' < T'$ such that $(H',T') \models_{\text{THT}} \varphi \wedge \psi_K$, meaning that (T',T') is a TEM of $\varphi \wedge \psi_K$.

Conversely, if $\varphi \wedge \psi_K$ admits a TEM, then an LTL trace constructed over the alphabet $A \cup Q$ exists which is a TEM of $\varphi \wedge \psi_K$. From T, its projection T' over the A alphabet, $T'_i \stackrel{\text{def}}{=} T_i \cap A$, can be obtained. By virtue of ψ_K, T' is a trace from K. Further, since φ is constructed over the A alphabet, $(T',T') \models_{\text{THT}} \varphi$ continues to hold. Finally, it can be argued that $\nexists H' < T'$ for which $(H',T') \models_{\text{THT}} \varphi$ holds. Hence an LTL trace T in K exists which is a TEM of φ, and that trace is T' itself. □

Using Lemma 8, the following can be concluded:

Theorem 6. TELKS∃ ∈ EXPSPACE.

Proof. To show TELKS∃ to belong to EXPSPACE, a Karp reduction $f : \Sigma_{\text{TELKS}\exists} \rightarrow \Sigma_{\text{TEL}}$ is constructed. Given that by [8] TEL belongs to EXPSPACE, TELKS∃ also results to belong to EXPSPACE.

Given an instance $(K,\varphi) \in \Sigma_{\text{TELKS}\exists}$, $f((K,\varphi)) \stackrel{\text{def}}{=} \varphi \wedge \psi_K$, where ψ_K is the K-quasiembedding of K. What needs to be shown is that f is a function from $\Sigma_{\text{TELKS}\exists}$ to Σ_{TEL}, that $(K,\varphi) \in$ TELKS∃ iff $\varphi \wedge \psi_K \in$ TEL, and that f is computable in polynomial time with respect to the size of the instance (K,φ).

The first and third points can be easily argued. For the second one, $(K,\varphi) \in$ TELKS∃ is first assumed. If $(K,\varphi) \in$ TELKS∃, then an LTL trace T within K such that (T,T) is a TEM of φ exists, and by Lemma 8 a TEM for $\varphi \wedge \psi_K$ exists, showing $f((K,\varphi))$ to belong to TEL. Vice versa, if $(K,\varphi) \in \Sigma_{\text{TELKS}\exists}$ is an instance of TELKS∃ such that $f((\varphi,K)) = \varphi \wedge \psi_K \in$ TEL, then a TEM of $\varphi \wedge \psi_K$ exists and by Lemma 8 an LTL trace T from K exists which is a TEM of φ, meaning that $(K,\varphi) \in$ TELKS∃. □

4 Fragments of the TELKS Problem

The complexity of fragments of the TELKS∀ and TELKS∃ problems can be analyzed by restricting the set of allowed temporal operators, or the *temporal* and *implication height* of a formula.

Given a THT formula φ, φ has a *temporal height* of value m if the number of nested temporal operators is m. For instance, $a \mathbb{U} \bigcirc b$ has a temporal height of value 2, whereas $\Box a \rightarrow \Diamond a$ has a temporal height of value 1. Similarly, φ has an *implication height* of value k if the number of nested implication operators $\rightarrow$ is k. For instance, $a \rightarrow (b \rightarrow c)$ has an implication height equal to 2. However, given that $\neg\psi$ is a syntactic sugar for $\psi \rightarrow \bot$, $a \rightarrow (b \rightarrow \neg c)$ has an implication height of value 3.

For $P \in \{$TELKS∀, TELKS∃$\}$, $P_m^k(O_1,\ldots,O_n)$ denotes the fragment of P where only the temporal operators $O_1,\ldots,O_n$ are allowed, and where formulas with a temporal height of value *at most m* and an implication height of value *at most k* are considered.

TELKS∀($\mathbb{R}$). TELKS∀($\mathbb{R}$) is the fragment of the TELKS∀ problem where only the temporal operator $\mathbb{R}$ is allowed, and like TELKS∀, deciding it is still PSPACE–complete. The PSPACE–hardness of this problem results from the fact that LTLKS∀($\mathbb{R}$) is still PSPACE–hard, and that since the $\mathbb{R}$ operator, and in particular the $\Box$ operator, is allowed, a reduction from LTLKS∀($\mathbb{R}$) to TELKS∀($\mathbb{R}$) in the style of Theorem 2 using the $\varphi_{\text{EM}}(A)$ formula is still possible. The membership of TELKS∀($\mathbb{R}$) to PSPACE continues to hold because TELKS∀($\mathbb{R}$) is a subset of TELKS∀:

Theorem 7. *Deciding* TELKS∀($\mathbb{R}$) *is* PSPACE*–complete.*

TELKS∃($\mathbb{R}$). TELKS∃($\mathbb{R}$) is the fragment of the TELKS∃ problem where only the $\mathbb{R}$ operator is allowed, and like TELKS∃, deciding it is also EXPSPACE–complete. Showing the EXPSPACE–hardness of the TELKS∃($\mathbb{R}$) problem can be done by readapting the proof of the EXPSPACE–hardness of the unconstrained TELKS∃ problem, by revising the definition of the L-transformation in a way that no $\bigcirc$ and $\mathbb{U}$ operators are used. For lack of a better name, this modified transformation is termed *M-transformation*:

Definition 14 (M-transformation). *The* M-transformation *is a function from THT formulas to THT formulas, defined by structural recursion as:*

$$\bot^M \stackrel{\text{def}}{=} \bot; \quad p_i^M \stackrel{\text{def}}{=} p_i \mathbb{R} \neg\beta; \quad (\varphi_1 \odot \varphi_2)^M \stackrel{\text{def}}{=} \varphi_1^M \odot \varphi_2^M, \odot \in \{\vee, \wedge, \to\};$$
$$(\varphi_1 \mathbb{R} \varphi_2)^M \stackrel{\text{def}}{=} \alpha \wedge \varphi_1^M \mathbb{R} \neg\alpha \vee \varphi_2^M.$$

By adapting Lemma 6 and Lemma 7, already used for the L-transformation, to the case of the M-transformation, the following can be concluded:

Theorem 8. *Deciding* TELKS∃($\mathbb{R}$) *is* EXPSPACE*–hard.*

Proof. Similarly to the proof of Theorem 5, a Karp reduction $f(\varphi) \stackrel{\text{def}}{=} (K(\varphi), \varphi')$ from TEL($\mathbb{R}$) to TELKS∃($\mathbb{R}$) is defined, where $\varphi' \stackrel{\text{def}}{=} \varphi^M \wedge \varphi_\alpha \wedge \varphi_\beta$. Since by [4, Theorem III.1] deciding $\text{TEL}_2^2(\Box)$, and in particular deciding TEL($\mathbb{R}$), is EXPSPACE–hard, deciding TELKS∃($\mathbb{R}$) also turns out to be EXPSPACE–hard. □

Since TELKS∃($\mathbb{R}$) ⊂ TELKS∃ and TELKS∃ ∈ EXPSPACE:

Corollary 1. TELKS∃($\mathbb{R}$) ∈ EXPSPACE.

Theorem 9. *Deciding* TELKS∃($\mathbb{R}$) *is* EXPSPACE*–complete.*

5 The TELT Problem

If the requirement that the transition relation $\to$ of K only form a single loop, like in Fig. 2, is imposed, a special instance of the TELKS problem results where only one trace is obtained by traversing K. Kripke structures satisfying this condition are termed *linear*. Deciding whether an input formula φ holds against a linear Kripke structure essentially corresponds to deciding whether φ holds over a single *periodically infinite* LTL trace T, a trace $T \stackrel{\text{def}}{=} T_1 T_2^\omega$ where T_1 and T_2 are LTL traces of *finite* length and T_2^ω represents the infinite concatenation of T_2. This restriction leads to the TELT *problem*:

Definition 15 (TELT). *The* MC problem for TEL over traces *is the language* TELT $\stackrel{\text{def}}{=}$ $\{(T, \varphi)\}$, *where* $T \stackrel{\text{def}}{=} T_1 T_2^\omega$ *is a periodically infinite LTL trace and* φ *a THT formula such that* T *is a TEM of* φ.

As only one trace can be obtained by traversing a linear Kripke structure K, asking whether a THT formula φ is a TEM for *all* of the traces in K is equivalent to asking whether φ is a TEM for *a single* trace in K. Therefore, in the case of TELT the universal and the existential semantics of the TELKS problem from Sect. 3 collapse into one and TELT can be seen to correspond to a subset of TELKS∀. In particular, this means that deciding TELT cannot be harder than deciding TELKS∀:

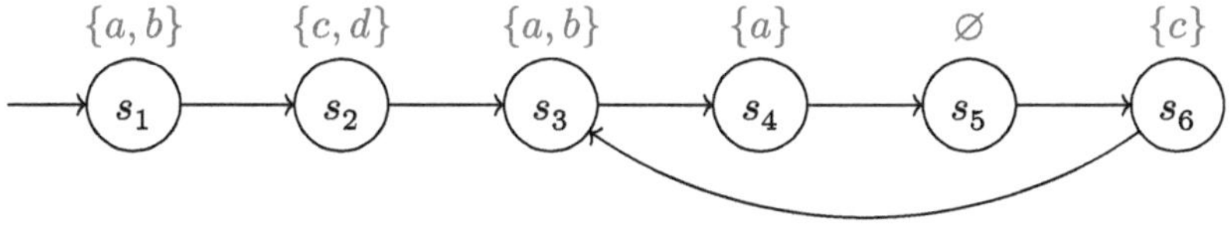

Fig. 2. A linear Kripke structure.

Proposition 4. TELT $\in$ PSPACE.

Deciding TELT is in fact not only at most as hard as TELKS$\forall$—it is *just as* hard as deciding TELKS$\forall$. For this problem, the following also holds:

Theorem 10. *Deciding* TELT *is* PSPACE*–hard.*

Due to the constraints imposed to the TELT problem, a different proof technique than the one used for the PSPACE–hardness proof of the TELKS$\forall$ problem has to be used:

Proof (abridged). To show the PSPACE–hardness of deciding TELT, it is shown how any language L in PSPACE can be reduced to $\overline{\text{TELT}}$ by proving the existence of a Karp reduction $f: \Sigma_L \to \Sigma_{\overline{\text{TELT}}}$ assigning to each word $x \in \Sigma_L$ a pair $(T, \varphi) \in \Sigma_{\overline{\text{TELT}}}$, where T is a periodically infinite LTL trace and φ a THT formula. As the complement of any PSPACE–hard problem is also PSPACE–hard, if deciding $\overline{\text{TELT}}$ is shown PSPACE–hard, deciding TELT also results to be PSPACE–hard.

If $L \in$ PSPACE, then a single-tape Turing machine $M = (Q, \Gamma, \delta, q_0, F)$ deciding L in deterministic polynomial space exists, where Q is the non-empty, finite set of states, Γ the tape alphabet, $\delta: (Q \setminus F) \times \Gamma \to Q \times \Gamma \times \{-1, 0, 1\}$ the transition function, $q_0 \in Q$ the initial state and $F = \{q_{\text{accept}}, q_{\text{reject}}\} \subseteq Q$ the set of halting states. $\{-1, 0, 1\}$ denotes the possible directions the tape head of M can move to, corresponding to left, no movement, and right, represented as integers to facilitate the construction of f.

Since M decides L in polynomial space, a polynomial $p(n)$ exists such that for any $x \in \Sigma_L$, M decides in $p(|x|)$ space whether x belongs to L or not, where $|x|$ is the number of symbols in x. Each configuration of M at step i is encoded by storing the state q at step i, the position of the head of M at step i and at most $p(|x|)$ tape symbols. M is encoded into the trace T in the following way:

- To encode the state q of M, a set of symbols Q is used, in such a way that for a $q \in Q$, $q \in T_i$ iff the state of M at time step i is q;
- To encode the head position of M at time step i, a set of variables h_k, $k \in [0..p(|x|))$ is used, so that $h_k \in T_i$ iff the head of M at time step i points to cell k;
- The tape content of M at time step i can be encoded into state T_i of T by the use of $|\Gamma| \cdot p(|x|)$ many propositional atoms;
- For each tape symbol $\gamma \in \Gamma$ and $k \in [0..p(|x|))$, the propositional variable $\sigma_{k,\gamma}$ is added to the alphabet A of φ to signify that at the tape position k, the symbol is γ.

The alphabet A over which φ is defined is $A \stackrel{\text{def}}{=} A_Q \cup A_h \cup A_\sigma$, where $A_Q \stackrel{\text{def}}{=} Q$, $A_h \stackrel{\text{def}}{=} \{h_k \mid 0 \leq k < p(|x|)\}$, and $A_\sigma \stackrel{\text{def}}{=} \{\sigma_{k,\gamma} \mid 0 \leq k < p(|x|),\ \gamma \in \Gamma\}$, showing in particular that the cardinality of A is polynomial with respect to the size of M and $p(|x|)$.

Given an arbitrary word $x \in \Sigma_L$, $f(x) \stackrel{\text{def}}{=} (T, \varphi)$, where $T \stackrel{\text{def}}{=} (2^A)^\omega$ and $\varphi \stackrel{\text{def}}{=} \bigwedge_{1 \leq i \leq 7} \varphi_i$ is the formula encoding the behavior of M, split into the subformulas φ_i for easier understanding:

$$\varphi_1 \stackrel{\text{def}}{=} q_0 \wedge h_0 \wedge \sigma_{0,x_0} \wedge \sigma_{1,x_1} \wedge \cdots \wedge \sigma_{|x|,x_{|x|}} \wedge \sigma_{|x|+1,\sqcup} \wedge \cdots \wedge \sigma_{p(|x|)-1,\sqcup},$$

$$\varphi_2 \stackrel{\text{def}}{=} \bigwedge_{q \in Q} \ \bigwedge_{0 \leq k < p(|x|)} \ \bigwedge_{\gamma \in \Gamma} \square(q \wedge h_k \wedge \sigma_{k,\gamma} \wedge \delta(q,\gamma) = (q', \gamma', \Delta) \rightarrow \bigcirc(q' \wedge h_{k+\Delta} \wedge \sigma_{k,\gamma'})),$$

$$\varphi_3 \stackrel{\text{def}}{=} \square\Big(\bigwedge_{0 \leq k < p(|x|)} \ \bigwedge_{\substack{0 \leq k' < p(|x|) \\ k' \neq k}} \ \bigwedge_{\gamma \in \Gamma} h_k \wedge \sigma_{k',\gamma} \rightarrow \bigcirc \sigma_{k',\gamma} \Big),$$

$$\varphi_4 \stackrel{\text{def}}{=} \Diamond\Big(\bigvee_{q \in Q} \ \bigvee_{q' \in Q \setminus \{q\}} q \wedge q' \Big) \rightarrow \varphi^{\uparrow}, \quad \varphi_5 \stackrel{\text{def}}{=} \Diamond\Big(\bigvee_{0 \leq k < p(|x|)} \ \bigvee_{\substack{0 \leq k' < p(|x|) \\ k' \neq k}} h_k \wedge h_{k'} \Big) \rightarrow \varphi^{\uparrow},$$

$$\varphi_6 \stackrel{\text{def}}{=} \Diamond\Big(\bigvee_{0 \leq k < p(|x|)} \ \bigvee_{\gamma \in \Gamma} \ \bigvee_{\gamma' \in \Gamma \setminus \{\gamma\}} \sigma_{k,\gamma} \wedge \sigma_{k,\gamma'} \Big) \rightarrow \varphi^{\uparrow}, \quad \varphi_7 \stackrel{\text{def}}{=} \Diamond\, q_{\text{reject}} \rightarrow \varphi^{\uparrow}.$$

The φ_i formulas make use of the auxiliary formula $\varphi^{\uparrow}$, defined as $\varphi^{\uparrow} \stackrel{\text{def}}{=} \square \bigwedge_{a \in A} a$ and used to induce a state of saturation over the TEMs of φ.

On the basis of this construction, it can be argued that f correctly maps x to a pair (T, φ), with T a periodically infinite LTL trace and φ a THT formula; that $x \in L$ iff T is not a TEM of φ; and that f is computable in polynomial time with respect to $|x|$. □

Theorem 11. *Deciding* TELT *is* PSPACE*–complete.*

Given that the φ_i formulas from the proof of Theorem 10 have a temporal height no greater than 2 and an implication height no greater than 1:

Corollary 2. *Deciding* TELT_2^1 *is* PSPACE*–complete.*

If formulas making no use of the $\mathbb{U}$ operator are considered, the $\text{TELT}(\bigcirc, \mathbb{R})$ fragment is obtained, for which the following holds:

Theorem 12. *Deciding* $\text{TELT}(\bigcirc, \mathbb{R})$ *is* PSPACE*–hard.*

Proof (abridged). To show the PSPACE–hardness of deciding $\text{TELT}(\bigcirc, \mathbb{R})$, a rewriting of the φ formula from the proof of Theorem 10 into a φ' formula using only the $\bigcirc$ and $\mathbb{R}$ operators is given. The way φ' can be defined is by adding a special atom $a^{\uparrow}$, referred to as the *saturation atom*, to the $A \stackrel{\text{def}}{=} A_Q \cup A_h \cup A_\sigma$ alphabet over which φ is defined, obtaining an $A' \stackrel{\text{def}}{=} A \cup \{a^{\uparrow}\}$ alphabet. Each φ_i subformula of φ can be subsequently rewritten into a subformula φ_i' of φ' in the following way:

$$\varphi_1' \stackrel{\text{def}}{=} \varphi_1, \quad \varphi_2' \stackrel{\text{def}}{=} \varphi_2, \quad \varphi_3' \stackrel{\text{def}}{=} \varphi_3, \quad \varphi_4' \stackrel{\text{def}}{=} \square\Big(\bigvee_{q \in Q} \ \bigvee_{q' \in Q \setminus \{q\}} q \wedge q' \rightarrow a^{\uparrow} \Big),$$

$$\varphi_5' \stackrel{\text{def}}{=} \square\Big(\bigvee_{0 \leq k < p(|x|)} \ \bigvee_{\substack{0 \leq k' < p(|x|) \\ k' \neq k}} h_k \wedge h_{k'} \rightarrow a^{\uparrow} \Big),$$

$$\varphi_6' \stackrel{\text{def}}{=} \square\Big(\bigvee_{0 \leq k < p(|x|)} \ \bigvee_{\gamma \in \Gamma} \ \bigvee_{\gamma' \in \Gamma \setminus \{\gamma\}} \sigma_{k,\gamma} \wedge \sigma_{k,\gamma'} \rightarrow a^{\uparrow} \Big), \quad \varphi_7' \stackrel{\text{def}}{=} \square(q_{\text{reject}} \rightarrow a^{\uparrow}).$$

An additional set of formulas, denoted by ψ_i, also needs to be used to govern the behavior of the saturation atom $a^\uparrow$:

$$\psi_1 \stackrel{\text{def}}{=} \Box(a^\uparrow \rightarrow \bigcirc a^\uparrow), \quad \psi_2 \stackrel{\text{def}}{=} \Box(\bigcirc a^\uparrow \rightarrow a^\uparrow), \quad \psi_3 \stackrel{\text{def}}{=} \Box a^\uparrow \rightarrow \varphi^\uparrow.$$

The $\varphi^\uparrow$ formula is rewritten into $\varphi^\uparrow \stackrel{\text{def}}{=} \Box \bigwedge_{a' \in A'} a'$ to take the $a^\uparrow$ atom into account. Finally, the φ' formula is defined as $\varphi' \stackrel{\text{def}}{=} \bigwedge_{1 \leq i \leq 7} \varphi'_i \wedge \bigwedge_{1 \leq i \leq 3} \psi_i$. □

Theorem 13. *Deciding* TELT($\bigcirc$, $\mathbb{R}$) *is* PSPACE*–complete.*

Corollary 3. *Deciding* $\text{TELT}_2^1(\bigcirc, \mathbb{R})$ *is* PSPACE*–complete.*

6 Conclusion

This work studied the MC problem for TEL under Kripke structures, specifically the universal and existential variants of it, and the same problem under linear Kripke structures, corresponding to linear LTL traces.

For reasons of space, a number of already proven results, planned to be included in future work, has not been discussed. These are the coNP–completeness of TELT_1; the coNP–completeness of TELT($\bigcirc$, $\mathbb{U}$), TELT($\bigcirc$) and TELT($\mathbb{U}$); the PSPACE–completeness of TELT($\mathbb{U}$, $\mathbb{R}$) and $\text{TELT}_2^1(\mathbb{U}, \mathbb{R})$; the coNP–completeness of TELT_f (the restriction of TELT where the input trace T is assumed to be finite) and the coNP–completeness of TELKS_0 (corresponding to MC over the atemporal EL). The coNP–completeness of TELT_f means, in particular, that MC for TEL in practical solvers like `telingo` is not computationally harder than for atemporal ASP.

Acknowledgments. This project received funding from the European Research Council (grant agreement no. 101034440), by the MOSAIC project (EU H2020-MSCA-RISE-2020 Project 101007627) and by the WWTF project ICT22-023.

References

1. Aguado, F., et al.: Linear-time temporal answer set programming. Theory Pract. Logic Program. (2023). https://doi.org/10.1017/S1471068421000557
2. Barreca, O.: On the Complexity of Model Checking for Temporal Equilibrium Logic. MSc thesis, Technische Universität Wien (2025). https://doi.org/10.34726/hss.2025.125771
3. Beck, H., Dao-Tran, M., Eiter, T.: LARS: a logic-based framework for analytic reasoning over streams. Artif. Intell. (2018). https://doi.org/10.1016/j.artint.2018.04.003
4. Bozzelli, L., Pearce, D.: On the complexity of temporal equilibrium logic. In: Proceedings of ACM/IEEE LICS-2015. IEEE (2015). https://doi.org/10.1109/LICS.2015.65
5. Bozzelli, L., Pearce, D.: On the expressiveness of temporal equilibrium logic. In: Proceedings of JELIA 2016. Springer (2016). https://doi.org/10.1007/978-3-319-48758-8_11
6. Brandt, S., Kalayci, E.G., Ryzhikov, V., Xiao, G., Zakharyaschev, M.: Querying log data with metric temporal logic. J. Artif. Intell. Res. (2018). https://doi.org/10.1613/jair.1.11229
7. Buss, S.R.: The boolean formula value problem is in ALOGTIME. In: Proceedings of ACM STOC 1987. Association for Computing Machinery (1987). https://doi.org/10.1145/28395.28409

8. Cabalar, P., Demri, S.: Automata-based computation of temporal equilibrium models. In: Logic-Based Program Synthesis and Transformation. Springer, Heidelberg (2012). https://doi.org/10.1007/978-3-642-32211-2_5
9. Cabalar, P., Diéguez, M., Hahn, S., Schaub, T.: Automata for dynamic answer set solving: preliminary report (2021)
10. Cabalar, P., Eiter, T., Soldà, D.: Contracted temporal equilibrium logic. In: Proceedings of KR 2024 (2024). https://doi.org/10.24963/kr.2024/21
11. Cabalar, P., Kaminski, R., Morkisch, P., Schaub, T.: Telingo = ASP + time. In: Proceedings of LPNMR 2019. Springer (2019). https://doi.org/10.1007/978-3-030-20528-7_19
12. Cabalar, P., Pérez Vega, G.: Temporal equilibrium logic: a first approach. In: Computer Aided Systems Theory – EUROCAST 2007 (2007). https://doi.org/10.1007/978-3-540-75867-9_31
13. Cadoli, M.: The complexity of model checking for circumscriptive formulae. Inf. Process. Lett. (1992). https://doi.org/10.1016/0020-0190(92)90049-2
14. Clarke, E.M., Emerson, E.A.: Design and synthesis of synchronization skeletons using branching time temporal logic. In: Logics of Programs. Springer (1982). https://doi.org/10.1007/BFb0025774
15. Demri, S., Schnoebelen, P.: The complexity of propositional linear temporal logics in simple cases. Inf. Comput. (2002). https://doi.org/10.1006/inco.2001.3094
16. Eiter, T., Faber, W., Fink, M., Pfeifer, G., Woltran, S.: Complexity of model checking and bounded predicate arities for non-ground answer set programming. In: Proceedings of KR 2004, pp. 377–387. AAAI Press (2004)
17. Eiter, T., Kiesel, R.: Weighted LARS for quantitative stream reasoning. In: Proceedings of ECAI 2020. SAGE Publications (2020). https://doi.org/10.3233/FAIA200160
18. Gelfond, M., Lifschitz, V.: The stable model semantics for logic programming. In: Proceedings of ICLP/ILPS 1988, pp. 1070–1080. MIT Press (1988)
19. Giordano, L., Martelli, A., Dupré, D.T.: Reasoning about actions with temporal answer sets. Theory Pract. Log. Program. (2013). https://doi.org/10.1017/S1471068411000639
20. Heyting, A.: Die formalen Regeln der intuitionistischen Logik. Sitzungsberichte der Preussischen Akademie der Wissenschaften Berlin, phys.-math. Klasse, pp. 42–56 (1930)
21. Kripke, S.A.: Semantical analysis of intuitionistic logic I. In: Studies in Logic and the Foundations of Mathematics. Elsevier (1965). https://doi.org/10.1016/S0049-237X(08)71685-9
22. Laroussinie, F.C., Leclercq, L., Sangnier, A.: QLTL model-checking. In: Proceedings of CSL 2024. LIPIcs, vol. 288 (2024). https://doi.org/10.4230/LIPICS.CSL.2024.35
23. Liberatore, P., Schaerf, M.: The complexity of model checking for propositional default logics. Data Knowl. Eng. (2005). https://doi.org/10.1016/j.datak.2005.03.002
24. Pearce, D.: A new logical characterisation of stable models and answer sets. In: Proceedings of NMELP 1996. Springer, Heidelberg (1997). https://doi.org/10.1007/BFb0023801
25. Pearce, D.: Equilibrium logic. Ann. Math. Artif. Intell. (2006). https://doi.org/10.1007/s10472-006-9028-z
26. Schnoebelen, P.: The complexity of temporal logic model checking. In: Advances in Modal Logic 4, pp. 393–436. King's College Publications (2002). http://www.aiml.net/volumes/volume4/Schnoebelen.ps
27. Sistla, A.P., Clarke, E.M.: The complexity of propositional linear temporal logics. J. ACM (1985). https://doi.org/10.1145/3828.3837
28. Sistla, A.P., Vardi, M.Y., Wolper, P.: The complementation problem for Büchi automata with applications to temporal logic. In: Proceedings of ICALP 1985. Springer (1985). https://doi.org/10.1007/BFb0015772
29. Van Dalen, D.: Logic and Structure. Springer (2013). https://doi.org/10.1007/978-1-4471-4558-5

Solving Configuration Problems with Unbounded Cardinalities in COOM

Joachim Baumeister[1,2], Konstantin Herud[1], Jan Heuer[3,4], Jochen Reutelshöfer[1], Nicolas Rühling[3,4](✉), Abdallah Saffidine[5], and Torsten Schaub[3,5]

[1] denkbares GmbH, Wurzburg, Germany
[2] University of Würzburg, Wurzburg, Germany
[3] University of Potsdam, Potsdam, Germany
[4] UP Transfer GmbH, Potsdam, Germany
nruehling@uni-potsdam.de
[5] Potassco Solutions GmbH, Werder, Germany

Abstract. Industrial product configuration often involves complex partonomic structures with intricate, interdependent constraints such that the number of required components is unknown in advance. This paper addresses the challenge of determining minimal bounds for unbounded cardinalities within the CoomSuite workbench. While previous methods relied on a "naive" single-shot approach, requiring grounding and solving from scratch for every iteration, we introduce an extended workflow that leverages *clingo*'s multi-shot capabilities. We evaluate our approach across three benchmark domains demonstrating the efficiency of our approach compared to traditional single-shot strategies.

1 Introduction

Industrial product configuration [8,12] problems typically have large partonomic structures with complex interdependencies. While some cardinalities are fixed, e.g., a bike has 2 wheels, others are dynamic and depend on constraints and requirements provided by the user. This impedes determining the exact (or even approximate) number of objects needed in advance [21]. As an example, consider a customer who wants to order a new bottling plant with a required minimal capacity of bottles per minute. Configuring this bottling plant consists of generating a number of instances of bottling robots together with parallel instances of conveyor belts matching the robots. Finding suitable lower and upper bounds is not trivial as the capacity of each robot depends on various factors and constraints and neighboring robot instances might restrict each other.

We started addressing this challenge in [4] in the context of the CoomSuite [5], a workbench for experimenting with industrial-scale product configuration problems formulated in the industrial configuration language Coom [6].[1] The CoomSuite contains various benchmark sets, Coom grammar definitions,

[1] Coom is developed by denkbares and used in numerous industrial applications.

W. Faber et al. (Eds.): LPNMR 2026, LNAI 16952, pp. 83–99, 2027.
https://doi.org/10.1007/978-3-032-38320-4_6

and further resources related to Answer Set Programming (ASP; [19]). While our basic workflow from [4] only allowed for solving problems with bounded cardinalities, we introduced a simple method for unbounded ones with two possible search strategies to determine minimal bounds. However, this approach does not make use of *clingo*'s multi-shot capabilities [17], and thus required grounding and solving from scratch at each iteration. We address this limitation here by (1) introducing an extended workflow for the CoomSuite with a new, general ASP multi-shot encoding, and (2) evaluating this workflow on three benchmark domains. Two of these were already evaluated in [4] in a non-incremental setting and have been adapted to contain unbounded cardinalities. This allows us to compare our incremental approaches with the previous one and shows that even when upper bounds exist, it can be beneficial to solve a problem incrementally.

The remainder of our paper is structured as follows: We start by providing the required background in Sect. 2 and then introduce our multi-shot encoding in Sect. 3. Finally, we discuss the results of our empirical evaluation in Sect. 4.

2 Background

In this section, we review all the necessary parts for introducing our multi-shot encoding in the next section. We start by giving a brief overview of *clingo*'s multi-shot solving capabilities [17,18] and then introduce the CoomSuite [4].

2.1 Multi-shot Solving in *clingo*

Multi-shot solving allows for solving continuously changing logic programs in an operative way through looping on grounding and solving while reacting, for instance, to any outside changes or previous solving results. This does not only avoid re-grounding previously added parts but also benefits solving through constraints learned over time. The basic building blocks needed for this are the possibility to split a (non-ground) logic program into subprograms (by means of the `#program` directive) and so-called *externals* (by means of the `#external` directive), which allow us to activate and/or deactivate ground rules on demand.

2.2 The Coom Language

Our language of choice for representing product configuration models is Coom. In [4], we distinguished between three Coom language fragments of increasing complexity plus corresponding extensions for two of them. We focus here on the language fragment Coom[X*] represented by the *CargoBike* example in Listing 1. This fragment is the unbounded extension of Coom[X], which allows for modelling various features like partonomies and a broad range of (mostly linear) numerical calculations and constraints.

The *CargoBike* has two features: The first one, `requestedVolume`, is numeric with range `0-200` and serves as input to the configuration problem (Line 2). The second one represents an unknown number of needed `bags` (Line 3) expressed

```
1   product {
2               num   0-200     requestedVolume
3       0..*    Bag             bags
4   }
5   structure Bag { Size size }
6   enumeration Size {
7       attribute num weight
8       attribute num volume
9       Small    = ( 10 12 )
10      Medium   = ( 15 16 )
11      Large    = ( 25 20 )
12  }
13  behavior { require sum(bags.size.volume) >= requestedVolume }
```

Listing 1. Representation of the *CargoBike* example in COOM

by the cardinality `0..*` where `*` represents an unknown upper bound. The type `Bag` (Line 5) is a *structure* with a single feature `Size`. Structures in COOM represent parts, and thus allow for building complex partonomies. The type `Size` is an *enumeration*, which represent discrete attributes, and provides a number of different options (`Small`, `Medium`, `Large`), each with an associated value for the `weight` and `volume` (Lines 6-12). For instance, a `Bag` with `size Small` has a `weight` of 10 and a `volume` of 12. Finally, the constraint in Line 13 ensures that the total `volume` of all `bags` is greater or equal to the `requestedVolume`.

2.3 Solving Unbounded COOM Product Models Incrementally

The workflow for solving COOM product models with unbounded cardinalities is depicted in Fig. 1.[2]

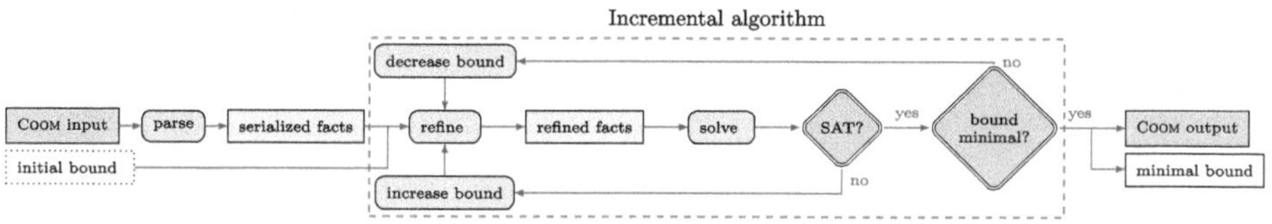

Fig. 1. Workflow for solving an unbounded COOM model incrementally

The input to the problem is a COOM product model and possibly an initial upper bound (0 by default). The output, if it exists, consists of a COOM configuration, i.e., a solution to the underlying configuration problem, plus the corresponding minimal upper bound. Since COOM product models can be unsatisfiable, the loop in Fig. 1 might not terminate.

Regarding the workflow, first, the COOM product model is parsed and converted into a "serialized" ASP fact format that closely resembles the COOM

[2] For more information on the general workflow, see [4].

language. The unspecified upper bound `*` (cf. Line 3 in Listing 1) is translated into *clingo*'s `#sup`[3] expression and used to automatically detect if an input model needs to be solved incrementally. Then, the serialized facts are processed using the current bound into a "refined" ASP fact format that is independent of COOM and captures the underlying configuration problem. Note that the bound does not necessarily equal the upper bound of unbounded cardinalities. Rather it is used to determine the range for any unbounded cardinality, e.g., for the bound n an unbounded cardinality `k..*` is replaced by `k..k+n`. This initiates a loop where, first, the upper bound is increased until the problem becomes satisfiable and, subsequently, decreased (and possibly increased again) until it converges to the minimal upper bound. For the incremental "single-shot" implementation this requires that the entire problem has to be refined and ground from scratch for every new bound. Lastly, the answer sets representing valid configurations are transformed back into COOM solutions. Currently, the COOMSUITE offers two search methods to determine the minimal upper bound: A linear and an exponential one [14], both of which are parametrizable by the user.

Given an *initial bound* β_i, the linear search method increases this bound by a fixed *step size* s. The exponential search method, in contrast, has a *base* parameter b from which a sequence $\beta_0, \beta_1, \beta_2, \dots$ is obtained with $\beta_k = \lceil b^k \rceil$. Note that the b^k are rounded up because b is not restricted to be an integer value. The search starts with the initial bound β_i and continues with β_{k_0}, where k_0 is the smallest value such that $\beta_{k_0} > \beta_i$. Subsequently, we continue with the β_k sequence, skipping any repeated values. The defaults values for the step size s and the base parameter b are 1 and 2, respectively.

When an upper bound β_u has been found for which the problem is satisfiable, it is not necessarily minimal. Therefore, we recursively converge β_u to a minimal bound β_m using binary search within the interval $(\beta_l, \beta_u]$, where β_l is the previous bound (for which the problem is unsatisfiable). We compute the (integer) midpoint $\beta = \lfloor(\beta_u + \beta_l)/2\rfloor$ and solve at this bound. If the problem is satisfiable with bound β, then β becomes the new upper bound, otherwise β becomes the new lower bound. The search terminates once β_l and β_u are consecutive integers. This strategy is the same for both search methods independent of the parameters.

2.4 Solving COOM Models with ASP

Fact Format. For the sake of brevity and as done in [4], we omit the "serialized" ASP fact format as it does not provide any further insights. We only give a brief overview of the intuition behind our "refined" ASP representation, as well as an introduction to the predicates needed for Sect. 3.

The essential concepts of our "refined" fact format are a partonomy with bounded cardinalities, attributes ranging over discrete and integer domains,

[3] The `#sup` expression is a *clingo* built-in representing the greatest element among all variable-free terms, cf. [16].

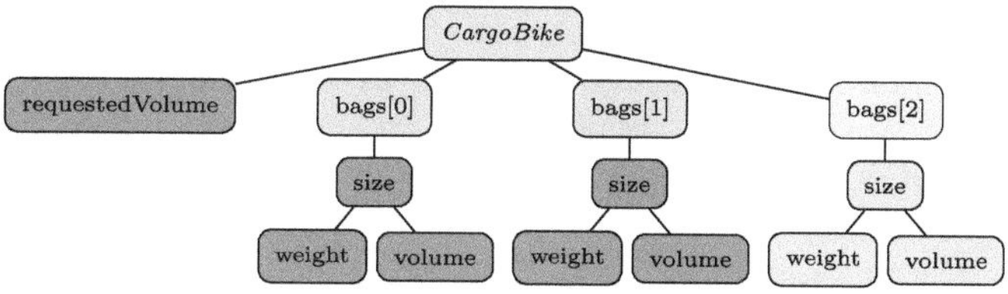

Fig. 2. The *CargoBike* example converted into a configuration tree

and Boolean as well as table constraints, where the former allow for arithmetic expressions and aggregate functions. This representation does not allow for unbounded cardinalities, i.e., all possible objects need to be stated explicitly, and thus an upper bound needs to be specified beforehand (compare with Fig. 1).

We represent a configuration as a tree such that each node represents a variable, and its root reflects the object to be configured.[4] Variables can be either parts or attributes. Solutions are represented as subtrees of this tree where values are assigned to any attribute variable included in the subtree. Thus, not all variables are necessarily included in the solution and an excluded variable renders all variables in its subtree excluded. Cardinalities are represented as constraints over sets of nodes in the tree.

The configuration tree for the *CargoBike* is shown in Fig. 2. This can be seen as an explicit representation of the COOM product model of Listing 1 where we assumed an upper bound of 3 for the `bags`. Nodes belonging to parts are highlighted in yellow and those belonging to attributes in green. Consider an example solution where the third `bag` is undefined, thus not included in the solution. We represent this in Fig. 2 by highlighting the corresponding variables in a lighter color. Note that undefined variables automatically render their subnodes undefined as well.

The structure of the configuration tree serves as the basis for our fact format, where all possible variables within the model are generated. For each variable, a unique (human-readable) identifier is assigned by leveraging the tree-like structure of the configuration. For example, the `volume` feature of the second instance of the `bags` feature in Listing 1 results in the variable `"bags[1].size[0].volume[0]"`. This is captured in ASP by three facts representing the type, index and parent of the variable as shown in Listing 2 for the example variable. As mentioned above, this requires that an upper bound for every variable has to be provided.

```
type("bags[1].size[0].volume[0]","Size.volume").
index("bags[1].size[0].volume[0]",0).
parent("bags[1].size[0].volume[0]","bags[1].size[0]").
```

Listing 2. A variable of the instantiated *CargoBike*

Boolean constraints, which include arithmetic formulas and aggregates, are encoded recursively. Listing 3 shows the `require` constraint from Listing 1. First,

[4] For a formal approach of this representation we refer the reader to [20].

the constraint is instantiated using a `constraint/2` predicate, where the first argument is the constraint identifier consisting of an index and the entire formula as a string, and the second argument denoting the type of the constraint. This could be any unique string but we opt for a human-readable format.

The formula of the constraint, which has operator $\geq$, is separated into its two sub-formulas by using a `binary/4` predicate. Next, the `sum` aggregate is encoded using a `function/3` predicate, where the first argument is the identifier of the entire aggregate, the second argument denotes its type, and the third argument denotes the set on which the aggregate is being applied. Lastly, the members of the aggregate set are encoded using `set/2` predicates. Following our example from Fig. 2, we assume that an upper bound of 3 has been provided.

```
constraint((0,"sum(bags.size.volume)>=requestedVolume[0]"),
"boolean").
binary("sum(bags.size.volume)>=requestedVolume[0]",
       "sum(bags.size.volume)",">=","requestedVolume[0]").
function("sum(bags.size.volume)","sum","bags.size.volume").
set("bags.size.volume","bags[0].size[0].volume[0]").
set("bags.size.volume","bags[1].size[0].volume[0]").
set("bags.size.volume","bags[2].size[0].volume[0]").
```

Listing 3. The constraint of the instantiated *CargoBike*

***clingo* encoding** Solutions are captured in terms of `include/1` predicates, stating that a variable is included in the solution, and `value/2` predicates, assigning values to attribute variables. Both are generated via the choice rules in Listing 4, where the fact `include("root")` and the integrity constraint in Line 2 ensure that each solution is a subtree with the same root.

```
1 { include(X) : type(X,_) }. include("root").
2 :- include(X), parent(X,P), not include(P).
3 { value(X,V) : domain(T,V) } = 1 :- include(X), type(X,T),
4                                      attribute(T).
```

Listing 4. Definedness of variables and generation of attribute values

Listing 5 shows the rules necessary to determine whether the constraint in Listing 3 is satisfied. For the `sum` calculation, we use *clingo*'s built-in `#sum` aggregates. Then, the integrity constraint in Line 5 enforces that a constraint cannot be violated. This happens if it is defined and its formula is not satisfied. For the sake of brevity, we omit the rules regarding definedness but, intuitively, a formula is defined if all variables in it have a value assigned.

```
1 value(F,V) :- function(F,"sum",P),
2               V = #sum{ V',X : set(P,X), value(X,V')}.
3 satisfied(F) :- binary(F,XL,">=",XR), VL >= VR,
4                 value(XL,VL), value(XR,VR).
5 :- constraint((ID,F),"boolean"), defined(F), not satisfied(F).
```

Listing 5. Subset of constraint checking rules

***flingo* encoding** An alternative encoding is provided using hybrid solver *flingo* [7], which is a prototype system for solving conditional linear constraints with integer variables in ASP. *flingo* uses CASP solver *clingcon* [3] as a backend, and therefore, is able to deal with large integer ranges and numerical calculations. The main difference, however, is that variables in *flingo* can stay undefined, while in *clingcon* all integer variables need to have a value assigned. As COOM allows for optional attributes, this is a crucial feature.

The encoding for *flingo* is identical in many parts to the *clingo* encoding, except for rules which treat integer variables and numerical constraints. Due to lack of space, we do not show them here and refer the reader to [4].

Coom solution An example solution, corresponding to the configuration tree in Fig. 2, and with user input `requestedVolume[0]=35`, is shown in Listing 6. Here, the ASP output facts have been converted back into COOM.

```
requestedVolume[0]=35
bags[0]
    bags[0].size[0]=Large
    bags[0].size[0].weight[0]=25
    bags[0].size[0].volume[0]=20
bags[1]
    bags[1].size[0]=Medium
    bags[1].size[0].weight[0]=15
    bags[1].size[0].volume[0]=16
```

Listing 6. A solution to the *CargoBike* example

3 A Multi-shot Approach to Solving COOM[X*]

As mentioned in the previous section, solving unbounded cardinalities using the "single-shot" approach involves preprocessing as well as grounding and solving the entire problem from scratch for every new bound. We now discuss an approach making use of *clingo*'s multi-shot capabilities. We start by introducing the COOMSUITE multi-shot workflow and then present some illustrative program parts of the ASP encoding.

The multi-shot workflow is very similar to the one of Fig. 1; however different from before, we construct the ground program step-by-step for every new bound. Due to lack of space, we omit a detailed description of this workflow and only discuss the *update_program* function (Algorithm 1). This function is responsible for constructing the extension of the ground program for a new bound and contains the main differences wrt the workflow of Fig. 1.

Its input are the serialized ASP facts (which are the same for every bound) as well as a tuple containing the previous and current upper bound. Its output is a ground program that is to be added to the current ground program. Even though our supported algorithms may increase the bound in larger steps, the addition of program parts and grounding is done in increments of 1. However, solving is only done for the bounds provided by the search algorithm.

For each bound increment, we first process the serialized facts and filter the resulting refined facts to remove facts obtained in previous steps. Next, the

Algorithm 1: Update program

```
Input: serialized_facts, bounds
Output: ground_program
ground_program ← { };
foreach bounds[0] < b ≤ bounds[1] do
    new_facts ← refine_and_filter(serialized_facts);
    program_parts ← { };
    foreach fact ∈ new_facts do
        program_parts ← program_parts ∪ get_program_part(fact, b);
    ground_program ← ground_program ∪ ground(program_parts);
    Set external active(b) to True;
Set external max_bound(bounds[0]) to False;
Set external max_bound(bounds[1]) to True;
```

program parts corresponding to each of the newly refined facts are collected and grounded. The values of externals are updated to activate/deactivate certain rules. We discuss the specific function of each of the externals, `active` and `max_bound`, below when introducing the multi-shot encoding.

3.1 Encoding

As not all facts and rules need to be treated in an incremental way, we split our ASP encoding and the corresponding fact format into two parts. First, a "base" part containing all facts and rules which correspond to variables with fixed, thus bounded, cardinalities,[5] and second, a multi-shot part containing facts and rules corresponding to variables with unbounded cardinalities.

This second part consists again of various program parts, one for each type of fact that can be added by an increased bound. These program parts were obtained by partitioning the rules of the single-shot encoding and adding some small modifications such as including externals. For reasons of space, we only demonstrate a few of these program parts together with their necessary modifications by the following example scenario.

Consider that our previous upper bound was 3 (cf. Figure 2) and that our new upper bound is 4. The new complete configuration tree is depicted in Fig. 3.

Variables. While, in general, a bound increase can add an arbitrarily complex subtree with many objects, here, the new variables are `"bags[3]"` and its corresponding attributes, e.g., `"bags[3].size[0]"` and so forth. These variables are added to the program using the program part shown in Listing 7(cf. Listing 4 for the single-shot case). Note that we present simplified versions of the encodings here to illustrate the concepts.

Line 1 defines the program part and its parameters: the `name` and `type` of the variable as well as the current `bound`. Line 2 defines an external to deactivate

[5] This part corresponds to the fact format and encoding from [4] which we partially discussed in Sect. 2.4.

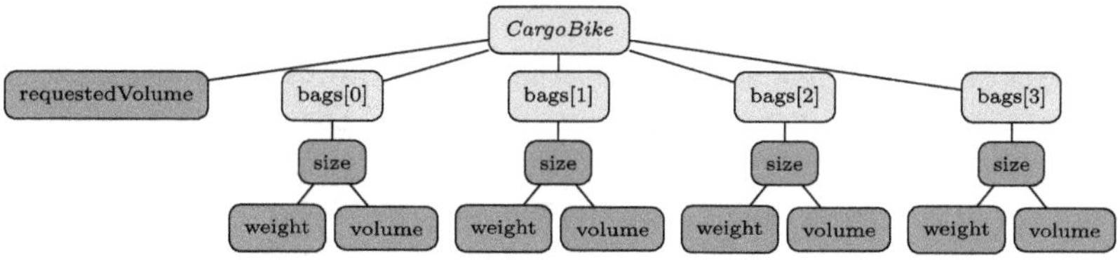

Fig. 3. The *CargoBike* example converted into a configuration tree with maximum upper bound 4

variables introduced at some specific bound. This is required for decreasing the bound when converging to the minimal bound.

Next, Line 3 defines a new fact recording the `bound` at which a variable was introduced. This auxiliary predicate is used for the evaluation of constraints later on. The remaining three rules correspond to the rules in Listing 4. A fact `type/2` represents the variable and its type and the two choice rules control whether the variable is included in the configuration and which value it receives (if it is an attribute). Note the inclusion of the external `active(bound)` in the body of the choice rule in Line 5 to prevent the inclusion of a variable when its corresponding bound is not active.

```
1 #program new_variable(name,type,bound).
2 #external active(bound).
3 bound(name,bound).
4 type(name,type).
5 { include(name) } :- active(bound).
6 { value(name,V) : domain(type,V) } = 1 :- include(name),
7                                type(name,type), attribute(type).
```

Listing 7. Simplified program part for adding new variables.

Constraints We differentiate between *simple* and *incremental* constraints. While the truth values of the former are not affected by additions of variables for higher bounds, the evaluation of the latter needs to be updated with each new bound.

As an example of a simple constraint, consider the extension of the *CargoBike* from Listing 1 by adding a color feature to the bags as shown in Listing 8.

```
1 ...
2 structure Bag {
3             Size         size
4             Color        color
5 }
6 enumeration Color { Green Blue Red }
7 ...
8 behavior Bag { require color = Blue }
```

Listing 8. Extension of the *CargoBike* example with colors for bags.

The constraint in Line 8 has to be added for each new instance of the type `Bag`; however, it is not affected by additional instances of `Bag` later on. Therefore, the addition of such a constraint is handled similarly to the addition of new variables discussed above. Importantly, the external `active(bound)` is used to enforce the constraint only while its corresponding bound is active.

On the other hand, consider the constraint in Line 13 of Listing 1. This constraint involves the aggregate `sum(bags.size.volume)`, thus reasons over the set of all `bags`. While it is only added once to the problem, its evaluation needs to be updated with each new instance of the type `Bag`.

We define incremental constraints or, more generally, incremental expressions recursively. A *set* is incremental if its cardinality is unbounded. A (set-based) *function* is incremental if its set argument is incremental. A *unary* or *binary* expression is incremental if it has a sub-expression which is incremental and a *Boolean constraint* is incremental if its corresponding expression is incremental.[6]

Returning to our example scenario, we would only obtain the new fact `set("bags.size.volume","bags[3].size[0].volume[0]")` after increasing the bound to 4. All other facts from Listing 3 had already been obtained for bound 3. To record the value (or satisfaction) of an expression in our single-shot encoding, we used the predicates `value/2` (or `satisfied/1`) (cf. Listing 5). However, for incremental expressions the truth values of these predicates now additionally depend on the bound as the underlying set of elements can change. As *clingo* does not allow the redefinition of existing atoms [17], we instead introduce new predicates, `value/3` and `satisfied/2`, with an additional bound parameter to record the value (or satisfaction) of an expression at a specific bound. Listing 9 shows some of the program parts for defining these new predicates (cf. Listing 5).

For incremental functions we define the value at a new bound using the value at the old bound. For example, the value of the `sum` function gets defind at bound `n+1` by taking its value at bound `n` and adding the values of all objects introduced at bound `n+1` that belong to the underlying set. In our example scenario only a single element is added to the set, however, in general an arbitrary number of objects may be added by a new bound. This addition is expressed by the rule in Lines 2-5 in the program part `update_incremental_function`. Here, we use the auxiliary `bound/2` predicate that records the bound of an object (see Listing 7). For "initializing" a new incremental function, we have a separate program part, which does not refer to any previous values.

```
1 #program update_incremental_function(f,agg,p,bound).
2 value(f,V+V',N+1) :- function(f,agg,p), agg = "sum",
3                      bound = N+1, value(f,V,N),
4                      V' = #sum{ Val,X : set(p,X), bound(X,bound),
5                                         value(X,Val) }.
6 #program incremental_binary_l(f,xl,op,xr,bound).
7 binary(f,xl,op,xr).
8 satisfied(f,bound) :- binary(f,xl,op,xr), VL >= VR, op = ">=",
```

[6] Coom also supports tables constraints whose treatment we omit but which are fully supported by the multi-shot encoding.

```
9    value(xl,VL,bound), value(xr,VR).
```

Listing 9. Subsets of the program parts for incremental expressions

Any incremental expression then refers to the value of its incremental sub-expression(s) by means of the `value/3` (or `satisfied/2`) predicate and in turn its own value is recorded using `value/3` (or `satisfied/2`). For binary expressions we need different program parts depending on whether only the left, only the right, or both sub-expressions are incremental. For instance, the expression "`sum(bags.size.volume)>=requestedVolume[0]`" has an incremental expression on the left side only. The corresponding rule checking its satisfaction is shown in Lines 8-9 and belongs to program part `incremental_binary_l`. Here, the value of the left sub-expression is fetched using a `value/3` predicate, while the right sub-expression is taken from a `value/2` predicate.

Finally, we consider the rules for incremental Boolean constraints shown in Listing 10(cf. Listing 5). Line 1 defines the program part with parameters for the constraint identifier `cons` as well as the current `bound`. Line 2 defines the external `max_bound`. This external is similar to `active` defined in Listing 7, however, `active` is true for every bound that is currently active (i.e. if the current bound is n, then `active` holds for $n, n-1, \ldots, 0$), whereas `max_bound` is only true for the current maximum bound and false for all others. This is because incremental constraints only need to hold for the current bound and not for earlier bounds. The constraint in lines 4-5 forbids the violation of a constraint as long as its associated bound is the maximum bound.

```
1  #program incremental_constraint(cons,bound).
2  #external max_bound(bound).
3  constraint(cons).
4  :- constraint(cons), cons = (C,F), max_bound(bound),
5     defined(F,bound), not satisfied(F,bound).
```

Listing 10. Program part for incremental constraints.

4 Benchmarks

We evaluate the multi-shot encoding on three different benchmark domains[7] (cf. Table 1) that are representative of typical industrial problems. That is, in a nutshell, some abstract structure is given over which attributes and constraints create non-trivial dependencies. Furthermore, the solution and the exact number of actual instances required depend on some (user-given) requirement.

While the *CargoBike* benchmark domain corresponds to an extended version of the example from Listing 1, the other two benchmark domains, *TravelBikeFleet* and *Restaurant*, were already part of the benchmark sets evaluated in [4].[8]

[7] https://github.com/potassco/coom-benchmarks.

[8] Some small adjustments were made to the instances for the sake of having a more balanced benchmark set.

Table 1. Incremental benchmark sets of the CoomSuite

Benchmark set	Language	Input	Scalable factor	# Instances
CargoBike	Coom[x*]	*minVolume*	#Bags	25
TravelBikeFleet	Coom[x] & Coom[x*]	*minVolume, maxPrice*	#Bikes	20
Restaurant	Coom[x] & Coom[x*]	*totalSeats*	#Tables	15

The configuration tasks of the *TravelBikeFleet* and *CargoBike* are similar but differ in a few details. First, the *TravelBikeFleet* configures a (possibly unbounded) number of bikes that each allows a limited number of bags, while the *CargoBike* configures only a single bike with an unbounded number of bags. Both problems take as input a requested minimal volume, however, for the *TravelBikeFleet* the user additionally can specify a maximum total price that must not be exceeded. Thus, the *TravelBikeFleet* instances do not only contain more arithmetic formulas but also can be unsatisfiable if a too low maximum price has been set. We adapted the parameters in the instance generation such that we allow for around 10% of unsatisfiable instances. Lastly, for the *Restaurant* domain, the aim is to configure tables with differing number of chairs such that we obtain an exact total number of requested seats. However, since in [4], only bounded versions in Coom[x] existed, we created incremental versions in Coom[x*] by adapting the respective cardinalities to unbounded ones. Note that the change to unbounded cardinalities adds an implicit minimization on the number of bikes (which could also have an effect on the solving time).

We ran all benchmark instances on a compute cluster with Intel Xeon E5-2650v4@2.9GHz CPUs with 64GB of memory running Debian Linux 10.[9] We used a timeout of 10 min and limited the memory to 20GB per instance. Furthermore, we used version v1.1.2 of the CoomSuite [5].

The bounded instances (Coom[x] versions of *TravelBikeFleet* and *Restaurant*) were run using the *clingo* and *flingo* single-shot encodings from [4]. Note that since the bounds in these instances just provide an upper bound for the number of objects, they might not be minimal. In fact, the single-shot encodings do not determine a minimal bound at all but just a single solution. All unbounded instances were run with both the naive "single-shot" incremental approach (cf. Section 2) and the multi-shot encoding presented in Sect. 3. For the rest of the paper we refer to the single-shot approaches as *single-shot clingo*, resp. *flingo*, and to the naive "single-shot" incremental approaches as simply *incremental clingo*, resp. *flingo*. The multi-shot encoding only works with *clingo* and is referred to as *multishot*. For all unbounded instances, we also evaluated the linear and exponential search algorithms with different parameters. More precisely, for the linear algorithm we used various integer step sizes in the range of 1 to 32, and for the exponential algorithm exponential bases in the range of 1.25, to 2.75. For the latter, as described in Sect. 2.3, the bound values are rounded up to obtain integer values and repeated bounds are skipped. We do

[9] https://www.cs.uni-potsdam.de/bs/research/labs.html#hardware.

not consider larger exponential bases as they performed worse in preliminary experiments.

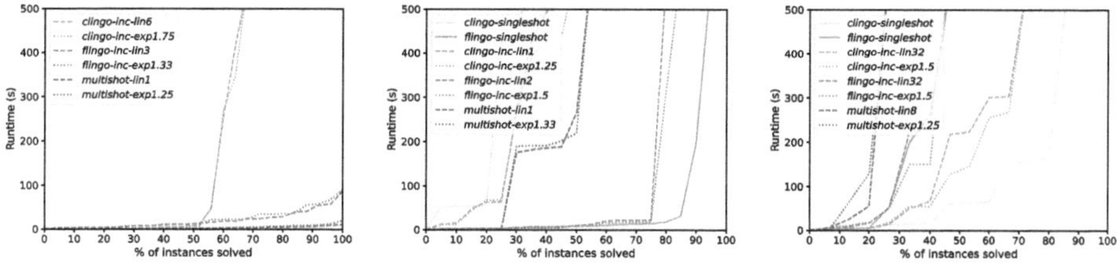

(a) *CargoBike* (b) *TravelBikeFleet* (c) *Restaurant*

Fig. 4. Benchmark results for three representative domains

The results per domain are presented in Fig. 4. For the sake of readability, we only show the best performing parameter for each combination of incremental approach (*clingo*, *flingo*, multishot) and search algorithm (linear, exponential). This selection was performed based on the minimum average runtime of all instances per parameter.

The results show that the performance of the different encodings strongly depends on the problem domain. For the *CargoBike*, the multi-shot encoding outperforms both incremental *clingo* and *flingo*, solving all instances within a few seconds. Meanwhile, incremental *flingo* has comparable but slower runtimes and incremental *clingo* is only able to solve about two thirds of the instances within the time limit. For the *TravelBikeFleet*, the multi-shot encoding is clearly slower than single-shot and incremental *flingo*, however, it performs better than single-shot and incremental *clingo*. The reason *flingo* performs better here could be due to its dedicated inference algorithm for linear constraints, which enables it to more efficiently solve the combination of minimal volume and maximum price constraints. Lastly, for the *Restaurant*, the multi-shot encoding performs worse than all *clingo* and *flingo* approaches and the *clingo* single-shot approach is able to solve most instances by a margin. For *flingo*, the single-shot and incremental approaches perform comparable but slower than incremental *clingo*.

One possible reason for the worse performance of the multi-shot encoding for instances of the *Restaurant* could be the approach of grounding in steps of 1 and the fact that the minimal upper bounds of its instances reach values of up to 600 (compared to bounds in the range of 5 to 25 for the two bike domains). In general, the multi-shot encoding produces a higher number of ground rules than the single shot encoding due to the representation of incremental constraints. Incremental functions are defined via chains of rules where the length of such a chain equals the bound (see Listing 9). Additionally, for all other types of incremental expressions there are rules defining their value at every possible bound. For the *CargoBike* domain the multi-shot encoding results in around 3 times as many rules for the largest instances. However, for the *Restaurant* domain this factor increases to around 25 due to the higher bounds of the domain. An alternative grounding approach that grounds according to the increments given by the respective algorithm may be advantageous for such domains.

Similarly, the ranges of the minimal upper bounds could explain why smaller linear step sizes perform best on the two bike domains but not for the *Restaurant* (here, for both linear incremental *clingo* and *flingo* a step size of 32 gave the best results). Lastly, note that for the exponential base parameters no clear pattern seems evident, other than a general preference for bases below 2.

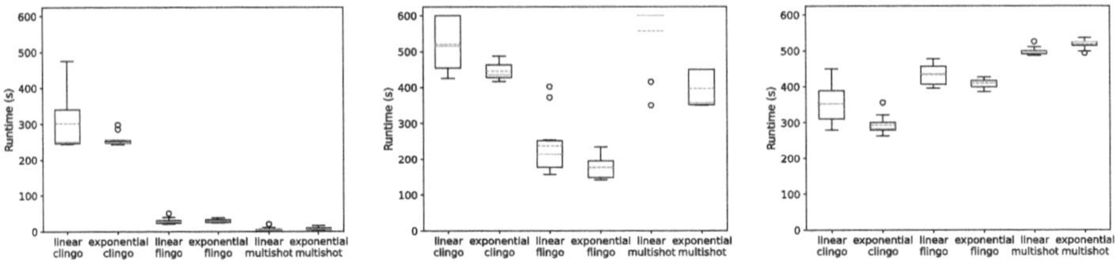

(a) *CargoBike* (b) *TravelBikeFleet* (c) *Restaurant*

Fig. 5. Average results for linear and exponential search parameters for three domains

Regarding the search algorithms, Fig. 4 shows that, generally, the linear and exponential search algorithms perform similarly for their best parameters on all domains. Another question that arises is how much the choice of parameter actually influences the runtime.

Figure 5 shows a boxplot of the average (dashed green line) and median (orange line) runtimes per algorithm and solver for each domain. Before plotting, the average runtimes over all instances had already been calculated and used as basis for the boxplot. Boxes extend from the first to the third quartile and whiskers extend from the box to the farthest data point lying within 1.5x the inter-quartile range. Outliers lying further outside are represented as small circles.

Generally, the variation of the average runtime for the exponential algorithm is rather small between the evaluated parameters with a minor exception of the *TravelBikeFleet* domain. The linear algorithm deviates more, especially for incremental *clingo* and, most notably, for the linear multi-shot approach on the *TravelBikeFleet*. Here, only for two parameter choices the average runtimes lie below the timeout of 600 seconds (these correspond to the smallest step sizes of 1 and 2). However, there are also many cases with almost no deviation at all.

5 Discussion

We presented a new and general *clingo* multi-shot encoding for the CoomSuite that works with all language constructs of Coom[x*]. This allows us to solve

COOM product models incrementally and offers an alternative to a naive approach, where grounding and solving have to be performed from scratch for each new bound. An evaluation of this approach on three different benchmark domains shows that the multi-shot encoding can increase the performance compared to pure single-shot or naive incremental approaches but that the performance also depends on the structure of the underlying problem. Especially when the minimal upper bounds are large, our current multi-shot encoding performed worse.

Due to their large and intricate nature, the need for solving industrial configuration problems incrementally arose early on [13]. Other approaches attempt to derive tight upper bounds from UML class diagrams before starting to solve [21] or to automatically infer upper bounds from logical axioms [1]. Note that we did not evaluate the approach from [21] as they only address cardinalities of UML class diagrams and do not consider more complex dependencies.

An ASP multi-shot approach that is similar to ours was introduced in [9] and refined in [2] for the object-oriented configuration language OOASP [11]. However, there, more complex constraints have to be formulated directly in ASP because OOASP does not provide specific constructs for modelling them. While this offers great flexibility, it also obliges the modeller to encode the constraint in the exact format of the given multi-shot encoding. In contrast, our multi-shot encoding supports all language constructs of fragment COOM[X*]. This follows the principle that the modeller should be able to formulate any knowledge independent of the underlying encoding.

Future work consists of extending our benchmark sets and adding refinements to our workflow. For the former, we would like to add language constructs and corresponding encoding parts to model arbitrary associations/connections as is possible for instance in OOASP [11]. This would allow us to evaluate our approach on the well-known industrial benchmarks from the *Racks* [10] and *House* [15] configuration domains.

Two concrete ideas for refinement of our workflow are implementing different grounding strategies (currently grounding is always done in increments of 1 even when the maximal bound is augmented in larger steps) and the addition of so-called "smart expansion" functions as done in [2]. These functions attempt to infer as much knowledge as possible for each iteration with the aim of guiding the search for minimal bounds. While the functions in [2] were mostly using information from cardinality constraints, the underlying methods should be general enough in order to be applicable to our use case. Furthermore, instead of just increasing a global bound, we would like to study more fine-grained strategies to increase bounds, which could be useful for incrementally solving problems that are already bounded but have very large cardinalities.

Acknowledgments. This work was partly funded by ZIM BMBK grants KK5291307GR4 and KK5394902GR4.

Disclosure of Interests. The authors have no competing interests to declare that are relevant to the content of this article.

References

1. Aschinger, M., Drescher, C., Gottlob, G., Vollmer, H.: LoCo - a logic for configuration problems. ACM Trans. Comput. Logic **15**(3), 20:1–20:25 (2014). https://doi.org/10.1145/2629454
2. Balázová, L., Comploi-Taupe, R., Hahn, S., Rühling, N., Schenner, G.: Smart expansion techniques for ASP-based interactive configuration. Theory Pract. Logic Program. **25**(4), 473–488 (2025)
3. Banbara, M., Kaufmann, B., Ostrowski, M., Schaub, T.: Clingcon: the next generation. Theory Pract. Logic Program. **17**(4), 408–461 (2017)
4. Baumeister, J., et al.: Towards industrial-scale product configuration. Theory Pract. Logic Programm., 1–31 (2026)
5. Baumeister, J., et al.: CoomSuite (2024). https://github.com/potassco/coom-suite
6. Baumeister, J., Herud, K., Reutelshöfer, J., Belli, V.: Coom language (2024). https://www.coom-lang.org/
7. Cabalar, P., Fandinno, J., Schaub, T., Wanko, P.: flingo — instilling asp expressiveness into linear integer constraints. Theory Pract. Logic Program. (2026)
8. Comploi-Taupe, R., Falkner, A.: Product Configuration - An Introduction for Practitioners. In: Springer Briefs in Computer Science, Springer-Verlag (2026)
9. Comploi-Taupe, R., Falkner, A., Hahn, S., Schaub, T., Schenner, G.: Interactive configuration with ASP multi-shot solving. In: Proceedings of the Twenty-fifth International Configuration Workshop (CONF'23), vol. 3509, pp. 95–103. CEUR Workshop Proceedings (2023). https://ceur-ws.org/Vol-3509/paper13.pdf
10. Falkner, A., Friedrich, G., Haselböck, A., Schenner, G., Schreiner, H.: Twenty-five years of successful application of constraint technologies at siemens. AI Mag. **37**(4), 67–80 (2016). https://doi.org/10.1609/aimag.v37i4.2688
11. Falkner, A., Ryabokon, A., Schenner, G., Shchekotykhin, K.: OOASP: connecting object-oriented and logic programming. In: Calimeri, F., Ianni, G., Truszczynski, M. (eds.) LPNMR 2015. LNCS (LNAI), vol. 9345, pp. 332–345. Springer, Cham (2015). https://doi.org/10.1007/978-3-319-23264-5_28
12. Felfernig, A., Hotz, L., Bagley, C.: Knowledge-Based Configuration: From Research to Business Cases (2014)
13. Fleishanderl, G., Friedrich, G., Haselbock, A., Schreiner, H., Stumptner, M.: Configuring large systems using generative constraint satisfaction. IEEE Intell. Syst. Appl. **13**(4), 59–68 (1998)
14. Francescutto, G., Schekotihin, K., El-Kholany, M.: Solving a multi-resource partial-ordering flexible variant of the job-shop scheduling problem with hybrid ASP. In: Proceedings of the Seventeenth European Conference on Logics in Artificial Intelligence (JELIA'21), pp. 313–328. Springer-Verlag, Cham (2021). https://doi.org/10.1007/978-3-030-75775-5_21
15. Friedrich, G., Ryabokon, A., Falkner, A., Haselböck, A., Schenner, G., Schreiner, H.: (re)configuration based on model generation. In: Proceedings of the Second International Workshop on Logics for Component Configuration (LoCoCo'11), pp. 26–35 (2011)
16. Gebser, M., et al.: Potassco User Guide (2019). version 2.2.0 edn
17. Gebser, M., Kaminski, R., Kaufmann, B., Schaub, T.: Multi-shot ASP solving with clingo. Theory Pract. Logic Program. **19**(1), 27–82 (2019)
18. Kaminski, R., Romero, J., Schaub, T., Wanko, P.: How to build your own ASP-based system?! Theory Pract. Logic Program. **23**(1), 299–361 (2023)
19. Lifschitz, V.: Answer Set Programming. Springer-Verlag (2019)

20. Rühling, N., Schaub, T., Wanko, P.: Formalizing ASP-based product configuration: Work in progress. In: Proceedings of the Eighth Workshop on Trends and Applications of Answer Set Programming (TAASP'25) (2025)
21. Taupe, R., Falkner, A., Schenner, G.: Deriving tighter component cardinality bounds for product configuration. In: Proceedings of the Eighteenth International Configuration Workshop (CONF'16), pp. 47–54 (2016)

Joint Air Traffic Flow and Capacity Management via Answer Set Programming

Alexander Beiser[1(✉)], Markus Hecher[2,3], Nysret Musliu[1], and Stefan Woltran[1]

[1] TU Wien, Vienna, Austria
alexander.beiser@tuwien.ac.at
[2] University of Potsdam, Potsdam, France
[3] CNRS, Artois University (CRIL), Lens, France

Abstract. Operational *Air Traffic Flow and Capacity Management* (ATFCM) balances flight demand with available sector capacity, to ensure safe and efficient operations. Mathematical models enhance operational ATFCM performance by framing demand-capacity balancing as an optimization problem, maximizing efficiency while adhering to safety constraints. However, state-of-the-art (SOTA) research optimizes the aircraft trajectories (called ATFM) or the sector configuration (called DAC) separately. This leaves a research gap of whether joint optimization of ATFM and DAC can bring benefits. We partially address this limitation by introducing a *joint ATFCM* model with an encoding in Answer Set Programming (ASP). The ASP implementation is evaluated against two baselines applied to our joint model: a SOTA Mixed Integer Programming (MIP) model and an iterative CASA-based heuristic. Computational experiments utilize an instance generator fitted to historical OpenSky Network flight data. Our results indicate that the ASP model outperforms the MIP model, while ASP remains competitive against heuristics on small instances. Furthermore, while DAC has the largest improvement on solving performance compared to rerouting and delaying, unrestricted variants of DAC or rerouting lead to search space thrashing.

Keywords: Answer Set Programming · Air Traffic Flow and Capacity Management · Dynamic Airspace Configuration · Joint Optimization

1 Introduction

Operational *Air Traffic Flow and Capacity Management* (ATFCM) is essential to maintaining safe and efficient air traffic. ATFCM aims to balance demand and capacity. Demand can be understood as the number of flights that wish to operate in a sector at a specific time, while capacity is the maximum number of flights a sector can handle in a time window [9]. Demand must be kept below

W. Faber et al. (Eds.): LPNMR 2026, LNAI 16952, pp. 100–116, 2027.
https://doi.org/10.1007/978-3-032-38320-4_7

capacity, as overloading a sector increases the risk of safety incidents. This is achieved by delaying or rerouting aircraft, or restructuring airspace.

However, at the time of writing, ATFCM faces unprecedented challenges due to multiple factors, including air traffic controller shortages and increasing traffic demand [19]. These challenges lead to an increase in demand, with a simultaneous decrease in capacity. Tackling this imbalance is non-trivial; however, scientific endeavors are making progress on mathematical models suitable for optimization. Existing ATFCM research can be split into work that focuses on increasing the efficiency of *Air Traffic Flow Management* (ATFM) and optimizing airspace via *Dynamic Airspace Configuration* (DAC). ATFM focuses on measures to keep demand below capacity by delaying aircraft or rerouting them. Their models assume a static or pre-determined airspace and methodologically often use Mixed Integer (linear) Programming (MIP) [3,10,12]. In contrast to this, DAC research uses methods based on geometric, graph-based, or trajectory-based approaches [17], but keeps flight plans fixed.

Nevertheless, gaps remain. First, *joint* optimization of ATFM and DAC can potentially yield performance improvements, due to higher degrees of freedom. Second, the dominance of MIP raises the question whether declarative logic programming methods such as Answer Set Programming (ASP) [13] can serve as a viable formalization language. From an ASP perspective, joint ATFCM is an interesting real-world setting with interacting hard and soft constraints (safety, efficiency, and fairness/stability).

Contributions. We address these gaps by proposing a novel ATFCM model:

- We present the first combined air traffic flow and capacity management model for simultaneous optimization in ASP.
- We provide an instance generator for small instances fitted to open flight data (including the OpenSky Network COVID-19 dataset), enabling controlled scaling studies across geographic regions.
- We present the first ATFCM ASP encoding, which we benchmark on data sampled from the instance generator. We compare the ASP encoding to simulated state-of-the-art (SOTA) MIP and heuristic algorithms, and finally perform an ablation study to investigate the impact of enabling / partially disabling/disabling actions. Our findings indicate (1) promising results of ASP, (2) that restricting the search spaces of DAC and rerouting improves results under a fixed compute budget, and (3) that computational bottlenecks in both solving and grounding remain for unbounded variants.

After the introduction (Sect. 1) and the preliminaries (Sect. 2), we present the ATFCM model with the ASP encoding in Sect. 3. Section 4 shows the data pipeline, Sect. 5 the experiments, and Sect. 6 our conclusions.

2 Preliminaries and Related Work

Answer Set Programming. ASP is a logic programming paradigm based on non-monotonic reasoning [13]. A program is a set of rules $p_1(\mathbf{X}_1) \vee \ldots \vee p_\ell(\mathbf{X}_\ell) \leftarrow p_{\ell+1}(\mathbf{X}_{\ell+1}), \ldots, p_m(\mathbf{X}_m), \neg p_{m+1}(\mathbf{X}_{m+1}), \ldots, \neg p_n(\mathbf{X}_n)$, where $p_i(\mathbf{X}_i)$ is a literal, l, m, n are non-negative integers s.t. $l \leq m \leq n$, and $\mathbf{X}_i = \langle x_1, \ldots, x_z \rangle$ is a term vector comprising constants and variables. *Grounding* refers to the instantiation of variables by all possible domain values, resulting in a ground program. Semantics of ground programs is defined via *Gelfond-Lifschitz reduct*. *Weak constraints* enable optimization [5]. ASP is attractive for ATFCM because it supports rapid modeling of constraints, and lexicographic optimization.
Setting. Air Traffic Flow and Capacity Management (ATFCM) is the layer of Air Traffic Management that aims to keep demand below capacity [9]. Capacity is primarily driven by controller workload: airspace is partitioned into *sectors* and each sector admits at most X flights per hour. For *filed* flights (requested/-planned operations), a network manager considers interventions that trade off safety (no overload) and efficiency (delay, fuel, distance, stability). In practice, common levers are (i) ground delay, (ii) rerouting within (constrained) acceptable trajectories, and (iii) *Dynamic Airspace Configuration* (DAC). While (i) and (ii) operate on a per-aircraft trajectory basis, (iii) operates on a sector level.

Related Work. In European operations, ATFM departure regulations are largely computed by the *Computer Assisted Slot Allocation* (CASA) algorithm, which follows a "First-Planned, First-Served" principle [6]. CASA is known to be efficiency-suboptimal; even early mathematical optimization models improved total delay and were later extended with additional criteria (e.g., fairness) [21]. Bertsimas and Patterson showed that the ATFM model for static airspaces and static routes, but dynamic delaying, is already NP-hard [3]. On the DAC side, many approaches construct sectorizations in continuous airspace using heuristics (e.g., genetic algorithms, Voronoi diagrams) [22] or exploit graph/flow and learning-based methods [7,8]. Model-wise, our approach occupies a middle ground between bottom-up sector construction by combining atomic sector structures and airspace partitioning. From a logic programming perspective, the aviation literature contains only isolated uses (e.g., drones/vertiports) [15,18]. Still, ASP is used in many other industrial domains [1,2,11]. We provide the first ASP encoding for joint ATFCM, compare it to SOTA methods, conduct an ablation study, and investigate whether ATFCM suffers from the grounding bottleneck.

3 Joint ATFCM Model via ASP

In this section, we present the basics of our ATFCM model by following a running example based on Fig. 1b. Our model is based on the basic structure of the *navpoint graph*. Aircraft fly between *navpoints* or *airports* along *airways* on the navpoint graph. We assume that flights can not take other maneuvers and must stay on the airways. With this, we can define our navpoint graph structure.

Definition 1 (Navpoint Graph). *The navpoint graph $G = (V, E)$ is undirected and labeled. Each $v \in V$ is either a navpoint or an airport and has an associated coordinate $(lat, lon, alt) \in \mathbb{R}^3$. Edges (airways) $e = (v_i, v_j) \in E$ connect vertices. Distances of airways are given by the geodesic distance $d : V^2 \rightarrow \mathbb{R}$.*

Example 1. G is defined according to Fig. 1b. Let $V' = \{v_0, v_1, v_2\}$, with $v_0 = (50, 14, 100)$, $v_1 = (48, 14, 100)$, $v_2 = (46, 14, 100)$, and $V_a = \{a_0, a_1\}$ with $a_0 = (48.3536, 11.7832, 0)$ and $a_1 = (48.1179, 16.5566, 0)$, so $V = V' \cup V_a$, and further, $E = \{(a_0, v_0), (a_0, v_1), (a_0, v_2), (v_0, a_1), (v_1, a_1), (v_2, a_1)\}$. For the sake of this running example, we approximate the distances to be $d(a_0, v_0) = d(a_0, v_2) = d(a_1, v_0) = d(a_1, v_2) = 290[km]$ and $d(a_0, v_1) = d(a_1, v_1) = 180[km]$.

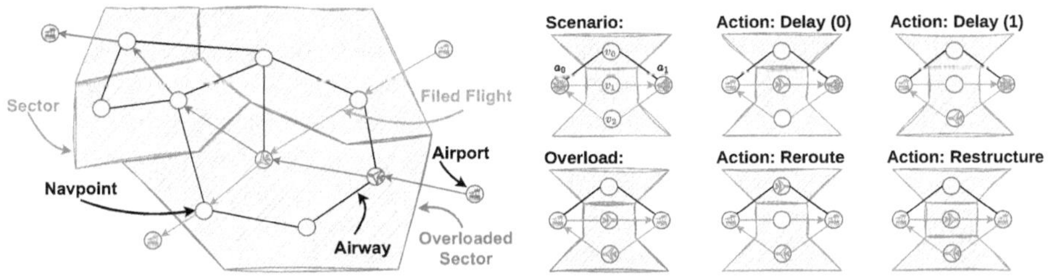

(a) Schematics of ATFCM for a time t. (b) Schematics with available actions.

Fig. 1. (a): Filed flights fly along airways (edges) on the navpoint graph, overlaid with a sector configuration with four sectors, where one sector is overloaded (red). (b): From left top to bottom right: two filed flights, delaying a flight, indication of an overload, rerouting, and restructuring. (Color figure online)

Definition 2 (Time Model). *Time is discretized into timesteps $t_i \in T$, with T_{gran} timesteps per hour where T_{gran} divides 60 such that the timestep length is defined in minutes by $T_s = \frac{60}{T_{gran}}$. The set of timesteps T, is for $dur \in \mathbb{N}$ given by $T = \{t \mid t \in \mathbb{N}, 1 \leq t \leq dur \cdot T_{gran}\} \cup \{0\}$.*

Example 2. We consider $T_{gran} = 1$ with $|T| = 25$, so $dur = 24$ (1h granularity). If $T_{gran} = 4$, with $|T| = 97$, then also $dur = 24$ (15 minutes granularity).

Definition 3 (Sector Configuration). *A* sector *at time t is a set of vertices (navpoints/airports). To keep the index set fixed across time, we represent each sector i by a distinguished* sector identifier *$i \in V$. We write $S = V$ for the set of all identifiers. The sector identified by i at time t is the set $sec(i, t) \subseteq V$. Formally, a* sector configuration *is a function $sec : S \times T \rightarrow 2^V$ such that for every $t \in T$: (i) $\{sec(i, t) \mid i \in S,\ sec(i, t) \neq \emptyset\}$ forms a partition of V; and (ii) every airport is a singleton sector. Conversely, $sec^{-1} : V \times T \rightarrow S$ denotes the inverse assignment. The initial sector configuration at timestep $t_s = 0$ is the atomic configuration, with atomic capacities $cap(i, 0) = c_i$. Due to operational constraints, merging sectors does not lead to an increase in overall capacity. We model this by defining $cap(i, t)$ for a composite sector to be the max function.*

Example 3. We define two sector models on G from Example 1 and let $T_{gran} = 4$ and $|T| = 97$. Let the atomic capacities be $cap(a_0, 0) = cap(a_1, 0) = 2$ and $cap(v_0, 0) = cap(v_1, 0) = cap(v_2, 0) = 1$. We define the static model as $\forall t > 0$: $sec(a_0, t) = \{a_0\}$, $sec(a_1, t) = \{a_1\}$, $sec(v_0, t) = \{v_0\}$, and $sec(v_1, t) = \{v_1, v_2\}$.

Definition 4 (Aircraft Model). *Let* $\mathtt{A}$ *be the set of aircraft where an aircraft* $p = (I_p, u_p, F_p) \in \mathtt{A}$ *is defined by its ID* I_p*, (time granularity normalized) velocity* u_p*, and its flights* F_p*. A flight* $f = (I_f, tr) \in F_p$ *is comprised of an ID* I_f *and a trajectory* $tr \in \mathcal{TR}_a$*. A trajectory* $tr \in \mathcal{TR}_a$ *is a (simple) path on* G *augmented with timestamps in the form* (v_i, t_i)*, where* $v_i \in V$ *and* $t_i \in T$*; for pairs* $(v_i, t_i), (v_{i+1}, t_{i+1}) \in tr$ *it holds* $t_i < t_{i+1}$ *s.t.* $t_{i+1} - t_i = \max\{\lceil \frac{d(v_i, v_{i+1})}{u_a} \rceil, 1\}$*. The set of flights is* $\mathcal{F}$ *and the set of flights w.r.t. a velocity* u_a *is* $\mathcal{F}_a$*.*

Example 4. Let G be as in Example 1, $T_{gran} = 4$, and $|T| = 97$. We assume that both aircraft $\mathtt{A} = \{p_0, p_1\}$ are typical single-piston engine aircraft, where $p_0 = (p_0, u_a, f_0)$ and $p_1 = (p_1, u_a, f_1)$. Therefore, we choose their velocity to be $u_a = 172.79[kts] = 0.08[\frac{km}{s}] = 80[\frac{km}{15 \cdot min}]$, where the last one is the time granularity normalized velocity. With this velocity, we obtain the flight times $\Delta t = 3$ for (a_0, v_1) and (v_1, a_1), and $\Delta t = 4$ for $(a_0, v_0), (v_0, a_1), (a_0, v_2)$, and (v_2, a_1). Finally, according to Fig. 1b the filed flights are: $\mathcal{F} = \{f_0, f_1\} = \{(0, ((a_0, 1), (v_1, 4), (a_1, 7))), (1, ((a_1, 1), (v_2, 5), (a_0, 9)))\}$.

Definition 5 (ATFCM Instance). *An instance is* $I = (G, T_{gran}, T, sec, cap, \mathtt{A})$*, comprising a navpoint graph* G*, time granularity* T_{gran}*, timesteps* T*, initial sector configurations* sec*, atomic capacities* cap*, and aircraft* $\mathtt{A}$*. All identifiers are unique.*

Definition 6 (ATFCM Solution). *A valid solution* $\mathbf{S} = (\mathbf{T}, \mathbf{SEC}, \mathbf{A})$ *defines solution timesteps* $\mathbf{T} \supseteq T$*, an updated DAC* $\mathbf{SEC}$*, and adjusted aircraft* $\mathbf{A}$*. We denote with* $\mathbf{F}$ *the set of adjusted flights stemming from* $\mathbf{A}$*. We require:*

- ***Flight Adjustments:*** *Flights* $f \in \mathbf{F}$*: we measure arrival delay as* d_f*; if* f *is delayed and/or rerouted, then* $r_f = 1$ *(else 0).*
- ***Sector Constraints:*** $\mathbf{SEC}$ *partitions navpoints over time (airports atomic).*
- ***Demand Routing:*** *A flight* f *traversing navpoints* v_a *to* v_b *in* $\Delta t = t_b - t_a$ *occupies* $sec^{-1}(v_a, t)$ *for* $t \in [t_a, t_a + \Delta t/2]$ *and* $sec^{-1}(v_b, t)$ *subsequently. We define* $over(f, i, t) \in \{0, 1\}$ *to indicate if* f *occupies sector* i *at* t*.*
- ***Capacity Constraints:*** *Sector demand* $q(i, t) = \sum_{f \in \mathbf{F}} over(f, i, t)$ *must satisfy* $q(i, t) \leq cap(i, t)$ *for all* $t \in \mathbf{T}$*,* $i \in V$*.*

Definition 7 (Optimization Problem). *Valid solutions are strictly ordered* $(\mathbf{S} \prec \mathbf{S}')$ *by a lexicographically minimized objective tuple* $(K_d, K_{\#s}, K_{ds}, K_r, K_c)$*, balancing efficiency and stability:*

- ***Arrival Delay:*** $K_d = \sum_{f \in \mathbf{F}} d_f$
- ***Active Sectors:*** $K_{\#s} = \sum_{t \in \mathbf{T}_{>0}} \sum_{i \in V} \mathbb{I}(|\mathbf{SEC}(i, t)| > 0)$
- ***Vertex-Sector Changes:*** $K_{ds} = \sum_{t \in \mathbf{T}_{\geq 1}} \sum_{v \in V} \mathbb{I}(\mathbf{SEC}^{-1}(v, t-1) \neq \mathbf{SEC}^{-1}(v, t))$
- ***Reroutes/Delays:*** $K_r = \sum_{f \in \mathbf{F}} r_f$
- ***Reconfigurations:*** $K_c = \sum_{t \in \mathbf{T}_{\geq 0}} \sum_{v \in V} \mathbb{I}(sec^{-1}(v, t) \neq \mathbf{SEC}^{-1}(v, t))$

3.1 ASP Encoding: Definition of Instance

Based on these definitions, we are ready to present the ASP instance and encoding. First, we are going to present the ASP instance with some preprocessing steps, followed by the encoding. In our prototype written in Python[1], the input as defined above is translated into an ASP instance, which we structure into three parts: *navpoint graph instance*, *initial DAC instance*, and *filed flights instance.* The navpoint graph instance defines the navpoint graph with the distinction between airports and navpoints. Additionally, we perform a preprocessing step which eases the computational load of ASP, by computing normalized distances w.r.t. T_{gran} based on aircraft velocities—so the distances are given in timesteps.

Navpoint Graph Instance

- arpt(<ID>): Indicates that a vertex is an airport.
- nvpt_e(<V_i>,<V_j>,<V_a>,<Δt>): For two connected vertices $e = (v_i, v_j) \in E$, we pre-compute the normalized travel duration Δt for all normalized velocities of aircraft u_a.

For the initial DAC instance we define atomic capacities and init configuration.

Initial DAC Instance

- atomic_s(<NVPT-ID>,<CAP>,<T>): Initial capacities (assumed static).
- nvpt_s(<NVPT-ID>,<SEC-ID>,<T=0 for FACTS>): The initial sector configuration for time $t = 0$.

The filed flights are given with the additional information about aircraft velocity and the mapping for multi-leg flights.

Filed Flights Instance

- acft(<ID>,<u_a>): Aircraft ID and its velocity u_a.
- acft_flt(<ACFT-ID>,<FLIGHT-ID>): The mapping between aircraft and flights; needed among others for multi-leg flights.
- nvpt_flt_pln(<FLT-ID>,<NVPT-ID>,<T>): The filed flight plan as 3-tuples of flight ids, navpoint ids, and time steps.

Example 5. The converted running example into the ASP instance:

```
arpt(a0). arpt(a1). nvpt_e(a0, v0, 80, 4). nvpt_e(a0, v1, 80, 3). nvpt_e(a0, v2, 80, 4).
nvpt_e(a1, v0, 80, 4). nvpt_e(a1, v1, 80, 3). nvpt_e(a1, v2, 80, 4).  atomic_s(a0,2,0). atomic_s(a1,2,0).
atomic_s(v0,1,0). atomic_s(v1,1,0). atomic_s(v2,1,0). nvpt_s(a0, a0, 0). nvpt_s(a1, a1, 0).
nvpt_s(v0, v0, 0). nvpt_s(v1, v1, 0). nvpt_s(v2, v1, 0).  acft(0,80). acft(1,80). acft_flt(0,0).
acft_flt(1,1). nvpt_flt_pln(0,a0,1). nvpt_flt_pln(0,v1,4). nvpt_flt_pln(0,a1,7). nvpt_flt_pln(1,a1,1).
nvpt_flt_pln(1,v2,5). nvpt_flt_pln(1,a0,9). atomic_s(N,C,T) ←atomic_s(N,C,0), t(T).
```

[1] GitHub: https://github.com/alexl4123/ASPaeroFlow-Optimizer/tree/main/02_ASP.

3.2 ASP Encoding: Actions

We continue to present the ASP encoding. The encoding is written in a way that enables us to perform an ablation study, which actions (*ground delaying*, *rerouting*, or *airspace restructuring*) are actually beneficial. For each action, we implement 3 versions, which gives us in total 27 possible ASP configurations for our ablation study. An ASP configuration is given by the 3-tuple (R, D, S), with $R \in \{r, r_p, \neg r\}$, $D \in \{d, d_p, \neg d\}$, and $S \in \{s, s_p, \neg s\}$. The Python wrapper translates a configuration (R, D, S) to a set of facts, which provides instructions to the encoding. Here, we focus on the definitions of these facts and how this is translated in the encoding. We start with D, followed by R, and lastly S.

Ground Delaying ($D \in \{d, d_p, \neg d\}$)

- d: Delaying along the entire considered time T
  - ASP atom: `reg_del`
- d_p: Partial delaying (only max. `<MAX-TIME>` $= 4$ timesteps)
  - ASP atom: `reg_rd`
  - ASP atom: `reg_dmd(<MAX-TIME>)`
- $\neg d$: Delaying is forbidden
  - ASP atom: `-reg_del`

Ground delaying means that we guess the actual departure time depending on the atom $(d, d_p, \neg d)$ present in the instance (Lines (1–4)). For d_p, we restrict the guess to a pre-defined selection (Line (3)).

```
1 p_dep_t(ID,T) ← flt_id(ID), T = #min{T':nvpt_flt_pln(ID,_,T')}.
2 1{a_dep_t(ID,T):t(T), T >= TP}1 ← p_dep_t(ID,TP), reg_del.
3 1{a_dep_t(ID,T):t(T),T>=TP,T<=TP+MD}1 ← p_dep_t(ID,TP),reg_dmd(MD),reg_rd
  .
4 a_dep_t(ID,TP) ← p_dep_t(ID,TP), -reg_del.
```

Rerouting ($R \in \{r, r_p, \neg r\}$)

- r: Full rerouting is allowed (ASP finds paths).
  - ASP atom: `reg_rer`
- r_p: Partial rerouting; pick best of 4 diverse precomputed shortest paths (Jaccard similarity at most 60%). Let `<FLT>` be the flight ID, `<NVPT>` be the navpoint at flight time `<FLT-T>` for a chosen path `<PTH>`.
  - ASP atom: `reg_restr_rer`
  - ASP atom: `reg_rrp(<FLT>,<NVPT>,<FLT-T>,<PTH>)`
- $\neg r$: Rerouting is forbidden.
  - ASP atom: `-reg_rer`

We continue with R. First, we combine the ATFM side, whether a flight is rerouted or delayed, into one atom `rer` (Lines (1–2)). If r is enabled we guess a set of vertices (Line (4)), if r_p is enabled then we guess one path of the provided ones (Lines (5)–(6)), and if rerouting is disabled ($\neg r$) or `rer` is not set, we require that the flight follows the vertices of the filed flight (Lines (3) and (7)).

```
{rer(ID)} ← nvpt_flt_pln(ID,_,_).
rer(ID) ← p_dep_t(ID,T), a_dep_t(ID,T'), T' > T.
nvpt_flt(ID,X,T) ← nvpt_flt_pln(ID,X,T), not rer(ID).
{nvpt_flt(ID,X,T):nvpt(X)}1 ← rer(ID),t(T),a_dep_t(ID,T'),T>=T',reg_rer.
1{nvpt_flt_cp(ID,P):reg_rrp(ID,_,_,P)}1 ← rer(ID),reg_restr_rer.
nvpt_flt(ID,X,T+T') ← reg_rrp(ID,X,T',P),rer(ID),a_dep_t(ID,T),
    nvpt_flt_cp(ID,P),reg_restr_rer.
nvpt_flt(ID,X,T+TT) ← nvpt_flt_pln(ID,X,T),a_dep_t(ID,TACT),p_dep_t(ID,
    TPLAN),TT=TACT-TPLAN,-reg_rer.
```

Airspace Restructuring ($S \in \{s, s_p, \neg s\}$)

- s: Full airspace restructuring is allowed (no explicit operational constraints).
  - ASP atom: `reg_dyn_sec_alloc`.
- s_p: Partial restructuring — 4 choices (`<D>`): (i) keep airspace structure, split into (ii) 2 or (iii) 4 connected sectors, or (iv) split into atomic structure. We enforce connected sectors in our partial restructuring to comply with typical operational needs of lowering the *sector complexity*. Let `<S>` be the original sector, `<NVPT>` be the navpoint, and `<S1>` the new sector.
  - ASP atom: `reg_rdsa`
  - ASP atom: `nvpt_restr_sec_alloc(<S>,<D>,<NVPT>,<S1>)`
- $\neg s$: Keep initial structure.
  - ASP atom: `-reg_dyn_sec_alloc`.

We continue with S. First, each airport sector is atomic (Line (1)). If s is enabled, then an arbitrary sectorization set is guessed (Line (2)), if s_p is enabled, then one of four choices is picked (Lines (3)–(5)), and if $\neg s$ is enabled, then we enforce the initial sectorization (Line (6)).

```
1 nvpt_s(SEC,SEC,T) ← nvpt(SEC), t(T), arpt(SEC).
2 1{nvpt_s(N,S,T):nvpt_s(_,S,0)}1← nvpt(N),t(T),not arpt(N),
      reg_dyn_sec_alloc.
3 isec(SEC) ← nvpt_s(_,SEC,0), reg_rdsa.
4 1{nvpt_dec(S,0..3,T)}1 ← isec(S),t(T),not arpt(S),reg_rdsa.
5 nvpt_s(N1,S1,T) ← nvpt_dec(S,D,T),nvpt_restr_sec_alloc(S,D,N1,S1),
      reg_rdsa.
6 nvpt_s(NAV,SEC,T) ← t(T), nvpt_s(NAV,SEC,0), -reg_dyn_sec_alloc.
```

3.3 ASP Encoding: Constraints

We require that the sectorization is a partition and adheres to our definition of a sectorization. Therefore, for each timestep, it must not be the case that a vertex is assigned to two sectors (Line (1)), a navpoint is assigned to an airport (Line (2)), an airport is assigned to a navpoint sector (Line (3)), or that a non-empty sector labeled by index i does not contain vertex i (Line (4)).

```
1 ← nvpt_s(NAV,SEC1,T), nvpt_s(NAV,SEC2,T), SEC1 ≠ SEC2.
2 ← nvpt_s(NAV,SEC,T), not arpt(NAV), arpt(SEC).
3 ← nvpt_s(NAV,SEC,T), arpt(NAV), not arpt(SEC).
4 ← nvpt_s(NAV1,SEC,T), NAV1 ≠SEC, not nvpt_s(SEC,SEC,T).
```

We further require that at any step the flight must not be operating before its planned departure time (Line (1)). Additionally, we require that for r the rerouting is an actual path, therefore the flight starts at the departure airport and lands at the destination airport (Lines (2–7)). A flight is finished if its destination is reached (Lines (8–9)).

```
1 ←rer(ID), nvpt_flt(ID,_,T), p_dep_t(ID,T'), T<T'.
2 planned_origin(ID,X) ←rer(ID),p_dep_t(ID,T),nvpt_flt_pln(ID,X,T).
3 nvpt_flt(ID,X,T) ←rer(ID), a_dep_t(ID,T), planned_origin(ID,X).
4 p_dest(ID,X) ←rer(ID),T=#max{T':nvpt_flt_pln(ID,_,T')},nvpt_flt_pln(ID,X
      ,T).
5 a_arr_t(ID,T) ←flt_id(ID), T=#max{T':nvpt_flt(ID,_,T')}.
6 ←flt_id(ID), not a_arr_t(ID,_).
7 ←flt_id(ID), p_dest(ID,X), a_arr_t(ID,T), nvpt_flt(ID,X',T), X ≠ X'.
8 a_dest_f_rch_t(ID,T) ←rer(ID), p_dest(ID,X), T=#min{T':nvpt_flt(ID,X,T')
      }.
9 ←rer(ID), nvpt_flt(ID,_,T), a_dest_f_rch_t(ID,T'), T > T'.
```

We require that a flight is a valid trajectory, so is a path with valid timesteps (Lines (1–4)), that a flight is never twice at the same location (Line (5)), that a flight actually occurs (Lines (6–7)), and ensure that multi-leg flights occur in the right order (Line (8)).

```
1 p_nvpt_seq(ID,T,TT) ←nvpt_flt(ID,_,T), nvpt_flt(ID,_,TT), T < TT.
2 n_nvpt_seq(ID,T,TT) ←p_nvpt_seq(ID,T,TT),T<TTT,TTT<TT,p_nvpt_seq(ID,T,
      TTT).
3 nvpt_seq(ID,T,TT) ←p_nvpt_seq(ID,T,TT), not n_nvpt_seq(ID,T,TT).
4 ←nvpt_seq(ID,T,TT), nvpt_flt(ID,X,T), nvpt_flt(ID,XX,TT), acft_flt(AID,
      ID), acft(AID,S), D=TT-T, not nvpt_e(X,XX,S,D).
5 ←nvpt_flt(ID,X,T), nvpt_flt(ID,X,T'), T ≠ T', not arpt(X).
6 flightOccurs(ID) ←nvpt_flt(ID,_,_).
7 ←flt_id(ID), not flightOccurs(ID).
8 ←acft_flt(AID,FID0), acft_flt(AID,FID1), FID0≠FID1, p_arr_t(FID0,T0),
      p_arr_t(FID1,T1), T0 < T1, a_arr_t(FID0, T0'),a_dep_t(FID1,T1'),T0
      '>=T1'.
```

3.4 ASP Encoding: Navpoint Flight Mapping

Due to the joint modeling of DAC and flow optimization, we are left to map navpoint reach times to travel times. We approximate sector occupancy by assigning the first half of the flight between two navpoints to the first navpoint sector, and the second half to the second navpoint sector: let $f \in \mathbf{F}$ be a flight reaching navpoint $v_a \in V$ at time t_a and then flying to navpoint $v_b \in V$, which it reaches at time t_b. Assuming that $\Delta t = t_b - t_a$, then f is in the timespan $t \in [t_a, t_a + \lfloor\frac{\Delta t}{2}\rfloor]$ in sector $sec^{-1}(v_a, t)$, and for $t' \in [t_a + \lfloor\frac{\Delta t}{2}\rfloor + 1, t_b]$ in sector $sec^{-1}(v_b, t')$. We encode this in Lines (1–5), while we forbid "holes" (Line (6)).

```
1 flight(ID,S,T) ←nvpt_flt(ID,X,T), nvpt_s(X,S,T).
2 flightT(ID,T,T',0) ←nvpt_seq(ID,T,TT),D=TT-T,t(T'),T'>T,T'<=T+D/2.
3 flightT(ID,TT,T',1) ←nvpt_seq(ID,T,TT),D=TT-T,t(T'),T'<TT,T'>T+D/2.
4 flight(ID,S,T') ←flightT(ID,T,T',0), nvpt_flt(ID,X,T), nvpt_s(X,S,T').
5 flight(ID,S,T') ←flightT(ID,TT,T',1), nvpt_flt(ID,XX,TT), nvpt_s(XX,S,T
      ').
6 ←t(T), a_dep_t(ID,T'), T > T', a_arr_t(ID,T''), T < T'', not flight(ID,_
      ,T).
```

3.5 ASP Encoding: Optimization

We map the optimization problem of Definition 7 into a multi-objective lexicographic optimization ASP program. Regarding specifics, we treat safety as a soft constraint in order to track its computational results in the experiment section. Still, only 0-overload solutions are valid solutions. Overall, we have then six optimization criteria: the total number of overloads followed by the criteria from Definition 7.

```
sec_len(SEC,T,CL) ← t(T),nvpt(SEC),CL=#count{NAV:nvpt_s(NAV,SEC,T)}.
sec(SEC,T,0) ← sec_len(SEC,T,CAP_LEN), CAP_LEN = 0.
sec(SEC,T,C) ← t(T), nvpt(SEC), C = #max{C',NAV:nvpt_s(NAV,SEC,T),
    atomic_s(NAV,C',T)}, sec_len(SEC,T,CAP_LEN), CAP_LEN > 0.
overload(X,T,LOAD-C) ← sec(X,T,C), #count{ID:flight(ID,X,T)}=LOAD, LOAD>C
.
:~ overload(X,T,OVER). [OVER@10,X,T] % PRIMARY WEAK CONSTRAINT
```

We use efficiency objectives as our secondary objectives, which follows common practice in the literature [3]. However, we expand the current practice by incorporating *airspace efficiency* metrics, which we partially take from the DAC literature. Generally speaking, DAC wants to have as few sectors as possible with as few changes as possible, while additionally minimizing sector complexity. As proxies for this, people may use minimization of excess capacity [16], or explicitly minimizing for controller communication overload [17]. We minimize the number of sector changes, while considering airspace complexity with our partial sectorization approach (s_p).

```
p_arr_t(ID,T) ← flt_id(ID), T = #max{T':nvpt_flt_pln(ID,_,T')}.
arrival_delay(ID,Y-T) ← p_arr_t(ID,T), a_arr_t(ID,Y).
sector_number(T,NUM) ← t(T), NUM = #count{SEC:sec_len(SEC,T,C), C > 0}.
nvpt_ch(NAV,T,1) ← nvpt_s(NAV,SEC0,T),nvpt_s(NAV,SEC1,T+1),SEC0≠SEC1.
nvpt_ch(NAV,T,0) ← nvpt_s(NAV,SEC0,T),nvpt_s(NAV,SEC0,T+1).
sector_diff(T,DIFF) ← t(T), DIFF = #sum{V,NAV: nvpt_ch(NAV,T,V)}.
:~ arrival_delay(ID,DIFF). [DIFF@9,ID]    % SECONDARY WEAK CONSTRAINT
:~ sector_number(T,NUM). [NUM@8,T]        % TERTIARY WEAK CONSTRAINT
:~ sector_diff(T,DIFF). [DIFF@7,T]        % OPTIMIZE FOR LEAST SECTOR
    CHANGES
```

Lastly, we optimize for fairness/stability to the original plan, where we follow the general plan of optimizing for flow first and then airspace.

```
reconfig(NAV,T) ← nvpt_s(NAV,SEC,0), nvpt_s(NAV,SEC2,T), SEC ≠ SEC2, T >
    0.
:~ rer(ID). [1@6,ID]              % OPTIMIZE FOR LEAST REROUTES/DELAYS
:~ reconfig(ID,T). [1@5,ID,T]        % OPTIMIZE FOR LEAST RECONFIGS
```

3.6 Finalizing the Example

Example 6. We show the results of the running example applied to the encoding above under the configuration (r, d, s):

```
max_t(96). reg_del. reg_dyn_sec_alloc. reg_rer.
```

Solving this instance leads to the following results: 0 overload, 0 arrival delay, 294 number of sectors, 3 sector-diffs, 1 rerouting, and 94 reconfigurations. The solution of the sectorization is: $\forall t > 0$: $sec(a_0, t) = \{a_0\}$ and $sec(a_1, t) = \{a_1\}$. For $t \leq 3$ and $t \geq 6$ it is: $sec(v_1, t) = \{v_0, v_1, v_2\}$, whereas for $t \in \{4, 5\}$ it is: $sec(v_0, t) = \{v_0\}$ and $sec(v_1, t) = \{v_1, v_2\}$. Further, the optimized flight trajectories are: $\mathcal{F}_a = \{(0, ((a_0, 1), (v_1, 4), (a_1, 7))), (1, ((a_1, 1), (v_0, 5), (a_0, 9)))\}$. The trajectory-sector mappings are: f_0 : $(a_0, 1), (a_0, 2), (v_1, 3), (v_1, 4)$, $(v_1, 5), (a_1, 6), (a_1, 7)$; f_1 : $(a_1, 1)$, $(a_1, 2), (a_1, 3), (v_0, 4)$, $(v_0, 5), (v_1, 6), (v_1, 7), (a_0, 8), (a_0, 9)$. The (total) number of sectors is also optimal: each airport must be a singleton sector, therefore their contribution is $96 \cdot 2$. The en-route sector contribution is $96 \cdot 1$ for v_1 and $2 \cdot 1$ for v_0 (for $t \in \{4, 5\}$). As the lowest possible number of en-route total sectors is 96, any lower number than $98 = 96 + 2$ would result in merging v_1 and v_0, which would lead to an overload. This results in a (total) number of sectors of 290 (for $t > 0$), which in addition with the initial configuration with 4 sectors for $t = 0$ yields in 294. The solution changes the assignment of navpoint v_0 three times: once between $t = 0$ and $t = 1$, between $t = 3$ and $t = 4$ and between $t = 5$ and $t = 6$, leading to sector diff of 3. Further, flight 1 is rerouted from flying over navpoint v_2 to flying via v_0 and finally, 94 reconfigurations results from reconfigurations of v_0 in 94 timesteps ($t \notin \{0, 4, 5\}$), yielding $97 - 3 = 94$.

3.7 Correctness

We briefly argue for correctness for $ASP(r, d, s)$. Let $\mathcal{I}$ be an arbitrary instance; let Π be the encoding, then Π' is the encoding without soft constraints, but with $c_1 := \{\leftarrow \texttt{overload}(X, T, OVER)\}$. Let $\mathcal{AS}$ be the answersets of Π'. For any flight $f \in \mathbf{F}$, let t^a_f be its actual arrival time. Let $c(\mathcal{I})$ be instance converted to ASP without $max\_t(t)$ (Sect. 3.1); for answersets $AS \in \mathcal{AS}$ let $c^{-1}(AS)$ be the converted corresponding solution $\mathbf{S}$ where $\mathbf{T}$ is chosen to be $\max_{f \in \mathbf{F}} t^a_f$. Let $\mathcal{S}_{=t}$ be the set of valid solutions for $\mathcal{I}$ s.t. $\forall \mathbf{S} \in \mathcal{S}_{=t} : \max\{\mathbf{T}\} = t$, where we require $\max_{f \in \mathbf{F}}\{t^a_f\} = t$; further $\mathcal{S}_{\leq t} = \bigcup_{t' \in \{0,\ldots,t\}} \mathcal{S}_{=t'}$. [$\star$]**Solution Space Equivalence.** For any $t \geq 24 \cdot T_{gran}$, the sets $\mathcal{S}_{AS} := \{c^{-1}(AS) \mid AS \in \mathcal{AS}(\Pi' \cup c(\mathcal{I}) \cup \{max\_t(t)\})\}$ and $\mathcal{S}_{\leq t}$ match.

Theorem 1 ($\star$). *Solution Existence.* *Let $\mathcal{I}$ be an instance and $t \geq 24 \cdot T_{gran}$. $\Pi \cup c(\mathcal{I}) \cup \{max\_t(t)\}$ has a 0-overload answerset iff there exists a solution $\mathbf{S} \in \mathcal{S}_{\leq t}$ for the optimization problem (Definition 7).*

Theorem 2 ($\star$). *Optimality.* *Let $\mathcal{I}$ be an arbitrary instance, let $t \geq 24 \cdot T_{gran}$, and let one of its best solutions $\mathbf{S}_{opt}$ be found within $\max\{\mathbf{T}\} = t : \mathbf{S}_{opt} \in \mathcal{S}_{\leq t}$. Then $\Pi \cup c(\mathcal{I}) \cup \{max\_t(t)\}$ is optimal.*

4 Pipeline Integration

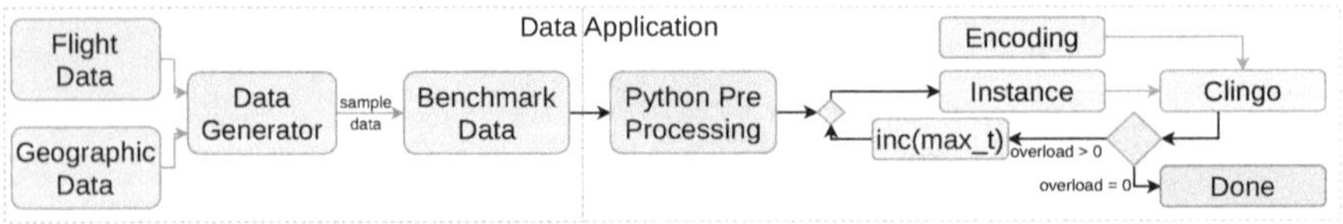

Fig. 2. Pipeline displaying the entire process, from data generation (left), over Python preprocessing to solving with ASP (right).

In Fig. 2 we show the integration of the encoding into the overall pipeline. Based on actual data, we developed an open source data generator, which enables us to sample data from different geographic regions and with an arbitrary number of flights. This benchmark data is then pre-processed in Python, which again starts the ASP solving loop: we start with a fixed maximum time (`max_t(t)`), which is iteratively expanded until a solution with 0 overload is found[2].

[2] See supplementary material for details: https://arxiv.org/abs/2606.22978.

4.1 An Open Source Data Generator

Data in ATM research is often closed source, due to privacy concerns or the fear of competitive disadvantage. Although these concerns are understandable from an economic perspective, they are disadvantageous for science—which leads to two common issues: (a) published research cannot be reproduced, thereby manifesting itself in a so-called reproducibility crisis; (b) researchers relying on open data are sometimes forced to use datasets that are ill-suited to the task. In order to circumvent this problem, movements have been initiated, such as the formation of the Open Science Alliance for ATM research [4]. However, open data for ATFCM research is still scarce. This paper takes a pro-open-data stance, by creating a data generator built from publicly available open data. Our data generator is available on GitHub[3] and we published the dataset used in the experiments on Zenodo[4]. The *Data Generator* executes three sequential internal phases to construct problem instances:

- **Graph Generation:** Constructs a configurable grid-graph of navpoints augmented with real-world airport coordinates using the public *OurAirports* dataset.
- **Flight Pair Generation:** Employs a stochastic point process [14] to sample flight operations. The underlying *Poisson model* is parameterized by historical departure and arrival intensities derived from the *OpenSky Network* COVID-19 surveillance dataset [20].
- **Trajectory & Sector Generation:** Computes baseline trajectories via *shortest-path routing* for origin-destination pairs. Initial airspace configurations are partitioned using a *Breadth-First Search (BFS)* algorithm to guarantee sectors are connected or geometrically convex.

5 Experiments

We conduct experiments on 5 graph scenarios, as shown in Table 1. Thereby, we enable a scaling study from 16 to 117 vertices. Further, we range flights from 10 to 100, with steps of 10. For each such combination of geographic and flight scenario, we generated 4 instances with different seeds. The size of these instances was chosen to be able to conduct experiments with exact solvers. Industry-sized instances largely depend upon the selected area of investigation and range from several hundreds of flights and sectors up to $30,000$ flights, $\approx 10^3$ sectors, and $\approx 10^5$ navpoints for European airspace. However, SOTA research using exact MIP models considers smaller instances which go up to approximately $\approx 3,000$ flights with bounded choices, while considering static sector configurations [12]. By enabling more degrees of freedom and dynamic alternative rerouting/delaying choices, we cannot expect to solve instances with thousands of flights.

Variants. We consider 27 variants of the ASP encoding, where each variant is defined by the previously defined 3-tuple (R, D, S). Our model implements a

[3] GitHub Link: https://github.com/alexl4123/ASPaeroFlow-DataGenerator.

[4] Zenodo DOI: https://doi.org/10.5281/zenodo.20782934.

Table 1. Scenario details for the navpoint graphs. Besides the instance and region, we show *En-route* vertices, *Airport* vertices, *Total* vertices, capacity per timestep, timestep granularity (T_{gran}), and the number of the initial sectors at $t = 0$.

Instance	Region	En-route	Airports	Total	Capacity	T_{gran}	Sec.-Num
EA-3x3	East-Asia	9	7	16	1	1	10
CE-5x5	Europe	25	7	32	1	1	12
IND-4x10	India	40	8	48	1	1	16
USA-7x7	USA	49	8	57	1	1	16
EUR-10x10	Europe	100	17	117	1	1	27

heuristic proxy for the CASA algorithm, iteratively assigning ground delays to aircraft to resolve sector capacity constraints. We denote the baseline solution as INITIAL, which are the values of the instance without any actions taken. Further, we simulate a SOTA dynamic MIP algorithm, that acts on delaying and rerouting aircraft, with bounded delay and reroute choices.

Technical Setup. Experiments were conducted on a cluster with 2x Intel Xeon Silver 4314 CPUs, 512GB RAM, and Ubuntu 22.04 (Kernel 5.15.0-131-generic). The compute budget is limited by a TIMEOUT of 1800s and a MEMOUT of 35GB. We use Python 3.13.7 with Clingo (5.8.0) API, which preprocesses and converts the input to an ASP instance. For MIP we use Gurobi (build v13.0.0rc1).

Table 2. Results aggregated by variant (across all scenarios and instances). ± denotes the SEM. Variants are sorted lexicographically.

Variant	Overload [#]	Arrival Delay [h]	Sector-Number [#]	Sector-Diff [#]	Reroute [#]	Reconfig [#]	Execution-Time [s]	Grounding-Time [s]	RAM-Usage [MB]
CASA	0.00 ± 0.00	2353.12 ± 185.87	1909.16 ± 83.14	0.00 ± 0.00	45.31 ± 1.99	0.00 ± 0.00	7.09 ± 0.16	–	214.59 ± 0.79
ASP (r_p, d, s_p)	23.27 ± 2.98	211.44 ± 15.19	1048.75 ± 50.01	434.03 ± 26.29	46.59 ± 2.13	858.01 ± 49.01	1800.20 ± 0.00	2.10 ± 0.10	487.27 ± 13.72
ASP (r_p, d_p, s_p)	29.55 ± 3.78	82.01 ± 5.21	1041.72 ± 49.92	441.54 ± 25.77	44.65 ± 2.09	838.51 ± 48.10	1800.19 ± 0.00	0.44 ± 0.02	291.44 ± 3.82
ASP $(\neg r, d, s_p)$	30.11 ± 3.33	244.55 ± 14.87	1046.53 ± 49.98	451.13 ± 25.80	46.95 ± 2.13	856.70 ± 48.86	1800.21 ± 0.00	1.54 ± 0.07	424.18 ± 9.76
ASP $(r_p, d, \neg s)$	32.25 ± 3.51	313.11 ± 15.99	448.44 ± 12.56	0.00 ± 0.00	48.99 ± 2.15	0.00 ± 0.00	1510.90 ± 45.87	1.63 ± 0.08	362.03 ± 10.12
ASP $(\neg r, d, \neg s)$	34.97 ± 3.53	327.61 ± 16.14	448.29 ± 12.62	0.00 ± 0.00	49.57 ± 2.14	0.00 ± 0.00	1537.20 ± 43.97	1.14 ± 0.06	313.56 ± 7.59
ASP $(\neg r, d_p, s_p)$	40.46 ± 4.12	94.37 ± 5.01	1043.82 ± 51.06	445.25 ± 24.93	44.53 ± 2.02	840.92 ± 48.76	1800.20 ± 0.00	0.38 ± 0.02	280.62 ± 3.33
ASP $(r_p, \neg d, s_p)$	45.58 ± 3.96	0.00 ± 0.00	986.67 ± 46.46	479.08 ± 28.64	17.84 ± 0.96	784.60 ± 44.74	1800.18 ± 0.00	0.27 ± 0.02	261.24 ± 3.01
ASP (r_p, d, s)	47.44 ± 3.98	273.53 ± 15.31	391.00 ± 10.57	693.67 ± 41.36	51.67 ± 2.06	983.91 ± 56.89	1800.24 ± 0.00	6.10 ± 0.40	965.09 ± 45.63
MIP	48.67 ± 4.43	128.52 ± 6.02	3619.49 ± 112.30	0.00 ± 0.00	30.35 ± 1.08	0.00 ± 0.00	1229.52 ± 55.54	–	269.51 ± 2.22
ASP $(\neg r, d, s)$	52.25 ± 4.07	297.90 ± 16.15	387.28 ± 10.83	683.91 ± 39.96	52.03 ± 2.17	1000.03 ± 56.25	1800.25 ± 0.00	5.14 ± 0.34	860.20 ± 38.15
ASP (r_p, d_p, s)	56.05 ± 4.69	110.06 ± 5.57	398.79 ± 11.02	698.25 ± 40.38	52.17 ± 2.13	985.38 ± 56.56	1800.22 ± 0.00	3.44 ± 0.31	631.39 ± 30.19
ASP $(\neg r, \neg d, s_p)$	63.02 ± 4.32	0.00 ± 0.00	944.65 ± 44.78	448.78 ± 30.93	0.00 ± 0.00	708.00 ± 44.16	1800.17 ± 0.00	0.24 ± 0.01	248.93 ± 3.42
ASP $(\neg r, d_p, s)$	65.50 ± 4.85	121.61 ± 5.72	392.37 ± 10.90	672.52 ± 39.77	51.08 ± 2.14	986.70 ± 56.45	1800.22 ± 0.00	3.34 ± 0.30	626.46 ± 30.18
ASP $(r_p, \neg d, s)$	66.90 ± 4.62	0.00 ± 0.00	381.69 ± 10.88	665.29 ± 38.59	26.53 ± 1.38	1010.56 ± 57.23	1794.55 ± 5.67	3.15 ± 0.30	589.37 ± 29.12
ASP $(r_p, d_p, \neg s)$	68.72 ± 4.74	94.05 ± 5.25	448.44 ± 12.56	0.00 ± 0.00	40.27 ± 2.18	0.00 ± 0.00	1398.07 ± 52.50	0.16 ± 0.01	202.86 ± 2.03
ASP $(r, \neg d, s_p)$	68.98 ± 5.33	21.90 ± 3.56	774.60 ± 30.21	223.72 ± 21.75	12.89 ± 1.30	619.86 ± 32.96	1795.13 ± 5.33	64.05 ± 6.61	5511.59 ± 527.30
ASP $(\neg r, d_p, \neg s)$	74.80 ± 4.94	84.88 ± 4.28	448.44 ± 12.56	0.00 ± 0.00	35.99 ± 1.90	0.00 ± 0.00	1437.50 ± 50.67	0.13 ± 0.00	196.70 ± 1.82
ASP $(\neg r, \neg d, s)$	80.83 ± 4.81	0.00 ± 0.00	386.35 ± 12.10	528.17 ± 29.14	0.00 ± 0.00	856.79 ± 43.54	1800.21 ± 0.00	3.10 ± 0.29	566.61 ± 26.05
ASP $(r, \neg d, \neg s)$	84.84 ± 5.48	38.55 ± 4.37	448.44 ± 12.56	0.00 ± 0.00	13.57 ± 1.38	0.00 ± 0.00	1489.11 ± 46.79	62.19 ± 6.55	4960.60 ± 487.43
ASP $(r_p, \neg d, \neg s)$	84.90 ± 4.94	0.00 ± 0.00	448.44 ± 12.56	0.00 ± 0.00	8.23 ± 0.57	0.00 ± 0.00	726.02 ± 60.64	0.05 ± 0.00	161.50 ± 1.06
ASP (r, d, s_p)	87.90 ± 7.27	173.85 ± 12.08	777.90 ± 36.72	396.43 ± 28.12	44.52 ± 2.34	590.65 ± 38.20	1795.14 ± 5.35	30.92 ± 2.85	5779.65 ± 540.39
Initial	92.39 ± 5.07	0.00 ± 0.00	448.44 ± 12.56	0.00 ± 0.00	0.00 ± 0.00	0.00 ± 0.00	0.00 ± 0.00	–	0.00 ± 0.00
ASP $(\neg r, \neg d, \neg s)$	92.39 ± 5.07	0.00 ± 0.00	448.44 ± 12.56	0.00 ± 0.00	0.00 ± 0.00	0.00 ± 0.00	6.01 ± 0.67	0.03 ± 0.00	144.03 ± 0.24
ASP (r, d_p, s_p)	96.32 ± 7.89	155.79 ± 10.14	781.05 ± 33.76	397.17 ± 26.98	47.29 ± 2.35	598.31 ± 35.86	1795.12 ± 5.36	33.62 ± 2.91	5827.82 ± 551.50
ASP $(r, \neg d, s)$	103.84 ± 6.43	37.56 ± 4.38	346.33 ± 7.65	359.92 ± 26.70	16.07 ± 1.54	864.26 ± 56.30	1762.82 ± 14.07	64.39 ± 6.31	6802.62 ± 627.52
ASP (r, d, s)	112.29 ± 8.93	180.80 ± 11.80	334.50 ± 8.72	512.28 ± 35.30	42.72 ± 2.13	665.04 ± 47.28	1762.68 ± 14.13	27.42 ± 2.30	6919.20 ± 633.03
ASP $(r, d_p, \neg s)$	124.30 ± 8.30	158.29 ± 8.21	438.62 ± 12.08	0.00 ± 0.00	50.45 ± 2.21	0.00 ± 0.00	1515.45 ± 45.23	54.26 ± 5.58	5041.34 ± 493.87
ASP $(r, d, \neg s)$	126.64 ± 8.58	209.50 ± 12.51	431.47 ± 11.68	0.00 ± 0.00	49.16 ± 2.19	0.00 ± 0.00	1528.53 ± 44.31	48.19 ± 4.73	5056.61 ± 493.95
ASP (r, d_p, s)	132.92 ± 8.79	151.88 ± 8.92	354.54 ± 8.27	522.28 ± 39.89	43.37 ± 2.24	794.71 ± 53.09	1762.79 ± 14.08	55.65 ± 6.18	6910.15 ± 632.98

Table 3. Ablation study aggregated over all scenarios, instances, and ASP variants. $\pm$ shows the standard error of the mean.

Option	Overload [#]	Arrival Delay [h]	Sector-Number [#]	Sector-Diff [#]	Reroute [#]	Reconfig [#]	Execution-Time [s]	Grounding-Time [s]	RAM-Usage [MB]
r	103.89 ± 2.53	121.59 ± 3.37	520.51 ± 8.27	253.88 ± 9.34	34.82 ± 0.76	445.11 ± 14.51	1689.64 ± 9.67	50.09 ± 1.82	5867.73 ± 186.23
r_p	50.51 ± 1.46	120.53 ± 4.12	621.68 ± 12.00	378.94 ± 11.45	37.44 ± 0.71	606.55 ± 17.52	1603.40 ± 13.05	1.93 ± 0.08	439.13 ± 9.16
$\neg r$	59.38 ± 1.53	129.99 ± 4.28	616.33 ± 11.93	359.06 ± 10.81	31.12 ± 0.78	583.56 ± 16.80	1531.33 ± 15.05	1.67 ± 0.07	406.81 ± 8.18
d	58.36 ± 1.95	251.73 ± 5.11	595.19 ± 11.62	348.76 ± 11.15	48.25 ± 0.72	549.46 ± 16.92	1703.93 ± 9.25	12.86 ± 0.74	2351.98 ± 123.41
d_p	75.33 ± 2.12	115.81 ± 2.29	594.91 ± 11.35	351.10 ± 11.13	45.52 ± 0.72	558.44 ± 16.88	1678.86 ± 10.41	15.95 ± 1.07	2223.20 ± 124.97
$\neg d$	76.71 ± 1.72	10.79 ± 0.87	574.84 ± 10.25	300.16 ± 9.86	10.54 ± 0.39	536.65 ± 15.80	1441.58 ± 16.73	21.76 ± 1.42	2138.50 ± 122.31
s	78.01 ± 2.01	129.04 ± 4.00	376.34 ± 3.49	597.17 ± 12.71	37.14 ± 0.76	913.98 ± 18.29	1787.11 ± 2.81	18.17 ± 1.12	2763.45 ± 139.60
s_p	52.56 ± 1.71	107.35 ± 3.68	944.18 ± 15.21	413.70 ± 9.04	33.51 ± 0.74	749.38 ± 14.96	1798.50 ± 1.03	14.20 ± 1.00	2123.64 ± 119.68
$\neg s$	80.09 ± 2.02	135.68 ± 4.20	445.54 ± 4.14	0.00 ± 0.00	32.77 ± 0.75	0.00 ± 0.00	1238.76 ± 19.35	18.40 ± 1.24	1826.58 ± 108.42

Results and Discussion. We evaluate the suitability of *ASP* for ATFCM (Tables 2 and 3; Figs. 3 and 4).

- **Lexicographic Performance:** CASA achieves strict feasibility (0 overload) but incurs massive arrival delay (2353.12 h). In contrast, *ASP* (r_p, d, s_p) provides a superior operational trade-off, achieving an overload of 23.27 with 211.44 h delay. Arguably, *ASP* (r_p, d_p, s_p) offers an even stronger operational balance; while its overload is slightly higher (29.55), its arrival delay (82.01 h) is strictly lower than the *MIP* baseline (48.67 overload, 128.52 h delay). All highlighted variants significantly outperform the unmodified Initial state (92.39 overload).
- **Computational Bottlenecks:** For heuristically bounded variants, solving time dominates the computational effort, leading to TIMEOUTs on larger instances. However, enabling unrestricted rerouting (r) triggers a grounding bottleneck. This manifests in drastically larger grounding times and a severe memory explosion (averaging 5867.73 MB and 50.09s grounding time) compared to partial (r_p, 439.13 MB and 1.93s grounding time) or no rerouting ($\neg r$, 406.81 MB and 1.67s grounding time).

These results demonstrate that shifting spatial routing and sectorization from the solver to a heuristic pre-processor is critical to bypass memory and time bottlenecks. We attribute the performance discrepancy between our exact *ASP* models and reported *MIP* literature to our looser model definitions and the treatment of rerouting alternatives as dynamic rather than static data.

TTF/TTB Analysis. Figure 4 visualizes the search dynamics by plotting Time to First Solution (TTF) against Time to Best Solution (TTB). We quantify the optimization phase using the median time gap $\Delta t = \text{TTB} - \text{TTF}$ and the median percentage reduction in initial overload o_m.

- **Search Space Thrashing:** The unbounded variant *ASP* (r, d, s) struggles to find initial feasibility and frequently terminates without improving the initial bound (clustering on the diagonal). It yields the lowest optimization impact ($\Delta t = 878.74$s, $o_m = 34.10\%$).
- **Fast Feasibility:** Tightly constrained variants rapidly establish initial upper bounds, efficiently utilizing the remaining budget to traverse the search space ($\Delta t > 1500$s, $o_m > 76\%$). Visual clustering differentiates their behavior: *ASP* (r_p, d_p, s_p) strictly clusters in the top-left (extremely fast TTF, sustained late TTB), whereas *ASP* $(\neg r, d, \neg s)$ clusters primarily in the center-top and left-mid, indicating earlier search space exhaustion.

- **Adequate Convergence:** The globally best-performing variant, *ASP* (r_p, d, s_p), is bounded in the scatter plot by the extremes of the other methods. It requires slightly more time to establish initial feasibility than fully constrained models but sustains a robust optimization phase ($\Delta t = 1644.49$s, $o_m = 74.88\%$).

Open Challenge: Frequent timeouts of ASP shows that exact solvers cannot yet prove optimality for large instances within operational time limits.

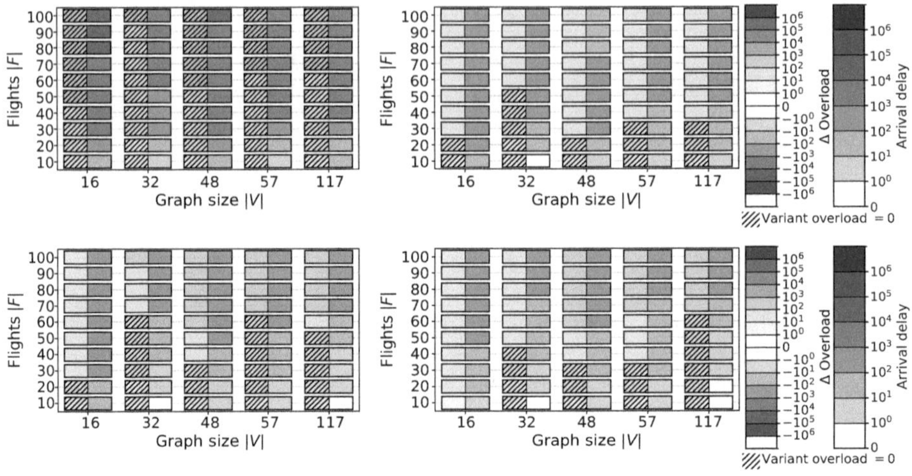

Fig. 3. Scaling results of CASA (top left), MIP (top right), ASP (r_p, d, s_p) (bottom left), and ASP (r_p, d_p, s_p) (bottom right). X-axis shows size of the considered geographical instance ($|V|$) and Y-axis shows number of flights. Each data point has four instances, where the hatching is shown iff all seeds achieve 0 overload.

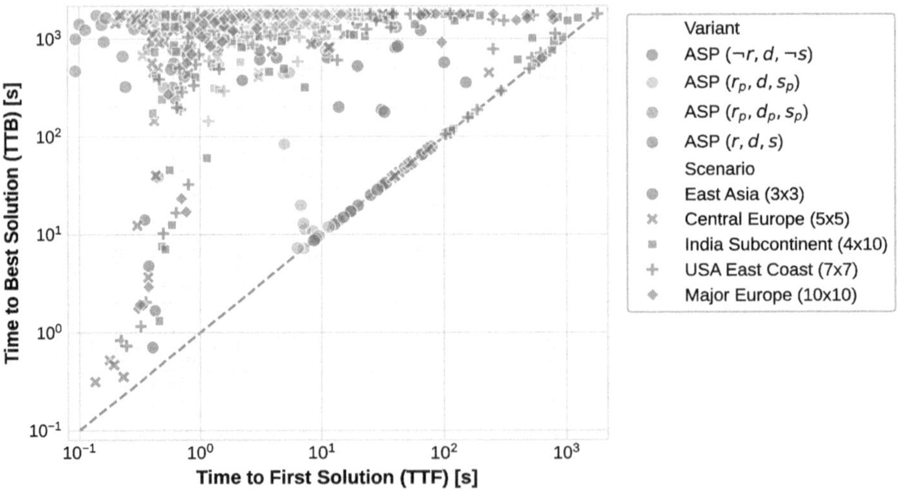

Fig. 4. Time to First Solution [TTF] vs. Time to Best Solution (TTB) scatter plot comparing four selected ASP variants.

6 Conclusion

We present a unified and extensible formalization of Air Traffic Flow and Capacity Management (ATFCM) that integrates flow management decisions and dynamic airspace configuration (DAC). Unlike existing formulations that treat these components in isolation or assume pre-defined sector changes, our model captures delaying, rerouting, and DAC within a single navpoint-graph-based framework. We develop an ASP encoding to investigate the feasibility of ASP in the ATFCM domain. Our ASP encoding is able to freely switch between full/partial/disabled actions, which enable the conduction of an ablation study, where we further compare our encoding to a simulation of the practical CASA algorithm and a simulation of a SOTA MIP model. Our results indicate that ASP with partial sectorization is able to achieve strong results, especially for smaller instance sizes. When the instance sizes grow larger, the computational budget does not suffice for ASP to finish the computation, which leads to the result that the CASA heuristics is the only tested variant able to solve all benchmarked instances to 0-overload—however, with the downside of having low efficiency (high delay), in comparison to ASP's solutions. Our ablation study of the ASP variants indicates, that the size of the search space should be "just big enough", as restrictions of the search space to a fixed number of alternatives lead to the best results. Several directions are promising for future work. First, the lack of theoretical analysis is a hindrance for abstract modelling, where we plan to analyze which modelling choices drive computational hardness. Second, we will investigate the combination of ASP into a hybrid heuristic solver for larger instances. Third, due to the inherent safety criticality of the domain, we will enable operational explainability by generating human-interpretable justifications for delays, reroutes, and reconfigurations.

Acknowledgments. This research was supported by Frequentis and the Austrian Science Fund (FWF), grant 10.55776/COE12. Hecher has been supported by the French National Research Agency (ANR), grant ANR-25-CE23-7647-01, and the Austrian Science Fund (FWF), grant 10.55776/J4656.

References

1. Abels, D., Jordi, J., Ostrowski, M., Schaub, T., Toletti, A., Wanko, P.: Train scheduling with hybrid answer set programming. TPLP **21**(3), 317–347 (2021)
2. Baumeister, J., et al.: Towards industrial-scale product configuration. In: LPNMR24, pp. 71–84 (2024)
3. Bertsimas, D., Patterson, S.S.: The air traffic flow management problem with enroute capacities. Oper. Res. **46**(3), 406–422 (1998)
4. Bolic, T., Cook, A., Koelle, R., Spinielli, E., Goens, Q., Strohmeier, M.: Roadmap for a European open science alliance for ATM research. EJTIR **24**(4), 18–40 (2024)
5. Buccafurri, F., Leone, N., Rullo, P.: Enhancing disjunctive datalog by constraints. IEEE Trans. Knowl. Data Eng. **12**(5), 845–860 (2000)

6. Bucuroiu, R., Vincent, S.: European network operations plan 2025/2026 - 2029. EUROCONTROL (2025)
7. Chandra, A., Hazra, S., Verma, A.: The integration of En route flow optimization, complex network clustering, and rule-based approach to airspace sub-sectorization for enhanced air traffic monitoring. JATRS **3**, 100036 (2024)
8. Chen, Y., Zhang, D.: Dynamic airspace configuration method based on a weighted graph model. Chin. J. Aeronaut. **27**(4), 903–912 (2014)
9. Cook, A.: European Air Traffic Management: Principles, Practices and Research (2007)
10. Dalmau, R., Gawinowski, G., Kopec, J.: Multi-objective air traffic flow management through lexicographic optimization. In: SID24 (2024)
11. Falkner, A., Friedrich, G., Schekotihin, K., Taupe, R., Teppan, E.C.: Industrial applications of answer set programming. Künstl. Intell. **32**(2–3), 165–176 (2018)
12. García-Heredia, D., Alonso-Ayuso, A., Molina, E.: A Combinatorial model to optimize air traffic flow management problems. Comput. Oper. Res. **112**, 104768 (2019)
13. Gelfond, M., Leone, N.: Logic programming and knowledge representation-the a-prolog perspective. Artif. Intell. **138**(1–2), 3–38 (2002)
14. Gerstner, W., Kistler, W.M., Naud, R., Paninski, L.: Neuronal Dynamics: From Single Neurons to Networks and Models of Cognition. Cambridge University Press, Cambridge (2014)
15. Kim, J., Kim, K.: Enhancing urban air mobility scheduling through declarative reasoning and stakeholder modeling. Aerospace **12**(7), 605 (2025)
16. Lui, G.N., Lulli, G., Carro, I.G.O., Martinez, R.L., De Giovanni, L., Galeazzo, M.: A robust optimization approach for dynamic airspace configuration. In: ATRDS25 (2025)
17. Lui, G.N., Lulli, G., Lema-Esposto, M.F., Martinez, R.L.: Airspace sector design: an optimization approach. In: SID24 (2024)
18. Nguyen, A.D., Pham, L., Lindsay, N., Sun, L., Tran, S.C.: Optimized eVTOL aircraft scheduling - an answer set programming based approach. In: AIAA Aviation Forum and Ascend 2024 (2024)
19. SESAR: SESAR Master Plan 2025 (2024)
20. Strohmeier, M., Olive, X., Lübbe, J., Schäfer, M., Lenders, V.: Crowdsourced air traffic data from the OpenSky Network 2019–2020. Earth Syst. Sci. Data **13**(2) (2021)
21. Vranas, P.B.M.: Optimal slot allocation for European air traffic flow management. Air Traffic Control Q. **4**(4), 249–280 (1996)
22. Yin, C.W.S., Venugopalan, T., Suresh, S.: A multi-objective approach for 3D airspace sectorization: a study on Singapore regional airspace. In: IEEE SSCI 2016, pp. 1–8 (2016)

BLAST: Benchmarking LLMs with ASP-Based Structured Testing

Manuel Santana Borroto[1](✉), Erica Coppolillo[2], Francesco Calimeri[1], Giuseppe Manco[2], Simona Perri[1], and Francesco Ricca[1]

[1] University of Calabria, Rende, Italy
{manuel.santana,francesco.calimeri,simona.perri, francesco.ricca}@unical.it

[2] ICAR-CNR, Rende, Italy
{erica.coppolillo,giuseppe.manco}@icar.cnr.it

Abstract. Large Language Models (LLMs) have demonstrated remarkable performance across a broad spectrum of tasks, including natural language understanding, dialogue systems, and code generation. Despite evident progress, less attention has been paid to their effectiveness in handling declarative paradigms such as Answer Set Programming (ASP), to date. In this paper we introduce BLAST: The first dedicated benchmarking methodology and associated dataset for evaluating the accuracy of LLMs in generating ASP code. BLAST provides a structured evaluation framework featuring two novel semantic metrics tailored to ASP code generation. The paper presents the results of an empirical evaluation involving ten well-established graph-related problems from the ASP literature and a diverse set of eight state-of-the-art LLMs.

1 Introduction

Large Language Models (LLMs) [58] have been showing remarkable performance across a broad spectrum of tasks, including natural language understanding [44], dialogue systems [42], and code generation [31]. More recently, some efforts have been made to encompass advanced reasoning, knowledge representation, and logical formalisms [15,34,48,53]. In this context, while several benchmarks have been proposed to assess LLM performance on imperative and web-oriented programming languages (e.g., C++, Java, HTML) [16,20,43], far less attention has been given to declarative paradigms such as Answer Set Programming (ASP) [9,27], despite some recent initial efforts [15,30,48,49].

Rooted in logic programming and nonmonotonic reasoning, ASP is well-suited for modeling and solving complex AI problems [9]. Over the years, ASP has become increasingly adopted for its expressive language and the availability of efficient and reliable solvers [26], notably Clingo [24] and DLV [3]. As a fully declarative paradigm, ASP has been successfully employed in both academic research and industrial applications, particularly in complex domains (e.g., scheduling, configuration, robotics, workforce planning, decision support) [19,21]. In recent years substantial effort has been devoted to developing

W. Faber et al. (Eds.): LPNMR 2026, LNAI 16952, pp. 117–132, 2027.
https://doi.org/10.1007/978-3-032-38320-4_8

programming environments and tools that support the creation of ASP specifications, including advanced editors, debuggers, testing frameworks, and utilities [4,10,11,23,29].

Motivation. Despite these advancements, writing ASP code often remains challenging, especially for newcomers without a solid background in logic and mathematics. In this context, LLMs represent a promising avenue for supporting, and even automating, ASP coding. Recent studies have highlighted significant limitations in the ability of general-purpose LLMs to generate correct and semantically sound ASP programs [15]. At the same time, other lines of research, including approaches specifically tailored to ASP encoding, demonstrate that the overall direction is viable and promising [15,30,48,49]. However, the field lacks systematic evaluations, standardized benchmarks, and well-defined metrics for assessing the ASP-coding capabilities of LLMs (and of any automatic approach).

Contributions. To fill this gap, we introduce **BLAST**, a benchmarking methodology specifically designed to assess the capability of LLMs in generating ASP code. BLAST provides a structured evaluation framework that measures program quality through two novel metrics specifically designed for ASP code generation. The methodology encompasses both evaluation *breadth* (covering a diverse set of problems) and *depth* (testing robustness across multiple natural-language paraphrases of each problem). Crucially, BLAST imposes no guidance or syntactic constraints on input/output formats for the evaluated models. Moreover, existing procedures mostly rely on manual evaluations of the automated encoding outcomes [15,48], resulting in time-consuming and potentially inconsistent assessments. In contrast, we propose a systematic approach that automates the evaluation process, reducing human intervention while improving scalability, reliability and reproducibility. We evaluate BLAST through an experimental study on ten well-known graph problems from the ASP literature using eight state-of-the-art LLMs. For the sake of reproducibility, the complete experimental setup, including code and evaluation data, is publicly available (https://github.com/EricaCoppolillo/BLAST).

2 Preliminaries

Large Language Models. A Large Language Model (LLM) is a function f that stochastically maps an input token sequence $x = [x_1, \dots, x_n]$ to an output sequence $y = [y_1, \dots, y_m]$, with $x \in V^*$ and $y \in W^*$, where V and W are token vocabularies. Formally, f defines the conditional probability $P(y|x)$, from which y is sampled, capturing the structure and semantics of natural language. Most LLMs are based on Transformer architectures [54], which encode token embeddings and generate outputs auto-regressively through distributions of the form $P(y_i|x, y_{:i-1})$. Although many architectural variants exist [36,45], these details are orthogonal to our focus. In practice, LLMs are typically used via *prompting*, where a textual input guides the generated output.

Answer Set Programming. Answer Set Programming (ASP) is a declarative formalism for Knowledge Representation and Reasoning [9,27]. In ASP, a problem is encoded as a finite set of logical rules, and solutions correspond to answer sets. Rather than presenting a formal introduction to the language, we provide a representative example to highlight its expressive power: the classical 3-colorability problem, which requires assigning one of three colors to each node of an undirected graph such that adjacent nodes receive different colors.

The following ASP encoding captures this specification. The input graph (nodes and edges) and the available colors are represented via facts. A choice rule assigns exactly one color to each node, and an integrity constraint eliminates colorings in which adjacent nodes share the same color:

```
col(red). col(green). col(black). node(1..4).
edge(1,2). edge(4,2). edge(1,3).
1 { colored(X,C) : col(C) } 1 :- node(X).
:- edge(X,Y), colored(X,C), colored(Y,C).
```

ASP also provides constructs for optimization via weak constraints, which allow specifying preferences among answer sets. For instance, to minimize the number of nodes assigned the color red: `:~ colored(X,red). [1@1,X].`

We assume the reader to be familiar with ASP, and limit our description to this example illustrating the declarative nature and expressiveness of ASP.

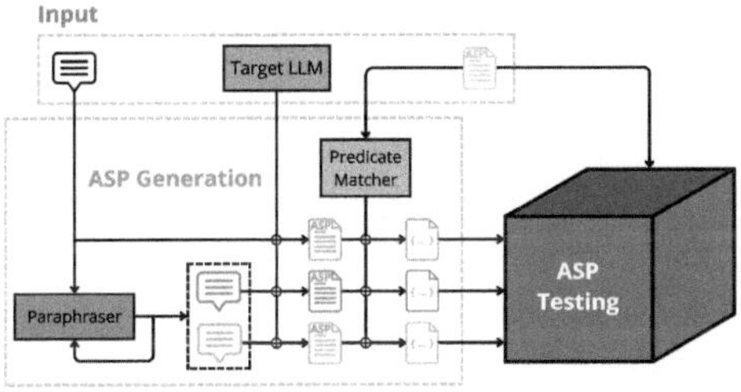

Fig. 1. Overview of the framework: the input includes the problem specification, target LLM, and gold ASP program. The ASP Generation module produces paraphrases and predicate mappings, which are passed with the gold encoding to the ASP Testing module for evaluation.

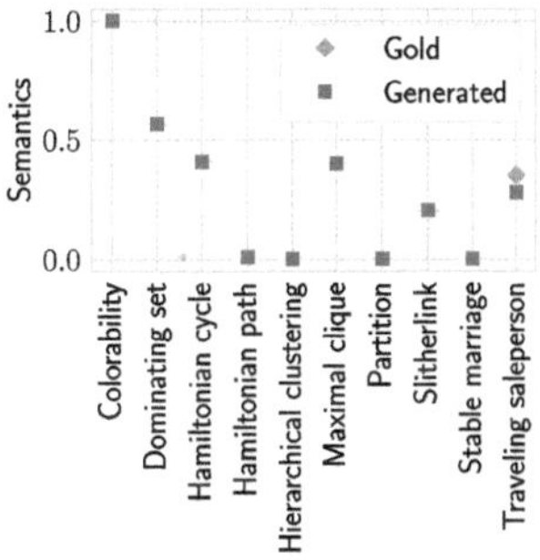

Fig. 2. Semantic comparison using gold vs. generated matching dictionaries, with DeepSeek-R1 as target LLM.

3 BLAST Methodology

The core of the approach consists in automatically testing the generation capabilities of a target LLM. To this end, we devise a methodology comprising two main components: *(i)* an **ASP Generation** framework that, starting from a specification in natural language, provides a set of encodings of the problem in ASP; *(ii)* an **ASP Testing** infrastructure aimed at evaluating the performance of the target LLM. The overall scheme of the approach is detailed in Fig. 1.

3.1 ASP Generation

The framework for generating ASP initiates with a natural language description of the problem intended for ASP encoding, alongside a *gold program* that exemplifies the ASP-based solution. The generation process is driven by the following elements: *(i)* the **target LLM**, serving as the generator under evaluation, in charge of encoding the problem into ASP; *(ii)* an LLM instructed to **paraphrase** the initial problem description to make it more human-readable; *(iii)* an LLM that semantically **matches** the predicates of the resulting program with those in the gold program.

Target LLM. As an initial step in our framework, the LLM under evaluation is prompted with the problem description and asked to provide an encoding in ASP language. Box 1 provides an example of the provided prompt. (Note that this component can be replaced by any method generating ASP programs from natural language specifications.)

Box 1: Target LLM Prompt Example

`[PROBLEM DESCRIPTION]`

Write an ASP program which models this problem, along with facts that make it instantiable. Generate the program only, without any additional text.

Predicate Matcher. It is important to remark that the target model is not given any instructions or constraints regarding the syntax, predicate names, or problem modeling to adopt. To normalize its output and enable comparison with the gold standard solution, we employ a further LLM, referred to as the Predicate Matcher. This model takes as input both the gold program and the encoding generated by the target model, and is prompted to perform a semantic match of the predicates used in the two programs. The result is returned as a Python dictionary mapping corresponding predicates. If no semantic similarity can be established, the model is instructed to return "No semantic match". Note that predicate matching is performed before the generated encoding is evaluated.

We emphasize three crucial aspects of the predicate matcher component. First, the predicate matching phase is independent of encoding correctness: the matcher LLM only semantically associates predicates between programs, without assessing their validity. Second, the matcher does not semantically alter a correct program. In other words, the quality of the target LLM performance (that is, its ability to generate a correct ASP program from a natural language problem description) remains consistent regardless of whether a "gold" predicate matching dictionary (manually crafted by the authors) or a generated one is used. Figure 2 compares the results obtained using gold and generated matching dictionaries, with DeepSeek-R1 serving as the representative target LLM. The only exception is the Traveling Salesperson problem, where performance is slightly better with the gold matching dictionary. By looking deeper into this problem, we realized that despite the better matching, the generated ASP programs were still incorrect, mainly because of erroneous constraints intended to ensure a valid path. Third, we remark that this result enables our methodology to achieve a high degree of generality, since it allows evaluating generated programs without imposing any prompting constraints on the LLMs. Indeed, we deliberately avoid penalizing encodings that differ only at the syntactic level, through the use of alternative predicate names. For instance, adopting `reach(X)` instead of `reached(X)` to represent the same concept should not negatively affect the evaluation, provided that the program is semantically correct. By abstracting away from superficial naming differences, our approach focuses on assessing genuine modeling and coding ability rather than sensitivity to arbitrary lexical choices.

Paraphraser. Beyond the original technical statements, we also test whether models can handle prompts written in a more human-relatable style. This evaluates not only *breadth* across diverse problems, but also *depth*, which is the ability to adapt to less technical descriptions for an "ASP layman". To this end, we use another LLM as a *paraphraser* to produce two variants of each initial description.

Paraphrasing is performed in two phases: A first variant is generated from the original problem statement, and a second variant is then derived from it. We remark that this step is *optional*: although we analyze its impact, the framework can also evaluate the target LLM using only the original encoding.

3.2 ASP Testing

To evaluate the ASP programs generated by the LLMs, we propose two methods: *(i)* a **test-suite**-based approach and *(ii)* a **model**-based approach. Both methods are associated with proper metrics that allow us to measure a form of semantic distance from the gold program. Both approaches assume that each problem has a fixed set of input and output predicates, corresponding to those in the gold program. This assumption is pragmatic, yet reasonably not too restrictive. Indeed, LLMs are expected to produce meaningful programs as written by a human; thus, syntactic variations of predicate names are very likely resolved by the predicate matcher. If not, we assume the program is not correct.

Test-Suite-Based Evaluation. This evaluation method relies on the unit testing mechanism implemented in the ASP-WIDE tool [5], which uses an annotation-based test specification language inspired by JUnit. The objective is to create a test suite that thoroughly checks the program functionality. A *test suite* is a collection of test cases, each comprising assertions that verify a number of conditions on the expected program output. Based on the test-suite results, we compute the **test case accuracy** as the ratio of passed test cases over the total.

To ensure this evaluation method is effective, it is crucial to design a robust test suite over most of the program's expected behavior. To this end, we developed a guideline for constructing meaningful test cases. The first step involves creating test cases to check for unsatisfiability. Specifically, given a set of input instances that violate the problem constraints, the program is expected to return no answer set for each instance. Next, we define test cases that verify the satisfiability of the problem constraints by checking if valid instances comply with them. If needed, we further refine the test suite by adding test cases that validate the correctness of the program's output atoms. For example, in the *Colorability* problem, it should never occur that a node remains uncolored. This is done by writing an ASP-WIDE test case with the following assertion:

```
@constraintForAll(constraint=":- node(U), not chosenColor(U,_).")
```

which ensures that every node U is assigned at least one color. Finally, we add tests to check if the program produces the expected number of answer sets.

Model-Based Testing. This method evaluates an ASP program P_t based on its ability to reproduce the *correct* (*gold*) (stable) *models* (GM) for a given set of instances provided via facts. The core idea relies on the assumption that, given a gold program P_g and a set of instances, the target program P_t is considered correct if and only if it produces the *same* (stable) models as P_g on those instances. To formalize this, we define the set of *target program models* (TPM) as the (stable) models of P_t, and the *covered gold models* (CGM) as the intersection of TPM and GM, i.e., CGM = GM ∩ TPM.

To quantify the accuracy of P_t, we use the standard (micro) F1-score computed as the harmonic mean of the standard measures of precision and recall [13].

Notably, we retrieve the CGM set with high efficiency by means of Algorithm 1, which leverages an ASP solver. Rather than relying on full answer set enumeration of the program under test, that might quickly become infeasible, we modify the ASP program to directly target specific solutions. In particular, we constrain the search space to gold models only, thereby avoiding the overhead of enumerating irrelevant answer sets. Clearly, we carefully crafted our instance set to be sure that the enumeration of gold program answers is instead feasible.

The algorithm takes as input the program to test P_t, a gold program P_g, and a set of instances Ins. For each instance $I \in Ins$, we compute the set of gold models AS_g by computing all answer sets of $P_g \cup I$ using an ASP solver (line 5). Then, for each gold model $M_g \in AS_g$, we create a set of constraints aimed at forcing M_g to be an answer set of P_t (line 8). Specifically, for each atom a over the output predicates, if $a \in M_g$ then we add the constraint *:- not a*; otherwise, we add the constraint *:- a*. For the sake of clarity, let us consider the Colorability problem with 3 nodes and 3 colors and a gold model M_g where node 1 is colored as *purple*, node 2 as *red*, and node 3 as *brown*. In this case, `create_model_constraints(M_g)` returns the following constraints:

```
:- not chosenColor(3,brown).   :- chosenColor(2,brown).
:- not chosenColor(2,red).     :- chosenColor(2,purple).
:- not chosenColor(1,purple).  :- chosenColor(3,red).
:- chosenColor(1,brown).       :- chosenColor(3,purple).
:- chosenColor(1,red).
```

Intuitively, in the answer set M_g, node 1 is colored as *purple* and so *:- not cho senColor*$(1, purple)$ is obtained. Conversely, node 1 is colored neither *red* nor *brown*, and so the constraints *:- chosenColor*$(1, red)$ and *:- chosenColor*$(1, brown)$ are obtained. Analogously, the remaining constraints are obtained for nodes 2 and 3. Note that if the gold program contains weak constraints, then `create _model_constraints(M_g)` does not return strong constraints as in the previous example but a set of weak constraints with cost 1 and a priority higher than the maximum priority used in P_t. This ensures that the solver prioritizes the inclusion of these gold atoms in the resulting answer sets. After obtaining the set of constraints C_g, the program $P_t \cup C_g \cup I$ is solved using the solver configured to return exactly one answer set M. This operation is performed by the function `solve_once` in line 9 of the algorithm. Then, the gold model M_g is considered *covered* if M_g exactly matches M. M and M_g exactly match if, for each atom a over output predicates, it holds that $a \in M$ if and only if $a \in M_g$.

The next step is to identify the set of models generated by P_t that differ from the gold models (i.e., wrong models). Note that this last step is necessary in order to properly calculate TPM. To this end, we first augment P_t with the set of facts encoding the gold models in AS_g. To do this, we used the predicate *trueInGold/2*, where the first term is an identifier (i.e., a positive integer) for a gold model $M_g \in AS_g$, and the second term is a true atom in M_g. Note that such facts are obtained considering only atoms over the output predicates. Then, the program P_t is further augmented with additional rules that discard all those models of P_t that exactly match one gold model. This augmented version of the program P_t is returned by the function `aug_program` and is denoted as P_{ta}. For example, let us consider again the Colorability problem and the gold model in which node 1 is colored as *purple*, node 2 as *red*, and node 3 as *brown*. Here the program P_{ta} is obtained by adding to the program P_t the rules in Listing 1.1.

Listing 1.1. Augment a program P_t for the Colorability problem.

```
1 trueInGold(1,chosenColor(2,red)).
2 trueInGold(1,chosenColor(1,purple)).
3 trueInGold(1,chosenColor(3,brown)).
4 ...
5 mod(X) :- trueInGold(X,_).
6 trueInTested(chosenColor(X,Y)) :- chosenColor(X,Y).
7 smallerMG(M) :- trueInGold(M, X), not trueInTested(X).
8 smallerMt(M) :- mod(M), trueInTested(X), not trueInGold(M, X).
9 :- mod(M), not smallerMG(M), not smallerMt(M).
```

Rules in lines 1–3 in Listing 1.1 represent the facts encoding the considered gold model (here we reported only one for the sake of readability, but all gold models are considered). The rule at line 6 is used to compute the true atoms in a model of P_t. Note that this rule is domain-specific, as the output predicate names vary across different domains. Then, rules in lines 7–8 compute for each gold model, the differences with a candidate model of P_t. Finally, the constraint

Algorithm 1 Finding P_t covered gold models and overall models.

Input: A program P_t, a program P_g, a set of instances Ins.
Output: the sets of models GM, CGM, and WM.
1: $GM = \emptyset$
2: $CGM = \emptyset$
3: $WM = \emptyset$
4: **for** $I \in Ins$ **do**
5:     $AS_g =$ `solve_all`$(P_g \cup I)$.
6:     $GM = GM \cup AS_g$.
7:     **for** $M_g \in AS_g$ **do**
8:         $C_g =$ `create_model_constraints`(M_g).
9:         $M =$ `solve_once`$(P_t \cup C_g \cup I)$.
10:         **if** $M = M_g$ **then**
11:             $CGM = CGM \cup \{M_g\}$
12:         **end if**
13:     **end for**
14:     $P_{ta} =$ `aug_program`(P_t, AS_g).
15:     $AS_w =$ `solve_all`$(P_{ta} \cup I)$.
16:     $WM = WM \cup AS_w$
17: **end for**
18: **return** GM, CGM, WM

at line 9 forces the program to discard a model if it matches a gold model. Once the program P_{ta} is obtained, the algorithm calls the solver to compute all models of $P_{ta} \cup I$ (i.e., `solve_all`($P_{ta}\cup$ I)). Obtained models are considered wrong. Finally, the algorithm returns the set of gold models over all instances GM, the set of covered gold models CGM $\subseteq$ GM, and the set of wrong models WM, which is disjoint from GM. The value |TPM| can then be calculated as the sum of the number of elements of CGM and WM.

Discussion on Metrics. The proposed metrics assess how well an ASP program semantically models a problem. The test-suite-based approach provides a more accurate, interpretable and targeted correctness measure through white-box testing, enabling inspection of the program's internal behavior. However, it requires expert-designed tests, and its reliability depends on test-suite quality. Conversely, the model-based approach is more automated, requiring only input instances and a gold program, but offers less insight into failures: it can reveal missing or incorrect answer sets, but not their causes, whereas targeted tests are directly linked to specific abilities and failure reasons.

4 Experimental Evaluation

This section presents an experimental evaluation of the proposed approach.

Dataset. To evaluate the proposed approach, we created a dataset comprising the following ten graph-related problems: **Colorability**, **(Connected) Dominating Set**, **Hamiltonian Cycle**, **Hamiltonian Path**, **Hierarchical Clustering**, **Maximal Clique**, **(Graph) Partitioning**, **Slitherlink**, **(Strong) Stable Marriage**, and **Traveling Salesperson**. We selected this set of tasks since they are standard problems used in many ASP competitions [2,25]. Each problem includes a formal natural language description and its corresponding gold standard program, as provided in the benchmarks from the competitions. For each problem, we provide the related test suite and the input instances required by the evaluation methods outlined earlier. Notably, the online repository provides all materials related to our approach, including detailed problem descriptions, test-suite design, and problem-specific instances.

Test Suite Validation. To ensure test-suite quality, we follow mutation-based ASP testing [5,38], relying on the small-scope hypothesis that many ASP errors emerge on small inputs [38]. For each gold program, we generate 15 mutants by randomly modifying rules, run the test suite on selected instances, and iteratively refine tests and inputs until no mutant obtains a perfect score. This process validates the suite's ability to detect behavioral deviations.

Tested Models. For the experimental evaluation, we adopt eight state-of-the-art LLMs from five distinct families: **o4-mini** [41], **Claude-3.5-Sonnet** [6], **DeepSeek-R1** [17], **Gemini-1.5-Pro** [52], **Gemini-2.5-Flash** [14], **GPT-4o** [39], **GPT-5** [40], and **LLaMa3.3-70B** [28]. All tested models have been invoked via the dedicated APIs of OpenAI, Anthropic, Google, and DeepSeek, with a temperature of 0.7 (when allowed). In the case of LLaMa3.3-70B, we used a self-hosted instance deployed through Ollama. The LLM-related and ASP-testing code has been implemented in Python. The interaction with the ASP-WIDE tool (developed in Spring Boot) was done through a RESTful API endpoint. The experiments have been conducted on an Intel(R) Xeon(R) CPU E7-8880 v4 @ 2.20 GHz, 512 GB of RAM, and running Debian 13 (6.1.0-32-amd64).

Predicate Matcher Accuracy. We evaluate predicate-matcher accuracy by manually scoring each generated predicate dictionary in $[0, 1]$, based on the fraction of correct associations. For each problem, we generate ten matches and report the average score. Figure 3 shows the results with GPT-4o, whose strong summarization and rephrasing abilities [1,59] also motivate its use as a *paraphraser*.

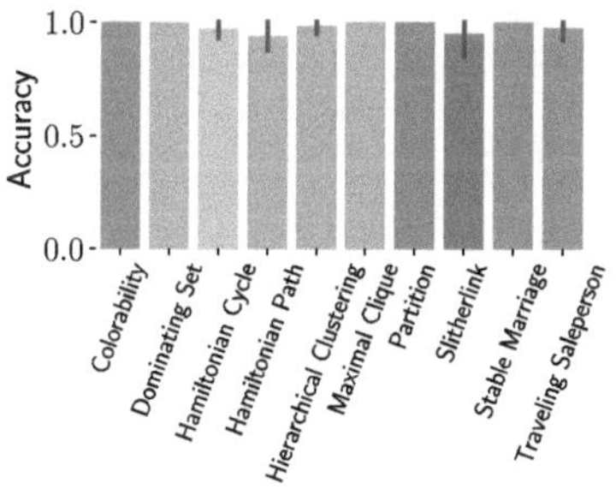

Fig. 3. Performance of GPT-4o as predicate matcher. Error bars represent confidence intervals on ten different runs.

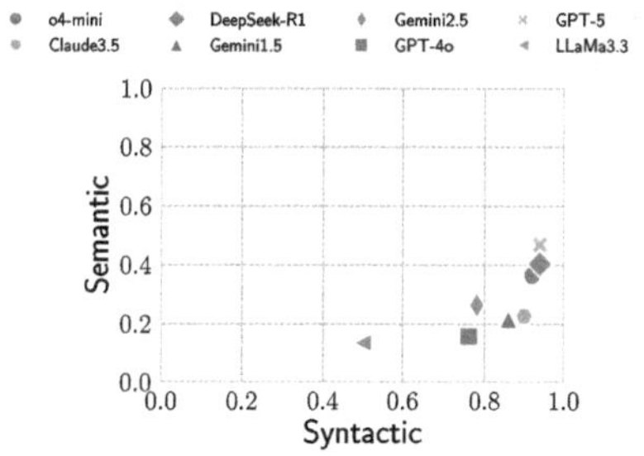

Fig. 4. Trade-off of the evaluated LLMs between syntactic (X-axis) and semantic accuracy (Y-axis), test suite-based method(see footnote 3). Results are averaged across all considered problems.

LLMs Performance. Further, we assess the effectiveness of the evaluated models concerning both syntactic and semantic accuracy. Figure 4 shows the average results for all examined problems, whereas Fig. 5 displays scores for each individual problem. At this stage, we concentrate solely on the initial problem statements, with more in-depth analyses discussed subsequently. Here, semantic accuracy is determined using test suite-based evaluation[1]. In comparison, syntactic correctness is evaluated by checking whether the input program results in any syntax errors during processing by the solver. To ensure results are statistically robust, each experiment is conducted by calling the target LLM five times, with outcomes then averaged. Two considerations can be made. First, as depicted in Fig. 4, while most LLMs show an impressive accuracy under the syntactic perspective (with the notable exception of LLaMa3.3), they perform poorly in terms of semantics. Secondly, Fig. 5 shows that, while simple problems such as Colorability or Dominating Set are easier to address, almost all LLMs fall short in encoding more complex tasks (e.g., Partition or Slitherlink). This suggests that state-of-the-art LLMs still struggle to effectively encode declarative paradigms, such as Answer Set Programming.

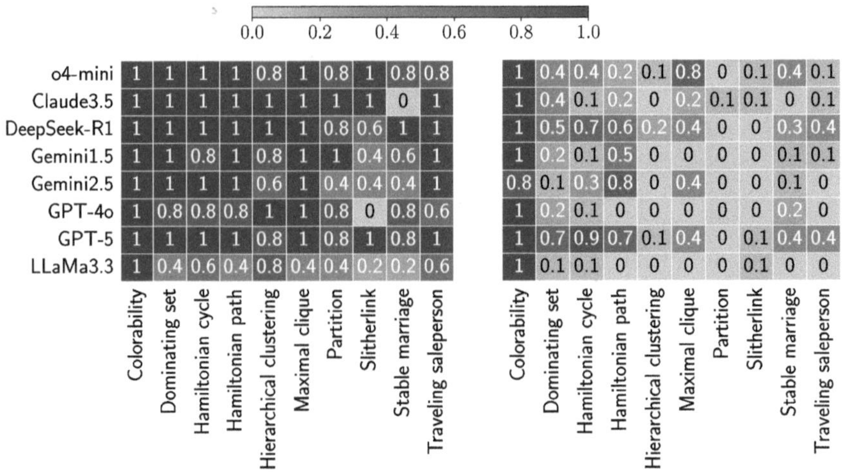

(a) **Syntactic** (b) **Semantic**

Fig. 5. Syntactic and semantic performance of the evaluated LLMs across problems. Semantic scores use the test-suite metric(see footnote 3); values are five-run averages.

Paraphrasing Impact. Further, we want to assess whether a more natural, human-like style of the textual description might help in increasing performance. To this end, we select DeepSeek-R1 as the representative LLM candidate, since

[1] For Maximal Clique, we use only the model-based metric due to ASPWIDE issues.

it achieves one of the best syntactic-semantic trade-offs while being comparatively inexpensive to evaluate. We compare its semantic accuracy when problem paraphrases are applied. Figure 6 depicts the test-suite-based evaluation score, averaged over five runs, along with the confidence intervals (CIs). We see that, in most cases, the original problem description generally yields better performance, despite some exceptions where the first paraphrase slightly improves the semantic accuracy of the model (notably, with Dominating set, Partition, Stable marriage).

LLM Error Analysis. For completeness, we summarize the most common error patterns observed in syntactically valid but semantically incorrect programs. A frequent issue is the omission of constraints. For example, in the Hamiltonian Path problem, LLMs often fail to correctly enforce the in-degree/out-degree constraints, including the special treatment of the path endpoints, which is required to guarantee a proper Hamiltonian path. In Stable Marriage, models sometimes omit bijectivity constraints ensuring that each man is matched with exactly one woman and vice versa. In optimization tasks involving weak constraints, mistakes in the specification of weights or priorities are also common. Another recurring problem concerns incorrect predicate signatures, such as wrong arity or mismatched arguments in input atoms. In some cases, additional constraints are introduced without a clear correspondence to the problem description; while not always harmful, they reveal a tendency to produce plausible but unjustified rules. Overall, LLMs tend to generate encodings that look reasonable at a superficial level, yet the formal rigor of ASP exposes subtle inaccuracies. Although such drafts may assist human programmers, our results indicate that fully automatic generation of correct ASP encodings remains challenging for current state-of-the-art models.

Test-Suite-Based vs Model-Based. Next, we compare the two proposed semantic metrics, both in terms of accuracy (Fig. 7) and efficiency (Fig. 8). Specifically, Fig. 7 shows the difference in performance computed via the test-suite- and the model-based metric. Therefore, a positive (resp., negative) score means that the performance is higher if the test-suite-based metric (resp., the model-based metric) is considered. Again, results are obtained by averaging five distinct runs, while the bars represent confidence intervals. We see that, across most problems and evaluated LLMs, the two metrics align. This alignment is also confirmed by the Pearson correlation coefficient $\rho = 0.865$.

We finally compare the two metrics in terms of efficiency. Figure 8 depicts the testing times (in seconds) across the considered problems, using DeepSeek-R1 as the reference LLM. In all problems (except for Hierarchical Clustering), the test-suite-based metric substantially reduces the computation time, making it the more efficient metric.

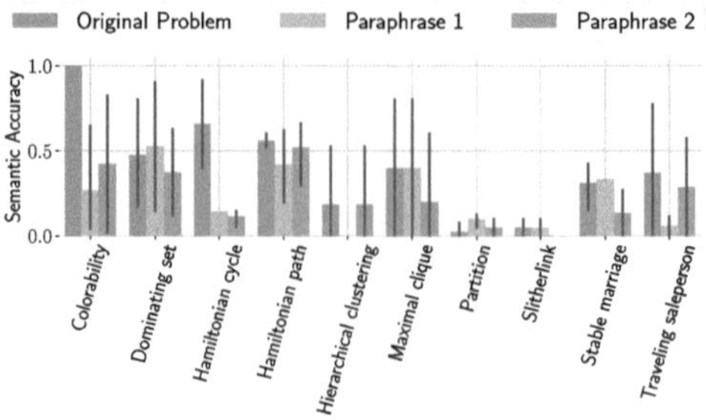

Fig. 6. Semantic accuracy under paraphrasing. Test-suite score and DeepSeek-R1. Five-run averages; error bars show CIs.

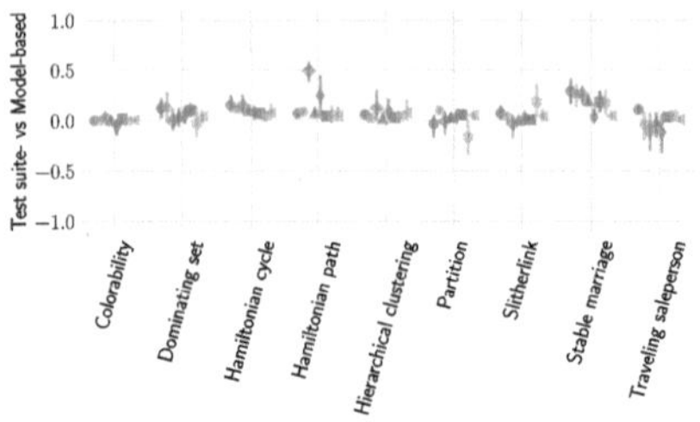

Fig. 7. Comparison of the two semantic metrics (see footnote 3) using DeepSeek-R1. Average score differences over five runs; error bars denote CIs.

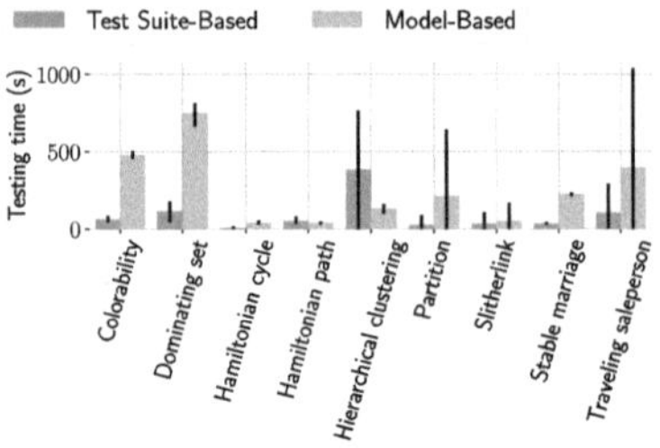

Fig. 8. Testing times(s) comparison of the two semantic metrics using DeepSeek-R1. Five-run averages; error bars indicate CIs.

5 Related Work

Automatic Code Synthesis. For declarative programming, a key goal is to automate ASP development by translating natural-language specifications into ASP code [12,22,50]. Early work translated simplified-English logic puzzles into ASP using λ-calculus and probabilistic combinatory categorial grammars [7]. Subsequent research focused on Controlled Natural Languages (CNLs) [33], including PENG^{ASP} [50] and the CNL2ASP tool [12].

ASP and LLMs. LLMs have been combined with ASP in several ways, including GPT-3-based semantic parsing with reasoning modules [37], few-shot translation from natural language to ASP logical forms [57], prompt-engineered solving of logic puzzles [30,35], and commonsense learning via LLM2LAS, which integrates LLMs with ILASP [32]. LLMASP integration has also been used for natural-language understanding in STAR [46] and Visual Graph Question Answering in NSGRAPH [8]. Beyond ASP, StreamLLM uses LLMs to generate MiniZinc streamlining constraints, yielding substantial speedups on benchmarks [55].

Closer to our setting, [47] benchmarked LLMs on ASP solving abilities, namely entailment, verification, and answer-set computation, whereas BLAST targets ASP code generation. NL2ASP translates natural-language specifications into CNL statements and then into ASP via CNL2ASP, using neural machine translation models with promising results [48]. Recent work evaluates LLMs on simple core ASP encodings, showing that they remain weak ASP coders but can benefit from fine-tuning, while providing no benchmark or methodology for systematic assessment of general ASP code generation [15]. Building on this potential, [49] introduced an ASP-solver-in-the-loop framework that improves LLM-based ASP generation through solver-feedback data curation, supervised fine-tuning, and solver-guided search with best-of-N sampling.

Evaluation Benchmarks. A substantial body of literature provides benchmarking datasets and test suites tailored to evaluating LLMs on imperative (e.g., Python, C++, Java) and web-oriented programming languages (e.g., HTML, CSS, JavaScript) such as [18,51,56]. We argue that far less attention has been devoted to declarative programming paradigms. A first benchmark for automatic translation from natural language to ASP was introduced by [48]. However, it primarily focuses on controlled natural language [12] and features input sentences with limited fluency. Recently, [47] proposed a methodology to assess whether state-of-the-art LLMs can solve programs coded in ASP, comparing their capabilities to standard solvers. However, their goal (computing answer sets with LLMs) is different from ours (testing LLMs' coding ability). To the best of our knowledge, no existing benchmark enables systematic *automatic* evaluation of LLMs' ability to *generate* ASP programs. This work addresses this gap.

6 Conclusions and Future Work

Although LLMs excel at language understanding and code synthesis, their ability to generate correct ASP programs remains underexplored. Existing evaluations often rely on manual inspection or restrictive input/output formats, making results sensitive to superficial choices such as predicate names. Thus, systematic benchmarks and rigorous metrics for ASP code generation are still needed.

We addressed this gap with **BLAST**, a benchmarking methodology and dataset for evaluating LLM-based ASP code generation. BLAST includes an ad-hoc benchmark, two testing methodologies, and correctness metrics that assess semantic distance from reference encodings without constraining predicate names or prompt structure. The two metrics provide consistent yet complementary assessments: one is more interpretable but requires human intervention, while the other is fully automatic but less explainable. Using BLAST, we evaluated eight state-of-the-art LLMs from five model families on ten standard graph problems. Results show that LLMs often achieve high syntactic accuracy but struggle with semantic correctness, degrade as task complexity increases, and do not consistently benefit from rephrased specifications.

As future work, we plan to address current limitations and explore several directions. Although our evaluation adopts zero-shot prompting to ensure a uniform and controlled comparison, more advanced strategies, e.g., few-shot prompting, prompt tuning, or retrieval-augmented generation, deserve systematic investigation, and could lead to better performance of LLMs in generating ASP code. Moreover, BLAST focuses on graph problems that are standard in ASP system testing. Extending the benchmark to additional domains would further strengthen its scope and representativeness. Finally, although here we evaluate general-purpose LLMs, our methodology is model-agnostic and could be employed to evaluate specialized techniques for ASP encoding.

References

1. Adams, G., Fabbri, A., Ladhak, F., Lehman, E., Elhadad, N.: From sparse to dense: GPT-4 summarization with chain of density prompting. In: Proceedings of the 4th New Frontiers in Summarization Workshop, pp. 68–74. ACL (2023)
2. Alviano, M., et al.: The fourth answer set programming competition: preliminary report. In: Cabalar, P., Son, T.C. (eds.) LPNMR 2013. LNCS (LNAI), vol. 8148, pp. 42–53. Springer, Heidelberg (2013). https://doi.org/10.1007/978-3-642-40564-8_5
3. Alviano, M., et al.: The ASP system DLV2. In: Balduccini, M., Janhunen, T. (eds.) LPNMR 2017. LNCS (LNAI), vol. 10377, pp. 215–221. Springer, Cham (2017). https://doi.org/10.1007/978-3-319-61660-5_19
4. Alviano, M., Cirimele, D., Reiners, L.A.R.: Introducing ASP recipes and ASP chef. In: ICLP Workshops. CEUR WP, vol. 3437. CEUR-WS.org (2023)
5. Amendola, G., Mazzotta, G., Ricca, F., Berei, T.: Unit testing in ASP revisited: language and test-driven development environment. Theory Pract. Log. Program. **24**(6), 1078–1108 (2024)
6. Anthropic: Claude 3.5 sonnet model card addendum (2024). https://api.semanticscholar.org/CorpusID:270667923
7. Baral, C., Dzifcak, J.: Solving puzzles described in English by automated translation to ASP and learning how to do that translation. In: KR. AAAI Press (2012)
8. Bauer, J.J., Eiter, T., Ruiz, N.H., Oetsch, J.: Visual graph question answering with ASP and LLMs for language parsing. In: ICLP. EPTCS, vol. 416, pp. 15–28 (2024)
9. Brewka, G., Eiter, T., Truszczynski, M.: Answer set programming at a glance. Commun. ACM **54**(12), 92–103 (2011)
10. Busoniu, P., Oetsch, J., Pührer, J., Skocovsky, P., Tompits, H.: SeaLion: an eclipse-based IDE for answer-set programming with advanced debugging support. Theory Pract. Log. Program. **13**(4–5), 657–673 (2013)
11. Calimeri, F., Germano, S., Palermiti, E., Reale, K., Ricca, F.: Developing ASP programs with ASPIDE and LoIDE. Künstliche Intell. **32**(2–3), 185–186 (2018)
12. Caruso, S., Dodaro, C., Maratea, M., Mochi, M., Riccio, F.: CNL2ASP: converting controlled natural language sentences into ASP. Theory Pract. Log. Program. **24**(2), 196–226 (2024)
13. Christen, P., Hand, D.J., Kirielle, N.: A review of the f-measure: Its history, properties, criticism, and alternatives. ACM Comput. Surv. **56**(3) (2023). https://doi.org/10.1145/3606367
14. Comanici, G., Bieber, E., et al.: Gemini 2.5: pushing the Frontier with advanced reasoning, multimodality, long context, and next generation agentic capabilities (2025). https://arxiv.org/abs/2507.06261
15. Coppolillo, E., Calimeri, F., Manco, G., Perri, S., Ricca, F.: LLASP: fine-tuning large language models for answer set programming. In: KR (2024)

16. Dakhel, A.M., Majdinasab, V., Nikanjam, A., Khomh, F., Desmarais, M.C., Jiang, Z.M.J.: GitHub copilot AI pair programmer: asset or liability? J. Syst. Softw. **203**, 111734 (2023)
17. DeepSeek: DeepSeek-R1: Incentivizing reasoning capability in LLMs via reinforcement learning (2025). https://arxiv.org/abs/2501.12948
18. Du, X., et al.: Evaluating large language models in class-level code generation. In: ICSE, pp. 81:1–81:13. ACM (2024)
19. Erdem, E., Gelfond, M., Leone, N.: Applications of answer set programming. AI Mag. **37**(3), 53–68 (2016)
20. Ernst, N.A., Bavota, G.: AI-driven development is here: should you worry? IEEE Softw. **39**(2), 106–110 (2022)
21. Falkner, A.A., Friedrich, G., Schekotihin, K., Taupe, R., Teppan, E.C.: Industrial applications of answer set programming. Künstliche Intell. **32**(2–3), 165–176 (2018)
22. Fang, M., Tompits, H.: An approach for representing answer sets in natural language. In: DECLARE. LNCS, vol. 10997, pp. 115–131. Springer (2017)
23. Febbraro, O., Reale, K., Ricca, F.: ASPIDE: integrated development environment for answer set programming. In: Delgrande, J.P., Faber, W. (eds.) LPNMR 2011. LNCS (LNAI), vol. 6645, pp. 317–330. Springer, Heidelberg (2011). https://doi.org/10.1007/978-3-642-20895-9_37
24. Gebser, M., Kaminski, R., Kaufmann, B., Ostrowski, M., Schaub, T., Wanko, P.: Theory solving made easy with Clingo 5. In: ICLP. OASIcs, vol. 52, pp. 2:1–2:15. Schloss Dagstuhl - Leibniz-Zentrum für Informatik (2016)
25. Gebser, M., Maratea, M., Ricca, F.: The sixth answer set programming competition. J. Artif. Intell. Res. **60**, 41–95 (2017)
26. Gebser, M., Maratea, M., Ricca, F.: The seventh answer set programming competition: design and results. Theory Pract. Log. Program. **20**(2), 176–204 (2020)
27. Gelfond, M., Lifschitz, V.: Classical negation in logic programs and disjunctive databases. New Gener. Comput. **9**(3/4), 365–386 (1991)
28. Grattafiori, A., et al.: The llama 3 herd of models (2024). https://arxiv.org/abs/2407.21783
29. Hahn, S., Sabuncu, O., Schaub, T., Stolzmann, T.: Clingraph: a system for ASP-based visualization (2023)
30. Ishay, A., Yang, Z., Lee, J.: Leveraging large language models to generate answer set programs. In: KR, pp. 374–383 (2023)
31. Jiang, J., Wang, F., Shen, J., Kim, S., Kim, S.: A survey on large language models for code generation (2024). https://arxiv.org/abs/2406.00515
32. Kareem, I., Gallagher, K., Borroto, M.A., Ricca, F., Russo, A.: Using learning from answer sets for robust question answering with LLM. In: LPNMR. LNCS, vol. 15245, pp. 112–125. Springer (2024)
33. Kuhn, T.: A survey and classification of controlled natural languages. Comput. Linguistics **40**(1), 121–170 (2014)
34. Lippolis, A.S., et al.: Ontology generation using large language models. In: ESWC (1). LNCS, vol. 15718, pp. 321–341. Springer (2025)
35. Mitra, A., Baral, C.: Addressing a question answering challenge by combining statistical methods with inductive rule learning and reasoning. In: AAAI, pp. 2779–2785. AAAI Press (2016)
36. Naveed, H., et al.: A comprehensive overview of large language models (2024)
37. Nye, M.I., Tessler, M.H., Tenenbaum, J.B., Lake, B.M.: Improving coherence and consistency in neural sequence models with dual-system, neuro-symbolic reasoning. In: NeurIPS, pp, 25192–25204 (2021)

38. Oetsch, J., Prischink, M., Pührer, J., Schwengerer, M., Tompits, H.: On the small-scope hypothesis for testing answer-set programs. In: KR. AAAI Press (2012)
39. OpenAI: GPT-4O system card (2024). https://arxiv.org/abs/2410.21276
40. OpenAI: Introducing GPT-5 (2025). https://openai.com/index/introducing-gpt-5/
41. OpenAI: Introducing OpenAI o3 and O4-mini (2025). https://openai.com/index/introducing-o3-and-o4-mini/
42. Ou, J., et al.: DialogBench: evaluating LLMs as human-like dialogue systems. In: NAACL-HLT. ACL (2024)
43. Peng, S., Kalliamvakou, E., Cihon, P., Demirer, M.: The impact of AI on developer productivity: evidence from GitHub copilot (2023)
44. Qin, L., et al.: LLM meet NLP: a survey (2024). https://arxiv.org/abs/2405.12819
45. Raiaan, M.A.K., et al.: A review on large language models: architectures, applications, taxonomies, open issues and challenges. IEEE Access **12**, 26839–26874 (2024)
46. Rajasekharan, A., Zeng, Y., Padalkar, P., Gupta, G.: Reliable natural language understanding with large language models and answer set programming. In: ICLP, pp. 274–287. EPTCS (2023)
47. Ren, L., Xiao, G., Qi, G., Geng, Y., Xue, H.: Can LLMs solve ASP problems? Insights from a benchmarking study. In: KR (2025)
48. Santana, M.A.B., Kareem, I., Ricca, F.: Towards automatic composition of ASP programs from natural language specifications. In: IJCAI, pp. 6198–6206 (2024)
49. Schrader, T.P., Lange, L., Kaminski, T., Razniewski, S., Friedrich, A.: A solver-in-the-loop framework for improving LLMs on answer set programming for logic puzzle solving. CoRR abs/2512.17093 (2025)
50. Schwitter, R.: Specifying and verbalising answer set programs in controlled natural language. Theory Pract. Log. Program. **18**(3–4), 691–705 (2018)
51. Shah, N., Genc, Z., Araci, D.: StackEval: benchmarking LLMs in coding assistance. In: NeurIPS (2024)
52. Team, G., et al., P.G.: Gemini 1.5: unlocking multimodal understanding across millions of tokens of context (2024). https://arxiv.org/abs/2403.05530
53. Valmeekam, K., Stechly, K., Gundawar, A., Kambhampati, S.: A systematic evaluation of the planning and scheduling abilities of the reasoning model o1. Trans. Mach. Learn. Res. **2025** (2025)
54. Vaswani, A., et al.: Attention is all you need. In: Advances in Neural Information Processing Systems, vol. 30, Curran Associates, Inc. (2017)
55. Voboril, F., Ramaswamy, V.P., Szeider, S.: Generating streamlining constraints with large language models. J. Artif. Intell. Res. **84** (2025)
56. Xu, K., Mao, Y., Guan, X., Feng, Z.: Web-bench: a LLM code benchmark based on web standards and frameworks (2025). https://arxiv.org/abs/2505.07473
57. Yang, Z., Ishay, A., Lee, J.: Coupling large language models with logic programming for robust and general reasoning from text. In: ACL, pp. 5186–5219 (2023)
58. Zhao, W.X., Zhou, K., et al.: A survey of large language models (2025). https://arxiv.org/abs/2303.18223
59. Zhou, Y., Ringeval, F., Portet, F.: Can GPT models follow human summarization guidelines? A study for targeted communication goals (2025). https://arxiv.org/abs/2310.16810

On Strong Equivalence Notions in Logic Programming and Abstract Argumentation

Giovanni Buraglio(✉), Wolfgang Dvořák, and Stefan Woltran

TU Wien, Vienna, Austria
{giovanni.buraglio, wolfgang.dvorak, stefan.woltran}@tuwien.ac.at

Abstract. Strong equivalence between knowledge bases ensures the possibility of replacing one with the other without affecting reasoning outcomes, in any given context. This makes it a crucial property in non-monotonic formalisms. In particular, the fields of logic programming and abstract argumentation provide primary examples in which this property has been subject to vast investigations. However, while (classes of) logic programs and abstract argumentation frameworks are known to be semantically equivalent in static settings, this alignment breaks in dynamic contexts due to differing notions of update. As a result, strong equivalence does not always carry over from one formalism to the other. In this paper, we carefully investigate this discrepancy and introduce a new notion of strong equivalence for logic programs. Our approach preserves strong equivalence under translation between certain classes of logic programs and both Dung-style and claim-augmented argumentation frameworks, thus restoring compatibility across these formalisms.

Keywords: Strong Equivalence · Abstract Argumentation · Logic Programming

1 Introduction

In the field of Knowledge Representation and Reasoning, the concept of equivalence between knowledge bases has been the subject of extensive studies. A primary motivation behind this research is the potential to exploit the equivalence between two knowledge bases to achieve a compact representation of the same information. Furthermore, the possibility to substitute a specific component of a given knowledge base $\mathcal{K}$ with an equivalent yet simplified alternative has been shown to ease the computational cost of reasoning over $\mathcal{K}$. While this advantageous behavior can be taken for granted in monotonic formalisms (e.g. classical logic), it is usually not the case in non-monotonic ones. For this, the notion of strong equivalence has been introduced in a dynamic environment, to capture the idea of equivalence under any possible update [4, 12, 17–20].

W. Faber et al. (Eds.): LPNMR 2026, LNAI 16952, pp. 133–149, 2027.
https://doi.org/10.1007/978-3-032-38320-4_9

In this paper, we consider two families of non-monotonic formalisms, namely logic programming and abstract argumentation. Logic programming is a declarative programming paradigm where a reasoning problem is specified by means of a so-called logic program (LP). This consists of a set of inference rules made of atoms, possibly preceded by a negation-as-failure operator. Negative literals are assumed to be true as long as their corresponding positive atom cannot be proven to hold. Abstract argumentation is a sub-field of symbolic Artificial Intelligence [1] that offers formal approaches to represent and reason over situations where conflicting information is present. An argumentative scenario is specified by means of an abstract argumentation framework, which is a directed graph where nodes represent arguments and edges their relation. The starting point in the field is the seminal work of Dung [8], where argumentation frameworks, which we call Dung-style AFs, contain only a relation of attack. Several semantics have been proposed for both of these formalisms, with the common purpose of extracting solutions for the given program or argumentation framework. These are respectively sets of atoms that satisfy each rule in the program (called *answer-sets*), and sets of arguments that are able to defend themselves against possible counter-arguments (called *extensions*). In this work, we focus on the stable model semantics for LPs [13] and the stable semantics for AFs [8].

Previous work has introduced a one-to-one mapping between Dung-style AFs and (a restricted class of) LPs under the stable model semantics [5,8]. Any problem can be either specified via a program P or an abstract argumentation framework F in such a way that their solutions coincide. Later, this mapping has been extended to a wider class of LPs and generalizations of Dung-style AFs, such as claim-augmented AFs [10]. Thus, equivalent LPs correspond to equivalent AFs.

However, such a semantic correspondence does not necessarily carry over to dynamic contexts, where strong equivalence is required. It is possible for two logic programs that are strongly equivalent to induce argumentation frameworks that are not, due to the incongruous notions of update (or expansion) in the two realms. To acknowledge such mismatch, consider the following example:

Example 1. Two suspects, X and Y, are under investigation for a murder proven by forensic analysis to have been committed by a single person. While questioning possible witnesses, the detective learns that X and Y have been seen far away from the crime scene at the time of the murder, and the case remains unsolved. We model the detective's knowledge via an Dung-style AF and an LP as follows:

F 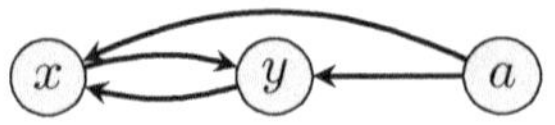 $P = \{x \leftarrow \texttt{not}\, y, \texttt{not}\, a.,\ y \leftarrow \texttt{not}\, x, \texttt{not}\, a.,\ a \leftarrow .\}$

where a means "has an alibi" and x (resp. y) means "X (resp. Y) is the murder". Later, another witness testifies that the first witness was drunk (d), falsifying the suspects' alibi. This information update is captured via:

F'  $P' = \{a \leftarrow \texttt{not}\, d.,\ d \leftarrow .\}$

In accordance with equivalence results between logic programs and argumentation frameworks, the two ways of modeling our knowledge base are consistent with each other when taken individually. However, this does not happen when they are combined. Incorporating the second pair of knowledge bases (F' and P') into the first one (resp. F and P) yields different result: in the case of F and F', their union returns the expected result in the form of two possible extensions $\{d, x\}$ and $\{d, y\}$. Indeed, since the first witness was drunk, this is compatible with either X or Y being the murder. On the other hand, the union of P and P' yields an unexpected prediction: the alibi '$a \leftarrow$' is not overwritten by the witness being drunk '$d \leftarrow$', leaving $\{a, d\}$ as the only possible solution.

Updating an existing program by simply adding rules may yield unexpected outcomes. Firstly, because facts (e.g. '$a \leftarrow$' in P) cannot be overwritten by incoming information, while their corresponding arguments (e.g. $a \in F$) can. This behavior of LPs is fundamentally in contrast with the way in which non-monotonicity is encoded in abstract argumentation: an argument can always be attacked by new ones. Moreover, rule addition may not account for situations where existing rules need to be refined by introducing further exceptions.

Example 2. Consider a self-driving vehicle being trained to learn safety policies. Initially the vehicle is tested in isolation, and learns the policy P: "Proceed (p) at the traffic light if the traffic light is not red (r)". Later, other objects are introduced in the environment to simulate the presence of humans on the street. The vehicle is then able to learn a more refined policy R: "Proceed (p) at the traffic light if the traffic light is not red (r) and no object is crossing the road (o)". The two policies and their union Q are represented below as logic programs:

$$P = \{p \leftarrow \texttt{not}\, r.\} \quad R = \{p \leftarrow \texttt{not}\, r, \texttt{not}\, o.\} \quad Q = \{p \leftarrow \texttt{not}\, r., p \leftarrow \texttt{not}\, r, \texttt{not}\, o.\}$$

Notice that, again, updating P with R does not account for the learning process exhibited by the vehicle: even if an object crossing the road is detected (i.e. '$o \leftarrow$' is added to Q), p remains derivable via the first rule. In fact, it has been observed that adding a rule that *subsumes* another one has no effect on the final solution of the program (i.e. it preserves strong equivalence) [11].

As Examples 1 and 2 show, the standard notion of LP update introduces new alternatives for the same head-atom, yielding a *disjunctive* interpretation of updates. Nonetheless, a *conjunctive* interpretation of updates, where rule bodies get merged, might be preferable to account for different forms of information expansion. Towards filling this gap, in this work we carefully analyze the relationship between logic programming and abstract argumentation, with a particular interest in dynamic contexts. As a first step, we recall and extend equivalence results for classes of logic programs and abstract argumentation frameworks. Subsequently, inspired by Dung-style AFs, we introduce a novel notion of update for a restricted class of LPs, called Rule Refinement, that resolves the issue by allowing disjunctive or conjunctive interpretations of updates. We further extend Rule Refinement to the wider class of atomic logic programs (where no positive literal occurs in the body), which is shown to capture strong equivalence in claim-augmented AFs. All proofs are available at https://arxiv.org/abs/2605.14721.

2 Preliminaries

Logic Programming. We consider normal logic programs with negation-as-failure $\texttt{not}$, consisting of rules r of the form '$n : c \leftarrow a_1, \ldots, a_k, \texttt{not}\, b_1, \ldots, \texttt{not}\, b_m$.' read as '$c$ if a_1 and ... and a_k and $\texttt{not}\, b_1$ and ... and $\texttt{not}\, b_m$'. Here, $n \in \mathbb{N}$ is the *identifier* of the rule r in the program; we refer to it with $id(r) = n$. Identifiers will become relevant in Sects. 3.2, 4.2 and 5.2. $\mathcal{L}(P)$ is the set of all atoms occurring in P. The atoms a_i and b_j are called positive and negative atoms, respectively denoted by $pos(r) = \{a_1, \ldots, a_k\}$ and $neg(r) = \{b_1, \ldots, b_m\}$. We use $head(r) = c$ and $body(r) = \{a_1, \ldots, a_k, \texttt{not}\, b_1, \ldots, \texttt{not}\, b_m\}$ for the head and body of r. With a slight abuse of notation, we extend *pos*, *neg*, *head*, *body* to sets of rules, e.g. $head(R) = \{head(r) \mid r \in R\}$. For a set of atoms S, we use $\texttt{not}\, S = \{\texttt{not}\, b \mid b \in S\}$. A rule r is called: *constraint* if $head(r) = \emptyset$; *fact* if $k = m = 0$; *atomic* if $k = 0$. A program P is *atomic* if all the rules in P are. The stable model semantics of normal LPs is defined in terms of answer sets [13].

Definition 1. *Let P be a normal logic program and $S \subseteq \mathcal{L}(P)$ a set of atoms. The* reduct *of P w.r.t. S is the negation-free program P^S obtained from P by: (i) deleting all rules $r \in P$ with $\texttt{not}\, b_j$ in the body for some $b_j \in S$, (ii) deleting all negated atoms from the remaining rules. S is an answer set of P iff S is the minimal model of P^S. The collection of answer sets of a program P is $AS(P)$.*

In this paper, whenever we write program we mean an atomic one. We further focus on sub-classes of atomic LPs: we call *strict* (resp. *h-unique*) a program P where each $p \in \mathcal{L}(P)$ occurs at least (resp. at most) once in the head of a rule.

Abstract Argumentation. We fix an infinite background set of arguments $\mathcal{U}$. A strict argumentation framework (strict AF[1]) is a directed graph $F = (A, R)$ where $A \subseteq \mathcal{U}$ is a finite set of arguments and $R \subseteq A \times A$ is an attack relation between them [8]. The union of any two strict AFs $F = (A, R)$ and $G = (A', R')$ is defined as $F \cup G = (A \cup A', R \cup R')$. For two arguments $a, b \in A$ we say that a attacks b if $(a, b) \in R$. Moreover, a set of arguments $E \subseteq A$ attacks b if $(a, b) \in R$ for some $a \in E$ and a attacks E if $(a, b) \in R$ for some $b \in E$. We use $E_R^+ = \{a \in A \mid E \text{ attacks } a\}$ and $E_R^- = \{a \in A \mid a \text{ attacks } E\}$ to denote the set of arguments respectively attacked by and attacking E. Further, $E_R^\oplus = E \cup E_R^+$ is called the *range* of E w.r.t. R. For a singleton $\{a\}$ we use a_R^+, a_R^- and $a_R^\oplus$.

E is conflict-free in F ($E \in cf(F)$) iff for no $a, b \in E$, $(a, b) \in R$. For any strict AF $F = (A, R)$, an argumentation semantics $\sigma : F \mapsto \sigma(F) \subseteq 2^A$ returns a set of subsets of A (called σ-extensions). Here we consider only *stable* semantics:

---

[1] We use this terminology for standard Dung AFs, to emphasize the fact that the attack relation is restricted to arguments in A. In Sect. 3, we will relax this requirement.

Definition 2. *Let $F = (A, R)$ be a strict AF and $E \in cf(F)$ a conflict-free set in F. We say that E is a stable extension of F ($E \in stb(F)$) iff $E_R^{\oplus} = A$.*

In recent years, more expressive abstract formalisms have been proposed that extend Dung-style AFs. Among these, *claim-augmented argumentation frameworks* (or CAFs) add claims to the abstract representation [9,10].

Definition 3. *Let C be a set (or universe) of claims. A claim-augmented argumentation framework (CAF) is a triple $\mathcal{F} = (A, R, \gamma)$ such that $F = (A, R)$ is a strict AF and $\gamma : A \mapsto C$ is a function that assigns claims to arguments.*

For a set of arguments E, we use $\gamma(E) = \{\gamma(a) \mid a \in E\}$ to denote the associated set of claims. By means of CAFs, it is possible to represent situations where different arguments have the same claim. In this paper we focus on *well-formed CAFs*, for which arguments with the same claim attack the same arguments. A CAF $\mathcal{F} = (A, R, \gamma)$ is well-formed iff for any two arguments a, b, $\gamma(a) = \gamma(b)$ implies $a_R^+ = b_R^+$. Stable semantics for a well-formed CAF $\mathcal{F} = (F, \gamma)$ can be defined as taking the claim-sets $\gamma(E)$ inherited from every stable extension E.

Definition 4. *For a well-formed CAF $\mathcal{F} = (F, \gamma)$, a set S is a stable (claim-)extension of $\mathcal{F}$ ($S \in stb_i(\mathcal{F})$) iff there is an $E \in stb(F)$ such that $S = \gamma(E)$.*

Strong Equivalence. Strong equivalence notions for logic programs and argumentation frameworks have been presented to capture equivalence under any possible updates. In the case of LPs, updates consist of expanding the original program with a set of rules. Two LPs P and Q are said to be equivalent, denoted $P \equiv Q$ whenever $AS(P) = AS(Q)$. Further, P and Q are strongly equivalent, denoted $P \equiv_s Q$, iff, for any LP R, the programs $P \cup R$ and $Q \cup R$ are equivalent, i.e. $P \cup R \equiv Q \cup R$ [17]. Here, we consider specific classes of LPs and adjust the relative notion of strong equivalence accordingly.

Definition 5. *Given a class Π of LPs, P and Q in Π, we say that P and Q are strongly equivalent in Π, written $P \equiv_s^{\Pi} Q$, iff for every program R: either (1) $P \cup R \notin \Pi$ and $Q \cup R \notin \Pi$ or (2) $P \cup R \equiv Q \cup R$.*

More recently, strong equivalence has been studied for other non-monotonic formalisms, in the field of abstract argumentation [18]. Two strict AFs F and G are equivalent under stable semantics, if $stb(F) = stb(G)$. Strong equivalence, denoted by $F \equiv_s G$, is satisfied whenever $stb(F \cup H) = stb(G \cup H)$ for any strict AF H. In this setting, strong equivalence admits a syntactic characterization in terms of so-called (semantics-dependent) kernels, obtained by syntactical modifications of the given frameworks. For stable semantics, such modification consists in the removal of out-going attacks from self-attacking arguments.

Definition 6 ([18]). *Let $F = (A, R)$ be an strict AF. The stable kernel of F is $F^{SK} = (A, R^{SK})$ with $R^{SK} = R \setminus \{(a, b) \mid a \neq b, (a, a) \in R\}$.*

A characterization of strong equivalence can be obtained via kernels [18].

Proposition 1. *For any two strict AFs F and G, $F \equiv_s G$ iff $F^{SK} = G^{SK}$.*

The idea of strong equivalence has been investigated for CAFs as well. In the literature only expansions among *compatible* CAFs are considered. Informally, two CAFs are compatible if and only if the arguments they share have the same claim. Moreover, AF kernels characterize strong equivalence for CAFs as well.

Proposition 2 ([2]). *Let $\mathcal{F} = (F, \gamma)$ and $\mathcal{G} = (G, \gamma')$ be two compatible well-formed CAFs. Then $\mathcal{F} \equiv_s^{stb_i} \mathcal{G}$ iff $F \equiv_s^{stb} G$.*

This kernel characterization applies when $\mathcal{F}$ and $\mathcal{G}$ are well-formed, for any common update $\mathcal{H}$ (possibly not well-formed). In Sect. 5.2 we follow a different path, since CAFs translated from LPs are guaranteed to be well-formed and the requirement of compatibility for expansions is not natural for logic programs.

3 From Abstract Argumentation to Logic Programming and Back

In this section we introduce translations between increasingly larger classes of logic programs and increasingly more expressive abstract argumentation frameworks. We recall the fact that strict h-unique atomic programs correspond to strict AFs [5]. Further, we show that by relaxing the strictness requirement for LPs we end up in the broader class of (possibly non-strict) AFs. Then, we consider the full class of atomic LPs and their correspondence to well-formed CAFs.

3.1 Logic Programs and Dung-Style AFs

We begin with strict h-unique atomic programs and strict AFs. Any strict AF can be transformed into an logic program by generating a rule r for every argument such that the head of r is the argument's name and the (negative) body contains the names of each attacker. The resulting program is atomic, strict and h-unique.

Definition 7 ([5]). *Let $F = (A, R)$ be an argumentation framework with $A = \{a_1, \ldots, a_n\}$. The corresponding logic program of F is:*

$$P_F = \{i : a_i \leftarrow \mathtt{not}\, b_1, \ldots, \mathtt{not}\, b_k. \mid a_i \in A \text{ and } \{b_1, \ldots, b_k\} = a_i^-\}$$

Example 3. Consider the following strict AF $F = (A, R)$ depicted below with $A = \{a, b, c\}$ and $R = \{(a, a), (a, b), (b, a), (b, c)\}$ and its corresponding LP P_F:

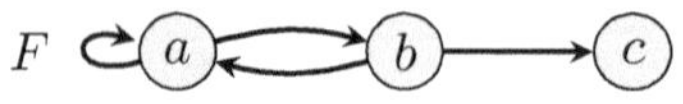

$$P_F = \{1 : a \leftarrow \mathtt{not}\, a, \mathtt{not}\, b., \quad 2 : b \leftarrow \mathtt{not}\, a., \quad 3 : c \leftarrow \mathtt{not}\, b.\}$$

For the other direction, the transformation only takes strict h-unique programs as input. For each rule, the head atom is associated to an argument with the same name and each negated atom (called *vulnerability*) in the body is associated with an attacker of the argument corresponding to the rule-head.

Definition 8 ([5]). *Let P be a strict h-unique program. The corresponding strict argumentation framework $F_P = (A_P, R_P)$ is defined by:*

- $A_P = \{a \mid a \in head(r),\ r \in P\}$,
- $R_P = \{(a, b) \mid b \in head(r),\ a \in neg(r),\ r \in P\}$.

It is easy to see that under translation, the program in Example 3 generates exactly the strict AF F. Indeed, the presented translation is a bijection.

Proposition 3 **([5]).** *For a strict AF F and its corresponding LP P_F, $F = F_{P_F}$.*

Moreover, the answer sets for a (strict h-unique) program correspond exactly to the stable extensions of its transformed strict AF.

Proposition 4 **([5]).** *For any strict AF F and h-unique atomic program P, $stb(F) = AS(P_F)$ and $AS(P) = stb(F_P)$.*

Given a certain program P, the attacks that are generated in F_P depend on two factors: the vulnerabilities and head-atoms. In [5] equivalence under transformation is studied in a static setting, where strictness becomes a crucial aspect to enforce in order to define a one-to-one mapping. In a dynamic setting, on the other hand, the vulnerabilities in P which do not occur as head-atoms may have an impact at the semantic level: new incoming attacks in F_P may arise.

Example 4. The programs $P = \{a \leftarrow \mathtt{not}\, b.\}$ and $P' = \{a \leftarrow .\}$ have the same unique answer set $\{a\}$. However, when concurrently updated with $P'' = \{b \leftarrow .\}$, their answer sets differ: $AS(P \cup P'') = \{\{b\}\}$ and $AS(P' \cup P'') = \{\{a, b\}\}$.

Motivated by these considerations, we relax the notion of strictness for logic program, i.e. we consider programs with negative literals that never occur as head-atoms. Indeed, the previously shown translation would relate non-strict programs to strict AFs only at the cost of losing the one-to-one mapping: several non-strict LPs correspond to the same strict AF. In order to maintain an exact mapping, we also relax the definition of attack relation, allowing incoming attacks from elements in the universe $\mathcal{U}$ outside of A. We use *ungrounded attacks* to refer to these relations. Further, we simply call argumentation framework (AF) any framework with possibly ungrounded attacks.

Definition 9 (AF). *An AF $F = (A, R)$ is a directed graph with $A \subseteq \mathcal{U}$ a non-empty set of arguments and $R \subseteq \mathcal{U} \times A$ a conflict relation. We call $R_{\downarrow A} = R \cap (A \times A)$ the set of (proper) attacks, and $R \setminus R_{\downarrow A}$ the set of ungrounded attacks.*

The strictness notion of logic programs and argumentation frameworks are indeed connected: every non-strict AF can be mapped to exactly one non-strict LP. The isomorphism of Proposition 3 between strict h-unique atomic LPs and strict AFs can be lifted to possibly non-strict programs and AFs.

Remark 1. For any AF F and corresponding logic program P_F, $F = F_{P_F}$. Conversely, for any h-unique atomic LP P and corresponding AF F, $P = P_{F_P}$.

Example 5.
Let $F = (A, R)$ be the AF below. In the program P_F, the ungrounded attack $(c, b) \in R \setminus R_{\downarrow A}$ is represented by the vulnerability $c \in neg(P_F)$.

F

$P_F = \{1 : a \leftarrow \mathtt{not}\, a, \mathtt{not}\, b.,\ 2 : b \leftarrow \mathtt{not}\, a, \mathtt{not}\, c.\}$

The notions of defense, conflict-freeness as well as stable semantics for AFs are defined over $R_{\downarrow A}$ and are thus identical to those introduced for strict AFs.

Definition 10. *Let $F = (A, R)$ be an AF. A set $E \subseteq A$ is conflict-free in F iff for no $a, b \in A$, $(a, b) \in R_{\downarrow A}$. Further, E is a stable extension of F iff $E^{\oplus}_{R_{\downarrow A}} = A$.*

Notice that the notion of stable-kernel characterizes strong equivalence between AFs. This follows straightforwardly from the fact that we fixed $R \subseteq \mathcal{U} \times A$. Hence, no ungrounded attack generates from a self-attacking argument. Moreover, ungrounded attacks have no influence on the evaluation of an AF.

Proposition 5. *For an AF $F = (A, R)$ and $F_{\downarrow A} = (A, R_{\downarrow A})$, $stb(F) = stb(F_{\downarrow A})$.*

For h-unique programs we observe a similar behavior. We can identify a set $S \subseteq neg(P)$ of *ungrounded vulnerabilities* that make a program P non-strict. Formally, the set of ungrounded vulnerabilities for P is $UV(P) = \{\mathtt{not}\, b \mid b \in neg(P) \setminus head(P)\}$. By removing such vulnerabilities, we obtain the strict program $P_{\downarrow head}$, defined as $P_{\downarrow head} = \{id(r) : head(r) \leftarrow body(r) \setminus UV(P). \mid r \in P\}$. Notice that transforming a non-strict atomic program into the corresponding strict one yields equivalent answer-sets, and vice-versa. Ungrounded vulnerabilities have no semantic impact, similarly to ungrounded attacks. Thus, answer-sets are preserved when restricting to strict programs.

Proposition 6. *For an atomic program P and $P_{\downarrow head}$, $AS(P) = AS(P_{\downarrow head})$.*

To show that semantic equivalence can be lifted to AFs and h-unique programs, we introduce the following lemma.

Lemma 1. *For any h-unique atomic logic program P, $F_{P_{\downarrow head}} = (F_P)_{\downarrow A_P}$. For any AF F, $P_{F_{\downarrow A}} = (P_F)_{\downarrow head}$.*

Proposition 7. *For any h-unique atomic program P and the corresponding AF F_P, it holds that $AS(P) = stb(F_P)$. Conversely, for any AF F and its corresponding program P_F, we have that $stb(F) = AS(P_F)$.*

3.2 Logic Programs and Well-Formed CAFs

We can now move one step forward and consider the wider class of atomic LPs and their relation to well-formed CAFs. For these, attacks are not arbitrary pairs of arguments, but depends on the attacker's claim. A translation has been introduced between *strict* atomic LPs and well-formed CAFs. In our setting, we provide a more general translation that considers possibly non-strict LPs. To do so, we give a definition of well-formed CAFs more suitable for a dynamic setting.

Definition 11. *A well-formed CAF is a triple $\mathcal{F} = (A, R^{\mathcal{C}}, \gamma)$ where A is a finite set of arguments, $R^{\mathcal{C}} \subseteq \mathcal{C} \times A$ is a set of claim-attacks with $\mathcal{C}$ the universe of claims and $\gamma : A \mapsto \mathcal{C}$ the claim function.*

One can easily retrieve the original definition of CAF by fixing $R = \{(x_i, x_j) \mid x_i, x_j \in A, \gamma(x_i) = c \text{ and } (c, x_j) \in R^{\mathcal{C}}\}$. As a result, we can utilize the definition of stable semantics for well-formed CAFs by means of this translation. By appealing to the universe of claims $\mathcal{C}$, we have a formulation that encompasses claim attacks from claims which do not label any argument, i.e. ungrounded attacks. Any atomic LP exactly corresponds to some well-formed CAF by taking an argument for each rule, a set of claims for each atom occurring as the head of some rule and attacks defined from claims to arguments.

Definition 12. *Given an atomic program P, we obtain the corresponding well-formed CAF $\mathcal{F}_P = (A_P, R^{\mathcal{C}}_P, \gamma_P)$ by fixing $A_P = \{x_i \mid id(r) = i, r \in P\}$, $R^{\mathcal{C}}_P = \{(c, x_i) \mid c \in neg(r), id(r) = i\}$, and $\gamma_P(x_i) = head(r)$ with $id(r) = i$.*

Example 6. Consider the atomic LP P below and its corresponding well-formed CAF. Notice that the claim-attack (c, x_2) is realized by an ungrounded attack.

$P = \{1 : a \leftarrow \texttt{not}\, b.,$
$\quad 2 : a \leftarrow \texttt{not}\, c., \; 3 : b \leftarrow \texttt{not}\, a.\}$

$\mathcal{F}_P$ 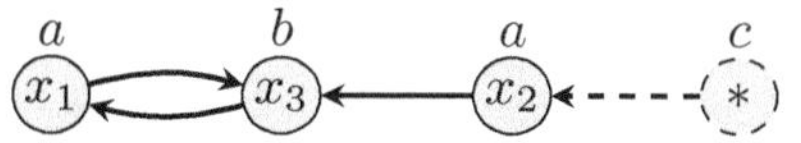

From a well-formed CAF, each argument x_i corresponds to a rule r with $id(r) = i$ and head $\gamma(x_i)$. Further, for each claim $c \in \mathcal{C}$ attacking the argument x_i, $\texttt{not}\, c$ appears in the body of the rule.

Definition 13. *For a well-formed CAF $\mathcal{F} = (A, R^{\mathcal{C}}, \gamma)$ with $A = \{x_1 \ldots, x_n\}$, $P_{\mathcal{F}} = \{i : \gamma(x_i) \leftarrow \texttt{not}\, b_1 \ldots \texttt{not}\, b_k. \mid x_i \in A, \{b_1 \ldots b_k\} = \gamma(x_i^-)\}$ is the corresponding LP.*

Any CAF $\mathcal{F}$ where different arguments share the same claim is associated with a non h-unique program $P_{\mathcal{F}}$. Thus, CAFs are isomorphic to atomic LPs.

Proposition 8 **([15]).** *For a CAF $\mathcal{F}$ and corresponding LP $P_{\mathcal{F}}$, $\mathcal{F} = \mathcal{F}_{P_{\mathcal{F}}}$.*

For well-formed CAFs and LPs, equivalence is preserved under translation.

Proposition 9 **([15]).** *For any well-formed CAF $\mathcal{F}$ and atomic program P, $stb(\mathcal{F}) = AS(P_{\mathcal{F}})$ and $AS(P) = stb(\mathcal{F}_P)$.*

In their original formulation, the propositions above consider only strict well-formed CAFs and atomic programs. However, they can be carefully adapted to our context based on the our relaxed notion of well-formed CAF.

3.3 Equivalence from Static to Dynamic Setting

Until now, we have considered equivalence within a static setting and provided translations that preserve it. Such a semantic correspondence does not carry over to dynamic scenarios, already within the class of strict AFs. Two strongly equivalent LPs may have corresponding AFs that are not strongly equivalent.

Proposition 10. *For two LPs P and Q, $P \equiv_s Q$ does not imply $F_P \equiv_s F_Q$.*

Example 7. Take two logic programs as follows:

$P = \{a \leftarrow \mathtt{not}\, b, \mathtt{not}\, c.,$
$b \leftarrow \mathtt{not}\, a, \mathtt{not}\, c., \; c \leftarrow .\}$

$Q = \{a \leftarrow \mathtt{not}\, c.,$
$b \leftarrow \mathtt{not}\, a, \mathtt{not}\, c., \; c \leftarrow .\}$

Since both P and Q contain the fact $c \leftarrow$ and $c \in neg(r)$ for every other rule in both programs, c occurs in any answer-set of $P \cup R$ and $Q \cup R$ for any R. Hence, they are strongly equivalent. The associated strict AFs are:

F_P

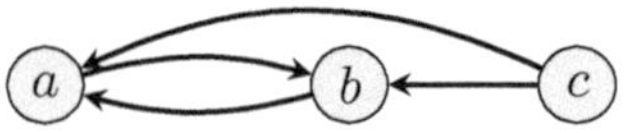

F_Q

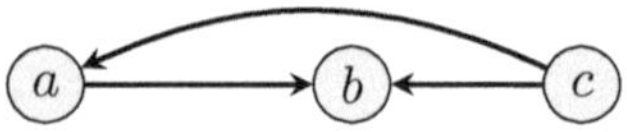

Both F_Q and F_P coincide with their own kernels, as they contain no self-attacking argument. Since they are different, they are not strongly equivalent.

4 Strong Equivalence Under Rule Refinement

As previously shown, equivalence among LPs and AFs does not carry over to strong equivalence: due to the incongruous definitions of update in the two realms, their evaluation changes when moving from a static to a dynamic setting. To solve this mismatch we look at LPs through the lenses of abstract argumentation. From the LP perspective, adding attackers on the corresponding AF means adding vulnerabilities to the rule whose head identifies the attacked argument. We call this operation *rule refinement*, defined as follows.

Definition 14 (rule refinement). *Let r and r' be two arbitrary LP rules. To express that r is refined by means of r', we use*

$$\mathtt{refine}(r, r') := \{id(r) : head(r) \leftarrow body(r) \cup body(r').\}.$$

In this section, we introduce a novel notion of strong equivalence for the class of (h-unique) atomic programs based on the rule refinement operator.

4.1 Rule Refinement for H-Unique LPs

We first consider the class Ξ of h-unique atomic programs. Within this class, each rule can be identified by means of its head-atom. Consequently, we can omit the explicit identifiers from rules and use the head-atoms instead. We can now introduce a novel notion of LP update, that we call Rule Refinement (RR, for brevity). Updating a program P with a rule r' via RR consists of two possible operations: if $head(r') \notin head(P)$, the update yields a set-union; otherwise, the rule-body of $r \in P$ for which $head(r) = head(r')$ is merged with that of r'.

Definition 15 ($\uplus$-update). *Let P be an h-unique atomic program and r a rule in P. The $\uplus$-update (or simply update) of P by means of an atomic rule r' is:*

$$P \uplus r' = \begin{cases} P \cup \{r'\} & \textit{if } head(r') \notin head(P) \\ P \setminus \{r\} \cup \mathtt{refine}(r, r') & \textit{otherwise} \end{cases}$$

Example 8. The $\uplus$-update of $P = \{a \leftarrow \texttt{not}\, b.,\ b \leftarrow \texttt{not}\, a.,\ c \leftarrow .\}$ via the rule $r = c \leftarrow \texttt{not}\, d.$ is: $P \uplus r = \{a \leftarrow \texttt{not}\, b.,\ b \leftarrow \texttt{not}\, a.,\ c \leftarrow \texttt{not}\, d.\}$.

Towards the generalization of $\uplus$ between sets of rules, notice that the consecutive applications of $\uplus$ preserve the result independently of the order of execution.

Lemma 2. *For an h-unique atomic program P and two rules r_1 and r_2 it holds that $(P \uplus r_1) \uplus r_2 = (P \uplus r_2) \uplus r_1$.*

Updating an h-unique program P with a program $Q = \{r_1, \ldots, r_n\}$ results in $P \uplus Q = P \uplus r_1 \uplus \cdots \uplus r_n$, which is guaranteed to be atomic and h-unique.

Proposition 11. *For an h-unique atomic program P and any atomic program Q, the program $P \uplus Q$ is h-unique and atomic.*

We can now introduce RR strong equivalence for h-unique atomic programs.

Definition 16. *Two h-unique atomic programs P and Q are strongly equivalent under Rule Refinement in Ξ, written $P \equiv_r^{\Xi} Q$, iff for any program R: either (1) $P \uplus R \notin \Xi$ and $Q \uplus R \notin \Xi$ or (2) $AS(P \uplus R) = AS(Q \uplus R)$.*

By the definition of RR-update, whenever $R \in \Xi$, condition (1) is never satisfied. Moreover, strongly equivalent programs under standard expansions are not guaranteed to be RR strong equivalent in Ξ.

Proposition 12. *For any two h-unique atomic programs P and Q, it holds that: (i) $P \equiv_s^{\Xi} Q$ does not imply $P \equiv_r^{\Xi} Q$; (ii) $P \equiv_s Q$ does not imply $P \equiv_r^{\Xi} Q$.*

Example 9. Consider the LPs $P = \{a \leftarrow \texttt{not}\, b, \texttt{not}\, c.,\ b \leftarrow \texttt{not}\, a, \texttt{not}\, c.,\ c \leftarrow .\}$ and $Q = \{a \leftarrow \texttt{not}\, b, \texttt{not}\, c.,\ b \leftarrow \texttt{not}\, c.,\ c \leftarrow .\}$. Let R be an (atomic) program. Since $c \leftarrow$ is contained in both $P \cup R$ and $Q \cup R$, c occurs in every answer-set of both programs. Thus, all the other rules in P and Q do not fire, making P and Q strongly equivalent, i.e. $P \equiv_s Q$ and $P \equiv_s^{\Xi} Q$. However, for the program $R' = \{c \leftarrow \texttt{not}\, d., d \leftarrow .\}$, we get: (1) $P \uplus R' \in \Xi$ and $Q \cup R' \in \Xi$ and (2) $AS(P \uplus R') \neq AS(Q \uplus R')$ since $\{a, d\}$ is not a common answer-set of the two.

4.2 Rule Refinement for LPs

In this section we consider a notion of strong equivalence under rule refinement for the whole class Λ of atomic LPs by dropping the requirement of h-uniqueness. We deal with (possibly non-strict) atomic programs, in which several rules with the same head might occur. Here, the information provided by rule identifiers becomes relevant when considering possible updates: identifiers allow to distinguish among updates that involve rules already contained in P or new ones. Indeed, updating a program with a new rule r' may result in the addition or refinement, irrespective of the head of r'. We then adapt the notion of update.

Definition 17 ($\uplus$-update). *Let P be an atomic program and r a rule in P. We define the $\uplus$-update (or simply update) of P by means of a new rule r' as:*

$$P \uplus r' = \begin{cases} P \cup \{r'\} & \textit{if } id(r') \notin id(P) \\ P \setminus \{r\} \cup \texttt{refine}(r, r') & \textit{otherwise} \end{cases}$$

Identifiers guide the update either towards the addition of the new rule or the refinement of an old rule with the same identifier.

Example 10. The $\uplus$-update of $P = \{1 : a \leftarrow \texttt{not}\, b., 2 : b \leftarrow \texttt{not}\, a., 3 : b \leftarrow .\}$ via $r = 3 : a \leftarrow \texttt{not}\, c.$ is: $P \uplus r = \{1 : a \leftarrow \texttt{not}\, b., 2 : b \leftarrow \texttt{not}\, a., 3 : b \leftarrow \texttt{not}\, c.\}$.

As before, to generalize the notion of $\uplus$-update between sets of rules, we note that associativity is preserved. Further, $P \uplus Q$ is atomic whenever P and Q are.

Lemma 3. *For an atomic program P and two rules r_1 and r_2 it holds that $(P \uplus r_1) \uplus r_2 = (P \uplus r_2) \uplus r_1$.*

Proposition 13. *For any two atomic programs P and Q, $P \uplus Q$ is atomic.*

We are now able to define strong equivalence under rule refinement.

Definition 18. *Two (atomic) programs P and Q are strongly equivalent under Rule Refinement in a class Π, written $P \equiv_{r+}^{\Pi} Q$, iff for any program R: either (1) $P \uplus R \notin \Pi$ and $Q \uplus R \notin \Pi$ or (2) $AS(P \uplus R) = AS(Q \uplus R)$.*

In the following we will consider $\Pi = \Lambda$. Then, in case P and Q are atomic, condition (1) is false iff $R \in \Lambda$, i.e., it is sufficient to check condition (2) for $R \in \Lambda$. For atomic programs, we inherit results from Proposition 12, i.e. $P \equiv_s^{\Lambda} Q$ does not imply $P \equiv_{r+}^{\Lambda} Q$ (see Example 9). Further this notion faithfully generalizes RR strong equivalence for h-unique programs.

Proposition 14. *For the class of h-unique atomic programs Ξ and $P, Q \in \Xi$, it holds that $P \equiv_{r+}^{\Xi} Q$ implies $P \equiv_r^{\Xi} Q$.*

5 Rule Refinement Captures Strong Equivalence in Abstract Argumentation

In the present section, we show that the notion of strong equivalence under Rule Refinement matches the one for abstract argumentation frameworks.

5.1 AFs and H-Unique Logic Programs

We first consider h-unique LPs and AF strong equivalence. Inspired by the syntactic characterization of strong equivalence for strict AFs [18], we define the notion of *kernel* for logic programs. Similarly to its AF counterpart, the ASP kernel of a program is obtained by deleting dispensable vulnerabilities from its rules. Each atom that is in conflict with itself, i.e. it occurs in the head as well as in the negative body of a rule, is removed from every other rule-body. We call such rules *loops* and define $loop(P) = \{r \in P \mid head(r) \in neg(r)\}$ for an LP P.

Definition 19. *Let* $loopH(Q) = \{\texttt{not}\, head(r) \mid r \in loop(Q)\}$*. The kernel of a h-unique program* P *is* $P^K = \{head(r) \leftarrow body(r) \setminus loopH(P \setminus \{r\}).\mid r \in P\}$*.*

Example 11. In what follows, we represent a program P and its kernel P^K.

$$P=\{a \leftarrow \texttt{not}\, a, \texttt{not}\, b.,\ b \leftarrow \texttt{not}\, a, \texttt{not}\, c.,\ c \leftarrow \texttt{not}\, c, \texttt{not}\, d.,\ d \leftarrow \texttt{not}\, a, \texttt{not}\, c.\} \qquad P^K=\{a \leftarrow \texttt{not}\, a, \texttt{not}\, b.,\ b \leftarrow .,\ c \leftarrow \texttt{not}\, c, \texttt{not}\, d.,\ d \leftarrow .\}$$

As a sanity check, observe that for our notions of LP and AF kernel, the order in which we apply the translation and construct the kernel does not matter.

Proposition 15. *For a h-unique atomic program* P*, it holds that* $(F_P)^{SK} = F_{P^K}$*. Analogously for an AF* F*, it holds that* $(P_F)^K = P_{F^{SK}}$*.*

Combining two programs P and Q through Rule Refinement and transforming the resulting program into an AF yields the same framework as taking the AF union of the transformed programs.

Lemma 4. *For two h-unique atomic programs* P *and* Q*, it holds that* $F_{P \uplus Q} = F_P \cup F_Q$*. Vice-versa, for two AFs* F *and* G*, it holds that* $P_{F \cup G} = P_F \uplus P_G$*.*

As illustrated for AFs, ASP kernels are equivalent to the original instance.

Proposition 16. *For any h-unique atomic program* P*,* $AS(P) = AS(P^K)$*.*

Two programs P and Q maintain the same kernel under any common update.

Proposition 17. *Let* P *and* Q *be two h-unique atomic programs with* $P^K = Q^K$*. Then for any h-unique atomic program* R*, it holds that* $(P \uplus R)^K = (Q \uplus R)^K$*.*

Finally, we show that Rule Refinement characterizes AF strong equivalence.

Theorem 1. *Let* P *and* Q *be two h-unique atomic programs, then the following conditions are equivalent:*

1. P *and* Q *have the same kernel, i.e.* $P_K = Q_K$*.*
2. *The AFs* F_P *and* F_Q *have the same stable-kernel, i.e.* $(F_P)^{SK} = (F_Q)^{SK}$*.*
3. *The AFs* F_P *and* F_Q *are strongly equivalent for stb semantics, i.e.* $F_P \equiv_s F_Q$*.*
4. P *and* Q *are strongly equivalent under Rule Refinement, i.e.* $P \equiv_r^{\Xi} Q$*.*

5.2 Atomic Programs and Well-Formed CAFs

First observe that the ASP-kernel is not helpful to characterize RR strong equivalence for atomic programs, e.g. for $P = \{1 : a \leftarrow \texttt{not}\, b.,\ 2 : b \leftarrow .,\ 3 : b \leftarrow \texttt{not}\, b.\}$ and $P^K = \{1 : a \leftarrow .,\ 2 : b \leftarrow .,\ 3 : b \leftarrow \texttt{not}\, b.\}$, we get $AS(P) \neq AS(P^K)$. Thus, we provide a direct characterization of RR strong equivalence and connect it to well-formed CAFs. Two programs are RR strongly equivalent if their rules' components pairwise coincide, with the possible exception of loop-rules' heads.

Lemma 5. *Let* P *be a program and* $r \in loop(P)$ *a loop-rule in* P*. Then,* r *gets removed when computing* P^S *for any* $S \in AS(P)$*.*

Theorem 2. *Two atomic programs P and Q are strongly equivalent under Rule Refinement, denoted* $P \equiv_{r+}^{A} Q$*, iff it holds that:*

1. $id(r) = id(r')$ *implies* $body(r) = body(r')$ *for all rules* $r \in P$ *and* $r' \in Q$*;*
2. $id(r) = id(r')$ *implies* $head(r) = head(r')$ *for all* $r \in P \setminus loop(P)$ *and* $r' \in Q \setminus loop(Q)$

As before, we analyze how this new notion of update is understood in terms of CAFs. On the one hand, simply adding a rule to a program P amounts to augmenting $\mathcal{F}_P$ with an argument and possibly new attacks. On the other hand, refining a rule corresponds to adding claim-attacks to $\mathcal{F}_P$.

Example 12. Consider the CAFs $\mathcal{F}_P$ (left), $\mathcal{F}_r$ (center) and $\mathcal{F}_{P \uplus r}$ (right) corresponding to P, r and $P \uplus r$ from Example 10:

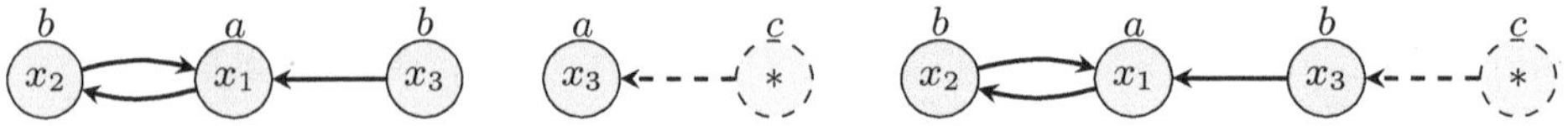

We define an update operator for well-formed CAFs that mimics $\uplus$-updates.

Definition 20. *Let* $\mathcal{F}_1 = (A_1, R_1^{\mathcal{C}}, \gamma_1)$ *and* $\mathcal{F}_2 = (A_2, R_2^{\mathcal{C}}, \gamma_2)$ *be two well-formed CAFs, the update of* $\mathcal{F}_1$ *via* $\mathcal{F}_2$ *is* $\mathcal{F}_1 \cup \mathcal{F}_2 = (A_1 \cup A_2, R_1^{\mathcal{C}} \cup R_2^{\mathcal{C}}, \gamma_1 \overrightarrow{\times} \gamma_2)$ *where:*

$$\gamma_1 \overrightarrow{\times} \gamma_2(a) = \begin{cases} \gamma_1(a) & \text{if } a \in A_1 \\ \gamma_2(a) & \text{if } a \in A_2 \setminus A_1 \end{cases}$$

Updating an atomic program with an atomic rule might result in a violation of compatibility in the corresponding CAFs. For instance, in Example 12 the argument x_3 is labelled with two different claims in $\mathcal{F}_P$ and $\mathcal{F}_r$. For such incompatible expansions, we operate a choice between the claim functions, prioritizing γ_1. Thus, when two CAFs are incompatible with respect to some arguments, we choose the original claim as it is done with the rule-head of any rule r that is refined via an $\uplus$-update. We can now define strong equivalence in this setting.

Definition 21. *Given any two well-formed CAFs* $\mathcal{F}$ *and* $\mathcal{G}$*, we say that* $\mathcal{F} \equiv_s \mathcal{G}$ *if and only if* $\sigma(\mathcal{F} \cup \mathcal{H}) = \sigma(\mathcal{G} \cup \mathcal{H})$ *for any well-formed CAF* $\mathcal{H}$*.*

This notion differs from the original in two respects: (1) it does not restrict to compatible updates only and (2) it requires updates to be well-formed. This notion of strong equivalence for CAFs corresponds to strong equivalence under rule refinement for atomic LPs. To show this, we use of the following lemma.

Lemma 6. *For any atomic programs P and Q, it holds that* $\mathcal{F}_{P \uplus Q} = \mathcal{F}_P \cup \mathcal{F}_Q$*. Conversely, for any two well-formed CAFs* $\mathcal{F}$ *and* $\mathcal{H}$*,* $P_{\mathcal{F} \cup \mathcal{H}} = P_{\mathcal{F}} \uplus P_{\mathcal{H}}$*.*

Theorem 3. *For any atomic programs P and Q, the following are equivalent:*

- *$\mathcal{F}_P$ and $\mathcal{F}_Q$ are strongly equivalent for stable semantics, i.e. $\mathcal{F}_P \equiv_s \mathcal{F}_Q$.*
- *P and Q are strongly equivalent under Rule Refinement, i.e. $P \equiv^{A}_{r+} Q$.*

Thus, characterizing strong equivalence on well-formed CAFs is now possible.

Corollary 1. *For two well-formed CAFs $\mathcal{F} = (A_\mathcal{F}, R^\mathcal{C}_\mathcal{F}, \gamma_\mathcal{F})$ and $\mathcal{G} = (A_\mathcal{G}, R^\mathcal{C}_\mathcal{G}, \gamma_\mathcal{G})$, we have $\mathcal{F} \equiv_s \mathcal{G}$ iff (1) $A_\mathcal{F} = A_\mathcal{G} = A$ and $R^\mathcal{C}_\mathcal{F} = R^\mathcal{C}_\mathcal{G}$, and (2) for each $x_i \in A$, it holds that either $\gamma_\mathcal{F}(x_i) = \gamma_\mathcal{G}(x_i)$ or $(\gamma_\mathcal{F}(x_i), x_i) \in R^\mathcal{C}_\mathcal{F}$ and $(\gamma_\mathcal{G}(x_i), x_i) \in R^\mathcal{C}_\mathcal{G}$.*

Having a characterization for strong equivalence under rule refinement, we now prove that it generalizes standard strong equivalence for atomic programs.

Proposition 18. *For any P and Q atomic programs, $P \equiv^{A}_{r+} Q$ implies $P \equiv_s Q$.*

6 Discussion

In this paper, we analyzed the correspondence between certain classes of logic programs and abstract argumentation frameworks. In the static setting, we extended existing semantic equivalence results from strict to non-strict programs and AFs, by appealing to the concept of ungrounded attack. Further, we adapted the definition of well-formed CAFs to align precisely with (possibly non-strict) atomic programs. We then examined how equivalence in dynamic contexts gets lost in translation, and identified the source of such misalignment in the diverging representations of expansions. To overcome the issue, we proposed a new notion of update for (h-unique) atomic programs, called rule refinement. We then introduced the notion of strong equivalence under Rule Refinement for (h-unique) atomic programs, studied its relation with the standard one, and proven that characterizes strong equivalence for AFs and well-formed CAFs. Overall, our notion defines equivalence under both disjunctive and conjunctive interpretation of successive updates. Hence, it extends standard strong equivalence for atomic programs and captures the corresponding notion for increasingly expressive AFs.

The notion of strong equivalence has been extensively investigated in both logic programming and argumentation. The misalignment has been noted before in the work of [3], that shares with ours the motivation of bridging the gap between strong equivalence notions across different formalisms. Indeed, they provide a general semantic framework for strong equivalence that is formally independent of specific formalism, and capable of subsuming both logic programs and Dung-style AFs. In contrast, by remaining on the syntactic level, our work is closer to original characterizations of strong equivalence and addresses the mismatch in a direct way. For logic programs, strong equivalence has been characterized using *SE*-models [17], which offer a semantic basis for comparing programs under arbitrary expansions. Building on this, [7] defined belief revision operators for LPs and established representation theorems for various program classes, connecting strong equivalence with stability after revisions. Studying the relation between revision and update operators in ASP [16] and our notion of rule refinement is subject of future investigations. Moreover, we aim at providing a characterization of RR strong equivalence for the entire class of normal logic programs, and connect this to possibly more expressive types of AFs. We anticipate that this could be achieved by encoding positive dependencies among atoms via some notion of support in the corresponding framework [6]. To this end, a comparative analysis of our notion of strong equivalence and those defined over argumentation formalisms related to normal LPs, such as abstract dialectical frameworks (ADFs), is needed [14]. Notice that the existing notion of strong equivalence for ADFs [14] allows for the conjunctive and disjunctive interpretation of updates via so-called and-or-assignments. Hence, it generalizes the strong equivalence notions for normal LPs and Dung-style AFs—and thus, RR-strong equivalence for h-unique atomic LPs. However, this is not the case for well-formed CAFs, since ADF expansions are restricted to compatible ones.

Acknowledgments. We are grateful to the anonymous reviewers for their valuable comments and suggestions on a preliminary version of this paper. This work has been supported by the European Union's Horizon 2020 research and innovation programme (under grant agreement 101034440) and by the Austrian Science Fund (FWF) project 10.557766/COE12.

Disclosure of Interests. The authors have no competing interests to declare that are relevant to the content of this article.

References

1. Baroni, P., Gabbay, D., Giacomin, M., van der Torre, L. (eds.): Handbook of Formal Argumentation. College Publications (2018)
2. Baumann, R., Rapberger, A., Ulbricht, M.: Equivalence in argumentation frameworks with a claim-centric view: classical results with novel ingredients. J. Artif. Intell. Res. **77**, 891–948 (2023). https://doi.org/10.1613/JAIR.1.14625
3. Baumann, R., Strass, H.: An abstract, logical approach to characterizing strong equivalence in non-monotonic knowledge representation formalisms. Artif. Intell. **305**, 103680 (2022). https://doi.org/10.1016/J.ARTINT.2022.103680
4. Cabalar, P.: A three-valued characterization for strong equivalence of logic programs. In: AAAI 2002, pp. 106–111. AAAI Press/The MIT Press (2002)
5. Caminada, M., Sá, S., Alcântara, J., Dvořák, W.: On the equivalence between logic programming semantics and argumentation semantics. Int. J. Approx. Reasoning **58**, 87–111 (2015). https://doi.org/10.1016/j.ijar.2014.12.004
6. Cayrol, C., Lagasquie-Schiex, M.C.: On the acceptability of arguments in bipolar argumentation frameworks. In: Godo, L. (ed.) ECSQARU 2005. LNCS (LNAI), vol. 3571, pp. 378–389. Springer, Heidelberg (2005). https://doi.org/10.1007/11518655_33
7. Delgrande, J., Peppas, P., Woltran, S.: AGM-style belief revision of logic programs under answer set semantics. In: Cabalar, P., Son, T.C. (eds.) LPNMR 2013. LNCS (LNAI), vol. 8148, pp. 264–276. Springer, Heidelberg (2013). https://doi.org/10.1007/978-3-642-40564-8_27
8. Dung, P.M.: On the acceptability of arguments and its fundamental role in nonmonotonic reasoning, logic programming and N-person games. Artif. Intell. **77**(2), 321–358 (1995)

9. Dvořák, W., Rapberger, A., Woltran, S.: On the different types of collective attacks in abstract argumentation: equivalence results for SETAFs. J. Log. Comput. **30**(5), 1063–1107 (2020). https://doi.org/10.1093/logcom/exaa033
10. Dvořák, W., Woltran, S.: Complexity of abstract argumentation under a claim-centric view. Artif. Intell. **285**, 103290 (2020)
11. Eiter, T., Fink, M., Tompits, H., Woltran, S.: Simplifying logic programs under uniform and strong equivalence. In: LPNMR 2004, pp. 87–99. Springer (2004)
12. Eiter, T., Fink, M., Woltran, S.: Semantical characterizations and complexity of equivalences in answer set programming. ACM Trans. Comput. Log. **8**(3) (2007)
13. Gelfond, M., Lifschitz, V.: The stable model semantics for logic programming. In: Logic Programming, Proceedings of the Fifth International Conference and Symposium, pp. 1070–1080. MIT Press (1988)
14. Heyninck, J., Kern-Isberner, G., Rienstra, T., Skiba, K., Thimm, M.: Revision, defeasible conditionals and non-monotonic inference for abstract dialectical frameworks. Artif. Intell. **317**, 103876 (2023). https://doi.org/10.1016/J.ARTINT.2023.103876
15. König, M., Rapberger, A., Ulbricht, M.: Just a matter of perspective – intertranslating expressive argumentation formalisms. In: COMMA 2022, vol. 353, pp. 212–223. IOS Press (2022). https://doi.org/10.3233/FAIA220154
16. Leite, J., Slota, M.: A brief history of updates of answer-set programs. Theory Pract. Log. Program. **23**(1), 57–110 (2023)
17. Lifschitz, V., Pearce, D., Valverde, A.: Strongly equivalent logic programs. ACM Trans. Comput. Log. **2**(4), 526–541 (2001). https://doi.org/10.1145/383779.383783
18. Oikarinen, E., Woltran, S.: Characterizing strong equivalence for argumentation frameworks. Artif. Intell. **175**(14–15), 1985–2009 (2011)
19. Truszczynski, M.: Strong and uniform equivalence of nonmonotonic theories - an algebraic approach. Ann. Math. Artif. Intell. **48**(3–4), 245–265 (2006)
20. Turner, H.: Strong equivalence for logic programs and default theories (made easy). In: Eiter, T., Faber, W., Truszczyński, M. (eds.) LPNMR 2001. LNCS (LNAI), vol. 2173, pp. 81–92. Springer, Heidelberg (2001). https://doi.org/10.1007/3-540-45402-0_6

Brief Temporal Equilibrium Logic

Pedro Cabalar[1], Thomas Eiter[2], David Pearce[3], and Davide Soldà[2(✉)]

[1] University of A Coruña, A Coruña, Spain
cabalar@udc.es
[2] Institute of Logic and Computation, Technische Universität Wien, Vienna, Austria
{thomas.eiter,davide.solda}@tuwien.ac.at
[3] Universidad Politécnica de Madrid, Madrid, Spain
david.pearce@upm.es

Abstract. Equilibrium Logic is a logical characterisation of Answer Set Programming (ASP) that is very successfully used for the study of ASP foundations and extensions. One of such extensions is Temporal Equilibrium Logic (TEL), that allowed for incorporating temporal modal operators from Linear Temporal Logic (LTL) into ASP. Following the steps of Equilibrium Logic, TEL is defined by selecting models from a temporal extension of the intermediate logic of Here-and-There (HT). The models have are traces obtained by some kind of truth minimisation alike the one performed in ASP. Recently, the variant called *contracted* TEL (cTEL) introduced an additional minimisation that may also shorten the length of the trace. Each contracted trace obtained with cTEL can be seen as a "summarisation" of a family of temporal stable models of a given theory. In absence of temporal operator cTHT models differ from THT ones, as the former is a weaker logic. Such a irregularity does not occur here. We propose a variant of TEL, called *brief TEL* (bTEL), that performs a different trace length minimisation in which traces become "shortest witnesses" of the formula or theory. The new variant bTHT collapses to HT for non-temporal theories and it allows for applying Kamp's translation of temporal logic into Monadic First Order Logic, interpreting the obtained formulas under Quantified HT with dynamic domains. Specifically, we provide the bTEL definition, illustrate its effect on some examples, and prove that Kamp's translation is sound.

1 Introduction

(Linear-time) *Temporal Equilibrium Logic* (TEL) [1,6] extends Answer Set Programming (ASP) [10–12] by providing a general semantics for arbitrary formulas in the syntax of Linear-time Temporal Logic (LTL) [9,14]. In the same way that *Equilibrium Logic* [13] captures (non-temporal) ASP by selecting some kind of minimal models from the intermediate logic of *Here-and-There* [8], TEL is also defined by a model selection criterion imposed on a temporal extension of HT (THT) [2], choosing those traces that are in *equilibrium* (a.k.a. stable traces). Recently, a contraction-based additional selection condition for equilibrium models has been investigated [5]: the idea is to discard candidate traces when a sequence of states in the "there" trace can be *contracted* into a single state in the "here" trace. The monotonic base studied in that work coincides, in the non-temporal case, with an intermediate logic (Bounded-Depth 2, BD2)

W. Faber et al. (Eds.): LPNMR 2026, LNAI 16952, pp. 150–166, 2027.
https://doi.org/10.1007/978-3-032-38320-4_10

strictly weaker than Here-and-There in terms of valid formulas: for example $\neg\neg p \vee \neg p$ is not a valid formula there.

In this work, we introduce a new, intrinsically logical selection criterion for TEL that we call *brief TEL* (bTEL). The goal is to semantically capture a typical feature of incremental temporal reasoning in (temporal, incremental) ASP: intuitively, the length of a trace must be *founded*, in the ASP sense, by what the program justifies. Brief TEL enforces this foundedness by preferring traces that advance only as required by the temporal connectives; informally, one may "hop" ahead unless a synchronous *next*-operator forces a step to the immediate successor, internalizing brevity in the trace via a semantic selection principle. At the same time, we propose an alternative definition for the *next*-operator which allows for "hops" ahead, while preserving the key intuitionistic property of *persistence*.

One interesting feature of bTEL is its strong connection to the well-known Kamp's translation [9] from LTL to (Monadic) First-Order Logic with a linear order relation '$<$'. Without any need of modification, Kamp's translation was already proved to be sound [4] for transforming THT formulas into (Monadic) Quantified HT plus '$<$' (QHT($<$)) and, respectively, to obtain stable traces in terms of first-order equilibrium models. In the paper, we prove that the same Kamp's translation still works to transform bTHT formulas into $\mathrm{QHT}^+(<)$, a generalisation of QHT that allows a different domain in the worlds "here" and "there", as happens in intuitionistic first-order interpretations in the general case. Moreover, we provide two different versions of the "next" operator that arise from two different, classically equivalent formulations that are not equivalent in $\mathrm{QHT}^+(<)$.

Trace selection by length has been previously addressed in the literature. For instance, the authors in [15] focus on selecting models by identifying the shortest counterexamples for model-checking purposes. In planning contexts, ASP solvers often operate up to a predetermined plan horizon to generate the shortest possible plans. Additional approaches involve minimization criteria applied to weighted atoms; for example, [7] addresses LTL over finite traces, among others.

The rest of the paper proceeds as follows. In Sect. 2 we introduce bTEL and its monotonic basis, brief THT (bTHT). In the next Section, we revisit the already mentioned first order extension of Here-and-There, $\mathrm{QHT}^+(<)$, we will use later for translating temporal formulas. Section 4 contains Kamp's translation from LTL into Monadic First Order Logic, and proves that the translation is sound when done between bTHT and $\mathrm{QHT}^+(<)$. Finally, Sect. 5 concludes the paper.

2 Brief THT and Brief TEL

All logics considered in this paper share the same syntax as for LTL. Given a (countable, possibly infinite) set $\mathcal{A}$ of propositional atoms (called *alphabet*), a *temporal formula* φ follows the grammar:

$$\varphi ::= a \mid \bot \mid \varphi_1 \otimes \varphi_2 \mid \circ\varphi \mid \circ_a\varphi \mid \varphi_1 \,\mathbf{U}\, \varphi_2 \mid \varphi_1 \,\mathbf{R}\, \varphi_2$$

where $a \in \mathcal{A}$ is an atom and $\otimes$ is any binary Boolean connective $\otimes \in \{\rightarrow, \wedge, \vee\}$. The last four cases correspond to the temporal connectives whose names are listed as follows: **U** for *until*; and **R** for *release*; $\circ$ and $\circ_a$ for synchronous and asynchronous *next*, where synchronicity can be seen as a constraint on the possible relation between here and there traces; such a constraint can be intuitively used, as later shown in Example 5 to force the fact that the next state cannot be skipped. A formula φ is said to be $\otimes$-*free* if it does not contain any occurrence of some connective $\otimes$. We also define common derived operators like the Boolean connectives $\neg\varphi \stackrel{df}{=} \varphi \rightarrow \bot$, $\top \stackrel{df}{=} \neg\bot$, $\varphi \leftrightarrow \psi \stackrel{df}{=} (\varphi \rightarrow \psi) \wedge (\psi \rightarrow \varphi)$, and the following temporal operators: *always* as $\Box\varphi \stackrel{df}{=} \bot \mathbf{R}\, \varphi$, *eventually* as $\Diamond\varphi \stackrel{df}{=} \top \mathbf{U}\, \varphi$, *final* as $\mathbf{F} \stackrel{df}{=} \neg \circ \top$, and the two *weak next* as $\widehat{\circ}\varphi \stackrel{df}{=} \circ\top \rightarrow \circ\varphi$ and $\widehat{\circ}_a\varphi \stackrel{df}{=} \circ_a\top \rightarrow \circ_a\varphi$. A *(temporal) theory* is a (possibly infinite) set of temporal formulas.

The semantics of formulas and theories is defined in terms of *traces*. We introduce the notation $x \in [a..b)$ to stand for $a \leq x < b$. An LTL-*trace* $\mathbf{T}$ is a sequence $\mathbf{T} = (T_i)$, $i \in [0..\lambda)$ of sets of atoms (or propositional interpretations) $T_i \subseteq \mathcal{A}$, where $\lambda \in \mathbb{N} \cup \{\omega\}$ is the *length* of the trace. As in contracted THT (cTHT) [5], we have two traces $\mathbf{H}$ and $\mathbf{T}$ of lengths $\lambda_h = |\mathbf{H}|$ and $\lambda_t = |\mathbf{T}|$ respectively, where $\lambda_h \leq \lambda_t \in \mathbb{N} \cup \{\omega\}$.

Definition 1. *An* HT-trace *is a triple* $\langle \mathbf{H}, \mathbf{T}, \rho\rangle$ *satisfying* $\lambda_h \leq \lambda_t$ *and* $\rho : [0..\lambda_h) \rightarrow [0..\lambda_t)$ *such that:*

- ρ *is strictly monotonic, that is, if* $j > i$ *then* $\rho(j) > \rho(i)$*;*
- $H_i \subseteq T_{\rho(i)}$. □

Intuitively, the function ρ selects reference points in the There-trace $\mathbf{T}$ that should be taken into account for evaluating a formula similarly as in an HT-trace for temporal HT-logic (we shall discuss this more in detail below). It can be compactly represented as a vector $[v_0, \ldots, v_{n-1}]$ of length $n = \lambda_h$ so that $\rho(i) = v_i$. An example of HT-trace is shown in Fig. 1. In the example, $\lambda_t = 7$, $\lambda_h = 4$ and $\rho = [0, 2, 3, 5]$. An HT-trace of the form $\langle \mathbf{T}, \mathbf{T}, id\rangle$ corresponds to a standard LTL trace $\mathbf{T}$. For this reason, we will sometimes write $\mathbf{T}$ instead of $\langle \mathbf{T}, \mathbf{T}, id\rangle$.

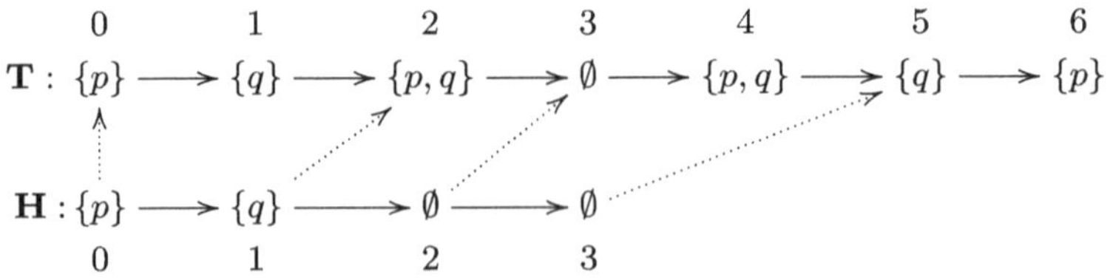

Fig. 1. Example of HT-trace.

We next define satisfaction of a formula in an HT-trace.

Definition 2 (Satisfaction). *Given* $\mathbf{M} = \langle \mathbf{H}, \mathbf{T}, \rho \rangle$ *and* $i \in [0, \lambda_h)$,

- $\mathbf{M}, i \models \top$, $\mathbf{M}, i \not\models \bot$
- $\mathbf{M}, i \models p$ *iff* $p \in H_i$
- $\mathbf{M}, i \models \varphi \wedge \psi$ *iff* $\mathbf{M}, i \models \varphi$ *and* $\mathbf{M}, i \models \psi$
- $\mathbf{M}, i \models \varphi \vee \psi$ *iff* $\mathbf{M}, i \models \varphi$ *or* $\mathbf{M}, i \models \psi$
- $\mathbf{M}, i \models \varphi \rightarrow \psi$ *iff both:*
  1. $\mathbf{M}, i \not\models \varphi$ *or* $\mathbf{M}, i \models \psi$ *and* 2. $\mathbf{T}, \rho(i) \not\models \varphi$ *or* $\mathbf{T}, \rho(i) \models \psi$
- $\mathbf{M}, i \models \circ\varphi$ *iff* $i + 1 < \lambda_h$ *and* $\rho(i+1) = \rho(i) + 1$ *and* $\mathbf{M}, i+1 \models \varphi$
- $\mathbf{M}, i \models \circ_a\varphi$ *iff* $i + 1 < \lambda_h$, 1. $\mathbf{M}, i+1 \models \varphi$ *and* 2. $\mathbf{T}, \rho(i) + 1 \models \varphi$
- $\mathbf{M}, i \models \varphi \, \mathbf{U} \, \psi$ *iff there exists* $j \in [i..\lambda_h)$ *such that* $\mathbf{M}, j \models \psi$ *and both*
  1. for all $k \in [i..j)$, $\mathbf{M}, k \models \varphi$
  2. for all $k \in [\rho(i)..\rho(j))$, $\mathbf{T}, k \models \varphi$
- $\mathbf{M}, i \models \varphi \, \mathbf{R} \, \psi$ *iff both:*
  1. for all $j \in [i..\lambda_h)$, $\mathbf{M}, j \models \psi$ *or there exists* $k \in [i..j)$, $\mathbf{M}, k \models \varphi$
  2. for all $j \in [\rho(i)..\lambda_t)$, $\mathbf{T}, j \models \psi$ *or there exists* $k \in [\rho(i)..j)$, $\mathbf{T}, k \models \varphi$

An important property in intermediate logics is *persistence*: it guarantees that anything true in a world is maintained true in all accessible worlds. In our context, this means that any formula φ true "here" $\mathbf{H}$ should still be true "there" $\mathbf{T}$. However, in the temporal setting, we must also specify the time point i at which φ is satisfied, and any time point i for $\mathbf{H}$ must be mapped into $\rho(i)$ for $\mathbf{T}$. As a consequence, we get the following formulation of the persistence property.

Theorem 1 (Persistence). *For any formula* φ*, any* HT*-trace* $\mathbf{M} = \langle \mathbf{H}, \mathbf{T}, \rho \rangle$*:* $\mathbf{M}, i \models \varphi$ *implies* $\mathbf{T}, \rho(i) \models \varphi$ *for every* $i \in [0..\lambda_h)$.

Proof. We proceed by structural induction on formula φ:

- If $\varphi = \bot$ both $\mathbf{M}, i \models \bot$ and $\mathbf{T}, \rho(i) \models \bot$ are false and the result trivially follows.
- If $\varphi = p$ is an atom, $\mathbf{M}, i \models p$ implies $p \in H_i \subseteq T_{\rho(i)}$ and so $\mathbf{T}, \rho(i) \models p$.
- If $\varphi = \alpha \wedge \beta$ then $\mathbf{M}, i \models \alpha \wedge \beta$ is equivalent to both $\mathbf{M}, i \models \alpha$ and $\mathbf{M}, i \models \beta$. Applying induction in both subformulas, we conclude $\mathbf{T}, \rho(i) \models \alpha$ and $\mathbf{T}, \rho(i) \models \beta$, and so, $\mathbf{T}, \rho(i) \models \alpha \wedge \beta$.
- If $\varphi = \alpha \vee \beta$ then $\mathbf{M}, i \models \alpha \wedge \beta$ is equivalent to $\mathbf{M}, i \models \alpha$ or $\mathbf{M}, i \models \beta$. Suppose $\mathbf{M}, i \models \alpha$: applying induction we conclude $\mathbf{T}, \rho(i) \models \alpha$ and this implies $\mathbf{T}, \rho(i) \models \alpha \vee \beta$. If $\mathbf{M}, i \models \beta$ instead, the result is analogous.
- If $\varphi = \alpha \rightarrow \beta$ then the definition of $\mathbf{M}, i \models \alpha \rightarrow \beta$ implies (in its second condition) $\mathbf{T}, \rho(i) \not\models \alpha$ or $\mathbf{T}, \rho(i) \models \beta$. But this immediately implies $\mathbf{T}, \rho(i) \models \alpha \rightarrow \beta$.
- If $\varphi = \circ\alpha$ then $\mathbf{M}, i \models \circ\alpha$ is equivalent to $i + 1 < \lambda_h$ and $\rho(i+1) = \rho(i) + 1$ and $\mathbf{M}, i+1 \models \alpha$. As $i + 1 < \lambda_h$, by induction we conclude $\mathbf{T}, \rho(i+1) \models \alpha$. As $\rho(i+1) = \rho(i) + 1$, we get $\mathbf{T}, \rho(i) + 1 \models \alpha$, and so, $\mathbf{T}, \rho(i) \models \circ\alpha$.
- If $\varphi = \circ_a\alpha$ then $\mathbf{M}, i \models \circ_a\alpha$ is equivalent to $i + 1 < \lambda_h$, $\mathbf{M}, i+1 \models \alpha$ and $\mathbf{T}, \rho(i) + 1 \models \alpha$. Therefore, we can conclude $\mathbf{T}, \rho(i) \models \circ_a\alpha$.

- If $\varphi = \alpha \mathbf{U} \beta$ then $\mathbf{M}, i \models \alpha \mathbf{U} \beta$ implies there exists some $j \in [i..\lambda_h)$ satisfying $\mathbf{M}, j \models \beta$ and (condition 2) for all $k \in [\rho(i)..\rho(j))$ we have $\mathbf{T}, k \models \alpha$. By induction, $\mathbf{M}, j \models \beta$ implies $\mathbf{T}, \rho(j) \models \beta$. Also, by the definition of ρ as monotonic function mapping to $[0..\lambda_t)$, $j \in [i..\lambda_h)$ implies $\rho(j) \in [\rho(i)..\lambda_t)$. This means we have obtained some $l = \rho(j)$ such that $\mathbf{T}, l \models \beta$ and for all $k \in [\rho(i)..l)$, $\mathbf{T}, k \models \alpha$, which is the condition for $\mathbf{T}, \rho(i) \models \alpha \mathbf{U} \beta$.
- If $\varphi = \alpha \mathbf{R} \beta$ then the second condition of the definition of $\mathbf{M}, i \models \alpha \mathbf{R} \beta$ directly corresponds to $\mathbf{T}, \rho(i) \models \alpha \mathbf{R} \beta$. □

Proposition 1. *Given* $\mathbf{M} = \langle \mathbf{H}, \mathbf{T}, \rho \rangle$*, we consequently get the following satisfaction conditions for derived operators:*

(i) $\mathbf{M}, i \models \neg\varphi$ *iff* $\mathbf{T}, \rho(i) \not\models \varphi$
(ii) $\mathbf{M}, i \models \widehat{\circ}\varphi$ *iff both:*

(a) if $i + 1 < \lambda_h$ *and* $\rho(i+1) = \rho(i) + 1$ *then* $\mathbf{M}, i+1 \models \varphi$
(b) if $\rho(i) + 1 < \lambda_t$ *then* $\mathbf{T}, \rho(i) + 1 \models \varphi$

(iii) $\mathbf{M}, i \models \widehat{\circ}_a\varphi$ *iff both:*

(a) if $i + 1 < \lambda_h$ *then* $\mathbf{M}, i+1 \models \varphi$
(b) if $\rho(i) + 1 < \lambda_t$ *then* $\mathbf{T}, \rho(i) + 1 \models \varphi$

(iv) $\mathbf{M}, i \models \Diamond\varphi$ *iff there exists* j, $i \le j < \lambda_h$ *such that* $\mathbf{M}, j \models \varphi$
(v) $\mathbf{M}, i \models \Box\varphi$ *iff both:*

(a) for all $j \in [i..\lambda_h)$, $\mathbf{M}, j \models \varphi$
(b) for all $j \in [\rho(i)..\lambda_t)$ $\mathbf{T}, j \models \varphi$

Proof. (Sketch) Conditions (ii)–(v) all follow immediately from the respective definition of the derived operator and the satisfaction relation. For (i), note that $\neg\varphi \stackrel{df}{=} \varphi \to \bot$ and $\mathbf{M}, i \models \varphi \to \bot$ amounts to the conjunction of $\mathbf{M}, i \not\models \varphi$ and $\mathbf{T}, \rho(i) \not\models \varphi$ but the first condition can be removed since, due to Persistence (Theorem 1), it is implied by the second condition.

Proposition 2. *Fixing* $\rho = id$ *collapses to* THT*-satisfaction. Furthermore, fixing* $\mathbf{H} = \mathbf{T}$ *(with* $\rho = id$*) collapses to LTL.*

Proof. (Sketch) This can be proven by structural induction on the formula φ. Note that $\langle \mathbf{H}, \mathbf{T}, id \rangle$ amounts to $\langle \mathbf{H}, \mathbf{T} \rangle$ in THT-logic, and if $\mathbf{H} = \mathbf{T}$, then $\langle \mathbf{H}, \mathbf{T} \rangle$ amounts to $\mathbf{T}$ in LTL.

Although neither THT nor LTL accept $\circ_a$ in their language, notice that the condition $\rho = id$ makes $\circ_a\varphi$ collapse to $\circ\varphi$ so, under that assumption, we may replace all occurrences of asynchronous next by occurrences of regular next.

Proposition 3. *For the syntax of non-temporal, propositional formulas,* bTHT *collapses to* HT*, that is, if* φ *does not contain temporal operators:* $\models \varphi$ *in* bTHT *iff* $\models \varphi$ *in* HT.

Proof. We prove both directions by contraposition. For the left to right direction, suppose for some HT-interpretation $\langle H, T\rangle \not\models \varphi$. Then, we can build the bTHT trace $\langle \mathbf{H}, \mathbf{T}, id\rangle$ where $\mathbf{H} = (H)$, $\mathbf{T} = (T)$, $\rho = id$ where $\lambda_h = \lambda_t = 1$ and we can easily see that $\langle H, T\rangle \not\models \varphi$ amounts to $\langle \mathbf{H}, \mathbf{T}, id\rangle, 0 \not\models \varphi$ by inspection of bTHT satisfaction of non-temporal operators. For the right to left direction, suppose there is some bTHT-trace $\langle \mathbf{H}, \mathbf{T}, id\rangle \not\models \varphi$. Then, we build the HT-interpretation $\langle H, T\rangle$ with $H = H_0$ and $T = T_{\rho(0)}$. Again, by inspection of bTHT satisfaction of non-temporal operators, we may easily see that $\langle \mathbf{H}, \mathbf{T}, id\rangle \not\models \varphi$ amounts to $\langle H, T\rangle \not\models \varphi$ in HT.

As well-known, the logic of HT does not satisfy the excluded middle axiom $\varphi \vee \neg\varphi$: for instance, the HT interpretation $\langle H, T\rangle = \langle \emptyset, \{p\}\rangle$ does not satisfy $p \vee \neg p$ since neither $\langle H, T\rangle \models p$, because $p \notin H$, nor $\langle H, T\rangle \models \neg p$ because $p \in T$. Adding the axiom schemata $p \vee \neg p$ for all atoms in the signature forces $H = T$ and makes HT collapse to classical, propositional logic. Analogously, THT does not satisfy excluded middle either, whereas adding the axiom schemata:

$$\Box(p \vee \neg p) \tag{EM}$$

for every $p \in \mathcal{A}$ forces $\mathbf{H} = \mathbf{T}$ and makes THT collapse to LTL. In bTHT, however, axiom (**EM**) does not suffice to guarantee $\mathbf{H} = \mathbf{T}$. Instead, the addition of (**EM**) only guarantees that $H_i = T_{\rho(i)}$, but traces $\mathbf{H}$ and $\mathbf{T}$ may still have different lengths. To put an example, trace $\mathbf{M} = \langle \mathbf{H}, \mathbf{T}, \rho\rangle$ with $\mathbf{T} = \emptyset \cdot \{p\} \cdot \emptyset$, $\mathbf{H} = \{p\}$ and $\rho(0) = 1$ is a model of (**EM**). This effect is somehow due to the fact that requiring (**EM**) on atoms does not suffice to satisfy the excluded middle for any formula φ. In particular, the formula $\circ\top \vee \neg \circ \top$ (which is a THT-tautology) is not bTHT-valid. As a counterexample, we may use the same example trace introduced above: on the one hand, we may easily see that $\mathbf{M}, 0 \not\models \circ\top$ since the $\mathbf{H}$ trace ends at state $H_0 = \{p\}$. On the other hand, $\mathbf{T}, \rho(0) \not\models \neg \circ \top$ because $\rho(0) = 1$ and, at trace $\mathbf{T}$, state $T_1 = \{p\}$ is followed by a next state $T_2 = \emptyset$. Let us define the axiom:

$$\Box(\circ\top \vee \neg \circ \top) \tag{EM$'$}$$

Note that $\mathbf{M}, i \models \neg \circ \top \vee \circ\top$ means: (1) either $\rho(i) + 1 = \lambda_t$ (and so $i + 1 = \lambda_h$) so both traces are at the end; or (2) $i + 1 < \lambda_h$ and $\rho(i + 1) = \rho(i) + 1$. In principle, one could expect that the addition of (**EM$'$**) forced $\rho = id$ (or if preferred $\rho(i) = i$), and so, bTHT-traces in that context would amount to THT-traces. However, in general, this does not hold. This is because we may build bTHT-traces where $\rho(0) \neq 0$, so that the $\mathbf{H}$ trace "starts" at a non-initial point $\rho(0) > 0$ in the $\mathbf{T}$ trace. As a result, the actual effect of axiom (**EM$'$**) is captured by following proposition:

Proposition 4. *The models of* (**EM$'$**) *are* bTHT*-traces* $\langle \mathbf{H}, \mathbf{T}, \rho\rangle$ *where* $\mathbf{T} = \gamma \cdot \mathbf{T}'$ *being* γ *an arbitrary prefix of finite length* $|\gamma|$ *and* $\rho(i) = i + |\gamma|$ *for every* $i \in [0..\lambda_h)$.

Notice that the states in the $\mathbf{T}$-prefix γ are never accessible through bTHT-satisfaction (defn. 2) since, in this paper, we do not consider temporal operators that can refer to time points in the past. Thus there is no possible additional axiom that could enforce $\rho = id$. However, although we have no one-to-one mapping between

THT-models of γ and bTHT-models of $\{\gamma\} \cup (\mathbf{EM}')$ we can still prove that bTHT plus $(\mathbf{EM}')$ collapses to THT.

Let us consider the following axiom:

$$\Box(\circ_a \top \vee \neg \circ_a \top) \qquad (\mathbf{EM}'_a)$$

Proposition 5. *The models of* $(\mathbf{EM}'_a)$ *are* bTHT*-traces* $\langle \mathbf{H}, \mathbf{T}, \rho \rangle$ *where* $\lambda_h = \omega$ *or* $\lambda_t = \rho(\lambda_h - 1) + 1$.

Proof. For each possible bTHT interpretation $\mathbf{M}$ we must satisfy at any index $i \in [0, \ldots \lambda_h)$, the disjunct $\circ_a \top \vee \neg \circ_a \top$. By satisfying the first one, we only require there is a next state in the here trace at position $i + 1$, and therefore, in the there trace as well, but at position $\rho(i) + 1$. While if the second disjunct is satisfied, then there is no successive state neither in the here, nor in the there trace.

This means that $(\mathbf{EM}'_a)$ only imposes a condition when $\mathbf{H}$ is finite, forcing that $\mathbf{T}$ is finite too and that the last position $\lambda_h - 1$ in trace H points to the last position $\lambda_t - 1$ in T. On the other hand, $\widehat{\circ}_a \top$ becomes a tautology, contrary to $\widehat{\circ} \top$, which instead imposes synchronicity.

Proposition 6 (bTHT$\subseteq$ THT)**.** *Any* bTHT*-tautology is also a* THT*-tautology.*

Proof. The result is trivial, since all THT-models are also bTHT-models.

Proposition 7 (THT$\subseteq$ bTHT+$(\mathbf{EM}')$)**.** *If* φ *is a* THT*-tautology then any* bTHT*-trace satisfying* $(\mathbf{EM}')$ *also satisfies* φ.

Proof. It follows from the fact that THT-models are also bTHT-models. Then, by contraposition, if $\mathbf{T}$ is not THT-stable, then there exists some THT-model $\langle \mathbf{H}, \mathbf{T} \rangle$ of Γ (with $\lambda_h = \lambda_t$) but the latter is also a bTHT-model and, thus, $\mathbf{T}$ is not bTHT-stable either.

Definition 3 (Temporal Equilibrium Model). *A trace* $\mathbf{M} = \langle \mathbf{T}, \mathbf{T}, id \rangle$ *is a* temporal equilibrium (TEL) model *of a theory* Γ *iff (1)* $\mathbf{M}$ *is a model of* Γ *and (2) there is no other different model of* Γ *of the form* $\langle \mathbf{H}, \mathbf{T}, \rho \rangle$*. When this holds, we also say that* $\mathbf{T}$ *is a* bTHT*-stable model of* Γ.

A first observation is that, as desired, bTHT-stable models are selected from the TEL-models.

Proposition 8. *Any* bTHT*-stable model of* Γ *is also a* THT*-stable model of* Γ.

Let us next look at a couple of examples.

Example 1. Take the formula $\Diamond p$. Its TEL models have the form $\emptyset^* \cdot \{p\} \cdot \emptyset^{*,\omega}$. Models of the form $\emptyset^+ \cdot \{p\} \cdot \emptyset^{*,\omega}$ or $\emptyset^* \cdot \{p\} \cdot \emptyset^{+,\omega}$ will not be stable because we can form the trace $\mathbf{H} = \{p\}$ and take $\rho(0) = k$ where k is the position of the leftmost state $\{p\}$ in $\mathbf{T}$. It is easy to see that $\langle \mathbf{H}, \mathbf{T}, \rho \rangle, 0 \models \Diamond p$. Thus, the only temporal stable model is the trace $\mathbf{T} = \{p\}$ of length $\lambda_t = 1$.

Example 2. Take the formula $\Box p$. Its TEL models have the form $\{p\}^{+,\omega}$. Models of the form $\{p\} \cdot \{p\}^{+,\omega}$ will not be stable because we can form the trace $\mathbf{H} = \{p\}$ and take $\rho(0) = 0$. Again, it is easy to see that $\langle \mathbf{H}, \mathbf{T}, \rho \rangle, 0 \models \Box p$. Thus, the only temporal stable model is the trace $\mathbf{T} = \{p\}$ of length $\lambda_t = 1$.

Example 3. Take the formula $\Diamond p \wedge \neg \Box p$. Its TEL models are traces containing at least one state $\{p\}$ and at least one $\emptyset$, namely:

$$\emptyset^* \cdot \{p\} \cdot \emptyset^* \cdot \emptyset^{+,\omega} \; + \; \emptyset^+ \cdot \{p\} \cdot \emptyset^{*,\omega}$$

The bTEL-models of this example are $\emptyset \cdot \{p\}$ and $\{p\} \cdot \emptyset$.

Example 4. Take the formula $\Box(p \vee \neg p) \wedge \Box(\circ\top \vee \neg\circ\top)$. This is a TEL-tautology in the sense that any LTL-trace is a TEL-model $(\emptyset + \{p\})^{+,\omega}$. Yet, take any LTL infinite trace $\mathbf{T}$: we can always form a smaller model with $\mathbf{H}$ by taking any suffix of $\mathbf{T}$, that is, $\mathbf{T} = \gamma \cdot \mathbf{H}$ with $|\gamma| > 0$ and $\rho(i) = i + |\gamma|$, so infinite traces do not form any bTEL-model in this example. For finite traces of length $n > 0$, we can always pick $\mathbf{H} = (T_{n-1})$ of length 1 with $\rho(0) = n - 1$ to form a bTHT-model for this example. This means that we only get two bTEL-models $(\emptyset)$ and $(\{p\})$, both of length 1. This example shows that the abbreviation of traces also takes place even in the presence of excluded middle for atoms and for $\circ\top$. Notice that this effect would be removed if we forced $\rho(0) = 0$ for all the bTHT models.

Example 5. Let us consider the following simplified action-based scenario. If *goal* is not reached, then execute either action a_1 or action a_2. Action a_2 derives the atom *goal*. Furthermore, we require *goal* to be eventually reached.

$$\pi \;:=\; \Box(\neg goal \rightarrow \circ(a_1 \vee a_2)) \quad \Box(a_2 \rightarrow goal) \quad \Box(\neg goal) \rightarrow \bot$$

$\mathbf{T} = \emptyset \cdot \{a_1\}\{a_1\}\{a_2, goal\}$ is a bTEL model of π, as the $\circ$ forces synchronization in the mapping when trying to obtain a smaller $\mathbf{H}$ trace. However, if the same scenario is expressed using the asynchronous next operator, i.e., as

$$\pi_a \;:=\; \Box(\neg goal \rightarrow \circ_a(a_1 \vee a_2)) \quad \Box(a_2 \rightarrow goal) \quad \Box(\neg goal) \rightarrow \bot$$

we can consider $\mathbf{H} = \emptyset \cdot \{a_2, goal\}$ as a smaller trace such that $\langle \mathbf{H}, \mathbf{T}, \rho \rangle \models \pi_a$, where $\rho(0) = 0, \rho(1) = 3$. Note that $\mathbf{H}$ is a bTEL model, as it cannot be minimized further.

3 Quantified Here-and-There with Dynamic Domains

A *first-order signature* is a tuple $\Sigma = \langle \mathcal{C}, \mathcal{F}, \mathcal{P} \rangle$, where $\mathcal{C}$ is the set of constants (or 0-ary functions), $\mathcal{F}$ is the set of (non-0-ary) function symbols and $\mathcal{P}$ is the set of predicate symbols. The function $arity : \mathcal{P} \cup \mathcal{F} \rightarrow \mathbb{N}$ denotes the number of arguments of each predicate in $\mathcal{P}$ and each function in $\mathcal{F}$.

Well-formed formulas follow the syntax of classical predicate calculus with equality $=$. We assume a countably infinite set of variables, connectives '$\bot$', '$\vee$', '$\wedge$', '$\rightarrow$', '$\exists$', '$\forall$' and auxiliary parentheses. Additionally, we define negation by $\neg\varphi \stackrel{df}{=} \varphi \rightarrow \bot$ and double implication by $\varphi \leftrightarrow \psi \stackrel{df}{=} (\varphi \rightarrow \psi) \wedge (\psi \rightarrow \varphi)$. We denote by $Atoms(\mathcal{C}, \mathcal{F}, \mathcal{P})$, or At for short, the set of ground predicate atoms over the language. We also write $Terms(\mathcal{C}, \mathcal{F})$ to stand for the set of ground terms formed with constants in $\mathcal{C}$ and functions in $\mathcal{F}$. As usual, a *sentence* is a formula where all its variables are bound by some quantifier. A set of sentences is called a *theory*.

Definition 4 (QHT$^+$**-Interpretation).** *A* QHT$^+$-interpretation *is a tuple* $\langle D_h, D_t, I, \sigma\rangle$ *where*

- $\emptyset \neq D_h \subseteq D_t$ *are the domains at the "here" and the "there" worlds, respectively.*
- I *is a function that maps each predicate* $p \in \mathcal{P}$ *with* $arity(p) = n$ *at each world* $w \in \{h, t\}$ *to a set of tuples* $I(p, w) \subseteq D_w^n$ *formed with elements from the domain of that world. It additionally satisfies* $I(p, h) \subseteq I(p, t)$ *for every predicate* $p \in \mathcal{P}$.
- $\sigma : Terms(\mathcal{C} \cup D_t, \mathcal{F}) \rightarrow D_t$ *is the interpretation of terms, satisfying the conditions:*
  - $\sigma(d) = d$ *for all* $d \in D_t$
  - *if* $\sigma(t) \in D_h$ *and* t' *is a subterm of* t *then* $\sigma(t') \in D_h$.

Given a tuple of terms $\mathbf{t} = \langle t_1, \ldots, t_n\rangle$, we write $\sigma(\mathbf{t})$ to stand for the tuple $\langle \sigma(t_1), \ldots, \sigma(t_n)\rangle$. For simplicity, a monadic tuple $\langle t\rangle$ is just written as t, omitting the angle brackets $\langle \cdot \rangle$.

The order relation between worlds is such that $h \leq t$ and $w \leq w$ for $w \in \{h, t\}$.

We say that a QHT^+ interpretation M is *total* when $M = \langle D_t, D_t, I, \sigma\rangle$ and $I(p, h) = I(p, t)$ for every predicate $p \in \mathcal{P}$. Given a QHT^+ interpretation $M = \langle D_h, D_t, I, \sigma\rangle$, we write M^t to stand for the corresponding total interpretation $\langle D_t, D_t, I', \sigma\rangle$ where $I'(p, h) = I'(p, t) = I(p, t)$ for every predicate $p \in \mathcal{P}$.

Definition 5. *A* QHT$^+$*-interpretation* $M = \langle D_h, D_t, I, \sigma\rangle$ *for signature* $\langle \mathcal{C}, \mathcal{F}, \mathcal{P}\rangle$ satisfies *a sentence* φ *at world* $w \in \{h, t\}$, *written* $M, w \models \varphi$, *recursively as follows:*

- $M, w \not\models \bot$,
- $M, w \models p(\mathbf{t})$ *iff* $\sigma(\mathbf{t}) \in I(p, w)$,
- $M, w \models t_1 = t_2$ *iff* $\sigma(t_1) = \sigma(t_2) \in D_w$,
- $M, w \models \varphi \wedge \psi$ *iff* $M, w \models \varphi$ *and* $M, w \models \psi$,
- $M, w \models \varphi \vee \psi$ *iff* $M, w \models \varphi$ *or* $M, w \models \psi$,
- $M, w \models \varphi \rightarrow \psi$ *iff* $M, w' \not\models \varphi$ *or* $M, w' \models \psi$ *for all* $w' \geq w$,
- $M, w \models \forall x\, \varphi(x)$ *iff* $M, w' \models \varphi(d)$ *for all* $w' \geq w$ *and* $d \in D_{w'}$.
- $M, w \models \exists x\, \varphi(x)$ *iff* $M, w \models \varphi(d)$ *for some* $d \in D_w$.

4 Kamp's Translation

We will deal with monadic QHT$^+(\leq)$ for signature $\langle \mathcal{C}, \mathcal{F}, \mathcal{P}\rangle$ where $\mathcal{C} = \{0\}$ has the unique constant 0, $\mathcal{F} = \emptyset$ and $\mathcal{P} = \mathcal{A} \cup \{\leq\}$ consists of a set of unary predicates $p \in \mathcal{A}$, $arity(p) = 1$, plus a binary predicate '$\leq$' that will satisfy the properties of a discrete linear order.

Relation '$\leq$' will be constrained by several axioms. First, we add the axioms for a total linear order whose minimum element is 0:

$$\forall x(x \leq x) \qquad \forall x\forall y\forall z(x \leq y \wedge y \leq z \rightarrow x \leq z)$$
$$\forall x\forall y(x \leq y \vee y \leq x) \qquad \forall x\forall y(x \leq y \wedge y \leq x \rightarrow x = y)$$
$$\forall x(x \geq 0)$$

Second, we force a discrete order by resorting to a *successor* predicate $succ(x, y)$. Note that we do not use a function $s(x) = y$ because in finite traces, the last point in the trace has no defined successor. We start defining the derived predicates:

$$x < y \stackrel{df}{=} x \leq y \wedge \neg(y \leq x)$$
$$succ(x, y) \stackrel{df}{=} x < y \wedge \neg\exists z(x < z \wedge z < y)$$

and then, we include the axioms

$$\forall x\forall y(x < y \rightarrow \exists x'(succ(x, x') \wedge x' \leq y)\,) \tag{1}$$
$$\forall x\forall y(x < y \rightarrow \exists y'(succ(y', y) \wedge x \leq y')\,) \tag{2}$$

These two axioms (1) and (2) respectively state that, if $x < y$, then there is a minimum element $x' \leq y$ strictly greater than x, and a maximum element $y' \geq x$ strictly smaller than y'.

Let $M = \langle D_h, D_t, I, \sigma\rangle$ be a QHT$^+(\leq)$ interpretation and $w \in \{h, t\}$. The expression $a \leq_w^M b$ represents $(a, b) \in I(\leq, w)$. Furthermore, for any world $w \in \{h, t\}$, we define the *level* of every element $d \in D_w$ at w as the function $level_{M,w} : D_w \rightarrow [0..|D_w|)$:

$$level_{M,w}(d) \stackrel{df}{=} \begin{cases} 0 & \text{if there is no } c \neq d \in D_w \text{ s.t. } c \leq_w^M d \\ level_{M,w}(c) + 1 & \text{otherwise, where} \\ & c = \max\{x \mid x \in D_w, x \neq d, x \leq_w^M d\}. \end{cases}$$

Notice that the maximum in the second case above is well-defined: the set is not empty (if empty, the level is 0 due to the first case) and there exists a maximum because $\leq_w^M$ is a discrete linear order relation. A second observation is that function $level_{M,w}(\cdot)$ is bijective, so it has an inverse $level^{-}_{M,w}(i)$ that, essentially, returns the element in D_w positioned at level i in the order relation.

Example 6. Consider the interpretation $M = \langle D_h, D_t, I, \sigma\rangle$ with domains $D_h = \{a, c, d, f\}$ and $D_t = \{a, b, c, d, e, f, g\}$, and predicates p and q interpreted as follows:

$$I(p, t) = \{a, c, e, g\} \quad I(q, t) = \{b, c, e, f\} \quad I(p, h) = \{a\} \quad I(q, h) = \{c\}$$

Let $I(\leq, t)$ correspond to the alphabetical order of the letters we used to represent the elements in D_t, namely $a \leq_t^M b \leq_t^M c \leq_t^M d \leq_t^M e \leq_t^M f \leq_t^M g$ plus the reflexive and transitive closure of those relations. The same relations $\leq_h^M$ apply among elements in D_h. The level of each element in world t corresponds to:

$$level_{M,t}(a) = 0, \;\; level_{M,t}(b) = 1, \;\; level_{M,t}(c) = 2, \;\; level_{M,t}(d) = 3,$$
$$level_{M,t}(e) = 4, \;\; level_{M,t}(f) = 5, \;\; level_{M,t}(g) = 6$$

whereas in world h we get

$$level_{M,h}(a) = 0, \;\; level_{M,h}(c) = 1, \;\; level_{M,h}(d) = 2, \;\; level_{M,h}(f) = 3.$$

Note that a has the same level 0 both in world h and world t while element f, for instance, appears at different levels, 3 and 5, respectively. Finally, note how the inverse of the level relation at some world w can be used to get the element positioned at some given level between 0 and $|D_w|$. For instance $level^{-}_{M,t}(2) = c$ whereas $level^{-}_{M,h}(2) = d$.

Given a QHT$^+(\leq)$ interpretation $M = (D_h, D_t, I, \sigma)$, we define its corresponding HT-trace $f(M) = \langle \mathbf{H}, \mathbf{T}, \rho \rangle$ as follows. The lengths of $\mathbf{H}$ and $\mathbf{T}$ respectively correspond to $\lambda_h = |D_h|$ and $\lambda_t = |D_t|$. The traces $\mathbf{H} = (H_i)$ with $i \in [0..\lambda_h)$ and $\mathbf{T} = (T_i)$ with $i \in [0..\lambda_t)$ are defined as follows:

$$H_i \stackrel{df}{=} \{p \in \mathcal{A} \mid level^{-}_{M,h}(i) \in I(p,h)\} \text{ and } T_i \stackrel{df}{=} \{p \in \mathcal{A} \mid level^{-}_{M,t}(i) \in I(p,t)\}$$

That is, for each state H_i we collect the names (becoming propositional atoms) of all those monadic predicates $p \in \mathcal{A}$ such that the element in D_h positioned at i belongs to the extension $I(p,h)$ of that predicate. The same applies for T_i with respect to world t. Finally, the mapping ρ is defined in the following way:

$$\rho(i) \stackrel{df}{=} level_{M,t}(level^{-}_{M,h}(i))$$

Example 7. For instance, if we take the interpretation M from Example 6, then $f(M)$ corresponds to the HT-trace $\langle \mathbf{H}, \mathbf{T}, \rho \rangle$:

$$\begin{aligned} H_0 &= \{x \in \mathcal{A} \mid a \in I(x,h)\} = \{p\} \\ H_1 &= \{x \in \mathcal{A} \mid c \in I(x,h)\} = \{q\} \\ H_2 &= \{x \in \mathcal{A} \mid d \in I(x,h)\} = \emptyset \\ H_3 &= \{x \in \mathcal{A} \mid f \in I(x,h)\} = \emptyset \end{aligned}$$

$$\begin{aligned} T_0 &= \{x \in \mathcal{A} \mid a \in I(x,h)\} = \{p\} \\ T_1 &= \{x \in \mathcal{A} \mid b \in I(x,h)\} = \{q\} \\ T_2 &= \{x \in \mathcal{A} \mid c \in I(x,h)\} = \{p,q\} \\ T_3 &= \{x \in \mathcal{A} \mid d \in I(x,h)\} = \emptyset \\ T_4 &= \{x \in \mathcal{A} \mid e \in I(x,h)\} = \{p,q\} \\ T_5 &= \{x \in \mathcal{A} \mid f \in I(x,h)\} = \{q\} \\ T_6 &= \{x \in \mathcal{A} \mid g \in I(x,h)\} = \{p\} \end{aligned}$$

with the mapping:

$$\begin{aligned} \rho(0) &= level_{M,t}(level^{-}_{M,h}(0)) = level_{M,t}(a) = 0 \\ \rho(1) &= level_{M,t}(level^{-}_{M,h}(1)) = level_{M,t}(c) = 2 \\ \rho(2) &= level_{M,t}(level^{-}_{M,h}(2)) = level_{M,t}(d) = 3 \\ \rho(3) &= level_{M,t}(level^{-}_{M,h}(3)) = level_{M,t}(f) = 5 \end{aligned}$$

To sum up, it can be easily observed that the HT-trace $f(M)$ we have obtained, which is shown in Fig. 2 corresponds to the one shown in Fig. 1.

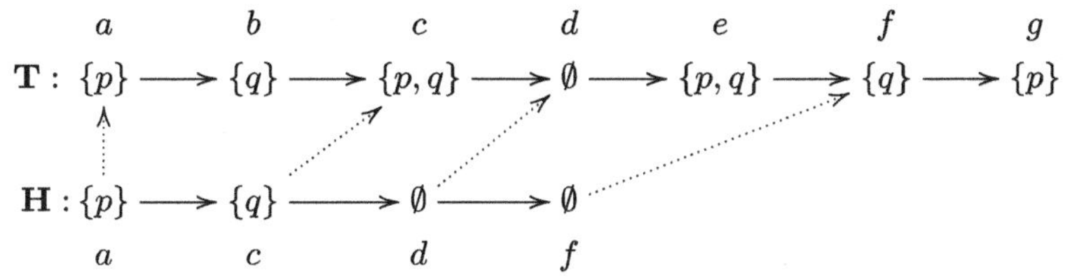

Fig. 2. HT-trace $f(M)$ for the interpretation M in Example 6.

The correspondence function $f(\cdot)$ is not injective: different interpretations $M \neq M'$ may produce the same HT-trace $f(M) = f(M')$. As an example of this situation, simply take M from Example 6 and another M' obtained by switching the roles of elements a and b everywhere in M. It is easy to see that the elements themselves are irrelevant, provided that we have the same number of them and keep their same roles in the domains and the order relations. On the other hand, function $f(\cdot)$ is surjective, as stated below.

Proposition 9. *Function $f(\cdot)$ is surjective: given any* HT*-trace* $\mathbf{M} = \langle \mathbf{H}, \mathbf{T}, \rho \rangle$ *there always exist some* $\mathrm{QHT}^+(\leq)$ *interpretation M such that $f(M) = \mathbf{M}$.*

Proof. We proceed to build one possible M such that $f(M) = \mathbf{M}$. To this aim, the domains will be subsets of rational numbers $D_h \subseteq D_t \subseteq \mathbb{Q}$ being:

$$D_h := [0..\lambda_h)$$
$$D_t := [0..\lambda_t) \cup \{\ \rho(i) + (1/k) \mid i, i+1 \in D_h,\ k \in [2..\rho(i+1) - \rho(i)]\ \}$$

and we take $\leq_h^M$ and $\leq_t^M$ to be the standard ordering for rationals $\mathbb{Q}$. As we can see, for D_h we just take the integers in the interval $[0..\lambda_h)$ with the standard ordering, so $level_{M,h}(i) = i$. For D_t, the idea is to include all the integer numbers in D_h and, between each pair i and $i+1$, add to i as many fractions like $1/2$, $1/3$, $1/4, \ldots$ as needed to keep the same distance as from $\rho(i)$ to $\rho(i+1)$. Doing this, we may also observe that $level_{M,t}(i) = \rho(i)$. For instance, if $\rho(3) = 6$ and $\rho(4) = 10$, we have $k \in [2..(10-6)] = [2..4]$ and we in D_t the three fractions:

$$3 + 1/2 = 7/2\ \geq\ 3 + 1/3 = 10/3\ \geq\ 3 + 1/4 = 13/4$$

all of them between 3 and 4. Starting with $level_{M,t}(3) = 6$, we then can see that $level_{M,t}(13/4) = 7$, $level_{M,t}(10/3) = 8$, $level_{M,t}(7/2) = 9$ and $level_{M,t}(4) = 10$. Finally, we define the extensions $I(p, w)$ of monadic predicates as follows:

$$I(p, h) \stackrel{df}{=} \{i \mid p \in H_i, i \in [0..\lambda_h)\}$$
$$I(p, t) \stackrel{df}{=} \{level^{-}_{M,t}(i) \mid p \in T_i, i \in [0..\lambda_t)\}$$

From here, it is then routine to check that $f(M) = \mathbf{M}$.

Thus, the correspondence between HT-traces and $\mathrm{QHT}^{+}(\leq)$ interpretations is actually one-to-many, and we can partition the set of $\mathrm{QHT}^{+}(\leq)$ interpretations into equivalence classes, each one consisting of the set of interpretations M that map to the same HT-trace $f(M)$.

We eventually consider Kamp's translation of linear temporal logic into first-order logic.

Definition 6 (Kamp's translation). *Given a temporal formula φ, we define its translation $\tau(\varphi)_x$ w.r.t. some domain element $x \in D_t$ into a first-order formula as follows:*

$$
\begin{aligned}
\tau(\bot)_x &\stackrel{df}{=} \bot \\
\tau(p)_x &\stackrel{df}{=} p(x) \qquad \textit{for any atom } p \\
\tau(\alpha \otimes \beta)_x &\stackrel{df}{=} \tau(\alpha)_x \otimes \tau(\beta)_x \quad \textit{for all } \otimes \in \{\wedge, \vee, \rightarrow\} \\
\tau(\circ\alpha)_x &\stackrel{df}{=} \exists y(succ(x,y) \wedge \tau(\alpha)_y) \\
\tau(\circ_a\alpha)_x &\stackrel{df}{=} \exists y(x < y) \wedge \forall y(x < y \rightarrow \tau(\alpha)_y \vee \exists z(x < z < y))) \\
\tau(\alpha \, \mathbf{U} \, \beta)_x &\stackrel{df}{=} \exists y(x \leq y \wedge \tau(\beta)_y \wedge \forall z(x \leq z \wedge z < y \rightarrow \tau(\alpha)_z)) \\
\tau(\alpha \, \mathbf{R} \, \beta)_x &\stackrel{df}{=} \forall y(x \leq y \rightarrow \tau(\beta)_y \vee \exists z(x \leq z \wedge z < y \wedge \tau(\alpha)_z))
\end{aligned}
$$

Additionally, from the definition of derived operators and some basic equivalences of QHT, it is not hard to see that we can abbreviate the translation of derived connectives as follows:

$$
\begin{aligned}
\tau(\top)_x &\equiv \top \\
\tau(\neg\alpha)_x &\equiv \neg\tau(\alpha)_x \\
\tau(\widehat{\circ}\alpha)_x &\stackrel{df}{=} \forall y(succ(x,y) \rightarrow \tau(\alpha)_y) \\
\tau(\widehat{\circ}_a\alpha)_x &\stackrel{df}{=} \forall y(x < y \rightarrow \tau(\alpha)_y \vee \exists z(x < z < y))) \\
\tau(\Diamond\alpha)_x &\stackrel{df}{=} \exists y(x \leq y \wedge \tau(\alpha)_y) \\
\tau(\Box\alpha)_x &\stackrel{df}{=} \forall y(x \leq y \rightarrow \tau(\alpha)_y)
\end{aligned}
$$

The main result of this section is then that Kamp's translation works beyond LTL also for bTHT. As a corollary, it holds using a static domain assumption also for THT, which was already proved in [4].

Theorem 2 (Soundness of Kamp's translation). *For every* $\mathrm{QHT}^{+}(\leq)$ *interpretation* $M = (D_h, D_t, I, \sigma)$, $f(M) = \langle \mathbf{H}, \mathbf{T}, \rho \rangle$ *and every* $i \in [0..\lambda_h)$, *it holds for* $d = level^{-}_{M,h}(i)$ *that*

$$f(M), i \models \varphi \text{ in THT iff } M, h \models \tau(\varphi)_d$$

Proof. Note that $d = level^{-}_{M,h}(i)$ iff $i = level_{M,h}(d)$. The missing cases in the induction step will be included the extended version. We proceed by structural induction on φ.

- If $\varphi = p \in \mathcal{A}$, then $\mathbf{M}, h \models \tau(p)_d = p(d)$ with $d = level^{-}_{M,h}(i)$, that is, $d \in I(p, h)$ and $level_{M,h}(d) = i$. By defn. of $f(M)$ it is equiv. to $p \in H_i$ so, to $f(M), i \models p$.
- If $\varphi = \alpha \to \beta$ then: $M, h \models \tau(\alpha \to \beta)_d \Leftrightarrow M, h \models \tau(\alpha)_d \to \tau(\beta)_d$

$$\begin{aligned}
&\Leftrightarrow (M, h \not\models \tau(\alpha)_d \text{ or } M, h \models \tau(\beta)_d) \text{ and } (M, t \not\models \tau(\alpha)_d \text{ or } M, t \models \tau(\beta)_d)\\
&\overset{\text{(IH)}}{\Leftrightarrow} (f(M), i \not\models \alpha \text{ or } f(M), i \models \beta) \text{ and } (f(M^t), \rho(i) \not\models \alpha \text{ or } f(M^t), \rho(i) \models \beta)\\
&\Leftrightarrow (f(M), i \not\models \alpha \text{ or } f(M), i \models \beta) \text{ and } (\mathbf{T}, \rho(i) \not\models \alpha \text{ or } \mathbf{T}, \rho(i) \models \beta)\\
&\Leftrightarrow f(M), i \models \alpha \to \beta
\end{aligned}$$

- If $\varphi = \circ_a \alpha$ then: $M, h \models \tau(\circ_a \alpha)_d$

$$\begin{aligned}
\Leftrightarrow\quad & M, h \models \exists y(x < y) \land \forall y(x < y \to \tau(\alpha)_y \lor \exists z(x < z < y)))\\
\Leftrightarrow\quad & \text{there exists } y \in D_h, d <^M_h y,\\
& \text{and for all } y \in D_h, \text{such that there is no } z \text{ such that } d <^M_h z, z <^M_h y\\
& M, h \models \tau(\alpha)_y\\
& \text{and for all } y \in D_t, \text{such that there is no } z \text{ such that } d <^M_t z, z <^M_t y\\
& M, t \models \tau(\alpha)_y\\
\Leftrightarrow\quad & \text{there exists } y \in D_h, M, h \models \tau(\alpha)_y\\
& \text{and } level_{M,h}(y) = level_{M,h}(d) + 1 = i + 1\\
& \text{there exists } y \in D_t, M, t \models \tau(\alpha)_y\\
& \text{and } level_{M,t}(y) = level_{M,t}(d) + 1 = \rho(i) + 1\\
\overset{\text{(IH)}}{\Leftrightarrow}\quad & \text{there exists } y \in D_h, f(M), i + 1 \models \alpha\\
& \text{and there exists } y \in D_t, f(M), \rho(i) + 1 \models \alpha\\
\Leftrightarrow\quad & i + 1 < \lambda_h, f(M), i + 1 \models \alpha, \text{and } f(M^t), \rho(i) + 1 \models \alpha\\
\Leftrightarrow\quad & f(M), i \models \circ_a \alpha
\end{aligned}$$

– If $\varphi = \alpha \,\mathbf{U}\, \beta$ then: $M, h \models \tau(\alpha \,\mathbf{U}\, \beta)_d$

$\Leftrightarrow$ $M, h \models \exists y(d \leq y \wedge \tau(\beta)_y \wedge \forall z(d \leq z \wedge z < y \rightarrow \tau(\alpha)_z))$

$\Leftrightarrow$ there is $y \in D_h, d \leq_h^M y, M, h \models \tau(\beta)_y$
and for all $z \in D_h$, s.t. $d \leq_h^M z$ and $z <_h^M y$ implies $M, h \models \tau(\alpha)_z$
and for all $z \in D_h$, s.t. $d \leq_t^M z$ and $z <_t^M y$ implies $M, t \models \tau(\alpha)_z$
and for all $z \in D_t$, s.t. $d \leq_t^M z$ and $z <_t^M y$ implies $M, t \models \tau(\alpha)_z$
(the last 'for all' implies the second one, that can be removed)

$\overset{(IH)}{\Leftrightarrow}$ there is $y \in D_h, d \leq_h^M y, f(M), j \models \beta$, with $j = \mathit{level}_{M,h}(y)$
and for all $z \in D_h$, s.t. $d \leq_h^M z$ and $z <_h^M y$ implies $f(M), k \models \alpha$,
with $k = \mathit{level}_{M,h}(z)$
and for all $z \in D_t$, s.t. $d \leq_t^M z$ and $z <_t^M y$ implies $f(M^t), k \models \alpha$,
with $k = \mathit{level}_{M,t}(z)$

$\Leftrightarrow$ there is $j \in [0..\lambda_h), i \leq j, f(M), j \models \beta$
and for all $k \in [0..\lambda_h)$, s.t. $i \leq k$ and $k < j$ implies $f(M), k \models \alpha$
and for all $k \in [0..\lambda_t)$, s.t. $\rho(i) \leq k$ and $k < \rho(j)$ implies $f(M^t), k \models \alpha$

$\Leftrightarrow$ there is $j \in [0..\lambda_h), i \leq j, f(M), j \models \beta$
and for all $k \in [0..\lambda_h)$, s.t. $i \leq k$ and $k < j$ implies $f(M), k \models \alpha$
and for all $k \in [0..\lambda_t)$, s.t. $\rho(i) \leq k$ and $k < \rho(j)$ implies $f(M^t), k \models \alpha$

$\Leftrightarrow$ there exists $j \in [i..\lambda_h)$ such that $f(M), j \models \beta$
and for all $k \in [i..j), f(M), k \models \alpha$
and for all $k \in [\rho(i)..\rho(j)), \mathbf{T}, k \models \alpha$

$\Leftrightarrow$ $f(M), i \models \alpha \,\mathbf{U}\, \beta$

As an illustration, take the formula $\varphi = \Box(\neg goal \rightarrow \circ(a_1 \vee a_2))$ from π in Example 5. Then, its translation at x corresponds to:

$$\begin{aligned}
\tau(\varphi)_x &= \forall y(x \leq y \rightarrow \tau(\neg goal \rightarrow \circ(a_1 \vee a_2)))_y\,) \\
&= \forall y(x \leq y \rightarrow (\tau(\neg goal)_y \rightarrow \tau(\circ(a_1 \vee a_2))_y)\,) \\
&= \forall y(x \leq y \rightarrow (\neg\tau(goal)_y \rightarrow \tau(\circ a_1)_y \vee \tau(\circ a_2)_y)\,) \\
&= \forall y(x \leq y \rightarrow (\neg goal(y) \rightarrow \exists z(succ(y,z) \wedge \tau(a_1)_z) \vee \exists z(succ(y,z) \wedge \tau(a_2)_z))\,) \\
&= \forall y(x \leq y \rightarrow (\neg goal(y) \rightarrow \exists z(succ(y,z) \wedge a_1(z)) \vee \exists z(succ(y,z) \wedge a_2(z)))\,)
\end{aligned}$$

Finally, this formula is $\text{QHT}^+(<)$-equivalent to:

$$\forall y(x \leq y \wedge \neg goal(y) \rightarrow \exists z(succ(y,z) \wedge (a_1(z) \vee a_2(z))\,)$$

namely, for every future (or present) state $y \geq x$ satisfying $\neg goal(y)$, there exists a successor state z, $succ(y,z)$ that satisfies either $a_1(z)$ or $a_2(z)$.

An interesting observation is that $\tau(\circ\alpha)_x$ and $\tau(\circ_a\alpha)_x$ are QHT equivalent (and so, LTL equivalent too). This corroborates the fact that, when we use a static domain, $\circ_a\alpha$ collapses to $\circ\alpha$. However, when we move to $\mathrm{QHT}^+(<)$ and dynamic domains, that equivalence no longer holds. For instance, the translation of $\psi = \square(\neg goal \rightarrow \circ_a(a_1 \vee a_2))$ (also from π_a in Example 5) where we have replaced $\circ$ by $\circ_a$ is:

$$
\begin{aligned}
\tau(\varphi)_x &= \forall y(x \leq y \rightarrow \tau(\neg goal \rightarrow \circ_a(a_1 \vee a_2))_y\,) \\
&= \forall y(x \leq y \rightarrow (\tau(\neg goal)_y \rightarrow \tau(\circ_a(a_1 \vee a_2))_y)\,) \\
&\equiv \forall y(x \leq y \wedge \neg\tau(goal)_y \rightarrow \tau(\circ_a a_1)_y \vee \tau(\circ_a a_2)_y\,) \\
&= \forall y(x \leq y \wedge \neg goal(y) \rightarrow \\
&\qquad\quad (\exists z(y < z) \wedge \forall z(y < z \rightarrow a_1(z) \vee \exists w(y < w < z))) \\
&\qquad\quad \vee (\exists z(y < z) \wedge \forall z(y < z \rightarrow a_2(z) \vee \exists w(y < w < z)))) \\
&= \forall y(x \leq y \wedge \neg goal(y) \rightarrow \exists z(y < z) \wedge \\
&\qquad\quad (\forall z(y < z \rightarrow a_1(z) \vee \exists w(y < w < z)) \\
&\qquad\qquad \vee\ \forall z(y < z \rightarrow a_2(z) \vee \exists w(y < w < z)))
\end{aligned}
$$

which is not $\mathrm{QHT}^+(<)$ equivalent to $\tau(\varphi)_x$ obtained before.

5 Conclusion

In this paper, we have introduced brief THT (bTHT) as a new variant of temporal Here-and-There logic that aims at shortening traces by disregarding states and gives rise to bTEL as a restriction of temporal equilibrium logic (TEL). Furthermore, we have shown that Kamp's translation of LTL into first-order logic can be applied to bTHT as well, and thus also to THT. Formulas that are equivalent under classical semantics, behave differently under QHT^+; such different encodings of temporal operators into QHT^+may yield to differences that have some clear intuition at the temporal level as in the case of the synchronicity of the *next*-operator.

Our ongoing work aims to elucidate the relationship between bTHT and contracted THT (cTHT) in depth, as well as of the ensuing brief TEL and contracted TEL logics. As we have seen, bTHT is closer to HT than cTHT, which means that more THT intuitions are available at the semantics level. Intuitively, bTEL tends to provide models where subsequences of states along the trace are justified, i.e., that cannot be skipped to obtain a smaller model. In contrast, cTEL models are traces whose segments cannot be contracted into a state, offering therefore a contraction-based justification to traces. A more detailed picture of the semantics and their properties remains to be drawn.

Furthermore, the computational properties and algorithms for efficient evaluation remain to be investigated. As a future work, we aim to provide an encoding of bTEL into $\exists\forall$LTL and obtaining so a Büchi automata construction, adapting the technique of [3]. Büchi automata accept only ω-regular languages, which are expressible as $\cup_{i \in I} U_i\ V_i$ with I finite and U and V regular languages; as a conclusion there are no infinite traces for the $\circ$-free fragments, however, the same does not happen in the finite case, where the intuition of traces with justified sub-traces is matched. Furthermore, fragments of the language close to the notion of temporal programs will be considered.

Acknowledgments. This project received funding from the European Research Council under the European Union's Horizon 2020 research and innovation programme (grant agreement no. 101034440), by the WWTF project ICT22-023, and by grant PID2023-148531NB-I00 funded by Spanish Ministry MCIU/AEI/10.13039/501100011033.

References

1. Aguado, F., et al.: Linear-time temporal answer set programming. TPLP **23**(1), 2–56 (2021)
2. Aguado, F., Cabalar, P., Diéguez, M., Pérez, G., Vidal, C.: Temporal equilibrium logic: a survey. J. Appl. Non-Classical Logics **23**(1–2), 2–24 (2013)
3. Cabalar, P., Demri, S.: Automata-based computation of temporal equilibrium models. In: Proceedings LOPSTR-2011 (2011)
4. Cabalar, P., Diéguez, M., Vidal, C.: An infinitary encoding of temporal equilibrium logic. In: Proceedings of the 31st International Conference on Logic Programming (ICLP'15) (2015)
5. Cabalar, P., Eiter, T., Soldà, D.: Contracted temporal equilibrium logic. In: Proceedings KR-2024 (2024). https://doi.org/10.24963/KR.2024/21
6. Cabalar, P., Pérez Vega, G.: Temporal equilibrium logic: a first approach. In: Moreno Díaz, R., Pichler, F., Quesada Arencibia, A. (eds.) EUROCAST 2007. LNCS, vol. 4739, pp. 241–248. Springer, Heidelberg (2007). https://doi.org/10.1007/978-3-540-75867-9_31
7. Dodaro, C., Fionda, V., Greco, G.: LTL on weighted finite traces: formal foundations and algorithms. In: Proceedings IJCAI-2022, pp. 2606–2612. ijcai.org (2022)
8. Heyting, A.: Die formalen Regeln der intuitionistischen Logik. Sitzungsberichte der Preussischen Akademie der Wissenschaften, Physikalisch-mathematische Klasse (1930)
9. Kamp, H.: Tense Logic and the Theory of Linear Order. Ph.D. thesis, UCLA (1968)
10. Lifschitz, V.: Answer set planning. In: Proceedings ICLP-1999, pp. 23–37. MIT Press (1999)
11. Marek, V., Truszczyński, M.: Stable Models and an alternative logic programming paradigm, pp. 169–181. Springer-Verlag (1999)
12. Niemelä, I.: Logic programs with stable model semantics as a constraint programming paradigm. Ann. Math. Artif. Intell. **25**(3–4), 241–273 (1999)
13. Pearce, D.: Equilibrium logic. Ann. Math. Artif. Intell. **47**(1–2), 3 (2006)
14. Pnueli, A.: The temporal logic of programs. In: Proceedings FOCS-1977, pp. 46–57. IEEE (1977)
15. Schuppan, V., Biere, A.: Shortest counterexamples for symbolic model checking of LTL with past. In: Halbwachs, N., Zuck, L.D. (eds.) TACAS 2005. LNCS, vol. 3440, pp. 493–509. Springer, Heidelberg (2005). https://doi.org/10.1007/978-3-540-31980-1_32

Deontic Equilibrium Logic with Paraconsistent Modality

Pedro Cabalar[1], Ovidio Manteiga[1(✉)], and Concepción Vidal[1,2]

[1] University of A Coruña, A Coruña, Spain
{cabalar, ovidio.manteiga, concepcion.vidalm}@udc.es
[2] CITIC, University of A Coruña, A Coruña, Spain

Abstract. Equilibrium Logic constitutes a well-established logical characterisation of Answer Set Programming (ASP) that has been recently extended to the deontic formalism called DELX. Focused on obligations of literals (built with explicit negation), DELX allows a certain degree of paraconsistency: a literal can be both obligatory and forbidden when one of those two norms is violated. This is convenient for contrary-to-duty situations, where a secondary obligation can coexist with a contradictory, primary one when the latter is violated. Unlike modal approaches, any DELX theory can be reduced to a normal form where deontic operators are only applied on atoms. This allows a direct translation into ASP and was exploited in the recent tool for normative reasoning `deolingo`. However, the simplicity and flexibility of DELX come at the price of its impossibility of a proper representation of disjunctive obligations like $\mathbf{O}(p \vee q)$ that become DELX-equivalent to $\mathbf{O}p \vee \mathbf{O}q$. A similar problem arises with conjunctive prohibitions. In this paper, we study a modal deontic extension of equilibrium logic, MDEL, that avoids these problems by treating obligations as proper modal operators, while preserving the same restricted paraconsistency of DELX. We prove some basic properties of the new formalism and illustrate its use with several examples. We show that the monotonic basis of MDEL is strictly weaker than the one of DELX and that, as a result, any DELX equilibrium model of a theory is also an MDEL equilibrium model. Finally, we prove that DELX reasoning is formally correct in MDEL for the syntactic fragment where modal operators are exclusively applied on explicit literals.

1 Introduction

The concerns about the legal and ethical implications of the widespread use of Artificial Intelligence have renewed interest in reasoning about norms and regulations. The formalisation of normative concepts such as obligation, permission or prohibition is the topic of study of *Deontic* systems [5,6] that evolved from the so-called *Standard Deontic Logic* (SDL) [22] (a.k.a. modal logic KD) to overcome some of its limitations. In the literature, several prototypical scenarios, also called 'paradoxes', were used to illustrate multiple features of deontic reasoning that could not be covered by SDL. For instance, the following well-known scenario can be used to illustrate both the need of *defeasible norms* versus the potential inconsistency in *contrary-to-duty* (CTD) obligations (namely, when a secondary norm is derived from the violation of a primary one):

W. Faber et al. (Eds.): LPNMR 2026, LNAI 16952, pp. 167–182, 2027.
https://doi.org/10.1007/978-3-032-38320-4_11

Example 1 (Cottage Fence [21]*).* A holiday cottage regulation consists of the norms:

(i) There must be no fence (f).
(ii) If, even so, there is a fence, it must be a white (w) fence.
(iii) If the cottage is by the sea (s), there may be a fence. □

Note how (iii) is an explicit permission to override the prohibition of fences (i), so the latter behaves as a defeasible norm that is *not effective* when the exception (being by the sea) is applicable. On the other hand, (ii) is a CTD obligation acquired when (i) is violated (a fence has been placed). In such a case, the secondary obligation of putting a white fence also implies the obligation to put a fence contradicts the prohibition of fences (i) that must be *still effective*. While it has been clear that defeasibility [13, 15, 18] requires introducing some form of *Non-Monotonic Reasoning* (NMR), the representation of CTDs has generated more controversy, leading to an heterogeneous umbrella of technical solutions to avoid the potential inconsistency between a primary and a secondary obligation. Some solutions establish formal differences between the two kinds of obligations, either by using different operators, establishing priorities or adding some kind of temporal precedence, but these normally imply further formalisation effort. Another alternative is to remove the **D** axiom $\neg(\mathbf{O}p \wedge \mathbf{O}\neg p)$ so that, for instance, the obligation of a fence $\mathbf{O}f$ and its prohibition $\mathbf{O}\neg f$ can coexist, forming in this way some sort of paraconsistency [4]. The usual problem with this kind of solution is that dilemmas (situations where we have equal instructions to do one thing *and* the opposite) are no longer inconsistent.

The recent *Deontic Equilibrium Logic with Explicit Negation* (DELX) [2] provided a solution to these and other problems in deontic reasoning by extending *Answer Set Programming* (ASP) [17] and in particular, its logical characterisation *Equilibrium Logic* [20], to incorporate deontic operators. DELX exploits the use of the two negations already present in ASP: on the one hand, defeasible norms are naturally represented using the standard ASP default negation (we will denote here as '$\neg$'). On the other hand, obligations in DELX are focused on literals built with an *explicit negation* [1] (written here as '$\sim$') allowing some degree of paraconsistency: $\mathbf{O}f$ and $\mathbf{O}{\sim}f$ are not inconsistent if one of them is violated. An important advantage of DELX is that any theory can be reduced to a normal form where deontic operators are only applied to atoms. This enables a direct translation into ASP without extra computational cost, something exploited by the deontic reasoning tool `deolingo` [3] built on top of the popular ASP solver `clingo` [7]. However, this normal form reduction is possible thanks to a quite radical treatment of disjunctive obligations. For instance, the imperative "fight in the army (a) or perform alternative civil (c) service" [16] formulated as $\mathbf{O}(a \vee c)$, is equivalent in DELX to the disjunction $\mathbf{O}a \vee \mathbf{O}c$ that, intuitively, is a stronger statement forcing one of the two atomic obligations to hold. The same counterintuitive behaviour arises with a prohibition of a conjunction:

Example 2. It is forbidden to drive (d) a car exceeding a limit of alcohol (a) in blood.□

If we formulate this prohibition as expected $\mathbf{O}{\sim}(d \wedge a)$ and we assume $\sim$ satisfies De Morgan laws, we again get a disjunctive obligation $\mathbf{O}({\sim}a \vee {\sim}d)$ that, in DELX, collapses to $\mathbf{O}{\sim}a \vee \mathbf{O}{\sim}d$ meaning that either we forbid driving or we forbid drinking alcohol, rather than forbidding the *simultaneous occurrence* of the two facts.

In this paper, we propose a new deontic extension of equilibrium logic, MDEL, where deontic connectives become proper modal operators under a Kripke semantics, while preserving the same paraconsistent treatment of obligations for literals formed with explicit negation. With respect to DELX, this new extension shows a more cautious behaviour for disjunctive obligations (analogously, conjunctive prohibitions) but, as a counterpart, its Kripke semantics does not allow a simple translation into ASP any more. We accompany the new definition with the proof of several basic properties. The main result is that MDEL collapses to DELX for the syntactic fragment where modal operators are exclusively applied on explicit literals.

The rest of the paper is organised as follows. The next section revisits the logic DELX from [2] and its monotonic basis DHTX. Then, Sect. 3 introduces the new formalism, MDEL, in terms of its monotonic basis, Modal Deontic HT (MDHT). Section 4 provides some properties connecting both MDEL and MDHT to the non-modal variants DELX and DHTX, respectively. Finally, Sect. 5 concludes the paper.

2 Background: Revisiting DELX

In this section, we revisit the definition of *Deontic Equilibrium Logic with eXplicit Negation* (DELX) [2] and its monotonic basis, *Deontic Here-and-There with eXplicit negation* (DHTX). Given a (countable) set of propositional atoms At, we define a *(deontic) formula* φ as any expression following the grammar:

$$\varphi ::= \bot \mid a \mid \varphi \wedge \varphi \mid \varphi \vee \varphi \mid \varphi \rightarrow \varphi \mid {\sim}\varphi \mid \mathbf{O}\varphi$$

where a is any atom in At. Operator '$\sim$' represents *explicit negation* whereas $\mathbf{O}$ stands for *obligation*. We define the derived operators $\neg\varphi := \varphi \rightarrow \bot$, $\top := \neg\bot$, $\mathbf{F}\varphi := \mathbf{O}{\sim}\varphi$, $\mathbf{P}\varphi := {\sim}\mathbf{F}\varphi$. The last two expressions are respectively read as "φ is *forbidden*" and "φ is *explicitly permitted*". Operator $\neg\varphi$ corresponds to *default negation* and is usually represented in ASP as '$not\ \varphi$'. A *(deontic) theory* is a set of (deontic) formulas. Given any set of atoms A, we define the corresponding set of *(explicit) literals* as $lit(A) := A \cup \{{\sim}p \mid p \in A\}$. A set $S \subseteq lit(A)$ is said to be *consistent* if it contains no pair $\{p, {\sim}p\}$ for any $p \in A$.

Definition 1 (DHTX-interpretation). *A DHTX-*interpretation *$\mathcal{I}$ is a pair $\mathcal{I} = \langle \mathcal{I}^h, \mathcal{I}^t \rangle$ of consistent sets of explicit literals where:*

(i) $\mathcal{I}^h \subseteq \mathcal{I}^t \subseteq lit(At')$ for the extended signature:
$At' := At \cup \{\mathbf{O}p \mid p \in At\} \cup \{\mathbf{F}p \mid p \in At\}$
(ii) $\{\mathbf{O}p, \mathbf{F}p\} \subseteq \mathcal{I}^t$ implies $\{p, {\sim}p\} \cap \mathcal{I}^t \neq \emptyset$, for any $p \in At$. □

The intuition about the two sets, $\mathcal{I}^h$ and $\mathcal{I}^t$, is that literals in $\mathcal{I}^h$ are considered to be "*founded*" whereas literals in $\mathcal{I}^t \setminus \mathcal{I}^h$ have less strength and are just "*assumed*" but not founded. The rest of literals in $lit(At') \setminus \mathcal{I}^t$ are just *not assumed*. For instance, take the signature $\{f, w, s\}$ for Example 1 and consider the interpretation I_0:

$$\mathcal{I}_0^h = \{s, {\sim}\mathbf{F}f\} \qquad \mathcal{I}_0^t = \mathcal{I}_0^h \cup \{\mathbf{O}w, {\sim}f\} \tag{1}$$

Then, literals s and $\sim\mathbf{F}f$ are founded, whereas $\mathbf{O}w$ and $\sim f$ are only assumed. On the other hand, the rest of possible literals not included in T, such as f, $\sim s$, w, $\sim w$, $\mathbf{F}f$, $\mathbf{O}f$, $\sim\mathbf{O}f$, etc., are not assumed. As we can see, in general, some literals can be assumed but not founded, as happened to $\mathbf{O}w$ and $\sim f$ above. The only situation in which this never happens is when $\mathcal{I}^h = \mathcal{I}^t$: in that case, we say that interpretation $\mathcal{I}$ is *total*. For simplicity, we will sometimes abbreviate $\langle \mathcal{I}^t, \mathcal{I}^t \rangle$ just as $\mathcal{I}^t$ when there is no ambiguity.

Condition (ii) allows the coexistence of an obligation $\mathbf{O}p$ and a prohibition $\mathbf{F}p$ of the same atom if one of them is violated, namely, either $p \in \mathcal{I}^t$ violates the prohibition or $\sim p \in \mathcal{I}^t$ violates the obligation. This condition corresponds to the axiom schemata:

$$\mathbf{O}p \wedge \mathbf{F}p \wedge \neg p \wedge \neg{\sim}p \rightarrow \bot \tag{wD}$$

that, for every atom p, forces a weaker version of the $\mathbf{D}$ axiom $\mathbf{O}p \wedge \mathbf{F}p \rightarrow \bot$. As we will see later, $\mathbf{F}p$ is DHTX-equivalent to $\mathbf{O}{\sim}p$ so DHTX introduces a kind of paraconsistency where, in general, $\mathbf{O}p \wedge \mathbf{O}{\sim}p \equiv \mathbf{O}(p \wedge {\sim}p) \not\equiv \mathbf{O}\bot \equiv \bot$. Axiom (**wD**) enforces consistency when none of the two obligations is violated, namely $\neg p \wedge \neg{\sim}p$ having no information about p. In that case, we face an unresolved *dilemma* situation, that is, we have both the obligation and the prohibition of a fact, something that becomes contradictory, as customary in the deontic reasoning literature.

The use of explicit negation leads to a three-valued semantics where, in addition to satisfaction of formulas $\models$, we also have a dual falsification relation $=\!\mid$. Besides, formulas will be evaluated with respect to one of the two HT "coordinates" $x \in \{h, t\}$ and will depend on a *context* $c \in \{\mathbf{r}, \mathbf{o}, \mathbf{f}\}$ standing for *real*, *obligatory* and *forbidden*, respectively. Each context c has a dual $\overline{c}$ defined as $\overline{\mathbf{r}} := \mathbf{r}$, $\overline{\mathbf{o}} := \mathbf{f}$ and $\overline{\mathbf{f}} := \mathbf{o}$. The satisfaction $\models$ and falsification $=\!\mid$ relations for DHTX are shown in Fig. 1. In the figure, M just stands for the interpretation $\mathcal{I} = \langle \mathcal{I}^h, \mathcal{I}^t \rangle$ but we keep that different name so that, later on, M will correspond to a richer structure that also contains $\mathcal{I}$.

A DHTX-interpretation $\mathcal{I}$ is a *model* of a theory Γ, written $\mathcal{I} \models \Gamma$, if $\mathcal{I}, \mathbf{r}, h \models \varphi$ for all $\varphi \in \Gamma$. A formula φ is a DHTX-*tautology* (or DHTX-*valid*), written $\models \varphi$, if any DHTX-interpretation is a model of φ. DHTX is the logic induced by all DHTX-tautologies.

Definition 2 (DHTX-Equilibrium model). *A total DHTX-interpretation $\mathcal{I}$ (when $\mathcal{I}^h = \mathcal{I}^t$) is a DHTX-*equilibrium model *of a theory Γ if $\mathcal{I} \models \Gamma$ and there is no model $\mathcal{J} \models \Gamma$ such that $\mathcal{J}^t = \mathcal{I}^t$ and $\mathcal{J}^h \subset \mathcal{I}^h$.*

DELX is the logic induced by the set of DHTX-equilibrium models of a deontic theory.

Example 3 (Example 1 continued). Example 1 can be represented as:

$$\neg{\sim}\mathbf{F}f \rightarrow \mathbf{F}f \tag{2}$$
$$f \wedge \mathbf{F}f \rightarrow \mathbf{O}w \tag{3}$$
$$s \rightarrow {\sim}\mathbf{F}f \tag{4}$$
$$(w \rightarrow f) \wedge (\mathbf{O}w \rightarrow \mathbf{O}f) \tag{5}$$

φ	$M, c, x \models \varphi$ **when**	$M, c, x =\!\!\mid \varphi$ **when**
$\top$ ($\bot$)	always (never)	never (always)
$\alpha \wedge \beta$	$M, c, x \models \alpha$ and $M, c, x \models \beta$	$M, c, x =\!\!\mid \alpha$ or $M, c, x =\!\!\mid \beta$
$\alpha \vee \beta$	$M, c, x \models \alpha$ or $M, c, x \models \beta$	$M, c, x =\!\!\mid \alpha$ and $M, c, x =\!\!\mid \beta$
$\alpha \to \beta$	for $y \in \{x, t\}$: $M, c, y \not\models \alpha$ or $M, c, y \models \beta$	$M, c, t \models \alpha$ and $M, c, x =\!\!\mid \beta$
$\sim\alpha$	$M, \bar{c}, x =\!\!\mid \alpha$	$M, \bar{c}, x \models \alpha$
p	$p \in \mathcal{I}^x$ if $c = \mathbf{r}$ $\mathbf{O}p \in \mathcal{I}^x$ if $c = \mathbf{o}$ $\sim\mathbf{F}p \in \mathcal{I}^x$ if $c = \mathbf{f}$	$\sim p \in \mathcal{I}^x$ if $c = \mathbf{r}$ $\sim\mathbf{O}p \in \mathcal{I}^x$ if $c = \mathbf{o}$ $\mathbf{F}p \in \mathcal{I}^x$ if $c = \mathbf{f}$
$\mathbf{O}\alpha$	$M, \mathbf{o}, x \models \alpha$	$M, \mathbf{o}, x =\!\!\mid \alpha$

Fig. 1. DHTX satisfaction and falsification relations where $M = \mathcal{I}$.

Formulas (2)–(4) respectively correspond to norms (i)–(iii) while (5) captures the commonsense knowledge that having a white fence implies there is a fence and that the obligation of a white fence implies the obligation of a having a fence. We may observe that (2)–(5) plus the axiom (**wD**) looks like an ASP program (with explicit negation), assuming we read formulas like '$\mathbf{O}a$' and '$\mathbf{F}a$' as ASP atoms. In fact, Cabalar et al. [2] proved that, in general, any DHTX theory is reducible to a syntactic fragment, called *Deontic Atom Normal Form* (DANF), where deontic operators are only applied on atomic expressions of the forms $\mathbf{O}a$ and $\mathbf{F}a$ where a is an atom. Once in DANF, the formula is then reducible to a logic program so that the answer sets of the latter correspond to the DHTX-equilibrium models of the former. Using this connection, it is easy to see that the only equilibrium model of (2)–(5) is a total interpretation $\mathcal{I}$ formed by $\mathcal{I}^h = \mathcal{I}^t = \{\mathbf{F}f\}$. If we add the fact f stating that we put a fence, then we get a new, unique equilibrium model formed by $\{\mathbf{F}f, f, \mathbf{O}w, \mathbf{O}f\}$ where we have derived the obligation to put a white fence $\mathbf{O}w$ and so, the obligation to put a fence $\mathbf{O}f$ too. The potential contradiction between $\mathbf{F}f$ and $\mathbf{O}f$ is cancelled by the fact that $\mathbf{F}f$ has been violated by f. Finally, if we extend the theory once more, stating that we are by the sea (2)–(5) $\cup \{f, s\}$, we obtain a unique equilibrium model $\{f, s, \sim\mathbf{F}f\}$ where we have derived the explicit permission $\sim\mathbf{F}f$ to put a fence, retracting the default prohibition $\mathbf{F}f$ derived before from (2). □

Cabalar et al. [2] illustrated the expressiveness of DELX with multiple examples combining CTD with dilemmas, defeasible obligations, explicit versus implicit permissions and defeasible deontic detachment. However, all these cases were focused on obligations of explicit literals, and left apart more complex formulas such as disjunctive obligations. Let us consider a classical example from the literature:

Example 4 (From [16]*).* An agent is constrained by the following two imperatives:

(i) Fight in the army (a) or perform alternative civil (c) service.
(ii) Do not fight in the army.

Intuitively, (i) corresponds to the disjunctive obligation $\mathbf{O}(a \vee c)$ whereas the second is a prohibition $\mathbf{F}a$ or equivalently $\mathbf{O}{\sim}a$. If we are given (i) alone, since $\mathbf{O}(a \vee c) \equiv \mathbf{O}a \vee \mathbf{O}c$ in DHTX, we obtain two equilibrium models $\{\mathbf{O}a\}$ and $\{\mathbf{O}c\}$ where we force (exclusively) one of the two obligations to occur. If we add (ii) to the theory, then $\mathbf{F}a$ forms a dilemma with $\mathbf{O}a$ according to (**wD**) since none of the two obligations has been violated. As a result, we obtain a unique equilibrium model $\{\mathbf{F}a, \mathbf{O}c\}$ where we derive the obligation to perform civil service, as expected. Let us elaborate the example by adding the following two premises:

(iii) If you fight in the army and violate (ii) then do not use firearms (f).
(iv) You fight in the army.

Our new theory would contain the formulas $\{\mathbf{O}(a \vee c), \mathbf{F}a, (\mathbf{F}a \wedge a \rightarrow \mathbf{F}f), a\}$ where $(\mathbf{F}a \wedge a \rightarrow \mathbf{F}f)$ states a CTD. In this case, the dilemma between $\mathbf{O}a$ with $\mathbf{F}a$ does no longer hold, because the prohibition has been violated. As a result, the two options from (i) are enabled and we obtain the two equilibrium models $\{\mathbf{O}a, \mathbf{F}a, a, \mathbf{F}f\}$ and $\{\mathbf{O}c, \mathbf{F}a, a, \mathbf{F}f\}$. □

Even though the previous example shows a reasonable behaviour in practice, the fact that $\mathbf{O}(a \vee c)$ is eventually treated as $\mathbf{O}a \vee \mathbf{O}c$ seems a rather radical assumption. This becomes perhaps clearer in the following case:

Example 5 (Example 2 revisited). Consider again the prohibition to drive drunk, that can be stated as $\mathbf{F}(d \wedge a)$. This formula is DHTX-equivalent to $\mathbf{F}d \vee \mathbf{F}a$ and produces the two equilibrium models $\{\mathbf{F}d\}$ and $\{\mathbf{F}a\}$, meaning that either we completely forbid driving or we completely forbid drinking alcohol (above the limit), a statement that is stronger than the original prohibition. If, for instance, we add evidence of driving without exceeding the alcohol limit $d \wedge {\sim}a$, we obtain an equilibrium model $\{\mathbf{F}a, d, {\sim}a\}$ where we fulfil a prohibition (no alcohol) but another one $\{\mathbf{F}d, d, {\sim}a\}$ where we make a violation of the prohibition to drive. □

In what follows, we study a possible way to *weaken* the DELX behaviour for disjunctive obligations (through a Kripke-based modal semantics) to better accommodate this kind of compound obligations.

3 Modal Deontic HT

We proceed now to define *modal deontic*-HT (MDHT). The syntax of MDHT extends DHTX formulas with a new operator $\widehat{\mathbf{O}}\varphi$ that will act as a dual of $\mathbf{O}\varphi$. We also define $\widehat{\mathbf{P}}\varphi := {\sim}\widehat{\mathbf{O}}{\sim}\varphi$ which will become a kind of stronger explicit permission. Given the propositional signature At, we define its corresponding *deontic signature* as $At_D := At \cup \{\overline{p} \mid p \in At\}$. Intuitively, atoms $\overline{p}$ will be used for prohibitions whereas literals ${\sim}\overline{p}$ will constitute explicit permissions. An HT-*world* I is a pair $\langle I^h, I^t\rangle$ of consistent sets of explicit literals $I^h \subseteq I^t \subseteq lit(At_D)$. As a notation remark, we will use non-calligraphic capital letters I, J for denoting HT-worlds formed over At_D, as a distinction from calligraphic $\mathcal{I}$, $\mathcal{J}$ for DHTX-interpretations over At' seen before.

Definition 3 (MDHT-interpretation). *An* MDHT-interpretation *is a pair* $\langle \mathbb{W}, I \rangle$ *where* I *is a distinguished HT-world (the "*actual*" world) for signature* At *and* $\mathbb{W} \neq \emptyset$ *is a set of HT-worlds for signature* At_D *such that, for all* $I, J \in \mathbb{W}$, *if* $I^t = J^t$ *then* $I^h = J^h$.

To increase readability, given a cluster $\mathbb{W} = \{J_1, J_2, \dots, J_n\}$ we will remove the commas and use square brackets, writing $[J_1\ J_2\ \dots\ J_n]$ instead. The intuition of $\langle \mathbb{W}, I \rangle$ is that the actual world I exclusively contains literals in $lit(At)$, that is, of the forms p or $\sim p$, meaning that we have evidence for p true or false, respectively. On the other hand, the set $\mathbb{W}$ will act as a cluster (like in modal logic S5) of HT-worlds over literals $lit(At_D)$, that is, of any of the forms p, $\sim p$, $\overline{p}$ or $\sim\overline{p}$, but their meaning now is slightly different: p will represent the obligation of p; $\overline{p}$ its prohibition; $\sim\overline{p}$ an explicit permission for p; and $\sim p$ an explicit permission for $\sim p$. This meaning will be combined with quantification: an obligation (or prohibition) must be satisfied in all worlds (as usual with modal *necessity* operators), whereas a permission must hold in at least one (as usual with modal possibility operators). Besides, as we can see, both the real world and each point J in the cluster have the two components J^h and J^t that, as before, are used for separating founded literals (those in J^h) from just assumed ones (those in $J^t \setminus J^h$).

Example 6. As an example of interpretation, take $M_0 = \langle \mathbb{W}_0, I_0 \rangle$ with $I_0^h = \{s\}$, $I_0^t = \{s, \sim f\}$ and the cluster:

$$\mathbb{W}_0 = [\quad \langle \{\sim\overline{f}\}, \{w, \sim\overline{f}\} \rangle \quad \langle \emptyset, \{w\} \rangle \quad \langle \{w, \overline{s}\}, \{w, \overline{s}\} \rangle \quad] \tag{6}$$

Let us respectively call J_1, J_2, J_3 to the three worlds above. In this cluster, the obligation for w is assumed, since $w \in J_i^t$ for all worlds $i = 1, 2, 3$. However, this obligation is not founded, since $w \notin J_1^h$ and $w \notin J_2^h$. On the other hand, the permission of f is founded, since we have at least one world $\sim\overline{f} \in J_1^h$. The last condition of Definition 3 implies that we cannot have new worlds in $\mathbb{W}$ like $\langle \cdot, \{w, \sim\overline{f}\} \rangle$, $\langle \cdot, \{w\} \rangle$ or $\langle \cdot, \{w, \overline{s}\} \rangle$ because those three t-components already occur in $\mathbb{W}$. □

An MDHT-interpretation $M = \langle \mathbb{W}, I \rangle$ is said to be *total* if all its HT-worlds are total, that is, $J^h = J^t$ for all $J \in \mathbb{W} \cup \{I\}$. Given any MDHT-interpretation $M = \langle \mathbb{W}, I \rangle$, we define its corresponding total interpretation as $M^t := \langle \mathbb{W}^t, \langle I^t, I^t \rangle \rangle$ where $\mathbb{W}^t := \{ \langle J^t, J^t \rangle \mid J \in \mathbb{W} \}$. Informally speaking, M^t overrides all the h-components in all the worlds in M to make them coincide with their corresponding t-components. As an example, $M_0^t = \langle \mathbb{W}_0^t, \langle I_0^t, I_0^t \rangle \rangle$ with I_0^t from (6) and the cluster:

$$\mathbb{W}_0^t := [\quad \langle \{w, \sim\overline{f}\}, \{w, \sim\overline{f}\} \rangle \quad \langle \{w\}, \{w\} \rangle \quad \langle \{w, \overline{s}\}, \{w, \overline{s}\} \rangle \quad]$$

As we did in DHTX, we will sometimes write total worlds $\langle J^t, J^t \rangle$ simply as J^t when there is no ambiguity: for instance, the above cluster becomes $[\ \{w, \sim\overline{f}\}\ \{w\}\ \{w, \overline{s}\}\ ]$. It is easy to see that M is total iff $M^t = M$.

The satisfaction $\models$ and falsification $=\!|$ relations for MDHT are shown in Fig. 2. Note that we reuse Fig. 1, but in the latter, we now take the liberty of reading M as the MDHT-interpretation $M = \langle \mathbb{W}, I \rangle$ instead of $M = \mathcal{I}$ we had before. We say that an MDHT-interpretation M is a *model* of a theory Γ, written $M \models \Gamma$ when $M, \mathbf{r}, h \models \varphi$ for every $\varphi \in \Gamma$. The following theorem proves an essential property in intermediate logics called *persistence*: in HT, it means that anything holding at h must still hold at t.

φ	$M, c, x \models \varphi$ **when**	$M, c, x =\!\!\mid \varphi$ **when**
$\bot \top \rightarrow$ $\wedge \vee \sim$	as in DHTX (Fig. 1)	as in DHTX (Fig. 1)
p	$p \in I^x$ if $c \neq \mathbf{f}$ $\sim\overline{p} \in I^x$ if $c = \mathbf{f}$	$\sim p \in I^x$ if $c \neq \mathbf{f}$ $\overline{p} \in I^x$ if $c = \mathbf{f}$
$\mathbf{O}\alpha$	$\forall J \in \mathbb{W}$: $\langle \mathbb{W}, J\rangle, \mathbf{o}, x \models \alpha$	$\exists J \in \mathbb{W}$: $\langle \mathbb{W}, J\rangle, \mathbf{o}, x =\!\!\mid \alpha$
$\widehat{\mathbf{O}}\alpha$	$\exists J \in \mathbb{W}$: $\langle \mathbb{W}, J\rangle, \mathbf{o}, x \models \alpha$	$\forall J \in \mathbb{W}$: $\langle \mathbb{W}, J\rangle, \mathbf{o}, x =\!\!\mid \alpha$
Derived		
$\neg\alpha$	$M, c, t \not\models \alpha$	$M, c, t \models \alpha$
$\mathbf{F}\alpha$	$\forall J \in \mathbb{W}$: $\langle \mathbb{W}, J\rangle, \mathbf{f}, x =\!\!\mid \alpha$	$\exists J \in \mathbb{W}$: $\langle \mathbb{W}, J\rangle, \mathbf{f}, x \models \alpha$
$\mathbf{P}\alpha$	$\exists J \in \mathbb{W}$: $\langle \mathbb{W}, J\rangle, \mathbf{f}, x \models \alpha$	$\forall J \in \mathbb{W}$: $\langle \mathbb{W}, J\rangle, \mathbf{f}, x =\!\!\mid \alpha$
$\widehat{\mathbf{P}}\alpha$	$\forall J \in \mathbb{W}$: $\langle \mathbb{W}, J\rangle, \mathbf{f}, x \models \alpha$	$\exists J \in \mathbb{W}$: $\langle \mathbb{W}, J\rangle, \mathbf{f}, x =\!\!\mid \alpha$

Fig. 2. MDHT satisfaction and falsification relations, being $M = \langle \mathbb{W}, I\rangle$.

Theorem 1 (Persistence). *For any formula α, any MDHT-interpretation $M = \langle \mathbb{W}, I\rangle$ and any context $c \in \{\mathbf{r}, \mathbf{o}, \mathbf{f}\}$:*

- *$M, c, h \models \alpha$ implies $M, c, t \models \alpha$.*
- *$M, c, h =\!\!\mid \alpha$ implies $M, c, t =\!\!\mid \alpha$.*

Proposition 1. *The semantics for derived operators $\neg$, $\mathbf{F}$, $\mathbf{P}$ and $\widehat{\mathbf{P}}$ correspond to the last four lines of the table in Fig. 2.*

We say that two formulas φ and ψ are *equivalent*, written $\varphi \equiv \psi$, when both (1) $M, c, x \models \varphi$ iff $M, c, x \models \psi$ and (2) $M, c, x =\!\!\mid \varphi$ iff $M, c, x =\!\!\mid \psi$, for all MDHT-interpretation M and any $c \in \{\mathbf{r}, \mathbf{o}, \mathbf{f}\}$, $x \in \{h, t\}$.

Note that MDHT is also paraconsistent, as happened in DHTX: in general, $\mathbf{O}p \wedge \mathbf{F}p = \mathbf{O}(p \wedge \sim p) \not\equiv \bot$. Moreover, even when $\mathbf{O}(p \wedge \sim p)$ does not hold, we may still have now that $\widehat{\mathbf{O}}(p \wedge \sim p)$, namely, both the obligation of p and its prohibition $\overline{p}$ may hold in *some* world in the cluster $J \in \mathbb{W}$. Thus, we propose a stronger variant of (**wD**) where a non-violated $\widehat{\mathbf{O}}(p \wedge \sim p)$ becomes a dilemma:

$$\widehat{\mathbf{O}}(p \wedge \sim p) \wedge \neg p \wedge \neg\sim p \rightarrow \bot \qquad \textbf{(wD')}$$

Proposition 2. *An MDHT-interpretation $M = \langle \mathbb{W}, I\rangle$ for signature At is a model of* $(\mathbf{wD}')$ *iff, for all $p \in At$: $p \in I^t$ or $\sim p \in I^t$ or there is no $J \in \mathbb{W}$ s. t. $\{p, \overline{p}\} \subseteq J^t$.*

In what follows, we will assume that (**wD'**) is satisfied. It must be noticed, however, that this axiom only applies to atoms and is not extrapolable to arbitrary formulas. As a counterexample, note that the formula $\widehat{\mathbf{O}}(\varphi \wedge \sim\varphi) \wedge \neg\varphi \wedge \neg\sim\varphi$ is consistent[1] for $\varphi = (a \vee c)$ even under the presence of (**wD'**).

We can now define the equilibrium models in this extended modal setting.

Definition 4 (MDHT-Equilibrium model). *A total MDHT-interpretation M, where $M = \langle \mathbb{W}, I \rangle$ and $M^t = M$, is an (MDHT)-*equilibrium model *of a theory Γ if it is a model of Γ and there is no other model M' of Γ such that $(M')^t = M$.*

MDEL is the logic induced by the set of MDHT-equilibrium models of a deontic theory.

Example 7 (Example 2 revisited). Suppose our theory only contains the formula $\mathbf{F}(d \wedge a) = \mathbf{O}\sim(d \wedge a)$. Following Fig. 2, this formula forces clusters $\mathbb{W}$ where all the worlds $J \in \mathbb{W}$ must satisfy either $\overline{d} \in J^h$ or $\overline{a} \in J^h$. It is not hard to see that, for deciding equilibrium models, only these two literals $\overline{d}$ and $\overline{a}$ are relevant in the set of worlds: the addition of any other literal d, $\sim d$, $\sim\overline{d}$, a, $\sim a$, $\sim\overline{a}$, in any J^t for $J \in \mathbb{W}$ or in I^t will never be in equilibrium, because we can always form a smaller M' with $(M')^t = M$ that removes these atoms making them unfounded. As a result, equilibrium models will have an empty real world $I^t = \emptyset$ (no literal is assumed). Similarly, the assumed literals for J^t in the cluster can only be either $\{\overline{a}\}$ or $\{\overline{d}\}$ since adding the two atoms $\{\overline{a}, \overline{d}\}$ together is unfounded (we can always remove one of them in J^h). This only leaves us three equilibrium models $M_1 = \langle \mathbb{W}_1, I \rangle$, $M_2 = \langle \mathbb{W}_2, I \rangle$ and $M_3 = \langle \mathbb{W}_3, I \rangle$ with $I^h = I^t = \emptyset$ and the clusters $\mathbb{W}_1 = [\ \{\overline{a}\}\ ], \mathbb{W}_2 = [\ \{\overline{d}\}\ ], \mathbb{W}_3 = [\ \{\overline{a}\}\ \{\overline{d}\}\ ]$. Interestingly, M_1 and M_2 correspond to the two equilibrium models we obtained in DELX, $\{\mathbf{F}a\}$ and $\{\mathbf{F}d\}$ respectively: in fact, we will see later that any DHTX-equilibrium model corresponds to an MDHT-equilibrium model. The novelty in MDEL is the third equilibrium model M_3. Notice that the equilibrium model minimisation works in a similar way as in ASP: the rest of literals are disregarded due to a lack of evidence and, in fact, the disjunction between $\overline{a}$ and $\overline{d}$ is also minimised, acting as an exclusive-or. If we add the information $d \wedge \sim a$ to our theory, we get again three equilibrium models formed by $\mathbb{W}_1$, $\mathbb{W}_2$ and $\mathbb{W}_3$ as before with a common actual world $I^h = I^t = \{d, \sim a\}$. □

In the previous example, we may observe that, when we add $d \wedge \sim a$, we still get an equilibrium model (formed by $\mathbb{W}_2$) where we violate the prohibition $\mathbf{F}d$. However, the situation now is weaker, since we also have now an equilibrium model with cluster $\mathbb{W}_3$ that contains "less information" since $\mathbb{W}_2 \subseteq \mathbb{W}_3$ (in fact, $\mathbb{W}_1 \subseteq \mathbb{W}_3$ too). In general, we may be sometimes interested in a preference relation among MDHT-equilibrium models using the following order:

Definition 5 (Relation $\preceq$). *Given two total MDHT-interpretations $M = \langle \mathbb{W}, I \rangle$ and $M' = \langle \mathbb{W}', I' \rangle$ we say that M is* less-preferred *than M', written $M \preceq M'$, when $I = I'$ and for all $J \in \mathbb{W}$ there exists some $J' \in \mathbb{W}'$ such that $(J')^t \subseteq J^t$.*

In the previous example, the only $\preceq$-maximal equilibrium model is $\mathbb{W}_3$ and $I^t = \{d, \sim a\}$. In that model, we are not violating any prohibition: moreover, we do fulfil the compound prohibition $\mathbf{F}(d \wedge a)$ because $\sim a$ holds and so $(d \wedge a)$ is falsified. We now illustrate relation $\preceq$ applied on permissions:

[1] As an example of a model, we may take a total interpretation $M = \langle \{J\}, I \rangle$ with $I^h = I^t = \{\sim a\}$ and $J^h = J^t = \{a, \overline{a}, \overline{c}\}$.

Example 8. Take the following pair of explicit permissions:

(i) A license gives you permission to drive (d).
(ii) Being adult, you can drink alcohol (a).

For simplicity, suppose you are adult and have a driving license, so $\mathbf{P}d \wedge \mathbf{P}a$ applies. The four equilibrium models of this conjunction are $M_i = \langle \mathbb{W}_i, \emptyset \rangle$ with $i = 1..4$ and:

$$\mathbb{W}_1 = [\ \{\sim\overline{d}, \sim\overline{a}\}\ ] \qquad \mathbb{W}_2 = [\ \{\sim\overline{d}, \sim\overline{a}\}\ \emptyset\ ]$$
$$\mathbb{W}_3 = [\ \{\sim\overline{d}\}\ \{\sim\overline{a}\}\ ] \qquad \mathbb{W}_4 = [\ \{\sim\overline{d}\}\ \{\sim\overline{a}\}\ \emptyset\ ]$$

In this case, we also have a unique $\preceq$-maximal equilibrium model formed by $\mathbb{W}_4$. Note how $\mathbb{W}_4$ does not allow concluding an explicit permission to drive and drink simultaneously. Such a permission would correspond to the formula $\mathbf{P}(d \wedge a)$ whose equilibrium models are $\mathbb{W}_1$ and $\mathbb{W}_2$, being the latter the only $\preceq$-maximal one in this case. Finally, if we combine the two permissions $\mathbf{P}a$ and $\mathbf{P}d$ with the prohibition to drive drunk $\mathbf{F}(d \wedge a)$ we get four equilibrium models M_5, M_6, M_7 and M_8 formed by a common actual world $I = \emptyset$ and the respective clusters:

$$\mathbb{W}_5 = [\ \{\overline{a}, \sim\overline{d}\}\ \{\overline{d}, \sim\overline{a}\}\ ] \qquad \mathbb{W}_6 = [\ \{\overline{a}, \sim\overline{d}\}\ \{\overline{d}, \sim\overline{a}\}\ \{\overline{a}\}\ ]$$
$$\mathbb{W}_7 = [\ \{\overline{a}, \sim\overline{d}\}\ \{\overline{d}, \sim\overline{a}\}\ \{\overline{d}\}\ ] \qquad \mathbb{W}_8 = [\ \{\overline{a}, \sim\overline{d}\}\ \{\overline{d}, \sim\overline{a}\}\ \{\overline{a}\}\ \{\overline{d}\}\ ]$$

being $\mathbb{W}_8$ the only $\preceq$-maximal one. On the other hand, if we take the formula $\mathbf{F}(d \wedge a) \wedge \mathbf{P}(d \wedge a)$ instead, we get no equilibrium models as expected – note that $\mathbf{P}(d \wedge a)$ amounts to $\sim\mathbf{F}(d \wedge a)$ by definition. □

Example 9 (Example 4 continued). Consider the first two premises (1)–(ii) from Example 4 modelled as the theory $\{\mathbf{O}(a \vee c), \mathbf{F}a\}$. Due to axiom (**wD'**), this theory produces a unique MDHT-equilibrium model $\langle [\ \{\overline{a}, c\}\ ], \emptyset \rangle$ where c becomes obligatory, as happened in DELX. If we extend the theory by covering premises (i)-(iv), that is $\{\mathbf{O}(a \vee c), \mathbf{F}a, (\mathbf{F}a \wedge a \rightarrow \mathbf{F}f), a\}$, then the dilemma is removed because $\mathbf{F}a$ is violated and we obtain now three MDHT-equilibrium models: $\langle [\ \{\overline{a}, c, \overline{f}\}\ ], \{a\} \rangle$, $\langle [\ \{\overline{a}, a, \overline{f}\}\ ], \{a\} \rangle$ and $\langle [\ \{\overline{a}, c, \overline{f}\}\ \{\overline{a}, a, \overline{f}\}\ ], \{a\} \rangle$. The first two cases correspond to the two DELX-equilibrium models we saw in Example 4, whereas the last one is the only $\preceq$-maximal equilibrium model and keeps $\mathbf{O}(a \vee c)$ without concluding neither $\mathbf{O}a$ nor $\mathbf{O}c$. Note how, in this model, paraconsistency only occurs in world $\{\overline{a}, a, \overline{f}\}$, where both the obligation a and prohibition $\overline{a}$ can coexist because of the violation of $\mathbf{F}a$. □

One interesting observation in the previous examples is that the DELX-equilibrium models seem to correspond to its MDHT-equilibrium models whose clusters are singletons. We will see next that, in fact, this is a general property.

4 Some Properties of MDHT

In this section, we study some properties of MDHT, starting with its relation to DHTX. In what follows, and for simplicity, we will use the same symbols $\models$ and $=\!|$ for evaluation of formulas both in DHTX and MDHT: ambiguity is resolved by the form of the interpretations used on the left, $\mathcal{I}$ with HT-interpretation over $lit(At')$ for DHTX and $M = \langle \mathbb{W}, I \rangle$ with $\mathbb{W} \cup \{I\}$ HT-worlds over $lit(At_D)$ for MDHT. We start identifying a kind of MDHT-interpretations that will have a strong relation to DHTX.

Definition 6 (Singleton MDHT-interpretation). *An MDHT-interpretation M, where $M = \langle \mathbb{W}, I \rangle$, is said to be* singleton *if its cluster is a singleton, that is $|\mathbb{W}| = 1$.* □

Notice that M is a singleton iff M^t is a singleton.

Theorem 2 *An MDHT-interpretation M is singleton iff M is a model of the axiom schemata, for every $\ell \in lit(At)$:*

$$(\widehat{\mathbf{O}}\ell \rightarrow \mathbf{O}\ell) \wedge (\sim\mathbf{O}\ell \rightarrow \sim\widehat{\mathbf{O}}\ell) \tag{S}$$

Under axiom (**S**), we can easily observe that $\widehat{\mathbf{O}}\varphi \equiv \mathbf{O}\varphi$ since the existential and universal quantification used in both operators collapse to a same condition when we have a singleton cluster. Therefore, if (**S**) holds, we also get that (**wD'**) collapses to (**wD**).

Definition 7 (Modal mapping μ). *Given a DHTX-interpretation $\mathcal{I}$ for signature At, we define $\mu(\mathcal{I})$ as the singleton MDHT-interpretation $\mu(\mathcal{I}) = \langle \{J\}, I \rangle$ where:*

$$\begin{aligned} I^x &:= \{p \mid p \in lit(At) \cap \mathcal{I}^x\} \\ J^x &:= \{p \mid \mathbf{O}p \in \mathcal{I}^x\} \cup \{\overline{p} \mid \mathbf{F}p \in \mathcal{I}^x\} \\ &\quad \cup \{\sim p \mid \sim\mathbf{O}p \in \mathcal{I}^x\} \cup \{\sim\overline{p} \mid \sim\mathbf{F}p \in \mathcal{I}^x\} \end{aligned}$$

for every $x \in \{h, t\}$. □

For instance, given $\mathcal{I}_0$ from Eq. (1), we get $\mu(\mathcal{I}_0) = \langle \{J_0\}, I_0 \rangle$ where $I_0 = \langle \{s\}, \{s, \sim f\} \rangle$ as in Example 6 and $J_0 = \langle \{\sim\overline{f}\}, \{\sim\overline{f}, w\} \rangle$. It is very easy to see that function μ is bijective, so it has an inverse μ^-: given any singleton $M = \langle \{J\}, I \rangle$, $\mu^-(M)$ corresponds to $\mathcal{I} = \langle \mathcal{I}^h, \mathcal{I}^t \rangle$ where:

$$\begin{aligned} \mathcal{I}^x := I^x &\cup \{\mathbf{O}p \mid p \in At, p \in J^x\} \cup \{\mathbf{F}p \mid p \in At, \overline{p} \in J^x\} \\ &\cup \{\sim\mathbf{O}p \mid p \in At, \sim p \in J^x\} \cup \{\sim\mathbf{F}p \mid p \in At, \sim\overline{p} \in J^x\} \end{aligned}$$

Theorem 3. *Let φ be any DHTX-formula (that is, not containing $\widehat{\mathbf{O}}$) over signature At, let $\mathcal{I}$ be a DHTX-interpretation over At and let $\mu(\mathcal{I}) = \langle \{J\}, I \rangle$ its corresponding singleton MDHT-interpretation. Then, for all $x \in \{h, t\}$ and all $c \in \{\mathbf{o}, \mathbf{f}\}$:*

(i) $\mathcal{I}, \mathbf{r}, x \models \varphi \Leftrightarrow \langle \{J\}, I \rangle, \mathbf{r}, x \models \varphi$
(ii) $\mathcal{I}, \mathbf{r}, x \mathrel{=\!\!|} \varphi \Leftrightarrow \langle \{J\}, I \rangle, \mathbf{r}, x \mathrel{=\!\!|} \varphi$
(iii) $\mathcal{I}, c, x \models \varphi \Leftrightarrow \langle \{J\}, J \rangle, c, x \models \varphi$
(iv) $\mathcal{I}, c, x \mathrel{=\!\!|} \varphi \Leftrightarrow \langle \{J\}, J \rangle, c, x \mathrel{=\!\!|} \varphi$ □

As a consequence, $\mathcal{I}, \mathbf{r}, h \models \varphi$ iff $\mu(\mathcal{I}), \mathbf{r}, h \models \varphi$ and, since μ is bijective for singleton interpretations, we conclude that DHTX is strictly stronger than MDHT:

Corollary 1. *Logic DHTX corresponds to MDHT restricted to singleton interpretations. In other words:* $DHTX = \text{MDHT} + (\mathbf{S})$. □

This can be used to prove that, in the non-monotonic setting, DELX is also strictly stronger than MDEL. In particular, DHTX-equilibrium models correspond exactly to MDHT-equilibrium models that are singleton, as stated below:

Theorem 4. *Let $\mathcal{I}$ be a total DHTX-interpretation and Γ a deontic theory (not containing $\widehat{\mathbf{O}}$). Then: $\mathcal{I}$ is a DHTX-equilibrium model of Γ iff $\mu(\mathcal{I})$ is a MDHT-equilibrium model of Γ.*

Recall that μ is bijective: for any singleton MDHT-equilibrium model M, this theorem guarantees that we can always get the corresponding DHTX-equilibrium model $\mathcal{I} = \mu^{-}(M)$.

In what follows, we will show that DHTX is a sound approximation of MDHT when restricted to formulas in the syntactic fragment of DANF. We recall that a deontic formula φ is in DANF if all the occurrences of deontic operators in φ are of the forms $\mathbf{O}a$ or $\mathbf{F}a$ where $a \in At$. Although DANF constitutes a normal form for DHTX, this is not the case in MDHT, though: for instance, the formula $\mathbf{O}(a \vee c)$ is not MDHT-reducible to DANF. We start defining, for any arbitrary MDHT-interpretation M, a particular singleton interpretation $\delta(M)$ assigned to M:

Definition 8. *Given an MDHT-interpretation $M = \langle \mathbb{W}, I \rangle$, we define the singleton interpretation $\delta(M) := \langle \{K\}, I \rangle$ where*

$$
\begin{aligned}
K^x := \quad & \{A \in J^x \mid A \in At_D, \textit{ for all } J^x \in \mathbb{W}\} \\
& \cup \{{\sim}A \in J^x \mid {\sim}A \in At_D, \textit{ for some } J^x \in \mathbb{W}\}
\end{aligned}
$$

for $x \in \{h, t\}$.

For instance, given M_0 defined before Eq. (6), we get $\delta(M) = \langle \{K_0\}, I_0 \rangle$ with I_0 as in M_0 and $K_0 = \langle \{{\sim}\overline{f}\}, \{{\sim}\overline{f}, w\} \rangle$ which coincides with J_0 seen after Definition 7. Moreover, $\mu^{-}(\delta(\mathcal{I}))$ is $\mathcal{I}_1$ from Eq. (1). It is obvious that, if M is already singleton, then $\delta(M) = M$. On the other hand, if M is any total interpretation $M^t = M$, then $\delta(M)$ is also total: $\delta(M)^t = \delta(M)$. The following result shows that the set of MDHT-models of a formula in DANF is completely characterised by its singleton models.

Theorem 5. *Let φ be a formula in DANF and M an MDHT-interpretation. Then:* $M, \mathbf{r}, h \models \varphi$ *iff* $\delta(M), \mathbf{r}, h \models \varphi$.

Corollary 2. *Checking MDHT-satisfiability (resp. MDHT-validity) of a formula φ in DANF can be reduced to checking its satisfiability (resp. validity) in MDHT+($\mathbf{S}$), or equivalently (Corollary 1) in DHTX.*

The correspondence at the non-monotonic level (i.e. with respect to equilibrium models) is stated in the following theorem:

Theorem 6. *If M is a MDHT-equilibrium model of a formula φ in DANF then $\delta(M)$ is also a MDHT-equilibrium model of φ.*

This result is weaker than in the monotonic case. Even if the formula is in DANF, we may obtain more MDHT-equilibrium models than in DHTX, as happens for arbitrary formulas after all. The novelty now is that if M is an equilibrium model, then the singleton $\delta(M)$ will also be in equilibrium. Moreover, these singleton equilibrium models are *sufficiently representative* in the sense that they suffice to cover the satisfaction/falsification of deontic atoms $\mathbf{O}a$ and $\mathbf{F}a$. As a result, singleton equilibrium models are enough to check equilibrium entailment when formulas are in DANF.

Theorem 7. *Let φ and ψ be two formulas in DANF. To check whether $M, \mathbf{r}, h \models \psi$ in all (resp. some) MDHT-equilibrium model of φ is equivalent to check it in all (resp. some) singleton MDHT-equilibrium model of φ, that is, all (resp. some) DHTX-equilibrium model of φ.*

Example 10 (Example 8 revisited). As an illustration, consider again the formula $\mathbf{P}d \wedge \mathbf{P}a$. This formula is an abbreviation of $\sim\mathbf{F}d \wedge \sim\mathbf{F}a$ that is in DANF. As we saw before, the formula has four MDHT-equilibrium models M_1, M_2, M_3 and M_4. We may observe that only one of them, M_1 with cluster $\mathbb{W}_1 = [\{\sim\overline{d}, \sim\overline{a}\}]$ is singleton and so, due to Theorem 4, $\mu^-(M_1) = \{\sim\mathbf{F}d, \sim\mathbf{F}a\}$ is the unique DHTX-equilibrium model of $\mathbf{P}d \wedge \mathbf{P}a$. Notice that, in M_1, we may derive the formula $\mathbf{P}(d \wedge a)$, that is, we have an explicit permission for both driving and drinking alcohol at the same time. This is no surprise, since $\mathbf{P}d \wedge \mathbf{P}a \equiv \mathbf{P}(d \wedge a)$ in DHTX. Remember, however, that the only $\preceq$-maximal MDHT-equilibrium model was M_4 where this simultaneous permission is not derived. Now, since φ is in DANF and M_1 is the only singleton equilibrium model, Theorem 6 further guarantees that $\delta(M_i) = M_1$ with $i = 1..4$, that is, for the four equilibrium models of φ. Finally, Theorem 7 tells us that, if we are only interested in equilibrium entailment of formulas in DANF, such as $\sim\mathbf{F}a$ or $\sim\mathbf{F}d$ (or in general, any propositional combination of deontic atoms) then M_1 suffices and there is no need to compute the rest of MDHT-equilibrium models. □

We conclude this section focusing on the fragment of MDHT induced by total models. In the case of regular HT, total models are enforced by the excluded middle axiom $p \vee \neg p$, which makes the logic collapse to classical propositional logic. Moreover, the same happens with Equilibrium Logic: the addition of excluded middle removes non-monotonicity and also makes equilibrium models collapse to classical models. In the case of MDHT, we can extend the excluded middle axiom as follows:

$$EM(p) \wedge \mathbf{O}(EM(p)) \wedge \widehat{\mathbf{P}}(EM(p)) \qquad \textbf{(EM)}$$

for any atom $p \in At$, where $EM(p) := (p \vee \neg p) \wedge (\sim p \vee \neg\sim p)$.

Theorem 8. *A MDHT-interpretation M is total iff M is a model of* (**EM**).

As we can see, forcing the excluded middle makes the "two-component" behaviour of HT disappear, leading to total interpretations. This is analogous to the non-modal setting, where adding the excluded middle to HT, makes it collapse to classical propositional logic. Note that $\widehat{\mathbf{P}}(EM(p))$ in (**EM**) amounts to $\sim\widehat{\mathbf{O}}\sim(EM(p))$ and that, if we remove this operator $\widehat{\mathbf{O}}$ from the language, it is no longer possible to characterise the set of total interpretations as in Theorem 8. The reason for this is that, by removing $\widehat{\mathbf{O}}$, we lose existential quantification for context **o**, and so, we lose universal quantification for context **f** over the worlds in the cluster. By examining the proof of Theorem 8 we can observe that any model $M = \langle \mathbb{W}, I \rangle$ of $EM(p)$ is forced to have a total actual world $I^h = I^t$, whereas the other part of the axiom $\mathbf{O}(EM(p)) \wedge \widehat{\mathbf{P}}(EM(p))$ enforces total clusters $\mathbb{W}^t = \mathbb{W}$. The fragment of total clusters can also be interesting: it removes non-monotonicity in deontic formulas, but keeps the logic programming behaviour for all the rest. To put an example, if we add the axiom $\mathbf{O}(EM(p)) \wedge \widehat{\mathbf{P}}(EM(p))$ to the formula $\mathbf{F}(d \wedge a)$ from Example 2, we obtain now 7 equilibrium models whose clusters are formed by all non-empty subsets of $[\{\sim\overline{a}, \sim\overline{d}\}\ \{\sim\overline{a}\}\ \{\sim\overline{d}\}]$.

5 Related Work and Conclusions

In this paper, we have introduced a modal variant of Deontic Equilibrium Logic with Explicit Negation [2] (DELX). This new variant, we called MDEL, allows a more cautious treatment of disjunctive obligations (resp. conjunctive prohibitions) avoiding the equivalence $\mathbf{O}(a \vee b) \equiv \mathbf{O}a \vee \mathbf{O}b$ imposed by DELX. DELX and MDEL are based on model selection criteria imposed on the monotonic logics DHTX and MDHT, respectively, both of them proper extensions of the logic of Here-and-There [14] (HT). MDHT interpretations have the form of Kripke models consisting of a cluster of HT worlds (that captures the meaning of deontic formulas) plus an isolated HT world that stands for the actual world. We have proved that, for any formula φ, there exists a one-to-one correspondence between its DHTX-models and MDHT-models where the cluster is a singleton. We also proved that any DHTX-equilibrium model is also an MDHT-equilibrium model but not vice versa. However, when the formula is in a given syntactic fragment where deontic operators are only applied to explicit literals, then MDEL collapses to DELX, if we are only interested in entailment of formulas in that syntactic fragment.

Apart from the relation to DELX extensively studied in this paper, other deontic extensions of ASP that have a clear connection to MDEL are *Deontic Logic Programs* (DLP) [10,11] and *Deontic Temporal ASP* (DTASP) [9]. While MDEL provides a full logical characterisation for arbitrary formulas (with no restrictions on connective nesting), both DLP and DTASP are defined in terms of a syntactic transformation extending the ASP program reduct [8]. Besides, the two formalisms rely on SDL (modal logic KD) and do not allow paraconsistent situations where $\mathbf{O}a \wedge \mathbf{F}a$, something that disables a suitable treatment of contrary-to-duty (e.g. Example 3). Another related approach is *Defeasible Deontic Logic* (DDL) [12] (extending *Defeasible Logic* [19]) that is not a proper extension of ASP, but has a similar syntax to logic programming. DDL introduces multiple types of rule implications (strict, defeasible and defeaters) that, again, act as meta-logical connectives and cannot be arbitrarily nested as in MDEL.

As immediate future work, we plan to study additional formal properties of MDHT (especially in relation to HT with explicit negation [1]), and the complexity of reasoning tasks associated to MDHT and MDEL, having in mind a modal extension of the current reasoning tool `deolingo` [3] based on DELX. Finally, we also plan to study a formal relation to the aforementioned formalisms DLP, DTASP and DDL.

Acknowledgements. We wish to thank Davide Soldà and Agata Ciabattoni for their useful comments on a previous version of this draft, and the anonymous reviewers for their suggestions. This research was partially supported by the Ministry of Science, Innovation and Universities (SPAIN) MICIU/AEI/10.13039/501100011033 grant PID2023-148531NB-I00. The CITIC center of UDC also receives funding from the Xunta of Galicia and the EU through the FEDER Galicia 2021-27 operational program (Ref. ED431G 2023/01).

References

1. Aguado, F., Cabalar, P., Fandinno, J., Pearce, D., Pérez, G., Vidal, C.: Revisiting explicit negation in answer set programming. Theory Pract. Logic Program. **19**(5–6), 908–924 (2019). https://doi.org/10.1017/S1471068419000267
2. Cabalar, P., Ciabattoni, A., van der Torre, L.: Deontic equilibrium logic with explicit negation. In: Gaggl, S.A., Martinez, M.V., Ortiz, M. (eds.) Logics in Artificial Intelligence - 18th European Conference, JELIA 2023, Dresden, Germany, 20–22 September 2023, Proceedings. LNCS, vol. 14281, pp. 498–514. Springer (2023)
3. Cabalar, P., Manteiga, O.: Deolingo: extending answer set programming with deontic reasoning. In: van Berkel, K., Ciabattoni, A., Horty, J.F. (eds.) Deontic Logic and Normative Systems - 17th International Conference, DEON 2025, Vienna, Austria, 1–3 July 2025, pp. 61–77. College Publications (2025)
4. da Costa Jr., N., Carnielli, W.: On paraconsistent deontic logic. Philosophia **16**, 293–305 (1986). https://doi.org/10.1007/BF02379748
5. Gabbay, D., Horty, J., Parent, X., van der Mayden, R., van der Torre, L. (eds.): Handbook of Deontic Logic and Normative Systems, vol. 2. College Publications (2021)
6. Gabbay, D., Horty, J., Parent, X., van der Meyden, R., van der Torre, L. (eds.): Handbook of Deontic Logic and Normative Systems. College Publications (2013)
7. Gebser, M., Kaminski, R., Kaufmann, B., Ostrowski, M., Schaub, T., Wanko, P.: Theory solving made easy with Clingo 5. In: Carro, M., King, A., Saeedloei, N., Vos, M.D. (eds.) Technical Communications of the 32nd International Conference on Logic Programming, ICLP 2016 TCs. OASIcs, vol. 52, pp. 2:1–2:15. Schloss Dagstuhl - Leibniz-Zentrum für Informatik (2016). https://doi.org/10.4230/OASIcs.ICLP.2016.2
8. Gelfond, M., Lifschitz, V.: The stable model semantics for logic programming. In: Proceedings of the 5th International Conference on Logic Programming (ICLP 1988), pp. 1070–1080 (1988)
9. Giordano, L., Martelli, A., Dupré, D.T.: Temporal deontic action logic for the verification of compliance to norms in ASP. In: Francesconi, E., Verheij, B. (eds.) International Conference on Artificial Intelligence and Law, ICAIL 2013, pp. 53–62. ACM (2013)
10. Gonçalves, R., Alferes, J.J.: An embedding of input-output logic in deontic logic programs. In: Ågotnes, T., Broersen, J.M., Elgesem, D. (eds.) DEON 2012, Proceedings. LNCS, vol. 7393, pp. 61–75. Springer (2012)
11. Gonçalves, R., Alferes, J.J.: Deontic logic programs. In: Gini, M.L., Shehory, O., Ito, T., Jonker, C.M. (eds.) International conference on Autonomous Agents and Multi-Agent Systems, pp. 1333–1334. IFAAMAS (2013)
12. Governatori, G., Olivieri, F., Rotolo, A., Scannapieco, S.: Computing strong and weak permissions in defeasible logic. J. Phil. Logic **42**(6), 799–829 (2013). https://doi.org/10.1007/s10992-013-9295-1
13. Governatori, G., Tosatto, S.C., Rotolo, A.: A defeasible deontic logic for pragmatic oddity. In: Liu, F., Marra, A., Portner, P., Putte, F.V.D. (eds.) Deontic Logic and Normative Systems - 15th International Conference, DEON 2020/21, pp. 239–254. College publications (2021)

14. Heyting, A.: Die formalen Regeln der intuitionistischen Logik. Sitzungsber. Preuss. Akad. Wiss., Phys.-Math. Kl, 42–56 (1930)
15. Horty, J.F.: Deontic logic as founded on nonmonotonic logic. Ann. Math. Artif. Intell. **9**(1–2), 69–91 (1993). https://doi.org/10.1007/BF01531262
16. Horty, J.F.: Moral dilemmas and nonmonotonic logic. J. Philos. Log. **23**(1), 69–91 (1994)
17. Lifschitz, V.: Action Languages, Answer Sets, and Planning, pp. 357–373. Springer (1999)
18. Nute, D. (ed.): Defeasible Deontic Logic. Kluwer, Dordrecht (1997)
19. Nute, D.: Defeasible logic. In: Handbook of Logic in Artificial Intelligence and Logic Programming. Oxford University Press (1993)
20. Pearce, D.: A new logical characterisation of stable models and answer sets. In: NMELP. LNCS, vol. 1216, pp. 57–70. Springer (1997)
21. Prakken, H., Sergot, M.: Dyadic deontic logic and contrary-to-duty obligations. In: Nute, D. (ed.) Defeasible Deontic Logic, pp. 223–262. Dordrecht (1997). https://doi.org/10.1007/978-94-015-8851-5_10
22. von Wright, G.H.: Deontic logic. Mind **60**(237), 1–15 (1951)

Operationalizing L-DINF in DALI2 for Trust and Probability-Aware Adaptive Scheduling

Stefania Costantini, Valentina Pitoni, and Lorenzo De Lauretis(✉)

Department of Information Engineering, Computer Science and Mathematics, University of L'Aquila, L'Aquila, Italy
{stefania.costantini, valentina.pitoni, lorenzo.delauretis}@univaq.it

Abstract. We present an executable operationalization of L-DINF, an epistemic logic for cooperative agents, in the DALI2 multi-agent system framework. Building on recent trust-aware and probabilistic extensions of L-DINF, we show how explicit beliefs, intentions, feasibility, preferences, inter-group delegation, trust thresholds, and probability-aware action selection can be represented through DALI2 beliefs, reactive rules, message passing, and execution traces. The implementation is demonstrated on a healthcare scheduling case study in which runtime disruptions trigger belief revision, local repair attempts, trust-sensitive decisions, mediated lending, and selection among equivalent actions according to reliability, preference, and cost. The resulting system produces explanation traces that connect DALI2 events with the corresponding L-DINF-style transitions, showing how an epistemic decision layer can be made executable in a practical multi-agent platform.

Keywords: Epistemic logic · Multi-agent systems · Logic programming · Probability · Trust · DALI2 · L-DINF

1 Introduction

Multi-agent systems operating in dynamic environments must revise their behaviour when the assumptions under which plans were generated no longer hold. In safety-sensitive or organizational domains, however, adaptation is not only a matter of finding another executable action. The system must also explain why an action remains admissible, why responsibility is delegated, or why a fallback procedure is activated. This requires an epistemic layer in which beliefs, intentions, feasibility, preferences, trust thresholds, and action-selection criteria are explicit and traceable.

L-DINF [9–11] is an epistemic logic for modelling cooperative agents. It provides formal constructs for explicit beliefs, background knowledge, intentions, action feasibility, qualitative preferences, equivalence classes of actions, and inter-group delegation, called *lending*. Its modular structure separates the epistemic

W. Faber et al. (Eds.): LPNMR 2026, LNAI 16952, pp. 183–198, 2027.
https://doi.org/10.1007/978-3-032-38320-4_12

core from packages describing executability, resources, costs, roles, preferences, equivalence classes, selection functions, and lending conditions. This modularity makes L-DINF particularly suitable for executable interpretations, since each package can be associated with a corresponding operational component.

In recent work, L-DINF has been extended along two complementary directions. The first direction introduces trust as a first-class regulatory component. Trust is not treated merely as an external score attached to agents, but as a constraint on practical agency. It can affect whether an agent is allowed to act autonomously, whether delegation is required, or whether the action must be blocked. The second direction introduces probability as an optional package for reasoning about uncertain beliefs, action reliability, and selection among equivalent feasible actions. Probability does not replace the original semantics of L-DINF; rather, it refines deliberation when alternatives differ in success probability, preference degree, and resource consumption.

A hybrid architecture coupling Answer Set Programming (ASP) [16] for baseline schedule generation with L-DINF for local runtime adaptation has also been proposed. In that view, ASP is used to compute a globally coherent initial schedule, while L-DINF provides a local epistemic layer that can react to runtime disruptions. In the present implementation, the ASP-generated baseline is treated as an offline input loaded into the agents' belief bases. DALI2 realizes the runtime adaptation layer, while full live integration with an ASP solver is left as future work.

This paper moves from the formal specification of L-DINF and its recent extensions to their executable operationalization. We implement a substantial operational fragment of L-DINF in DALI2 [1], the evolution of the DALI multi-agent system framework [12,13]. DALI2 runs on SWI-Prolog, uses a process-per-agent architecture with Redis-based pub/sub communication, and provides DALI-compatible syntax for reactive rules, internal events, goals, and beliefs. This makes it a natural operational substrate for L-DINF, since both frameworks are rooted in logic programming and share the principle that agent behaviour should be declaratively specified and formally traceable.

Contribution and Novelty. To clarify the scope of the present contribution, we distinguish what is inherited from prior work, what is new in this paper, and what remains future work.

- **Inherited:** the L-DINF epistemic core [9–11], its trust-aware and probabilistic extensions, the DALI2 runtime engine [1], and the idea of a hybrid ASP+agent architecture.
- **New:** (i) the compositional operational mapping $\mathcal{T}_D$ from L-DINF constructs to DALI2 patterns (Sect. 4); (ii) the executable multi-agent implementation with nine interacting agents realizing belief revision, trust-sensitive decisions, a mediated lending protocol, and a probability-aware selector (Sect. 5); (iii) the operational soundness and trace correspondence result (Theorem 1); (iv) a parameterized benchmark generator and quantitative evaluation on five scenarios of increasing complexity, including a structurally diverse scenario with raised trust thresholds (Sect. 7).

- **Future work:** mental-action budgets, live ASP integration, dynamic probability updates, and larger-scale empirical evaluation.

The paper is structured as follows. Section 2 discusses related work. Section 3 recalls the L-DINF constructs and the DALI2 features used in the implementation. Section 4 defines the operational mapping. Section 5 presents the agent system. Section 6 walks through the disruption scenario. Section 7 reports a quantitative evaluation on parameterized scenarios of increasing complexity. Section 8 discusses explanation traces and implementation choices. Section 9 concludes.

2 Related Work

The present work is connected to several research areas, including BDI agent programming, dynamic epistemic logic, trust-aware multi-agent systems, probabilistic reasoning, ASP-based scheduling, and agent-oriented logic programming. Classical BDI approaches provide a foundational model of intentional agency, while frameworks such as AgentSpeak/Jason [6] offer established tools for programming rational agents. However, these approaches do not natively provide a trust-sensitive semantics in which trust explicitly constrains intention adoption, execution feasibility, or delegation. Our work complements this tradition by relying on the epistemic and cooperative structure of L-DINF, where beliefs, intentions, preferences, feasibility, and group interaction are represented as explicit logical components.

L-DINF is also related to research on dynamic epistemic logic and belief dynamics for resource-bounded agents [4,5,17]. These works provide formal tools for modelling cognitive change, explicit beliefs, and epistemic attitudes. L-DINF extends this perspective toward cooperative agency, action feasibility, preferences, resource constraints, equivalence classes of actions, and group-level interaction. In recent work, this framework has been further enriched with trust-aware and probabilistic components. Trust is used as a regulatory condition for autonomous execution, delegation, and inhibition, while probability refines action selection by considering success probability, preference satisfaction, and resource consumption. The contribution of the present paper is not to introduce a new logical semantics, but to show how these L-DINF-style mechanisms can be operationalized in DALI2.

The paper is also related to the broad literature on trust in multi-agent systems, especially in distributed and security-sensitive domains [3,15]. Much of this literature focuses on trust evaluation, trust management, or application-level policies. By contrast, the approach adopted here treats trust as part of the practical decision layer: trust thresholds directly affect whether an agent may act autonomously, whether delegation is required, or whether an action must be blocked. Similarly, the probabilistic component is related to probabilistic epistemic logics and probabilistic approaches to BDI reasoning, but it is used here in a lightweight and modular way, as an instance of the L-DINF action selector rather than as a separate monolithic probabilistic agent logic.

Finally, our work is connected to ASP-based scheduling and to the DALI family of agent-oriented logic programming languages. ASP has been successfully applied to scheduling and allocation problems, including healthcare and workforce scheduling [2,7,14], and is well suited for generating globally coherent baseline schedules. In our architecture, such a baseline is treated as an offline input, while DALI2 provides the runtime epistemic adaptation layer. DALI2 [1], building on the original DALI framework [8,12,13], offers reactive rules, dynamic beliefs, communication, and event memory, making it a suitable operational substrate for implementing trust-aware and probability-aware L-DINF agents.

3 Background

3.1 L-DINF

L-DINF [11] is an epistemic logic composed of a static component, called L-INF, and a dynamic component. The static part models agents with explicit beliefs $B_i\phi$, background knowledge $K_i\phi$, intentions $intend_i(\varphi_A)$, feasibility $can\_do_i(\varphi_A)$, preferences $pref\_do_i(\varphi_A, d)$, equivalence classes $Cl(\varphi_A, \varphi'_A)$, and inter-group delegation $lend_G(i, H, \varphi_A)$. The dynamic part captures mental actions such as $+\phi$, $\downarrow(\phi, \psi)$, $\cap(\phi, \psi)$, $\dashv(\phi, \psi)$, and $\vdash(\phi, \psi)$, which model explicit belief formation, inference, conjunction, removal, and derivation from working memory. The present operational fragment uses $+\phi$ and $\dashv(\phi, \psi)$; the remaining dynamic operators ($\downarrow, \cap, \vdash$) concern higher-level epistemic processing that is not needed for the runtime adaptation chain addressed here.

The L-DINF model has a modular organization. The core epistemic model is separated from packages describing specific dimensions of agent behaviour. These packages include executability functions A and E, budgets B_1 and B_2, cost functions C_1 and C_2, a role-based enabling function H, a preference function P, an equivalence-class function Q, a selector function F, and a lending function L. This separation is important for the present paper because it allows each formal component to be mapped to a corresponding DALI2 representation without collapsing the whole logic into a monolithic program.

Trust-Aware Extension. Recent work has introduced a trust-aware layer for L-DINF. The extension adds a predicate $trust_K(i, \tau)$, where K is the evaluator, i is the evaluated agent, and τ belongs to a finite ordered scale of trust levels:

$$very\_low < low < medium < high < very\_high.$$

A possibly distinct policy authority fixes action-dependent thresholds for intention adoption, feasibility, lending, blocking, and autonomy. We denote them by τ_I, τ_C, τ_L, τ_B, and τ_A, respectively, with $\tau_B < \tau_A$.

The resulting decision policy partitions the trust scale into three outcomes. If the trust value reaches the autonomy threshold, the action is allowed autonomously. If the trust value is above the blocking threshold but below the autonomy threshold, the action is delegated. If the trust value is at or below the blocking threshold, the action is blocked. Thus, delegation is not treated as a mere implementation fallback, but as the formal outcome associated with an intermediate trust region.

Probabilistic Package. Recent work has also introduced a probabilistic package for L-DINF. A probabilistic extension of a model contains a package

$$\mathcal{P}_M^{prob} = (\mu, \rho, \theta),$$

where $\mu(i, w)$ is a probability measure over the epistemic alternatives of agent i at world w, $\rho(i, w, \varphi_A) \in [0, 1]$ is the probability that physical action φ_A succeeds when executed by agent i at world w, and $\theta(i, w)$ is an acceptance threshold.

At the epistemic level, the package can express probabilistic explicit beliefs of the form $B_i^{\geq q}\phi$, meaning that agent i believes ϕ with probability at least q. At the practical level, it refines executability by requiring not only ordinary executability, role-enabling, and affordability, but also a sufficient success probability. In the implementation presented below, we focus on the operational part of this package, namely probability-aware selection among feasible equivalent actions.

Given a decision policy $\pi = (\lambda_\rho, \lambda_P, \lambda_C)$, the probabilistic instance of the L-DINF selector ranks feasible equivalent actions by the following score:

$$score_i^{w,\pi}(\psi_A) = \lambda_\rho \cdot \rho(i, w, \psi_A) + \lambda_P \cdot \frac{P(i, w, \psi_A)}{P_{\max}} - \lambda_C \cdot \frac{sum(C_2(i, \psi_A, w))}{sum(B_2(i, w))},$$

where $P_{\max}$ is the upper bound of the preference scale (set to 1 when preferences are normalized to $[0, 1]$). The selected action is therefore explainable as equivalent to the intended one, feasible, affordable, and optimal according to an explicit policy combining reliability, preference, and resource preservation.

3.2 DALI2

DALI2 [1] is the evolution of the DALI [12,13] multi-agent system framework. It runs on SWI-Prolog with a process-per-agent architecture, uses Redis pub/sub for communication, and supports DALI-compatible syntax.

From the perspective of L-DINF, the relevant point is that DALI2 separates reactive rules, internal events, beliefs, communication, and memory. These elements provide natural operational counterparts for belief revision, event-triggered adaptation, inter-agent lending protocols, and explanation traces. The key constructs used in our implementation are the following:

- **Reactive rules** of the form `eventE(X) :> Body.`, which fire when an external event arrives.
- **Internal events**, which fire proactively when their conditions are satisfied.
- **Beliefs**, represented through `believes(Fact)`, `assert_belief`, and `retract_belief`.
- **Communication**, implemented by `send(Agent,Content)` over Redis.

- **Condition monitors**, used for level-triggered checks (e.g., instability warnings in the logger).
- **Helper predicates**, used for local utility definitions.
- **Past memory**, used to record events with timestamps and to query previous actions.

Agents are defined in a single `.pl` file and each directive `:- agent(name, [options]).` sets the context for subsequent rules.

4 Mapping L-DINF to DALI2

We now define the operational passage from L-DINF to DALI2. We denote the translation function by $\mathcal{T}_D$, where the subscript recalls the target language DALI2. The goal of $\mathcal{T}_D$ is not to encode the full possible-worlds semantics of L-DINF in DALI2, but to preserve the executable content of the constructs involved in runtime adaptation: belief update, intention management, feasibility checking, trust-sensitive decision making, lending, action execution, past-action recording, and probability-aware selection.

4.1 Operational Translation

Let $\mathcal{L}_{\mathsf{op}}$ be the operational fragment of L-DINF considered in this paper. It contains explicit beliefs $B_i\phi$, background knowledge $K_i\phi$, intentions $intend_i(\varphi_A)$, individual and group feasibility $can\_do_i(\varphi_A)$ and $can\_do_G(\varphi_A)$, preferences $pref\_do_i(\varphi_A, d)$, equivalence classes $Cl(\varphi_A, \psi_A)$, action execution $do_i(\varphi_A)$, past-action information $do_i^P(\varphi_A)$, trust assessments $trust_K(i, \tau)$, trust thresholds Θ, lending conditions $lend_G(i, H, \varphi_A)$, and the probabilistic selector F_π^{prob}.

An operational state is represented as a tuple

$$s = (\mathsf{Bel}, \mathsf{Int}, \mathsf{Avail}, \mathsf{Mem}, \mathsf{Pref}, \mathsf{Trust}, \Theta, \mathsf{Eq}, \mathsf{Prob}, \mathsf{Cost}, \mathsf{Past}),$$

where the components respectively store explicit beliefs, pending intentions, availability and feasibility-relevant facts, group membership, preferences, trust values, thresholds, action equivalence, success probabilities, costs, and completed actions.

The translation $\mathcal{T}_D$ maps the operational constructs of L-DINF into DALI2 beliefs, rules, messages, and trace events. The mapping is compositional: each construct has a local DALI2 counterpart, and the global adaptive behaviour emerges from event propagation, guarded rules, message exchange, and logging. Table 1 summarizes the main clauses of $\mathcal{T}_D$.

The transitions of $\mathcal{L}_{\mathsf{op}}$ are labelled by the observable runtime effects that the DALI2 implementation must preserve:

- $\mathsf{bel}^+(i, \phi)$ and $\mathsf{bel}^-(i, \phi)$ for belief assertion and removal;
- $\mathsf{int}^+(i, \varphi_A)$ and $\mathsf{int}^-(i, \varphi_A)$ for intention adoption and discharge;
- $\mathsf{loss}(i, \varphi_A)$ for the loss of feasibility of an intended or planned action;

Table 1. Operational mapping $\mathcal{T}_D$ from L-DINF constructs to DALI2 patterns.

L-DINF construct	DALI2 implementation pattern
$B_i(\phi)$	Dynamic belief represented by `believes(phi)`.
$K_i(\phi)$	Static predicates and background rules.
$intend_i(\varphi_A)$	Intention belief, e.g. `believes(intend(action))`.
$can\_do_i(\varphi_A)$	Guarded rule checking availability, role, and constraints.
$can\_do_G(\varphi_A)$	Manager-level query over group members.
$pref\_do_i(\varphi_A, d)$	Preference fact used in candidate ranking.
$do_i(\varphi_A)$	Execution event followed by completion recording.
$do_i^P(\varphi_A)$	Past-event memory or explicit completion fact.
$+\phi$	Belief assertion through `assert_belief(phi)`.
$\dashv(\phi, \psi)$	Belief removal through `retract_belief(psi)`.
$trust_K(i, \tau)$	Trust fact plus order-preserving numeric encoding.
Θ	Threshold facts for autonomy, blocking, and lending.
$lend_G(i, H, \varphi_A)$	Mediated lending protocol among managers, mediator, and lent agent.
$Cl(\varphi_A, \psi_A)$	Equivalence facts between actions.
F_π^{prob}	Candidate generation, score computation, and deterministic ranking.
Trace	Logger events recording decisions, lending, selection, and execution.

- $\mathsf{dec}(i, \varphi_A, o)$ for a trust-sensitive decision, where $o \in \{\mathsf{allow}, \mathsf{delegate}, \mathsf{block}\}$;
- $\mathsf{lend}(G, H, j, \varphi_A)$ for the authorized lending of an agent j from group H to group G for action φ_A;
- $\mathsf{exec}(i, \varphi_A)$ and $\mathsf{past}(i, \varphi_A)$ for action execution and past-action recording;
- $\mathsf{select}(i, \varphi_A, \psi_A)$ for the selection of an equivalent feasible action ψ_A for an intended action φ_A.

This labelling does not introduce a new semantics for L-DINF. It only identifies the part of the formal transition structure that is observable in the DALI2 execution trace.

The translation preserves a representation invariant. If an L-DINF operational state s is represented by a DALI2 configuration c, then every belief, intention, availability fact, group-membership fact, preference, trust value, threshold, equivalence relation, probability, cost, and past action occurring in s has its corresponding DALI2 representation in c. We write this invariant as $\mathcal{I}_D(s, c)$.

4.2 Trust, Lending, and Selection

The non-trivial clauses of $\mathcal{T}_D$ concern trust, lending, and probability-aware selection. Trust values are stored symbolically and compared numerically. The ordered scale $very\_low < low < medium < high < very\_high$ is encoded by an order-preserving function ν.

Given a trust value τ, a blocking threshold τ_B, and an autonomy threshold τ_A, the implemented decision policy has three outcomes: allow if $\nu(\tau) \geq \nu(\tau_A)$; $\mathsf{delegate}$ if $\nu(\tau_B) < \nu(\tau) < \nu(\tau_A)$; and block if $\nu(\tau) \leq \nu(\tau_B)$. Since ν preserves the ordering of the trust scale, the DALI2 comparison implements the same three-valued policy as the trust-aware L-DINF extension.

Lending is implemented as a mediated protocol. The mediator checks source-group membership, availability, role or capability enabling, and the lending threshold τ_L. If these conditions hold, the selected agent is temporarily allowed to act for the requesting group and is then returned to its original group after completion. Thus, lending is represented as an authorized group-sensitive transition rather than as unstructured message forwarding.

The probabilistic selector is implemented by generating equivalent feasible candidates, computing their scores according to the policy π, and selecting the maximal candidate. In the current implementation, success probability is used as a soft component of the score. A stricter variant can be obtained by adding a hard admissibility condition of the form $\rho(i, w, \psi_A) \geq \theta(i, w)$ before candidate ranking. Ties are resolved deterministically, first by maximal success probability, then by minimal cost, and finally by a fixed order on action names.

4.3 Operational Soundness

The following result should be read as an implementation-level correspondence property. It does not aim to provide a new semantic characterization of L-DINF, nor a completeness result for its full possible-worlds semantics. Rather, it states that the DALI2 program obtained by the translation preserves the observable runtime effects of the L-DINF constructs that are actually implemented in the adaptive scheduling prototype.

Theorem 1 (Operational soundness and trace correspondence for the implemented fragment). *Let S be a well-formed specification in the operational fragment $\mathcal{L} * \mathsf{op}$ considered in this paper, let s_0 be its initial operational state, and let P_D be the DALI2 program obtained from S by $\mathcal{T} * !D$. Assume that external events are delivered to the addressed agents, DALI2 rule execution is fair and serialized at the level of each agent, the probabilistic selector uses deterministic tie-breaking, and the logger records only events generated by translated rules or by logging rules attached to them.*

If S admits a finite operational transition sequence

$$s_0 \xrightarrow{\alpha_1} s_1 \xrightarrow{\alpha_2} \cdots \xrightarrow{\alpha_n} s_n,$$

where each α_k is one of the observable labels of $\mathcal{L}{*}\mathsf{op}$, namely belief update, intention update, feasibility loss, trust-sensitive decision, lending, execution, past-action recording, or probability-aware selection, then there exists a fair DALI2 execution of P_D whose explanation trace contains the corresponding translated sequence

$$\mathcal{T} * !D(\alpha_1), \mathcal{T} * !D(\alpha_2), \ldots, \mathcal{T} * !D(\alpha_n),$$

possibly interleaved with internal communication events required by the DALI2 implementation. Conversely, every event logged by P_D corresponds to one of the observable operational labels of $\mathcal{L}_{\mathsf{op}}$.

Proof. The proof proceeds by induction on the length of the operational transition sequence.

For the base case, the initial operational state s_0 is translated by $\mathcal{T} * !D$ into the initial DALI2 configuration c_0. In particular, beliefs, intentions, availability facts, group-membership facts, trust values, thresholds, preferences, equivalence relations, probability values, costs, and past-action facts occurring in s_0 are represented in c_0 by the corresponding DALI2 beliefs, predicates, rules, and initial facts. Hence the representation invariant $\mathcal{I} * D(s_0, c_0)$ holds.

For the inductive step, assume that $\mathcal{I} * D(s_k, c_k)$ holds after the first k translated steps, and suppose that $s_k \xrightarrow{\alpha * k+1} s_{k+1}$ is an operational transition of $\mathcal{L} * \mathsf{op}$. By construction of $\mathcal{T} * !D$, each possible label α_{k+1} has a corresponding executable mechanism in DALI2. Belief assertion and removal are implemented by assertion and retraction of DALI2 beliefs; intention adoption and discharge are represented by updates of intention facts; loss of feasibility is implemented by changes in availability or executability-related facts and by the propagation of disruption events; trust-sensitive decisions are implemented by order-preserving comparisons between trust values and policy thresholds; lending is implemented by the mediated protocol involving the requesting manager, the source manager, the mediator, and the lent agent; execution and past-action recording are implemented by completion events and memory facts; and probability-aware selection is implemented by candidate generation, policy-based score computation, and deterministic tie-breaking.

Therefore, whenever the operational transition α_{k+1} is enabled in s_k, the translated DALI2 program contains an enabled rule, event handler, or message-driven protocol step that produces the corresponding trace item $\mathcal{T} * !D(\alpha * k + 1)$ and updates the DALI2 configuration so as to represent s_{k+1}. Fairness and event delivery ensure that enabled translated rules and addressed events are eventually processed. Thus the representation invariant is restored for s_{k+1}, and the trace contains the translated counterpart of the operational transition. Repeating the argument for all transitions in the finite sequence proves the forward direction.

For the converse direction, the logger records only events produced by rules generated by $\mathcal{T} * !D$ or by logging rules directly attached to them. Since each such rule is associated by construction with one of the observable operational labels of $\mathcal{L} * \mathsf{op}$, every logged DALI2 event has a corresponding operational label in the implemented fragment.

This result is intentionally limited to the executable fragment $\mathcal{L}_{\mathsf{op}}$ considered in this paper. It establishes operational soundness and trace correspondence for the implemented runtime adaptation mechanisms, but it does not establish completeness with respect to the full possible-worlds semantics of L-DINF, nor does it claim to operationalize all mental-action operators of the original logic. The proof assumes serialized event processing per agent, which is consistent with the DALI2 execution model where each agent processes one reactive rule at a time. When multiple disruptions are injected concurrently, as in the benchmark scenarios discussed later, the resulting per-agent event sequences are still serial, and the theorem applies to each such sequence. Under these assumptions, the

DALI2 implementation preserves the observable runtime effects of the L-DINF constructs used for adaptive scheduling, namely belief revision, intention management, feasibility checking, trust-sensitive decision making, lending, execution, memory update, and probability-aware action selection.

5 Implementation

5.1 System Architecture

The implementation consists of nine DALI2 agents defined in a single file, running as separate OS processes communicating via Redis pub/sub, with SWI-Prolog as execution engine. Conceptually, the architecture has three layers: (1) an offline scheduling layer (ASP baseline pre-loaded as initial beliefs); (2) an epistemic adaptation layer (patient, doctor, manager, mediator agents); (3) an explanation layer (logger agent). Trust and probability act as decision filters inside layer (2). The same initial beliefs and disruption event always produce the same trace, ensuring reproducibility.

5.2 Agent Descriptions

Patient Agents. `alice` illustrates trust-aware disruption handling: a reactive rule `local_repairE` compares the proposed doctor's trust against τ_A and τ_B, producing the three-valued outcome `allow`/`delegate`/`block`. The lending threshold τ_L is checked separately by the mediator. `bob` illustrates probability-aware selection: rule `select_actionE` collects equivalent feasible candidates within budget, scores them using $\pi = (\lambda_\rho, \lambda_P, \lambda_C)$ from Sect. 3.1, and asserts the best action.[1]

Doctor Agents. `doc_jones` triggers the disruption; `doc_lee` is a local alternative (trust `medium`, below τ_A); `doc_smith` (`clinic_b`, trust `high`) participates in lending with temporary group transition.

Managers and Mediator. Two clinic managers implement group-level feasibility (rank local candidates by preference, send offers). The mediator implements the institutional lending protocol: on delegation request it queries the source manager, checks τ_L, coordinates temporary reassignment, and restores membership after completion.

Logger. Records all events as an explanation trace (type, source, data), providing the observable counterpart of L-DINF transitions.

6 Disruption Scenario Walkthrough

This section validates the mapping of Sect. 4 by showing that the DALI2 implementation realizes the expected L-DINF adaptation chain under a concrete disruption.

[1] https://github.com/lollix91/L-DINF-DALI2—annotated rule listings in README.

DALI2 Execution Model (Brief Overview). Each agent is a separate process whose behaviour is defined by *reactive rules* of the form `eventE(Args) :> Body.` When a message matching `event(Args)` arrives, the rule fires, executing goals left to right. Beliefs are dynamic facts (`assert_belief`/`retract_belief`); communication uses `send(Agent, Content)`. Annotated code examples are in the repository.

Initial State. The baseline assigns `alice` to `doc_jones` at slot t_1 in `clinic_a`:

$$B_{alice}(assigned\_doctor(doc\_jones)), \quad intend_{alice}(consultation(t_1)).$$

Additional beliefs encode group membership, trust assessments, preferences, and thresholds.

Step 1: Disruption. `doc_jones` becomes unavailable, retracting its feasibility fact for the consultation at t_1 and notifying `clinic_a_mgr`, which propagates the disruption to `alice`. The disruption first changes the explicit belief state and only then activates repair reasoning.

Step 2: Local Repair Attempt. `clinic_a_mgr` checks $can\_do_{clinic\_a}(consultation)$ and finds `doc_lee` (trust level `medium`, preference degree 5). Feasibility alone is insufficient: the trust-aware layer must determine admissibility.

Step 3: Trust Evaluation. `alice` evaluates the repair offer. Since $T(doc\_lee) = medium$, $\tau_A = high$, and $\tau_B = very\_low$, we have $\tau_B < T < \tau_A$, so the decision is `delegate`—the intermediate trust region where the candidate is neither trusted enough for autonomous execution nor untrusted enough for inhibition.

Step 4: Lending Protocol. `alice` sends a lending request to the mediator, which queries `clinic_b_mgr` and obtains `doc_smith` ($T = high$). Since $T(doc\_smith) \geq \tau_L = high$, lending is approved:

$$lend_{clinic\_a}(doc\_smith, clinic\_b, consultation(t_1)).$$

The threshold τ_L is checked independently of τ_A (they may differ in general).

Step 5: Execution and Completion. `doc_smith` temporarily joins `clinic_a`, performs the consultation, and returns. `alice` records:

$$do^P_{alice}(consultation\_with(doc\_smith, t_1))$$

and retracts the pending intention, closing the intention–execution–memory loop.

Explanation Trace. The logger records a structured trace where each entry maps to an L-DINF operational counterpart: belief loading, feasibility loss, group update, trust decision, lending request/approval/execution, past-action recording, group restoration, and probabilistic selection. The full trace output is available in the repository.

Probability-Aware Action Selection. In a separate step, bob triggers the selector with $\pi = (100, 10, 20)$ over three equivalent affordable actions (Table 2).

Table 2. Probabilistic selection: score $= \lambda_\rho \cdot \rho + \lambda_P \cdot \mathit{Pref} - \lambda_C \cdot \mathit{CostRatio}$.

Action	ρ	Pref.	Cost ratio	Score
`visit_standard`	0.90	0.80	0.417	**89.67**
`visit_home`	0.85	0.70	0.667	78.67
`visit_telemedicine`	0.75	0.60	0.167	77.67

Operational Coverage. The scenario exercises all main components of the mapping: beliefs and intentions, belief revision, group feasibility, the trust-sensitive three-valued policy, inter-group lending, execution with intention discharge, and probability-aware selection.

7 Quantitative Evaluation

7.1 Methodology

To assess behaviour at increasing scale, we executed a parameterized benchmark with five scenario configurations and three independent runs each. A Python generator produces DALI2 scenario files from a configuration specifying clinics, doctors per clinic, patients, disruptions, equivalent actions per patient, and trust parameters (Table 3). Each scenario uses the same agent types from Sect. 5, instantiated over larger groups. Trust levels, preferences, probabilities, and costs are drawn pseudo-randomly from realistic ranges with a fixed seed. Scenarios S1–S4 use a minimum trust of *low*, exercising local repair and inter-group lending. Scenario S5 introduces structural diversity: more clinics with fewer doctors per clinic, a raised blocking threshold ($\tau_B = \mathit{low}$), and the possibility of *very_low* trust values, so that the system must rely almost entirely on the mediated lending protocol when local candidates fail the trust check. For each configuration, the benchmark runner starts a fresh DALI2 server, injects disruptions via the HTTP API, waits for repair chains to settle, triggers probabilistic selection for every patient, and collects results. Metrics are extracted from deduplicated TRACE lines. Each configuration is run three times; Table 4 reports averages. Patient-perceived disruptions may exceed injected ones because each doctor unavailability is propagated to all assigned patients.

7.2 Discussion of Results

Decision Patterns. In S1, the single injected disruption propagates to both patients (2 patient-perceived disruptions) but no repair or lending is triggered in the measurement window, confirming that the system correctly propagates unavailability events even when local candidates remain available. As

Table 3. Scenario configurations used in the benchmark.

Scenario	Clinics	Docs/cl.	Patients	Agents	Disr.	Eq. Act.	τ_B
S1 (small)	2	2	2	10	1	3	1 (v.low)
S2 (medium)	3	3	6	20	3	4	1 (v.low)
S3 (large)	3	4	8	25	5	5	1 (v.low)
S4 (xlarge)	4	3	10	28	8	6	1 (v.low)
S5 (diverse)	5	2	12	29	6	4	2 (low)

Table 4. Quantitative results (averages over 3 runs).

Scen.	Pat. Disr.	Repairs	Lendings	Repair (s)	Lend. %	Sel. (ms)
S1	2	0	0	—	0	7.3
S2	12	3	4	15.6	33	5.8
S3	30	7	18	18.3	60	7.2
S4	38	18	34	22.9	89	9.5
S5	22	3	21	11.7	97	4.1

disruption density grows, *lending* dominates: in S4, 34 lendings are triggered across 38 patient-perceived disruptions (89%), because locally trusted candidates become exhausted after cascading unavailability. Patient-perceived disruptions exceed injected ones in all scenarios due to propagation to all assigned patients; in S4, 8 injected disruptions produce 38 patient-level events. The lending rate (Lend. %, computed as lendings over patient-perceived disruptions) grows monotonically from S1 to S5: 0%, 33%, 60%, 89%, 97%.

S5 and Structural Diversity. Scenario S5 is structurally different: it uses five clinics with only two doctors per clinic, raises the blocking threshold to $\tau_B =$ *low* (numeric value 2), and allows *very_low* trust values. This configuration produces very few local repairs (3 on average) but 21 lendings, confirming that when local candidates have insufficient trust, the system relies on inter-group delegation. The lending rate of 97% demonstrates that the mediated lending protocol handles the vast majority of disruptions. The low number of repairs relative to lendings indicates that most local candidates fail the trust check, causing the patient to escalate to lending rather than accepting a local repair.

Latency and Overhead. Repair latency grows from 0 s (S1, no repair) to ~23 s (S4), driven by longer message chains and the number of concurrent disruptions; S5 (11.7 s) shows lower latency than S3–S4 despite having more agents, because many decisions are resolved quickly through direct escalation to lending. The probabilistic selector adds only 4–10 ms per selection, confirming negligible overhead. Patient-perceived disruptions and lending counts were stable across runs; repair counts and latency showed minor variation due to message ordering and OS scheduling. Scenario files, scripts, and raw logs are in the public repository.

8 Discussion

The implementation shows that the main operational components of L-DINF can be represented in DALI2 while preserving a declarative and traceable style: explicit beliefs become dynamic facts, group feasibility is implemented through manager queries, lending is a mediated protocol, and probability-aware selection uses candidate generation with score-based ranking. The quantitative evaluation confirms that these mechanisms remain effective and reproducible at increasing scale.

Three design choices are relevant. First, trust levels are stored symbolically but compared numerically, preserving the ordered scale while keeping the three-valued policy executable. Second, probability contributes as a soft component of the selection score; a stricter variant could add a hard reliability threshold. Third, the ASP schedule is an offline input, sufficient to validate the runtime adaptation layer but not yet completing the full hybrid loop. The current prototype assumes stable trust values, probabilities, and thresholds during each run. Other disruption types (resource loss, patient cancellation, conflicting priorities) would require additional event rules but not a different mapping principle.

9 Conclusion and Future Work

We presented an executable DALI2 implementation of a substantial operational fragment of L-DINF, enriched with trust-aware decision making, mediated inter-group lending, and probability-aware action selection. The healthcare scheduling case study shows how a runtime disruption can trigger belief revision, local repair, trust-sensitive delegation, lending, execution, and explanation tracing. A quantitative evaluation on five parameterized scenarios with up to 29 agents and 8 simultaneous disruptions confirmed that the system scales predictably: lending rates grow from 0% to 97% as disruption density and trust constraints increase, repair latency scales with scenario complexity (up to 23 s for S4 with 38 patient-level disruptions), and probabilistic selection overhead remains negligible (4–10 ms). Scenario S5, with a raised blocking threshold and very-low trust values, demonstrates that the mediated lending protocol handles nearly all disruptions when local candidates lack sufficient trust. The implementation provides an operational validation of recent trust-aware and probabilistic developments of L-DINF, showing how their main decision mechanisms can be represented through DALI2 beliefs, reactive rules, message passing, and execution traces.

Future work will address the implementation of mental-action budgets, live integration with an ASP solver for global re-optimization, dynamic probability updates driven by observation and learning, larger empirical evaluation under replayable disruption streams, and an explicit executable tie-breaking policy for the probabilistic selector.

The implementation is publicly available at https://github.com/lollix91/L-DINF-DALI2.

Acknowledgments. This work was partially supported by the Italian Ministry of University and Research (MUR).

Disclosure of Interests. The authors have no competing interests to declare that are relevant to the content of this article.

References

1. AAAI-DISIM-UnivAQ: AAAI-DISIM-UnivAQ/DALI2. Zenodo (2026). https://doi.org/10.5281/zenodo.19858727
2. Alviano, M., Dodaro, C., Maratea, M.: Nurse (re)scheduling via answer set programming. Intelligenza Artificiale **12**, 109–124 (2019)
3. Amaral, G., Sales, T.P., Guizzardi, G., Porello, D.: Towards a reference ontology of trust. In: Panetto, H., Debruyne, C., Hepp, M., Lewis, D., Ardagna, C.A., Meersman, R. (eds.) OTM 2019. LNCS, vol. 11877, pp. 3–21. Springer, Cham (2019). https://doi.org/10.1007/978-3-030-33246-4_1
4. Balbiani, P., Fernández-Duque, D., Lorini, E.: A logical theory of belief dynamics for resource-bounded agents. In: AAMAS 2016, pp. 644–652. ACM (2016)
5. Balbiani, P., Fernández-Duque, D., Lorini, E.: The dynamics of epistemic attitudes in resource-bounded agents. Stud. Logica. **107**(3), 457–488 (2019)
6. Bordini, R.H., Hübner, J.F.: BDI agent programming in agentspeak using *Jason*. In: Toni, F., Torroni, P. (eds.) CLIMA 2005. LNCS (LNAI), vol. 3900, pp. 143–164. Springer, Heidelberg (2006). https://doi.org/10.1007/11750734_9
7. Cappanera, P., Gavanelli, M., Nonato, M., Roma, M.: Logic-based Benders decomposition in ASP for chronic outpatients scheduling. TPLP **23**, 848–864 (2023)
8. Costantini, S., De Gasperis, G., Pitoni, V., Salutari, A.: DALI: a multi agent system framework for the web, cognitive robotic and complex event processing. In: CILC 2017. CEUR Workshop Proceedings, vol. 1949, pp. 286–300 (2017)
9. Costantini, S., Formisano, A., Pitoni, V.: An epistemic logic for multi-agent systems with budget and costs. In: Faber, W., Friedrich, G., Gebser, M., Morak, M. (eds.) JELIA 2021. LNCS (LNAI), vol. 12678, pp. 101–115. Springer, Cham (2021). https://doi.org/10.1007/978-3-030-75775-5_8
10. Costantini, S., Formisano, A., Pitoni, V.: Cooperation among groups of agents in the epistemic logic L-DINF. In: RuleML+RR 2022. LNCS, vol. 13752, pp. 280–295. Springer (2022)
11. Costantini, S., Formisano, A., Pitoni, V.: An epistemic logic for formalizing group dynamics of agents. Interact. Stud. **23**, 391–426 (2023). https://doi.org/10.1075/is.22019.cos
12. Costantini, S., Tocchio, A.: A logic programming language for multi-agent systems. In: Flesca, S., Greco, S., Ianni, G., Leone, N. (eds.) JELIA 2002. LNCS (LNAI), vol. 2424, pp. 1–13. Springer, Heidelberg (2002). https://doi.org/10.1007/3-540-45757-7_1
13. Costantini, S., Tocchio, A.: The DALI logic programming agent-oriented language. In: Alferes, J.J., Leite, J. (eds.) JELIA 2004. LNCS (LNAI), vol. 3229, pp. 685–688. Springer, Heidelberg (2004). https://doi.org/10.1007/978-3-540-30227-8_57

14. Dodaro, C., Galatà, G., Maratea, M., Porro, I.: Operating room scheduling via answer set programming. J. Log. Comput. **34**, 1556–1579 (2024)
15. Li, W., Meng, W., Kwok, L.F.: Surveying trust-based collaborative intrusion detection: State-of-the-art, challenges and future directions. IEEE Commun. Surv. Tutor. **24**, 280–305 (2021)
16. Lifschitz, V.: Answer Set Programming. Springer (2019). https://doi.org/10.1007/978-3-030-24658-7
17. Lorini, E.: Reasoning about cognitive attitudes in a qualitative setting. In: JELIA 2019, pp. 726–743 (2019)

Multi-shot Solving and Domain Heuristics for CASP-Based Traffic Signal Optimisation

Francesco Doria[1], Gabriele Ramagnano[2,3], Alice Tarzariol[2(✉)], Marco Maratea[1], and Mauro Vallati[4]

[1] DeMaCS, University of Calabria, Arcavacata, Italy
[2] AICS, University of Klagenfurt, Klagenfurt, Austria
alice.tarzariol@aau.at
[3] DMIF, University of Udine, Udine, Italy
[4] School of Computing and Engineering, University of Huddersfield, Huddersfield, UK

Abstract. Traffic signal optimisation is a key approach to urban traffic control and aims to mitigate congestion in urban areas by adjusting the green-light durations of traffic signals. While prior work has shown the viability of Constraint Answer Set Programming (CASP) for this task, specifically with the system *clingcon*, limitations remain in terms of scalability and solution quality. In this paper, we extend the existing CASP-based approach by incorporating multi-shot solving to enable incremental reasoning, together with two domain-specific heuristics designed to guide the search more effectively towards high-quality solutions. We evaluate our approach on real-world benchmark instances, including more challenging settings that were not addressed in previous work. Overall, our enhancements represent a substantial advancement over the previous *clingcon* encoding, both in terms of coverage and solution quality, and compares favourably to PDDL+ methods.

Keywords: Applications · Constraint Answer Set Programming · Urban Traffic Control

1 Introduction

Traffic signal optimisation plays a key role in urban traffic control, where the objective is to regulate traffic flows to reduce congestion and improve overall network efficiency [31]. The problem is challenging, as it involves dynamic, interdependent processes subject to both physical constraints (e.g., link capacities, stage durations) and operational requirements imposed by existing traffic control infrastructure. In this context, developing optimisation techniques that are both effective and deployable remains a key research challenge.

Recent work has explored the use of Constraint Answer Set Programming (CASP) as a viable framework for traffic signal optimisation. The approach

W. Faber et al. (Eds.): LPNMR 2026, LNAI 16952, pp. 199–214, 2027.
https://doi.org/10.1007/978-3-032-38320-4_13

introduced by Tarzariol et al. [28] demonstrated that CASP, and specifically the *clingcon* system, can model traffic dynamics while capturing constraints and optimisation objectives within a unified formalism. Despite its expressiveness, however, this approach exhibits limitations in scalability when addressing longer planning horizons and larger instances, as well as variability in solution quality when the search space becomes increasingly complex. At the same time, the general-purpose heuristics embedded in ASP solvers can be insufficient to effectively guide the search [9].

In this paper, we address these challenges by extending the existing CASP-based model along two complementary directions. First, we introduce a multi-shot solving strategy, exploiting the incremental solving capabilities of *clingo* to decompose the optimisation horizon into smaller windows. Second, we design two domain-specific heuristics, one of which inspired by a domain heuristic proposed for the PDDL+-based solution to the problem [10], that up to now constitutes the state-of-the-art solution. We also present a revised encoding which further strengthens performance. We empirically demonstrate the capabilities of the introduced approaches on real-world instances derived from historical data collected from a major traffic corridor in the United Kingdom. The experimental results show that multi-shot solving significantly improves coverage on challenging instances, while the proposed heuristics lead to substantial gains in terms of solution quality. Remarkably, our best option compares favourably to the state-of-the-art PDDL+ method.

2 Answer Set Programming and Its Extensions

Answer Set Programming (ASP) [2,6,15,22] is a declarative programming paradigm that applies non-monotonic reasoning and relies on the stable model semantics. In the following, we describe a fragment of the ASP syntax and semantics, and refer to [7] for more details. An ASP program P is a set of *rules* r of the form: `h:- b`$_1$`,...,b`$_n$`.`, where `h` is an atom and each `b`$_i$, for $1 \leq i \leq n$, is a literal, a comparison, or an aggregate. An *atom* is an expression of the form `p(t`$_1$`,...,t`$_m$`)`, where `p` is a predicate and `t`$_i$, for $1 \leq i \leq m$, are terms. A *literal* `c` is either an atom `a`$_i$ or its negation `not a`$_i$. A comparison is of the form `t`$_1 \circ$ `t`$_2$, where `t`$_1$ and `t`$_2$ are terms and $\circ \in$ {`<=`, `<`, `=`, `>`, `>=`}. An aggregate is of the form `t=#count{t`$_1$`:c`$_1$`,···, t`$_n$`:c`$_n$`}` or `t=`f`{v`$_1$`,t`$_1$`:c`$_1$`,··· , v`$_n$`,t`$_n$`:c`$_n$`}` where f is `#max` or `#sum`, `t` and each `v`$_i$ are integers, `t`$_i$ are terms and `c`$_i$ are literals, for $1 \leq i \leq n$. A rule r is called a *fact* when $n = 0$, and a *constraint* if `h` is not present. The left side of the symbol `:-` in a rule is called *head*, while the right side is called *body*. The semantics of a program P is given in terms of the answer sets of its *ground instantiation* P_{grd}, computed by replacing each (first-order) rule $r \in P$ with ground rules obtained by substituting the variables in r by constants occurring in P and evaluating arithmetical expressions. An *answer-set* is a collection of (true) ground atoms such that all rules of P_{grd} are satisfied and allow for deriving each of the atoms in the head of some rule whose body is satisfied.

Constraint Answer Set Programming (CASP). Mellarkod et al. [21] integrate ASP and Constraint Programming. Among its various dialects, we focus in this paper on the one of *clingcon* [1], which is the one used by Tarzariol et al. [28]. It extends the ASP system *clingo* by introducing theory atoms in its language and augmenting the solver with propagators for linear constraints, allowing it to deal with integer domains of considerable size. Among its language extensions, *clingcon* defines theory atoms as expressions such as $\texttt{\&sum\{t}_1\texttt{;t}_2\texttt{;...;t}_n\texttt{\}=t}_0$, where each $\texttt{t}_i$ for $\texttt{i} \in [\texttt{0..n}]$ is a constraint variable or an integer. After grounding, these expressions become linear constraint atoms requiring $\sum_{i\in[1..n]}\texttt{t}_i = \texttt{t}_0$.

Multi-shot Solving. allows for dynamically grounding and solving logic programs [13]. To do so, *clingo* enhances the ASP language with the directive `#program` that allows to structure the ASP program into subprograms, making the solving process modular. Each subprogram has a name and an optional list of parameters, and it gathers all the rules up to the next `#program` directive. A special subprogram *base* collects all the rules not preceded by any `#program` directive. The `#external` directives are used within sub programs to set external atoms to some truth value via the *clingo* API. Lastly, an imperative programming interface allows a continuous assembly of the program and gives control over the grounding and solving functions.

Heuristics allows for driving the solving process of an ASP program, leaving unchanged its answer sets [14]. In this work, we tested domain-specific heuristics activated with the option `--heuristic=Domain`, specified in the encoding by directives of the form: `#heuristic a. [w,m]`, where `a` is a (non-theory) atom, `w` is an integer, and `m` can be either `true` or `false`. The value of `m` defines the first truth assignment to test for `a`, while `w` defines in which order the solver follows for propagating it, deciding first upon atoms of the highest level. Note that, to the best of our knowledge, it is not possible to define heuristics that effects the constraint variables.

3 Problem Description and CASP Baseline

In this section, we describe the elements and constraints of the traffic signal optimisation problem and briefly recap the idea of the modelling introduced in [28]. The considered formalism relies on a mesoscopic representation of traffic [12], in which the number of vehicles in road links are considered rather than representing individual vehicles.

A road network consists of a graph whose nodes are *junctions* and whose arcs are road *links*. The number of vehicles in road link defines its *occupancy*, which ranges from zero to the maximal *capacity* of the link. Note that, as a result of the mesoscopic representation, the occupancy of a link is approximated and thus represented with a floating-point number with five significant digits (which are normalised to integer for the ASP representation). Each junction contains traffic signals defining whether vehicles on certain incoming roads are allowed to proceed through to other outgoing ones. The traffic signals in a junction are abstracted as *stages*, each representing a set of simultaneous traffic movements. A *cycle* is a complete sequence of all stages, defining their order. Moreover, stages are always interleaved by *intergreen* times, i.e., times where no traffic movement occurs in the junction. This occurs when all the junction's traffic signals are on red to allow pedestrians to cross and vehicles still transiting in the junction to leave the area before the next stage begins. Constraints on the problem include the legal and practical restrictions on the minimum and maximum duration of each stage, and the minimum and maximum length of the overall traffic signal cycle. The order of stages in a cycle cannot be modified.

Traffic signal optimisation aims to minimise the average traffic delay for a region of interest. In particular, it can focus on specific scenarios, such as alleviating the extreme delays of traffic exiting major city events and passing through the region, or dealing with accidents or unusual events. To simulate historical conditions and test potential strategies for the specific scenarios, we can extract sensor data and operational information derived from SCOOT [27], a traffic reactive control mechanism operating in the focus areas. Thus, for a given scenario, we represent with the *turnrate* the average traffic flows between links in number of PCU[1] per second. More precisely, each turnrate represents the number of vehicles flowing through a particular junction in the considered scenario, when the corresponding traffic signal stage is green. This allows for the use of external tools, e.g., ASP and PDDL+ solvers, to generate and evaluate signal control strategies that can be deployed in the region. However, to allow deployment on heritage traffic control infrastructure [18], the traffic signal optimisation problem needs to be redefined by considering the following additional constraints: (i) the length of the stages cannot be modified arbitrarily; instead, for each junction, the *configuration* of cycles (i.e., the specification of the length of every stage in the cycle) can only be selected from a predefined set, and (ii) the cycles considered for the junctions in the controlled region should have approximately the same duration – to avoid synchronisation issues and ensure that green waves are preserved. Lastly, to minimise the average traffic delay, the problem formalisation uses the concept of *counter* to measure the number of vehicles that navigated through the link over a considered period of time, and was introduced in [23] to support the heuristic reasoning of the planning engine. Increasing the number of vehicles that navigate the region in a given period of time is a proxy for minimising average delay, as it aims at increasing the throughput of the network, hence reducing time wasted queuing.

3.1 Traffic Signal Optimisation with Clingcon

We now briefly describe the idea of the model introduced by Tarzariol et al. [28], focusing on describing only the atoms used in the heuristics proposed in our paper, while we refer to the original paper for more details on the encoding. A problem instance introduces a set of atoms describing the network elements and

[1] PCU stands for "passenger car units", a standard unit for measuring traffic flows.

considered scenario, while the encoding can be divided in two main components: the former containing only ASP atoms, while the latter including also the language extensions of *clingcon*. More precisely, the former selects for each junction a configuration at the end of its cycle, while the latter deduces deterministically at each time point the active stage for each junction and the occupancy (and counter) of each link. We deal with integer domains of considerable size since the numbers have a precision of five decimal digits and are normalised in ASP by multiplying each number by 10^5. Differently from the PDDL+ models [18], where the heuristics of the planner are used to return a promising sequence of configurations to reach a target value for every counter, with ASP we can define an optimisation statement aiming to maximise the values of counters for a set of target links within a given horizon expressed in seconds, defined by a constant `horizon`.

Problem Instance. Among the atoms defined in each problem instance we have: `available_conf(J,C)`, defining the available configurations `C` for a junction `J`; `phase_limit(P,C,D)` defining for each configuration `C` the duration `D` of the phase `P` (where `P` is either a stage or an intergreen); while, the atoms `turnrate(S,L1,L2,U)` contain the PCU `U` that transits from a link `L1` to link `L2` during the stage `S` per unit of time (i.e., second). The goal links for which we aim to maximise their *counters*, are specified in the instance by atoms of the form `counter(0,L,C)` (where `L` is a link and `C` is the initial value of the counter).

ASP Encoding. Among the ASP atoms defined in the encoding, `time(T)` represents the time point considered in the model, defined for each instant `T` ranging from `1` to the constant `horizon`. The solver searches for the configuration `A` that is assigned at the end of the `C`-th cycle (occurring a time `T`) for the junction `J`, expressed through the atom `configuration(J,C,T,A)`. To identify the moments when a change of configuration occurred, we introduced the auxiliary predicate `change/4` projecting a subset of the atoms of `configuration/4`, where the configuration selected at the end of a cycle differs from the one selected at the end of the previous cycle. These auxiliary atoms were used to impose restrictions on the configuration-change policy, as defined by Kouaiti et al. [18].

Theory Atoms and Optimization Statement. Lastly, the two constraint variables appearing in the theory atoms of *clingcon* are `occupancy(T,L)` describing the occupancy of link `L` at time `T`, and `counter(T,L)`, containing the counter value for a set of goal links. The considered encoding requires maximising the value of each variable `counter(horizon,L)`. Optionally, a constraint can be activated to produce only solutions improving a given threshold.

4 Approach

In the following, we describe the two main techniques applied to the model of Tarzariol et al. [28], i.e., multi-shot and domain-heuristics.

4.1 Multi-shot

We implemented a multi-shot solving approach using the *clingo* API, decomposing the horizon into a sequence of fixed time windows and solving each incrementally, where each horizon is defined with `t`. This addresses cases where solving the problem in a single shot becomes too expensive for larger values of `horizon`, and allows us to investigate whether conflicts learned in earlier windows propagate and benefit solving in later ones.

We converted the original *clingcon* encoding [28] into a multi-shot version by replacing the grounding over `time(1..horizon)` with a modular structure defining: `#program base`, `#program step(t)`, and `#program check(t)` for each time window `t`. We moved all time-independent rules, including those defining the initial state, into the `base` part, and all time-dependent rules into the `step(t)` part. We also added the `#external` atom `fixed_configuration(J,C,T,A)` to allow the control script to fix configuration decisions. When set to true, a rule derives `configuration(J,C,T,A)` forcing junction `J` to use configuration `A` at cycle `C` and time `T`. Finally, we moved the goal constraints and optimisation into the `check(t)` part. The control script advances through the horizon by grounding and solving `step(t)` at each time step, and evaluating `check(t)` only at the end of each window. For each time window, it selects the model with the highest objective value and fixes its configuration decisions via `fixed_configuration/4`. The final solution contains the configurations changes accumulated over all windows.

4.2 Domain Heuristics

We design two domain heuristics, bearing in mind lessons learnt from deployable approaches in terms of robustness of the generated solutions [18]. In particular, our heuristics are aiming at minimising the number of times configurations are changed, to reduce the overhead on the existing traffic control infrastructure.

h^{phase}. The characteristic of h^{phase} is guiding the selection of configurations that allocate the most green time to stages serving goal links. To do so, we derive for each stage the unique configuration that maximises its green time, and if that stage serves a goal link, we identify the configuration as promising. The heuristic then biases the solver towards those promising configurations. More precisely, the heuristic and auxiliary predicates are defined in Listing 1. The predicate `max_phase_limit(S,M)` (Line 1) computes for each stage `S` the maximum green time `M` across all the available configurations involving `S` (note that the stage `S` uniquely identify its junction, and by specifying that `S` is a stage, we ignore the *intergreen*, which are fixed among the available configurations). The atoms of the form `max_stage(C,S)` (Line 4) identifies all configurations `C` that achieve this maximum, while `unique_max_conf(C, S)` (Line 7) retains only those where this maximum is achieved by exactly one configuration[2]. The atoms `stage_fill(S,L)` and `stage_empty(S,L)` (Lines 10–11) identify whether the stage

[2] We focused on configurations identified by `unique_max_conf/2` as preliminary experiments suggest that it yields better results than considering those in `max_stage/2`.

`S` fills or drains a link `L`, respectively. From these, `max_conf_empty(C,L)` (Line 13) identifies, for each goal link `L` the unique configuration that maximises the phase limit of the stage responsible for draining it, while `max_conf_fill(C,L)` (Line 15) does the same for the stage responsible for filling it. These are then joined with `configuration(J,C,_,A)` to associate each selected configuration `A` with its junction `J` and cycle `C` via `promising_conf_empty(J,C,A)` (Line 18) and `promising_conf_fill(J,C,A)` (Line 20). The three `#heuristic` directives (Lines 23–25) encode a two-level preference. At lower priority, `promising_conf_empty/3` and `promising_conf_fill/3` receive a bias towards true, leading the solver towards configurations that maximise the phase limit of stages affecting goal links. At higher priority, any `change/4` atom is biased towards false, discouraging configuration changes.

```
1  max_phase_limit(stage(J,N),M) :-  stage(J,N),
2      M=#max{L : phase_limit(stage(J,N),_,L)}.
3
4  max_stage(C,stage(J,N)) :- available_conf(_,C),
5      phase_limit(stage(J,N),C,L),
6      max_phase_limit(stage(J,N),L).
7  unique_max_conf(C,stage(J,N)) :- max_stage(C,stage(J,N)),
8      #count{C1 : max_stage(C1,stage(J,N))}=1.
9
10 stage_fill(stage(J,N), L) :- turnrate(stage(J,N),_,L,_).
11 stage_empty(stage(J,N), L) :- turnrate(stage(J,N),L,_,_).
12
13 max_conf_empty(C,L) :- counter(0,L,_),
14     stage_empty(S,L), unique_max_conf(C,S).
15 max_conf_fill(C,L) :- counter(0,L,_),
16     stage_fill(S,L), unique_max_conf(C,S).
17
18 promising_conf_empty(J,C,A) :- configuration(J,C,_,A),
19     max_conf_empty(A,L).
20 promising_conf_fill(J,C,A) :- configuration(J,C,_,A),
21     max_conf_fill(A,L).
22
23 #heuristic change(J,C,T,A). [3, false]
24 #heuristic promising_conf_empty(J,C,A). [1, true]
25 #heuristic promising_conf_fill(J,C,A). [1, true]
```

Listing 1. Domain-heuristic h^{phase}.

$\boldsymbol{h^{link}}$**.** Inspired by the flow estimation approach of the heuristic *cafe* [10], h^{link} guides the selection of configurations that maximise vehicle throughput at goal links, prioritising those that do so across the greatest number of links. To do so, we estimate for each goal link the combined inflow and outflow under every pair of configurations assignable to the junctions managing that link, and identify the pairs that maximise this combined flow. We then rank configurations by how many of these pairs they appear in, and the heuristic biases the solver towards those with the highest count. It is worth noting that *cafe* is value-driven (wrt the sum of the *counters*), while h^{link} guides the search with preference on the truth assignments. More precisely, the heuristic and auxiliary predicates are defined in Listing 2. Predicates `total_enter(L,A,S)` and `total_exit(L,A,S)` (Lines 1–11) compute for every goal link `L` the estimated inflow and outflow during a cycle under configuration `A`. From these, `enter_exit_pairs (L,A1,A2,S)` (Line 13) combines every distinct pair of configurations `A1` and `A2`, where `A1` is assigned to the junction managing inflow to `L` and `A2` to the junction managing outflow from it, summing their flow estimates into `S`. The atoms `max_pair_sum(L,S)` (Line 16) derive the maximum such sum for each link `L`, and `best_enter_exit_pair(L,A1,A2,S)` (Line 19) retains only configurations pairs achieving this value. The atoms `appears_in_pair(A, L)` (Lines 22–23) identify every configuration `A` appearing in a best pair for link `L`, and `pair_link_count(A,N)` (Line 25) counts the number of links for which configuration `A` belongs to a best pair. Subsequently, `best_enter_count(L,N)` (Line 28) and `best_exit_count(L,N)` (Line 32) derive, for each link `L`, the highest such count among entry and exit configurations, respectively. Lastly, `promising_enter(L,A)` (Line 36) and `promising_exit(L,A)` (Line 39) select configurations that belong to a best pair for link `L` and appear in best pairs for the greatest number of links. These are then joined with `configuration(J,C,_,A)` to associate each selected configuration `A` with its junction `J` and cycle `C` via `promising_conf(J,C,A)` (Line 45). The two `#heuristic` directives (Lines 48–49) encode a two-level preference. At lower priority, `promising_conf/3` receives a bias towards true, expressing preference for configurations that maximise vehicle throughput across the most goal links. At higher priority, any `change/4` atom is biased towards false, discouraging configuration changes.

```
1  total_enter(L, A, S) :- counter(0, L, _),
2      available_conf(J, A), turnrate(stage(J,_), _, L, _),
3      S = #sum{ R*D, stage(J,N) :
4          turnrate(stage(J,N), _, L, R),
5          phase_limit(stage(J,N), A, D)}.
6
7  total_exit(L, A, S) :- counter(0, L, _),
8      available_conf(J, A), turnrate(stage(J,_), L, _, _),
9      S = #sum{ R*D, stage(J,N) :
10     turnrate(stage(J,N), L, _, R),
11     phase_limit(stage(J,N), A, D)}.
12
13 enter_exit_pairs(L, A1, A2, S) :- total_enter(L, A1, Ein),
14     total_exit(L, A2, Eout), S = Ein + Eout, A1!=A2.
15
16 max_pair_sum(L, S) :- counter(0,L,_),
17     S = #max { V,A1,A2 : enter_exit_pairs(L, A1, A2, V) }.
18
19 best_enter_exit_pair(L, A1, A2, S) :- max_pair_sum(L, S),
20     enter_exit_pairs(L, A1, A2, S).
21
22 appears_in_pair(A, L) :- best_enter_exit_pair(L, A, _, _).
```

```
appears_in_pair(A, L) :- best_enter_exit_pair(L, _, A, _).

pair_link_count(A, N) :- appears_in_pair(A, _),
    N = #count { L : appears_in_pair(A, L) }.

best_enter_count(L, N) :- best_enter_exit_pair(L, _, _, _),
    N = #max { C, A : best_enter_exit_pair(L, A, _, _),
    pair_link_count(A, C) }.

best_exit_count(L, N) :-  best_enter_exit_pair(L, _, _, _),
    N = #max { C, A : best_enter_exit_pair(L, _, A, _),
    pair_link_count(A, C) }.

promising_enter(L, A) :- best_enter_exit_pair(L, A, _, _),
    pair_link_count(A, N), best_enter_count(L, N).

promising_exit(L, A) :- best_enter_exit_pair(L, _, A, _),
    pair_link_count(A, N), best_exit_count(L, N).

promising_conf(J, C, A) :- configuration(J, C, _, A),
    promising_enter(_, A).

promising_conf(J, C, A) :- configuration(J, C, _, A),
    promising_exit(_, A).

#heuristic change(J,C,T,A). [3, false]
#heuristic promising_conf(J, C, A). [1, true]
```

Listing 2. Domain-heuristic h^{link}.

5 Experiments

Similarly to the work of Kouaiti et al. [18] and Tarzariol et al. [28], to test our work we use a benchmark of real-world instances derived from historical data. Specifically, we focused on a major 1.3 kilometres long corridor in the Kirklees council area within West Yorkshire, United Kingdom. The corridor allows traffic from the Huddersfield ring road to reach the M62 and M1 highways, and vice versa. Further, it also serves people joining or leaving events hosted at the nearby John Smith's Stadium. The corridor includes 6 junctions and 34 road links. Following the structure detailed in our previous work [28], we considered different configurations and number of goal links, combined in 7 scenarios in order to provide variability in terms of traffic volumes, directions, and conditions. We set the constant `horizon` to different values, starting from 600 up to 900 s, with a step size of 60 (i.e., from 10 min to 15 with a step size of one minute). Moreover, we extended the original benchmark, consisting of 70 instances, by 35 more challenging ones, which cover the same scenarios but consider a configuration set generating more decision points with respect to the others (within the same time horizon). We obtained this by considering shorter cycles, which then cause more decision points defining the active configurations.

The aim of our experiments is to assess the potential for improving the performance of the original *clingcon* encoding, both in terms of the number of instances for which a solution is found (without considering the proof of optimality) and in terms of the actual improvement in the quality of the solutions found (measured by the sum of the counters defined by the goal links). To evaluate these parameters, we compared the results obtained with the modifications proposed in this paper against the original *clingcon* encoding. Moreover, to assess the significance of the results obtained, we compared our setting against a solution produced by the PDDL+ model [18] used in our previous work, considering also the recent use of domain-heuristics [10].

We run our experiments on an AMD EPYC 9354 (4) @ 3.2 GHz machine with 32 GB of memory under Linux (Ubuntu 22.04.5 LTS), using the system *clingcon* (v5.2.1) with the *libclingo* v5.8.0. Furthermore, we run *clingcon* with the flag `--config=crafty` since this is the option that obtained the best performance in our experiments, and set a time-out of 10 minutes for each run, after which the last solution found is returned. To run the PDDL+ solver, *enhsp* [26], we use *java openjdk* (v21.0.6). The instances, *clingcon* encoding, as well as the experiment setup and results can be found at: https://github.com/GabrieleRamagnano/Multi-Shot_Heuristic_Traffic_Sign_Opt.

5.1 Single-shot vs Multi-shot

We first compare our original single-shot encoding with the revised multi-shot version across all horizons in terms of solved instances (Fig. 1a) and solution quality (Fig. 1b). In terms of solved instances, multi-shot performs similarly to single-shot at lower horizons, but outperforms it at higher horizons, where single-shot solves only 75 out of the 105 instances compared to an average of 99 instances for multi-shot. On the other hand, Fig. 1b illustrates the relative improvement projected on the instances that where solved by both single and multi-shot approach for each horizon. For each pair of instances, the relative improvement is calculated as the difference between the sums of the corresponding counters, where the difference is credited to the encoding with the larger total counter value. We can see that, despite being able to solve more instances at higher horizons, the use of multi-shot brings a general reduction in solution quality.

5.2 Domain Heuristics

After seeing the results with multi-shot approach, we experimented the usage of domain heuristics on the single-shot approach. Figure 2a shows the comparison of the performance of the original encoding without domain heuristics (refereed as *clingcon*), and of each of the two domain heuristics we designed, i.e., h^{phase} and h^{link}. We can see that, without heuristics, the quality of the solutions is

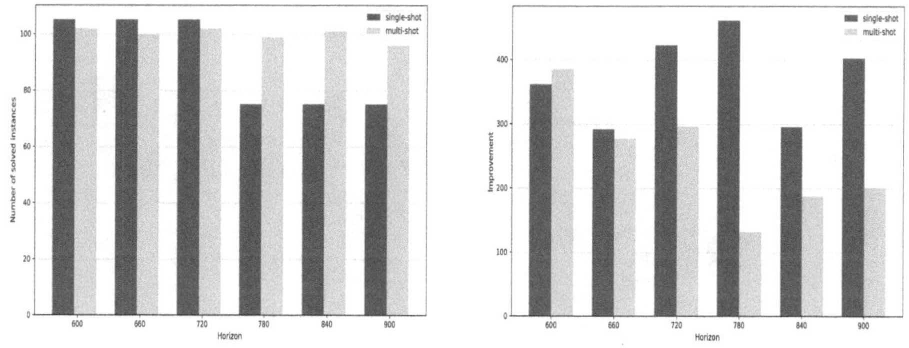

(a) Number of solved instances (b) Relative improvement (aggregated)

Fig. 1. Comparison of multi-shot and single-shot with at different horizons.

lower than with either h^{phase} or h^{link}, where the latter obtained the highest results. Regarding the number of instances covered, *clingcon* struggles to find a solution for the 35 new challenging instances, when the horizon is greater than 720 s, while h^{phase} and h^{link} manages to cover a couple of challenging instances with high horizons, but still struggles with the majority of them.

Revised Encoding. By analysing the original encoding [28], we identified a possible rewriting of the rules defining the increments/decrements in the occupancy of each link at each time step. More precisely, the occupancy of each link is determined by the contributions of all the incoming and outgoing links that have a stage active during the simulation. The number of vehicles entering and leaving the link is expressed in PCUs and calculated for each time point recursively by ASP rules and stored in auxiliary atoms `delta/4`. Noting the limited amount of possible values for `delta/4` at each time point and link, we decided to directly include the amount into the occupancy expression as follows:

```
&sum{occupancy(T,L); I+O} = occupancy(T+1,L) :-time(T+1), link(L),
 I = #sum{R*E*F,L1: precedes(J,L), status(J,S), active(T,S), in_ord(L,L1,N),
      turnrate_gez(S,L1,L,R), empty_link(T,L1,E), full_link(T,L,F)},
 O = #sum{-R*E*F,L1: follows(J,L), status(J,S), active(T,S), out_ord(L,L1,N),
      turnrate_gez(S,L,L1,R), empty_link(T,L,E), full_link(T,L1,F)}.
```

Intuitively, the idea is to aggregate in the variable `I` the turnrate of links sending vehicles to `L`; while `O` sums the turnrate of links receiving vehicles from it, where both variables are defined with respect to the traffic conditions at time `T`[3]. Similarly, we can redefine the rule defining the value of the variables `counter`, where the negative sum of outgoing links, identified with `O`, is not included.

Figure 2b shows the results obtained by applying the rewriting on the encoding and repeating the previous experiments. It turned out that all the three

[3] The variables `E` and `F` contain binary values (i.e., 0 or 1) representing whether the link is not empty or not full, respectively.

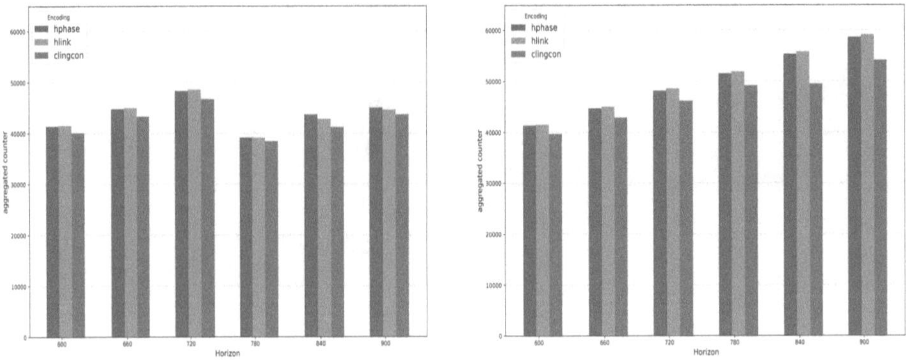

(a) Original encoding. (b) Revised encoding: no `delta` atoms.

Fig. 2. Comparison between the encoding without heuristics (clingcon) and with heuristics (h^{phase} and h^{link}).

versions benefits from the rewriting, changing the ranking between the heuristic models, namely, h^{link} has the best performance, followed by h^{phase}, while *clingcon* (i.e., no heuristics) has the worst results for each horizon considered. The rewriting allows for covering all the 105 instances for each horizon, except for *clingcon* which reaches a total of 99 and 103 instances solved for the horizons 840 and 900 respectively. This contributed in a visible improvement of the aggregated results, especially in the last three horizons: for instance, h^{link} with horizon 900 reached 59.107 PCUs (an improvement of about 37% w.r.t. *clingcon* in Fig. 2a).

5.3 Comparison to PDDL+ Model

To fully appreciate the advantages of rewriting and heuristics, we have compared the results obtained by h^{link} with FIRE, the PDDL+ model that obtained the best performance among the proposed alternatives in the work of Kouaiti et al. [18]. This model has the same solution space of ours, but it is not limited to a certain time horizon. Indeed, PDDL+ planning engines focus on generating satisfying solutions, with no guarantees on the quality of the solution found. In practice, this can lead to traffic signal optimisation plans that show extremely long time horizons – potentially reducing the ability of plans to cope with identified issues. For this reason, to evaluate the plans found by PDDL+ model, it is necessary to cut the horizons up to 900 seconds (i.e., 15 minutes), since when considering horizons greater than 15 minutes, the results diverge from the simulations because of the shifting of underlying turn rates [5]. Despite this limitation, a clear advantage of the PDDL+ model is that it is relatively easy to find a solution, whereas the CASP model we presented has shown limitations in finding solutions or improving upon the one initially found by PDDL+, particularly with long time horizons [28].

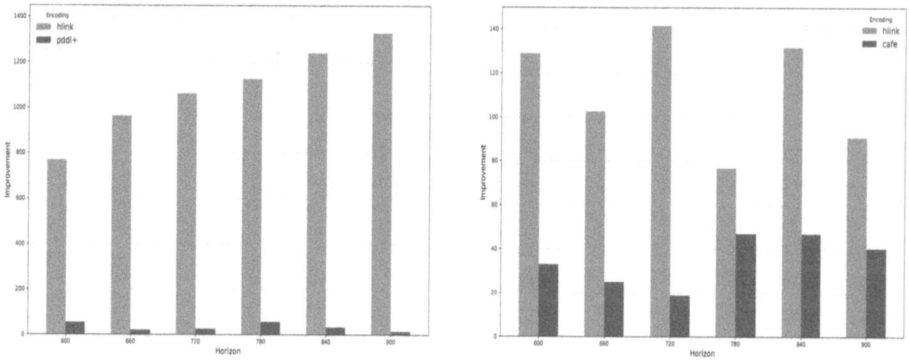

(a) h^{link} vs PDDL+ model. (b) h^{link} vs PDDL+ model (with *cafe*).

Fig. 3. Comparison between our best setting (h^{link}) and the PDDL+ model (with and without heuristics).

Figure 3a shows the relative improvement between the PDDL+ model and h^{link}, where it is clear to see that our approach generate overall better solutions. Here, the relative improvement is considered on all the 105 instances. Furthermore, as proposed in our previous work, we combined the two approaches, first using PDDL+ to find an initial solution and then our CASP model to improve upon it. Without heuristics, only 32% of the initial solutions were improved; in particular, for the higher horizons (i.e., 780, 840 and 900 s), an improvement was found in only 27–21 instances out of 105. In contrast, with the h^{link} heuristic, it is possible to find a strictly better solution than the one returned by the PDDL+ model in 85% of all cases, with 86 to 93 instances out of 105 being improved for the higher horizons (i.e., 780, 840 and 900 s).

Lastly, the recent work of Doria et al. [10] identified a domain heuristic for PDDL+, called *cafe*, which has been shown to improve performance over the baseline model. Figure 3b shows the relative improvement between the PDDL+ model with *cafe* and the CASP encoding with h^{link}. We can see that even with a heuristic, our approach generally finds higher quality solutions than PDDL+.

6 Related Work

A large number of planning approaches have been developed for centralised traffic signal optimisation. Gulić et al. [16] proposed a system that integrates an AI planning engine with the SUMO simulator, and is based on abstracting away individual vehicle counts to enhance scalability. The work by Pozanco et al. [25] builds upon this approach, introducing also the ability for continuous learning and knowledge model evolution for improved network adaptation.

On a different line of work, Vallati et al. [29] and McCluskey and Vallati [20] exploit PDDL+ for encoding a flow model of vehicles through traffic-light controlled junctions. Those initial works have then been extended, proposing approaches that have been extensively validated with historical data from urban regions of the United Kingdom [10,18,24]. These works take into account the constraints of the existing infrastructure and are hence suitable for deployment.

Instead, there are far fewer approaches to problems related to traffic signal optimisation that use ASP. Besides the work that underpinned this paper [28], the work of Eiter et al. [11] introduces an approach to optimise the coupling of traffic movements at junctions, according to expected traffic demand in the area, and to simulate using a mesoscopic-level representation. The experiments considered a realistic area with two junctions and are compared to the microscopic traffic simulator SUMO [19]. In the wider area of traffic control, Cardellini et al. [8] deals with the problem of dynamic traffic distributions in urban areas. As a part of a framework defined for solving such problem, they employed ASP for the computation of the best possible routes for all the vehicles in the network, starting from a set of candidate routes for all vehicles within the framework. On other directions in traffic research, ASP has been employed to manage the inconsistency in traffic regulations in Smart Cities [3,4], and as a component in a situation awareness system for maritime traffic control [30].

7 Conclusion

In this paper, we investigate possible extensions for CASP-based traffic signal optimisation, addressing key limitations of prior *clingcon*-based approaches in terms of scalability and solution quality. Multi-shot solving improves scalability and coverage on challenging instances, but introduces a degradation of the solution quality. On the other hand, domain-specific heuristics substantially improve solution quality by guiding the search towards effective and stable configurations. A revised encoding further strengthens performance, shedding some light on the impact of modelling alternatives. Overall, the proposed approach outperforms the baseline and compares favourably to PDDL+ methods, confirming the effectiveness of combining tailored heuristics and modelling refinements. Future work will include the evaluation of the combination of multi-shot solving and domain heuristics, and the usage of alternative CASP dialects, e.g., *clingo-lpx* [17].

Acknowledgments. This research was funded in part by the Austrian Science Fund (FWF) project 10.55776/PAT1599524. Mauro Vallati was supported by a UKRI Future Leaders Fellowship [grant number MR/Z00005X/1]. We thank the "Knowledge Representation and Reasoning" group at the University of Potsdam, for the feedback provided. We are also grateful to the anonymous reviewers for their feedback and suggestions that helped us improving the paper's readability.

Disclosure of Interests. The authors have no competing interests to declare that are relevant to the content of this article.

References

1. Banbara, M., Kaufmann, B., Ostrowski, M., Schaub, T.: Clingcon: the next generation. Theory Pract. Logic Program. **17**(4), 408–461 (2017)

2. Baral, C.: Knowledge Representation, Reasoning and Declarative Problem Solving. Cambridge University Press, Cambridge (2003)
3. Beck, H., Eiter, T., Krennwallner, T.: Inconsistency management for traffic regulations. In: Proc. of Semantic Cities, Papers from the 2012 AAAI Workshop, AAAI Technical Report, vol. WS-12-13. AAAI Press (2012)
4. Beck, H., Eiter, T., Krennwallner, T.: Inconsistency management for traffic regulations: formalization and complexity results. In: Proc. of JELIA, pp. 80–93 (2012)
5. Bhatnagar, S., Mund, S., Scala, E., McCabe, K., McCluskey, T.L., Vallati, M.: On-the-fly knowledge acquisition for automated planning applications: challenges and lessons learnt. In: Proceedings of the International Conference on Agents and Artificial Intelligence, ICAART, pp. 387–397 (2022)
6. Brewka, G., Eiter, T., Truszczynski, M.: Answer set programming at a glance. Commun. ACM **54**(12), 92–103 (2011)
7. Calimeri, F., et al.: ASP-Core-2 input language format. Theory Pract. Logic Program. **20**(2), 294–309 (2020)
8. Cardellini, M., Dodaro, C., Maratea, M., Vallati, M.: Optimising dynamic traffic distribution for urban networks with answer set programming. Theory Pract. Log. Program. **24**(4), 825–843 (2024)
9. Dodaro, C., Gasteiger, P., Leone, N., Musitsch, B., Ricca, F., Schekotihin, K.: Combining answer set programming and domain heuristics for solving hard industrial problems (application paper). Theory Pract. Log. Program. **16**(5–6), 653–669 (2016)
10. Doria, F., Percassi, F., Maratea, M., Vallati, M.: A domain-specific heuristic for PDDL+-based traffic signal optimisation. In: Proc. of AAAI, pp. 36207–36216 (2026)
11. Eiter, T., Falkner, A.A., Schneider, P., Schüller, P.: ASP-based signal plan adjustments for traffic flow optimization. In: ECAI 2020 - 24th European Conference on Artificial Intelligence, pp. 3026–3033. IOS Press (2020)
12. Ferrara, A., Sacone, S., Siri, S., Ferrara, A., Sacone, S., Siri, S.: Microscopic and mesoscopic traffic models. Freeway Traffic Modelling Control **1**, 113–143 (2018)
13. Gebser, M., Kaminski, R., Kaufmann, B., Schaub, T.: Multi-shot ASP solving with clingo. Theory Pract. Log. Program. **19**(1), 27–82 (2019)
14. Gebser, M., Kaufmann, B., Romero, J., Otero, R., Schaub, T., Wanko, P.: Domain-specific heuristics in answer set programming. In: Proc. of AAAI, pp. 350–356 (2013)
15. Gelfond, M., Lifschitz, V.: Classical negation in logic programs and disjunctive databases. New Gener. Comput. **9**(3/4), 365–386 (1991)
16. Gulić, M., Olivares, R., Borrajo, D.: Using automated planning for traffic signals control. PROMET-Traffic&Transportation **28**(4), 383–391 (2016)
17. Janhunen, T., Kaminski, R., Ostrowski, M., Schellhorn, S., Wanko, P., Schaub, T.: Clingo goes linear constraints over reals and integers. Theory Pract. Log. Program. **17**, 872–888 (2017)
18. Kouaiti, A.E., Percassi, F., Saetti, A., McCluskey, T.L., Vallati, M.: PDDL+ models for deployable yet effective traffic signal optimisation. In: Proceedings of ICAPS, pp. 168–177 (2024)
19. López, P.Á., et al.: Microscopic traffic simulation using SUMO. In: Proc. of ITSC, pp. 2575–2582. IEEE (2018)
20. McCluskey, T., Vallati, M.: Embedding automated planning within urban traffic management operations. In: Proc. of ICAPS, pp. 391–399 (2017)
21. Mellarkod, V.S., Gelfond, M., Zhang, Y.: Integrating answer set programming and constraint logic programming. Ann. Math. Artif. Intell. **53**(1–4), 251–287 (2008)

22. Niemelä, I.: Logic programs with stable model semantics as a constraint programming paradigm. Ann. Math. Artif. Intell. **25**(3–4), 241–273 (1999)
23. Percassi, F., Bhatnagar, S., Guo, R., McCabe, K., McCluskey, T.L., Vallati, M.: An efficient heuristic for AI-based urban traffic control. In: Proc. of MT-ITS (2023)
24. Percassi, F., Scala, E., Vallati, M.: A practical approach to discretised PDDL+ problems by translation to numeric planning. J. Artif. Intell. Res. **76**, 115–162 (2023)
25. Pozanco, A., Fernández, S., Borrajo, D.: On-line modelling and planning for urban traffic control. Expert Syst. J. Knowl. Eng. **38** (2021)
26. Scala, E., Haslum, P., Thiébaux, S., Ramirez, M.: Subgoaling techniques for satisficing and optimal numeric planning. J. Artif. Intell. Res. **68**, 691–752 (2020)
27. Taale, H., Fransen, W., Dibbits, J.: The second assessment of the SCOOT system in Nijmegen. IEEE Road Transp. Inf. Control, 21–23 (1998)
28. Tarzariol, A., Maratea, M., Vallati, M.: A CASP-based solution for traffic signal optimisation. Theory Pract. Log. Program. **25**(4), 794–812 (2025)
29. Vallati, M., Magazzeni, D., De Schutter, B., Chrpa, L., McCluskey, T.: Efficient macroscopic urban traffic models for reducing congestion: a PDDL+ planning approach. In: Proc. of AAAI, pp. 3188–3194 (2016)
30. Vaseqi, Z., Delgrande, J.: An application of answer set programming for situational analysis in a maritime traffic domain. In: Zaïane, O.R., Zilles, S. (eds.) AI 2013. LNCS (LNAI), vol. 7884, pp. 315–322. Springer, Heidelberg (2013). https://doi.org/10.1007/978-3-642-38457-8_32
31. Wei, H., Zheng, G., Gayah, V., Li, Z.: A survey on traffic signal control methods. arXiv preprint arXiv:1904.08117 (2019)

Bayesian Hyperparameter Optimization with ALASPO

Thomas Eiter, Tobias Geibinger(✉), and Dave Pfliegler

Institute of Logic and Computation, TU Wien, Vienna, Austria
{thomas.eiter,tobias.geibinger}@tuwien.ac.at, dave@pfliegler.at

Abstract. The ALASPO framework applies Large Neighbourhood Search (LNS) to Answer Set Programming (ASP), which has proven to be effective in tackling a number of different optimization problems. To control the behaviour of the LNS, ALASPO offers many configuration options that in combination with all solving and grounding parameters of the underlying ASP solver result in a vast configuration space. Choosing a best from it poses a challenge, which we address by integrating the SMAC3 framework for Bayesian Optimization into ALASPO in order to enable the automatic tuning of ALASPO configurations. In addition, we cluster the provided problem instances based on their characteristics, allowing one to obtain multiple optimal configurations, one for each cluster of similar instances. After tuning, the result can be used for future ALASPO runs on unseen instances to automatically select and apply an appropriate configuration based on the characteristics of the given instance. We evaluate our methodology on a set of four benchmark problems and show that tuning can yield significant gains over using the default configuration for some of them, while also demonstrating its limitations in case of insufficient opportunities for advancement.

1 Introduction

Answer Set Programming (ASP) [3] is a widely used declarative problem solving paradigm rooted in logic programming, and aims, unlike procedural languages, not at encoding an algorithm for solving a problem but instead at describing its solutions. ASP in combination with the Large Neighbourhood Search (LNS) [26,30] metaheuristic, which iteratively destroys and repairs parts of a solution to find an overall better result, in particular the Adaptive Large-Neighbourhood ASP Optimiser *ALASPO* [6], has already proven to be effective in tackling typical optimization problems. The latter involve various criteria that contribute to an objective value which reflects the quality of candidate solutions. Optimization is then usually conducted by iteratively finding, given an initial candidate, multiple solutions that are better than the previous one, i.e., with higher objective value.

ALASPO uses an ASP solver internally to facilitate both the finding of an initial solution as well as the repair step of the LNS. This solver offers an extensive range of solving and grounding parameters that can greatly influence its

W. Faber et al. (Eds.): LPNMR 2026, LNAI 16952, pp. 215–230, 2027.
https://doi.org/10.1007/978-3-032-38320-4_14

performance. In addition, ALASPO offers numerous configuration options that control the behaviour of the LNS process, which results in a vast configuration space. Consequently, an exhaustive exploration of different parameters and their combinations to manually identify an optimal configuration is infeasible and calls for using a (semi-)automated approach. To this end, Hyperparameter Optimization (HPO) [19] is a well-known process of identifying the best performing parameters for a given function, by evaluating them on trials, thereby reducing the effort of manual experimentation, improving reproducibility, and potentially improving performance through more thorough exploration.

The area of Hyperparameter Optimization has gained traction primarily due to the rise of machine learning algorithms and the fact that their performance strongly depends on suitable parameter choices [7]. Basic forms of HPO are Grid Search and Random Search [1], which evaluate the function with all possible combinations of parameters or a random subset thereof, require an extensive number of trials. In contrast, Bayesian Optimization [24] takes advantage of a surrogate model and may reduce the number of required function evaluations by balancing both exploration and exploitation using learned knowledge from previous function calls [7].

A natural question is thus whether and how HPO, and in particular Bayesian Optimization, can be fruitfully exploited for ASP with LNS. We address it in the realm of ALASPO with the following contributions.

- We design a customizable Bayesian Hyperparameter Optimization approach for ASP with LNS and integrate it into the ALASPO framework using SMAC3.
- We develop customizable clustering of problem instances based on their characteristics, exploiting their similar optimization behaviour, for an overall heterogeneous set of instances.
- We conduct a comprehensive experimental evaluation of the newly integrated features on a suite of four benchmark problems of high industrial relevance. The results show that our hyperparameter tuning may yield significant performance gains, i.e., finding better solutions in the same time frame, for some problems even with a small number of trials. Specifically, for one benchmark problem, average gains in solution quality of 28% over the non-tuned configuration are achieved, while for two others of 5% and 7%, respectively. For the fourth problem, tuning could not provide meaningful improvements over the ALASPO default configuration, which suggests that the latter is well-suited for this problem.

In conclusion, our results show that HPO and in particular Bayesian Optimization has high potential to advance the performance of ASP with LNS. As the tuning setup requires relatively little effort, and can already indicate whether performance gains are possible with just a few trials, it is inexpensive to evaluate whether benefits can be obtained for a given problem. Further details, experimental results, and discussion can be found in the Master thesis of the main author [25].

2 Preliminaries

Answer Set Programming (ASP) [3] provides a declarative modelling language that allows one to succinctly represent search and optimization problems, for which solutions can be computed using dedicated ASP solvers.

ASP is a compact relational, in essence propositional, formalism where variables in the input language are replaced by constant symbols in a preprocessing step called *grounding*. An ASP program is a set of rules r of the form

$$p_1 \mid \ldots \mid p_k \;\texttt{:-}\; q_1, \ldots, q_m, \texttt{not}\, r_1, \ldots, \texttt{not}\, r_n\,.$$

where all p_i, q_j, and r_l are atoms. The head are all atoms before the implication symbol `:-`, and the body are all the atoms and negated atoms afterwards. The intuitive meaning of r is that if all atoms $q_1, \ldots, q_m$ can be derived and there is no evidence for any of the atoms $r_1, \ldots, r_n$ (i.e., the rule fires) then at least one of $p_1, \ldots, p_k$ has to be derived. An *interpretation* I is a set of ground (variable-free) atoms. It is an *answer set*, if all its rules are satisfied in a minimal and consistent way [9]; intuitively, I must be a $\subseteq$-minimal model of all rules that fire.

A ground rule with an empty body is called a *fact* (with `:-` usually omitted), while a rule with empty head is a *constraint*. Facts express knowledge that is unconditionally true; the body of a constraint cannot be satisfied by any answer set and is used to prune away unwanted solution candidates.

The *ASP-Core-2 Input Language Format* [4] defines several language extensions; most are syntactic sugar but commonly used and convenient in practice. Furthermore, the language also allows for optimization statements.

Weak constraints are of the form $:\sim B.\ [w, t_1, \ldots, t_m]$, where B is a set of literals, the t_i are terms, and w is the *weight*. They incur penalty w if B is satisfied, i.e., the constraint instance is violated. An answer set is then assigned the sum of all such penalties; it is *optimal*, if it has minimal penalty. More elaborated versions have priority levels.

Large Neighbourhood Search (LNS) [30] is a local search heuristic often used in optimization problems. It proceeds with continuous relaxation and re-optimization as follows. First, an *initial solution* to the current problem must be obtained, for example, by using a construction heuristic that produces a sub-optimal or even trivial solution. Next, a subset, called the *neighbourhood*, of the current *incumbent solution* is destroyed (or relaxed). The resulting partial solution is then *rebuilt* in an attempt to find a new feasible solution of better quality. If this new solution is closer to the optimum, it becomes the new incumbent (otherwise it is discarded). Subsequently, the destroy and repair operations are repeated in a loop until some stopping criterion is met or an optimum is found.

Naturally, the effectiveness of the LNS optimization is highly dependent on the neighbourhood selection: If it is too small, the search may get stuck in a local optimum due to its limited exploration of the search space; if it is too

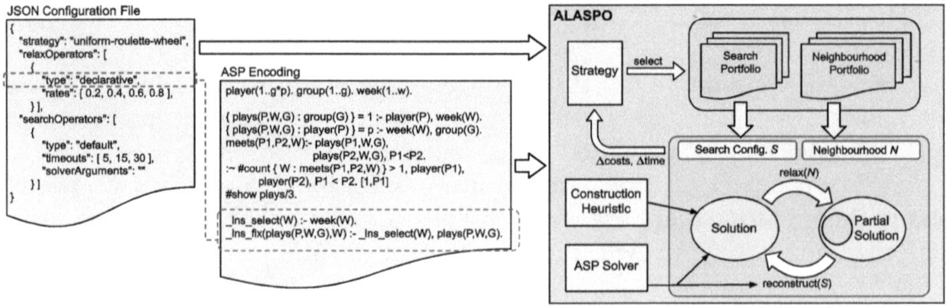

Fig. 1. Overview of the ALASPO system [6].

large, the heuristic may repeat certain optimizations at each step, resulting in poor efficiency or poor solution quality.

Adaptive Large Neighbourhood Search (ALNS) [28] extends regular LNS by allowing for multiple destroy and repair operators in one search. The operators are dynamically selected throughout the optimization based on their associated weight, which is continuously updated after each iteration based on their performance, e.g., success rate. The degree to which each operator's weight is affected after each iteration can be controlled by a *decay* parameter.

The Adaptive Large Neighbourhood ASP Optimiser *ALASPO*[1] [6] is a system implementing ALNS for ASP optimization problems. It supports the ASP solver *clingo* and its extensions *clingcon* and *clingo-dl* of the Potsdam Answer Set Solving Collection *Potassco*.[2] ALASPO provides a portfolio of different search and neighbourhood (relax) operators, implements different operator selection strategies, and allows for the integration of custom operators and strategies. It can be configured in detail through a JSON configuration. Figure 1 shows the architecture and the workflow of the ALASPO system; for further details on ALASPO, we refer to [6].

2.1 Hyperparameter Optimization

Hyperparameter Optimization (HPO) [19] is the process of identifying best performing parameters for a given function by evaluating them on a number of trial runs. Automating this procedure is a natural approach to reduce the effort of manual experimentation, improve reproducibility, and improve the performance of the examined function by exploring the configuration space more thoroughly.

The basic forms of HPO are the well-known Grid Search and Random Search [1]. The former evaluates the given function with all possible parameter combinations, resulting in a considerable number of required trials. This is an obstacle for complex configuration spaces, since increasing the dimensionality of the space

[1] https://gitlab.tuwien.ac.at/kbs/BAI/alaspo/.
[2] https://potassco.org.

leads to an exponential growth in the number of function evaluations. Random Search samples the configuration space at random until a given budget is exhausted; it is proven to work better than Grid Search for applications where the performance impact of parameters is very uneven [7].

The field of Algorithm Configuration (AC) – which focuses on finding the correct parameter settings, i.e., configurations, for a given algorithm on a set of different problem instances – has developed various methods to effectively solve AC scenarios: (1) Racing algorithms evaluate multiple candidate configurations sequentially, and discard worse performing ones as soon as they fall too far behind. (2) Stochastic Local Search (SLS) [16] algorithms use local search in the configuration space. (3) Sequential Model-Based Optimization (SMBO) [14] uses an internal model to estimate the performance of parameter settings.

SMAC3 [20] falls into SMBO and is a Bayesian Optimization framework for hyperparameter tuning written in Python. By default, it uses Random Forests as surrogate model for hyperparameter optimization, implements several so-called *facades* tailored to specific use cases and allows for custom combinations of different modules. In addition, it is capable of optimizing a function based on a given set of instances, evaluating the performance of a configuration based on trials with multiple instances. To enable the parallelization of trials, SMAC3 can make use of custom DASK [27] clients. DASK is a Python library that can be used to efficiently implement parallel computing; DASK clients can be passed to SMAC3 to parallelize its trials, including across high performance computing (HPC) clusters [20].

To identify the best performing parameter configurations, SMAC3 uses an aggressive racing algorithm [17] that, if provided with multiple instances, discards less promising candidates as soon as possible by evaluating them on only a few instances. Furthermore, SMAC3 can also be supplied with a feature vector for each instance which will then be incorporated in the surrogate model.

3 Automated Tuning for ASP with LNS

In addition to the extensive range of solving and grounding parameters of the underlying ASP solver, ALASPO offers numerous configuration options that control the behaviour of its LNS process, both resulting in a considerable configuration space. Consequently, an exhaustive exploration of different parameters and their combinations to identify optimal configurations is infeasible.

To address this, we integrate the SMAC3 framework for Bayesian Hyperparameter Optimization into ALASPO to automatically tune ALASPO configurations for a varied set of instances. Our implementation was incorporated into ALASPO and can be found in the respective repository.

We aim to allow for a workflow where a small, representative set of diverse instances for a problem is given and supplied to the tuning process. ALASPO then clusters these instances based on their characteristics, and produces a best configuration for each cluster. Furthermore, upon completion, the tuning process produces an artifact that can be used in future invocations of ALASPO with new instances to automatically select a fitting configuration.

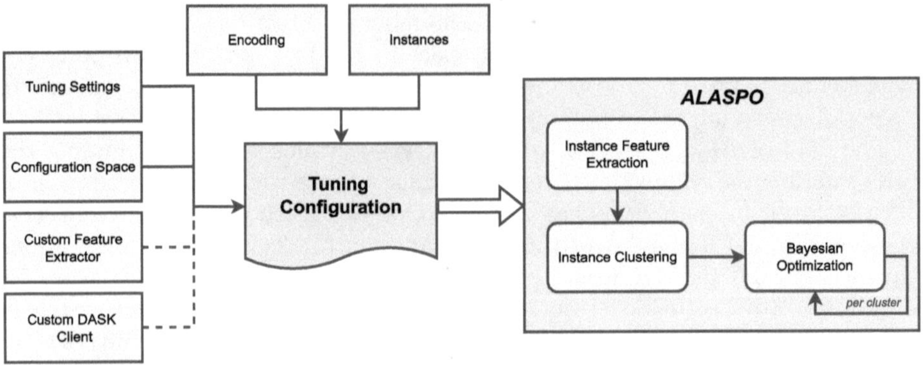

Fig. 2. Overview of automated tuning in ALASPO.

Figure 2 shows the general tuning approach in ALASPO. The tuning configuration file contains general settings including (i) the total trial budget, (ii) the time limit per run, (iii) the configuration space for the optimization, (iv) the problem encoding, and (v) the instances to be considered. Optionally, a custom feature extractor or a custom DASK configuration can be provided. ALASPO then uses its feature extractor (either the default or a custom one) to obtain a set $F = \{f_1, ..., f_n\}$ of features for each instance. The resulting dataset D is then used to cluster the provided instances into clusters $C_1, ..., C_k$, in a way that instances with similar characteristics are grouped together. Finally, Bayesian Optimization is performed on each instance cluster C_i, resulting in a best found configuration c_i^* for each of them. ALASPO will return a `clustering.dill` file after tuning, which can be used for future invocations, automatically applying a best found configuration c_i^* based on the given (unseen) instance.

3.1 Feature Extraction

For the clustering of the provided instances, each instance must be associated with a set $F = \{f_1, ..., f_n\}$ of features which are extracted by a *feature extractor*. The features f_i should capture the instance properties that affect their solving behaviour, enabling the tuning process to tailor configurations more effectively to each cluster.

Default Feature Extractor. Since the default method needs to be problem agnostic, we opted for counting the number of occurrences of different facts in an instance. However, the success of this approach is very dependent on the particular problem and its encoding, as the number of facts may, in the worst case, be identical across all instances, whereas their characteristics could differ significantly depending on the unaccounted-for terms of the predicates.

Custom Feature Extractor. To enable problem-specific instance feature extraction, a custom feature extractor can be passed to ALASPO. This custom feature extractor is a method that takes the path to an instance file as parameter, and must return a list $v_1, \ldots, v_n$ of numeric values (floats) v_i that best represent the characteristics of the instance. The extracted features will subsequently be used to produce a clustering that can better reflect the structure of the problem.

3.2 Clustering

We cluster the instances based on their characteristics and use SMAC3 to find best performing configurations for each cluster separately. We do this in the hope of exploiting similarities between instances to improve the quality of configurations by tailoring them to related groups of instances.

For the clustering, we use the K-means algorithm [13] on the dataset of extracted instance features. To determine the best number of clusters, we use the Silhouette Coefficient [29] to evaluate the quality of the clustering. It ranges from -1 to 1, with the upper bound indicating that samples are far from neighbouring clusters, i.e., a good clustering, while values around 0 and below indicate that clusters overlap. We therefore find the number of clusters that maximizes the Silhouette Coefficient of the resulting clustering. Alternatively, the number of clusters can be specified using a corresponding parameter in the tuning configuration.

3.3 Tuning

We perform the hyperparameter optimization with SMAC3 for each cluster of instances. Specifically, we use its `HyperparameterOptimizationFacade`, which in turn uses a Random Forest as the surrogate model. For the initial design – the component that determines which configurations are evaluated before the Bayesian Optimization loop – we use the `DefaultInitialDesign` instead of the `SobolInitialDesign` used by the selected facade. This ensures that the actual provided default configuration is evaluated initially, rather than a *random* set sampled from the configuration space.

For the serialisation of the tuning results, we use the *dill* [22] library, as it allows us to serialize complete functions, such as the feature extractor, which is needed for future ALASPO runs on new instances.

Tuning Configuration. To start the hyperparameter tuning described above, a tuning configuration has to be passed to ALASPO. This can be done using either a JSON file or directly through Python. For a complete list and description of available parameters as well as examples we refer to the tuning README[3].

The JSON configuration file extends a standard ALASPO configuration file by adding an additional `tuning` node, under which all tuning related parameters are specified. To be valid, it must contain (i) a time or trial budget, (ii) a time limit for each trial, (iii) a problem encoding, (iv) instances, and (v) a configuration space. The remaining standard part of the file serves as the default configuration for the tuning process.

[3] https://url.tuwien.at/bgwwk.

```
{
    "strategy": {
        "name": "dynamic", "unsatStrikes": 3, "timeoutStrikes": 1
    },
    "relaxOperators": [
        { "type": "randomAtoms", "sizes": [ 0.1, 0.2, 0.4, 0.6, 0.8 ] },
        { "type": "randomConstants", "sizes": [ 0.1, 0.2, 0.3, 0.5 ] } ],
    "searchOperators": [ { "name": "default", "timeouts": [ 5, 15, 30, 60 ] } ],
    "tuning": {
        "trials": 1000,
        "trialTimeLimit": 600,
        "encoding": [ "./encoding.lp" ],
        "instances": "./instances.txt",
        "configurationSpace": {
            "strategy": [
                { "name": "dynamic",
                  "unsatStrikes": [ 1, 2, 3, 4 ],
                  "timeoutStrikes": [ 1, 2, 3, 4 ] },
                { "name": "powerlaw",
                  "alpha": "$eval:(-5.0, 5.0)"  },
                { "name": "roulette",
                  "alpha": "$eval:(0.0, 1.0)"  },
                { "name": "random" } ]
        }
    }
}
```

Fig. 3. An example JSON tuning configuration for ALASPO.

The configuration space is configured as a JSON node where a *key* represents the JSONPath [12] to a specific property of the default configuration, and the associated *value* is an array (or range) of candidate values to be tested for that property. The tuning configuration allows the user to give a set of potential selection strategies along with their settings. The different strategies and their attributes are essentially flattened to regular hyperparameters, while the settings are resolved as conditional hyperparameters.

Figure 3 shows an example JSON tuning configuration file. In the configuration space shown, the various available ALASPO strategies are tuned along with their respective settings. The purpose of the tuning is to find out which strategy and parameters should be chosen for the given problem and instances.

To use a custom feature extractor, the path to a Python file has to be provided. This file must contain a function named `extractFeatures` that takes the path to an instance as parameter and returns a list of numeric values (float or integer) that best characterize it. Note that import statements required by the provided function must be written inside the function itself for it to work after deserialisation.

Usage. To use the tuning integrated into ALASPO, one of two dependency groups needs to be installed using `pip`: either `tuning` or `tuning-viz`, where the latter includes additional packages for cluster visualization. ALASPO can then be used for tuning by passing a configuration file with the argument `--tuning-config tuningConfig.json`. The resulting `clustering.dill` file can be used as input for an (unseen) instance with the `--use-clustering` argument.

4 Experiments

With our experimental evaluations, we want to investigate the following hypotheses about the tuning of ALASPO configurations:

(H1) The resulting configuration of a tuning run should perform better than the default ALASPO configuration, which uses the dynamic strategy.
(H2) Clustering problem instances based on their characteristics should result in multiple best configurations achieving better objective values for the validation instance set than a single configuration.
(H3) The custom feature extractor produces better features and, in turn, better configurations.
(H4) Tuning approaches without clustering may perform better if the instances are quite similar in their optimization behaviour.
(H5) Increasing the number of trials run by the tuning should yield configurations of better quality, and consequently improve overall performance.

Baseline. We compare the results to ALASPO with its default selection strategy as the baseline and depict their objective values as relative differences. The time limit for the baseline and for the tuned configurations is always the same, and we compare the objective values of the best found solution in that time frame. As ALASPO is inherently non-deterministic, this baseline and every experiment are run five times and subsequently averaged. For each problem, we divide the instances into a smaller tuning set and a test set.

Platform. Experiments were run on a SLURM [18] cluster of 10 nodes, each equipped with two Intel Xeon Silver 4314 CPUs and 512 GB of RAM, running Ubuntu 22.04 (Kernel 5.15.0-131-generic). We used Python v3.9.19, clingo v5.6.2, clingcon v5.2.0, SMAC v2.3.0, and ALASPO 0.3.Several steps were taken to ensure repeatability of the experiments [8]. CPU frequency was fixed to 2.4 GHz and memory limit to 25600 MB, Used encodings, instances, instance generators and experiment logs are available on Zenodo.[4]

4.1 Benchmark Problems

We consider four benchmark problems of industrial relevance: *Valves Location*, *Test Laboratory Scheduling*, *Travelling Salesman*, and *Multi-Agent Path Finding.*

(1) The *Test Laboratory Scheduling Problem* (TLSPS) [23] is a computationally intensive scheduling task that extends the well-known *Resource-Constrained Project Scheduling Problem* (RCPSP). It consists of multiple given projects, each involving multiple jobs that need to be completed. Every job requires various resources, such as employees, workbenches and equipment, that are shared across all jobs. A job can be carried out in multiple different modes that affect its requirements and duration, and must be completed in a given time window. The

[4] https://doi.org/10.5281/zenodo.15252026.

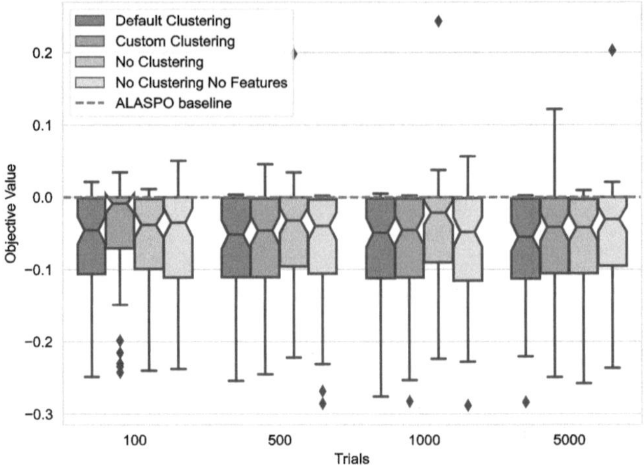

Fig. 4. Tuning results for TLSPS. Objective values are relative differences to the ALASPO baseline.

objective is to find an optimal schedule, i.e., one assigning each job a mode, the resources needed, and a start time while minimizing violations of soft constraints, such as due date violations, and the overall time to complete each project.

For the evaluation, we use the set of randomly generated instances created by Mischek et al. [23] and set a time limit of 600 s for the tuning trials, and 1800 s for the validation runs. Half of the instances were modelled as close to *real-world* test laboratories as possible, the others with more varied features. In addition, the set contains three anonymized *real-world* instances of an industry partner. For the tuning, we select 31 instances and one real-world instance, and use 74 of the remaining instances for the validation.

Figure 4 shows the results of our experiments for TLSPS. The boxes show the relative improvement of the objective value when compared to default configuration of ALASPO. Hence, negative values indicate improvements over the default and in general lower is better. Across the different clustering strategies, even a small number of trials could improve the objective values by ≈7% over our baseline, with the default clustering performing best and most consistent with increasing number of trials. Particularly at 5000 trials, the default tuning found a configuration that is almost strictly better than the baseline, except for two instances.

(2) The *Valves Location Problem* (VLP) [10] involves placing a limited number of valves in a water distribution network such that when specific pipes need to be isolated for maintenance, disruption to the network as a whole is minimal.

We use the instances provided with the VLP encoding[5] and set a time limit of 600 secs. The instance set contains 318 instances, the upper half of which we select 112 instances for the validation, and 48 for the tuning.

[5] https://www.mat.unical.it/aspcomp2014.

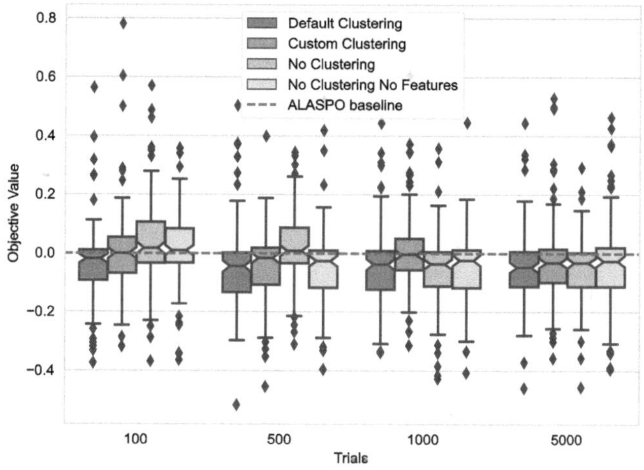

Fig. 5. Tuning results for the Valves Location Problem (VLP). Objective values are relative differences to the ALASPO baseline.

The tuning results for the VLP are shown in Fig. 5. They reveal that the tuning of the ALASPO selection strategies was not very effective for this problem, producing rather volatile results. Over the increasing number of trials, the default clustering performed the most consistently and also better than the other clustering strategies. Particularly at 5000 trials, all four strategies performed similarly, with average objective values 2.7% to 5.5% better than the baseline, and about 73 out of the total 112 instances performing better than default ALASPO. However, around 36 instances performed worse than the baseline, including significant outliers.

(3) For the *Travelling Salesman Problem* (TSP) [5], we created our own set of random instances using a generator written in R and the tspgen library [2], which implements a set of creative mutation operators to generate diverse instances. We generated 96 instances in total, with sizes chosen from 40, 60, 80, and 100 vertices, and set a time limit of 300 secs. For each size, we start with a random graph, and use one of four distinct mutations: (i) the `AxisProjectionMutation` of tspgen, (ii) the `GridMutation` of tspgen, (iii) a single cluster mutation, that clusters all points into a single group, and (iv) a triple cluster mutation, which splits the points into three separate clusters. Finally, the resulting instance is perturbed multiple times to obtain different instances with similar global characteristics. For the experiments, we then split the set, selecting the first instance of each size and type for tuning, while using the rest to validate the tuning results. This resulted in 16 instances for tuning and 80 for validation.

Figure 6 shows the tuning results for TSP. The tuning yielded significant performance improvements. At 5000 trials, all four clustering strategies performed almost identically and strictly better than the ALASPO baseline, with average improvements of around 28%. For this problem, our custom clustering strategy outperformed the default strategy; however, the overall best clustering approach was *No Clustering No Features*, as the power law ALASPO selection strategy with a large alpha value performed best across all instances.

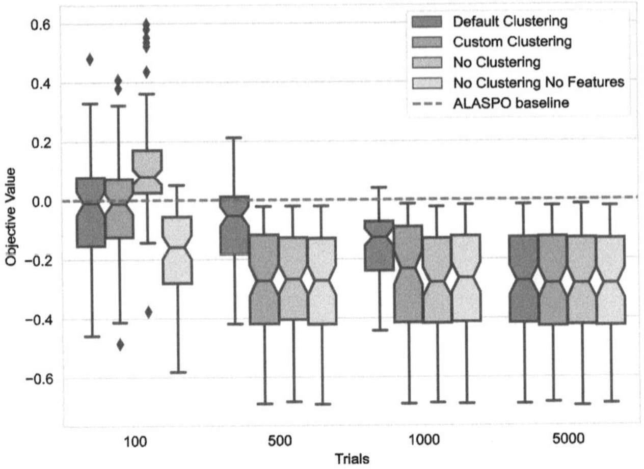

Fig. 6. Tuning results for TSP. Objective values are relative differences to the ALASPO baseline.

(4) *Multi-Agent Path Finding* (MAPF) [32] involves finding conflict-free paths for multiple agents that share the same environment. The goal is to find a plan in which every agent reaches their goal position with minimal time steps.

For our experiments, we implemented an instance generator which creates random instances with characteristics close to those used by Gomez et al. [11]: We created *random* and *warehouse* instances, with varying sizes, percentages of obstacles, and number of agents. *Random* instances were created for grids of size 8×8 and 20×20, with number of agents from [10,21] and [16,29] in increments of 2, respectively, with 0%, 10%, and 25% of obstacles. For the *warehouse* instances, we generated 15×15 and 21×18 grids with number of agents from [16,29] in increments of 2. For each combination of parameters, we generated three instances randomly. Without the unsatisfiable instances (due to the generation process or insufficient time limit), we were left with 39 instances for tuning and 81 for validation. The time limit for the validation runs was 600 secs.

Figure 7 presents the tuning results for MAPF. Tuning could not provide meaningful improvements over the default configuration, suggesting that the ALASPO baseline configuration is already the best fit for this problem.

4.2 Discussion

Overall, we found that tuning the available ALASPO strategies and their corresponding parameters yielded significant performance gains for ALASPO on TLSPS and TSP, while moderate improvements for the VLP and none for

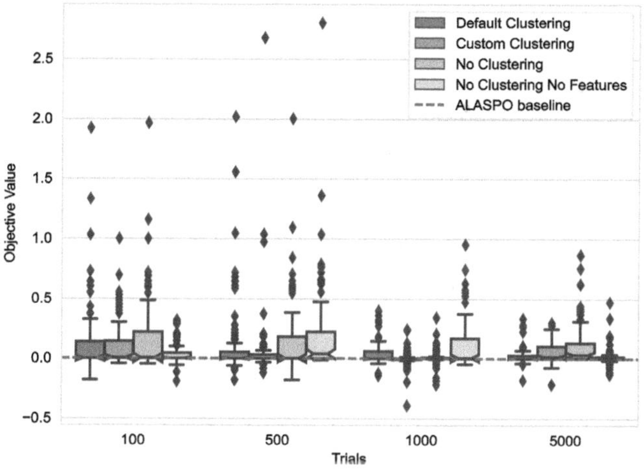

Fig. 7. Tuning results for MAPF.

MAPF. These findings are generally in support of our original hypothesis (H1), particularly for the TLSPS and the TSP, while highlighting that it is not applicable to the MAPF, where the default configuration already performs best.

A key observation is that with a small number of trials, the clustered approaches may perform worse than the unclustered methods whenever there is a single best configuration for all instances. This can be seen at 100 trials for both TSP and MAPF, where the *power law* and *dynamic* strategies, respectively, perform best for all types of instances. The reason is that the clustered variants have to share the trial budget for each cluster, whereas in absence of clusters SMAC3 has more trials available to find the overall best configuration. In those cases, hypothesis (H2) is directly contradicted as the implicit assumption of heterogeneous instances does not hold, which in turn supports (H4).

It is evident that the performance of the custom clustering is highly dependent on the implementation of the custom feature extractor, whereas the default clustering is highly dependent on the structure of the instances. The former is illustrated by the fact that it performs worse than the default clustering for the VLP. While the TSP instances prove to be the worst case for the latter, providing virtually no information about their characteristics. These results show that hypothesis (H3) can only hold if the custom features extracted from instances are successful in capturing distinct optimization behaviours.

We also observed that tuning with 5000 trials almost always gives the best objective values. However, custom clustering for TLSPS and *No Clustering No Features* for VLP performed worse than with fewer trials. A possible reason for this, and by extension why hypothesis (H5) does not hold universally, could be overfitting on the tuning dataset.

Tuning the selection strategies for MAPF also highlights the obvious fact that when the default strategy performs best, tuning is of little use.

5 Related Work

Sugimori et al. [33] presented the *heulingo* ASP solver akin to ALASPO, which implements Large Neighbourhood Prioritized Search (LNPS), which differs from LNS by allowing to change the usually fixed, undestroyed part of the solution in the reconstruction step using prioritized search, aiming to rely less on the destroy operator and offering more flexible search. As ALASPO and heulingo share the same underlying ASP solver and allow configuration of the used heuristic, our approach and methodology should transfer easily to the latter.

Related systems are *claspfolio* [15] and *ME-ASP* [21], which also perform automated configuration for ASP. In the case of claspfolio this concerns the settings of the ASP solver, whereas ME-ASP selects an ASP solver based on the given instance. In difference, we focus on the configuration of the outer ALNS. Furthermore, both claspfolio and ME-ASP only use general ASP program features and do not support custom feature extraction as we do. However, it is possible to use solver level configuration in our approach as a second level of configuration, or even integrate it into our SMAC-based tuning.

Xia et al. [34] explored the problem of SAT-based tree decomposition with the TW-SLIM (treewidth SAT-based local improvement method) framework. Instead of solving a large encoding of the problem into SAT, TW-SLIM uses multiple SAT calls to find decompositions for trees of smaller width. Unlike our work, this is not LNS but a distinct decomposition method and built upon SAT. Similar to our work, the authors investigated how best to choose and apply configurations for their framework. To find the best configurations, instances are clustered based on their features and the SMAC3 framework employed to find the best configuration for each cluster separately.

Similarly, Song et al. [31] proposed an AC method and also utilise SMAC3 but their target is Mixed-Integer Programming (MIP). Furthermore, their feature extraction does not use problem-specific knowledge but rather detected structural features from the graph representation of the instance.

6 Conclusion

We presented a Bayesian Hyperparameter Optimization approach for ASP with Large Neighbourhood Search and described its integration via the SMAC3 framework into ALASPO for automated tuning of ALASPO configurations. In addition, we provide customizable clustering of instances based on their characteristics, which allows one to obtain multiple optimal configurations – one for each cluster. The artifacts resulting from successful tunings run can be stored and passed to future invocations of ALASPO in order to automatically select and apply a configuration that fits the problem instance at hand. We investigated the effectiveness of our tuning approach on four benchmark problems of industrial relevance, using different clustering methods and varying the number of trials. Apparently, tuning may yield significant gains but its success is problem-specific, while clustering is most beneficial for diverse sets of instances.

Outlook. For future work, it would be interesting to further investigate the performance of the clustered approach on further benchmarks with more diverse sets of instances. As the custom clustering is highly dependent on the features selected by a custom feature extractor, testing and comparing the performance of several such implementations could be interesting. Finally, it may be worthwhile to explore more extensively whether tuning besides the selection strategies also other parts of the solver configuration can further increase the performance gains.

Acknowledgements. This work was supported by funding from the Bosch Center for AI at Renningen. Tobias Geibinger is a recipient of a DOC Fellowship of the Austrian Academy of Sciences at the Institute of Logic and Computation at the TU Wien.

References

1. Bergstra, J., Bengio, Y.: Random search for hyper-parameter optimization. JMLR **13**, 281–305 (2012)
2. Bossek, J., Kerschke, P., Neumann, A., Wagner, M., Neumann, F., Trautmann, H.: Evolving diverse TSP instances by means of novel and creative mutation operators. In: Proceedings of the FOGA, pp. 58–71. ACM (2019)
3. Brewka, G., Eiter, T., Truszczynski, M.: Answer set programming at a glance. Commun. ACM **54**(12), 92–103 (2011)
4. Calimeri, F., et al.: ASP-Core-2 input language format. TPLP **20**(2), 294–309 (2020)
5. Dantzig, G.B., Fulkerson, D.R., Johnson, S.M.: Solution of a large-scale traveling-salesman problem. OR **2**(4), 393–410 (1954)
6. Eiter, T., et al.: Adaptive large-neighbourhood search for optimisation in answer-set programming. AIJ **337**, 104230 (2024)
7. Feurer, M., Hutter, F.: Hyperparameter optimization. In: Hutter, F., Kotthoff, L., Vanschoren, J. (eds.) Automated Machine Learning. TSSCML, pp. 3–33. Springer, Cham (2019). https://doi.org/10.1007/978-3-030-05318-5_1
8. Fichte, J.K., Geibinger, T., Hecher, M., Schlögel, M.: Parallel empirical evaluations: resilience despite concurrency. In: Proceedings of theAAAI, pp. 8004–8012. AAAI Press (2024)
9. Gelfond, M., Lifschitz, V.: Classical negation in logic programs and disjunctive databases. N. Gener. Comput. **9**(3–4), 365–385 (1991)
10. Giustolisi, O., Savic, D.: Optimal design of isolation valve system for water distribution networks. In: Water Distribution Systems Analysis 2008, pp. 1–13. American Society of Civil Engineers (2009)
11. Gómez, R.N., Hernández, C., Baier, J.A.: Solving sum-of-costs multi-agent pathfinding with answer-set programming. In: Proceedings of the AAAI, pp. 9867–9874. AAAI Press (2020)
12. Gössner, S., Normington, G., Bormann, C.: Jsonpath: query expressions for JSON. RFC **9535**, 1–62 (2024)
13. Hartigan, J.A., Wong, M.A.: Algorithm as 136: a k-means clustering algorithm. J. Roy. Stat. Soc. **28**(1), 100–108 (1979)

14. Hoos, H.H.: Automated algorithm configuration and parameter tuning. In: Hamadi, Y., Monfroy, E., Saubion, F. (eds.) Autonomous Search, pp. 37–71. Springer, Heidelberg (2011). https://doi.org/10.1007/978-3-642-21434-9_3
15. Hoos, H.H., Lindauer, M., Schaub, T.: claspfolio 2: advances in algorithm selection for answer set programming. TPLP **14**(4–5), 569–585 (2014)
16. Hoos, H.H., Stützle, T.: Stochastic local search algorithms: an overview. In: Kacprzyk, J., Pedrycz, W. (eds.) Springer Handbook of Computational Intelligence, pp. 1085–1105. Springer, Heidelberg (2015). https://doi.org/10.1007/978-3-662-43505-2_54
17. Hutter, F., Hoos, H.H., Leyton-Brown, K., Stützle, T.: ParamILS: an automatic algorithm configuration framework. JAIR **36**, 267–306 (2009)
18. Jette, M.A., Wickberg, T.: Architecture of the slurm workload manager. In: Revised Selected Papers JSSPP. LNCS, pp. 3–23. Springer (2023)
19. Kohavi, R., John, G.H.: Automatic parameter selection by minimizing estimated error. In: Proceedings of the ICML, pp. 304–312. Morgan Kaufmann (1995)
20. Lindauer, M., et al.: SMAC3: a versatile Bayesian optimization package for hyperparameter optimization. JMLR **23**, 54:1–54:9 (2022)
21. Maratea, M., Pulina, L., Ricca, F.: A multi-engine approach to answer-set programming. TPLP **14**(6), 841–868 (2014)
22. McKerns, M.M., Strand, L., Sullivan, T., Fang, A., Aivazis, M.A.G.: Building a framework for predictive science. In: Proceedings of the SciPy, pp. 76–86. scipy.org (2011)
23. Mischek, F., Musliu, N.: The test laboratory scheduling problem. CD-TR 2018/1 Technical report (2018)
24. Mockus, J.: Application of bayesian approach to numerical methods of global and stochastic optimization. JGO **4**(4), 347–365 (1994)
25. Pfliegler, D.: Bayesian hyperparameter optimization with ALASPO and applications. Master's thesis, Technische Universität Wien, Wien (2025)
26. Pisinger, D., Ropke, S.: Large neighborhood search. In: Gendreau, M., Potvin, J.-Y. (eds.) Handbook of Metaheuristics. ISORMS, vol. 272, pp. 99–127. Springer, Cham (2019). https://doi.org/10.1007/978-3-319-91086-4_4
27. Rocklin, M.: Dask: parallel computation with blocked algorithms and task scheduling. In: Proceedings of the SciPy, pp. 126–132. scipy.org (2015)
28. Ropke, S., Pisinger, D.: An adaptive large neighborhood search heuristic for the pickup and delivery problem with time windows. TS **40**(4), 455–472 (2006)
29. Rousseeuw, P.J.: Silhouettes: a graphical aid to the interpretation and validation of cluster analysis. JCAM **20**, 53–65 (1987)
30. Shaw, P.: Using constraint programming and local search methods to solve vehicle routing problems. In: Maher, M., Puget, J.-F. (eds.) CP 1998. LNCS, vol. 1520, pp. 417–431. Springer, Heidelberg (1998). https://doi.org/10.1007/3-540-49481-2_30
31. Song, W., Liu, Y., Cao, Z., Wu, Y., Li, Q.: Instance-specific algorithm configuration via unsupervised deep graph clustering. EAAI **125**, 106740 (2023)
32. Stern, R., et al.: Multi-agent pathfinding: definitions, variants, and benchmarks. In: Proceedings of the SOCS, pp. 151–158. AAAI Press (2019)
33. Sugimori, I., et al.: Large neighborhood prioritized search for combinatorial optimization with answer set programming. In: Proceedings of the KR (2024)
34. Xia, H., Szeider, S.: Sat-based tree decomposition with iterative cascading policy selection. In: Proceedings of the AAAI, pp. 8191–8199. AAAI Press (2024)

Finding Counterexamples for External Equivalence

Jorge Fandinno[1], Jan Heuer[2(✉)], Tomi Janhunen[3], Javier Romero[2], and Torsten Schaub[2]

[1] University of Nebraska Omaha, Omaha, USA
[2] University of Potsdam, Potsdam, Germany
jan.heuer@uni-potsdam.de
[3] Tampere University, Tampere, Finland

Abstract. Refactoring is a common practice to improve code quality and maintainability while preserving external behavior. In Answer Set Programming, the *anthem* system supports this process by verifying the external equivalence of two encodings through a translation into first-order formulas, which are subsequently processed by automated theorem provers. However, while theorem proving is often successful for established equivalences, it frequently fails to terminate when programs are non-equivalent, leaving developers without actionable feedback during iterative refactoring. In this paper, we address this shortcoming by developing an approach for the automated generation of counterexamples for external equivalence. We extend an existing transformation for propositional programs to a first-order setting that covers a substantial subset of the *clingo* language, including non-tight encodings and aggregates. Furthermore, we generalize the transformation to handle private predicates through a novel guess-and-check formulation. Our approach is implemented in the *anthem-cx* system, providing developers with concrete witnesses of non-equivalence to facilitate the rapid identification of logical flaws in ASP encodings.

1 Introduction

Refactoring is the process of restructuring existing code to improve its internal properties without altering its external behavior. In the context of Answer Set Programming (ASP [14]), the *anthem* system [6] supports this practice by verifying *external equivalence* [7], which ensures that two encodings exhibit identical behavior relative to a specified interface. To this end, *anthem* translates non-ground (locally-tight) ASP programs into first-order formulas, leveraging off-the-shelf theorem provers to establish their external equivalence.

In practice, this approach faces a limitation stemming from the semi-decidability of first-order theorem proving. While valid equivalence properties can often be proven in reasonable time, automated theorem provers may diverge when two programs are not equivalent, effectively running "forever" and leaving

W. Faber et al. (Eds.): LPNMR 2026, LNAI 16952, pp. 231–247, 2027.
https://doi.org/10.1007/978-3-032-38320-4_15

the equivalence question open. This lack of termination is particularly detrimental during iterative refactoring, which relies on rapid, fail-fast feedback.. Furthermore, an inconclusive proof attempt provides no actionable insight into the underlying error. By shifting the focus to the generation of counterexamples, we address both of these practical issues. Although finding counterexamples remains generally undecidable, it naturally complements the theorem proving approach. In practice, counterexample search is highly effective precisely when equivalence does not hold. Not only does this provide a means to swiftly identify non-equivalence, but it also yields concrete witnesses, through specific input instances and their diverging output models, that allow developers to pinpoint logical flaws.

In this paper, we develop and implement an approach for finding counterexamples to external equivalence problems, specifically targeting the verification tasks addressed by the *anthem* system. While designed to complement *anthem*'s theorem-proving capabilities, our approach significantly expands its practical scope by accommodating a large subset of *clingo*'s input language [9], including non-tight encodings and aggregates. Our approach builds upon a transformation introduced in [10] for verifying weak equivalence of propositional programs. We extend this technique to verify the external equivalence of non-ground *clingo* encodings. In doing so, we generalize the account of private predicates, which provide local auxiliary definitions not subject to the equivalence check. Our counterexample generator is implemented in the *anthem-cx* tool and freely available.[1]

The rest of this paper is structured as follows. We introduce necessary background in Sect. 2. We discuss the complexity of external equivalence in Sect. 3. We define our transformation for generating counterexamples in Sect. 4 and discuss its correctness in a simplified setting that does not include private predicates. We extend the correctness discussion to account for private predicates in Sect. 5. While the transformation remains correct for restricted use of private predicates, we also discuss a novel adaptation accounting for arbitrary use of private predicates, as well as practical conditions to decide when this more general approach is necessary. In Sect. 6, we outline the design of the *anthem-cx* system, discuss its use as a companion tool to *anthem* and evaluate the combination of tools on a benchmark set. Finally, we discuss related work in Sect. 7 and conclude in Sect. 8.

2 Background

We consider a reduced fragment of the language of Abstract Gringo [8] and ASP-Core-2 [2]: non-disjunctive programs with non-recursive aggregates without conditional literals and pools.

Syntax. A *term* is either a *constant*, a *variable*, an *arithmetic term* or a *functional term*. A constant is either a *numeral* or a *symbolic constant*. A variable starts with an upper-case letter. An arithmetic term has the form $(t_1 \circ t_2)$ where t_1

[1] Available at: https://github.com/potassco/anthem-cx.

and t_2 are terms and $\circ$ is one of the *operation names* '..', '+', '−', '×', '/', '\'. A functional term has the form $f(\boldsymbol{t})$ where f is a symbolic constant and $\boldsymbol{t}$ is a tuple of terms.

An *atom* has the form $p(\boldsymbol{t})$ where p is a predicate and $\boldsymbol{t}$ is a tuple of terms. A *symbolic literal* is an atom possibly preceded by one or two occurrences of *not*. An *arithmetic literal* has the form $t_1 \prec t_2$ where t_1 and t_2 are terms and $\prec$ is one of the *relations* '=', '≠', '<', '>', '≤', '≥'.

An *aggregate atom* has the form $f\{\boldsymbol{t}_1 : L_1; \ldots; \boldsymbol{t}_n : L_n\} \prec u$, where f is one of *#count*, *#sum*, *#min*, *#max*, each $\boldsymbol{t}_i$ is a tuple of terms, each L_i is a (possibly empty) conjunction of symbolic literals, $\prec$ is a relation, and u is a term. An *aggregate literal* is an aggregate atom possibly preceded by one or two occurrences of *not*. A *literal* is a symbolic literal, an arithmetic literal or an aggregate literal. It is *negative* if it starts with one or two occurrences of *not*, and *positive* otherwise.

A *rule* has the form $h \leftarrow B$, where the head h is either $\bot$ or a symbolic atom, and the body B is a (possibly empty) conjunction of literals. We consider a choice rule $\{p(\boldsymbol{t})\} \leftarrow B$, where p is a predicate, $\boldsymbol{t}$ a tuple of terms and B as above, as an abbreviation for the rule $p(\boldsymbol{X}) \leftarrow B \wedge \boldsymbol{X} = \boldsymbol{t} \wedge \mathit{not\ not}\, p(\boldsymbol{X})$, where $\boldsymbol{X}$ is a tuple of fresh variables of the same length as $\boldsymbol{t}$. A *program* is a finite set of rules.

As in [2], we restrict the aggregates to be non-recursive. Further language constructs, such as head aggregates and choices with multiple elements and conditions, can be regarded as syntactic abbreviations, since they can be reduced to this fragment.

Semantics. The semantics for non-ground programs in our language is given in [8] by a transformation into infinitary propositional theories [27].

External Equivalence. A primary mode of *anthem* checks *external equivalence* [7], which is closely related to relativized uniform equivalence with projection [19,20].[2] In this setting, programs are associated with a user guide $(\mathcal{I}, \mathcal{O}, \mathcal{D})$ consisting of disjoint finite sets $\mathcal{I}$ and $\mathcal{O}$ of predicate symbols, called *input* and *output predicates*, respectively, and a collection $\mathcal{D}$ of *finite*[3] sets of ground atoms over $\mathcal{I}$, representing the admissible sets of *input atoms* for the programs.[4] Inputs not belonging to $\mathcal{D}$ fall outside the scope of the user guide. An *output atom* is a ground atom whose predicate belongs to $\mathcal{O}$.

[2] External equivalence allows for more fine grained control of considered inputs. As in relativized uniform equivalence with projection we specify the input predicates but we can additionally restrict the set of possible inputs. E.g., we can specify that the first argument of the predicate $p/2$ is an integer between 1 and 50, or that an input graph (via *node*/1 and *edge*/2) can not contain self loops. Another difference is that external equivalence forbids the use of input predicates in rule heads.

[3] The omission of this condition is an oversight in [7]. The restriction is due to the semantics of Abstract Gringo [8] which is defined for finite sets of rules only.

[4] This is a simplified version of user guides from [7], which additionally involve placeholders and their valuations.

A program adheres to a user guide if no input predicate appears in its rule heads. The predicate symbols in a program that are neither input nor output predicates are considered *private*. When comparing programs relative to a user guide, we assume their sets of private predicate symbols are disjoint. Given a program P, a user guide $(\mathcal{I}, \mathcal{O}, \mathcal{D})$, and an input $I \in \mathcal{D}$, the *external behavior* of P under input I is the set of all stable models of $P \cup I$ restricted to output atoms. Two programs P and Q are *externally equivalent* with respect to $(\mathcal{I}, \mathcal{O}, \mathcal{D})$ if they exhibit identical external behavior for every input in $\mathcal{D}$.

A *counterexample* to the external equivalence of P and Q with respect to $(\mathcal{I}, \mathcal{O}, \mathcal{D})$ is a pair of sets (I, O) where $I \in \mathcal{D}$ and O is an external behavior of either P or Q but not both. We say that a counterexample is for the *forward direction* if O is an external behavior of P, and for the *backward direction* otherwise. We define the *size* of a counterexample as the number of constants occurring in I.

We illustrate the definition of external equivalence with the orphan problem introduced in [7]. The set of input predicates is $\mathcal{I} = \{\mathit{father}, \mathit{mother}, \mathit{living}\}$, where *father* and *mother* are binary predicates and *living* is a unary predicate. The set of output predicates is $\mathcal{O} = \{\mathit{orphan}\}$, where *orphan* is a unary predicate. The domain $\mathcal{D}$ of the user guide is the collection of all sets of input atoms.

The first program, P_O, uses a private predicate *parentLiving* to define *orphan*

$$\begin{aligned} \mathit{parentLiving}(X) &\leftarrow \mathit{father}(Y, X) \wedge \mathit{living}(Y), \\ \mathit{parentLiving}(X) &\leftarrow \mathit{mother}(Y, X) \wedge \mathit{living}(Y), \\ \mathit{orphan}(X) &\leftarrow \mathit{living}(X) \wedge \mathit{not}\ \mathit{parentLiving}(X). \end{aligned}$$

While the second program, Q_O, defines *orphan* directly

$$\begin{aligned} \mathit{orphan}(X) \leftarrow\ & \mathit{living}(X) \wedge \mathit{father}(Y,X) \wedge \mathit{mother}(Z,X) \wedge \\ & \mathit{not}\ \mathit{living}(Y) \wedge \mathit{not}\ \mathit{living}(Z). \end{aligned}$$

The two programs are not externally equivalent, as we have the counterexample $(\{\mathit{living}(0)\}, \{\mathit{orphan}(0)\})$ of size 1 in the forward direction. Note that there is no counterexample in the backwards direction. If we instead take the domain $\mathcal{D}'$ as the collection of all inputs such that every living person has exactly one father and mother, then the programs are externally equivalent with respect to $(\mathcal{I}, \mathcal{O}, \mathcal{D}')$.

3 Complexity of External Equivalence

Before defining our transformation, we briefly discuss the complexity of external equivalence. Clearly for our full input language external equivalence is undecidable due to the undecidability of arithmetic.

We instead consider the subset of our language that only includes constants and variables as terms and does not include aggregates. Even for very restricted classes of this language fragment external equivalence remains undecidable as stated in the following theorem. The proof of the theorem relies on a similar technique as the proof of undecidability for query equivalence in Datalog from [25].

Theorem 1. *Assuming that the set of inputs is recursively enumerable and that programs do not have arithmetic terms, functional terms nor aggregates, the problem of deciding whether two logic programs are externally equivalent is co-recursively enumerable. It is undecidable even if we restrict the problem as follows:*

1. *both programs are positive, do not contain constraints, all rules contain at most two literals in the body, and all predicates are binary;*
2. *all rules contain at most two literals in the body, all predicates are binary, negation only occurs in a single constraint, and there are no private predicates;*
3. *both programs are tight, do not contain constraints, all rules contain at most three literals in the body, and all predicates are at most ternary.*

4 Basic Transformation

Our approach builds on an early method for testing the equivalence of logic programs [10]. We first outline the idea and then formulate it within a first-order setting. Here, we assume that the programs do not contain private predicates. We consider private predicates in Sect. 5.

Given two programs P and Q with a user guide $(\mathcal{I}, \mathcal{O}, \mathcal{D})$, we construct a program that is satisfiable if P exhibits an external behavior not shared by Q. Intuitively, this program performs the following four tasks:

1. Guess an input $I \in \mathcal{D}$.
2. Compute a stable model M of $P \cup I$.
3. Compute the minimal model M' of the reduct of $Q \cup I$ with respect to M.
4. Check whether the projections of M and M' onto $\mathcal{O}$ differ.

If the preceding check reveals a discrepancy, we have found a counterexample that reflects a difference in the external behaviors of P and Q.

In our setting, the program $E_d(P, Q)$ is parametrized by the input size d. It consists of one module for each task: a generator $G(d)$ enumerating inputs, the program P, a modified copy $Q^\star$ of Q addressing Task 3, and a discrepancy checker C.

Before defining $G(d)$, note that we cannot represent $\mathcal{D}$ explicitly as the set of admissible inputs may be infinite. Instead, following [7], we specify $\mathcal{D}$ by a set $\mathcal{A}$ of assumptions. A finite set of input atoms belongs to $\mathcal{D}$ iff it satisfies all assumptions in $\mathcal{A}$. In this work, assumptions are constraints over input predicates[5]. For example, the domain $\mathcal{D}$ of the orphan example is represented by $\mathcal{A} = \emptyset$, while the domain $\mathcal{D}'$ is represented by

$$\begin{aligned}\mathcal{A}' = \{&\bot \leftarrow \mathit{living}(X) \land \mathit{not}\ \#\mathit{count}\{Y : \mathit{mother}(Y, X)\} \neq 1,\\ &\bot \leftarrow \mathit{living}(X) \land \mathit{not}\ \#\mathit{count}\{Y : \mathit{father}(Y, X)\} \neq 1\}.\end{aligned}$$

[5] In [7], assumptions are first-order formulas over input predicates.

Given a natural number d, the component $G(d)$ contains the facts $dom(0)$, $\dots$, $dom(d-1)$ as well as the fact $dom(c)$ for every constant c occurring in P or Q. For every n-ary input predicate $p \in \mathcal{I}$ and $n \geq 0$, $G(d)$ contains a choice rule

$$\{p(X_1,\dots,X_n)\} \leftarrow dom(X_1) \wedge \cdots \wedge dom(X_n).$$

In addition, $G(d)$ contains the assumptions $\mathcal{A}$.

To accomplish Tasks 2 and 3 within the same encoding, we introduce a new starred copy $q^\star$ for each output predicate $q \in \mathcal{O}$.[6] The component $Q^\star$ is then obtained by replacing in Q every positive literal $q(\boldsymbol{t})$ such that $q \in \mathcal{O}$ by $q^\star(\boldsymbol{t})$, and every occurrence of $\bot$ by the fresh atom bot. Observe that all rule heads in $Q^\star$ are free of $\bot$ and predicates from $\mathcal{I} \cup \mathcal{O}$.

Lastly, the component C uses a fresh atom diff to indicate a discrepancy between models. Specifically, C contains the rules

$$\begin{aligned}
\bot &\leftarrow not\ \mathit{diff},\\
\mathit{diff} &\leftarrow bot,\\
\mathit{diff} &\leftarrow p(X_1,\dots,X_n) \wedge not\ p^\star(X_1,\dots,X_n), \text{ and}\\
\mathit{diff} &\leftarrow not\ p(X_1,\dots,X_n) \wedge p^\star(X_1,\dots,X_n)
\end{aligned}$$

for every n-ary output predicate $p \in \mathcal{O}$ with $n \geq 0$.

Altogether, for a natural number d, we obtain

$$E_d(P,Q) = G(d) \cup P \cup Q^\star \cup C.$$

The part $G(d) \cup P$ generates stable models M of $P \cup I$, where I is an input from $\mathcal{D}$. In $Q^\star$, negative literals are left unchanged. As a result, they are evaluated with respect to M, simulating the reduct of $Q \cup I$ with respect to M. The atoms derived from $Q^\star$, together with I, form a minimal model M' of this reduct. Finally, C checks whether the output atoms of M and M' differ (via diff), or some constraint from $Q^\star$ is violated (via additionally bot).

We return to the orphan example with the original domain $\mathcal{D}$. Even though the program P_O contains a private predicate, we can still use our method as for $E_d(P_O, Q_O)$ only Q_O needs to be free of private predicates.

The $\cdot^\star$ transformation only changes the rule head of Q_O:

$$\begin{aligned}
orphan(X)^\star \leftarrow\ & living(X) \wedge father(Y,X) \wedge mother(Z,X) \wedge\\
& not\ living(Y) \wedge not\ living(Z).
\end{aligned}$$

The program $E_1(P_O, Q_O)$ has the stable model $\{living(0), orphan(0), \mathit{diff}\}$ representing the previously mentioned counterexample.

[6] We do not need copies of input predicates as they cannot occur in rule heads.

4.1 Correctness

We discuss the correctness of $E_d(P, Q)$ by considering its parts separately.

The generator program $G(d)$ contains the constants occurring in P or Q as well as the set $\{0, \ldots, d-1\}$ as domain elements (via *dom*). Since $G(d)$ contains the assumptions $\mathcal{A}$, every input generated by $G(d)$ belongs to $\mathcal{D}$.

However, $G(d)$ does not generate all possible inputs. The generated inputs have size at most $d+n$ where n is the number of constants occurring in P and Q. But not all inputs of this size are generated because we consider only a fixed set of domain elements. In particular, we do not obtain inputs containing negative integers or symbolic constants not occurring in P or Q, even after increasing the parameter d.

In the following, let $\mathcal{U} = (\mathcal{I}, \mathcal{O}, \mathcal{D})$ be the user guide of the external equivalence problem. For a set $\mathcal{P}$ of predicates, let $\mathcal{P}^\star$ be the set $\{p^\star \mid p \in \mathcal{P}\}$. Similarly, for a set A of atoms, let $A^\star$ be the set $\{p^\star(\mathbf{t}) \mid p(\mathbf{t}) \subset A\}$. Let $\mathcal{U}^\star$ be the user guide with input predicates $\mathcal{I} \cup \mathcal{O}$, output predicates $\mathcal{O}^\star \cup \{bot\}$, and domain consisting of all sets of atoms over $\mathcal{I} \cup \mathcal{O}$.

We state two properties related to $Q^\star$: correctness and uniqueness. Correctness states that $Q^\star$ captures the external behavior of Q.

Lemma 1. *Let I and O be an input and an output of $\mathcal{U}$, respectively. The set O is an external behavior of Q with respect to $\mathcal{U}$ under input I iff the set $O^\star$ is an external behavior of $Q^\star$ with respect to $\mathcal{U}^\star$ under input $I \cup O$.*

This lemma justifies checking whether O is an external behavior of Q under input I by checking whether $O^\star$ is an external behavior of $Q^\star$ under input $I \cup O$.

We say that Q satisfies *uniqueness* with respect to $\mathcal{U}$ if for every input $I \in \mathcal{D}$ and every set of atoms O over $\mathcal{O}$, the program $Q^\star \cup I \cup O$ has a unique stable model.

Lemma 2. *If Q does not contain private predicates then it satisfies uniqueness with respect to $\mathcal{U}$.*

The reason is that $Q^\star$ is a stratified program: aggregates are not recursive, and negative symbolic literals use only predicates from $\mathcal{I} \cup \mathcal{O}$, which do not occur in the rule heads of $Q^\star$.

The program C receives as input the outputs of P and $Q^\star$. The former is some set of atoms O over $\mathcal{O}$, while the latter is a set of atoms U over $\mathcal{O}^\star \cup \{bot\}$. C is satisfied iff the atom *diff* is derived. This is the case if (i) $bot \in U$ or (ii) there is some $p(\mathbf{t})$ with $p \in \mathcal{O}$ such that either $p(\mathbf{t}) \in O$ and $p^\star(\mathbf{t}) \notin U$ or $p^\star(\mathbf{t}) \in U$ and $p(\mathbf{t}) \notin O$. It follows that C is satisfied iff $O^\star \neq U$.

Finally, we put the results of the individual program parts together. $G(d)$ generates some input I of size $d+n$ of the user guide $\mathcal{U}$ where n is the number of constants occurring in P and Q. P has some external behavior O under input I. By uniqueness of Q (Lemma 2), $Q^\star$ has a unique external behavior U under input $I \cup O$. By correctness of $Q^\star$ (Lemma 1), $O^\star = U$ iff O is an external behavior of Q. Then we have that C is satisfied iff $O^\star \neq U$ which is the case iff O is not an external behavior of Q.

Theorem 2. *If Q has no private predicates, and $E_d(P, Q)$ is satisfiable for a natural number d, then P and Q are not externally equivalent with respect to $\mathcal{U}$.*

From the stable model M of $E_d(P, Q)$ we obtain the sets I and O defining the counterexample by projecting M to $\mathcal{I}$ and $\mathcal{O}$, respectively.

5 Private Predicates

5.1 Correctness of $E_d(P, Q)$

The presence of private predicates in Q does not affect our discussion from Sect. 4.1 about the correctness of $G(d)$ or C. We only have to consider whether we can lift the two properties related to $Q^\star$.

It turns out that correctness (Lemma 1) lifts directly to this extended setting, but uniqueness (Lemma 2) does not. In the presence of private predicates, the program $Q^\star$ simulates a partial reduct where the literals over private predicates are left unchanged. This may generate many stable models and break the approach. For example, consider the problem where $P = \{\{x\}, p \leftarrow x\}$, $Q = \{\{y\}, p \leftarrow y\}$, and the user guide has $\mathcal{I} = \emptyset$, $\mathcal{O} = \{p\}$, and $\mathcal{D} = \{\emptyset\}$. Clearly, P and Q are externally equivalent. But the program $Q^\star = \{\{y\}, p^\star \leftarrow y\}$ has two stable models, and for each model of P it can generate the wrong one. Thus, although the program $E_d(P, Q)$ should be unsatisfiable, it has two stable models: $\{x, p, \mathit{diff}\}$ and $\{y, p^\star, \mathit{diff}\}$.

Theorem 2 remains correct whenever P and Q satisfy the uniqueness property.[7]

Theorem 3. *If Q satisfies the uniqueness property with respect to $\mathcal{U}$, and $E_d(P, Q)$ is satisfiable for some natural number d, then P and Q are not externally equivalent with respect to $\mathcal{U}$.*

For example, in the orphan problem the program P_O satisfies uniqueness. Thus, if $E_d(Q_O, P_O)$ has a stable model, we obtain a correct counterexample. But as the orphan problem does not have a counterexample in the backwards direction, $E_d(Q_O, P_O)$ is unsatisfiable for every value d.

5.2 Guess-and-Check Transformation

For programs that do not satisfy the uniqueness criterion, we adapt our transformation using guess-and-check answer set programming.

A *guess-and-check problem* is a pair (G, C) of logic programs G and C. A solution to such a problem is a stable model X of G such that $X \cup C$ is unsatisfiable. The approach was introduced in [5]. We use an implementation for non-disjunctive logic programs[8] based on techniques described in [13].

[7] In [12] uniqueness is called *enough visible atoms (EVA)* in the context of private predicates.

[8] Available at: https://github.com/potassco/guess_and_check.

Our guess program is $E_d^{\mathcal{G}}(P, Q) = G(d) \cup P$. It generates an input I of size $d + n$ (where n is the number of constants occurring in P and Q) and an external behavior O of P. Its correctness follows from the correctness of $G(d)$ discussed in Sect. 4.1.

Our check program is $E^{\mathcal{C}}(P, Q) = Q^\star \cup C'$, where C' is obtained from C by replacing the constraint $\bot \leftarrow$ *not diff* by $\bot \leftarrow$ *diff*. It searches for an external behavior of Q (under input I) that coincides with O (the external behavior of P). If such an external behavior exists, then, by Lemma 1, $O^\star$ is an external behavior of $Q^\star$ under input $I \cup O$. In this case, *diff* is not derived in C', the constraint $\bot \leftarrow$ *diff* is satisfied, and the check program is satisfiable. Hence, the stable model of the guess program is not a solution for the guess-and-check problem. On the other hand, if no such external behavior of Q exists, the check program is unsatisfiable, and the stable model of the guess program is a solution.

Let $E_d^{\mathcal{GC}}(P, Q)$ denote the guess-and-check problem $(E_d^{\mathcal{G}}(P, Q), E^{\mathcal{C}}(P, Q))$.

Theorem 4. *If $E_d^{\mathcal{GC}}(P, Q)$ has a solution for some natural number d, then P and Q are not externally equivalent with respect to $\mathcal{U}$.*

For example, recall the externally equivalent programs from Sect. 5.1. While the program $E_d(P, Q)$ finds an incorrect counterexample, the guess-and-check program $E_d^{\mathcal{GC}}(P, Q)$ has no solution.

5.3 Verifying Uniqueness

Since guess-and-check problems are solved using disjunctive logic programs, it is useful to identify programs that satisfy the uniqueness condition, to avoid the additional complexity of disjunctive ASP. However, deciding whether a program satisfies uniqueness is already coNP-hard in the propositional case [12, Proposition 4.14]. We therefore consider two sufficient criteria below.

Stratification. Checking whether the program $Q^\star$ is stratified is a sufficient syntactic criterion for uniqueness. This can be checked directly on the signed dependency graph [4] of Q, after removing the edges induced by negative literals over output predicates. For the orphan example, this criterion establishes uniqueness.

Local Uniqueness. If $E_d(P, Q)$ finds a potential counterexample and we do not know whether Q satisfies uniqueness, we may consider a local notion of uniqueness to check the validity of the counterexample. We say that Q is *locally unique* for a potential counterexample (I, O) if $Q^\star$ has a unique stable model under input $I \cup O$. If this condition holds, then (I, O) is a valid counterexample, even if Q does not satisfy uniqueness in general.

This suggests the following method. Start searching for potential counterexamples using $E_d(P, Q)$. If one is found, then check whether Q is locally unique for it. If that is the case, return the counterexample; otherwise, switch to the guess-and-check approach. If $E_d(P, Q)$ has no stable models, then the method can stop, provided that $Q^\star$ is call-consistent [4], i.e., its signed dependency graph has no loops containing an odd number of negative edges.[9]

Theorem 5. *For every natural number d, if $E_d(P,Q)$ has no stable models and $Q^\star$ is call-consistent, then $E_d^{\mathcal{GC}}(P,Q)$ has no solution.*

This condition is often satisfied in practice. Note that Q may include constraints, but in $Q^\star$ they are translated into normal rules and do not affect call-consistency. But if $Q^\star$ is not call-consistent, we need to use the guess-and-check approach. For example, consider the problem with $P = \emptyset$, $Q = \{x \leftarrow \mathit{not}\, x\}$, and the user guide $\mathcal{I} = \emptyset$, $\mathcal{O} = \emptyset$, and $\mathcal{D} = \{\emptyset\}$. The program $Q^\star = Q$ is not call-consistent. It is also unsatisfiable under every input. Hence, the program $E_d(P,Q)$ will not find a potential counterexample for any value of d. But the guess-and-check program $E_0^{\mathcal{GC}}(P,Q)$ has a solution, the empty set, which corresponds to the counterexample $(\emptyset, \emptyset)$.

6 The *anthem-cx* System

We have implemented the transformations $E_d(P,Q)$ and $E_d^{\mathcal{GC}}(P,Q)$ in the tool *anthem-cx*.[10] The implementation uses *clingo*'s python API to obtain and transform the abstract syntax trees of P and Q.

For the user guide we follow the syntax of *anthem*. While *anthem* supports the declaration of placeholders in a user guide, our method currently does not support placeholders and thus ignores them.[11] For *anthem* assumptions are declared as first-order formulas in the user guide. Such declarations are also ignored by our tool. Instead, assumptions can be passed as a separate file containing ASP constraints (only using input predicates) to *anthem-cx*.

Before transforming the programs, *anthem-cx* renames any conflicting private predicates. Additionally, *anthem-cx* ensures that the introduced auxiliary predicates (such as *diff*) are new by renaming them in case of conflicts.

After obtaining the counterexample programs our tool automatically invokes *clingo* to solve them. For this, the size parameter d is increased until a counterexample is found. The initial value of d can be adjusted (by default 0) and optionally a maximum value can be provided.

Regarding the uniqueness condition, we have implemented the two checks described in Sect. 5.3. We provide options to adjust which check(s) are used or alternatively disable or force the use of the guess-and-check method.

Finally, we note that our implementation includes experimental support for an even larger input language. In particular, syntactic shortcuts such as head

---

[9] Here we consider edges induced by literals starting with two occurrences of *not* as *positive*. This differs from the treatment of such literals when checking stratification (where we consider such edges as *negative*)

[10] Available at: https://github.com/potassco/anthem-cx.

[11] A possible approach to support placeholders is to introduce a new predicate encoding the value of a placeholder. The programs are then adjusted to use this predicate and assumptions are added ensuring that each placeholder has exactly one value.

aggregates are unfolded and features such as conditionals and pools are supported.

6.1 Using *anthem-cx* in Conjunction with *anthem*

Our tool complements the functionality of *anthem* for investigating whether an external equivalence holds or not. We illustrate this with the *orphan* example from Sect. 2. The user guide (with domain $\mathcal{D}$) is represented by the following:

```
input: father/2.    input: mother/2.    input: living/1.
output: orphan/1.
```

Running *anthem* to verify the external equivalence of the programs P_O and Q_O results in a timeout as the programs are not externally equivalent. By running our system using the command

```
anthem-cx orphan.1.lp orphan.2.lp orphan.ug
```

we obtain a counterexample of size 1 in the forward direction as indicated by the output of *anthem-cx*:

```
Found a counterexample of size 1 in the forward direction
  Input for the counterexample: living(0)
  External behavior of left: orphan(0)
```

Under the input `living(0)` the first program, P_O, has the external behavior `orphan(0)` which is not an external behavior of the second program, Q_O.

As mentioned in Sect. 2, the programs are externally equivalent if we restrict the domain to $\mathcal{D}'$. If we add the assumptions $\mathcal{A}'$ from Sect. 4 (characterizing $\mathcal{D}'$) to *anthem-cx* by appending the following option

```
--assumptions orphan-assumptions.lp
```

to the previous command, the counterexample search no longer terminates. After adding these assumptions to the user guide as first-order formulas[12] *anthem* successfully verifies the external equivalence.

As a second example, we consider path finding on a graph. The user guide of this problem is defined as follows:

```
input: start/1.    input: goal/1.    input: edge/2.
output: path/2.
```

The first program computes a path by starting from the `start` node and consecutively choosing a successor node until the `goal` node is reached.

```
visit(X) :- start(X).
{ path(X,Y) : edge(X,Y) } = 1 :- visit(X), not goal(X).
visit(Y) :- visit(X), path(X,Y).
:- not visit(X), goal(X).
```

[12] The translation into first-order formulas needs to be performed manually here. In cases where the constraints are in the input language of *anthem* it is possible to use the translation mode of *anthem* to automatically obtain the first-order formulas.

The second program follows a similar approach but computes the path in a backward manner. I.e., starting from the `goal` node, a predecessor node is consecutively chosen until the `start` node is reached.

```
reach(X) :- goal(X).
{ path(Y,X) : edge(Y,X) } = 1 :- reach(X), not start(X).
reach(Y) :- reach(X), path(Y,X).
:- not reach(X), start(X).
```

Running *anthem-cx*, we obtain a counterexample of size 1 in the forward direction with input `edge(0,0)` and `start(0)`, under which the first program has the external behavior `path(0,0)`. The second program does not have this external behavior, as it does not generate paths due to the lack of a `goal` node and is thus unsatisfiable.

Under the additional assumption that any input contains exactly one `start` and one `goal` node, the two programs become externally equivalent. However, we cannot verify this using *anthem* as the programs use aggregates and non-tight rules, which are not supported by *anthem*.

6.2 Experiments

Following the outlined approach, we test the combination of *anthem-cx* and *anthem* on a benchmark set of external equivalence examples. As our example problems, we use the benchmark problems from [6] complemented by a variation of one of those problems (tiling') as well as some new examples (path, transitive, independent, coloring).

For the problems from [6] we disregard any assumptions defined in the user guide as well as any supplementary proof outlines (a feature of *anthem* to assist the proof process). The reason for this is that assumptions are usually not obvious initially and only added after unsuccessful proof attempts and careful consideration of the problem. Similarly, proof outlines are constructed after failed proof attempts. In this way, our setup reflects a user's initial attempt to verify the equivalence of their programs.

As some of the problems from [6] use placeholders we modify them to replace the placeholders by new input predicates and additional assumptions.[13] One of the problems from [6] is incompatible with *anthem-cx* due to the use of an unsafe rule in one of the programs. For the newly added problems we note that some of them are not supported by *anthem* as the programs are not in the input language of *anthem* or are not (locally) tight.

Table 1 contains for each problem the runtime of *anthem-cx* and *anthem* in seconds. The experiments were run on Ubuntu 24.04.4 LTS, Intel(R) Core(TM) Ultra 7 265U, 32 GB RAM with a 300 s time limit and 8 cores for *anthem* (i.e., its underlying theorem prover *vampire*). Problems not compatible with a tool are indicated by "–" for the runtime. Symbols ">>" and "<<" indicate that the complementary tool found a proof or counterexample, respectively. In these cases

[13] We note that this modification may impact the runtime (of *anthem*) negatively.

the tool must necessarily timeout as no counterexample or proof, respectively, exists. The problems are partitioned into equivalent and non-equivalent ones.

Table 1. Evaluating the combination of *anthem-cx* and *anthem*

Problem	*anthem-cx* Runtime	*anthem* Runtime
Cover	>>	0.197
Tiling	Timeout	Timeout
Primes (1v2)	–	3.612
Primes (2v3)	Timeout	Timeout
Frame	0.309	<<
Orphan	0.269	<<
Path	0.285	–
Transitive	0.284	–
Tiling’	0.361	–
Independent	0.320	<<
Coloring	0.317	<<

For 9 out of the 11 problems one of the tools terminates within in a few seconds. The two problems where neither tool terminates are equivalent but require the addition of a proof outline for *anthem* to find a proof. For the seven non-equivalent problems, *anthem-cx* finds a counterexample in under a second. Using just *anthem* it would not be clear whether the non-termination (of *anthem*) is due to the difficulty of the proof task or due to non-equivalence.

We note that *vampire*, the theorem prover used by *anthem*, has a portfolio mode, `casc_sat`, for showing satisfiability of a problem corresponding to a counterexample of the problem posed by *anthem*. Using this mode still results in timeouts for all problems that timeout for *anthem*.

As a second benchmark set we use a set of query equivalence problems from the SPARQL query language [3]. The *SparqLog* system [1] provides a translation from SPARQL to Datalog. We modified the translation to obtain ASP rules instead, resulting in a set of 41 external equivalence problems. Of the 41 problems all but 2 are not equivalent. For each non-equivalent problem, *anthem-cx* finds a counterexample in around 0.3 s. For the two equivalent problems, *anthem* is able to find proofs in a similar time.

7 Related Work

As explained in Sect. 4, our work builds upon an earlier approach for verifying (weak) equivalence of propositional logic programs [10]. The method is implemented by a translator *lpeq* [11] for combining ground logic programs so that the actual verification task can be carried out by an ASP solver. This work is part of a series of investigations on different notions of equivalences [10,12,23,24] and their implementation using native ASP solvers as back-end solvers. There are further generalizations for disjunctive logic programs [22] and translators [11] also supporting the verification of classical and strong equivalence.

Concepts related to program interfaces and encapsulation are taken increasingly into account, e.g., in terms of private predicates [12] and by splitting public predicates into input and output predicates [23,24] for program modules.[14] The input language of all these approaches is limited to propositional (ground) programs with more restricted forms of aggregates. Furthermore, the transformations (and the respective implementations) of all aforementioned works accounting for private predicates are limited to programs fulfilling uniqueness. Any modifications to lift this restriction, such as our method from Sect. 5.2, are not considered.

For the common language fragment, our transformation behaves almost exactly like the one from [24] but there is a key difference in the treatment of private predicates. The original translation $E(P, Q)$ of [24] introduces a second copy of every private predicate of Q, and a second copy of every rule of Q defining a private predicate such that this second copy only refers to the joint input and the external behaviour of P. Moreover, the translation contains additional rules to derive the *diff* predicate for differences in these two versions of the private predicates. In contrast, our translation does not duplicate the private predicates of Q (and their rules). Under uniqueness, any differences in the two copies of private predicates must result from differences in the output predicates of P and Q. Therefore, as all output predicates are checked for differences the additional copies of private predicates become unnecessary.

Another closely related approach [17,19,21,26] reduces equivalences of disjunctive propositional programs without aggregates to QBFs. These works are based on so-called *correspondence frames*, providing a general framework for specifying equivalence relations, with weak or uniform equivalence (optionally with relativization and projection) as particular instances of this framework. The transformation to QBFs encodes arbitrary correspondence frames. Due to the expressiveness of QBFs, private predicates (even in disjunctive programs) are fully supported. While a follow-up study [18] discusses potential adaptations to the non-ground case no concrete implementation exists.

The overall approach of testing on small inputs corresponds to the so-called *small-scope hypothesis*: a general principle from software testing stating that most errors can be found by testing a program for all inputs of some small size. For ASP, an empirical evaluation of the small-scope hypothesis was conducted in [16]. The idea is to check the equivalence of a program and its mutated version, obtained by introducing small modifications to the program such as dropping literals, adding negation or renaming variables. The empirical evaluation confirmed that the small scope hypothesis holds in this setting. While such an approach

[14] The notions of equivalence in [12,23,24] also take into account the numbers of stable models in one-to-one correspondence. However, due to the limitation to programs fulfilling the uniqueness property, this aspect need not be accounted for.

of testing on small inputs may hold empirically it is incomplete even for simple classes of programs as follows directly from the results in Sect. 3.

8 Discussion

We have developed a transformation to generate counterexamples to external equivalence problems by extending an earlier method [10] for verifying weak equivalence of propositional programs. As the input language we consider non-ground programs with non-recursive aggregates corresponding to a large fragment of Abstract Gringo [8] and ASP-Core-2 [2]. Our approach allows for the unrestricted use of private predicates (i.e., predicates not subject to equivalence), lifting a restriction from earlier ASP-based verification work.

We have implemented our approach in the *anthem-cx* tool. First experiments show that our method is effective for identifying non-equivalence by quickly computing concrete counterexamples. This complements existing work on verifying external equivalence using *anthem* [6].

For simplicity, we have restricted the use of aggregates to be non-recursive. However, our results remain valid for unrestricted monotone aggregates (under Ferraris semantics). For general recursive aggregates (and disjunctive programs) this is no longer the case, although Lemma 1 and Theorem 3 continue to hold.

We plan to extend our transformation to account for the full Abstract Gringo language in future work. Furthermore, we plan to adapt the related method from [11] for verifying strong equivalence of propositional programs to the Abstract Gringo language as well.

Acknowledgments. This work was partly funded by DFG grant SCHA 550/15, Germany, and by the National Science Foundation CAREER award 2338635, USA. Any opinions, findings, and conclusions or recommendations expressed in this material are those of the authors and do not necessarily reflect the views of the National Science Foundation.

Disclosure of Interests. The authors have no competing interests to declare that are relevant to the content of this article.

References

1. Angles, R., Gottlob, G., Pavlovic, A., Pichler, R., Sallinger, E.: SparqLog: a system for efficient evaluation of SPARQL 1.1 queries via datalog. Proc. VLDB Endowment **16**(13), 4240–4253 (2023)
2. Calimeri, F., et al.: ASP-Core-2 input language format. Theory Pract. Logic Program. **20**(2), 294–309 (2020)
3. Wudage Chekol, M., Euzenat, J., Genevès, P., Layaïda, N.: Evaluating and benchmarking SPARQL query containment solvers. In: Alani, H., et al. (eds.) ISWC 2013. LNCS, vol. 8219, pp. 408–423. Springer, Heidelberg (2013). https://doi.org/10.1007/978-3-642-41338-4_26

4. Dung, P.: On the relations between stable and well-founded semantics of logic programs. Theoret. Comput. Sci. **105**(1), 7–25 (1992)
5. Eiter, T., Polleres, A.: Towards automated integration of guess and check programs in answer set programming: a meta-interpreter and applications. Theory Pract. Logic Program. **6**(1–2), 23–60 (2006)
6. Fandinno, J., et al.: ANTHEM 2.0: automated reasoning for answer set programming. Theory Pract. Logic Program. **25**(4), 668–684 (2025)
7. Fandinno, J., Hansen, Z., Lierler, Y., Lifschitz, V., Temple, N.: External behavior of a logic program and verification of refactoring. Theory Pract. Logic Program. **23**(4), 933–947 (2023)
8. Gebser, M., Harrison, A., Kaminski, R., Lifschitz, V., Schaub, T.: Abstract Gringo. Theory Pract. Logic Program. **15**(4–5), 449–463 (2015)
9. Gebser, M., Kaminski, R., Kaufmann, B., Schaub, T.: Multi-shot ASP solving with clingo. Theory Pract. Logic Program. **19**(1), 27–82 (2019)
10. Janhunen, T., Oikarinen, E.: Testing the equivalence of logic programs under stable model semantics. In: Flesca, S., Greco, S., Ianni, G., Leone, N. (eds.) JELIA 2002. LNCS (LNAI), vol. 2424, pp. 493–504. Springer, Heidelberg (2002). https://doi.org/10.1007/3-540-45757-7_41
11. Janhunen, T., Oikarinen, E.: LPEQ and DLPEQ — translators for automated equivalence testing of logic programs. [15], pp. 336–340
12. Janhunen, T., Oikarinen, E.: Automated verification of weak equivalence within the smodels system. Theory Pract. Logic Program. **7**(6), 697–744 (2007)
13. Kaminski, R., Romero, J., Schaub, T., Wanko, P.: How to build your own ASP-based system?! Theory Pract. Logic Program. **23**(1), 299–361 (2023)
14. Lifschitz, V.: Answer Set Programming. Springer (2019)
15. Lifschitz, V., Niemelä, I. (eds.): Proceedings of the Seventh International Conference on Logic Programming and Nonmonotonic Reasoning (LPNMR 2004). Springer (2004)
16. Oetsch, J., Prischink, M., Pührer, J., Schwengerer, M., Tompits, H.: On the small-scope hypothesis for testing answer-set programs. In: Proceedings of the Thirteenth International Conference on Principles of Knowledge Representation and Reasoning (KR 2012). AAAI (2012)
17. Oetsch, J., Seidl, M., Tompits, H., Woltran, S.: CCT: a correspondence-checking tool for logic programs under the answer-set semantics. In: Fisher, M., van der Hoek, W., Konev, B., Lisitsa, A. (eds.) JELIA 2006. LNCS (LNAI), vol. 4160, pp. 502–505. Springer, Heidelberg (2006). https://doi.org/10.1007/11853886_47
18. Oetsch, J., Seidl, M., Tompits, H., Woltran, S.: CCT on Stage: generalised uniform equivalence testing for verifying student assignment solutions. In: Erdem, E., Lin, F., Schaub, T. (eds.) LPNMR 2009. LNCS (LNAI), vol. 5753, pp. 382–395. Springer, Heidelberg (2009). https://doi.org/10.1007/978-3-642-04238-6_32
19. Oetsch, J., Seidl, M., Tompits, H., Woltran, S.: Beyond uniform equivalence between answer-set programs. ACM Trans. Comput. Logic **22**(1), 2:1–2:46 (2020)
20. Oetsch, J., Tompits, H.: Program correspondence under the answer-set semantics: the non-ground case. In: Garcia de la Banda, M., Pontelli, E. (eds.) ICLP 2008. LNCS, vol. 5366, pp. 591–605. Springer, Heidelberg (2008). https://doi.org/10.1007/978-3-540-89982-2_49
21. Oetsch, J., Tompits, H., Woltran, S.: Facts do not cease to exist because they are ignored: Relativised uniform equivalence with answer-set projection. In: Proceedings of the Twenty-second National Conference on Artificial Intelligence (AAAI 2007), pp. 458–464. AAAI (2007)

22. Oikarinen, E., Janhunen, T.: Verifying the equivalence of logic programs in the disjunctive disjunctive case. [15], pp. 180–193
23. Oikarinen, E., Janhunen, T.: Modular equivalence for normal logic programs. In: Proceedings of the Seventeenth European Conference on Artificial Intelligence (ECAI 2006), pp. 412–416. IOS (2006)
24. Oikarinen, E., Janhunen, T.: A translation-based approach to the verification of modular equivalence. J. Log. Comput. **19**(4), 591–613 (2009)
25. Shmueli, O.: Equivalence of datalog queries is undecidable. J. Log. Program. **15**(3), 231–241 (1993)
26. Tompits, H., Woltran, S.: Towards implementations for advanced equivalence checking in answer-set programming. In: Gabbrielli, M., Gupta, G. (eds.) ICLP 2005. LNCS, vol. 3668, pp. 189–203. Springer, Heidelberg (2005). https://doi.org/10.1007/11562931_16
27. Truszczynski, M.: Connecting first-order ASP and the logic FO(ID) through reducts. In: Erdem, E., Lee, J., Lierler, Y., Pearce, D. (eds.) Correct Reasoning. LNCS, vol. 7265, pp. 543–559. Springer, Heidelberg (2012). https://doi.org/10.1007/978-3-642-30743-0_37

Theory-Level Heuristics and Multi-level Optimization for `clingon`

Giray Havur[1,3](✉), Francesco Zuccato[2], Rafael Philipp Bankosegger[1], Richard Comploi-Taupe[1], and Patrick Rodler[2](✉)

[1] Siemens AG Österreich, Vienna, Austria
{giray.havur,rafael-philipp.bankosegger,richard.taupe}@siemens.com
[2] University of Klagenfurt, Klagenfurt, Austria
{francesco.zuccato,patrick.rodler}@aau.at
[3] St. Pölten University of Applied Sciences, St. Pölten, Austria

Abstract. `clingcon` extends the Answer Set Programming (ASP) solver `clingo` with linear constraints over finite-domain integer variables and is one of the most prominent systems of this kind. Two practical limitations remain: users cannot declaratively control how the solver explores the integer variables, and optimization is restricted to a single objective. We address both with three problem-independent extensions: a `&heuristic` directive that specifies which integer variable to branch on next and which value to try first, including a cooperative mode that only adjusts value selection and leaves variable selection to the solver; a `@priority` annotation for `&minimize` that enables lexicographic multi-objective optimization, solved either level by level or via an equivalent single weighted objective; and a `--bound-step` option that accelerates branch-and-bound by shrinking the objective bound in larger steps, e.g., by bisection. On hard scheduling benchmarks, these extensions prove optimality on instances where the default configuration proves none, raising proven optima from zero to nine out of ten on an industrial scheduling problem. A mismatched strategy, however, can also degrade performance; we characterize when each extension helps.

Keywords: Answer Set Programming (ASP) · Constraint Answer Set Programming (CASP) · `clingcon` · Solver Extensions · Search Heuristics · Lexicographic Optimization · Branch and Bound

1 Introduction

Answer Set Programming (ASP) [19] is a declarative problem-solving paradigm grounded in stable model semantics [14]. Modern ASP solvers such as `clingo` [10] solve the propositional (Boolean) part of a logic program using Conflict-Driven Nogood Learning (CDNL) [12,29]. However, problems that involve numerical reasoning, such as scheduling with time windows [13,32], resource allocation with capacities [5], and packing with geometric constraints [18], require integer

W. Faber et al. (Eds.): LPNMR 2026, LNAI 16952, pp. 248–264, 2027.
https://doi.org/10.1007/978-3-032-38320-4_16

variables and arithmetic constraints, which traditional ASP struggles to model efficiently, not least due to the grounding bottleneck.

The solver `clingcon` [5] addresses this gap by combining ASP with finite-domain integer constraints. Integer variables are encoded as *order literals* of the form $x \leq v$, providing the core mechanism through which CDNL communicates with a theory propagator in the integer domain [24]. Branching on these literals tightens integer bounds, and constraint propagation feeds back into CDNL via learned nogoods. While `clingcon` provides an expressive modeling language and effective solving techniques, two limitations restrict its use, particularly on hard problems: **(1) No declarative search control for integer variables.** Branching choices can change solving times by orders of magnitude, so ASP systems let users influence them: `clingo` offers built-in branching heuristics, most notably VSIDS [22], and problem-specific guidance over Boolean atoms through its `#heuristic` directive [11]. No comparable mechanism exists for `clingcon`'s integer variables, whose order literals are indistinguishable from ordinary Boolean literals to these heuristics. Users cannot, for example, direct the search to the variable with the smallest remaining domain, or make it try small values before large ones. Such control is standard in Constraint Programming (CP) solvers [26] and specified declaratively in MiniZinc [23] through search annotations. **(2) Optimization is limited to a single objective.** Many real-world problems call for lexicographic optimization; a scheduling problem may need to minimize tardiness first, then energy, and then makespan [32]. At the Boolean level, `clingo`'s `#minimize` directive supports such priority levels, but `clingcon`'s theory-level `&minimize` does not, so multi-level optimization over integer variables requires manually orchestrating a sequence of solver calls.

We address these limitations with three problem-independent extensions to `clingcon` 5: **(i)** a theory-level `&heuristic` directive specifying variable selection, value selection, and tie-breaking for integer variables, including a cooperative mode where VSIDS keeps picking the variable and the directive only decides which value to try first; **(ii)** the `@priority` annotation for `&minimize`, reintroduced from `clingcon` 3, with two lexicographic solving strategies selectable via `--lex-opt`: multi-shot, optimizing one priority level at a time, and weighted, which exploits the linearity of `&minimize` objectives to combine all levels into one equivalent objective compatible with parallel solving; and **(iii)** a `--bound-step` option that controls how branch-and-bound tightens the objective bound after each improving solution, with linear, bisection, and hybrid strategies.

We experimentally assess the impact of these extensions on seven benchmark problems, including four `clingcon` benchmarks from [5,18] and two industrial scheduling applications, i.e., the energy-aware double-flexible job-shop scheduling problem (E-DFJSP) [32] and the test laboratory scheduling problem (TLSP) [13]. The results show that the proposed extensions can enable the solver to prove optimality for hard instances unsolved with `clingcon`'s default configuration. For example, using bisection-based bound stepping raises the proportion of proven optima on E-DFJSP instances from 0 % to 90 %. Conversely, we also identify conditions under which an ill-suited strategy degrades performance. Section 2 introduces preliminaries; Sects. 3 and 4 present our extensions; Sects. 5–7 report the evaluation, related work, and conclusions.

2 Preliminaries

In this section, we introduce our notation and review the order-literal encoding as well as the CDNL search strategy underpinning `clingo` and `clingcon`.

ASP with Constraint Solving. The `clingcon` system [5] extends ASP with integer variables and linear arithmetic constraints through `clingo`'s theory propagator interface. The theory language enables domain declarations (e.g., `&dom{0..100} = x.`), linear constraints (e.g., `&sum{ 2*x; -y } $<$= 10.`), disjoint constraints, and minimize statements (e.g., `&minimize{ cost }.`). Integer variables are represented internally via the *order encoding*: for a variable x with domain $D = \{lb, lb+1, \ldots, ub\}$, where lb and ub denote its lower and upper bound, the solver creates on demand a Boolean atom ℓ_v for each $v \in \{lb, \ldots, ub-1\}$ encoding $x \leq v$ (none is needed for $v = ub$ since $x \leq ub$ necessarily holds), together with the implication chain $\ell_{lb} \Rightarrow \ell_{lb+1} \Rightarrow \cdots \Rightarrow \ell_{ub-1}$. These atoms are called *order atoms*; an order atom or its negation is an *order literal*. Asserting ℓ_v enforces $x \leq v$, whereas asserting $\neg\ell_v$ enforces $x \geq v+1$; in particular, $\neg\ell_{ub-1}$ implies $x = ub$. Unless stated otherwise, lb and ub denote a variable's current bounds, which tighten as its order atoms get assigned.

CDNL Search and Heuristics. CDNL [12] is the search procedure employed by modern ASP solvers and is closely related to CDCL (Conflict-Driven Clause Learning) in SAT solving [29]; in `clingo`, it is implemented by the solver component `clasp`. Starting from an empty assignment, the solver repeatedly executes three phases: (i) *decision*, in which an unassigned atom and a polarity (i.e., the truth value to try first) are selected via heuristics; (ii) *propagation*, in which consequences are derived through unit propagation on the program's nogoods (i.e., sets of literals that cannot jointly be true); and (iii) *conflict analysis*, which is triggered when propagation reaches a contradiction. In this phase, the solver learns a new *nogood* summarizing the conflict, backjumps to an earlier decision level determined by the learned nogood, and then resumes the search.

Two important heuristics govern the decision phase. First, *VSIDS* [22] maintains an activity score per Boolean atom, incremented whenever the atom is involved in the derivation of a learned nogood and decayed periodically; each decision selects an unassigned atom with maximal score. Second, the *phase saving* heuristic [25] records the most recent truth value assigned to each atom and reuses it as the polarity at later decisions.

In `clingcon`, the CDNL-based search is expanded to include order literals: they join the regular literals as valid decision choices, and branching on an order literal tightens an integer bound. VSIDS and phase saving extend naturally to order atoms, which are ordinary Boolean atoms from `clasp`'s perspective. In addition, a *theory propagator* participates in the search via callbacks: `propagate()` derives integer-bound consequences from the current assignment and passes them to CDNL, `undo()` rolls back the propagator's bound records on backjumps, and `decide()` can redirect a decision. Whenever `clasp` is about to branch on a literal, the propagator may return a different literal instead.

Two existing mechanisms in `clingcon` can influence branching: the option `--heuristic=Domain` enables `clasp`'s *domain* heuristic, which makes decisions according to the priorities and preferred truth values stated for atoms in `#heuristic` [11] directives; and `clingcon`'s `--order-heuristic` option can replace a decision on an order literal by a decision on another order literal of the same integer variable, following a single policy set on the command line that applies to all integer variables in the same way. Neither of these, however, lets users declaratively control variable and value selection for integer theory variables.

Example 1. Consider the `clingcon` program:

```
{a}.        &dom{0..3}=x.        &sum{x}<=1 :- a.        &minimize{x}.
```

with one Boolean atom a and an integer variable x encoded by order atoms ℓ_v for $v \in \{0,1,2\}$. The solver can make a propositional decision (on a) or a theory-level decision (on an order literal of x). Suppose it decides $a \mapsto \mathbf{T}$ first. Theory propagation then activates the constraint in the head of the third rule and asserts $\ell_1 \equiv x \leq 1$, tightening x's upper bound from 3 to 1. The `&minimize` statement drives branch-and-bound: once a first solution with, say, $x = 1$ is found, the new bound $x \leq 0$ is added, forcing the solver to find a strictly better solution than the current one, and the search continues; after a solution with $x = 0$ is found, the new bound $x \leq -1$ makes the problem unsatisfiable, proving $x = 0$ optimal. Note that the optimum is independent of the decision on a; the decision only affects the path by which the solver finds and proves it.

3 Heuristic Directives for Integer Variables

We introduce the `&heuristic` directive for `clingcon`, inspired by search annotations in CP [23] and adapted to `clingcon`'s order-literal encoding.

Syntax. A heuristic directive has the form:

```
&heuristic(P, VarSel, ValSel [, Tie] [, Lvl]) [{ vars }].
```

where `P` is a non-negative integer priority among directives (lower values are consulted first), and `VarSel` and `ValSel` are variable and value selection strategies, respectively. `Tie` is an optional tie-breaker. `Lvl` optionally scopes the directive to a single `@`-priority level of a `&minimize` statement (cf. Sect. 4.1); we call such directives *per-level*, and their semantics are described as part of the lexicographic solving strategies (cf. Sect. 4.2). The optional variable set `vars` restricts the directive to the listed integer variables. A directive that omits both `Lvl` and `vars` is *global*, applying to all integer variables of the program, on all levels.

Variable Selection. Variable selection strategies pick the "best" unassigned variable from the directive's variable set using one of the following metrics, each evaluated on the solver's current state: `input_order` takes the first unassigned variable in the set (in creation order when the set is omitted). `first_fail` and `anti_first_fail` pick the variable with the smallest and largest current domain width $ub - lb$, respectively; `smallest` picks the variable with the smallest lower bound, and `largest` the one with the largest upper bound. `degree` picks the variable involved in the largest number of constraints; `dom_deg` picks the variable with the smallest ratio of domain width to degree, preferring variables that are both tightly bounded and heavily constrained (a static variant of the `dom/wdeg` heuristic of Boussemart et al. [6]). `vsids` is the cooperative mode described in more detail in Section 3.1.

Tie-Breaking. When several variables achieve the best metric value under the variable selection strategy in use, an optional tie-breaker selects among them. In principle, any variable selection strategy can be combined with any metric as a tie-breaker. The current implementation supports one tie-breaker, the `degree` metric introduced above, which selects among the tied variables one with the highest degree. MiniZinc, e.g., offers the combination of `first_fail` with this tie-breaker as its *most_constrained* annotation, where the `degree` metric is called *occurrence* [31]. Ties that remain after tie-breaking, as well as ties in directives without a tie-breaker (`none`, the default), are broken by the order in which the directive iterates over its variable set.

Value Selection. Once a variable x is chosen, the value selection strategy returns an order literal to CDNL: `indomain_min` returns ℓ_{lb} (prefer lower bound), `indomain_max` returns $\neg\ell_{ub-1}$ (prefer upper bound), and `indomain_split` (`indomain_reverse_split`) returns ℓ_m ($\neg\ell_m$) for a split at the current domain midpoint $m = \lfloor (lb + ub)/2 \rfloor$ while considering the lower (upper) half first. Without an `&heuristic` directive, decisions on order literals are left to `clasp`, whose sign heuristic (including phase saving, where enabled) determines the polarity.

3.1 VSIDS-Cooperative Mode

A directive that selects variables by a fixed metric bypasses VSIDS and discards its accumulated conflict knowledge (Sect. 2), a key driver of CDNL performance. We therefore introduce the `vsids` strategy, which *cooperates* with VSIDS rather than replacing it: the propagator inspects the literal chosen by VSIDS. If that literal belongs to an integer variable within the directive's scope, the directive keeps this variable but applies its own value selection strategy; otherwise, the directive does not intervene. Variable selection thus remains conflict-driven, while value selection becomes domain-aware wherever the directive applies.

Example 2. Continuing Example 1, whenever VSIDS picks an order literal ℓ_i of x, the `decide()` callback can redirect the decision to another order literal of x, picked by the value selection strategy of an applicable directive. For instance, `&heuristic(0, vsids, indomain_min) {x}.` biases the propagator to return

$\ell_0 \equiv x \leq 0$; the solver then yields a model with x minimal on the first try, which the next branch-and-bound step proves optimal.

We call this instantiation (`vsids` with `indomain_min`, scoped to the variables in the objective) the *cost-first* scheme; it plays a central role in Sect. 5.

3.2 Implementation

Directives are registered as theory atoms; at initialization, they are sorted by priority and distributed across per-thread solver instances; omitted variable sets default to all integer variables. At each decision, the `decide()` callback consults the directives in increasing order of their priority value `P`; the first one with an unassigned variable in its scope selects a variable, derives an order literal via its value selection strategy, and returns it to CDNL. A directive with the `vsids` strategy selects no variable itself: if `clasp`'s chosen literal is an order literal of a variable in the directive's scope, it applies its value selection to that variable; otherwise, consultation proceeds with the next directive. If no directive applies, the decision falls back to the `--order-heuristic` option. Its pre-existing values are `none` (the default), which keeps `clasp`'s decision unchanged, and `max-chain`, which changes the decision to an extreme order literal of the decided variable, pushing the variable to its lowest or highest value depending on the chosen polarity. We add `earliest-start` and `tightest-window`, which, respectively, assign the decided variable its lower bound (as in `indomain_min`) and split its domain at the midpoint (as in `indomain_split`). All four values are problem-independent; the names of the added two reflect the scheduling use that motivated them [32]. All fallbacks apply only to decisions on order literals.

4 Optimization Extensions

We add priorities for objectives, lexicographic modes, and bound stepping.

4.1 The `@priority` Annotation for `&minimize`

The `#minimize` directive in `clingo` supports lexicographic priorities via the `@` operator: e.g., `#minimize{ cost @2 }` assigns the term `cost` to priority level 2. A higher number k in `@`k means a higher priority for the corresponding objective; terms without an explicit `@`-level default to level 0; and multiple terms at the same level are summed into a single per-level objective. `clingcon` 3 already supported such priorities for the theory-level `&minimize` [5], but the feature was removed in `clingcon` 5.[1] We restore it by extending the theory definition to recognize the `@` operator in `&minimize`, for example, `&minimize{ totalTardiness @3; totalEnergy @2; totalMakespan @1 }.` Terms may also carry integer coefficients, as in `&minimize{ 2*x; 3*y @1 }.`, where `2*x` defaults to level 0, giving `3*y` priority.

[1] For details, see https://github.com/potassco/clingcon/issues/96.

4.2 Multi-level Lexicographic Optimization

When multiple @-levels are present, we extend `clingcon` with three `--lex-opt` modes, namely two solving strategies and an automatic selector:

Multi-shot mode (`--lex-opt=multi-shot`). Each level is assigned its own minimize constraint. The solver optimizes the highest-priority level to proven optimality, fixes the level with a hard upper-bound constraint at its optimal value, and proceeds to the next level. An outer driver re-invokes `solve()` after each level, in the style of `clingo`'s multi-shot solving [10], seeding the next level's bound from the previous model. This guarantees exact lexicographic semantics, but the sequential per-level solve calls limit parallelization to individual levels.

Weighted Mode (`--lex-opt=weighted`). This mode flattens all levels into one objective. Since `&minimize` supports only linear objectives, the objective at level k can be written as $obj_k = \sum_i c_i^{(k)} \cdot x_i^{(k)}$, where the $x_i^{(k)}$ are integer variables and the $c_i^{(k)}$ their user-supplied coefficients; we index the m levels $1, \ldots, m$ in increasing order of priority. Level k is assigned the weight $w_k = 1 + \sum_{j<k} w_j\, r_j$ with base case $w_1 = 1$ [28], where $r_j = \sum_i |c_i^{(j)}| \cdot (ub_i^{(j)} - lb_i^{(j)})$ is computed from the variable bounds at initialization and bounds the maximal possible change of obj_j: no matter how the variables of level j change within their domains, obj_j varies by at most r_j. The combined objective[2] $\sum_k w_k \cdot obj_k$ is passed to a single minimize constraint. Intuitively, the per-level objectives form a mixed-radix number with higher-priority levels as more significant digits. This construction preserves lexicographic optimality: improving level k by one unit decreases the combined objective by w_k, whereas the maximal change towards minimization of *all* lower levels decreases it by at most $\sum_{j<k} w_j r_j = w_k - 1$. Thus, a higher-priority improvement always outweighs all lower-priority improvements combined.

Such weighting schemes are classical in multicriteria optimization [28] and have been applied to Boolean lexicographic optimization in MaxSAT [2,21]; our contribution is their automatic, domain-derived instantiation at `clingcon`'s theory level, which keeps the entire problem in a single solver call, so parallel solving applies to the whole multi-objective problem rather than individual levels. Per-level `&heuristic` directives (Sect. 3) are active only while multi-shot optimization works on their level and inactive under the weighted mode.

Automatic Mode (`--lex-opt=auto`). This default mode selects `multi-shot` for single-threaded and `weighted` for multi-threaded solving: multi-shot's sequential per-level solve calls benefit little from a portfolio of threads, whereas the weighted formulation exposes the entire problem to parallel exploration.

---

[2] The combined cost must fit into a 64-bit integer. As the weights grow exponentially [21], an overflow may occur during initialization. If so, a warning is issued and the lexicographic guarantee no longer holds; use `--lex-opt=multi-shot` instead.

4.3 Bound Stepping

In branch-and-bound optimization, each improving model with cost c yields a new upper bound on the optimum, and `clingcon` requires the next solution to improve on it. The default, *linear stepping*, uses the bound $c - 1$: strict improvement is ensured, but the bound is only guaranteed to shrink by one unit per improving model, requiring up to $O(n)$ improving models, where n denotes the gap between the first solution and the optimum. To accelerate convergence, we introduce the `--bound-step` option, providing two additional strategies inspired by established SAT-based optimization techniques [3]: bisection (`--bound-step=bisect`) [15] and a hybrid strategy (`--bound-step=hybrid[:K]`).

Bisect (`--bound-step=bisect`). Bisect treats optimization as a binary search over the objective value. It maintains a proven lower bound lb, initially derived from the variable domains (minimum values for positive, maximum values for negative coefficients). After a model with cost c is found, the next bound is set to the midpoint $lb + \lfloor (c - 1 - lb)/2 \rfloor$ instead of $c - 1$. If a model with cost at most the midpoint exists, the upper bound is reduced accordingly; otherwise, the midpoint is proven infeasible, lb is raised to the midpoint plus one, and the search continues in the upper half of the interval. Bisection thus shrinks the optimality gap logarithmically, at the cost of potentially expensive unsatisfiability proofs.

This trade-off becomes unfavorable when lb is far below the optimum: most midpoints are then infeasible, and each costs an unsatisfiability proof. Multi-shot lexicographic optimization is prone to this, because the domain-derived lb of a later level ignores the constraints fixing the already optimized levels. `--bound-step=bisect` therefore includes a safeguard: on levels after the first, a non-positive lb is typically just the trivial domain-derived default (for the non-negative objectives common in practice, it excludes nothing), so the solver replaces the bisection midpoint by a linear step while the upper bound exceeds 1; below that, the remaining gap is trivial. A positive but underestimated lb cannot be distinguished from a tight one without further solving, so the safeguard does not cover this case, and bisection can remain less effective there.

Hybrid(`--bound-step=hybrid[:K]`). Hybrid combines the two approaches: bisection is used while the gap $c - 1 - lb$ exceeds the threshold K (default 10); once it is at most K, the algorithm switches to linear stepping, which avoids the overhead of repeated unsatisfiability proofs in the small-gap regime.

5 Experimental Evaluation

We next evaluate the contributions of Sects. 3 and 4. Encodings, instances, and raw results are available at https://git-ainf.aau.at/saeling/publications.

Research Questions. The evaluation addresses three research questions, one for each of the proposed `clingcon` extensions:

(RQ1) What is the impact of `&heuristic` on solving performance and solution quality for decision and single-objective optimization problems?
(RQ2) What is the impact of `@priority` and `--lex-opt` on solving performance and solution quality for multi-objective lexicographic optimization?
(RQ3) What is the impact of `--bound-step` settings on solving performance and solution quality?

Benchmarks. We consider seven benchmark problems, each comprising ten instances: four established `clingcon` benchmarks from [5,18], graph coloring (GC) under both a basic and an improved encoding, the test laboratory scheduling problem (TLSP) from [13], and a real-world energy-aware double-flexible job-shop scheduling problem (E-DFJSP) from the metal industry [32]. Among those, three are *decision problems* and four are *optimization problems*. The `clingcon` benchmarks comprise three decision problems (incremental scheduling, reverse folding, and weighted sequence) and one academic single-objective optimization problem, 2D strip packing (2SP), with the objective of minimizing strip height. The remaining optimization problems are GC, seeking to minimize the number of colors; TLSP, optimizing employee preference, project preference, delay, and duration; and E-DFJSP, optimizing tardiness, energy consumption, and makespan. For GC, we evaluate two encodings on the same ten graph instances (nine random graphs and one 13-clique): a *basic* Boolean per-(vertex, color) indicator encoding, and an *improved* variant that adds canonical-order symmetry breaking, making it a more challenging encoding for bound stepping.

Optimization objectives are encoded as `&minimize{max_color}` (GC), `&minimize{height}` (2SP), and, for TLSP and E-DFJSP, a single `&minimize` statement over the sum of all objectives, yielding an *aggregated* encoding without priorities. The lexicographic variants annotate E-DFJSP's three objectives with `@3/@2/@1` and TLSP's four objectives with `@4/@3/@2/@1`.

Setup. Instances run single-threaded (`-t1`) on Google Cloud `e2-medium` VMs (1 vCPU, 4 GiB RAM, Ubuntu 22.04) with a 600 s timeout, five runs per (instance, configuration) pair under different random seeds.

Metrics. For each configuration on each problem (ten instances), we report: *OPT*, the number of instances on which optimality is proven for all five seeds (on lexicographic problems, optimality of the full tuple of objectives); *SOL*, the number of instances where a solution is found for at least one seed, but optimality is not proven for some seeds; and *TO*, the number of instances for which no solution is found for any seed. $t^\star$ is the median solving time over the OPT instances only. PAR-2 is the penalized average runtime, the standard ranking metric of recent SAT competitions [9]: each instance receives a score, namely its median solving time if it counts toward OPT and twice the timeout otherwise; PAR-2 is the average of these ten scores, so it evaluates speed and coverage in terms of a single number.

Configurations. The *default* is `clingcon` 5 without our extensions. For (RQ1), *cost-first* applies the cost-first scheme of Section 3.1 to the objective variables (e.g., `height` for 2SP, `max_color` for GC); *per-job cost-first* (E-DFJSP) extends this scope with per-job tardiness variables; *vsids cooperative* applies the same directive to all integer variables (variable set omitted); and the decision benchmarks also use non-cooperative `first_fail` directives with the `degree` tie-breaker. For (RQ2), the *aggregated baseline* solves the aggregated encoding (a single summed objective without `@`-levels) in the *default* configuration; all other configurations use the `@priority` encodings, named by their `--lex-opt` mode (`weighted`, `multi-shot`). For configurations combining lexicographic optimization with heuristics, *global directive* denotes the same global *vsids cooperative* directive as in (RQ1), covering all integer variables and tied to no specific cost or level; *per-level* denotes directives with `Lvl` (Sect. 3); *schedule bias* denotes per-level directives that bias operation start variables toward early values while the tardiness and energy levels are optimized, and end variables while the makespan level is optimized; and *default branching* denotes runs without any active directive, leaving all decisions to `clasp`. For (RQ3), `--bound-step` takes `linear`, `bisect`, or `hybrid:10` on the single-objective encodings, without heuristic directives. Since `linear` is `clingcon`'s default strategy, the *default* and *linear* rows differ only in seeds.

5.1 RQ1: Heuristics

Results for optimization problems are presented in Tab. 1, whereas those for decision problems are discussed only in the text.

Optimization Problems. The clearest effect appears on E-DFJSP's aggregated encoding. The *vsids cooperative* configuration proves optimality on five of ten instances (median 21 s), whereas neither the default nor the *per-job cost-first* configuration proves any optimum. This reflects a depth-versus-breadth trade-off: *vsids cooperative* finds no solution within 600 s on four instances (depth over breadth), while *per-job cost-first* finds a solution on all instances but never proves optimality (breadth over depth). On six instances, the latter improves the default solution by at least 50% (median 70%), although it performs substantially worse on two. By contrast, the directives have little effect on 2SP and both GC encodings (the basic encoding is omitted from Tab. 1 and evaluated only with *cost-first*): the timing differences are small, except that *vsids cooperative* times out on one 2SP instance where the other configurations still find a solution. These problems leave the directives little room to influence the search, as solving is dominated by satisfiability reasoning (2SP) or tight propagation of the objective bounds (GC).

Decision Problems. On the three decision benchmarks, we evaluate four generic directives, combining the variable selection strategies `vsids` (the strategy behind *vsids cooperative*) and `first_fail` (with the `degree` tie-breaker) with the value selection strategies `indomain_min` and `indomain_split`. The cooperative variants are comparable with the default configuration, solving all instances, mostly within seconds. The non-cooperative variants, however, solve only five of ten incremental scheduling instances and, depending on the value selection, six

Table 1. Results for the optimization problems (ten instances per problem, five seeds per instance). Column headers are defined in the paragraph "Metrics" in Sect. 5. Bold: best configuration per problem (highest OPT, then lowest PAR-2, then highest SOL); no row is bold if there is no unique winner.

Problem	Configuration	OPT	SOL	TO	$t^{\star}$ (s)	PAR-2
RQ1 – Heuristics						
2SP	default	3	5	2	<1	840
	cost-first	3	5	2	<1	840
	vsids cooperative	3	4	3	<1	840
E-DFJSP	default	0	10	0	–	1200
	per-job cost-first	0	10	0	–	1200
	vsids cooperative	**5**	1	4	**21**	**616**
GC (impr.)	default	6	4	0	29	516
	cost-first	6	4	0	24	515
	vsids cooperative	**6**	4	0	**24**	**512**
RQ2 – Lexicographic Optimization						
E-DFJSP	aggregated baseline	0	10	0	–	1200
	multi-shot, global directive	5	1	4	24	618
	weighted, global directive	**5**	1	4	**22**	**616**
	multi-shot, per-level schedule bias	0	7	3	–	1200
	multi-shot, per-level cost-first	0	10	0	–	1200
TLSP	weighted, global directive	0	4	6	–	1200
	weighted, default branching	0	**10**	0	–	1200
RQ3 – Bound Stepping						
E-DFJSP	linear	0	10	0	–	1200
	bisect	9	1	0	111	218
	hybrid:10	**9**	1	0	**77**	**212**
GC	linear	6	4	0	2.1	483
	bisect	**7**	3	0	**4.3**	**373**
	hybrid:10	6	4	0	2.2	486
GC (impr.)	**linear**	**6**	4	0	**24**	**512**
	bisect	5	5	0	6.4	619
	hybrid:10	6	4	0	25	517

(`indomain_min`) or seven (`indomain_split`) of ten weighted sequence instances, and even fail on a relatively simple reverse folding instance.

Answer to **(RQ1)**. A cooperative directive can enable optimality proofs that are out of reach for the default configuration, at the price of finding no solution on some instances. Where the problem structure is not amenable to heuristics, cooperative directives and the default remain closely comparable.

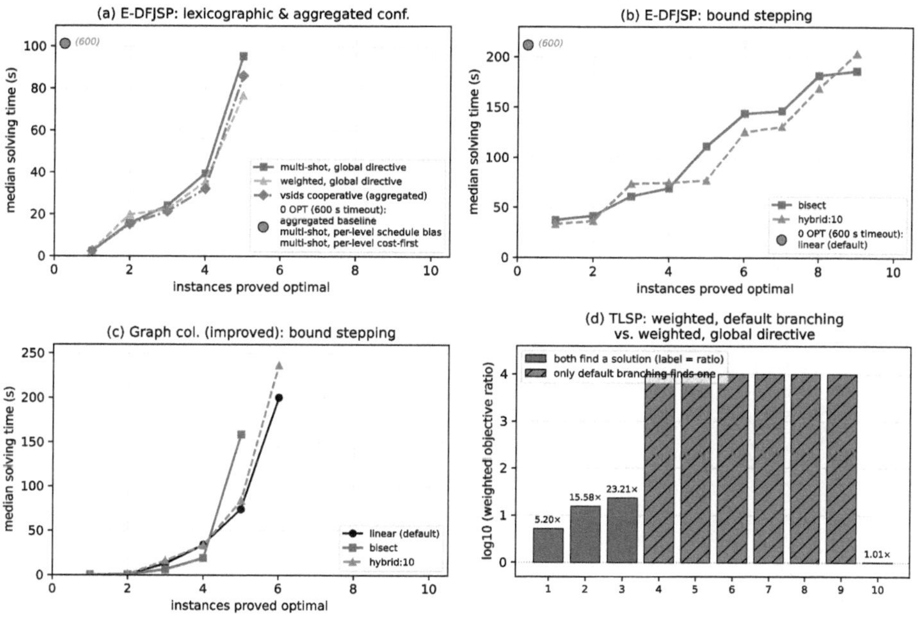

Fig. 1. Results for selected configurations of Tab. 1. Panels (a)–(c) are cactus plots: for each configuration, the instances proven optimal (the full lexicographic tuple for the RQ2 configurations, the global optimum elsewhere) are shown; the marker at the top left lists configurations that prove no optimum within the timeout. Panel (d) compares the two TLSP configurations of the RQ2-section of Tab. 1 instance by instance: bars show the factor by which the configuration *weighted with default branching* improves the combined weighted objective of the best found solution over the configuration *weighted with global directive*; hatched bars indicate instances where only the former finds a solution at all; they are drawn at the axis cap because no ratio exists.

Replacing VSIDS's variable selection entirely, however, discards the learned conflict structure and consistently degrades performance.

5.2 RQ2: Lexicographic Optimization

We evaluate `@priority` with `--lex-opt` on E-DFJSP and TLSP, the two problems with multiple objectives. Figure 1(a,d) and the RQ2-section of Tab. 1 report the results. Since the multi-shot and weighted modes implement the same lexicographic semantics (Sect. 4.2), we expect them to prove the same optima.

E-DFJSP. With the global directive, both modes prove optimality of the full lexicographic tuple on the same five out of ten instances, at nearly identical median times (24 s multi-shot, 22 s weighted). The aggregated baseline, the only option without `@priority`, solves a different, single-objective problem; it proves no optimum and cannot express the priority structure at all. The two per-level configurations isolate the effect of directive scoping under multi-shot.

Per-level schedule bias finds solutions on seven instances but proves no optimum: the early-start schedule chosen at the highest-priority tardiness level constrains the subsequent energy and makespan levels. Per-level cost-first finds a solution on every instance (one instance exhausts the 4 GiB memory limit on all seeds) but also proves no optimum. Per-level scoping thus sacrifices all five proofs that the global directive obtains.

TLSP. No configuration proves optimality on any TLSP instance, so we compare the quality of the best found solutions by their combined weighted objective, which, by construction, is dominated by the highest-priority level (Fig. 1(d)). Both configurations run the weighted mode on the same encoding (multi-shot attempts on earlier TLSP encodings exhausted the budget). The encoding also contains per-level directives, but these have no effect under the weighted mode (Sect. 4.2). The two configurations therefore differ only in the global directive. The outcome is unambiguous. Default branching finds a solution on all ten instances, whereas the global directive, the same scheme that wins on E-DFJSP, finds one on only four. Where both succeed, default branching is better by factors of 5 to 23, with one near-tie. Notably, the lexicographic encoding also yields solutions on two instances where the aggregated encoding yields none (cf. (RQ3)). This difficulty is consistent with the original study's reliance on adaptive large neighborhood search at this scale [13].

***Answer to* (RQ2).** `@priority` with `--lex-opt` makes lexicographic structure expressible and provable in `clingcon`. On E-DFJSP, the one problem with both modes evaluated, multi-shot and weighted perform almost identically. The heuristic dominates the outcome. The global directive is essential on E-DFJSP, yet counterproductive on TLSP, where *weighted, default branching* wins.

5.3 RQ3: Bound Stepping

We evaluate the three `--bound-step` strategies on the single-objective encodings of the four optimization problems (Fig. 1(b,c) and the RQ3-section of Tab. 1).

E-DFJSP. It shows the largest effect: linear stepping proves no optimum within 600 s, whereas bisect and hybrid both prove nine of ten (median times 111 s and 77 s, PAR-2 218 and 212), and, on the single unproven instance, both find solutions about 75% better than the solution obtained by linear stepping. The first solution is far from the optimum: unit steps exceed the time budget; bisection closes the gap logarithmically.

GC. The two GC encodings expose the trade-off. On the basic encoding, bisect proves one instance more than linear and hybrid (seven vs. six). On the improved encoding, the reverse holds: bisect drops to five and its PAR-2 rises to 619, since the static lower bound is loose there and bisect wastes time proving infeasibility at hopeless midpoints; the safeguard of Section 4.3 cannot intervene, as it applies only during multi-shot lexicographic optimization and for non-positive bounds. With hybrid stepping, six instances are proven optimal on the improved encoding, as with linear stepping, and nine on E-DFJSP, as with bisection.

2SP and TLSP. On these two problems, bound stepping makes no difference; the counts are identical under all three strategies and therefore not shown in Tab. 1. In 2SP, almost all time is spent on satisfiability reasoning, and the first solutions found are already near-optimal (OPT/SOL/TO =3/5/2 at $t^\star < 1$ s); on TLSP, no strategy proves any optimum (0/8/2).

***Answer to* (RQ3).** Bisection helps when the gap between the first solution and the optimum is large, but can perform worse than linear stepping when its initial lower bound is loose. Hybrid stepping combines most of the gains observed for bisection with the robustness of linear stepping and thus appears to be a reasonable default strategy.

5.4 Discussion

First, heuristic directives are powerful but double-edged. The *vsids cooperative* directive is essential on E-DFJSP but counterproductive on TLSP ((RQ2)), and replacing VSIDS's variable selection entirely degrades performance even on easy decision problems ((RQ1)). A directive thus helps only if its bias fits the problem structure. Among the evaluated schemes, cooperation with VSIDS is the most robust. Indeed, on E-DFJSP, excluding (RQ3), every optimality proof is obtained using *vsids cooperative*. It proves optima on five instances, both on the aggregated encoding ((RQ1)) and combined with either lexicographic mode ((RQ2)).

Second, on E-DFJSP, the main value of `--lex-opt` is not additional optimality proofs but stronger guarantees. The aggregated encoding and both lexicographic modes prove optimality on the same instances since the objectives are tightly coupled. However, `--lex-opt` proves the optimum of the full priority tuple, whereas the aggregated encoding proves only the minimum of an unweighted sum. TLSP shows this alignment is not general: the aggregated encoding finds no solution on two instances that the lexicographic encoding solves.

Third, the benefit of bisection depends not on the problem family but on the gap between the first solution and the optimum. It substantially improves performance on E-DFJSP and leaves 2SP unchanged. Within GC, it helps one encoding but hurts the other, depending on the tightness of the initial lower bound. Hybrid stepping sacrifices bisection's small gain on the basic encoding, avoids its loss on the improved encoding, and fully preserves its benefit on E-DFJSP.

All results are based on single-threaded execution. The parallel setting motivating the weighted and automatic modes for `--lex-opt` remains future work.

6 Related Work

Gebser et al. [11] introduced domain-specific heuristics for `clingo` via the `#heuristic` directive, which controls branching over Boolean atoms. Teppan and Friedrich [30] extended heuristic guidance to integer variables for configuration problems within Constraint Answer Set Programming (CASP), but their approach relies on a specialized solver architecture rather than a native, declarative theory extension; our `&heuristic` directive fills this gap, exposing `#heuristic`-style declarative control at the integer-variable level through order literals.

On the CP side, MiniZinc [23] provides declarative search annotations: `int_search` specifies variable and value selection for integer variables and is implemented natively by backends such as Gecode and Chuffed. Our directive adopts this strategy vocabulary but executes it inside a CDNL solver by rewriting order-literal decisions rather than in a dedicated CP engine, supports scoping to optimization levels, and adds the cooperative mode, whose closest relative, Chuffed's free search [7], alternates programmed and activity-based search across restarts instead of combining them within each decision. Unlike delegation- and translation-based CASP systems (EZCSP [4], EZSMT [27], `asp-fzn` [8], `mingo` [20]), which detach search from the ASP solver, and theory-extension systems that leave all branching to the ASP solver's decision heuristic (`clingo[DL]`, `clingo[LP]` [16]), our `&heuristic` directive is, to the best of our knowledge, the first mechanism in a CDNL-based CASP solver [17] letting users declaratively specify both variable and value selection for integer variables; the cooperative mode has no counterpart in existing systems.

On the optimization side, our bound stepping strategies adapt standard techniques from SAT-based optimization [3,15]; core-guided optimization in `clasp` [1] is complementary. Reducing lexicographic optimization to a single objective via dominance-preserving weights is classical in multicriteria optimization [28] and has been studied for Boolean optimization [2,21]; `clingo` supports lexicographic optimization natively for Boolean cost functions [10]. Our extensions lift these techniques to `clingcon`'s integer objectives, with automatically derived weights.

7 Conclusion

We extended `clingcon` 5 with three problem-independent mechanisms: a `&heuristic` directive with a VSIDS-cooperative mode, a `@priority` annotation for `&minimize` supporting multi-shot and weighted lexicographic optimization, and a `--bound-step` option providing linear, bisect, and hybrid stepping.

Empirically, these extensions substantially expand the range of problems `clingcon` can solve. On an industrial job-shop scheduling problem, bisection-based bound stepping increases the number of proven optima from zero to nine out of ten instances, the cooperative directive proves optimality where the default configuration cannot, and `--lex-opt` extends these proofs to full priority tuples. On an industrial laboratory scheduling problem with four objective levels, the weighted mode finds solutions on every instance, whereas the heuristic that excels on the job-shop problem is counterproductive. Overall, the effectiveness of each extension depends on how well it matches the problem structure.

Future work includes integrating `&heuristic` with `clingo`'s `#heuristic` [11], conflict-driven variable selection such as `dom/wdeg` [6], adaptive bound tightening for `--bound-step=bisect` [1], studying interactions among the proposed extensions, and evaluating `--lex-opt=weighted` in multi-threaded portfolios.

Acknowledgments. This research was funded in whole or in part by the Austrian Science Fund (FWF) 10.55776/COE12 and the Austrian Research Promotion Agency (FFG) FO999910235 (SAELING).

Disclosure of Interests. The authors have no competing interests to declare that are relevant to the content of this article.

References

1. Andres, B., Kaufmann, B., Matheis, O., Schaub, T.: Unsatisfiability-based optimization in clasp. In: Tech. Comm. of ICLP (2012)
2. Argelich, J., Lynce, I., Marques-Silva, J.P.: On solving Boolean multilevel optimization problems. In: IJCAI (2009)
3. Bacchus, F., Järvisalo, M., Martins, R.: Maximum satisfiability. In: Handbook of Satisfiability, 2nd edn. IOS Press (2021)
4. Balduccini, M., Lierler, Y.: Constraint answer set solver EZCSP and why integration schemas matter. TPLP **17**(4) (2017)
5. Banbara, M., Kaufmann, B., Ostrowski, M., Schaub, T.: Clingcon: the next generation. TPLP **17**(4) (2017)
6. Boussemart, F., Hemery, F., Lecoutre, C., Sais, L.: Boosting systematic search by weighting constraints. In: ECAI (2004)
7. Chu, G.G.: Improving Combinatorial Optimization. Ph.D. thesis, University of Melbourne (2011)
8. Eiter, T., Geibinger, T., Musliu, N., Oetsch, J., Kaminski, T.: ASP-FZN: a translation-based constraint answer set solver. TPLP **25**(4) (2025)
9. Froleyks, N., Heule, M.J.H., Iser, M., Järvisalo, M., Suda, M.: SAT competition 2020. AIJ **301** (2021)
10. Gebser, M., Kaminski, R., Kaufmann, B., Schaub, T.: Multi-shot ASP solving with clingo. TPLP **19**(1) (2019)
11. Gebser, M., Kaufmann, B., Romero, J., Otero, R., Schaub, T., Wanko, P.: Domain-specific heuristics in answer set programming. In: AAAI (2013)
12. Gebser, M., Kaufmann, B., Schaub, T.: Conflict-driven answer set solving: from theory to practice. AIJ **187** (2012)
13. Geibinger, T., Mischek, F., Musliu, N.: Constraint logic programming for real-world test laboratory scheduling. In: AAAI (2021)
14. Gelfond, M., Lifschitz, V.: The stable model semantics for logic programming. In: ICLP/SLP (1988)
15. Giunchiglia, E., Maratea, M.: Solving optimization problems with DLL. In: ECAI (2006)
16. Janhunen, T., Kaminski, R., Ostrowski, M., Schaub, T., Schellhorn, S., Wanko, P.: Clingo goes linear constraints over reals and integers. TPLP **17**, 5–6 (2017)
17. Lierler, Y.: Relating constraint answer set programming languages and algorithms. AIJ **207** (2014)
18. Lierler, Y., Smith, S., Truszczynski, M., Westlund, A.: Weighted-sequence problem: ASP vs CASP and declarative vs problem-oriented solving. In: PADL (2012)

19. Lifschitz, V.: Conclusion. In: Answer Set Programming, pp. 147–147. Springer, Cham (2019). https://doi.org/10.1007/978-3-030-24658-7_9
20. Liu, G., Janhunen, T., Niemelä, I.: Answer set programming via mixed integer programming. In: KR (2012)
21. Marques-Silva, J., Argelich, J., Graça, A., Lynce, I.: Boolean lexicographic optimization: algorithms & applications. AMAI **62**(3-4) (2011)
22. Moskewicz, M.W., Madigan, C.F., Zhao, Y., Zhang, L., Malik, S.: Chaff: engineering an efficient SAT solver. In: DAC (2001)
23. Nethercote, N., Stuckey, P.J., Becket, R., Brand, S., Duck, G.J., Tack, G.: MiniZinc: towards a standard CP modelling language. In: CP (2007)
24. Ohrimenko, O., Stuckey, P.J., Codish, M.: Propagation via lazy clause generation. Constraints **14**(3) (2009)
25. Pipatsrisawat, K., Darwiche, A.: A lightweight component caching scheme for satisfiability solvers. In: SAT (2007)
26. Rossi, F., van Beek, P., Walsh, T. (eds.): Handbook of Constraint Programming. Elsevier (2006)
27. Shen, D., Lierler, Y.: SMT-based constraint answer set solver EZSMT+ for non-tight programs. In: KR (2018)
28. Sherali, H.D.: Equivalent weights for lexicographic multi-objective programs: Characterizations and computations. EJOR **11**(4) (1982)
29. Silva, J.P.M., Lynce, I., Malik, S.: Conflict-driven clause learning SAT solvers. In: Handbook of Satisfiability, 2nd edn. IOS Press (2021)
30. Teppan, E.C., Friedrich, G.: Heuristic constraint answer set programming. In: ECAI (2016)
31. The MiniZinc Team: The MiniZinc handbook (2026). https://docs.minizinc.dev
32. Zuccato, F., Rodler, P., Friedrich, G., Schekotihin, K., Comploi-Taupe, R.: Energy-aware double-flexible job shop scheduling with machine modes and setup times: a real-world industrial case study using constraint programming. In: CAIPI (2025)

Equivalence Under Stable-Unstable Semantics

Tomi Janhunen(✉)

Mathematics Research Centre, Tampere University, Tampere, Finland
tomi.janhunen@tuni.fi

Abstract. The stable-unstable semantics of normal logic programs lifts their expressive power to cover decision problems from the second level of polynomial time hierarchy (PH). Under this semantics, each stable model of a main program is approved by oracle programs that are not supposed to have stable models given the stable model as input. If this idea is applied recursively, any level of PH can be reached with normal logic programs only, in analogy to quantified Boolean formulas (QBFs). In this article, we are interested in program development under stable-unstable semantics and verification problems that result, e.g., from the revision of programs. To create premises for formal verification in this setting, we introduce basic notions of equivalence for normal logic programs subject to stable-unstable semantics and study the computational complexity of the respective decision problems. Based on this analysis, we develop highly modular translations to implement equivalence checking in practice, aiming to use native answer set solvers for back-end reasoning tasks. Finally, we bridge the gap with respect to explicit quantification over stable models so that decisions about equi-coherence can be made using the method devised for stable-unstable semantics.

1 Introduction

The answer set programming paradigm (see, e.g., [8,25] for an overview) deploys logic programs under a declarative semantics based on *stable models* [18,19] also known as *answer sets. Normal* logic programs (NLPs) and *disjunctive* logic programs (DLPs) form the basic classes of logic programs and, as established in [10,33], they respectively cover decision problems from the first two levels of polynomial time hierarchy (PH). However, when programming with native DLPs, the second level of PH is typically reached using a saturation technique [10] that embeds the required coNP-oracles in such a way that it is quite difficult to recognize and maintain them as subprograms of the main program.

As a partial solution, the *guess-and-check* paradigm [11] separates the main program from the oracle(s) and given a stable model for the main program (the guess part) insists on the instability of the oracle(s) in the context of that model (the check part). The *stable-unstable semantics* [5] generalizes this idea for *combined programs* that are recursively constructed using NLPs as subprograms. In this way, any level of PH can be covered in analogy to *quantified Boolean*

W. Faber et al. (Eds.): LPNMR 2026, LNAI 16952, pp. 265–281, 2027.
https://doi.org/10.1007/978-3-032-38320-4_17

formulas (QBFs). But, if we wish to use existing answer set solvers for reasoning, the remedy is only partial in the sense that either meta-programming techniques [30] or translations toward DLPs [24] must be deployed. On the other hand, the application programmer need not understand the details of transformations such as saturation already mentioned. Moreover, the explicit treatment of oracles as subprograms facilitates modular program development in general.

Since the introduction of stable-unstable semantics [5], the related research has evolved in several directions. First, because stable-unstable semantics leaves quantification implicit, parallel approaches with explicit quantifiers emerged, e.g., where quantification is formulated over answer sets [2,34] or over propositional atoms [14] similarly to QBFs. Regardless explicit quantifications, connections to stable-unstable semantics are inherent. Second, stable model semantics has been generalized for higher-order logic programming using approximation fixpoint theory [4]. Third, several efforts on efficient implementations have been made in the context of quantified approaches and stable-unstable semantics [3,9,12,24,30]. As a result, the scope of logic programming has expanded to the higher levels of PH in general [1] and, more specifically, in the representation of novel application problems such as abstract argumentation [7], epistemic logic programming [13], electoral control [16], and explainable AI [20].

The goal of this article is to continue the research line of stable-unstable semantics, concentrating on the aspects of modular program development. Although the construction of combined programs [5] is highly modular and the component programs can be further modularized under stable semantics [36], the ultimate questions about program equivalence have not been thoroughly addressed so far. It is to be expected that programming under stable-unstable semantics gives rise to versions of programs as usual and there is a need to establish that particular programs of interest are either equivalent or not. To develop the required theoretical framework, we take some existing notions of equivalence as the starting point and generalize them to the setting of stable-unstable semantics where the main program is combined with oracles in order to eliminate particular stable models. Besides such conceptual contributions, we carry out complexity analysis, which is an essential prerequisite for the development of methods for equivalence checking. As a result, we obtain a highly modular method that can be implemented with native answer set solvers when comparing normal programs having normal programs as their oracles.

The rest of this article is organized as follows. Section 2 recalls the syntax and semantics of logic programs, including basic notions of equivalence, concepts related to modular programming, and stable-unstable semantics. In addition, an existing method for equivalence checking is elaborated further in Sect. 3. In particular, we distinguish a part of a translation acting as a program-level complement. In Sect. 4, we generalize basic notions of equivalence for stable-unstable semantics and classify the respective decision problems in terms of computational complexity. The modular translation for equivalence checking is gradually developed in Sect. 5. The interconnection to explicit quantification over stable models is refined in Sect. 6 where the coherence of quantified programs is linked to the existence of stable-unstable models. Section 7 explains how the existing translators in the ASPTOOLS collection[1] can be used to construct logic programs for equivalence checking. Finally, we present our conclusions in Sect. 8.

2 Preliminaries

In this section, we review the syntax and semantics of logic programs and, in particular, the fragments of normal and disjunctive programs in the propositional case. Moreover, we recall some basic notions related to program modules.

As regards syntax, a *logic program* is a set of *rules* of form[2]

$$a_1 \mid \ldots \mid a_k \leftarrow b_1, \ldots, b_n, \text{not } c_1, \ldots, \text{not } c_m. \tag{1}$$

where $a_1, \ldots, a_k$, $b_1, \ldots, b_n$, and $c_1, \ldots, c_m$ are (propositional) atoms and "not" denotes negation by default. *Literals* are either atoms "a" or their negations "not a", also called *positive* and *negative* literals, respectively. Using shorthands A, B, and C for the sets of atoms involved in (1), the rule can be abbreviated as $A \leftarrow B, \text{not } C$ where "not C" stands for the set of negative conditions $\{\text{not } c \mid c \in C\}$. The intuition behind a rule is that some atom from the *head* A of the rule can be inferred true whenever the *body* of the rule is satisfied, i.e., when all atoms of B are true and no atom of C is true by any other rules in the program.

A rule (1) is *proper disjunctive*, if $k > 1$, *normal*, if $k = 1$, and a *constraint* if $k = 0$. A rule (1) is a *fact*, if $k > 0$, $n = 0$, and $m = 0$ and then $\leftarrow$ is typically omitted. A *normal (logic) program* (NLP) consists of normal rules and constraints.[3] A *disjunctive (logic) program* (DLP) allows for any number of head atoms in its rules. Additionally, a program is *positive* if $m = 0$ for each rule (1).

2.1 Minimal and Stable Models

Turning our attention to semantics, we let $\text{At}(P)$ denote the *signature* of a DLP P, i.e., $A \cup B \cup C \subseteq \text{At}(P)$ for every rule $A \leftarrow B, \text{not } C$ of P.[4] An *interpretation* $I \subseteq \text{At}(P)$ is simply any subset of atoms considered to be true under I. A rule $A \leftarrow B, \text{not } C$ of P is satisfied in an interpretation $I \subseteq \text{At}(P)$ of P, if $B \subseteq I$ and $C \cap I = \emptyset$ imply $A \cap I \neq \emptyset$. A (classical) *model* of P is an interpretation $M \subseteq \text{At}(P)$ satisfying all rules of P. A model M of a positive DLP P is a (subset) *minimal* model of P if there is no other model M' of P such that $M' \subset M$. The set of minimal models of P is denoted by $\text{MM}(P)$. By the definitions above, a positive DLP may have no minimal models at all,

---

[1] https://github.com/asptools.

[2] The syntax of logic programs has been generalized, e.g., with choice, cardinality, and weight rules in [37], but such extensions can be translated back to normal rules [6].

[3] Or, constraints are cast as normal rules with a new head f and 'not f' in the body.

[4] Typically, $\text{At}(P)$ is selected to be minimal in this respect, i.e., it only contains atoms that actually appear in P. But larger sets might be used, e.g., if P resulted from rewriting and certain atoms were removed, but the semantics of P is unaffected.

a unique minimal model, or several minimal models as witnessed by programs $P_1 = \{a. \leftarrow a.\}$, $P_2 = \{a \leftarrow a.\}$, and $P_3 = \{a \mid b.\}$, respectively.

As a special case, a positive *normal* program P without constraints has always a unique minimal model, the *least model* denoted by $\mathrm{LM}(P)$. A widely agreed semantics of logic programs is given by their stable models [18,19] based on the Gelfond-Lifschitz reduct of a program P with respect to an interpretation $M \subseteq \mathrm{At}(P)$ understood as a model candidate. The reduced program is

$$P^M = \{(A \leftarrow B) \mid (A \leftarrow B, \mathrm{not}\ C) \in P,\ A \neq \emptyset,\ B \subseteq M, \text{ and } C \cap M = \emptyset\}. \quad (2)$$

Definition 1 (Gelfond and Lifschitz [18,19]). *A model M of a disjunctive logic program P is* stable *if and only if $M \in \mathrm{MM}(P^M)$.*

Note that for NLPs, the condition of Definition 1 is equivalent to a fixpoint $M = \mathrm{LM}(P^M)$. We let $\mathrm{SM}(P)$ denote the set of stable models of P. Definition 1 covers constraints (1) with $k = 0$ by the requirement that M is a *model* of P, i.e., for each constraint $\leftarrow B, \mathrm{not}\ C$ in the program, $B \not\subseteq M$, or $C \cap M \neq \emptyset$.

Example 1. Consider the following NLP P_{abcd}:

$$a \leftarrow \mathrm{not}\ b, \mathrm{not}\ c. \quad a \leftarrow d. \quad b \leftarrow \mathrm{not}\ a, \mathrm{not}\ c. \quad b \leftarrow d. \quad c \leftarrow \mathrm{not}\ a, \mathrm{not}\ b.$$

There are three stable models for P_{abcd}: $M_1 = \{a\}$, $M_2 = \{b\}$, and $M_3 = \{c\}$. E.g., the reduct with respect to M_1 consists of $a \leftarrow d$, $b \leftarrow d$, and the fact a. ■

2.2 Basic Notions of Equivalence

Obviously, the comparison of logic programs goes back to the stable semantics.

Definition 2. *Logic programs P and Q are (i)* weakly equivalent *(denoted $P \equiv Q$) iff $\mathrm{SM}(P) = \mathrm{SM}(Q)$ and (ii)* strongly equivalent *[38] (denoted $P \equiv_s Q$) iff for all context programs R, $\mathrm{SM}(P \cup R) = \mathrm{SM}(Q \cup R)$.*

Weak equivalence concerns entire programs while strong equivalence is typically applied more locally, e.g., to justify rule-level modifications to programs. For instance, rules like $a \leftarrow a$ and $a \leftarrow b, \mathrm{not}\ b$ can be safely removed in any context as they are strongly equivalent to an empty program. As shown in [32], strong equivalence (SE) is characterized by SE-models $\langle N, M\rangle$ where $N \subseteq M$, $M \models P$, and $N \models P^M$, associated with a logic program P. Thus we may reason about $P \equiv_s Q$ without considering arbitrary contexts R as per Definition 2. It is also practical to distinguish when P and Q are *classically equivalent* (denoted $P \equiv_c Q$) iff they have the same classical models. Classical equivalence is a prerequisite for strong equivalence, because $M \models P$ iff $\langle M, M\rangle$ is an SE-model of P. Thus $P \not\equiv_c Q$ implies $P \not\equiv_s Q$. Analogously, $P \not\equiv Q$ implies $P \not\equiv_s Q$ by $R = \emptyset$.

2.3 Modularity

For the purposes of this work, it is sufficient to present the module architecture of [29] in the case of NLPs only. The idea is to view a logic program P as a *module* and to partition its signature $\mathrm{At}(P)$ of into three pairwise disjoint sets of *input*, *output*, and *hidden* atoms, respectively. We introduce the respective notations $\mathrm{At}^{\mathrm{i}}(P)$, $\mathrm{At}^{\mathrm{o}}(P)$, $\mathrm{At}^{\mathrm{h}}(P)$ for these subsets of $\mathrm{At}(P)$. Moreover, the *visible* part $\mathrm{At}^{\mathrm{v}}(P) = \mathrm{At}^{\mathrm{i}}(P) \cup \mathrm{At}^{\mathrm{o}}(P)$ is the interface of P for interacting with other modules whereas the hidden part $\mathrm{At}^{\mathrm{h}}(P)$ is reserved for the internal (auxiliary) concepts of P. An essential restriction is that input atoms $a \in \mathrm{At}^{\mathrm{i}}(P)$ are not allowed as rule heads and thus every rule of a module P must contribute to the *definition* of at least one atom in $\mathrm{At}^{\mathrm{o}}(P) \cup \mathrm{At}^{\mathrm{h}}(P)$. As an example, we could view the program P_{abcd} from Example 1 as a module by setting $\mathrm{At}^{\mathrm{i}}(P_{abcd}) = \{d\}$, $\mathrm{At}^{\mathrm{o}}(P_{abcd}) = \{a, b\}$, and $\mathrm{At}^{\mathrm{h}}(P_{abcd}) = \{c\}$. The first two rules define a.

On the semantic side, each interpretation $I \subseteq \mathrm{At}(P)$ of a module P partitions into $I_{\mathrm{v}} = I \cap \mathrm{At}^{\mathrm{v}}(P) = I \setminus \mathrm{At}^{\mathrm{h}}(P)$, $I_{\mathrm{i}} = I \cap \mathrm{At}^{\mathrm{i}}(P)$, $I_{\mathrm{o}} = I \cap \mathrm{At}^{\mathrm{o}}(P)$, and $I_{\mathrm{h}} = I \cap \mathrm{At}^{\mathrm{h}}(P)$. Analogous notations are used for sets of interpretations in the sequel. A module P reduces to a conventional logic program when $\mathrm{At}^{\mathrm{i}}(P) = \emptyset = \mathrm{At}^{\mathrm{h}}(P)$ and then its semantics is given by $\mathrm{SM}(P)_{\mathrm{v}} = \mathrm{SM}(P)$ directly. Otherwise, the definition of stable models must be adjusted to take input atoms into account. This can be achieved in a number of ways. (i) The *input reduct* [29] $P^{M,M_{\mathrm{i}}}$ includes a positive rule $a \leftarrow (B \setminus M_{\mathrm{i}})$ for each normal rule $a \leftarrow B, \mathrm{not}\ C$ for which $B \subseteq M$ and $C \cap M = \emptyset$. For stability, we require that $M_{\mathrm{o}} \cup M_{\mathrm{h}} = \mathrm{LM}(P^{M,M_{\mathrm{i}}})$. (ii) Alternatively [31], we add M_{i} as facts to P, giving rise to an equation $M = \mathrm{LM}(P^{M} \cup M_{\mathrm{i}})$. For more general use cases in the sequel, we write $P@N$ for a program P extended by the set of facts $\{a \mid a \in \mathrm{At}(P) \cap N\}$ based on any interpretation N. (iii) Yet another option [36] is to add an *input generator* P_{i} with rules $a \leftarrow \mathrm{not}\ \overline{a}$ and $\overline{a} \leftarrow \mathrm{not}\ a$ for every $a \in \mathrm{At}^{\mathrm{i}}(P)$ and a new atom $\overline{a} \notin \mathrm{At}(P)$. Then, stability is captured by $M = \mathrm{LM}((P \cup P_{\mathrm{i}})^{M})$.

Example 2. Let $\mathrm{At}^{\mathrm{i}}(P_{abcd}) = \{d\}$, $\mathrm{At}^{\mathrm{o}}(P_{abcd}) = \{a, b\}$, and $\mathrm{At}^{\mathrm{h}}(P_{abcd}) = \{c\}$ for the program P_{abcd} of Ex. 1. Due to input atom d, there are now four stable models $M_1 = \{a\}$, $M_2 = \{b\}$, $M_3 = \{c\}$, and $M_4 = \{a, b, d\}$. The last one is reconstructed by an input reduct with a and b as a facts. Alternatively, d could be added as a fact, or as the reduct of $d \leftarrow \mathrm{not}\ \overline{d}$ with respect to M_4. Also, we note that $\mathrm{SM}(P_{abcd})_{\mathrm{v}} = \{\emptyset, \{a\}, \{b\}, \{a, b, d\}\}$ gives the semantics of P_{abcd} when comparing it against other programs, e.g., in terms of *visible equivalence* [21]. ■

Two modules P and Q can be merged if they define different atoms and respect each other's hidden atoms, i.e., $\mathrm{At}^{\mathrm{o}}(P) \cap \mathrm{At}^{\mathrm{o}}(Q) = \emptyset$, $\mathrm{At}^{\mathrm{h}}(P) \cap \mathrm{At}(Q) = \emptyset$, and $\mathrm{At}(P) \cap \mathrm{At}^{\mathrm{h}}(Q) = \emptyset$. The *composition* $P \oplus Q$ of P and Q [29] is effectively $P \cup Q$ based on signatures $\mathrm{At}^{\mathrm{o}}(P \cup Q) = \mathrm{At}^{\mathrm{o}}(P) \cup \mathrm{At}^{\mathrm{o}}(Q)$ and $\mathrm{At}^{\mathrm{h}}(P \cup Q) = \mathrm{At}^{\mathrm{h}}(P) \cup \mathrm{At}^{\mathrm{h}}(Q)$, but the input signature is reduced to $\mathrm{At}^{\mathrm{i}}(P \cup Q) = (\mathrm{At}^{\mathrm{i}}(P) \setminus \mathrm{At}^{\mathrm{o}}(Q)) \cup (\mathrm{At}^{\mathrm{i}}(Q) \setminus \mathrm{At}^{\mathrm{o}}(Q))$ as input atoms may get defined by P and Q. The union $P \cup Q$, as defined above, does not guarantee compositional semantics in general. To this end, conditions can be tightened using the *positive dependency graph* $\mathrm{DG}^{+}(P \cup Q)$ having the set of nodes $\mathrm{At}^{\mathrm{o}}(P \cup Q) \cup \mathrm{At}^{\mathrm{h}}(P \cup Q)$ and a dependency $b \leq a$ whenever there is a rule $a \leftarrow B, \mathrm{not}\ C$ in $P \cup Q$ such that $b \in B$. A *strongly connected component* (SCC) S of $\mathrm{DG}^+(P \cup Q)$ is a maximal set S of nodes that depend positively on each other. Programs P and Q are *mutually independent* in $P \cup Q$ iff $\mathrm{DG}^+(P \cup Q)$ has no SCC S properly intersecting with both $\mathrm{At^o}(P)$ and $\mathrm{At^o}(Q)$. If so, the *join* $P \sqcup Q$ in the sense of [29] is defined. Such a restriction is assumed about the joins/unions of programs in the sequel.

Theorem 1. (Module Theorem *[29]***).** *If P and Q are mutually independent programs or program modules, then* $\mathrm{SM}(P \cup Q) = \mathrm{SM}(P) \bowtie \mathrm{SM}(Q)$.

The operation $\bowtie$ is the *natural join* of *compatible* stable models, i.e., $M_1 \cup M_2$ belongs to $\mathrm{SM}(P) \bowtie \mathrm{SM}(Q)$ iff $M_1 \in \mathrm{SM}(P)$, $M_2 \in \mathrm{SM}(Q)$, and $M_1 \cap \mathrm{At^v}(Q) = M_2 \cap \mathrm{At^v}(P)$. Theorem 1 generalizes for finite joins by $\mathrm{SM}(P_1 \cup \ldots \cup P_n) = \mathrm{SM}(P_1) \bowtie \ldots \bowtie \mathrm{SM}(P_n)$ when modules P_i are pairwise mutually independent.

2.4 Programs with Enough Visible Atoms (EVA)

A potential side effect of hiding is that the set $\mathrm{SM}(P)_\mathrm{v}$ of *visible projections* can have elements for which there are at least two corresponding stable models $M \neq N$ in $\mathrm{SM}(P)$, i.e., $M \cap \mathrm{At^v}(P) = N \cap \mathrm{At^v}(P)$. Such hidden non-determinism can be avoided by setting restrictions on the hidden parts of programs [36].

Definition 3 (Hidden Part). *Given an NLP P, the* hidden part P_h *of P contains all rules $a \leftarrow B, \mathrm{not}\ C \in P$ such that $a \in \mathrm{At^h}(P)$. Moreover, we set* $\mathrm{At^i}(P_\mathrm{h}) = \mathrm{At^i}(P) \cup \mathrm{At^o}(P) = \mathrm{At^v}(P)$, $\mathrm{At^o}(P_\mathrm{h}) = \emptyset$, *and* $\mathrm{At^h}(P_\mathrm{h}) = \mathrm{At^h}(P)$.

Definition 4 (The EVA Property). *A normal logic program P has* enough visible atoms *if for every interpretation $M \subseteq \mathrm{At}(P)$, the program $P_\mathrm{h}@M_\mathrm{v}$ has a unique stable model $N \subseteq \mathrm{At}(P_\mathrm{h}) = \mathrm{At}(P)$ such that $N_\mathrm{i} = N \cap \mathrm{At^v}(P) = M_\mathrm{v}$.*

Since $\mathrm{At^h}(P) = \emptyset$ guarantees the EVA property, it can be enforced by revealing sufficiently many atoms. However, this may not be feasible if programs under consideration are based on different auxiliary concepts. The EVA property can also be established if the hidden part P_h is kept essentially *stratified*. Unstratified negation can be removed [35] if non-deterministic choices can be made visible. In general, checking if P_h has the EVA property is at least a coNP-hard decision problem [28]. In certain applications, such as *probabilistic reasoning*, the multitude of stable models encodes essential information and the EVA property is not worth pursuing. Such applications fall outside the scope of this paper.

Proposition 1. *If P is a normal logic program with the EVA property, and $M \in \mathrm{SM}(P)$, then* $\mathrm{SM}(P_\mathrm{h}@M_\mathrm{v}) = \{M\}$.

Example 3. Consider the following logic program P_{abce}:

$$b \leftarrow \mathrm{not}\ c. \quad c \leftarrow \mathrm{not}\ b. \quad b \leftarrow a. \quad c \leftarrow \mathrm{not}\ a. \quad e \leftarrow b. \quad e \leftarrow \mathrm{not}\ c.$$

Then, let $\mathrm{At}^{\mathrm{i}}(P_{abce}) = \{a\}$, $\mathrm{At}^{\mathrm{o}}(P_{abce}) = \{e\}$, and $\mathrm{At}^{\mathrm{h}}(P_{abce}) = \{b, c\}$. The hidden part $(P_{abce})_{\mathrm{h}}$ is formed by the four first rules. By definition, $\mathrm{At}^{\mathrm{i}}((P_{abce})_{\mathrm{h}}) = \{a, e\}$. Since e does not appear as an actual input atom, the relevant sets of input atoms are $\emptyset$ and $\{a\}$. They induce unique stable models $\{c\}$ and $\{a, b\}$, respectively. Thus, P_{abce} has the EVA property. The entire P_{abce} has two stable models $M_1 = \{c\}$ and $M_2 = \{a, b, e\}$ where the choice regarding a is visible. ■

2.5 Stable-Unstable Semantics

The original definition of stable-unstable semantics [5] adds one subprogram as an *oracle* to a main program. To cater for more flexible use cases, we adopt the generalized definition [24] with any fixed number $n \geq 0$ of oracles. While there is no real reason to restrict the main program P, it is assumed that oracles P_i are effectively NLPs containing no rule $a \leftarrow B, \mathrm{not}\ C$ such that $a \in \mathrm{At}(P)$. Thus oracles may not *define* any concepts for the main program P, they simply receive some facts as input for each stable model of P. Using concepts from Sect. 2.3, we assume that each oracle P_i is interfaced by $\mathrm{At}^{\mathrm{i}}(P_i) \subseteq \mathrm{At}^{\mathrm{v}}(P)$, $\mathrm{At}^{\mathrm{o}}(P_i) = \emptyset$, and $\mathrm{At}^{\mathrm{h}}(P_i) = \mathrm{At}(P_i) \setminus \mathrm{At}^{\mathrm{i}}(P_i)$. We write $P[P_1 \cdots P_n]$ for a *combined program* that connects the main program P to its oracles $P_1, \ldots, P_n$.

Definition 5. *A model M of a program P is* stable-unstable *with respect to oracle programs $P_1, \ldots, P_n$ iff $M \in \mathrm{SM}(P)$ and for $1 \leq i \leq n$, $\mathrm{SM}(P_i@M) = \emptyset$. The set of stable-unstable models of $P[P_1 \cdots P_n]$ is denoted by $\mathrm{StUn}(P[P_1 \cdots P_n])$.*

Note that input atoms $a \in \mathrm{At}^{\mathrm{i}}(P_i)$ such that $a \notin M$ will remain false by default in the context of the oracle P_i. This is why no constraints are required in $P_i@M$ in contrast with [31]. Definition 5 is applicable to an arbitrary depth $k \geq 1$. A k-combined program has an NLP P as its main program and $k-1$-combined programs as its oracles. On the other hand, if $k = 1$ or $n = 0$, Definition 5 reduces back to Definition 1. Also, Theorem 1 is not applicable to $P[P_1 \cdots P_n]$ as the respective sets $\mathrm{SM}(P_1@M) = \ldots = \mathrm{SM}(P_n@M) = \emptyset$ when M is stable-unstable.

Example 4. Consider the following oracles for the NLP P_{abcd} from Example 1:

$$P_f\colon\quad f \leftarrow \mathrm{not}\ a, \mathrm{not}\ b, \mathrm{not}\ c, \mathrm{not}\ f.$$
$$P_{f2}\colon\quad f \leftarrow a, \mathrm{not}\ f. \qquad f \leftarrow b, \mathrm{not}\ f.$$

Now M_1, M_2, and M_3 are not stable-unstable with respect to P_f since adding one of a, b, and c as a fact will cancel the only rule of P_f so that $\mathrm{SM}(P_f@M_j) = \{M_j\} \neq \emptyset$. On the other hand, M_1 and M_2 are stable-unstable with respect to P_{f2}, since adding a or b as a fact will pre-empt any stable models for P_{f2}. ■

3 Equivalence Checking via Complementation

The method for checking the equivalence of logic programs (or program modules) [36] translates the logic programs P and Q of interest into a single logic program

$\mathrm{Tr}_{\mathrm{EQ}}(P, Q)$ that has a stable model iff there is $M \in \mathrm{SM}(P)$ such that $M \notin \mathrm{SM}(Q)$. By this arrangement, the programs (or modules) P and Q are equivalent if $\mathrm{Tr}_{\mathrm{EQ}}(P, Q)$ and $\mathrm{Tr}_{\mathrm{EQ}}(Q, P)$ have no stable models. The required checks are feasible using an answer-set solver for actual computations.

The latter translation $\mathrm{Tr}_{\mathrm{EQ}}(Q, P)$ can be understood as $Q \cup \mathrm{Tr}_{\mathrm{C}}(P)$ where Q captures a stable model $M \in \mathrm{SM}(Q)$ and the subprogram $\mathrm{Tr}_{\mathrm{C}}(P)$ checks that $M \notin \mathrm{SM}(P)$. Therefore, the translation $\mathrm{Tr}_{\mathrm{C}}(P)$ essentially encodes the program-level *complement* of P that has as its stable models interpretations $M \subseteq \mathrm{At}(P)$ which are not stable models of P. This is also an interesting primitive from modelling perspective, since one can concentrate on describing either (the set of) *solutions* or *non-solutions* to a problem. The other set will be available through complementation if desired. The complement $\mathrm{Tr}_{\mathrm{C}}(P)$ detailed below introduces a new atom $a^\bullet$ for each atom $a \in \mathrm{At}(P)$ in the input program P. We generalize such renaming (i) for sets of atoms $A \subseteq \mathrm{At}(P)$ by setting $A^\bullet = \{a^\bullet \mid a \in A\}$ and (ii) for positive NLPs P by setting $P^\bullet = \{a^\bullet \leftarrow B^\bullet \mid a \leftarrow B \in P\}$. In addition, a special auxiliary atom $d \notin \mathrm{At}(P)$ is used to capture reasons of instability.

Definition 6. *For a normal logic program P, the complement $\mathrm{Tr}_{\mathrm{C}}(P)$ contains:*

1. *Each rule $a \leftarrow B, \mathrm{not}\ C \in P_{\mathrm{h}}$ of the hidden part of P.*
2. *For each rule $a \leftarrow B, \mathrm{not}\ C \in P$, the rule $a^\bullet \leftarrow B^\bullet, \mathrm{not}\ C$.*
3. *For each $a \in \mathrm{At}^{\mathrm{i}}(P)$, the rule $a^\bullet \leftarrow a$.*
4. *For each constraint $\leftarrow B, \mathrm{not}\ C \in P$, the rule $d \leftarrow B, \mathrm{not}\ C$.*
5. *For each $a \in \mathrm{At}^{\mathrm{o}}(P) \cup \mathrm{At}^{\mathrm{h}}(P)$, the rules $d \leftarrow a, \mathrm{not}\ a^\bullet$ and $d \leftarrow a^\bullet, \mathrm{not}\ a$.*
6. *The constraint $\leftarrow \mathrm{not}\ d$.*

The signature $\mathrm{At}(\mathrm{Tr}_{\mathrm{C}}(P)) = \mathrm{At}(P) \cup \mathrm{At}(P)^\bullet \cup \{d\}$ *where* $\mathrm{At}^{\mathrm{i}}(\mathrm{Tr}_{\mathrm{C}}(P)) = \mathrm{At}^{\mathrm{v}}(P)$, $\mathrm{At}^{\mathrm{o}}(\mathrm{Tr}_{\mathrm{C}}(P)) = \emptyset$, *and* $\mathrm{At}^{\mathrm{h}}(\mathrm{Tr}_{\mathrm{C}}(P)) = \mathrm{At}^{\mathrm{h}}(P) \cup \mathrm{At}(P)^\bullet \cup \{d\}$.

Given an interpretation $M \subseteq \mathrm{At}(P)$ and its visible part M_{v} as input, the purpose of the complement $\mathrm{Tr}_{\mathrm{C}}(P)$ is to check that M_{v} cannot be extended to a stable model of P. This is to be witnessed by a unique stable model N of $\mathrm{Tr}_{\mathrm{C}}(P)$ such that $M = N \cap \mathrm{At}(P)$. The reasons for the instability of M are two-fold: either $M \neq \mathrm{LM}(P^{M,M_{\mathrm{i}}})$ or some constraint of P is violated by M. The hidden part P_{h} is included in $\mathrm{Tr}_{\mathrm{C}}(P)$ as such to fix the interpretation M_{h} via the unique stable model of $P_{\mathrm{h}}@M_{\mathrm{v}}$ as to be guaranteed by the EVA property.

The translation of Definition 6 can be understood as a reduced version of the translation EQT [36] for modules. Our version is restricted to NLPs and the new atoms a° used to encode the hidden part P_{h} in [36] are reverted back to original hidden atoms $a \in \mathrm{At}^{\mathrm{h}}(P)$. A copy of the input is created using rules of the form $a^\bullet \leftarrow a$ for $a \in \mathrm{At}^{\mathrm{i}}(P)$. This simplifies the representation of the least model $\mathrm{LM}(P^{M,M_{\mathrm{i}}})$. In analogy to [36], the translation $\mathrm{Tr}_{\mathrm{C}}(P)$ can be split into P_{h}, $\mathrm{Tr}_{\mathrm{L}}(P)$ (Items 2–3 in Definition 6), and $\mathrm{Tr}_{\mathrm{D}}(P)$ (Items 4–6). Based on such a modularization of $\mathrm{Tr}_{\mathrm{C}}(P)$, the proof of correctness may rest on Theorem 1.

Theorem 2. *Let P be an NLP with the EVA property and $\mathrm{Tr}_{\mathrm{C}}(P)$ its complement. Then, for all interpretations $M \subseteq \mathrm{At}(P)$ such that $M \in \mathrm{SM}(P_{\mathrm{h}}@M_{\mathrm{v}})$, $M \notin \mathrm{SM}(P)$ iff there is a unique $N \in \mathrm{SM}(\mathrm{Tr}_{\mathrm{C}}(P)@M_{\mathrm{v}})$ with $N_{\mathrm{i}} = M_{\mathrm{v}}$.*

Example 5. Consider an NLP P_{ab} with $\mathrm{At}^{\mathrm{v}}(P_{ab}) = \{a, b\}$ and the rules

$$a \leftarrow \mathrm{not}\ b. \quad b \leftarrow \mathrm{not}\ a.$$

The complement $\mathrm{Tr}_{\mathrm{C}}(P_{ab})$ has the following rules:

$$a^\bullet \leftarrow \mathrm{not}\ b. \quad b^\bullet \leftarrow \mathrm{not}\ a.$$
$$d \leftarrow a, \mathrm{not}\ a^\bullet. \quad d \leftarrow a^\bullet, \mathrm{not}\ a. \quad d \leftarrow b, \mathrm{not}\ b^\bullet. \quad d \leftarrow b^\bullet, \mathrm{not}\ b. \quad \leftarrow \mathrm{not}\ d.$$

While $\mathrm{SM}(P) = \{\{a\}, \{b\}\}$, the complement $\mathrm{Tr}_{\mathrm{C}}(P_{ab})$ has two stable models $N_1 = \{a^\bullet, b^\bullet, d\}$ and $N_2 = \{a, b, d\}$ corresponding to inputs $\emptyset$ and $\{a, b\}$. By Theorem 2, the projections of N_1 and N_2 on $\mathrm{At}^{\mathrm{v}}(P_{ab}) = \{a, b\}$ capture the non-stable interpretations $M_1 = \emptyset$ and $M_2 = \{a, b\}$ for the program P_{ab}. ∎

After isolating the complement transformation $\mathrm{Tr}_{\mathrm{C}}(\cdot)$, the correctness of the translation-based verification method [36] follows from Theorems 1 and 2.

Corollary 1. *If NLPs P and Q have the EVA property, then $P \equiv Q$ holds iff* $\mathrm{Tr}_{\mathrm{EQ}}(P, Q) = P \cup \mathrm{Tr}_{\mathrm{C}}(Q)$ *and* $\mathrm{Tr}_{\mathrm{EQ}}(Q, P) = Q \cup \mathrm{Tr}_{\mathrm{C}}(P)$ *have no stable models.*

Proposition 2. *If a normal logic program P has the EVA property, so does its complement* $\mathrm{Tr}_{\mathrm{C}}(P)$.

Example 6. For the program P_{abce} of Ex. 3, the complement $\mathrm{Tr}_{\mathrm{C}}(P_{abce})$ is:

$$b \leftarrow \mathrm{not}\ c. \quad c \leftarrow \mathrm{not}\ b. \quad b \leftarrow a. \quad c \leftarrow \mathrm{not}\ a. \quad a^\bullet \leftarrow a.$$
$$b^\bullet \leftarrow \mathrm{not}\ c. \quad c^\bullet \leftarrow \mathrm{not}\ b. \quad b^\bullet \leftarrow a^\bullet. \quad c^\bullet \leftarrow \mathrm{not}\ a. \quad e^\bullet \leftarrow b^\bullet. \quad e^\bullet \leftarrow \mathrm{not}\ c.$$
$$d \leftarrow e^\bullet, \mathrm{not}\ e. \quad d \leftarrow e, \mathrm{not}\ e^\bullet. \quad \leftarrow \mathrm{not}\ d.$$
$$d \leftarrow b^\bullet, \mathrm{not}\ b. \quad d \leftarrow b, \mathrm{not}\ b^\bullet. \quad d \leftarrow c^\bullet, \mathrm{not}\ c. \quad d \leftarrow c, \mathrm{not}\ c^\bullet.$$

There are two stable models for $\mathrm{Tr}_{\mathrm{C}}(P_{abce})$: $N_1 = \{a, a^\bullet, b, b^\bullet, e^\bullet, d\}$ and $N_2 = \{c, c^\bullet, e, d\}$. Therefore, $M_1 = \{a, b\}$ and $M_2 = \{c, e\}$ are not stable for P_{abce}. ∎

4 Notions of Equivalence for Stable-Unstable Semantics

The weak equivalence of normal/disjunctive logic programs can be generalized for stable-unstable semantics by focussing on the stable models of the main programs, but only those accepted by the respective sets of oracles. In this section, we present the ideas on a general level for ordinary programs with $\mathrm{At}(P) = \mathrm{At}^{\mathrm{o}}(P)$ and deploy their modular variants in later sections.

Definition 7. *Let P be a main program with oracles $P_1, \ldots, P_n$ and Q a main program with oracles $Q_1, \ldots, Q_m$ such that* $\mathrm{At}(P) = \mathrm{At}(Q)$. *Then, P and Q are stable-unstable equivalent with respect to their oracles, denoted $P[P_1 \cdots P_n] \equiv_{su} Q[Q_1 \cdots Q_m]$, if and only if* $\mathrm{StUn}(P[P_1 \cdots P_n]) = \mathrm{StUn}(Q[Q_1 \cdots Q_m])$.

Given Definition 7, it is also possible to distinguish the respective *inclusions* of witnessing stable-unstable models, e.g., $P[P_1 \cdots P_n] \sqsubseteq_{su} Q[Q_1 \cdots Q_m]$ when

$$\mathrm{StUn}(P[P_1 \cdots P_n]) \subseteq \mathrm{StUn}(Q[Q_1 \cdots Q_m]). \qquad (3)$$

Then $P \equiv_{su} Q$ holds iff $P[P_1 \cdots P_n] \sqsubseteq_{su} Q[Q_1 \cdots Q_m]$ and $Q[Q_1 \cdots Q_m] \sqsubseteq_{su} P[P_1 \cdots P_n]$, which reveals that checking weak equivalence reduces to solving two inclusion problems. Given the first inclusion, two kinds of counter-examples may arise in relation to a stable-unstable model $M \in \mathrm{StUn}(P[P_1 \cdots P_n])$:

1. either $M \notin \mathrm{SM}(Q)$, or
2. $M \in \mathrm{SM}(Q)$ but for some oracle Q_i with $1 \leq i \leq m$, $\mathrm{SM}(Q_i@M) \neq \emptyset$.

In the sequel, the counter-examples distinguished in the two items above are called counter-examples of *types* 1 and 2, T1 and T2 for short.

Note that $P[P_1 \cdots P_n] \equiv_{su} Q[Q_1 \cdots Q_m]$ may hold even if $P \not\equiv Q$ when P and Q are understood as ordinary logic programs, i.e., the oracles of P and Q may exclude all differentiating stable models of the main programs. On the other hand, even if $P \equiv Q$ holds for P and Q as ordinary logic programs, their oracles could make a difference so that $P[P_1 \cdots P_n] \not\equiv_{su} Q[Q_1 \cdots Q_m]$ holds. Thus, checking $P \equiv Q$ does not help with checking $P[P_1 \cdots P_n] \equiv_{su} Q[Q_1 \cdots Q_m]$.

Theorem 3. *Deciding the weak stable-unstable equivalence of two k-combined programs consisting of normal logic programs is a Π_k^P-complete decision problem.*

In the sequel, we are mainly interested in 2-combined programs, called *normal oracle programs* whose main program and oracle programs are NLPs. This is not very restrictive as many syntactic extensions can be removed via normalization [6] and properties captured by proper DLPs can be encoded with NLP oracles.

Corollary 2. *Deciding the weak stable-unstable equivalence of normal oracle programs is a Π_2^P-complete decision problem.*

This result supports the goal of following sections, i.e., implementing the respective equivalence check using translations toward DLPs [24]. As regards *strong* equivalence [32], it can be applied to the components of k-combined programs in the usual way, e.g., to modify individual rules. However, even stronger versions can be introduced by taking oracles into account. An SE-model $\langle N, M\rangle$ of P is accepted by $P[P_1 \cdots P_n]$ if $\mathrm{SM}(P_i@M) = \emptyset$ for all $1 \leq i \leq n$. Thus, the oracles $P_1, \ldots, P_n$ of P act as special constraints excluding SE-models.

Definition 8. *k-combined programs $P[P_1 \cdots P_n]$ and $Q[Q_1 \cdots Q_m]$ are strongly equivalent with respect to their oracles, iff the SE-models of P accepted by oracles $P_1, \ldots, P_n$ and the SE-models of Q accepted by oracles $Q_1, \ldots, Q_m$ coincide.*

This is analogous to P and Q being strongly equivalent in a particular context R, i.e., $P \cup R \equiv_s Q \cup R$ but $P \not\equiv_s Q$ might not hold in general. The definition for classical equivalence is similar: a classical model M is accepted iff the corresponding SE-model $\langle M, M\rangle$ is. Also, a translation $\mathrm{Tr}_{\mathrm{CL}}(P)$ for capturing the classical models of P is obtained by adding for every atom $a \in \mathrm{At}(P)$, a rule $a \leftarrow \mathrm{not}\ \mathrm{not}\ a$. The one $\mathrm{Tr}_{\mathrm{SE}}(P)$ for the SE-models of P extends $\mathrm{Tr}_{\mathrm{CL}}(P)$ with (i) a rule $a^{\bullet} \leftarrow a, \mathrm{not}\ \mathrm{not}\ a^{\bullet}$ and a constraint $\leftarrow a^{\bullet}, \mathrm{not}\ a$ for every atom $a \in \mathrm{At}(P)$ and (ii) rules $a^{\bullet} \leftarrow B^{\bullet}, \mathrm{not}\ C$ for every $a \leftarrow B, \mathrm{not}\ C$ in P. Finally, the stable models of P can be captured with classical models through a more complex reduction to SAT [21] and back to NLPs. For these reasons, we observe:

Corollary 3. *Deciding the classical and strong equivalence of normal oracle programs (relative to their oracles) are* Π_2^P*-complete decision problems.*

5 Modular Translations for Equivalence Checking

In this section, we devise translations for checking the equivalence of k-combined programs and, more specifically, that of normal oracle programs ($k = 2$). As a further objective, we aim at a highly modular translation that exploits the structure offered by the main programs and oracles as far as possible. Moreover, we divide the equivalence check into the respective inclusion problems and concentrate on finding counter-examples of two types separately. Type 1 concerns the level of main programs while type 2 takes the effect of oracles into account.

Definition 9. *Let* $P[P_1 \cdots P_n]$ *be a* k*-combined logic program and* Q *an NLP with the EVA property such that* $\mathrm{At}^{\mathrm{v}}(Q) = \mathrm{At}^{\mathrm{v}}(P)$*,* $\mathrm{At}(P) \cap \mathrm{At}^{\mathrm{h}}(Q) = \emptyset$*, and* $\mathrm{At}^{\mathrm{h}}(P) \cap \mathrm{At}(Q) = \emptyset$*. The translation for counter-examples of type 1 is*

$$\mathrm{Tr}_{\mathrm{T1}}(P[P_1 \cdots P_n], Q) = (P \cup \mathrm{Tr}_{\mathrm{C}}(Q))[P_1 \cdots P_n]. \tag{4}$$

Theorem 4. *Given a* k*-combined logic program* $P[P_1 \cdots P_n]$ *and an NLP* Q *satisfying the conditions of Definition 9, the translation* $\mathrm{Tr}_{\mathrm{T1}}(P[P_1 \cdots P_n], Q)$ *has a stable-unstable model iff there is a stable-unstable model* M *of* $P[P_1 \cdots P_n]$ *and there is no* $M' \notin \mathrm{SM}(Q)$ *such that* $M \cap \mathrm{At}^{\mathrm{v}}(Q) = M' \cap \mathrm{At}^{\mathrm{v}}(P)$*.*

The next translation presumes that counter-examples of type 1 have been checked and further checks are carried out only if such counter-examples were not found. Under this assumption, the weak equivalence of P and Q is not preempted by the stable models of the main programs but it remains to be shown that the models are equally accepted by the oracles $P_1, \ldots, P_n$ and $Q_1, \ldots, Q_n$.

Definition 10. *Let* $P[P_1 \cdots P_n]$ *and* $Q[Q_1 \cdots Q_m]$ *be* k*-combined logic programs and* Q_i *an oracle of* Q *with* $1 \leq i \leq m$*. The translation for counter-examples of type 2 is* $\mathrm{Tr}_{\mathrm{T2}}(P[P_1 \cdots P_n], Q_i) = (P \cup Q_i)[P_1 \cdots P_n]$*.*

Theorem 5. *Given* k*-combined logic programs* $P[P_1 \cdots P_n]$ *and* $Q[Q_1 \cdots Q_m]$ *and the* i*:th oracle* Q_i*, the translation* $\mathrm{Tr}_{\mathrm{T2}}(P[P_1 \cdots P_n], Q_i)$ *has a stable-unstable model iff there is a stable-unstable model* M *of* $P[P_1 \cdots P_n]$ *excluded by* Q_i*.*

Corollary 4. *Let* $P[P_1 \cdots P_n]$ *and* $Q[Q_1 \cdots Q_m]$ *be* k*-combined logic programs such that* $\mathrm{At}^{\mathrm{v}}(P) = \mathrm{At}^{\mathrm{v}}(Q)$*,* $\mathrm{At}(P) \cap \mathrm{At}^{\mathrm{h}}(Q) = \emptyset$*,* $\mathrm{At}^{\mathrm{h}}(P) \cap \mathrm{At}(Q) = \emptyset$*, and* P *and* Q *have the EVA property. Then,* $P[P_1 \cdots P_n] \equiv_{su} Q[Q_1 \cdots Q_m]$ *iff translations*

1. $\mathrm{Tr}_{\mathrm{T1}}(P[P_1 \cdots P_n], Q)$ *has no stable-unstable models;*
2. $\mathrm{Tr}_{\mathrm{T1}}(Q[Q_1 \cdots Q_m], P)$ *has no stable-unstable models;*
3. $\mathrm{Tr}_{\mathrm{T2}}(P[P_1 \cdots P_n], Q_i)$ *have no stable-unstable models for* $1 \leq i \leq m$*; and*
4. $\mathrm{Tr}_{\mathrm{T2}}(Q[Q_1 \cdots Q_m], P_i)$ *have no stable-unstable models for* $1 \leq i \leq n$.

The modular method formalized above performs $n+m+2$ coNP-queries in the worst case when $P[P_1 \cdots P_n]$ and $Q[Q_1 \cdots Q_m]$ turn out to be equivalent. Note that any shared oracle $Q_i \in \{P_1, \ldots, P_n\}$ need not be checked with $\mathrm{Tr}_{\mathrm{T2}}(\cdot)$. Therefore, if P and Q have identical oracles, at most two coNP-queries are needed. The method can be readily used to check classical and strong equivalence by first applying translations $\mathrm{Tr}_{\mathrm{CL}}(\cdot)$ and $\mathrm{Tr}_{\mathrm{SE}}(\cdot)$ from Sect. 4 to P and Q.

6 Relationship with Quantified Programs

The higher levels of polynomial-time hierarchy can also be covered using explicit quantifiers in the context of ASP. In the following, we relate the approach based on quantification over answer sets [2] to stable-unstable semantics. The program-level complement $\mathrm{Tr}_{\mathrm{C}}(\cdot)$ introduced in Sect. 3 turns out to be a useful primitive in this respect, as it enables a modular embedding of ASP(Q) into k-combined logic programs under stable-unstable semantics. We present ASP(Q) in the case where quantification takes place over stable models of normal programs. Intuitively, given a normal program P, the quantifier $\exists^{\mathrm{st}} P$ (resp. $\forall^{\mathrm{st}} P$) states that some stable model (resp. all stable models) of P satisfies (resp. satisfy) some further condition of interest. Subsequent quantifications up to depth k give rise to quantified answer-set (ASP(Q)) programs as follows.

Definition 11 (ASP(Q)-programs [2]). *An ASP(Q)-program P is an expression of the form $\Box_1 P_1 \ldots \Box_k P_k : C$ where each quantifier $\Box_i \in \{\exists^{\mathrm{st}}, \forall^{\mathrm{st}}\}$, each P_i is an NLP, and C is a stratified NLP with constraints.*

If $\Box_i = \Box_{i+1}$ in the sequence, the latter quantifier can be dropped by replacing P_i with the join $P_i \sqcup P_{i+1}$ which is defined, since P_i can only provide input for P_{i+1}, not vice versa. For this reason, we assume that the quantifiers in the sequence $\Box_1, \ldots, \Box_k$ alternate between $\exists^{\mathrm{st}}$ and $\forall^{\mathrm{st}}$ and the first quantifier in the sequence determines the type of the program: *existential* ones start with $\exists^{\mathrm{st}}$ whereas the *universal* ones with $\forall^{\mathrm{st}}$. The semantics of ASP(Q)-programs is based on the inductive notion of *coherence* [2] which captures ASP(Q)-programs that satisfy the requirements enforced by the alternating quantifications over answer sets and the eventual constraints imposed by C. Since C it is a stratified normal logic program, when augmented by an input M to a program $C@M$, it will have either a unique stable model or no stable models at all, if some of its constraints is violated. In other words, C has the EVA property.

Definition 12 (Coherence [2]). *Given the depth of quantification $k > 1$,*

1. $\exists^{\mathrm{st}} P : C$ *is coherent, iff for some* $M \in \mathrm{SM}(P)$, $\mathrm{SM}(C@M) \neq \emptyset$*;*
2. $\forall^{\mathrm{st}} P : C$ *is coherent, iff for all* $M \in \mathrm{SM}(P)$, $\mathrm{SM}(C@M) \neq \emptyset$*;*

3. *$\exists^{\text{st}} P_1 \Box_2 P_2 \ldots \Box_k P_k : C$ is coherent, iff for some $M \in \text{SM}(P_1)$, the ASP(Q)-program $\Box_2 P_2 @M \Box_3 P_3 \ldots \Box_k P_k : C$ is recursively coherent; and*
4. *$\forall^{\text{st}} P_1 \Box_2 P_2 \ldots \Box_k P_k : C$ is coherent, iff for all $M \in \text{SM}(P_1)$, the ASP(Q)-program $\Box_2 P_2 @M \Box_3 P_3 \ldots \Box_k P_k : C$ is recursively coherent.*

It is implicitly assumed that the input M passed to a quantifier $\Box_i P_i$ does not interfere with the definitions of atoms in the programs $P_i, \ldots, P_k$ nor the program C with constraints. Let us now explicate how ASP(Q)-programs with $1 \leq k \leq 2$ can be captured by stable-unstable semantics. Intuitively, incoherence statements on universal quantification over answer sets translate to the existence of stable (or stable-unstable) models that act as witnessing counter-examples.

Proposition 3. *Coherence and stable-unstable semantics relate as follows:*

1. *$\exists^{\text{st}} P : C$ is coherent iff $P \cup C$ has a stable model;*
2. *$\forall^{\text{st}} P : C$ is incoherent iff $P \cup \text{Tr}_{\text{C}}(C)$ has a stable model;*
3. *$\exists^{\text{st}} P \forall^{\text{st}} Q : C$ is coherent iff $P[Q \cup \text{Tr}_{\text{C}}(C)]$ has a stable-unstable model; and*
4. *$\forall^{\text{st}} P \exists^{\text{st}} Q : C$ is incoherent iff $P[Q \cup C]$ has a stable-unstable model.*

Proof. Items **1** and **2** follow directly from definitions and Theorems 1 and 2. For Item **3**, note that $\exists^{\text{st}} P \forall^{\text{st}} Q : C$ is coherent $\iff$ for some $M \in \text{SM}(P)$, $\forall^{\text{st}} Q@M : C$ is coherent $\iff$ for some $M \in \text{SM}(P)$, $\forall^{\text{st}} Q@M : C$ is not incoherent $\iff$ for some $M \in \text{SM}(P)$, $Q@M \cup \text{Tr}_{\text{C}}(C)$ has no stable models $\iff$ for some $M \in \text{SM}(P)$, $(Q \cup \text{Tr}_{\text{C}}(C))@M$ has no stable models $\iff$ $P[Q \cup \text{Tr}_{\text{C}}(C)]$ has a stable-unstable model. For Item **4**, $\forall^{\text{st}} P \exists^{\text{st}} Q : C$ is incoherent $\iff$ for some $M \in \text{SM}(P)$, $\exists^{\text{st}} Q@M : C$ is incoherent $\iff$ for some $M \in \text{SM}(P)$, $(Q@M) \cup C$ has no stable models $\iff$ for some $M \in \text{SM}(P)$, $(Q \cup C)@M$ has no stable models $\iff$ $P[Q \cup C]$ has a stable-unstable model. □

Proposition 3 has important consequences. Firstly, it shows that ASP(Q)-programs of quantifier depth $k \in \{1, 2\}$ can be captured with k-combined programs, i.e., the constraints formalized by C can be checked without increasing the depth of oracle calls. The complement $\text{Tr}_{\text{C}}(C)$ plays a key role in this respect because it effectively substitutes an oracle call with a linear-size translation. It is only needed in the embedding towards stable-unstable semantics if the last quantifier in the sequence is $\forall^{\text{st}}$. As regards cases $k > 2$, the removal of universal quantifiers $\forall^{\text{st}}$ is feasible[5] in favour of (recursive) incoherence over existential quantifiers $\exists^{\text{st}}$—providing the link toward stable-unstable semantics. Secondly, the latter two interconnections provide a systematic way to implement coherence checking through stable-unstable semantics and the translations developed in [24]. The resulting (ground) disjunctive logic programs can be solved directly using Clingo. Thirdly, the equi-coherence of ASP(Q)-programs can be addressed indirectly via stable-unstable semantics and Definition 7.

[5] The effect is present in the first-order equivalence $\forall x \exists y \forall z \exists v\, \phi \equiv \neg\exists x \neg\exists y \neg\exists z \neg\exists v\, \phi$.

7 Implementation

Our implementation of the method developed in Sect. 5 is based on an existing modular method [24] for computing stable-unstable models. The earlier method deploys translators from the ASPTOOLS collection [23] and uses Clingo as the back-end solver. The translation of an oracle program P is effectively $\mathrm{Tr}_{\mathrm{UNSAT}}(\mathrm{Tr}_{\mathrm{SAT}}(P))$ where the first translation $\mathrm{Tr}_{\mathrm{SAT}}(P)$ can be any translation from logic programs under stable model semantics to propositional clauses [21]. In practice, it is a composition of several transformations such as removing aggregates in favour of normal rules [6], instrumenting SCCs with rules that enforce the acyclicity of support [17], and producing the completion of the program in CNF [21]. The second translation $\mathrm{Tr}_{\mathrm{UNSAT}}(\cdot)$ is the saturation transformation [10]. The output is a DLP which has a (unique) stable model iff the translated CNF is unsatisfiable given truth values for its own input atoms. Finally, the method of [24] integrates the translations of oracles with the main program using a linker LPCAT [22]. The result is a DLP, ready to be solved with Clingo.

The method presented in Sect. 5 deploys the complement transformation $\mathrm{Tr}_{\mathrm{C}}(\cdot)$ that is historically implemented by a translator SMCOMPL in the context of structural testing [26]. Alternatively, the dedicated translator LPEQ for equivalence checking [27] can be used to produce the translations of the form $P \cup \mathrm{Tr}_{\mathrm{C}}(Q)$. If desired, the complement $\mathrm{Tr}_{\mathrm{C}}(Q) = \mathrm{Tr}_{\mathrm{EQ}}(\emptyset, Q)$ can be computed using an empty program $\emptyset$ with an input signature $\mathrm{At}^{\mathrm{i}}(\emptyset) = \mathrm{At}^{\mathrm{v}}(Q)$.

As regards the translation $\mathrm{Tr}_{\mathrm{T1}}(P[P_1 \cdots P_n], Q)$ in (4), it can be constructed by extending $\mathrm{Tr}_{\mathrm{EQ}}(P, Q)$ with the translations $\mathrm{Tr}_{\mathrm{UNSAT}}(\mathrm{Tr}_{\mathrm{SAT}}(P_i))$ of the oracles P_i as described above. The disjunctive version of LPEQ, namely DLPEQ, is not really usable since hiding the internal structure of oracles compromises the EVA property. The joins $P \cup Q_i$ as parts of the translations $\mathrm{Tr}_{\mathrm{T2}}(P[P_1 \cdots P_n], Q_i)$ in Definition 10 can be computed using the linker LPCAT. A further observation is that the programs involved in Proposition 3 can also be produced using the tools discussed above. In summary, the method presented for the verification of weak equivalence is readily implemented using existing tools, but the use cases arising in the translations above are novel, such as the one elaborated next.

Example 7. Suppose that we want to study the equivalence of quantified programs $\forall^{\mathrm{st}} P_1 : C_1$ and $\forall^{\mathrm{st}} P_2 : C_2$. Their counter-examples (if any) are captured by the NLPs $Q_1 = P_1 \cup \mathrm{Tr}_{\mathrm{C}}(C_1)$ and $Q_2 = P_2 \cup \mathrm{Tr}_{\mathrm{C}}(C_2)$ by Proposition 3. If the sets of stable models of these programs are equally empty or non-empty, then the programs are strictly speaking *equi-coherent*. But a more fine-grained analysis is possible if the sets of counter-examples are cross-checked. This is possible by computing translations $\mathrm{Tr}_{\mathrm{EQ}}(Q_1, Q_2)$ and $\mathrm{Tr}_{\mathrm{EQ}}(Q_2, Q_1)$ to capture differentiating counter-examples and by computing stable models for them. ■

8 Conclusion

In this article, we investigate the basic notions of equivalence proposed for normal/disjunctive logic programs in the case of stable-unstable semantics. The latter equips a main program P with oracles $P_1, \ldots, P_n$ whose role is to accept a stable model M of the main program only when none of the oracles P_i has a stable model given (a part of) M as input. As the main conceptual contribution, we present the generalized notions of weak, strong, and classical equivalence in the presence of oracles. Moreover, on the theoretical side, we show that the main decision problems related to these generalizations are Π_k^P-complete for k-combined programs that allow the recursive incorporation of oracles to depth k. Based on this, we present highly modular translations for checking the equivalence of k-combined programs using the program-level complement $\mathrm{Tr}_{\mathrm{C}}(\cdot)$ as a central primitive. The resulting method localizes the key factors of equivalence: the main programs should have the same stable models in the context of their oracles, and the oracles should accept stable models on equal basis. In view of related work, we show how quantified logic programs can be reduced to stable-unstable semantics in a systematic way. Finally, as a further technical contribution, we describe how the translations for equivalence checking are constructed in practice using existing translators from the ASPTOOLS collection.

The proofs of the main results are included in extended versions of this article. Furthermore, the practical side is illustrated, e.g., using the examples of [24]. As regards future work, there are further notions of equivalence that could be generalized in a similar way by incorporating oracles. While the connection between k-combined *ground* logic programs and QBFs has already been investigated [5], the case of *non-ground* logic programs and their semantic characterization in terms of second-order logic [15] may yield analogous results. Finally, if native answer-set solvers supporting stable-unstable semantics are eventually developed, the translations presented in Sect. 5 remain applicable, but all oracles involved in the equivalence checks can be provided as is for the solving phase.

Disclosure of Interests. The author has no competing interests to declare that are relevant to the content of this article.

References

1. Amendola, G., Cuteri, B., Ricca, F., Truszczynski, M.: Solving problems in the polynomial hierarchy with ASP(Q). In: LPNMR 2022, pp. 373–386 (2022)
2. Amendola, G., Ricca, F., Truszczynski, M.: Beyond NP: quantifying over answer sets. Theory Pract. Log. Program. **19**(5–6), 705–721 (2019)
3. Azzolini, D., Leone, N., Mazzotta, G., Ricca, F.: Solving hard combinatorial optimization problems with PyQASP. In: PADL 2026, pp. 199–217 (2026)
4. Bogaerts, B., Charalambidis, A., Chatziagapis, G., Kostopoulos, B., Pollaci, S., Rondogiannis, P.: The stable model semantics for higher-order logic programming. Theory Pract. Log. Program. **24**(4), 737–754 (2024)

5. Bogaerts, B., Janhunen, T., Tasharrofi, S.: Stable-unstable semantics: beyond NP with normal logic programs. Theory Pract. Log. Program. **16**(5–6), 570–586 (2016)
6. Bomanson, J., Gebser, M., Janhunen, T.: Improving the normalization of weight rules in answer set programs. In: Fermé, E., Leite, J. (eds.) JELIA 2014. LNCS (LNAI), vol. 8761, pp. 166–180. Springer, Cham (2014). https://doi.org/10.1007/978-3-319-11558-0_12
7. Brewka, G., Diller, M., Heissenberger, G., Linsbichler, T., Woltran, S.: Solving advanced argumentation problems with answer set programming. Theory Pract. Log. Program. **20**(3), 391–431 (2020)
8. Brewka, G., Eiter, T., Truszczynski, M.: Answer set programming at a glance. Commun. ACM **54**(12), 92–103 (2011)
9. Cuteri, A., Mazzotta, G., Ricca, F.: 2-ASP(Q) solving based on CEGAR. In: AAAI 2026, pp. 19030–19038 (2026)
10. Eiter, T., Gottlob, G.: On the computational cost of disjunctive logic programming: propositional case. Ann. Math. Artif. Intell. **15**(3–4), 289–323 (1995)
11. Eiter, T., Polleres, A.: Towards automated integration of guess and check programs in answer set programming: a meta-interpreter and applications. Theory Pract. Log. Program. **6**(1–2), 23–60 (2006)
12. Faber, W., Mazzotta, G., Ricca, F.: An efficient solver for ASP(Q). Theory Pract. Log. Program. **23**(4), 948–964 (2023)
13. Faber, W., Morak, M.: Evaluating epistemic logic programs via answer set programming with quantifiers. In: AAAI 2023, pp. 6322–6329 (2023)
14. Fandinno, J., Laferrière, F., Romero, J., Schaub, T., Son, T.C.: Planning with incomplete information in quantified answer set programming. Theory Pract. Log. Program. **21**(5), 663–679 (2021)
15. Ferraris, P., Lee, J., Lifschitz, V.: A new perspective on stable models. In: IJCAI 2007, pp. 372–379 (2007)
16. Fitzsimmons, Z., Hemaspaandra, E., Hoover, A., Narváez, D.E.: Very hard electoral control problems. In: AAAI 2019, pp. 1933–1940 (2019)
17. Gebser, M., Janhunen, T., Rintanen, J.: Answer set programming as SAT modulo acyclicity. In: ECAI 2014, pp. 351–356. IOS Press (2014)
18. Gelfond, M., Lifschitz, V.: The stable model semantics for logic programming. In: ICLP, pp. 1070–1080. MIT Press (1988)
19. Gelfond, M., Lifschitz, V.: Classical negation in logic programs and disjunctive databases. New Gener. Comput. **9**(3/4), 365–386 (1991)
20. Jaakkola, R., Janhunen, T., Kuusisto, A., Rankooh, M.F., Vilander, M.: Explainability via short formulas: the case of propositional logic with implementation. J. Artif. Intell. Res. **83** (2025)
21. Janhunen, T.: Some (in)translatability results for normal logic programs and propositional theories. J. Appl. Non Class. Logics **16**(1–2), 35–86 (2006)
22. Janhunen, T.: Modular construction of ground logic programs using lpcat. In: The 3rd International Workshop on Logic and Search (LaSh 2010), (2010)
23. Janhunen, T.: Cross-translating answer set programs using the ASPTOOLS collection. Künstliche Intell. **32**(2–3), 183–184 (2018)
24. Janhunen, T.: Implementing stable-unstable semantics with ASPTOOLS and Clingo. In: PADL 2022, pp. 135–153 (2022)
25. Janhunen, T., Niemelä, I.: The answer set programming paradigm. AI Mag. **37**(3), 13–24 (2016)
26. Janhunen, T., Niemelä, I., Oetsch, J., Pührer, J., Tompits, H.: On testing answer-set programs. In: ECAI 2010, pp. 951–956 (2010)

27. Janhunen, T., Oikarinen, E.: LPEQ and DLPEQ - translators for automated equivalence testing of logic programs. In: LPNMR 2004, pp. 336–340 (2004)
28. Janhunen, T., Oikarinen, E.: Automated verification of weak equivalence within the SMODELS system. Theory Pract. Log. Program. **7**(6), 697–744 (2007)
29. Janhunen, T., Oikarinen, E., Tompits, H., Woltran, S.: Modularity aspects of disjunctive stable models. J. Artif. Intell. Res. **35**, 813–857 (2009)
30. Kaminski, R., Romero, J., Schaub, T., Wanko, P.: How to build your own ASP-based system?! Theory Pract. Log. Program. **23**(1), 299–361 (2023)
31. Lierler, Y., Truszczynski, M.: On abstract modular inference systems and solvers. Artif. Intell. **236**, 65–89 (2016)
32. Lifschitz, V., Pearce, D., Valverde, A.: Strongly equivalent logic programs. ACM TOCL **2**(4), 526–541 (2001)
33. Marek, V., Truszczyński, M.: Autoepistemic logic. J. ACM **38**(3), 588–619 (1991)
34. Mazzotta, G., Ricca, F., Truszczynski, M.: Quantifying over optimum answer sets. Theory Pract. Log. Program. **24**(4), 716–736 (2024)
35. Niemelä, I.: Answer set programming without unstratified negation. In: Garcia de la Banda, M., Pontelli, E. (eds.) ICLP 2008. LNCS, vol. 5366, pp. 88–92. Springer, Heidelberg (2008). https://doi.org/10.1007/978-3-540-89982-2_15
36. Oikarinen, E., Janhunen, T.: A translation-based approach to the verification of modular equivalence. J. Log. Comput. **19**(4), 591–613 (2009)
37. Simons, P., Niemelä, I., Soininen, T.: Extending and implementing the stable model semantics. Artif. Intell. **138**(1–2), 181–234 (2002)
38. Turner, H.: Strong equivalence for logic programs and default theories (made easy). In: Eiter, T., Faber, W., Truszczyński, M. (eds.) LPNMR 2001. LNCS (LNAI), vol. 2173, pp. 81–92. Springer, Heidelberg (2001). https://doi.org/10.1007/3-540-45402-0_6

Lightweight Language Models for Encoding ASP from Natural Language

Irfan Kareem, Manuel Borroto Santana, Francesco Ricca, and Michele Vitale(✉)

University of Calabria, Rende, Italy
{irfan.kareem,manuel.borroto,francesco.ricca,michele.vitale}@unical.it

Abstract. Translating natural language into formal knowledge representation languages such as Answer Set Programming (ASP) remains a challenging task, particularly with respect to faithful semantic interpretation and robust reasoning. Recent state-of-the-art approaches rely on large, resource-intensive Large Language Models (LLMs), thereby leaving the potential of smaller, more accessible models largely underexplored. In this paper, we investigate the use of compact, open-weight LLMs for this task. We build on prior NL2ASP work, where a transformer generates a controlled natural language (CNL) representation that is then translated into ASP. We replace the original components with fine-tuned "small" LLMs, and redesign the dataset to support a natural and realistic inputs. Our evaluation spans twelve lightweight models across three LLM families and compares two execution pipelines: one following the NL2ASP paradigm and one that bypasses the CNL intermediate representation. Results show that fine-tuned small LLMs consistently outperform the original NL2ASP approach, offering an effective and cheaper alternative to methods relying on larger, costlier models.

Keywords: Natural Language Processing · Answer Set Programming · LLMs

1 Introduction

Recent advances in Natural Language Processing (NLP) have transformed human-computer interaction by automating tasks that previously required substantial manual effort, time, and expertise. This phenomenon is particularly evident in software development, where tools such as Github Copilot [10,22] and Claude Code [2] have significantly modified programming workflows. As a result, the role of developers is increasingly shifting from manually writing code to reviewing, refining, and automatically generating solutions. Knowledge representation (KR) formalisms are no exception, and the automatic generation of formal specifications has recently attracted increasing attention [1,9,21,29,32,33]. In this paper we focus on the problem of translating natural language descriptions into Answer Set Programming (ASP) [5,16] specifications. This problem

W. Faber et al. (Eds.): LPNMR 2026, LNAI 16952, pp. 282–297, 2027.
https://doi.org/10.1007/978-3-032-38320-4_18

has been explored in a number of recent approaches [1,9,29,33], showing encouraging results under specific assumptions and application settings. Nevertheless, designing general and reliable methods for this task remains challenging.

A first step toward the automatic composition of ASP programs was made by Borroto et al. [29], who proposed NL2ASP, an encoder–decoder transformer-based tool. NL2ASP follows a two-step pipeline: natural language specifications are first translated into Controlled Natural Language (CNL) [7], and the corresponding ASP code is then generated automatically. NL2ASP was able to encode graph problems from mathematically oriented formulations with limited linguistic variation. In subsequent work, the potential of fine-tuning Large Language Models (LLMs) to generate specific patterns of elementary ASP subprograms [9] was explored. However, the resulting tool LLASP remains limited in terms of the expressiveness of the supported ASP fragment. More recently, agentic approaches [28,32] based on LLMs have demonstrated acceptable performance on the NL-to-ASP task by combining multi-step reasoning with tool-augmented pipelines. However, these methods typically rely on very large, computationally expensive models, and use reasoning-optimized LLMs, that increase output tokens and are unlikely to be run on-premise on cheap hardware.

In this paper, we investigate whether lightweight open-weight LLMs can provide an effective and accessible alternative for NL-to-ASP translation. Our work builds on NL2ASP [29], revisiting its architecture with fine-tuned lightweight LLMs. To this end, we redesign the original dataset into a more natural and realistic corpus, replacing rigid mathematical formulations with representative natural language inputs. To this end, we adopted LLM-as-a-judge techniques for automatic dataset validation and iterative refinement, together with data expansion strategies aimed at improving coverage, robustness, and generalization. Moreover, we implemented a simplified one-step translation architecture, based on the same dataset, that bypasses CNL generation and produces ASP code directly from natural language.

Our goal is to demonstrate empirically that lightweight models, namely LLMs with fewer than 10B parameters and deployable on on-premise hardware, can be effectively fine-tuned for automatic ASP code generation, and we provide a dedicated dataset supporting this task. In addition, we investigate whether the two-step translation pipeline of NL2ASP, based on an intermediate Controlled Natural Language representation is beneficial, or whether direct translation from natural language to ASP can achieve comparable performance.

To this end, we conducted an experimental evaluation comparing the original NL2ASP approach with twelve lightweight models from three LLM families, namely LLama, Qwen, and Ministral. The results show that the proposed LLM-based approach substantially improves on the original transformer-based NL2ASP framework, achieving higher syntactic and semantic accuracy on more natural and diverse inputs. The experiments also indicate that, while the intermediate CNL representation can still help in the translation process, direct NL-to-ASP generation achieves comparable performance. Also, we show that fine-tuned lightweight LLMs can constitute a practical alternative to other approaches of automatic ASP coding that rely on large proprietary models.

2 Preliminaries

We recall some basic concepts that will be useful in the paper.

Answer Set Programming. (ASP) [5,17] is a declarative, logic-based paradigm for knowledge representation and reasoning. In ASP, users encode a problem as a set of logical rules describing the properties of its solutions, which correspond to the program's *answer sets* [24]. A rule is of the form:

$$a_1 \mid \dots \mid a_n \ :- \ b_1, \dots, b_k, \ not\ b_{k+1}, \dots, not\ b_m \tag{1}$$

here, a_i $(1 \leq i \leq n)$ are *atoms*, while b_i $(1 \leq i \leq k)$ are positive *literals* and $not\ b_j$ $(k+1 \leq j \leq m)$ are negative *literals*. Informally, this rule can be interpreted as: "at least one of the head atoms a_i must hold whenever all positive literals b_i in the body hold, and all negative literals b_j do not hold". A rule with an empty body is referred to as a *fact*, while a rule with an empty head is called a *constraint*. Hereafter, we assume readers to be familiar with ASP, for more details about ASP, we refer readers to the dedicated literature [5,6,15,17,24].

Controlled Natural Language (CNL). (CNLs) are carefully restricted subsets of natural language, designed with limited grammar and vocabulary to reduce ambiguity [23]. A comprehensive CNL definition for ASP is provided by CNL2ASP [7], which supports most of the language constructs. In CNL2ASP, specifications are expressed as propositions structured into clauses that are combined through connectives to capture concepts, relations, and conditions in a precise and unambiguous form. The main proposition types in CNL2ASP can be grouped into: *definitions, negative and strong constraints, quantified choice rules, and weak constraints* [7]. As an example, we use CNL2ASP to encode the 3 Colorability problem as follows:

```
A node is identified by an id.
A color is identified by an id.
A node goes from 1 to 4.
A color is one of red, green, black.
Node 1 have an edge node X, where X is one of 2, 3.
There is an edge with node equal to 4, and with node equal to 2.
Every node can be assign exactly 1 color.
It is required that when node X is edge node Y then node X is
not assign color C and also node Y is not assign color C.
```

which gives rise to the ASP program:

```
node(1..4).
color(red). color(green). color(black).
edge(1,2). edge(4,2). edge(1,3).
1 { assign(X,C) : color(C) } 1 :- node(X).
:- edge(X,Y), assign(X,C), assign(Y,C).
```

To see the details of the CNL2ASP tools and examples, please refer to the dedicated paper [7] and NL2ASP tool [29].

Large Language Models. LLMs are neural network models, typically based on the Transformer architecture [34], composed of billions of parameters. They have shown strong performance not only in natural language processing, but also in semantic parsing, code generation, multimodal understanding, and decision-making, making them general-purpose models for structured generation tasks.

Formally, an LLM can be viewed as a function f that takes an input token sequence $x = [x_1, \ldots, x_n]$ and probabilistically generates an output sequence $y = [y_1, \ldots, y_m]$, where $x_i, y_i \in V$ and V is the model vocabulary. Most modern LLMs adopt a decoder-only architecture and generate text sequentially by token, conditioned on the input and previously generated tokens.

LLMs are commonly used through *prompting* [37,38], where instructions and examples guide generation. However, complex prompts may increase inference cost and latency. When prompting alone is insufficient, models can be specialized through fine-tuning on task-specific data. In particular, Parameter-Efficient Fine-Tuning (PEFT) [19,35] adapts pre-trained models by updating only a small subset of parameters while keeping the remaining weights frozen. Prominent PEFT methods include LoRA [18] and QLoRA [11], which reduce memory and computation while preserving performance.

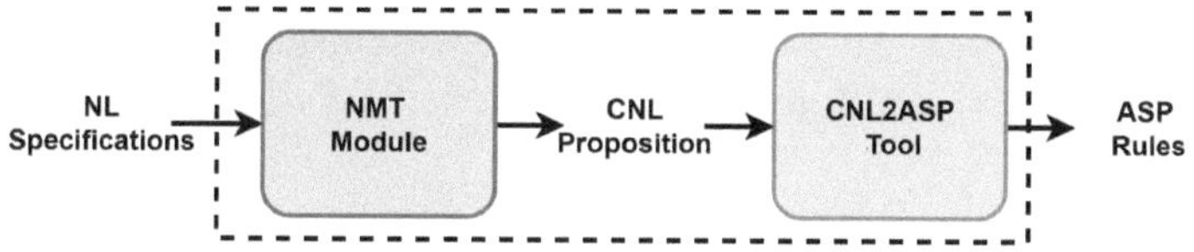

Fig. 1. NL2ASP architecture for automatic composition of ASP programs.

3 Approach and Dataset

We overview the base framework and detail the dataset creation procedure, which represents the core of our methods.

3.1 NL2ASP via LLM

Our work is based on NL2ASP [29], a two-step framework for translating natural language specifications into Answer Set Programming (ASP) programs. NL2ASP first maps natural language statements into an ASP-oriented Controlled Natural Language (CNL) using transformer-based encoder–decoder models, namely T5-small and BART-base. The resulting CNL statements are then deterministically converted into ASP code by the CNL2ASP tool [7], as shown in Fig. 1.

We revisit the NL2ASP approach [29] by replacing their NMT Module, originally implemented by a transformer-based NL-to-CNL translation with lightweight LLMs performing the same task.[1]

[1] Our approach is based on the same problem formulation and assumptions of [29].

3.2 Dataset Creation

A major practical limitation of the original NL2ASP approach [29] lies in its NL2CNL dataset. The input specifications are often unnaturally phrased, strongly influenced by mathematical jargon, and explicitly mention variables that would not normally appear in user-written natural language descriptions. As a result, the dataset only partially reflects the linguistic variability and ambiguity expected in realistic NL-to-ASP scenarios. To overcome these limitations, we replace both the original dataset and its template-based construction methodology. Instead of relying on predefined templates, which are time-consuming to design, introduce linguistic redundancy, and constrain the resulting language, we build a new dataset from scratch. We start from a manually curated set of paired natural language and CNL specifications, selected to provide semantically faithful examples while better reflecting natural language usage. We then expand this initial seed dataset through a controlled augmentation pipeline based on LLMs. In particular, LLMs are used to generate linguistically diverse variants while preserving the intended meaning of the original specifications. To improve the reliability of the resulting corpus, LLMs are also employed as judges to identify potential semantic mismatches between natural language inputs and their corresponding CNL representations. Detected inconsistencies are then manually inspected and corrected. The overall process is summarized in Fig. 2, with additional details on the main steps provided below.

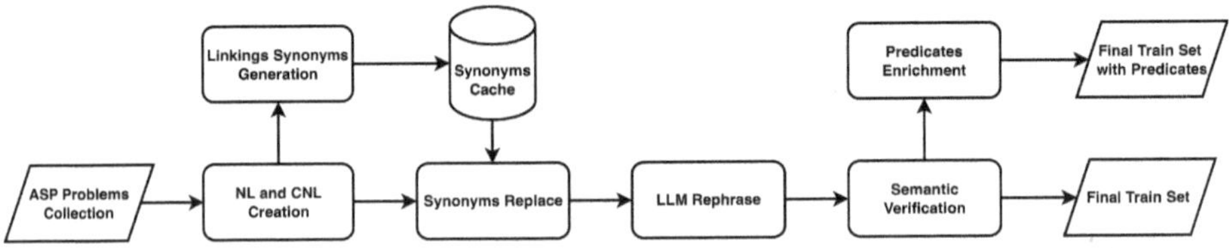

Fig. 2. Dataset Construction Pipeline.

NL and CNL Creation. We collected ASP encodings from competitions, books, NL2ASP repository, and well-known problems in the literature, obtaining an initial set of 534 representative rules covering different ASP constructs. For each rule, we produced a CNL sentence with the support of ASP2CNL [7] and manually provided a few alternative NL descriptions. This process yielded 1,310 tuples of the form $\langle NL, CNL, ASP, Category\rangle$, which we call the *Starting Set.*

We categorized each statement by rule type in CNL [7], namely: [*Definition Const/Compound, Negative Strong Constraint, Positive Strong Constraint, Quantified Choice Rule, Definition When, Definition Whenever, Weak Constraint*]. To reduce redundancy and limit overfitting to repeated ASP outputs, we retained only one manually selected NL description to be used during augmentation (only 534 over 1,310 statements remained). The selection favors linguistic diversity and avoids overly similar formulations. The remaining NL descriptions are set aside and reintroduced as explained later in the final stage of the pipeline. The augmentation phase is done in multiple steps: Linking and replacement of synonyms, rephrasing and semantic verification.

Linking and Synonyms Generation. Each example in the *Starting Set* is processed by an LLM to map the NL and CNL sentences to key–value pairs representing their semantic constructs. These mappings, called *linkings*, are manually verified for all examples. The resulting $\langle CNL, NL\rangle$ pairs form the *Linkings* set. For each unique linking pair, OpenAI GPT-5-mini was used to generate three synonym pairs $\langle CNL\_synonym, NL\_synonym\rangle$, stored in a *Synonyms Cache.* This cache is later used to replace terms with semantically equivalent alternatives while preserving the sentence structure.

Synonyms Replacement. Using the *Synonyms Cache*, we augment each unique tuple $\langle NL, CNL, ASP, Linkings\rangle$ by sampling three distinct synonym combinations and replacing the corresponding terms in the NL and CNL sentences while preserving correct grammatical inflection. The resulting CNLs are then recompiled into ASP with CNL2ASP [7] to maintain consistency with any modified predicate names. We also apply variable replacement: each ASP variable is systematically renamed across all its occurrences in the ASP rule and, when present, in the CNL and NL sentences. These steps reduce overfitting to the original lexical choices and encourage the model to focus on predicate semantics and variable relations. After this augmentation stage, the selected subset contains 2,136 elements.

LLM Rephrase. Each instance is then rephrased to further increase linguistic diversity. We prompt OpenAI GPT-5.2 with tuples $\langle NL, ASP, Linkings\rangle$, instructing the model to preserve both rule semantics and the linked semantic terms. Each input yields three rephrasings, except for *Definition Whenever* instances, which are rephrased once to balance the dataset, as this is the most frequent category in the *Starting Set.* The rephrased examples are merged with the previous augmentation outputs, yielding 6,408 instances. Finally, the NL sentences held out prior to the augmentation phase are reintroduced, resulting in a final training set of 7,151 instances.

Semantic Verification. The quality and semantic coherence of the resulting tuples are assessed through manual inspection and LLM-as-a-Judge evaluation [25]. Instances are reviewed by three independent annotators, while the LLM judge evaluated each tuple against its ASP rule. Low-scoring examples (only a minority) were manually corrected. Table 1 summarizes the dataset construction data.

Predicates Enrichment. The resulting dataset was also used to create a sibling version in which predicate-structure information was manually added to half of the examples. Informally, predicate structure means predicate name and arity, and which term is an identifier (like a key in databases). This variant allows us to assess whether providing such additional information in the prompt can be beneficial.

Test Set. For evaluation purposes, we manually constructed a test set consisting of 200 instances (see Table 1). To this end, we selected a subset of the rules used to build the training set and rewrote their natural language descriptions using substantially different linguistic formulations. This was intended to ensure that the fine-tuned models were evaluated on syntactic patterns that differs from those encountered during training. To increase semantic variability, we also included rules from other graph-related problems not considered in the training set. Overall, this construction strategy ensured both syntactic and semantic diversity, making the test set more suitable for evaluation than one obtained by randomly selecting statements from the training set. Finally, we created a sibling predicate-information-enriched version of the test set to evaluate the effect of providing predicate definitions at inference time.

Table 1. Dataset statistics for each step of the Dataset construction pipeline.

Categories	Starting Set	Unique Rules	Augmented	Rephrased	Final Dataset	Test Set
Definition Const/Compound	303	46	184	736	993	48
Definition When	60	25	100	400	435	20
Definition Whenever	609	271	1084	2168	2506	50
Positive Strong Constraint	97	54	216	864	906	23
Negative Strong Constraint	125	71	284	1136	1190	32
Weak Constraint	45	34	136	544	555	12
Quantified Choice Rules	71	33	132	528	566	15
Total	1310	534	2136	6376	7151	200

4 Experiments

We conducted an experimental analysis to empirically assess the practical viability of our approach and evaluate it against related methods. Specifically, the study investigated: (*i*) whether lightweight models can be effectively fine-tuned to generate CNL from natural language, and which models are the best-performing within three families; (*ii*) whether LLM-based NL2ASP outperforms the previous T5-based implementation; (*iii*) whether injecting predicate-structure information (i.e., whether more informative prompting) improves performance; (*iv*) the impact of using CNL as an intermediate representation; (*v*) the contribution of fine-tuning, assessed by comparing fine-tuned models with non-fine-tuned baselines; and (*vi*) whether agentic approaches are competitive when based on lightweight LLMs.The dataset and code are available at https://github.com/IrfanKareem/nl2asp/tree/LPNMR26.

4.1 Experiment Setup

Software and Hardware Details. For the experiments, we considered several lightweight LLMs from three model families: Llama, Ministral, and Qwen. In particular, we evaluated Qwen3 8B, Qwen3.5 9B, Llama3.1 8B, and Ministral 8B. For comparison with the NL2ASP pipeline in [29], we also include T5 models in three configurations, varying by parameter size: *T5-small* (60M), *T5-large* (770M), and *T5-3B* (3B).

The experiments were run on an AMD Instinct MI210 GPU (GFX90a architecture) equipped with 64 GB of VRAM, using Python 3.12.12 and the Hugging Face Transformers library (v4.57.3), in conjunction with Parameter-Efficient Fine-Tuning (PEFT) (v0.18.0) and Transformer Reinforcement Learning (TRL) (v0.25.1). The training pipeline was implemented with PyTorch (v2.10.0.dev2025 1123 + rocm7.0) configured for ROCm 7.0. For the Qwen3.5 9B model, we require Transformers library version 5.3.0 or later, along with the corresponding PyTorch 2.11.0.dev20260206+rocm7.0 release.

Evaluation Measures. We consider two evaluation criteria that were also used in previous analyses [29], namely *syntactic accuracy* and *semantic accuracy*. Syntactic accuracy, defined in Eq. 2, measures the proportion of generated sentences that comply with either the CNL2ASP grammar specification (for CNL generation) or with clingo syntax (for ASP generation).

$$SynA = \frac{\#\text{syntactically correct sentences}}{\#\text{total generated sentences}} \tag{2}$$

Analogously, semantic accuracy is defined as the proportion of sentences corresponding to ASP encodings that are also semantically correct.

$$SemA = \frac{\#\text{semantically correct sentences}}{\#\text{total generated sentences}} \tag{3}$$

Note that, $SynA \geq SemA$ since semantically correct statements are also syntactically correct. Syntactic correctness was checked automatically using CNL2ASP and Clingo, whereas semantic correctness was assessed manually by three human evaluators that analyzed separately all the produced encodings.

4.2 Results

Fine-Tuning and Model Selection. The LLMs Qwen3 8B, Ministral 8B, Qwen3.5 9B, and Llama3.1 8B were fine-tuned with LoRA ranks $r \in \{8, 16, 32\}$. As shown in Table 2, all models achieved high syntactic accuracy. The best result was obtained by Ministral 8B with $r = 32$ (99%), followed by Qwen3.5 9B with $r = 16$ (98%) and $r = 32$ (96.5%), while Llama3.1 8B reached 95.5%. Syntactic performance was generally stable across rule categories, with constraints being the most challenging cases.

Semantic accuracy, reported in Table 3, is more discriminative. The best overall result was achieved by Qwen3.5 9B with $r = 16$ (82%), followed by Qwen3 8B with $r = 16$ (75%). Ministral 8B and Llama3.1 8B obtained their best semantic

Table 2. Syntactic accuracy (%) per rule category and model configuration across the test set. Models are grouped by family; LoRA rank $r \in \{8, 16, 32\}$ for each decoder-only model. For T5 models SM = small, LG = large. Best overall score per model family is shown in **bold**, while "*" highlights the best model.

Rule Category	N	Qwen3 8B			Ministral 8B			Qwen3.5 9B			Llama3.1 8B			T5		
		$r=8$	$r=16$	$r=32$	$r=8$	$r=16$	$r=32$	$r=8$	$r=16$	$r=32$	$r=8$	$r=16$	$r=32$	SM	LG	3B
Def. Const./Compound	48	93.75	97.92	100.00	93.75	97.92	100.00	100.00	100.00	100.00	100.00	97.92	95.83	97.92	97.92	97.92
Def. When	20	95.00	95.00	95.00	100.00	90.00	90.00	90.00	100.00	100.00	100.00	95.00	90.00	95.00	100.00	100.00
Def. Whenever	50	84.00	88.00	96.00	92.00	92.00	100.00	92.00	96.00	90.00	94.00	96.00	96.00	100.00	92.00	96.00
Neg. Strong Constraint	32	93.75	96.88	90.63	93.75	96.88	100.00	93.75	100.00	96.88	90.63	90.63	100.00	81.25	100.00	90.63
Pos. Strong Constraint	23	95.65	95.65	95.65	95.65	95.65	100.00	91.30	95.65	95.65	91.30	91.30	91.30	91.30	95.65	91.30
Quantified Choice Rules	15	93.33	100.00	100.00	93.33	100.00	100.00	93.33	100.00	100.00	100.00	100.00	100.00	93.33	100.00	100.00
Weak Constraint	12	100.00	83.33	100.00	91.67	100.00	100.00	83.33	91.67	91.67	91.67	100.00	91.67	91.67	100.00	100.00
Average	200	92.00	94.00	**96.50**	94.00	95.50	**99.00***	93.50	**98.00**	96.00	**95.50**	**95.50**	**95.50**	94.00	**97.00**	96.00

scores with $r = 8$, reaching 71% and 69.5%, respectively. The most difficult categories were quantified choice rules and positive/negative constraints, although Qwen3.5 9B with $r = 16$ performed comparatively well on constraints.

Overall, Ministral 8B with $r = 32$ is the best model for syntactic accuracy, while Qwen3.5 9B with $r = 16$ is the best model for semantic accuracy and the strongest configuration overall. Interestingly, the best model on syntax accuracy is not the one producing the majority of meaningful statements.

Comparison with T5-Based Models. We compared LLM-based implementations of NL2ASP with the original T5-based models used in NL2ASP. In particular, we considered T5-small, the best-performing model reported in the NL2ASP paper [29], as well as larger encoder-decoder variants, namely T5-large and T5-3B. We trained these encoder-decoder models on the new NL-to-CNL translation corpus and evaluated their performance. The results reported in Tables 2 and 3 show that T5-large is the strongest instantiation of this approach, achieving good 97% syntactic accuracy but poor 60% semantic accuracy. Thus, it performs worse than the best LLM-based models, achieving from 69.5% to 82% in semantic accuracy.

Table 3. Semantic accuracy (%) per rule category and model. Models are grouped by family, including LoRA ranks for decoder-only models and size variants for T5 models.

Rule Category	N	Qwen3 8B			Ministral 8B			Qwen3.5 9B			Llama3.1 8B			T5		
		$r=8$	$r=16$	$r=32$	$r=8$	$r=16$	$r=32$	$r=8$	$r=16$	$r=32$	$r=8$	$r=16$	$r=32$	SM	LG	3B
Def. Const./Compound	48	87.50	91.67	87.50	87.50	85.42	72.92	95.83	91.67	89.58	91.67	89.58	85.42	83.33	87.50	85.42
Def. When	20	95.00	85.00	95.00	100.00	85.00	60.00	95.00	95.00	80.00	80.00	75.00	65.00	0.00	70.00	80.00
Def. Whenever	50	54.00	64.00	62.00	58.00	46.00	46.00	64.00	76.00	52.00	70.00	62.00	36.00	6.00	40.00	44.00
Neg. Strong Constraint	32	56.25	65.63	62.50	62.50	65.63	43.75	56.25	87.50	65.63	50.00	46.88	37.50	28.13	50.00	50.00
Pos. Strong Constraint	23	65.22	69.57	60.87	60.87	60.87	60.87	65.22	82.61	69.57	56.52	69.57	47.83	34.78	60.87	56.52
Quantified Choice Rules	15	53.33	66.67	60.00	46.67	66.67	46.67	40.00	46.67	46.67	33.33	60.00	53.33	20.00	40.00	33.33
Weak Constraint	12	66.67	83.33	50.00	83.33	50.00	41.67	83.33	75.00	58.33	83.33	66.67	41.67	16.67	66.67	50.00
Average	**200**	68.50	**75.00**	70.50	**71.00**	66.00	55.00	73.00	**82.00***	68.00	**69.50**	68.50	54.00	32.50	**60.00**	59.50

Effect of More Informative Prompting. We then focus on the best model from each family and assess whether enriching the input with CNL-derived predicate definitions brings further gains. We build predicate-enriched versions of the training and test sets, as described in Sect. 3.2, and evaluate four configurations depending on whether predicate definitions are used during fine-tuning (by using the enriched training set) and/or inference (by providing predicates to prompts). As shown in Tables 4 and 5, predicate enrichment provides limited benefits. Qwen3.5 9B does not improve and, in some configurations, performs substantially worse. T5-Large reaches comparable results only when predicates are used both during fine-tuning and testing. Llama3.1 8B improves by 4% when fine-tuned with predicates but tested without them, while Ministral 8B gains only 0.5% when predicates are used in both phases. Overall, predicate definitions do not provide a reliable advantage. The plain-input configuration remains the most robust choice.

Table 4. Syntactic accuracy (%) for models under fine-tuning inputs (with and without predicate identifiers) and test conditions (plain NL vs. NL augmented with predicates).

Fine-tuning/testset	Qwen3.5 9B		Llama3.1 8B		Ministral 8B		T5-large	
	w/o pred.	w/ pred.	w/o pred.	w/ pred.	w/o pred.	w/ pred.	w/o pred.	w/ pred.
w/o identifiers	**98.0***	96.5	**95.5**	95.0	**94.0**	91.5	**97.0**	93.5
w/ identifiers	95.5	96.0	88.0	85.0	88.5	88.0	84.0	83.5

Table 5. Semantic accuracy (%) for models under fine-tuning inputs (with and without predicate identifiers) and test conditions (plain NL vs. NL augmented with predicates).

Fine-tuning/testset	Qwen3.5 9B		Llama3.1 8B		Ministral 8B		T5-large	
	w/o pred.	w/ pred.	w/o pred.	w/ pred.	w/o pred.	w/ pred.	w/o pred.	w/ pred.
w/o identifiers	**82.0***	71.0	69.5	70.0	71.0	66.5	**60.0**	43.5
w/ identifiers	68.0	65.5	**73.5**	69.5	67.5	**71.5**	56.0	59.0

Impact of CNL. In this phase, we remove the intermediate CNL layer and fine-tune the selected models directly from NL to ASP. In this way we assess whether direct rule generation can match the CNL-based pipeline.

We consider the best models from the previous phases: Qwen3.5 9B with $r = 16$, Ministral 8B with $r = 8$, Llama3.1 8B with $r = 8$, and T5-Large. Each model is fine-tuned on NL-to-ASP data (ignoring the CNL data, and providing ASP code). As shown in Table 6, direct NL-to-ASP fine-tuning yields strong syntactic accuracy for the LLMs. Llama3.1 8B achieves the best result, reaching 99%, followed closely by Ministral 8B with 98.5%. Qwen3.5 9B also performs well, reaching up to 97%. In contrast, T5-Large remains substantially weaker, at about 70.5%. Regarding semantic accuracy, the results are generally lower compared to those obtained in the setting using CNL as an intermediate representation. Llama3.1 8B and Ministral 8B achieve the best semantic performance, both reaching 78.5%, while Qwen3.5 9B follows closely with 78.0%. In contrast, T5-Large performs clearly worse, obtaining 46.0% semantic accuracy. Overall, direct NL-to-ASP generation is effective for LLMs, but the CNL-based pipeline still provides an advantage, with the best model reaching 82% of semantic accuracy.

Table 6. Syntactic and semantic accuracy (%) for the direct NL-to-ASP approach, without predicate identifiers during fine-tuning.

Model	Syntactic	Semantic
Qwen3.5 9B	95.0	78.0
Llama3.1 8B	96.0	**78.5**
Ministral 8B	**97.5**	**78.5**
T5-large	70.5	46.0
CNL-based best model		
Qwen3.5 9B	**98.0***	**82.0***

Effect of Fine-Tuning. In this phase, we assess the impact of fine-tuning by comparing the selected fine-tuned models with their corresponding base models on the natural language specifications from the test set. As reported in Table 7, base models exhibit substantially lower syntactic and semantic accuracy than all fine-tuned models considered in our evaluation (see Tables 2, 3, and 6). Among the base models, the reasoning-based Qwen3.5 9B variant achieves the best performance, reaching 64% syntactic accuracy and 47% semantic accuracy. This suggests that reasoning capabilities can improve zero-shot NL-to-ASP generation. However, these results remain far below those achieved by the fine-tuned models; in particular, the best fine-tuned model reaches 98% syntactic accuracy and 82% semantic accuracy. These findings confirm that fine-tuning is beneficial for reliable NL-to-ASP translation with lightweight LLMs. T5 is not included in this evaluation because it is not a general-purpose LLM; rather, it was originally pre-trained for natural language generation and translation tasks.

Comparison with Agentic Approaches. For completeness, we also evaluate how recent agentic approaches perform when using lightweight LLMs. Specifically, we considered the approach by Szeider [33], substituting the original larger models by lightweight models without any fine-tuning. For the evaluation we used four graph-related problems, namely: Traveling Salesman Problem (TSP), Maximal Clique, Connected Dominating Set and Maximum Independent Set. Notably, the latter is included in the ASP-Bench [33] problems by Szeider. To ensure

Table 7. Semantic and syntactic accuracy (%) for models without fine-tuning, under the plain NL test-set (w/o predicates).

Model	Syntactic	Semantic
Qwen3.5 9B	59.0	27.5
Llama3.1 8B	54.0	19.5
Ministral 8B	46.0	15.0
Qwen3.5 9B (with thinking)	**64.0**	**47.0**
CNL-based best model		
Qwen3.5 9B	**98.0***	**82.0***

comparability with our setting, we simplified the original problem descriptions by providing the specification together with the required rules in natural language, thus reducing the need for problem decomposition. We considered a timeout threshold of 20 min, since agentic reasoning might run for a long time.

After execution of the agentic approach, we observed particularly poor performance when using Llama3.1 8B and Ministral 8B, which generated only a very limited number of correct rules, with no problem being completely solved. Moreover, these models did not produce any tool calls in the allotted time, preventing them from exploiting the feedback provided by the agentic framework. Regarding the reasoning models, Qwen3.5 9B generated correct programs for Maximal Clique and Independent Set. For TSP, however, the produced solution did not correctly add the rules preventing forks in the path, while for Connected Dominating Set the execution timed out. In the case of Qwen3 8B, a correct solution was obtained only for the Independent Set problem. Additionally, we evaluated the Szeider approach on the easy variants of problems 33 and 34 from ASP-Bench [33], using the original problem statements. None of the models produced solutions that were syntactically or semantically valid.

Finally, we evaluated the agentic approach using (the large, commercial, cloud-based) GPT-5.2 on the same problems considered in this section, obtaining correct solutions in all cases, while all executions terminated successfully and gracefully. These results highlight the strong dependence of such agentic approaches on large-scale models for effective performance.

5 Related Work

The benefits of automating code generation have been widely acknowledged in the literature [10,13,22,26], and most mainstream programming languages are now supported by automatic code generation tools [8]. In this landscape, Large Language Models (LLMs) play a central role, and their performance in code generation tasks has been thoroughly benchmarked [27,36,39]. Beyond general-purpose programming languages, the challenge of bridging natural language and formal knowledge representation languages has also received considerable attention. In particular, reducing the impedance mismatch between natural language specifications and Answer Set Programming (ASP) source code has been recognized as a valuable research direction [12,14,29]. Most recently, agentic approaches have shown promising results in generating ASP code [20,32].

NL2ASP by Santana et al. [29] introduced one of the first approaches for generating ASP programs from natural language specifications. In NL2ASP, Controlled Natural Language (CNL) [7,31] serves as a promising intermediate representation in the coding pipeline. Building on this framework, our work replaces the translation component with fine-tuned lightweight open-source models and introduces a redesigned dataset with more natural linguistic variations, constructed through LLM-as-a-judge and human verification. Experimental results show improved performance over NL2ASP, both in terms of flexibility of natural language, quality of the training data, and output accuracy.

Before the recent NLP-based approaches, intermediate representations were already used for ASP generation. Baral et al. [3] translated simplified English descriptions of logic puzzles into ASP through structured semantic representations based on λ-calculus and probabilistic combinatorial categorial grammars, showing the importance of controlled intermediate languages for ASP generation.

Recent work [9] demonstrated the feasibility of fine-tuning LLMs for ASP code generation, although the approach was limited to restricted ASP fragments and recurring subprogram patterns. Our work, also leverages fine-tuning, but uses it within the NL2ASP architecture, resulting in a more general approach that is not confined to specific ASP fragments.

Latest approaches, such as ASP-Bench [33] and CP-Agent [32] evaluate NL-to-ASP generation using advanced coding agents and iterative solver-feedback refinement on large-scale models, including GPT-5 and Claude. Similarly, ALM-ASP [28] adopts a multi-agent construct–validate architecture for ASP synthesis. While these approaches achieve strong results, they rely on very large pre-trained models, whereas our work specifically targets lightweight fine-tuned models, a setting in which such systems are less effective.

Several other works combine LLMs with ASP for related tasks. Yang et al. [40] explored few-shot semantic parsing from natural language to ASP logical forms using GPT-3, while [30] combined LLMs and inductive logic programming for question answering, using LLMs to extract facts and ILASP to learn rules. Ishay et al. [21] applied prompt-engineered LLMs to generate ASP encodings for logic puzzles. Bauer et al. explored the combination for visual question answering [4]. Although these works do not focus on rule translation as in NL2ASP, they show the effectiveness of neurosymbolic combinations of LLMs and ASP.

6 Conclusion

In this paper, we investigated the use of lightweight open-weight LLMs for translating natural language specifications into Answer Set Programming. Building on the NL2ASP paradigm, we evaluated both CNL-mediated and direct NL-to-ASP pipelines, assessing the role of fine-tuning, predicate-structure information, intermediate CNL translation, and agentic alternatives.

Our results show that fine-tuning is a key requirement for reliable NL-to-ASP translation with compact LLMs. Moreover, direct NL-to-ASP fine-tuning emerges as an almost equally effective setting, suggesting that modern lightweight LLMs can possibly successfully bypass the CNL intermediate representation. At the same time, our analysis shows that CNL still provides strong syntactic guidance and measurable advantages. Agentic approaches currently appear poorly suited to lightweight models, as they require reasoning and coordination capabilities that these models do not yet provide reliably without task-specific adaptation. Overall, our findings demonstrate that compact fine-tuned LLMs constitute a practical and cost-effective alternative to larger, resource-intensive models for NL-to-ASP translation, when resources are limited or on-premise execution is a requirement.

Future work will focus on extending the system to further improve semantic robustness by fine-tuning reasoning-based LLMs, and study enhancements needed for their integration in agentic approaches.

Acknowledgments. This work was supported by the Italian Ministry of Enterprises and Made in Italy under PON RIC project ASVIN "Assistente Virtuale Intelligente di Negozio" (CUP B29J24000200005); by MOZART "Modelli e tecniche di mOdernizzazione di applicaZioni e data silos a supporto di clienti esterni, field force e impiegati di backoffice basati su AI GeneRativa e apprendimento auTomatico" (CUP J49I24001740005); by SIGENERA "Large Language Models (LLM) per il controllo di SIstemi informativi, la GENERazione automatica di testo, e l'accesso a basi di conoscenzA" (CUP J29I24001770005). Francesco Ricca is a member of Gruppo Nazionale Calcolo Scientifico-Istituto Nazionale di Alta Matematica (GNCS-INdAM).

AI Declaration. Large language models were used to check spelling and grammar, and to support improvements in text quality. All experimental design choices, analysis, and conclusions are the author's responsibility.

References

1. Alviano, M., Scudo, F.L., Grillo, L., Reiners, L.A.R.: Answer set programming and large language models interaction with YAML: second report. In: KoDis+CAKR+SYNERGY@KR. CEUR Workshop Proceedings, CEUR-WS.org (2024)
2. Anthropic: Claude code (2025). https://claude.com/product/claude-code. Accessed 17 Feb 2026
3. Baral, C., Dzifcak, J.: Solving Puzzles Described in English by Automated Translation to Answer Set Programming and Learning How to do that Translation. In: KR. AAAI Press (2012)
4. Bauer, J.J., Eiter, T., Ruiz, N.H., Oetsch, J.: Visual graph question answering with ASP and LLMs for language parsing. In: ICLP, pp. 15–28. EPTCS (2024)
5. Brewka, G., Eiter, T., Truszczynski, M.: Answer set programming at a glance. Commun. ACM **54**(12), 92–103 (2011)
6. Calimeri, F., et al.: Asp-core-2 input language format. Theory Pract. Log. Program. **20**(2), 294–309 (2020)

7. Caruso, S., Dodaro, C., Maratea, M., Mochi, M., Riccio, F.: CNL2ASP: converting controlled natural language sentences into ASP. Theory Pract. Log. Program. **24**(2), 196–226 (2024)
8. Chen, M., Tworek, J., et al., H.J.: Evaluating large language models trained on code. CoRR abs/2107.03374 (2021)
9. Coppolillo, E., Calimeri, F., Manco, G., Perri, S., Ricca, F.: LLASP: fine-tuning large language models for answer set programming. In: KR (2024)
10. Dakhel, A.M., Majdinasab, V., Nikanjam, A., Khomh, F., Desmarais, M.C., Jiang, Z.M.J.: Github copilot AI pair programmer: asset or liability? J. Syst. Softw. **203**, 111734 (2023)
11. Dettmers, T., Pagnoni, A., Holtzman, A., Zettlemoyer, L.: Qlora: efficient finetuning of quantized LLMs. In: NeurIPS (2023)
12. Erdem, E., Yeniterzi, R.: Transforming controlled natural language biomedical queries into answer set programs. In: BioNLP@HLT-NAACL, pp. 117–124 (2009)
13. Ernst, N.A., Bavota, G.: AI-driven development is here: should you worry? IEEE Softw. **39**(2), 106–110 (2022)
14. Fang, M., Tompits, H.: An approach for representing answer sets in natural language. In: DECLARE. LNCS, vol. 10997, pp. 115–131. Springer (2017)
15. Gebser, M., Kaminski, R., Kaufmann, B., Schaub, T.: Answer Set Solving in Practice. Morgan & Claypool Publishers, Synthesis Lectures on Artificial Intelligence and Machine Learning (2012)
16. Gelfond, M., Lifschitz, V.: The stable model semantics for logic programming. In: ICLP/SLP, pp. 1070–1080. MIT Press (1988)
17. Gelfond, M., Lifschitz, V.: Classical negation in logic programs and disjunctive databases. New Gener. Comput. **9**(3/4), 365–386 (1991)
18. Hu, E.J., et al.: Lora: low-rank adaptation of large language models. In: ICLR (2022)
19. Hu, Z., et al.: LLM-adapters: an adapter family for parameter-efficient fine-tuning of large language models. In: EMNLP, pp. 5254–5276. ACL (2023)
20. Ishay, A., Lee, J.: LLMs as asp programmers: self-correction enables task-agnostic nonmonotonic reasoning. arXiv:2604.27960 arXiv preprint (2026)
21. Ishay, A., Yang, Z., Lee, J.: Leveraging large language models to generate answer set programs. In: KR, pp. 374–383 (2023)
22. Kalliamvakou, E.: Research: quantifying github copilot's impact on developer productivity and happiness. The GitHub Blog (2022)
23. Kuhn, T.: A survey and classification of controlled natural languages. Comput. Linguistics **40**(1), 121–170 (2014)
24. Lifschitz, V.: Answer Set Programming. Springer (2019)
25. Liu, Y., Iter, D., Xu, Y., Wang, S., Xu, R., Zhu, C.: G-eval: NLG evaluation using GPT-4 with better human alignment. In: EMNLP, pp. 2511–2522. Association for Computational Linguistics (2023)
26. Peng, S., Kalliamvakou, E., Cihon, P., Demirer, M.: The impact of AI on developer productivity: evidence from github copilot. CoRR abs/2302.06590 (2023)
27. Raihan, N., et al.: On the performance of large language models on introductory programming assignments. J. Intell. Inf. Syst. **64**(1), 239–263 (2026)
28. Reiners, L.A.R., Tarzariol, A., Alviano, M., Borroto, M., Schekotihin, K.: ALM-ASP: a functional agentic architecture for answer set programming. In: KR. Lisbon, Portugal (2026). to appear
29. Santana, M.A.B., Kareem, I., Ricca, F.: Towards automatic composition of ASP programs from natural language specifications. In: IJCAI, pp. 6198–6206 (2024)

30. Santana, M.A.B., Gallagher, K., Ielo, A., Kareem, I., Ricca, F., Russo, A.: Question answering with LLMs and learning from answer sets. In: TPLP, pp. 1–25 (2025)
31. Schwitter, R.: Specifying and verbalising answer set programs in controlled natural language. Theory Pract. Log. Program. **18**(3–4), 691–705 (2018)
32. Szeider, S.: Asp-bench: from natural language to logic programs. CoRR abs/2508.07468 (2025)
33. Szeider, S.: Asp-bench: from natural language to logic programs. CoRR abs/2602.01171 (2026)
34. Vaswani, A., et al.: Attention is all you need. CoRR abs/1706.03762 (2017)
35. Wang, L., et al.: Parameter-efficient fine-tuning in large language models: a survey of methodologies. Artif. Intell. Rev. **58**(8), 227 (2025)
36. Wang, Y., Le, H., Gotmare, A., Bui, N.D.Q., Li, J., Hoi, S.C.H.: Codet5+: open code large language models for code understanding and generation. In: EMNLP, pp. 1069–1088. Association for Computational Linguistics (2023)
37. Wei, J., et al.: Finetuned language models are zero-shot learners. In: ICLR (2022)
38. Wei, J., et al.: Chain-of-thought prompting elicits reasoning in large language models. In: NeurIPS (2022)
39. Xu, F.F., Alon, U., Neubig, G., Hellendoorn, V.J.: A systematic evaluation of large language models of code. In: MAPS@PLDI, pp. 1–10. ACM (2022)
40. Yang, Z., Ishay, A., Lee, J.: Coupling large language models with logic programming for robust and general reasoning from text. In: ACL (Findings), pp. 5186–5219. ACL (2023)

Computational Complexity of Disjunctive Answer Set Programming with Quantifiers

Giuseppe Mazzotta[1(✉)], Francesco Ricca[1], and Mirek Truszczynski[2]

[1] University of Calabria, Arcavacata, Italy
{giuseppe.mazzotta,francesco.ricca}@unical.it
[2] University of Kentucky, Lexington, USA
mirek@cs.uky.edu

Abstract. Answer set programming (ASP) is a well-known logic-based formalism enabling modeling hard combinatorial problems in a natural and compact way. Recently, an extension of ASP, answer set programming with quantifiers, or ASP(Q), has been introduced. By alternating existential and universal quantifiers over different ASP programs, ASP(Q) can model problems from the entire PH even without disjunctions in program rule heads. A crucial and so far unresolved question concerning ASP(Q) regards the power of disjunction: how much does expressive power of "disjunctive" ASP(Q) grow over that of the "normal" ASP(Q)? In this paper, we answer this question by providing exact complexity results for ASP(Q) programs with disjunction. Interestingly, we show that the presence of disjunction leads to only a limited increase in complexity (expressive power).

Keywords: Answer Set Programming · ASP with Quantifiers · Complexity

1 Introduction

Answer Set Programming (ASP) [10] is a widely adopted logic-based programming paradigm for modeling and solving hard combinatorial search and optimization problems [1,15,17,21]. It features an intuitive syntax of Prolog-style rules enriched with specialized modeling constructs, and a well-understood *stable-model* semantics [23], often called *answer-set* semantics [24], as in this paper.

Computational complexity analysis shows that ASP based on normal programs with extensions such as choice rules can be used to model all problems in the class NP. Allowing disjunction in the heads of rules in programs offers a *significant* jump in expressive power.[1] Namely, "disjunctive" ASP captures all problems in the class Σ_2^P [14]. While this class covers a wide range of practically relevant problems, there are important decision problems that lie at higher levels of the Polynomial Hierarchy (PH) [26,27].

[1] Assuming, as is commonly believed, that the Polynomial Hierarchy does not collapse.

W. Faber et al. (Eds.): LPNMR 2026, LNAI 16952, pp. 298–314, 2027.
https://doi.org/10.1007/978-3-032-38320-4_19

To address this limitation, several extensions of the ASP language have been proposed [3,9,22]. Among them, Answer Set Programming with Quantifiers, or ASP(Q), introduced quantification over the answer sets of ASP programs [3]. Expressions of the form

$$\exists^{st} P_1 \forall^{st} P_2 \ldots \Box P_n : C$$

and

$$\forall^{st} P_1 \exists^{st} P_2 \ldots \Box P_n : C,$$

are examples of ASP(Q) programs, where P_i are standard (disjunctive) logic programs (possibly with extensions such as choice rules), $\Box$ is either $\exists^{st}$ or $\forall^{st}$ depending on the parity of n) and C is a (normal) stratified program with constraints (we give precise definitions of these classes of programs in the next section). In these examples, quantifiers alternate but this is not required in general. Informally, ASP(Q) programs express statements of the form: "there exists an answer set of a program P_1 such that, for every answer set of P_2, and so on, a constraint component C encoding a global condition is coherent". They also support dual statements starting with universal quantification. The precise meaning is given by the formal definition of *coherence* of an ASP(Q) program [3].

The ASP(Q) formalism is expressive enough to capture all levels of the PH. That is, *existential* ASP(Q) programs $\exists^{st} P_1 \forall^{st} P_2 \ldots \Box P_n : C$, where all programs P_i are *normal*, model any decision problem in Σ_n^P [27], and *universal* ASP(Q) programs $\forall^{st} P_1 \exists^{st} P_2 \ldots \Box P_n : C$, with all programs P_i being *normal*, model all problems in Π_n^P.

This points to potential for interesting applications, especially since recently designed and implemented solvers [2,13,18] facilitate practical uses of ASP(Q). Domains where ASP(Q) has been successfully used include outlier detection [7], probabilistic reasoning [4–6] and others [3,19,20,25]. That said, ASP(Q) is still a fledgling formalism, and several key theoretical questions remain open.

A particularly important one concerns the use of disjunction in programs P_i used to construct ASP(Q) programs. The complexity results we mentioned above apply to ASP(Q) based on normal logic programs. Since ASP(Q) in general allows us to use disjunction in programs, it is natural to ask what effect disjunction has on expressive power of ASP(Q) programs with n alternating quantifiers. We address this question in our paper. While it might seem that using disjunctive programs in ASP(Q) programs with n quantifiers could extend the expressive power from the level n of the PH to the level $2n$ (eliminating disjunction at each level replaces one quantifier with two), it turns out the effect is much less dramatic. The expressive power grows, but only by *one* level.

In this paper we prove this result by establishing the complexity of deciding coherence of general ASP(Q) programs. To this end, we establish some useful technical properties of ASP(Q) programs. In particular, we present a coherence preserving translation of disjunctive ASP(Q) programs into normal ASP(Q) programs, as well as a translation of QBFs into disjunctive ASP(Q) programs so that the truth of the QBF corresponds to coherence of the target program. We use these results to establish complexity of reasoning with (disjunctive) ASP(Q) programs.

2 Preliminaries

2.1 Answer Set Programming

We consider the propositional case only. We assume *atoms* come from some fixed infinite set σ (often referred to as *signature* or *vocabulary*). A *literal* l is either an atom a or its negation $not\ a$ where not represents negation as failure. A *rule* is an expression of the form $h_1|\dots|h_n \leftarrow b_1,\dots,b_m$, where $n, m \geq 0$, $h_1|\dots|h_n$ is a disjunction of atoms referred to as the *head*, and $b_1,\dots,b_m$ is a conjunction of literals referred to as the *body*. A rule is said to be a *fact* if $m = 0$ (i.e., it is of the form $h_1|\dots|h_n$); a *constraint* if $n = 0$ (i.e., it is of the form $\leftarrow b_1,\dots,b_m$; *normal* if $n = 1$ (i.e., it is of the form $h \leftarrow b_1,\dots,b_m$). For a rule r, we write $B(r)$ and $H(r)$ for the body and the head of r, respectively. A *disjunctive program* (or, simply, a program) is a set of rules. A program is *normal* if it contains normal rules only. Given a program P, we denoted by $\mathcal{B}_P$, the set of atoms appearing in P. The *dependency graph* of P, denoted by G_P, is a labeled directed graph whose nodes are atoms in $\mathcal{B}_P$ and there is a *positive* (resp. *negative*) edge from an atom b to an atom h if there exists $r \in P$ such that b (resp. $not\ b$) appears in $B(r)$ and h appears in $H(r)$. A program P is said to be *stratified* if G_P does not contain loops involving negative edges.

The semantics of a program is defined in terms of answer sets [24]. More precisely, given a program P, then an interpretation I (i.e., a subset of $\mathcal{B}_P$) is said to be a *model* of P if for each rule $r \in P$ the $H(r)$ is true w.r.t. I whenever $B(r)$ r is true w.r.t. I. Let M be a model of P, then P^M denotes the *reduct* [23] of P w.r.t. M. More precisely, the reduct P^M is obtained from P by (i) removing all those rules having at least one negative literal $not\ a$ in $B(r)$ that is false w.r.t. I; and (ii) removing all negative body literals from the body of the remaining rules. Then, M is an *answer set* of P if there is no $M' \subset M$ such that M' is model of P^M. We denote by $AS(P)$ the set of answer sets of P. A program P is *coherent* if $AS(P) \neq \emptyset$; otherwise P is *incoherent*. For further details on the ASP semantics, we refer the reader to the dedicated literature [12,24].

2.2 ASP with Quantifiers

ASP(Q) [3] extends the ASP language by introducing the concept of existential and universal quantifiers over answer sets. We denote them by $\exists^{st}$ and $\forall^{st}$, respectively. More precisely, an ASP(Q) program is an expression of the form:

$$\Box_1 P_1 \cdots \Box_n P_n : C \tag{1}$$

where C is a stratified ASP program possibly with constraints, for each $i \in \{1,\dots,n\}$, $\Box_i \in \{\exists^{st}, \forall^{st}\}$, and P_i is an ASP program. An ASP(Q) program Π is *existential* if $\Box_1 = \exists^{st}$; otherwise it is *universal*. Moreover, Π is *normal* if each P_i is a normal program possibly with constraints; otherwise Π is *disjunctive*.

Let $\mathcal{B}$ be a set of atoms and $M \subseteq \mathcal{B}$ an interpretation. We define

$$fix_{\mathcal{B}}(M) = M \cup \{\leftarrow a \mid a \in \mathcal{B} \setminus M\}.$$

Intuitively, $fix_{\mathcal{B}}(M)$ is a program (in this case, a set of facts and constraints) that determines which atoms in $\mathcal{B}$ are true and which ones are false w.r.t. M.

Let Π be an ASP(Q) program of the form (1). We write $\Pi_{\mathcal{B},M}$ for the ASP(Q) program of the form

$$\Box_1 P_1 \cup fix_{\mathcal{B}}(M) \Box_2 P_2 \cdots \Box_n P_n : C.$$

We now define the *coherence* of an ASP(Q) program of the form (1) inductively as follows:

1. Base case, $n = 0$ (no quantifiers): C) is coherent if C has an answer set.
2. Inductive case, $n \geq 1$:
   - $\exists^{st} P_1 \Sigma$ is coherent if for some $M \in AS(P_1)$, $\Sigma_{\mathcal{B}_{P_1},M}$ is coherent;
   - $\forall^{st} P_1 \Sigma$ is coherent if for each $M \in AS(P_1)$, $\Sigma_{\mathcal{B}_{P_1},M}$ is coherent.

In the case when $\Pi = \exists^{st} P_1 \Sigma$, we say that $M \in AS(P_1)$ is a *quantified answer set* of Π if $\Sigma_{P_1,M}$ is coherent. Moreover, we denote by $QAS(\Pi)$ the set of quantified answer sets of Π.

3 From Disjunctive ASP(Q) to Normal ASP(Q)

In this section, we show how to translate disjunctive ASP(Q) programs into ASP(Q) programs built of programs consisting of normal rules and choice rules. The choice rules offer brevity and simplify notation. However, they are not essential here. As is well known, they can be compiled away into normal rules at a cost of introducing fresh atoms (with only linear growth in size).

The general idea behind the translation from disjunctive to normal ASP(Q) programs is that disjunction can be translated away from each subprogram by exploiting the subsequent quantifiers to check whether a candidate model is minimal. To present this transformation, we introduce some notation.

Let P be a program (possibly disjunctive). Let $\mathcal{B}$ be a set of atoms, some of which may belong to $\mathcal{B}_P$. For each atom $a \in \mathcal{B} \cup \mathcal{B}_P$, we introduce a fresh atom a'. For every rule r over $\mathcal{B} \cup \mathcal{B}_P$, say

$$r = \quad h_1 | \ldots | h_k \leftarrow a_1, \ldots, a_m,\ not\, b_1, \ldots, not\, b_n,$$

we define

$$cs(r) = \quad \leftarrow not\, h_1, \ldots, not\, h_k,\ a_1, \ldots, a_m,\ not\, b_1, \ldots, not\, b_n.$$

and

$$cs'(r) = \quad \leftarrow not\, h'_1, \ldots, not\, h'_k,\ a'_1, \ldots, a'_m,\ not\, b_1, \ldots, not\, b_n.$$

Next, we define $\mathcal{M}(P, \mathcal{B})$ to be a program:

$$\begin{array}{rl} \{a\} & a \in \mathcal{B}_P \setminus \mathcal{B} \\ cs(r) & r \in P \end{array}$$

and $\mathcal{R}(P, \mathcal{B})$ to be a program:

$$\begin{array}{rl} cs'(r) & r \in P \\ \{a'\} & a \in \mathcal{B}_P \setminus \mathcal{B} \\ \leftarrow a', not\, a & a \in \mathcal{B}_P \setminus \mathcal{B} \\ bad \leftarrow a, not\, a' & a \in \mathcal{B}_P \setminus \mathcal{B} \\ a' \leftarrow a & a \in \mathcal{B} \end{array}$$

where the atom *bad* is fresh. We note that both programs use *choice* rules of the form $\{x\}$ to simplify notation. Again, this simplifies notation but is not essential. It is well known that a choice choice rule $\{x\}$ can be simulated by two normal rules $x \leftarrow not\, nx$ and $nx \leftarrow not\, x$, where an atom nx is fresh [12].

Intuitively, let P be a program, $\mathcal{B}$ be a set of atoms (possibly with some appearing in $\mathcal{B}_P$, as well), and $I \subseteq \mathcal{B}$ be an interpretation of atoms in $\mathcal{B}$. When evaluating coherence of an ASP(Q) program Π, in which P is one of the sub-programs, we consider answer sets of $P \cup fix_{\mathcal{B}}(I)$, where $\mathcal{B}$ is the set of atoms appearing in the programs preceding P in Π, and I ranges over some collection of subsets of $\mathcal{B}$ (this collection consists of the unions of answer sets of programs considered before). By one of the well-known definitions of answer sets [23], an answer set of $P \cup fix_{\mathcal{B}}(I)$ is an interpretation M over atoms in $\mathcal{B} \cup \mathcal{B}_P$ such that M satisfies all the rules in $P \cup fix_{\mathcal{B}}(I)$ and no $M' \subset M$ exists such that M' is model of $[P \cup fix_{\mathcal{B}}(I)]^M$. Thus, $I \subseteq M$ because otherwise facts introduced by $fix_{\mathcal{B}}(I)$ would not be satisfied, and none of the atoms in $\mathcal{B} \setminus I$ are true w.r.t. M because otherwise constraints introduced by $fix_{\mathcal{B}}(I)$ would not be satisfied. So, M is obtained by extending I with an interpretation of atoms in $\mathcal{B}_P \setminus \mathcal{B}$ in such a way that (*i*) all the rules in P are satisfied and (*ii*) the minimality condition is met (i.e., no smaller model M' of $[P \cup fix_{\mathcal{B}}(I)]^M$ exists). The programs $\mathcal{M}(P, \mathcal{B})$ and $\mathcal{R}(P, \mathcal{B})$ are used to compute, respectively, extensions M of I that satisfy all rules in P and all models M' of $[P \cup fix_{\mathcal{B}}(I)]^M$ that are subsets of M. To better understand, let us consider the following example.

Example 1. Let P be the following program:

$$\begin{array}{l} a|b \leftarrow e \\ c \leftarrow a \\ \leftarrow e, not\ c \end{array}$$

Let us now consider $\mathcal{B} = \{e, f\}$ and $I = \{e\} \subseteq \mathcal{B}$. In this case $P \cup fix_{\mathcal{B}}(I)$ admits only one answer set that is $M = \{e, a, c\}$. In particular, M can be computed by looking at answer sets of $\mathcal{M}(P, \mathcal{B})$ and $\mathcal{R}(P, \mathcal{B})$. In this case $\mathcal{M}(P, \mathcal{B})$ is of the form:

$$
\begin{array}{l}
\{a\} \quad \{b\} \quad \{c\} \\
\leftarrow not\ \ a, not\ \ b, e \\
\leftarrow not\ \ c, a \\
\leftarrow e, not\ \ c
\end{array}
$$

So, answer sets of $\mathcal{M}(P, \mathcal{B}) \cup fix_{\mathcal{B}}(I)$ are $M_1 = \{e, b, c\}$, $M_2 = \{e, a, b, c\}$, and $M_3 = \{e, a, c\}$. As it can be observed, each answer set of $\mathcal{M}(P, \mathcal{B}) \cup fix_{\mathcal{B}}(I)$ is a model of $P \cup fix_{\mathcal{B}}(I)$ as it corresponds to an extension of I with atoms in $\mathcal{B}_P \setminus \mathcal{B} = \{a, b, c\}$ that satisfies all rules in P.

Thus, to compute answer sets of $P \cup fix_{\mathcal{B}}(I)$ we have to check stability condition for each M_i. Specifically, this can achieved by looking at answer sets of $\mathcal{R}(P, \mathcal{B}) \cup fix_{\mathcal{B} \cup \mathcal{B}_P}(M_i)$, for each $i \in \{1, 2, 3\}$.

The program $\mathcal{R}(P, \mathcal{B})$ is of the following form:

$$
\begin{array}{lll}
\leftarrow not\ \ a', not\ \ b', e' & \leftarrow not\ \ c', a' & \leftarrow e', not\ \ c \\
\{a'\} & \{b'\} & \{c'\} \\
e' \leftarrow e & f' \leftarrow f & \\
\leftarrow a', not\ \ a & \leftarrow b', not\ \ b & \leftarrow c', not\ \ c \\
bad \leftarrow a, not\ \ a' & bad \leftarrow b, not\ \ b' & bad \leftarrow c, not\ \ c'
\end{array}
$$

As can be observed, the constraints introduced by $cs'(r)$, for each $r \in P$, simulate the reduct of the program by using a primed signature (e.g., a') for atoms appearing in the head of r and for positive literals in its body, while retaining the original signature for negative literals. As a result, facts and constraints introduced by $fix_{\mathcal{B} \cup \mathcal{B}_P}(M_i)$, for each $i \in \{1, 2, 3\}$, simplify constraints in $\mathcal{R}(P, \mathcal{B})$ in such they coincide with $cs(r)$, for each $r \in P^{M_i}$.

Specifically, let us consider $M_1 = \{e, b, c\}$. Then, P^{M_1} is of the form

$$
\begin{array}{l}
a|b \leftarrow e \\
c \leftarrow a.
\end{array}
$$

Indeed, c is true w.r.t. M_1. Therefore, the constraint $\leftarrow e, not\ c$, containing a false negative literal in the body, is removed in the reduct. At the same time, since c is true w.r.t. M_1, $fix_{\mathcal{B} \cup \mathcal{B}_P}(M_1)$ introduces the fact $c \leftarrow$ which makes the constraint $\leftarrow e', not\ c$ trivially satisfied and so it can be removed, as well. Conversely, rules $a|b \leftarrow e$ and $c \leftarrow a$ do not contain any negative literals and so they appear in their original form in the program reduct. Similarly, the corresponding constraints in $\mathcal{R}(P, \mathcal{B})$ contain only primed atoms and so they cannot be simplified by facts and constraints introduced by $fix_{\mathcal{B} \cup \mathcal{B}_P}(M_1)$.

The choice rules $\{a'\}$, $\{b'\}$, $\{c'\}$ are used to guess a candidate interpretation over the primed atoms. This interpretation is then extended with atoms from $\mathcal{B}$ according to I via the rules $e' \leftarrow e$ and $f' \leftarrow f$. Then, if this interpretation satisfies all constraints $cs'(r)$, with $r \in P$, then it corresponds to a model of the reduct of $P \cup fix_{\mathcal{B}}(I)$ w.r.t. some M_i, with $1 \leq i \leq 3$. Finally, the remaining rules enforce that the guessed interpretation is a subset of M_i and derive the atom *bad* whenever the inclusion is strict, i.e., when the interpretation is a proper subset of M_i.

Let us now consider $M_1 = \{e, b, c\}$. In this case, $\mathcal{R}(P, \mathcal{B}) \cup fix_{\mathcal{B} \cup \mathcal{B}_P}(M_1)$ admits an answer set $M_1' = M_1 \cup \{e', b', bad\}$. This indicates that $\{e, b\}$ is a model of $[P \cup fix_{\mathcal{B}}(I)]^{M_1}$ and that $\{e, b\} \subset M_1$ (since $bad \in M_1'$). Therefore, M_1 is not an answer set of $P \cup fix_{\mathcal{B}}(I)$. Similarly, for $M_2 = \{e, a, b, c\}$, the program $\mathcal{R}(P, \mathcal{B}) \cup fix_{\mathcal{B} \cup \mathcal{B}_P}(M_2)$ admits an answer set $M_2' = M_2 \cup \{e', b', bad\}$, showing that M_2 is not an answer set of $P \cup fix_{\mathcal{B}}(I)$.

Conversely, for $M_3 = \{e, a, c\}$, the program $\mathcal{R}(P, \mathcal{B}) \cup fix_{\mathcal{B} \cup \mathcal{B}_P}(M_3)$ admits a unique answer set $M_3' = M_3 \cup \{e', a', c'\}$. This means that M_3 is the only model of $[P \cup fix_{\mathcal{B}}(I)]^{M_3}$ and, therefore, M_3 is the only answer set of $P \cup fix_{\mathcal{B}}(I)$. $\triangleleft$

Starting from this intuitive explanation, we can formalize two important properties of $\mathcal{M}(\cdot, \cdot)$ and $\mathcal{R}(\cdot, \cdot)$ transformations.

Lemma 1. *For every set of atoms $I \subseteq \mathcal{B}$, M is a model of $P \cup fix_{\mathcal{B}}(I)$ if and only if M is an answer set of $\mathcal{M}(P, \mathcal{B}) \cup fix_{\mathcal{B}}(I)$.*

Lemma 2. *For every set of atoms $I \subseteq \mathcal{B}$ and every model M of $P \cup fix_{\mathcal{B}}(I)$, S is an answer set of $\mathcal{R}(P, \mathcal{B}) \cup fix_{\mathcal{B} \cup \mathcal{B}_P}(M)$ if and only if at least one of the following holds:*

1. *$S = \{bad\} \cup M \cup \{a' \colon a \in I \cup R\}$, where $I \cup R$ is a model of the reduct $[P \cup fix_{\mathcal{B}}(I)]^M$ and $I \cup R$ is a* proper *subset of M.*
2. *$S = M \cup \{a' \colon a \in M\}$.*

Lemma 2 has an important corollary that follows directly from the definition of an answer set of a disjunctive logic program.

Corollary 1. *For every set of atoms $I \subseteq \mathcal{B}$, M is an answer of $P \cup fix_{\mathcal{B}}(I)$ if and only if M is an answer set of $\mathcal{M}(P, \mathcal{B}) \cup fix_{\mathcal{B}}(I)$ and $\mathcal{R}(P, \mathcal{B}) \cup fix_{\mathcal{B} \cup \mathcal{B}_P}(M)$ has a unique answer set, namely $M \cup \{a' \mid a \in M\}$.*

For a program P and a fresh atom a, we write $P, not\, a$ for a program obtained from P by appending each rule in P with $not\, a$. Further, for an ASP(Q) program Π and a fresh atom a, we write $\Pi, not\, a$ for an ASP(Q) program obtained from Π by replacing each "quantified" program P in Π with $P, not\, a$.

Let us consider an ASP(Q) program of the form

$$\Box_1 P_1 \ldots \Box_k P_k \ \Pi$$

where

$$\Pi = \Box P \ \Sigma : C$$

and $\Sigma : C$ is an ASP(Q) program. We define $\mathcal{B} = \mathcal{B}_{P_1} \cup \ldots \cup \mathcal{B}_{P_k}$. We denote by Π' the ASP(Q) program

$$\Box \mathcal{M}(P, \mathcal{B}) \ \Box' \mathcal{R}(P, \mathcal{B}) \ \Sigma, not\, bad : C^*,$$

where $\Box'$ is the "dual" quantifier to $\Box$, and where $C^* = C \cup \{\leftarrow bad\}$ if $\Box$ is existential, and $C^* = C, not\, bad$ if $\Box$ is universal, and also we assume that all fresh atoms used to construct $\mathcal{R}(P, \mathcal{B})$ are fresh wrt to the entire program $\Box_1 P_1 \ldots \Box_k P_k\ \Pi$. Let us now see an example to show how this transformation works.

Example 2. Let P be the program from Example 1. Then we consider the ASP(Q) $\forall^{st} P_1\ \Pi$, where P_1 is made of two choice rules $\{e\}$ and $\{f\}$ and

$$\Pi = \exists^{st} P\ \forall^{st} Q : C,$$

with Q being the program containing only the choice rule $\{g\}$, and $C = \{\leftarrow g, b\}$.

In this case, $\mathcal{B} = \mathcal{B}_{P_1} = \{e, f\}$ and Π' is of the form

$$\exists^{st} \mathcal{M}(P, \mathcal{B}) \forall^{st} \mathcal{R}(P, \mathcal{B}) \forall^{st} Q, not\ \ bad : C \cup \{\leftarrow bad\}.$$

Let us now consider an answer set $I = \{e\}$ of the program P_1.

Here it is possible to observe that $\Pi_{\mathcal{B},I} = \exists^{st} P \cup fix_{\mathcal{B}}(I) \forall^{st} Q : C$ is coherent since $P \cup fix_{\mathcal{B}}(I)$ admits only one answer set $M = \{e, a, c\}$ and $\forall^{st} Q \cup fix_{\mathcal{B} \cup \mathcal{B}_P}(M) : C$ is coherent.

Let us now check the coherence of $\Pi'_{\mathcal{B},I}$. Specifically, $\Pi'_{\mathcal{B},I}$ is of the form:

$$\exists^{st} \mathcal{M}(P, \mathcal{B}) \cup fix_{\mathcal{B}}(I) \forall^{st} \mathcal{R}(P, \mathcal{B}) \forall^{st} Q, not\ \ bad : C \cup \{\leftarrow bad\}.$$

From Example 1, we know that $\mathcal{M}(P, \mathcal{B}) \cup fix_{\mathcal{B}}(I)$ admits three answer sets $M_1 = \{e, b, c\}$, $M_2 = \{e, a, b, c\}$, and $M_3 = \{e, a, c\}$.

Let us now see if one of these can be used to prove the coherence of $\Pi'_{\mathcal{B},I}$. For M_1 we know, there exists $M_1' = M_1 \cup \{e', b', bad\}$ among answer sets of $\mathcal{R}(P, \mathcal{B}) \cup fix_{\mathcal{B} \cup \mathcal{B}_P}(M_1)$. M_1' is such that $Q, not\ \ bad \cup fix_{\mathcal{B} \cup \mathcal{B}_P \cup \mathcal{B}' \cup \mathcal{B}_{P'}}(M_1')$ admits only one answer set that is M_1' itself but M_1' violates the constraint $\leftarrow bad$ in the constraint program. So M_1 cannot be used to prove coherence of $\Pi'_{\mathcal{B},I}$.

For the same reason, M_2 cannot be used to prove coherence of $\Pi'_{\mathcal{B},I}$ due to the answer set $M_2' = M_2 \cup \{e', b', bad\}$ among answer sets of $\mathcal{R}(P, \mathcal{B}) \cup fix_{\mathcal{B} \cup \mathcal{B}_P}(M_2)$.

Whereas, for M_3 the only answer set of $\mathcal{R}(P, \mathcal{B}) \cup fix_{\mathcal{B} \cup \mathcal{B}_P}(M_3)$ is $M_3 \cup M_3'$. At this point we can observe that M_3 is equal to M (i.e., the only answer set of $P \cup fix_{\mathcal{B}}(I)$); *bad* is false w.r.t. M_3; and atoms over the primed signature do not appear neither in Q nor in C. So, this means that $\forall^{st} Q, not\ \ bad \cup fix_{\mathcal{B} \cup \mathcal{B}_P \cup \mathcal{B}' \cup \mathcal{B}_{P'}}(M_3') : C \cup \{\leftarrow bad\}$ is coherent since $\forall^{st} Q \cup fix_{\mathcal{B} \cup \mathcal{B}_P}(M) : C$ is coherent.

So thanks to this translation those answer sets of $\mathcal{M}(P, \mathcal{B}) \cup fix_{\mathcal{B}}(I)$ that are not answer sets of $P \cup fix_{\mathcal{B}}(I)$ cannot be used to prove that the coherence of $\Pi'_{\mathcal{B},I}$. Similarly, they are not taken into account when verifying the coherence of $\Pi_{\mathcal{B},I}$. Conversely, answer sets of $\mathcal{M}(P, \mathcal{B}) \cup fix_{\mathcal{B}}(I)$ that are answer set of $P \cup fix_{\mathcal{B}}(I)$ can be used as witness for the coherence of $\Pi'_{\mathcal{B},I}$ if and only if they are also witness for the coherence of $\Pi_{\mathcal{B},I}$. $\lhd$

Based on this exemplified explanation the following lemma can be established.

Lemma 3. *An ASP(Q) program of the form $\Box_1 P_1 \ldots \Box_k P_k\ \Pi$ is coherent if and only if the program $\Box_1 P_1 \ldots \Box_k P_k\ \Pi'$.*

Proof. The coherence of both programs might already be determined by the properties of the programs in the prefix $\Box_1 P_1 \ldots \Box_k P_k$. In such case, either both programs are coherent or both are incoherent, and the assertion follows.

Otherwise, the coherence of the two programs depends on the properties of Π and Π', respectively. More specifically, the coherence of the first program is determined by checking the coherence of the program

$$\Box P \cup fix_{\mathcal{B}}(I)\ \Sigma : C,$$

where I ranges over all sets from a certain family $\mathcal{I}$ of subsets of $\mathcal{B}$ ($\mathcal{I}$ consists of the unions of answer sets of programs P_i extended by atoms and constraints implied via the *fix* operation by answer sets of similarly modified programs P_j, with $j < i$). The coherence of the second program is determined similarly by checking the coherence of the programs

$$\Box \mathcal{M}(P, \mathcal{B}) \cup fix_{\mathcal{B}}(I)\ \Box' \mathcal{R}(P, \mathcal{B})\ \Sigma, not\, bad : C^*,$$

where I ranges over all sets from the *same* family $\mathcal{I}$ of subsets of $\mathcal{B}$ (because the prefixes preceding Π and Π' are the same).

Let us assume first that $\Box = \exists^{st}$. By definitionn, $\exists^{st} P \cup fix_{\mathcal{B}}(I)\ \Sigma : C$ is coherent if and only if there exists an answer set M of $P \cup fix_{\mathcal{B}}(I)$ such that $(\Sigma : C)_{\mathcal{B} \cup \mathcal{B}_P, M}$ is coherent. By Lemma 1, M is an answer set of $\mathcal{M}(P, \mathcal{B}) \cup fix_{\mathcal{B}}(I)$. We will prove that M can be used to show the coherence of the program

$$\exists^{st} \mathcal{M}(P, \mathcal{B}) \cup fix_{\mathcal{B}}(I)\ \forall^{st} \mathcal{R}(P, \mathcal{B})\ \Sigma, not\, bad : C \cup \{\leftarrow bad\}.$$

That is, we will show that the program

$$\forall^{st} \mathcal{R}(P, \mathcal{B}) \cup fix_{\mathcal{B} \cup \mathcal{B}_P}(M)\ \Sigma, not\, bad : C \cup \{\leftarrow bad\} \tag{2}$$

is coherent. By Corollary 1, $\mathcal{R}(P, \mathcal{B}) \cup fix_{\mathcal{B} \cup \mathcal{B}_P}(M)$ has exactly one answer set, namely $M \cup \{a' : a \in M\}$. Thus, the program (2) is coherent if and only if the program

$$(\Sigma, not\, bad : C \cup \{\leftarrow bad\})_{\mathcal{B} \cup \mathcal{B}' \cup \mathcal{B}_P \cup \mathcal{B}'_P, M \cup M'} \tag{3}$$

is coherent. Since the "primed" atoms do not belong to Σ and C, and since $bad \notin M \cup M'$ (3) is coherent if and only if the program $(\Sigma : C)_{\mathcal{B} \cup \mathcal{B}_P, M}$ is coherent. But this one is coherent under our assumption.

Conversely, let us assume that the program

$$\exists^{st} \mathcal{M}(P, \mathcal{B}) \cup fix_{\mathcal{B}}(I)\ \forall^{st} \mathcal{R}(P, \mathcal{B})\ \Sigma, not\, bad : C \cup \{\leftarrow bad\}$$

is coherent. It follows that for some answer set M of $\mathcal{M}(P, \mathcal{B}) \cup fix_{\mathcal{B}}(I)$, the program (2) is coherent. This M is a model of $P \cup fix_{\mathcal{B}}(I)$ (cf. Lemma 1). Assume that M is not an answer set of $P \cup fix_{\mathcal{B}}(I)$. Then, at least one answer set of $\mathcal{R}(P, \mathcal{B}) \cup fix_{\mathcal{B} \cup \mathcal{B}_P}(M)$ contains *bad* (cf. Corollary 1). When this answer set is passed on forward, all programs reduce to programs of the form $fix_B(X)$, for some Herbrand base B and some interpretation X, with *bad* being one of the atoms in those programs. Such programs have exactly one answer set (the set of facts in respective sets of the form $fix_B(X)$). Consequently, the coherence of Π is determined at the very last stage, when checking the coherence of $C \cup \{\leftarrow bad\}$. Since the program passed on from earlier stages contains *bad*, incoherence of $\Box P \cup fix_{\mathcal{B}}(I)\ \Sigma : C$ follows, contrary to our assumption.

Thus, M is an answer set of $P \cup fix_{\mathcal{B}}(I)$ and no answer set of $\mathcal{R}(P, \mathcal{B}) \cup fix_{\mathcal{B} \cup \mathcal{B}_P}(M)$ contains *bad*. In fact, $\mathcal{R}(P, \mathcal{B}) \cup fix_{\mathcal{B} \cup \mathcal{B}_P}(M)$ has only one answer set, $M \cup M'$. It follows that the program (3) is coherent. Reasoning as before, we show that the program $(\Sigma : C)_{\mathcal{B} \cup \mathcal{B}_P, M}$ is coherent. Since M is an answer set of $P \cup fix_{\mathcal{B}}(I)$, the program $\Box P \cup fix_{\mathcal{B}}(I)\ \Sigma : C$ is coherent.

The case when $\Box$ is universal can be handled similarly. $\Box$

Let us assume that Π is an ASP(Q) program

$$\Box_1 P_1 \ldots \Box_n P_n : C$$

with alternating quantifiers. Using our results, we can rewrite it, preserving coherence, to the program

$$\Gamma = \Box_1 \mathcal{M}(P_1, \mathcal{B}_0) \Box_2 \mathcal{R}(P_1, \mathcal{B}_0) \Box_2 \mathcal{M}(Q_2, \mathcal{B}_1) \Box_3 \mathcal{R}(Q_2, \mathcal{B}_1) \ldots$$

$$\ldots \Box_n \mathcal{M}(Q_n, \mathcal{B}_{n-1}) \Box_{n+1} \mathcal{R}(Q_n, \mathcal{B}_{n-1}) : C' \qquad (4)$$

where

- $\mathcal{B}_0 = \emptyset$;
- for each $i \in \{1, \ldots, n\}$, $\mathcal{B}_i = \mathcal{B}_{P_i} \cup \bigcup_{0 \le j < i} \mathcal{B}_j$;
- for each $i \in \{2, \ldots, n\}$, $Q_i = (((P_i, not\ bad_1), \ldots), not\ bad_{i-1})$; and
- C' is obtained from C by repeatedly applying the $(\cdot)^*$ operation when removing disjunctions from the programs $P_1, \ldots, P_n$.

Clearly, none of the programs in Γ is disjunctive and the size of Γ is polynomial in the size of Π. Moreover, consecutive pairs of identical quantifiers can be collapsed into a single quantifier of the same type while preserving coherence of Γ (cf. [25]). Since the collapse involves only polynomial growth in size of the program, the following result holds.

Theorem 1. *Every ASP(Q) program Π with n quantifiers can be rewritten in polynomial time to a normal ASP(Q) program Δ with $n+1$ quantifiers so that Π is coherent if and only if Δ is coherent. Moreover, if the innermost program in Π is non-disjunctive, the rewriting produces a program with only n quantifiers.*

4 From QBF to Disjunctive ASP(Q)

Quantified Boolean Formulas (QBF) [8] extend Boolean formulas by allowing quantification over variable assignments. Specifically, a QBF is an expression of the form $Q_1X_1 \ldots Q_nX_n\phi$, where each Q_i stands for $\exists$ or $\forall$, each X_i is a set of propositional variables, and ϕ is boolean formula over variables in $X_1, \ldots, X_n$. The concepts of a *truth* of a QBF Φ naturally corresponds to an intuitive reading of Φ (we refer to dedicated literature for further details [8]). A QBF Φ is *false* if it is not true. In this paper, without loss of generality, we consider QBFs with ϕ being either a formula in Conjunctive Normal Form (CNF) or Disjunctive Normal Form (DNF).

As it has been shown by Amendola et al. [3], the truth of QBF can be modeled as a normal ASP(Q) by using the same number of quantifiers. Interestingly, if we allow the usage of disjunction within ASP(Q) programs this encoding can be simplified by avoiding one quantifier. To illustrate how this encoding works we start from the base case that is QBF formulae made of two quantifiers.

Definition 1. *Let Π be a 2-QBF of the form $\exists X \forall Y \phi$, where ϕ is boolean formula in DNF. Then $ASPQ(\Phi) = \exists^{st} P_1 : C$ where*

$$P_1 = \left\{ \begin{array}{ll} x|nx & \forall x \in X \\ y|ny & \forall y \in Y \\ sat \leftarrow \sigma(l_1), \ldots, \sigma(l_n) & \forall l_1 \wedge \ldots \wedge l_n \in \phi \\ y \leftarrow sat & \forall y \in Y \\ ny \leftarrow sat & \forall y \in Y \\ \leftarrow not\ \ sat & \end{array} \right\}$$

$C = \emptyset$, and $\sigma(l) = nv$ if $l = \neg v$; otherwise $l = v$ and $\sigma(l) = v$.

Definition 1 is based on the encoding proposed by Eiter and Gottlob [16] to decide the truth of 2-QBF formula directly in ASP. More precisely, given a 2-QBF Φ of the form $\exists X\ \forall Y \phi$, where ϕ is boolean formula in DNF, by applying the encoding by Eiter and Gottlob [16] to Φ, we obtain the program P_1 that is coherent if and only if Φ is true. Thus, in this case we do not need to perform additional checks in the constraint program C and so it can be left empty which means C is always coherent. As a result, $ASPQ(\Phi)$ is coherent if and only if P_1 is coherent that is if and only if Φ is true.

Lemma 4. *Let Φ be a 2-QBF of the form $\exists X \forall Y \phi$, where ϕ is boolean formula in DNF. Then Φ is true if and only if $ASPQ(\Phi)$ is coherent.*

In the same spirit, we could also decide the truth of 2-QBF formulae starting with a universal quantifier (i.e., $Q_1 = \forall$).

Definition 2. *Let Π be a 2-QBF of the form $\forall X \exists Y \phi$, where ϕ is boolean formula in CNF then $ASPQ(\Phi) = \forall^{st} P_1 : C$ where*

$$P_1 = \left\{ \begin{array}{ll} x|nx & \forall x \in X \\ y|ny & \forall y \in Y \\ sat \leftarrow \sigma(l_1), \ldots, \sigma(l_n) & \forall l_1 \wedge \ldots \wedge l_n \in \neg\phi \\ y \leftarrow sat & \forall y \in Y \\ ny \leftarrow sat & \forall y \in Y \\ \leftarrow not \;\; sat & \end{array} \right\}$$

$C = \{\leftarrow not \;\; ok\}$, with ok being a fresh atom not appearing anywhere else, and $\sigma(l) = not \;\; v$ if $l = \neg v$; otherwise $l = v$ and $\sigma(l) = v$.

As can be observed, the main difference with Definition 1 lies in the fact that, instead of searching for a witness for Φ to be true, the proposed encoding searches for a witness for Φ to be false. More precisely, let Φ be of the form $\forall X_1 \exists X_2 \, \phi$. Then, Φ is false if and only if it is not true, which means there exists an assignment to the variables in X_1 such that no assignment to the variables in X_2 satisfies ϕ. Thus, Φ is false if and only if the formula $\exists X_1 \forall X_2 \neg\phi$ is true.

The truth of $\exists X_1 \forall X_2 \neg\phi$ can be verified with a disjunctive program, and so, we construct the program P_1 by applying the encoding of Eiter and Gottlob [16] to the formula $\exists X_1 \forall X_2 \neg\phi$. As a consequence, if Φ is true, then P_1 is incoherent. Since P_1 is universally quantified, it follows that $ASPQ(\Phi)$ is coherent, as $AS(P_1) = \emptyset$ and thus the universal quantifier is trivially satisfied. Conversely, since Φ is false, then P_1 is coherent, and so there exists $M_1 \in AS(P_1)$. In this case $C \cup fix_{\mathcal{B}_{P_1}}(M_1)$ is incoherent as C contains only the constraint $\leftarrow not \;\; ok$, and the atom ok does not appear in P_1. Therefore, $ASPQ(\Phi)$ is also incoherent as well.

Lemma 5. *Let Π be a 2-QBF of the form $\forall X \exists Y \phi$, where ϕ is boolean formula in CNF. Then Φ is true if and only if $ASPQ(\Phi)$ is coherent.*

Now that we have defined the transformation for the base cases (existential and universal ones) we can extend it to an arbitrary number of quantifiers.

Definition 3. *Let Φ be a QBF formula of the form $Q_1 X_1 \ldots Q_n X_n \phi$, where $n > 2$, $Q_i \neq Q_{i+1}$, with $1 \leq i < n$, and ϕ is boolean formula in DNF if $Q_n = \forall$; otherwise ϕ is in CNF. Then $ASPQ(\Phi) = \Box_1 P_1 \ldots \Box_{n-2} P_{n-2} \Pi$, where*

- *$\Box_i = \exists^{st}$ if $Q_i = \exists$, otherwise $\Box_i = \forall^{st}$, for each $i \in \{1, \ldots, n-2\}$;*
- *$P_i = \{x_i | nx_i \leftarrow$ such that $x_i \in X_i\}$, for each $i \in \{1, \ldots, n-2\}$*
- *$\Pi = ASPQ(\Phi')$, with $\Phi' = Q_{n-1} X_{n-1} Q_n X_n \phi$;*

Intuitively, Definition 3 generalizes Definitions 1 and 2 to arbitrary QBF of the form $Q_1 X_1 \ldots Q_n X_n \phi$, with $n > 2$. The idea is rather straightforward as the first $n-2$ quantifiers in $ASPQ(\Phi)$ map one-to-one to the first $n-2$ quantifiers of Φ. Specifically, answer sets of each program P_i, with $1 \leq i \leq n-2$, map to possible truth assignments for variables X_i and each $\Box_i$ corresponds to Q_i; whereas the suffix $Q_{n-1} X_1 Q_n X_n \; \phi$ is encoded according to Definitions 1 and 2.

Theorem 2. *Let Φ be a QBF formula of the form $Q_1X_1 \ldots Q_nX_n\phi$, where $n \geq 2$, $Q_i \neq Q_{i+1}$, with $1 \leq i < n$, and ϕ is a boolean formula in DNF if $Q_n = \forall$; otherwise ϕ is in CNF. Then Φ is true if and only if $ASPQ(\Phi)$ is coherent.*

5 Complexity Results

In this section we study the complexity of the coherence problem for ASP(Q) programs possibly containing disjunction. To this end we use our results from Sects. 3 and 4. They allow us to derive membership and hardness results for this class of ASP(Q) programs. We start by establishing membership.

Theorem 3. *Deciding the coherence of an ASP(Q) program Π possibly containing disjunction made of n quantifiers is in Σ^P_{n+1} if Π is existential; otherwise deciding coherence is in Π^P_{n+1}.*

Proof. Let Π be a disjunctive ASP(Q) program with n quantifiers. By Theorem 1, it is possible to construct in polynomial time a normal ASP(Q) program Δ with $n+1$ quantifiers that is coherent if and only if Π is coherent. Deciding the coherence of Δ is Σ^P_{n+1}-complete if Δ is existential; otherwise is Π^P_{n+1}-complete [3]. Thus, the assertion follows. □

Next, we establish the matching hardness result.

Theorem 4. *Deciding the coherence of an ASP(Q) program Π possibly containing disjunction made of n quantifiers is hard for Σ^P_{n+1} if Π is existential; and hard for Π^P_{n+1} otherwise.*

Proof. Let Φ be a QBF formula of the form $Q_1X_1 \ldots Q_nX_nQ_{n+1}X_{n+1}\phi$, where $n \geq 2$, $Q_i \neq Q_{i+1}$, with $1 \leq i < n$, and ϕ is boolean formula in DNF if $Q_{n+1} = \forall$; otherwise ϕ is in CNF.

Specifically, if $Q_1 = \exists$ then verifying the truth of Φ is Σ^P_{n+1}-complete. At the same time, by Theorem 2, Φ is true if and only if $ASPQ(\Phi)$ is coherent. Since, from Definition 3, $ASPQ(\Phi)$ is an existential disjunctive ASP(Q) program with n quantifiers then the thesis follows for the existential case.

Similarly, if $Q_1 = \forall$ then verifying the truth of Φ is Π^P_{n+1}-complete. By Theorem 2, Φ is true if and only if $ASPQ(\Phi)$ is coherent. Since, from Definition 3, $ASPQ(\Phi)$ is a universal disjunctive ASP(Q) program made of n quantifiers then the assertion follows also for the universal case. □

We can now establish the completeness result for the coherence program of ASP(Q) program possibly containing disjunction.

Corollary 2. *Deciding the coherence of an ASP(Q) program Π possibly containing disjunction made of n quantifiers is Σ^P_{n+1}-complete if Π is existential; it is Π^P_{n+1}-complete, otherwise.*

Proof. The proof follows from Theorems 3 and 4. □

Note that, the transformation introduced before (cfr. Γ, Eq. (4)) rewrites any disjunctive ASP(Q) program with n quantifiers into an equivalent program with at most $n+1$ quantifiers. The reduct computation for intermediate quantifiers can be "absorbed" by merging consecutive quantifiers of the same type. Only the last program may require an additional quantifier when it is disjunctive, going one step up in the PH.

Corollary 3. *Deciding the coherence of an ASP(Q) program Π possibly containing disjunction made of n quantifiers where the innermost program is not disjunctive is Σ_n^P-complete if Π is existential; it is Π_n^P-complete, otherwise.*

Proof. (Membership) From Theorem 1, since the innermost program of Π is not disjunctive then Π can be translated into a normal ASP(Q) program Δ with the same number of quantifiers, such that Π is coherent if and only if Δ is coherent. Deciding coherence of a normal ASP(Q) program with n quantifiers is Σ_n^P-complete for existential programs, and Π_n^P-complete, otherwise [3]. Thus, membership follows.
(Hardness) Here the results follows directly from the complexity of deciding the coherence of normal ASP(Q) programs [3]. Indeed, a normal ASP(Q) program is a particular case of an ASP(Q) program with the innermost program being normal, and so the thesis follows.

6 Related Work

The use of disjunction in ASP introduces an additional source of computational complexity, thus enabling modeling of problems up to the second level of the PH [14,16]. To further increase the expressiveness of ASP, several language extensions have been proposed over the years [3,9,22].

ASP(Q) [3], which we study in this paper, supports nested quantification over answer sets of programs. This feature allows us to model problems across the entire PH [3]. However, the exact complexity of *disjunctive* ASP(Q) has not been established before.

Recently, we investigated the effect of introducing weak constraints [11] into ASP(Q) programs [25]. Our results show that weak constraints may cause a jump in complexity for specific classes of ASP(Q) programs, while in other cases they can be translated away without introducing additional computational overhead. However, disjunction was not considered in that study. The results of the present paper might serve as a stepping stone for extending existing complexity results on ASP(Q) with weak constraints to the disjunctive setting.

Besides ASP(Q), the formalisms most closely related to our work are the stable-unstable semantics [9] and quantified answer set programming (QASP) [22].

Stable-unstable semantics [9] introduces combined logic programs as an alternative to disjunctive logic programming. In that framework, problems at the second level of the PH can be modeled using two normal logic programs: the first program is responsible for guessing candidate solutions, while the second program acts as an oracle used to validate them. By recursively nesting combined programs, the formalism can capture arbitrary levels of the PH. Although originally introduced for normal programs, the framework also admits the use of disjunction; however, to the best of our knowledge, no dedicated complexity analysis for the disjunctive case has been carried out so far.

Finally, Quantified Answer Set Programming (QASP) [22] extends ASP in a way analogous to how Quantified Boolean Formulas extend propositional logic. More specifically, QASP introduces quantification over propositional atoms, that is, over interpretations of atoms, while coherence is checked with respect to normal ASP programs. To the best of our knowledge, no extension of QASP explicitly supporting disjunctive programs has been proposed, nor has the computational impact of disjunction in this setting been investigated.

7 Conclusion

In this paper, we studied the computational cost of disjunction in ASP(Q). Our main result shows that disjunction introduces, in the worst case, a jump in complexity of one level in the PH. To establish this result, we introduced a translation from disjunctive ASP(Q) programs into normal ASP(Q) programs, and reductions from QBFs to disjunctive ASP(Q) programs. These constructions allowed us to characterize the complexity of disjunctive ASP(Q) and prove completeness results for the corresponding classes of programs.

Our work opens several directions for future research on the theoretical foundations of ASP(Q). In particular, we plan to study the computational complexity of ASP(Q) programs containing both disjunction and weak constraints as well as studying alternative semantics definition for ASP(Q) to provide more intuitive modeling and support the development of efficient solving techniques.

Acknowledgments. This work has been partially funded by the Italian Ministry of Industrial Development (MISE) under project EI-TWIN n. F/310168/05/X56 CUP B29J24000680005 and also partially by projects SIGENERA (CUP J29I24001770005) and MOZART (J49I24001740005) selected within the framework of the PR FESR–FSE Calabria 2021/2027 and implemented with the support of the Italian State and the Calabria Region.

References

1. Alviano, M., et al.: Answer set programming in healthcare: extended overview. In: IPS and RCRA 2020. CEUR Workshop Proceedings, vol. 2745. CEUR-WS.org (2020)
2. Amendola, G., Cuteri, B., Ricca, F., Truszczynski, M.: Solving problems in the polynomial hierarchy with ASP(Q). In: Proceedings of LPNMR. LNCS, vol. 13416, pp. 373–386. Springer (2022). https://doi.org/10.1007/978-3-031-15707-3_29
3. Amendola, G., Ricca, F., Truszczynski, M.: Beyond NP: quantifying over answer sets. Theory Pract. Log. Program. **19**(5–6), 705–721 (2019). https://doi.org/10.1017/S1471068419000140

4. Azzolini, D., Mazzotta, G., Ricca, F., Riguzzi, F.: Most probable explanation in probabilistic answer set programming. In: Proceedings of the Thirty-Fourth International Joint Conference on Artificial Intelligence, IJCAI 2025, pp. 9049–9057. ijcai.org (2025). https://doi.org/10.24963/IJCAI.2025/1006
5. Azzolini, D., Mazzotta, G., Ricca, F., Riguzzi, F.: A novel framework for reasoning over optimization problems in probabilistic answer set programming. In: KR (2025)
6. Azzolini, D., Riguzzi, F.: Probabilistic answer set programming with discrete and continuous random variables. Theory Pract. Log. Program. **25**(1), 1–32 (2025)
7. Bellusci, P., Mazzotta, G., Ricca, F.: Modelling the outlier detection problem in ASP(Q). In: Cheney, J., Perri, S. (eds.) PADL 2022. LNCS, vol. 13165, pp. 15–23. Springer, Cham (2022). https://doi.org/10.1007/978-3-030-94479-7_2
8. Beyersdorff, O., Janota, M., Lonsing, F., Seidl, M.: Quantified boolean formulas. In: Biere, A., Heule, M., van Maaren, H., Walsh, T. (eds.) Handbook of Satisfiability - Second Edition, pp. 1177–1221. Frontiers in Artificial Intelligence and Applications. IOS Press (2021). https://doi.org/10.3233/FAIA201015
9. Bogaerts, B., Janhunen, T., Tasharrofi, S.: Stable-unstable semantics: beyond NP with normal logic programs. Theory Pract. Log. Program. **16**(5–6), 570–586 (2016). https://doi.org/10.1017/S1471068416000387
10. Brewka, G., Eiter, T., Truszczynski, M.: Answer set programming at a glance. Commun. ACM **54**(12), 92–103 (2011)
11. Buccafurri, F., Leone, N., Rullo, P.: Enhancing disjunctive datalog by constraints. TKDE **12**(5), 845–860 (2000)
12. Calimeri, F., et al.: Asp-core-2 input language format. Theory Pract. Log. Program. **20**(2), 294–309 (2020). https://doi.org/10.1017/S1471068419000450
13. Cuteri, A., Mazzotta, G., Ricca, F.: 2-asp(q) solving based on CEGAR. In: AAAI, pp. 19030–19038. AAAI Press (2026)
14. Dantsin, E., Eiter, T., Gottlob, G., Voronkov, A.: Complexity and expressive power of logic programming. ACM Comput. Surv. **33**(3), 374–425 (2001)
15. Dodaro, C., Leone, N., Nardi, B., Ricca, F.: Allotment problem in travel industry: a solution based on ASP. In: ten Cate, B., Mileo, A. (eds.) RR 2015. LNCS, vol. 9209, pp. 77–92. Springer, Cham (2015). https://doi.org/10.1007/978-3-319-22002-4_7
16. Eiter, T., Gottlob, G.: On the computational cost of disjunctive logic programming: propositional case. Ann. Math. Artif. Intell. **15**(3–4), 289–323 (1995)
17. Erdem, E., Gelfond, M., Leone, N.: Applications of answer set programming. AI Mag. **37**(3), 53–68 (2016)
18. Faber, W., Mazzotta, G., Ricca, F.: An efficient solver for ASP(Q). Theory Pract. Log. Program. **23**(4), 948–964 (2023). https://doi.org/10.1017/S1471068423000121
19. Faber, W., Morak, M.: Evaluating epistemic logic programs via answer set programming with quantifiers. In: HYDRA/RCRA@LPNMR. CEUR Workshop Proceedings, vol. 3281, pp. 78–89. CEUR-WS.org (2022)
20. Faber, W., Morak, M., Chrpa, L.: Determining action reversibility in STRIPS using answer set programming with quantifiers. In: PADL. Lecture Notes in Computer Science, vol. 13165, pp. 42–56. Springer (2022)
21. Falkner, A.A., Friedrich, G., Schekotihin, K., Taupe, R., Teppan, E.C.: Industrial applications of answer set programming. Künstliche Intell. **32**(2–3), 165–176 (2018). https://doi.org/10.1007/S13218-018-0548-6
22. Fandinno, J., Laferrière, F., Romero, J., Schaub, T., Son, T.C.: Planning with incomplete information in quantified answer set programming. TPLP **21**(5), 663–679 (2021). https://doi.org/10.1017/S1471068421000259

23. Gelfond, M., Lifschitz, V.: The stable model semantics for logic programming. In: ICLP/SLP, pp. 1070–1080. MIT Press (1988)
24. Gelfond, M., Lifschitz, V.: Classical negation in logic programs and disjunctive databases. New Gener. Comput. **9**(3/4), 365–386 (1991)
25. Mazzotta, G., Ricca, F., Truszczynski, M.: Quantifying over optimum answer sets. Theory Pract. Log. Program. **24**(4), 716–736 (2024). https://doi.org/10.1017/S1471068424000395
26. Schaefer, M., Umans, C.: Completeness in the polynomial-time hierarchy: a compendium. SIGACT news **33**(3), 32–49 (2002)
27. Stockmeyer, L.J.: The polynomial-time hierarchy. Theor. Comput. Sci. **3**(1), 1–22 (1976). https://doi.org/10.1016/0304-3975(76)90061-X

Step-Wise Explanations for Sudoku Puzzles Using ASP(Q)

Maximilian Moeller[1(✉)], Alexander Ek[1,2], and Bart Bogaerts[1,3]

[1] Department Computer Science, KU Leuven, Leuven, Belgium
{maximilian.moeller,alexander.ek,bart.bogaerts}@kuleuven.be
[2] ARC Training Centre OPTIMA, Melbourne, Australia
[3] Vrije Universiteit Brussel, Brussels, Belgium

Abstract. One avenue to increase trustworthiness and transparency of *constraint satisfaction problem* (CSP) solvers is that of *step-wise explanations.* A step-wise explanation bridges the gap between a CSP and its solution through a series of reasoning steps that are "simple" enough for a human to understand and verify. In prior work, the computational task of finding an explanation has been reduced to finding certain kinds of cost-optimal unsatisfiable subsets, called OCUSs, of a set of Boolean formulae. In this paper, we show how the recently proposed framework of *answer set programming with quantifiers* (ASP(Q)) can be used to compute such OCUSs and hence step-wise explanations. We demonstrate this for Sudoku puzzles and show how our declarative approach facilitates experimentation with various OCUS problem formulations. Finally, we empirically compare the ASP(Q)-based approach with the state of the art, and observe that ASP(Q) solves more puzzles to completion, and does so faster for many explanation steps, while the state-of-the-art approach is faster on high-cost explanation steps.

Keywords: Answer set programming · Constraint satisfaction · Optimal constrained unsatisfiable subsets

1 Introduction

As constraint solvers are becoming increasingly powerful and widely used in areas such as logistics, healthcare, and finance, the need for *explainability* is growing, both for legal reasons and to increase trustworthiness for the users of these solvers. State-of-the-art constraint solvers are highly optimized and employ specialized reasoning techniques from solving technologies such as *(integer) linear programming* ((I)LP) [24], *Boolean satisfiability* (SAT) [3], or *constraint programming* (CP) [23], involving search, backtracking, and constraint learning. While these techniques are sound and highly efficient when properly implemented, they lack explanatory power suitable for humans, regarding *why* a particular decision was made, *why* a particular decision was ruled out, or *how* the solver progressed in the solving process. Further, the problems addressed often involve hundreds to

W. Faber et al. (Eds.): LPNMR 2026, LNAI 16952, pp. 315–331, 2027.
https://doi.org/10.1007/978-3-032-38320-4_20

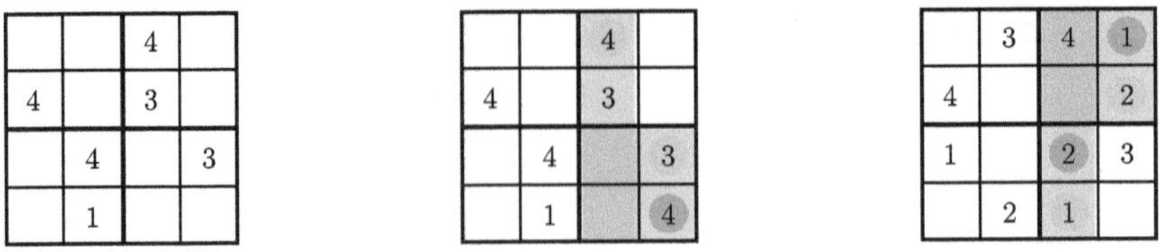

Fig. 1. Left: a typical 4 × 4 Sudoku puzzle with six given digits. Middle: an optimal first explanation step for this puzzle. Using the constraints associated with column three and box four (highlighted in gray), and two given digits (highlighted in blue), one can derive that the bottom right cell must contain the digit four (highlighted in orange). Right: an explanation step from another Sudoku instance in which two facts can be derived simultaneously. (Color figure online)

millions of variables. As a result, it is difficult for humans to verify the solutions provided by these solvers, and to understand the reasoning behind them.

These decision problems can each be formalized as a *constraint satisfaction problem* (CSP), with finite-domain variables and constraints over them. Explanations in the context of CSPs take various forms and shapes (see, e.g. the recent survey of Gupta et al. [17]). We focus here on explanations that are sequences of logically valid reasoning steps, that, starting from the CSP, arrive at the conclusion to be explained and are "easy" to follow. In particular, this kind of explanations aims *not* to interpret what the solver was doing, but rather to illustrate how a human could have found the solution themselves. Figure 1 exemplifies what explanation steps could look like for the logic puzzle Sudoku.

Prior Work. Much attention in SAT and CP research has been devoted to explaining why a problem instance is *unsatisfiable*, e.g. through the use of *minimal unsatisfiable subsets* (MUSs) [18–20]. In computer-assisted scheduling tasks, for example, human planners might be interested in *why* a partial assignment of workers to tasks makes the remaining problem unsatisfiable or necessarily results in a suboptimal schedule [4]. More recently, Bogaerts et al. [6] proposed a framework for explaining satisfiable CSPs, called *step-wise explanations* and applied it to logic grid puzzles. Within this context, an *explanation step* consists of some puzzle constraints and some previously derived facts that together derive a new fact in the puzzle. Several explanation steps can then be chained into an *explanation sequence* that starts from the initially given puzzle clues and constraints and derives the (unique) solution to the puzzle. Pen-and-paper puzzles such as logic grid puzzles or Sudoku lend themselves to this particular explanation technique, because they are constructed to be simple enough to solve without search. Each fact in the solution should be derivable through the use of previously derived facts and puzzle constraints alone, i.e. through (a powerful form of) *constraint propagation* that possibly combines multiple constraints. While these explanations were originally used to explain such logic puzzles, they have later also been applied to optimization problems [5] and can be of value for explaining a MUS in more detail: instead of just showing the user a set of constraints that together are unsatisfiable, an explanation sequence illustrates how these constraints interact with each other to derive the contradiction.

In following research, Gamba et al. [14] gained insight into the computational problem that lies at the heart of finding a "simple" explanation step and called it the *optimal constrained unsatisfiable subset* (OCUS) problem. They showed that the OCUS problem lies at the second level of the polynomial hierarchy and devised an *implicit hitting set* (IHS) based algorithm for it.

Logic programming [25] is a paradigm in which knowledge is expressed declaratively rather than imperatively through the use of *rules*. A set of such rules is commonly called a (logic) program. There are various logic programming frameworks which differ in syntax, semantics or underlying philosophies. One successful approach that has been primarily developed for NP-hard (search) problems is called *answer set programming* (ASP) [21]. ASP is based on the *stable model semantics* that, very roughly speaking, requires each fact in a model to the program to be "justified" by derivation through some rule in the program. There have been proposals to extend ASP's modelling capabilities to the second level of the polynomial hierarchy, most famously through so-called *disjunctive* rules and a technique called *saturation* [11]. However, these are widely regarded as unintuitive in the scientific community. More recently, proposals have been made to extend classical ASP to capture arbitrary levels in the polynomial hierarchy in a more natural way by combining multiple programs. This idea was first introduced as *stable-unstable semantics* [7] and later as *ASP with quantifiers* (ASP(Q)) [1]. The idea is to allow nesting answer set programs with alternating uses of quantification. E.g. in ASP(Q) notation, programs P_1, P_2 and P_3 could be nested into program $C = \exists P_1 \forall P_2{:}P_3$. Intuitively, the answer sets to C are the stable models of P_1 such that for all stable models of P_2 there is at least one stable model to P_3, where programs "deeper" inside the nesting can make use of predicates defined in programs "higher up" than them.

Motivation and Contributions. One strength of the framework proposed by Bogaerts et al. [6] is how agnostic it is of the concrete problem being explained. We are motivated, however, by the presumption that further augmenting the problem formulation with actual domain-specific knowledge might help to (1) guide the solver(s) towards more favorable explanation steps and sequences and (2) improve run times through a reduction of the search space. Since it might not be immediately clear which additions to the problem formulation might lead to the desired effects some prototyping might be required. However, encoding this knowledge in the IHS approach requires considerable insight into the inner workings of the solvers and/or the overall algorithm, and might therefore be also prone to errors. In this article we propose a different paradigm for computing OCUSs for explanation sequences that is based on recent developments in logic programming, and argue that our technique allows us to declaratively express and modify the problem formulation without encoding this knowledge deep inside an imperative procedure.

The **main contributions** of this paper are threefold. First, we show how the task of computing an explanation step (and by iterative application, an explanation sequence) can be mapped to ASP(Q). Second, we highlight the need for more effective optimization techniques for ASP(Q). In particular, we show that the standard solution-improving optimization implemented for ASP(Q) is insufficient for this problem, and easily outperformed by a naïve bound-driven method. Third, using recent developments in ASP(Q) solvers [10], we evaluate our approach against the previously proposed IHS algorithm on the well-known Sudoku puzzle. We observe that ASP(Q) performs better in many cases, while the IHS approach is still faster on some high-cost explanation steps.

Although our ASP(Q) encoding contains problem-specific components, it can be easily modified to accommodate other problems. Further, many high-level CSP modeling frameworks, such as MiniZinc [22], CPMpy [16], or Essence [13] have the capability to translate their models to other formalisms. Currently, ASP is not widely supported as a target formalism, but we hope that our work can contribute to the motivation for its adoption. We also hope that our use-case promotes further research and development of ASP(Q) and associated solvers, and maybe even contribute to benchmark datasets for ASP(Q).

The rest of the paper is structured as follows. First, we discuss relevant preliminaries in Sect. 2. We show how the OCUS problem can be mapped to ASP(Q) in Sect. 3 and highlight advantages of the declarative approach. We experimentally evaluate our approach against the previously proposed IHS algorithm in Sect. 4 and conclude in Sect. 5.

2 Preliminaries

As a running example, we use the well-known puzzle *Sudoku*. In a conventional Sudoku puzzle, we are given a 9×9 grid of cells to be filled with digits from 1 to 9, with some cells already filled with digits. The task is to fill the empty cells such that each digit from 1 to 9 appears exactly once in every row, column, and given 3×3 box. It is customary to number the rows, columns, and boxes from 1 to 9 in left-to-right, top-to-bottom order. Enough digits are given such that there is a unique solution to the puzzle. The (perceived) difficulty of a puzzle varies with the number of given digits and their placement. Sudoku can be generalized to an arbitrary $n \times n$ grid with "digits" from 1 to n and $\sqrt{n} \times \sqrt{n}$ boxes, such that $\sqrt{n}$ is an integer. Here, we will consider the 4×4 and 9×9 variants.

2.1 Constraint Satisfaction Problems

A *constraint satisfaction problem* (CSP) is a triple (X, D, C) where X is a set of *variables*, D is a set of initial *domains* mapping each variable $x \in X$ to its finite set of possible values $x \mapsto D(x)$, and C is a set of *constraints* over the variables X. An *assignment* $\mathcal{A}$ is a (partial) mapping from the variables $x \in X$ to values in their domains, i.e. $\mathcal{A}(x) \in D(x)$. If $\mathcal{A}(x)$ is undefined for any $x \in X$, we say it is a *partial* assignment, otherwise it is a *total* assignment. We denote the support of an assignment $\mathcal{A}$, i.e. the set of variables for which it is defined, by $\text{dom}(\mathcal{A})$. We call assignment $\mathcal{A}'$ *more precise* than assignment $\mathcal{A}$ if $\text{dom}(\mathcal{A}) \subseteq \text{dom}(\mathcal{A}')$ and both interpretations agree on $\text{dom}(\mathcal{A})$. If, additionally, $\text{dom}(\mathcal{A}') \neq \text{dom}(\mathcal{A})$, we call $\mathcal{A}'$ *strictly more precise* than $\mathcal{A}$. If for any $x \in X$, we have $|D(x)| = 1$, we say that every $\mathcal{A}$ contains the variable assignment $x \mapsto d$ for the unique $d \in D(x)$. Each constraint $c \in C$ is a set of assignments over a subset of variables called the *scope* of c, denoted $\text{vars}(c) \subseteq X$. An assignment $\mathcal{A}$ *satisfies* constraint c if $\{x \mapsto \mathcal{A}(x) \mid x \in \text{vars}(c)\} \in c$. An assignment $\mathcal{A}$ *violates* constraint c if there is no total assignment $\mathcal{A} \cup \{x \mapsto d \mid d \in D(x),\ x \notin \text{dom}(\mathcal{A})\}$ that satisfies c. A total assignment that satisfies all constraints C is a *solution*.

For example, in Sudoku, the variables are the cells in the grid, the domains are the possible values for each cell (initially $\{1, \ldots, 9\}$ for empty cells and a singleton set for given digits) and the constraints are the row, column, and box constraints denoting that their numbers are all distinct.

A *fact* is any constraint forcing some assignment to a variable, i.e. a constraint of the form $\{x \mapsto d\}$ for some variable x and value $d \in D(x)$. Further, we view an assignment $\mathcal{A}$ as a set of facts $\{x \mapsto \mathcal{A}(x)\}$ for $x \in \text{dom}(\mathcal{A})$. We write $\textsc{DeriveFacts}(C, \mathcal{A})$ for the set of all facts that can be derived from the constraints C (possibly already including facts) and the assignment $\mathcal{A}$, i.e. the *maximal consequence* of C and $\mathcal{A}$. Note that this includes facts previously in C or $\mathcal{A}$. For the rest of the paper we use *constraint* to mean any constraint that is not a fact.

2.2 Explanations

Using the CSP viewpoint, we describe the task of computing a step-wise explanation [6] for a CSP (X, D, C) and a given solution $\mathcal{A}^*$ to this CSP. An *explanation step* from assignment $\mathcal{A}$ to a strictly more precise assignment $\mathcal{A}'$ is a triple (F, S, N) of non-empty sets, where $F \subseteq \mathcal{A}$ is a set of known facts, $S \subseteq C$ is a constraint subset, and $N = \mathcal{A}' \setminus \mathcal{A}$ is a set of newly derived facts such that the CSP $(X, D, F \cup S \cup \{\overline{n}\})$ is unsatisfiable for each $n \in N$ (where $\overline{n}$ denotes the negation of n). This guarantees that the facts F and constraints S entail each new fact in N. The step-wise explanation algorithm, shown in Algorithm 1, computes a sequence of such steps, explaining all facts in $\mathcal{A}^*$. We thereby obtain a sequence of assignments $\mathcal{A}_0 \subsetneq \mathcal{A}_1 \subsetneq \ldots \subsetneq \mathcal{A}_k$, where $\mathcal{A}_0$ is the initial state, i.e. $\mathcal{A}_0 = \{x \mapsto d \mid x \in X,\ D(x) = \{d\}\}$, and $\mathcal{A}_k = \mathcal{A}^*$. The algorithm also receives a function g assigning to each explanation step a cost

Algorithm 1. Explanation Generation

```
1: function EXPLAIN(X, D, C, A*, g)
2:     i := 0
3:     A_0 := {x ↦ d | x ∈ X, D(x) = {d}}
4:     while A_i ≠ A* do
5:         (F_i, S_i, N') := EXPLAIN-ONE-FACT(A_i, A*, g)
6:         N_i := DERIVEFACTS(S_i, F_i) \ (A_i ∪ F_i)    all new facts derivable in this step
7:         i += 1
8:     return [(F_j, S_j, N_j)]_{j=0}^{i}
```

representing the difficulty of that step. Notice that $(\mathcal{A}_0, C, \mathcal{A}^* \setminus \mathcal{A}_0)$ is a valid explanation step from $\mathcal{A}_0$ to $\mathcal{A}^*$, but perhaps no more insightful than the solution $\mathcal{A}^*$ was in the first place. Hence, on line 5, we make use of the function EXPLAIN-ONE-FACT$(\mathcal{A}, \mathcal{A}', g)$, which is described in more detail in Sect. 3. It returns an explanation step (F, S, N) from $\mathcal{A}$ to some strictly more precise assignment such that $N \subseteq \mathcal{A}'$, $|N| = 1$ and (F, S, N) is g-minimal among all such steps. Using the function DERIVEFACTS(S, F) on line 6, we compute all new facts that can be derived from the constraints and facts used in the explanation step, and add those to N_i. This allows us to derive multiple facts in one step without increasing the cost of the step. See Fig. 1 (right) for an example step deriving multiple facts.

2.3 Optimal Constrained Unsatisfiable Subsets

Gamba et al. [14] presented a generalization of the problem of finding a MUS, called the *optimal constrained unsatisfiable subset* (OCUS) problem, and showed that it captures the problem of finding an optimal explanation step. In general, the OCUS problem, asks for a specific unsatisfiable *set* of constraints. In practice, an approach with *indicator variables* is commonly used as it lends itself well to implementation, using, e.g. an incremental solver. We present the indicator-perspective of the OCUS problem directly, since it also fits our needs better.

Definition 1. *Let $\mathcal{S}$ be a set of literals, called* soft literals, *and R be a set of* reified constraints, *i.e. of the form "$s \rightarrow c$", where $s \in \mathcal{S}$ and c is a constraint. Let $\mathcal{P}$ be a (CNF) formula over the variables in $\mathcal{S}$ and $g\colon 2^{\mathcal{S}} \rightarrow \mathbb{N}$ be a function associating each subset of $\mathcal{S}$ with a cost. The OCUS problem consists of finding a subset $\mathcal{O} \subseteq \mathcal{S}$ such that (1) $R \cup \mathcal{O}$ is unsatisfiable, (2) $\mathcal{O}$ satisfies $\mathcal{P}$, and (3) $\mathcal{O}$ is g-minimal among all subsets of $\mathcal{S}$ satisfying conditions (1) and (2).*

We will use the function EXPLAIN-ONE-FACT$(\mathcal{A}, \mathcal{A}', g)$ to refer to the special case of the OCUS problem as follows. The soft literals $\mathcal{S}$ contain the facts in $\mathcal{A}$, fresh indicator variables, and the negation of the facts in $\mathcal{A} \setminus \mathcal{A}'$. The set R contains the reified constraints (e.g. reified versions of the row, column, and box constraints in Sudoku), and $\mathcal{P}$ encodes the restriction that exactly one fact should be explained in this step. The function g is a weighted sum over the literals in $\mathcal{S}$, representing the cost of using facts and constraints in the explanation.

2.4 Answer Set Programming (with Quantifiers)

We recall some basic notions of *answer set programming* (ASP) and refer the reader to further literature [8,15] for a more detailed introduction. In ASP, *constants* can be integers or strings starting with lowercase letters, and *variables* are written as strings starting with uppercase letters. For *predicate symbols* we use camelCase. An *atom* is of the form $p(t_1, \ldots, t_n)$, where p is an n-ary predicate symbol, and each t_i is a constant or variable. A *literal* is an atom a or its negation not a. A (normal) *answer set program* P is a finite set of (normal) *rules* of the form

$$a \leftarrow b_1, \ldots, b_k, \text{not}\, b_{k+1}, \ldots, \text{not}\, b_m.$$

The *head* a of the rule is a positive literal, and the expression $b_1, \ldots, \text{not}\, b_m$ is called the *body* of the rule. A rule with an empty body is called an *ASP-fact* (not to be confused with the 'fact' defined above for CSPs; to disambiguate, we will always use the term *ASP-fact*). A literal in which no variables appear is called *ground*, and a rule consisting of only ground literals is also called ground. The *Herbrand Base* B_P of program P is the set of all ground atoms that can be formed from predicates and constants appearing in P. A *stable model* or *answer set* of a program P is a subset $A \subseteq B_P$ such that A is the least model of the reduct of P with respect to A (which is the program obtained from P by removing all rules with a false body and all negative literals). We also use the common syntactic sugar for *integrity constraints*, *choice rules*, and *cardinality rules* in our listings; as well as the language extension *weak constraints* allowing optimization [9]. We give a short example in Listing 1.1 to explain the syntax informally. Line 1 is a choice rule, which intuitively says that when the fact that the cell at row `X`, column `Y` has a digit `Z` in it is to be explained, and this cell lies in the `N`th constraint of type `T` (row, column, box), then this constraint can either be used or not. Line 2 is an integrity constraint, stating that it cannot be the case that fewer than two facts are used in an explanation (for 4 × 4 Sudokus, see Sect. 3.3). Finally, line 3 is a weak constraint, which states that each instantiation of `T` and `N` such that the predicate `useConstraint(T,N)` holds, incurs a cost of 10 at the first lexicographic optimization level. Note that the rule operator is written as ":-" and that weak constraints are written using ":~".

```
1  {useConstraint(T,N)} :- explainFact(X,Y,Z), in(X,Y,T,N).
2  :- {useFact(X,Y,Z) : fact(X,Y,Z)} < 2.
3  :~ useConstraint(T,N). [10@1,T,N]
```

Listing 1.1. Example of ASP syntax in CLINGO

ASP with quantifiers (ASP(Q)) [1] offers the extension to quantify over answer sets of ASP programs. An ASP(Q) program Π is of the form

$$\Box_1 P_1 \Box_2 P_2 \ldots \Box_n P_n : C : C_w,$$

where, for $1 \leq i \leq n$, P_i is a normal ASP program, $\Box_i \in \{\exists, \forall\}$, C is a stratified normal ASP program, i.e. the head predicates of C do not appear in the bodies of C in a way that would form a loop involving negation; and C_w is a program containing only weak constraints. The predicates defined in a program P_i, can appear in the rule bodies of programs P_j for $j \geq i$, C and C_w, but not in the heads, i.e. the programs define disjoint sets of predicates. For a stable model A_i to program P_i and a program P_j with $i < j$, we write $P_j \uplus_{P_i} A_i$ to mean the program $P_j \cup \{a. \mid a \in A_i\} \cup \{\leftarrow a. \mid a \in B_{P_i} \setminus A_i\}$.

For this paper, we will only consider programs of the form $\exists P_1 \forall P_2 : C : C_w$. We will call P_1 the *existential program*, P_2 the *universal program*, C the *checking program* (instead of the conventional *constraint program* used in ASP(Q) literature and software to avoid confusion with *constraint programming*) and C_w the *optimization program*. The semantics of such a program is defined as a stable model A_1 to P_1 such that, for each stable model A_2 of $P_2 \uplus_{P_1} A_1$, all rules in $C \uplus_{P_1} A_1 \uplus_{P_2} A_2$ hold; and A_1 is optimal w.r.t. C_w among all those answer sets.

3 Problem Formulation and Encoding

We use a series of ASP(Q) programs to compute step-wise explanations for a given Sudoku puzzle and its unique solution $\mathcal{A}^*$. Each program is of the form $\Pi = \exists P_1 \forall P_2 \colon C \colon C_w$ and encodes a single explanation step. As is customary, we split the description of Π into a *problem formulation* part, encoding the computational problem of finding an explanation step; and an *instance* part, encoding the current state in the explanation process using only ASP-facts.

3.1 Instance Encoding

We encode an intermediate assignment $\mathcal{A}$ into ASP-facts `fact(X, Y, Z)` for each $\{x \mapsto \texttt{Z}\} \in \mathcal{A}$, where x denotes the cell in row `X` and column `Y` and `Z` is the digit that is assigned to that cell. Analogously, we encode the missing digits $\mathcal{A}^* \setminus \mathcal{A}$ using the predicate `remains(X, Y, Z)`. We also state the size of the Sudoku instance here using the predicate `size`. The instance part is merged with the existential program P_1 before solving.

Example 1. Consider the 4 × 4 Sudoku puzzle shown in Fig. 1. The initial configuration of the puzzle is encoded as follows:

```
size(4).
remains(1,1,1). remains(1,2,3). fact(1,3,4).     remains(1,4,2).
fact(2,1,4).     remains(2,2,2). fact(2,3,3).     remains(2,4,1).
remains(3,1,2). fact(3,2,4).     remains(3,3,1). fact(3,4,3).
remains(4,1,3). fact(4,2,1).     remains(4,3,2). remains(4,4,4).
```

3.2 The Problem Formulation

As mentioned above, the problem formulation is split into the existential (P_1), the universal (P_2), the checking (C), and the optimization (C_w) program. Naïvely, one could encode our problem as follows. The existential program picks a single fact-to-explain and the constraints and facts to use in the explanation step, i.e. a subset $\mathcal{O} \subseteq \mathcal{S}$ that satisfies $\mathcal{P}$ (following Definition 1). The universal program goes over all possible assignments to the puzzle where the fact-to-explain is not part of the assignment but the other chosen facts are. Recall that we check for entailment of the fact-to-explain by the used facts and constraints via unsatisfiability when combining the latter with the negation of the fact-to-explain. The checking program verifies that the chosen assignment violates at least one Sudoku constraint. Since this has to hold for all answer sets of the universal program (i.e. all assignments to the puzzle), this means that $R \cup \mathcal{O}$ (as in Definition 1) is unsatisfiable. Lastly, the optimization program calculates the cost of the choices in the existential program, i.e. the function g in Definition 1, forcing subsequent search to find cheaper explanations.

Notice, however, how a lot of work is "wasted" by the way the universal program picks an assignment, because no information on obvious contradictions is available at this level. Internally, an ASP(Q) solver would therefore need to make unnecessarily many calls to an underlying solver. We circumvent this by "pushing up" the assignment checking to the universal program. This improved solving time drastically in preliminary experiments. More specifically, we add rules enforcing that the chosen assignment *satisfies* all selected constraints and change the checking program to just contain a contradiction. In other words, instead of checking that all assignments violate at least one selected constraint, we say that all assignments that *do* satisfy all constraints also satisfy a contradiction. This means that there is no assignment that satisfies all constraints.

We now present the problem formulation shown in Listing 1.2 using CLINGO syntax and following the Generate-Define-Test methodology. The comments in lines 1, 13, 33, and 35, which start with `%@`, demarcate the four subprograms for the ASP(Q) solver. In the existential program P_1, we define the Sudoku digits (line 2), predicates `row` denoting rows and `col` denoting columns (line 3), and constraint types (line 4; i.e. `r`(ow), `c`(olumn) and `b`(ox) constraints) appearing in the puzzle in a way that facilitates further machine processing of ASP(Q) solver output. To keep our problem formulation agnostic of the puzzle size, we define `boxSize` (line 5) and `boxIndex` (line 6) based on the `size` predicate from the instance part. The latter is used in the following (lines 7–9) to associate each box with an identifier. We use the predicate `box(B, X, Y)` to encode that the cell in row `X`, column `Y` is part of box `B` (when numbered in left-to-right top-to-bottom order). Lines 10–12 generate a candidate OCUS. They express that we want to explain exactly one fact (denoted by predicate `explainFact(X,Y,Z)`: the fact that row `X` column `Y` contains the digit `Z`), using some subset of the available facts (`fact(X,Y,Z)`: defined analogously) and constraints (`useConstraint(T,N)`: the `N`th constraint of type `T`). As such, the stable models of P_1 correspond to candidate explanation steps.

In the universal program, we use predicates `sol(X, Y, Z)` and `nsol(X, Y, Z)`, respectively denoting what is part of the assignment and what is not, to encode a total assignment to the puzzle. Lines 14–15 enforce that all the facts used in our explanation are part of the assignment and that the fact-to-explain is *not* part of the assignment. We define useful projection predicates of the assignment in lines 18–21. As described above, we also force the chosen assignment to satisfy all Sudoku constraints, namely that each Sudoku cell has exactly one digit in it (lines 22–23), and that all row (lines 24–25), column (lines 26–27), and box (lines 28–32) constraints are satisfied.

As described above, the checking program C (lines 33–34) just contains a contradiction. In the optimization program C_w, we choose a cost of 10 for each used constraint (line 36) and a cost of 1 for each used fact (line 37). This follows the reasoning by Bogaerts et al. that facts should be easier to use than constraints [6]. Of course, the weights can be adjusted to the user's preference; for instance building on research on how to learn these weights from user feedback [12].

```
1  %@exists
2  num(1..X) :- size(X).                              ▷Define domain predicates
3  row(X) :- num(X). col(X) :- num(X).
4  conType(r). conType(c). conType(b).
5  boxSize(B) :- B = #max{X: num(X), num(X*X)}.
6  boxIndex(1..B) :- boxSize(B).
7  box(B*(N-1) + M, X, Y) :- boxSize(B), row(X), col(Y),
8          boxIndex(N), boxIndex(M),
9          B*(N-1) < X < B*N + 1, B*(M-1) < Y < B*M + 1.
10 {useFact(X,Y,Z) : fact(X,Y,Z)}.                    ▷Generate candidate OCUS
11 {useConstraint(T,N) : conType(T), num(N)}.
12 1 <= { explainFact(X,Y,Z) : remains(X,Y,Z) } <= 1.
13 %@forall
14 sol(X,Y,Z)  :- useFact(X,Y,Z).                     ▷Generate total assignment
15 nsol(X,Y,Z) :- explainFact(X,Y,Z).
16 sol(X,Y,Z)  :- row(X), col(Y), num(Z), not nsol(X,Y,Z).
17 nsol(X,Y,Z) :- row(X), col(Y), num(Z), not sol(X,Y,Z).
18 hasVal(X,Y) :- sol(X,Y,Z).                         ▷Define auxiliary predicates
19 inRow(X,N) :- sol(X,Y,N).
20 inCol(Y,N) :- sol(X,Y,N).
21 inBox(S, N) :- sol(X, Y, N), box(S, X, Y).
22 :- sol(X,Y,Z), sol(X,Y,Z'), Z>Z'.                  ▷Test Sudoku constraints
23 :- row(X), col(Y), not hasVal(X,Y).
24 :- useConstraint(row,X), num(N), not inRow(X,N).
25 :- useConstraint(row,X), sol(X,Y,Z), sol(X,Y',Z), Y > Y'.
26 :- useConstraint(col,Y), num(N), not inCol(Y,N).
27 :- useConstraint(col,Y), sol(X,Y,Z), sol(X',Y,Z), X > X'.
28 :- useConstraint(box,S), num(N), not inBox(S, N).
29 :- useConstraint(box,S), box(S,X,Y), box(S,X',Y'),
30         X'>X, sol(X,Y,N), sol(X',Y',N).
31 :- useConstraint(box,S), box(S,X,Y), box(S,X',Y'),
32         Y'>Y, sol(X,Y,N), sol(X',Y',N).
33 %@constraint
34 contradiction. :- contradiction.
35 %@global
36 :~ useConstraint(T,X).    [10@1, T,X]               ▷OCUS weights
37 :~ useFact(X,Y,Z).        [1@1, X,Y,Z]
```

Listing 1.2. ASP(Q) problem formulation

3.3 Adding Redundant Constraints

We can improve our encoding with redundant constraints. We incorporate the following observations into the existential program by replacing the choices for used facts and constraints (lines 10–11) with Listing 1.3. First, all used facts and the fact-to-explain must appear in a constraint that is used in the explanation. Otherwise, such a fact could be dropped, contradicting optimality. Second, the set of used constraints must all be *connected* (either directly by sharing a joint variable or indirectly through other constraints). To encode these observations, we define a helper predicate `chooseFactIn` representing that some fact in a constraint is used (lines 1–2). Further, we define that constraints `overlap` when they share a cell (lines 3–4). We then recursively choose constraints to be used among those that either mention the fact-to-explain (line 5), or overlap with a used constraint (line 6) and we choose facts to be used among those appearing in chosen constraints (line 7). Further, if we use a constraint without using a fact in it, then it must "bridge" two other constraints (lines 8–9). Notice that these improvements apply to all CSPs, not only Sudoku puzzles.

To showcase, how problem specific information is easily represented in our approach, we also introduce a redundant, Sudoku-specific constraint in lines 10–11. For an $n \times n$ Sudoku, an explanation step must contain at least $2(\sqrt{n}-1)$ facts. To illustrate, notice that $\sqrt{n}$ is both the size of a box and the number of boxes per row or column. An explanation placing a digit somewhere in a specific box constraint must therefore rule it out from the $\sqrt{n}-1$ other rows and $\sqrt{n}-1$ other columns it could have gone into. Figure 1 (middle) shows such an explanation step. Analogously, the same holds for row and column constraints.

```
1  chooseFactIn(T,N) :- useConstraint(T,N),                          ▷Define
2          useFact(X,Y,Z), in(X,Y,T,N).
3  overlap(T,N,T',N') :- in(X,Y,T,N), in(X,Y,T',N'), T>T'.
4  overlap(T,N,T',N') :- overlap(T',N',T,N).
5  {useConstraint(T,N)} :- explainFact(X,Y,Z), in(X,Y,T,N).          ▷Generate
6  {useConstraint(T,N) : overlap(T,N,T',N')} :- useConstraint(T',N').
7  {useFact(X,Y,Z)} :- fact(X,Y,Z), useConstraint(T,N), in(X,Y,T,N).
8  2 <= {useConstraint(T,N) : overlap(T,N,T',N')} :-
9          useConstraint(T',N'), not chooseFactIn(T',N').
10 factsNeeded(X) :- boxSize(B), X=2(B-1).        ▷Sudoku specific constraint
11 :- {useFact(X,Y,Z) : fact(X,Y,Z) } < N, factsNeeded(N).
```

Listing 1.3. Improvements to the existential program P_1

3.4 Bound-Driven Search

The default search strategy in ASP(Q) solvers is solution-improving search, which we observed spends a lot of time incrementally improving suboptimal solutions. Convergence to an optimal solution is slow, because there are many candidate explanation steps of high cost. To alleviate this, we use a simple, bound-driven search strategy. As the cost of an explanation step is dominated by the number of constraints it uses, we make calls to the ASP(Q) solver with an additional restriction that it should search for an optimal explanation step that uses a fixed number of constraints. This number of constraints is initially 1 and is increased until no optimal solution can exist with strictly more constraints (i.e. as soon as we have found a solution with cost below or equal to $10 \cdot n$, we know that we should never consider explanation steps that use n or more constraints). To achieve this, we add the following line to the existential program:

```
:- {useConstraint(T,X)} != CONSTRAINT_COUNT.
```

where `CONSTRAINT_COUNT` denotes the number of constraints currently allowed. Notice that when a returned explanation step contains strictly more than 10 facts, the search will continue to the next level, as a better solution might still be possible (given that constraints have cost 10 and facts have cost 1).

4 Experiments

In this section, we first evaluate the proposed improvements regarding redundant constraints and bound-driven search. Then, we will compare our best encoding against the previous IHS-based approach.

Conveniently, the python library CPMPY [16] provides means for manipulation of literals, facts and constraints according to Algorithm 1, as well as a built-in IHS-based OCUS procedure. CPMPY also provides a translation of any CSP modelled in it to a CNF formula. Using this translation, we initially attempted to obtain an ASP(Q) encoding that was *fully agnostic* of the application CSP, i.e. the instance part would encode precisely the reified constraints R and soft literals $\mathcal{S}$ according to Definition 1, and the problem formulation part would encode conditions (1)-(3) specialized to the function EXPLAIN-ONE-FACT. The allocation of tasks to subprograms in our attempt was identical to the encoding presented above, and the addition of redundant constraints could be done in similar ways. However, even with sophisticated modeling techniques, we could not compensate for the increase in size in the instance encoding and complexity in the problem formulation. While the approach was feasible for 4 $\times$ 4 instances, it was completely unable to scale to 9 $\times$ 9 Sudokus, with some explanation steps requiring more than 20 h of compute time. We therefore choose to exclude this method here from our further discussion. Rather unexpectedly, we found the built-in OCUS method of CPMPY to work remarkably well with this CNF translation of the high-level Sudoku modeling. Below, we compare our approach to the previously developed OCUS method in both a high-level formulation that we call "N-IHS" (for "natural"), and its CNF translation "CNF-IHS".

All our experiments[1] were run on identical machines equipped with 12th Gen Intel® Core ™ i7-12700 CPUs and 64GB of memory running Linux 5.15. We use existing puzzle instances for our experiments [14], picking all nine 4 $\times$ 4 puzzles and the five first 9 $\times$ 9 puzzles of each difficulty level. We added a tenth randomly generated 4 $\times$ 4 instance of our own. For computing a complete explanation sequence we set a time limit of 15 min (resp. 90 min) for 4 $\times$ 4 (resp. 9 $\times$ 9) puzzles. As ASP(Q) solver, we use CASPER [10]. We let explanation sequences diverge, i.e. the compared techniques do not necessarily compute the same explanation sequences. This means that the nth explanation step is not necessarily comparable across methods for the same Sudoku puzzle if the previous steps differ. Thus, we compare methods on whole explanation sequences, rather than on individual explanation steps.

[1] The source code is available at: https://doi.org/10.5281/zenodo.21070133.

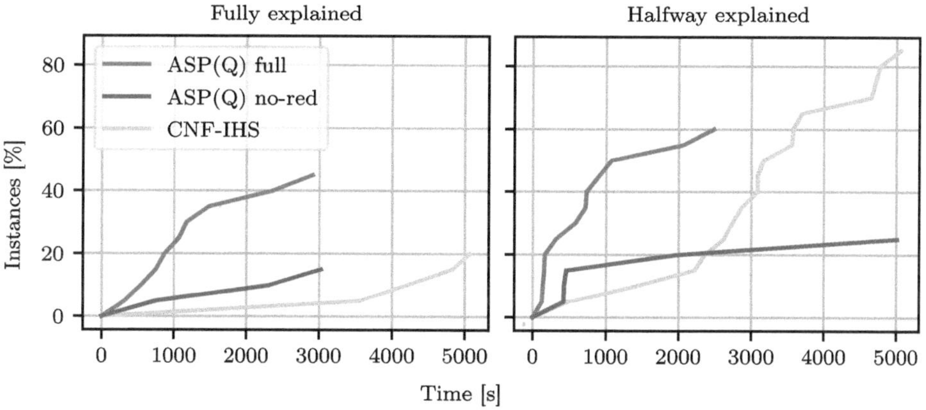

Fig. 2. The share of 9 × 9 Sudokus that could be fully explained (left) and "halfway" (right), i.e. to 40 filled cells before timeout, using ASP(Q) and IHS methods, respectively. Both, the no-bds ASP(Q) variant and the N-IHS variant did not explain a single instance even halfway and are hence not shown.

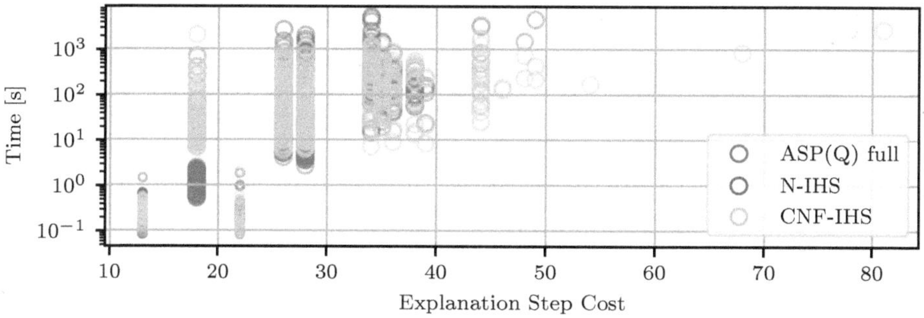

Fig. 3. Times to compute calls to EXPLAIN-ONE-FACT depending on the optimal cost of that step and the method used. Steps across all 4 × 4 (resp. 9 × 9) instances are shown as small (resp. big) circles.

4.1 Comparison of ASP(Q) Variations

We test our encoding presented in Sect. 3, which we call the "full" encoding, against the two variations in which we either *retract the redundant constraints addition* ("no-red") or *disable the bound-driven search strategy* ("no-bds"). For 4 × 4 instances we observed that the no-red variant finished only 4 out of 10 instances within the given time limit, whereas both other encodings explained all instances fully. For the 9 × 9 case, the no-bds encoding did not achieve more than 3 explanations steps for any instance, while the no-red and full encodings finished 3 and 9 complete explanation sequences, respectively. Figure 2 shows how many puzzles could be fully and "halfway" explained, respectively.

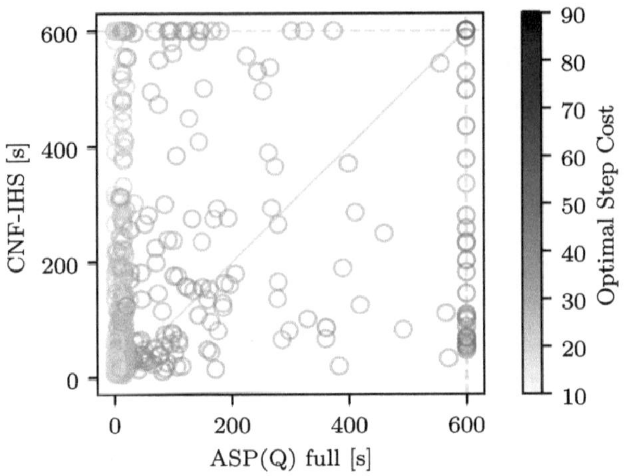

Fig. 4. Comparison of runtimes to compute optimal explanations steps using ASP(Q) and CNF-IHS, respectively. Histograms show distributions with bucket sizes of 3 s. The optimal cost of an explanation step is indicated by color.

4.2 Comparison to the Previous Approach

Our observation that the larger instance size in the CNF encoding drastically slows down the ASP(Q) solver, does not seem to transfer to the IHS based methods. In fact, out of 20 9×9 instances, our "full" ASP(Q) approach explained 9 fully, CNF-IHS finished 4 sequences, and N-IHS none. ASP(Q) struggles on instances of high cost and hence either breezes through the whole sequence if it only contains easy steps or gets stuck on a hard step. On the other hand, CNF-IHS takes longer to find easy steps, but manages to also compute hard steps without timing out (c.f. Fig. 3). Interestingly, this leads to CNF-IHS explaining fewer instances fully, but more instances to the midway point (c.f. Fig. 2).

For each 9×9 instance, we recorded the explanation sequences that explained the most facts and later *re-played* it using both the full ASP(Q) and CNF-IHS methods. By this we mean that sequences no longer diverge, i.e. regardless of the explanation step found by the respective method, we update the current state in the explanation process using the previously recorded step. Thereby, we can (1) validate that both sequences indeed find the same optimal cost and (2) draw meaningful comparisons regarding their respective runtimes on the level of explanation steps (instead of whole sequences). For these experiment we chose a timeout of 10 min per explanation step, (over-)estimating a maximum user patience. Our results are visualized in Fig. 4. A clear majority ($\approx 85\%$) of steps are solved faster using our proposed approach, especially relatively easy steps. For the few harder steps we encountered, ASP(Q) routinely times out, while CNF-IHS is more likely to yield an explanation in acceptable time.

5 Discussion and Conclusion

In this paper, we presented a novel application of ASP with quantifiers. We showed that it is feasible to use ASP(Q) to compute optimal explanation steps for constraint satisfaction problems, with a specific focus on Sudoku puzzles. We presented a direct encoding of the Sudoku problem in ASP that is competitive with the previously proposed IHS-based approach and even outperforms it on several instances in our empirical evaluation. We also discussed a more general encoding that can be applied to any problem that can be translated to a CNF formula, allowing it can be integrated directly into a library such as CPMpy which supports translations into CNF. Unfortunately, this generic approach did not scale well to realistically sized puzzles.

This work highlights opportunities for future work. First, designing translators of high-level constraint models into ASP could result in fully-general and efficient explanation computation methods, circumventing the need for translation to CNF. Second, the performance of our hand-crafted optimization compared to the standard solution-improving search stresses the need for programmable search strategies directly in ASP(Q) solvers. Third, we conjecture that our approach would benefit greatly from an ASP(Q)-specific core-guided optimization algorithm [2]. Finally, our optimization loop makes use of repeated calls to the solver with only a single constraint changing, meaning a lot of work probably needs to be redone. As such, we conjecture that an incremental solving interface for ASP(Q) would be beneficial.

Acknowledgments. This work was partially supported by Fonds Wetenschappelijk Onderzoek—Vlaanderen (project G064925N) and the European Union (ERC, CertiFOX, 101122653). Views and opinions expressed are however those of the author(s) only and do not necessarily reflect those of the European Union or the European Research Council. Neither the European Union nor the granting authority can be held responsible for them.

Disclosure of Interests. The authors have no competing interests to declare that are relevant to the content of this article.

References

1. Amendola, G., Ricca, F., Truszczynski, M.: Beyond NP: quantifying over answer sets. Theory Pract. Log. Program. **19**(5–6), 705–721 (2019). https://doi.org/10.1017/S1471068419000140
2. Andres, B., Kaufmann, B., Matheis, O., Schaub, T.: Unsatisfiability-based optimization in clasp. ICLP (Techn. Commun.). LIPIcs **17**, 211–221. Schloss Dagstuhl(2012). https://doi.org/10.4230/LIPIcs.ICLP.2012.211
3. Biere, A., Heule, M., van Maaren, H., Walsh, T. (eds.): Handbook of Satisfiability - Second Edition, FAIA, vol. 336. IOS Press (2021). https://doi.org/10.3233/FAIA336

4. Bleukx, I., Boumazouza, R., Guns, T., Laage, N., Povéda, G.: Modeling and explaining an industrial workforce allocation and scheduling problem. In: CP. LIPIcs, vol. 340, pp. 6:1–6:24. Schloss Dagstuhl (2025). https://doi.org/10.4230/LIPICS.CP.2025.6
5. Bleukx, I., Devriendt, J., Gamba, E., Bogaerts, B., Guns, T.: Simplifying step-wise explanation sequences. In: CP. LIPIcs, vol. 280, pp. 11:1–11:20. Schloss Dagstuhl (2023). https://doi.org/10.4230/LIPICS.CP.2023.11
6. Bogaerts, B., Gamba, E., Guns, T.: A framework for step-wise explaining how to solve constraint satisfaction problems. Artif. Intell. **300**, 103550 (2021). https://doi.org/10.1016/j.artint.2021.103550
7. Bogaerts, B., Janhunen, T., Tasharrofi, S.: Stable-unstable semantics: beyond NP with normal logic programs. Theory Pract. Log. Program. **16**(5–6), 570–586 (2016). https://doi.org/10.1017/S1471068416000387
8. Brewka, G., Eiter, T., Truszczynski, M.: Answer set programming at a glance. Commun. ACM **54**(12), 92–103 (2011). https://doi.org/10.1145/2043174.2043195
9. Calimeri, F., et al.: ASP-Core-2 input language format. Theory Pract. Log. Program. **20**(2), 294–309 (2020). https://doi.org/10.1017/S1471068419000450
10. Cuteri, A., Mazzotta, G., Ricca, F.: 2-ASP(Q) solving based on CEGAR. In: AAAI, pp. 19030–19038. AAAI Press (2026). https://doi.org/10.1609/AAAI.V40I23.38975
11. Eiter, T., Gottlob, G.: On the computational cost of disjunctive logic programming: propositional case. Ann. Math. Artif. Intell. **15**(3–4), 289–323 (1995). https://doi.org/10.1007/BF01536399
12. Foschini, M., Defresne, M., Gamba, E., Bogaerts, B., Guns, T.: Preference elicitation for step-wise explanations in logic puzzles. In: AAAI, pp. 14225–14233. AAAI Press (2026). https://doi.org/10.1609/AAAI.V40I17.38436
13. Frisch, A.M., Harvey, W., Jefferson, C., Hernández, B.M., Miguel, I.: Essence: a constraint language for specifying combinatorial problems. Constraints An Int. J. **13**(3), 268–306 (2008). https://doi.org/10.1007/s10601-008-9047-y
14. Gamba, E., Bogaerts, B., Guns, T.: Efficiently explaining CSPs with unsatisfiable subset optimization. J. Artif. Intell. Res. **78**, 709–746 (2023). https://doi.org/10.1613/JAIR.1.14260
15. Gebser, M., Kaminski, R., Kaufmann, B., Schaub, T.: Answer Set Solving in Practice. Morgan & Claypool Publishers, Synthesis Lectures on Artificial Intelligence and Machine Learning (2012). https://doi.org/10.2200/S00457ED1V01Y201211AIM019
16. Guns, T.: Increasing modeling language convenience with a universal n-dimensional array, CPpy as python-embedded example. In: ModRef. vol 19 (2019)
17. Gupta, S.D., Genc, B., O'Sullivan, B.: Explanation in constraint satisfaction: a survey. In: IJCAI, pp. 4400–4407. ijcai.org (2021). https://doi.org/10.24963/IJCAI.2021/601
18. Junker, U.: QuickXplain: preferred explanations and relaxations for over-constrained problems. In: AAAI, pp. 167–172. AAAI Press/The MIT Press (2004). http://www.aaai.org/Library/AAAI/2004/aaai04-027.php
19. Leo, K., Tack, G.: Debugging unsatisfiable constraint models. In: Salvagnin, D., Lombardi, M. (eds.) CPAIOR 2017. LNCS, vol. 10335, pp. 77–93. Springer, Cham (2017). https://doi.org/10.1007/978-3-319-59776-8_7
20. Liffiton, M.H., Sakallah, K.A.: Algorithms for computing minimal unsatisfiable subsets of constraints. J. Autom. Reason. **40**(1), 1–33 (2008). https://doi.org/10.1007/S10817-007-9084-Z

21. Lifschitz, V.: What is answer set programming? In: AAAI, pp. 1594–1597. AAAI Press (2008). http://www.aaai.org/Library/AAAI/2008/aaai08-270.php
22. Nethercote, N., Stuckey, P.J., Becket, R., Brand, S., Duck, G.J., Tack, G.: MiniZinc: towards a standard CP modelling language. In: Bessière, C. (ed.) CP 2007. LNCS, vol. 4741, pp. 529–543. Springer, Heidelberg (2007). https://doi.org/10.1007/978-3-540-74970-7_38
23. Rossi, F., van Beek, P., Walsh, T. (eds.): Handbook of Constraint Programming, Foundations of Artificial Intelligence, vol. 2. Elsevier (2006). https://www.sciencedirect.com/science/bookseries/15746526/2
24. Sierksma, G.: Linear and Integer Programming - Theory and Practice, Pure and Applied Mathematics, vol. 198. Dekker (1996). https://doi.org/10.1201/b16939
25. van Emden, M.H., Kowalski, R.A.: The semantics of predicate logic as a programming language. J. ACM **23**(4), 733–742 (1976). https://doi.org/10.1145/321978.321991

Reasonable Motion
A General ASP Foundation for Environment Constrained Movement Trajectory Computation

Julius Monsen[1,3(✉)], Jakob Suchan[2,3], Mehul Bhatt[1,3], and Lars Karlsson[1,3]

[1] Örebro University, Örebro, Sweden
{julius.monsen,mehul.bhatt,lars.karlsson}@oru.se
[2] Constructor University, Bremen, Germany
jsuchan@constructor.university
[3] CoDesign Lab EU, Örebro, Sweden
https://codesign-lab.org/cognitive-vision/

Abstract. We present a general *answer set programming* based hybrid quantitative-qualitative method for computing constrained branching trajectory modes for moving objects in real-world settings. The method performs constrained traversal of an environment graph, enumerating geometrically admissible motion behaviours as stable models, each constituting a distinct trajectory mode characterised by both domain-dependent and independent factors such as derived event sequence, map topology, and domain norms. The hybrid trajectory computation method is generally applicable across motion characteristics typically encountered in diverse dynamic domains with moving objects, e.g., autonomous driving. We demonstrate applicability and highlight how computed trajectories are traceable to their underlying stable model, thereby affording verifiable interpretability that purely learned approaches cannot provide. We also perform an empirical evaluation with Argoverse 2, a large-scale real-world autonomous driving benchmark representative of the class of dynamic domains within the scope of the proposed method.

1 Motivation

Autonomous systems operating in embodied **in-the-wild** situations are confronted with the challenge of *interactive sensemaking*, i.e., interleaved multimodal perception, interpretation, and decision-making requiring coordination of attention, integration of sensory inputs, and dynamic exploration of possible futures and interactive outcomes [1,16]. Such capabilities, referred to as **physical AI**, are gaining renewed traction as a major challenge for contemporary AI/ML research, and will be critical for deploying trustworthy technologies in safety-critical dynamic domains such as social robotics and autonomous driving.

Motion in Structured Environments. Many real-world domains in which autonomous agents operate are structured: roads constrain vehicle motion to lanes and require normative compliance in intersections and roundabouts; indoor

W. Faber et al. (Eds.): LPNMR 2026, LNAI 16952, pp. 332–348, 2027.
https://doi.org/10.1007/978-3-032-38320-4_21

environments constrain robot navigation to corridors, doorways, and rooms; social spaces impose normative constraints on pedestrian flow. This structure is not merely a backdrop; it is a rich source of information about what motions are geometrically admissible, physically plausible, and normatively appropriate. For instance, a human driver approaching an intersection does not reason over a continuous positional space; rather, they reason over a small set of symbolically distinct possibilities (*go straight*, *turn left*, *change lane*) that are immediately grounded in the geometry of the road ahead. Capturing this kind of geometry-constrained, commonsense qualitative inference [1,4,5] in a principled, transparent, and formally verifiable manner remains an open challenge, particularly in view of emerging AI regulation and the need for retrospective diagnosability in safety-critical deployments [6].

Limits of End-to-End Motion Prediction. Purely end-to-end stochastic approaches for the prediction of motion trajectories (of dynamic interacting objects) often focus on learning functional mappings from scene observations to future positions [13], without explicit representations of the environmental structure, admissible behaviours, or the events that characterise them. Such end-to-end approaches emphasise purely geometric accuracy on benchmarks, prioritising *where* agents may move, offering little insight into *why* a particular motion trajectory was generated or prioritised, or *which* aspects of the environment constrained it [9,13,21,22]. Qualitatively distinct behaviours (e.g., going straight versus turning at an intersection) may be represented as overlapping geometric trajectories, and there might not be a systematic semantic mechanism by which such distinctions can be inspected, explained, verified, or evaluated at scale.

Key Contributions. We present an answer set programming (ASP) [2,7] based *hybrid quantitative-qualitative* method for computing 'reasonable' motion trajectory modes for moving objects in real-world dynamic settings, that are geometrically admissible and normatively preferred with respect to the structured environment representation and domain constraints. The developed hybrid method consists of: **1)** an ASP encoding qualitatively modelling the environment as a typed directed graph, and performing constrained traversal to systematically enumerate geometrically admissible, branching motion trajectory modes; and **2)** a trajectory generation component that converts each qualitatively distinct motion mode into a smooth, continuous motion trajectory via environmental geometry-guided centerline construction and constant-speed following.

Our modular hybrid qualitative-quantitative characterisation ensures separation of concerns between the high-level commonsense and low-level numerical levels of representation of motion. Furthermore, we emphasise that following our approach, each computed motion trajectory is characterised by a verifiable path and a high-level event sequence capturing domain-dependent and independent factors such as map topology, norms/preferences. To highlight real-world relevance, we empirically evaluate the method in the autonomous driving domain using the Argoverse 2 community benchmark [19]. Here, we also demonstrate how every computed motion trajectory is fully traceable to its underlying stable model, thereby affording verifiable interpretability that most purely learned approaches lack. We posit that the proposed method is a principled—i.e., domain-independent, modular, and elaboration tolerant—and transparent alternative to monolithic end-to-end predictors in domains where explainability and geometric admissibility are critical requirements.

2 Computing 'Reasonable' Motion: A Hybrid Qualitative-Quantitative Method

The proposed *hybrid qualitative-quantitative method* for computing (reasonable) motion trajectories is illustrated in Fig. 1. Operationally, the method consists of four stages from a higher-level viewpoint: **(1)** Grounding the *answer set program*[1] from the scene description and deriving reachability over the environment graph; **(2)** Path selection via a choice rule and integrity constraints; **(3)** Grouping the resulting stable models by event sequence; and **(4)** Converting each mode group into a continuous trajectory. *A formal characterisation of the method follows*:

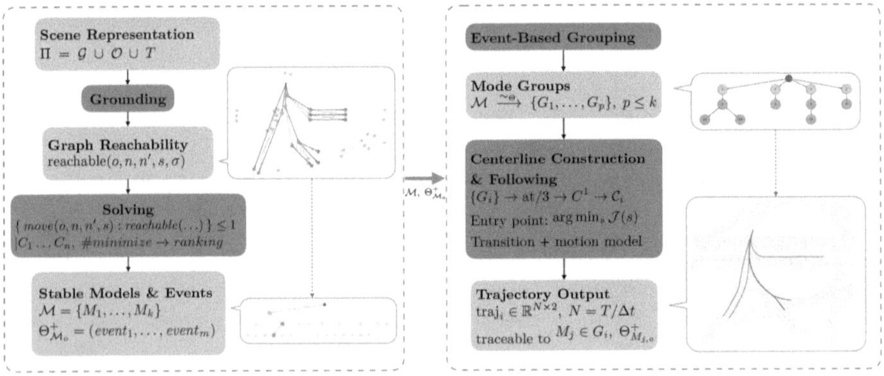

Fig. 1. Hybrid Qualitative-Quantitative Motion Trajectory Computing Method: Overview of the proposed pipeline. *Left:* ASP grounding and solving yield stable models, each representing a path annotated trajectory influencing events. *Right:* stable models are grouped and geometrical features constructed such that paths can be followed continuously according to a domain-specific motion model and yield a trajectory $\text{traj}_i \in \mathbb{R}^{N\times 2}$ per mode group.

2.1 Scene Representation

Let $\mathcal{O} = \{o_1, \ldots, o_n\}$ be a set of domain objects (e.g., moving entities), each associated with a state o^{state} comprising position, velocity, and heading at a

[1] Answer Set Programming (ASP) is an established declarative programming paradigm rooted in the stable model semantics; we refer readers to [2,7,10] for an introduction and further pointers.

given timestep. The environment is characterised by a finite set of discrete spatial regions $\mathcal{N}$, a set of time steps $\mathcal{T} = \{t_0, \ldots, t_m\}$, and a prediction horizon $T \subset \mathcal{T}$ over which trajectory modes are computed. The ASP program encoding the scene is then: $\Pi = \mathcal{G} \cup \mathcal{O} \cup T$, where $\mathcal{G} = (\mathcal{N}, \mathcal{E})$ is a typed directed graph whose nodes and edges are grounded as facts, while $\mathcal{O}$ and T are collections of facts encoding object states and time steps, respectively. Nodes $n \in \mathcal{N}$ represent discrete spatial regions and edges $(n_1, n_2, \delta) \in \mathcal{E}$ carry typed relations $\delta \in \Delta$ encoding navigational affordances (e.g., *successor* for sequential region transitions, *lateral* for side-by-side transitions such as lane changes, and *entry* for access relations into junctions or restricted zones). Each node is annotated with domain-dependent attributes such as region type (e.g., vehicle lane, bike lane, intersection), geometric extent (e.g., arc length or bounding polygon), or normative constraints (e.g., permitted crossing directions encoded in lane markings). A *trajectory mode* for object o is characterised by a derived event sequence Θ_o^+ capturing qualitatively distinct behavioural events, grounded in a supporting node sequence $(n_0, n_1, \ldots, n_k)$ through $\mathcal{G}$, constituting a commonsense / qualitative hypothesis about the future behaviour of o.

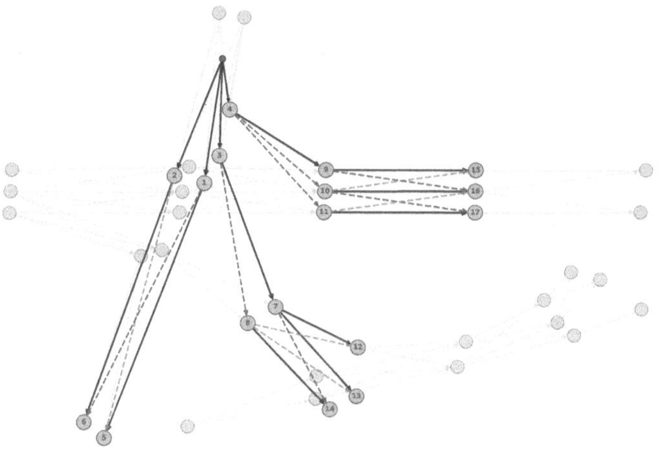

Fig. 2. Reachability over $\mathcal{G}$; Example: • *current agent position*; • *potential start node*; • *reachable nodes.* Solid arrows denote successor transitions; dashed arrows denote two-hop lateral relations (as used in Sect. 3.1).

2.2 Graph Reachability

Reachability over $\mathcal{G}$ is computed as a derived relation that tracks, for each object o, the set of nodes reachable within the prediction horizon, together with a *traversal state* σ recording accumulated progress and the history of any mode-changing transitions relevant to the domain (e.g., distance travelled and lateral manoeuvre history in driving, or floor level and door transitions in indoor navigation): reachable(o, n, n', s, σ). Rather than embedding recursive traversal directly inside the choice rule, reachability is defined separately as an inductively derived relation over the environment graph. This follows a modelling pattern used for recursively defined concepts such as graph reachability [2], where auxiliary Horn rules derive the transitive structure independently of the non-deterministic path selection. Operationally, this yields a relatively flat search problem for the solver. Rather than resolving recursive path dependencies during search, the solver operates over a pre-instantiated set of independent ground transitions, reducing backtracking and conflict depth. The traversal state σ and its propagation rules remain domain-dependent. An illustration of reachability in a concrete graph is shown in Fig. 2, where an agent is positioned at the red marker.

2.3 Constrained Mode Hypothesis Generation

Mode hypotheses are generated by selecting a path through the reachable set via an ASP choice rule:

$$\left\{ \text{move}(o, n, n', s) : \text{reachable}(o, n, n', s, \sigma) \right\} \leq 1 \qquad \forall\, s \in \text{steps}(o) \tag{1}$$

The set of stable models of Π under this rule is denoted $\mathcal{M} = \{M_1, \ldots, M_k\}$, each constituting a distinct, internally consistent trajectory mode hypothesis. Path validity (physical and normative) is enforced by the following integrity constraints, which hold across all domain instantiations:

C1. Mandatory Start: $\leftarrow \neg\, \text{move}(o, \cdot, \cdot, 0)$

Every object must be assigned a transition at step $s = 0$, grounding the trajectory in the object's observed state at the first prediction timestep.

C2. Temporal Consistency: $\leftarrow \text{move}(o, \cdot, n', s),\ \text{move}(o, n, \cdot, s{+}1),\ n \neq n'$.

The destination node at step s must equal the origin node at step $s{+}1$, enforcing that selected transitions form a connected path through $\mathcal{G}$.

C3. Continuity: $\leftarrow \neg\, \text{move}(o, \cdot, \cdot, s),\ \text{move}(o, \cdot, \cdot, s{+}1)$.

A transition at step $s{+}1$ is only permitted if a transition was chosen at step s. Together with C2, this ensures the selected path is contiguous: once a path terminates, no further transitions are admitted.

Additional domain-dependent constraints, e.g., bounding the number and spacing of mode-changing transitions, can be incorporated per domain. Stable models may furthermore be ranked via ASP weak constraints encoding domain-dependent preferences $\mathcal{W}$—such as penalising lane changes across solid lane markings or favouring paths requiring fewer lateral transitions—yielding an ordered set of trajectory mode hypotheses from which downstream components can select or sample. Each move(o, n, n', s) atom additionally derives at(o, n', s), recording the node occupied by o at step s, used for event derivation in Sect. 2.4. Exemplary ASP implementation of both domain-specific constraints and preference ranking is included in Sect. 3.1.

2.4 Event-Based Grouping

Following solving, the resulting stable models are grouped as a post-processing step based on their derived event sequences. To provide interpretable characterisations of each mode and enable grouping of behaviourally equivalent stable models, high-level events are derived directly from the selected path:

$$\text{event}(e(o,\ldots),s) \leftarrow \text{at}(o,n,s),\ \phi(o,n,s) \tag{2}$$

where $\phi(o,n,s)$ is a domain-supplied condition on the current node and step. The ordered tuple of event atoms derived from each stable model $M_i \in \mathcal{M}$ serves as a qualitative (event) fingerprint $\Theta^+_{\mathcal{M}_o} = (event_1, \ldots, event_m)$, ordered by step index s so that simultaneous events at the same step are canonically sorted. Models sharing the same fingerprint, i.e., $M_i \sim_\Theta M_j \iff \Theta^+_{M_i} = \Theta^+_{M_j}$, are collapsed into a single mode group G_i via the equivalence relation $\sim_\Theta$:

$$\mathcal{M} \xrightarrow{\sim_\Theta} \{G_1,\ldots,G_p\}, \quad p \leq k \tag{3}$$

This grouping serves two purposes: **(1)** reduction of the mode space to a manageable set of behaviourally distinct hypotheses (the number of stable models can be large in complex scenarios with many reachable nodes and permitted transitions); and **(2)** enabling an interpretable high-level description of each mode (e.g., *lane change left, go straight,* or *turn right at intersection*) that can be inspected for transparency and used to guide downstream trajectory generation together with the resulting lane occupation information.

2.5 From Commonsense Qualitative Modes to Continuous Geometric Trajectories

Given the grouped stable models, each mode group G_i is converted into a single continuous trajectory in two steps.

(1). Geometric Mode Construction. Each stable model $M_j \in G_i$ yields an ordered sequence of nodes, from which geometric representations (e.g., centerlines or region boundaries) are retrieved. Within a group, different models may follow geometrically distinct but behaviourally equivalent paths. To preserve the qualitative behaviour while reducing mode redundancy, a single representative, approximate geometric path $\mathcal{C}_i$ is obtained by stitching and averaging the node geometries across all models in G_i, ensuring C^1-continuity at junctions. Since all models in G_i share the same event fingerprint $\Theta^+_{G_i}$ by construction, the averaged path preserves the qualitative behavioural identity of the group while geometrically centralising across lane-level variations within it. For instance, if two models both perform a left lane change but at adjacent lane steps, the averaged path will execute the change at an intermediate position. The specific stitching and averaging procedure is domain-dependent and described in Sect. 3.2.

(2). Trajectory Following. Given $\mathcal{C}_i$ and the object's observed state o^{state}, a trajectory is produced over the prediction horizon T. If the object is not already

Algorithm 1: Hybrid Trajectory Mode Computation

Input: $\Pi = \mathcal{G} \cup \mathcal{O} \cup T$, constraints $\{C_1, \ldots, C_n\}$, preferences $\mathcal{W}$, agent state o^{state}, horizon T, Δt
Output: $\mathcal{Y} = \{(\text{traj}_i, \Theta^+_{G_i})\}_{i=1}^{p}$

$\mathcal{R} \leftarrow \text{ground}(\Pi)$ `// derive all reachable(`$o, n_{\text{prev}}, n, s, \sigma$`) at ground time`
`// Mode Hypothesis Generation`
$P_{\text{move}} = \left\{\{\text{move}(o, n, n', s) : \text{reachable}(o, n, n', s, \sigma)\}1\right\}$
$P \leftarrow \mathcal{R} \cup P_{\text{move}} \cup \{C_1, \ldots, C_n\} \cup \mathcal{W}$; $\mathcal{M} \leftarrow \text{optAnswerSets}(P)$
`// Event-Based Grouping`
$\mathcal{F} \leftarrow \{\}$
foreach $M_i \in \mathcal{M}$ **do**
  $E_i \leftarrow \emptyset$
  foreach (o, n, s) *s.t.* $\text{at}(o, n, s) \in M_i$ **do**
    if $\phi(o, n, s)$ *holds* **then**
      $E_i.\text{add}((e(o, \ldots), s))$
  $\Theta^+_{M_i} \leftarrow \text{sort}(E_i)$; $\mathcal{F}[\Theta^+_{M_i}].\text{add}(M_i)$
$\{G_1, \ldots, G_p\} \leftarrow \text{values}(\mathcal{F})$
`// Trajectory generation`
$\mathcal{Y} \leftarrow \emptyset$
foreach G_i **do**
  $\mathcal{P} \leftarrow \emptyset$
  foreach $M_j \in G_i$ **do**
    $n_1, \ldots, n_k \leftarrow$ at-sequence of M_j
    $\mathcal{P}.\text{add}(\text{stitch}(n_1, \ldots, n_k, \mathcal{G}))$
  $\mathcal{C}_i \leftarrow \text{arc\_length\_average}(\mathcal{P})$; $s^* \leftarrow \arg\min_s \mathcal{J}(s; o^{\text{state}}, \mathcal{C}_i)$
  $\text{traj}_i \leftarrow \text{follow}(\mathcal{C}_i, s^*, o^{\text{state}}, N{=}T/\Delta t)$; $\mathcal{Y}.\text{add}((\text{traj}_i, \Theta^+_{G_i}))$
return $\mathcal{Y}$

on $\mathcal{C}_i$, a smooth transition curve connects the current position and heading to an entry point on $\mathcal{C}_i$. The entry point is selected by minimising an angular cost penalising misalignment between the object's heading and the straight line to the entry point, and between that line and the path tangent at entry, with a distance regularisation term:

$$\mathcal{J}(s) = (1 - \cos\theta_{\text{depart}}) + (1 - \cos\theta_{\text{arrive}}) + \lambda \frac{\|p(s) - p_0\|}{L}, \tag{4}$$

where θ_{depart} is the angle between the object's heading and the line to entry point $p(s)$, θ_{arrive} is the angle between that line and the path tangent at $p(s)$, L is the total path length, and λ is a distance weight. The object then follows $\mathcal{C}_i$ from the entry point under a chosen motion model for the remainder of T, yielding:

$$\text{traj}_i \in \mathbb{R}^{N \times 2}, \quad N = T/\Delta t \tag{5}$$

Each trajectory traj_i is fully traceable to its underlying stable models $\{M_j \in G_i\}$ and event sequence Θ^+_o, affording verifiable interpretability over the complete pipeline. In Algorithm 1 we highlight the flow of the overall system and each functional component as outlined in this section.

3 Reasonable Motion in Autonomous Driving

We apply and practically demonstrate an encoding of the proposed (reasonable) motion trajectory computation method (Sect. 2) for the domain of autonomous driving, where a typical requirement[2] is to compute motion trajectories of dynamic entities. By *reasonable* motion, we allude to computed solutions that are both formally well-founded and behaviourally well-justified. Here, two connotations are implied: **(1)** in the manner of non-monotonic commonsense reasoning, our model derives motion trajectories that are "reasoned about": each motion hypothesis is grounded in a stable model, fully traceable to its supporting ASP derivation, and thereby is amenable to inspection and explanation; and **(2)** we also allude to "reasonableness" as a solution criterion, i.e., only trajectories satisfying explicit geometric, physical, and contextual or norm-respecting constraints—encoded as integrity constraints and ranked by preference minimisation—are admitted.

3.1 High-Level Commonsense Mode Hypothesis Generation

Given an ASP problem specification for a motion trajectory computation task in the domain of driving, it is desired that each stable model correspond to a distinct trajectory mode—a high-level behavioural hypothesis capturing the sequence of lanes a vehicle may occupy and the discrete events arising along it (e.g., *go straight, turn left, change lane then go straight*)—guiding downstream trajectory generation (Sect. 3.2).

Lane Graph. The environment graph $\mathcal{G}$ is instantiated with lane segments $\mathcal{L} = \{\ell_1, \ldots, \ell_n\}$ as nodes. Each edge $(\ell_1, \ell_2, \delta) \in \mathcal{E}$ carries a relation type $\delta \in \{\text{successor}, \text{left}, \text{right}\}$, and each lane ℓ is annotated with its arc length $\text{dist}(\ell) \in \mathbb{R}^+$, its type (vehicle, bus, bike), and its lane markings on each side. A subset $\mathcal{L}_I \subseteq \mathcal{L}$ of intersection lanes are tagged with a turn direction $\text{dir}_I(\ell) \in \{\text{left}, \text{right}, \text{straight}\}$.

Lane changes, the domain instantiation of mode-changing transitions, are derived as two-hop paths in $\mathcal{G}$ (Eqs. (6)–(7)). A third case (Eq. (8)) captures the common manoeuvre where a turning vehicle drifts into an adjacent parallel exit lane upon leaving an intersection. Let ℓ_1 be the turning lane with direction τ, m its primary exit, and ℓ_2 the adjacent lane in opposite direction $\bar{\tau}$ relative to the turn direction. Then a connection to ℓ_2's continuation ℓ_3 is admitted.

[2] Section 4 includes an empirical evaluation with the *in-the-wild* Argoverse 2 [19] motion forecasting community benchmark consisting of complex urban driving scenarios together with corresponding motion data from LIDAR and RGB signals. Here, the motion prediction task operates over a 6-second horizon at 10 Hz.

$$\mathrm{lc}(\ell_1, \ell_2, \delta) \leftarrow (\ell_1, m, \delta) \in \mathcal{E},\ (m, \ell_2, \mathrm{succ}) \in \mathcal{E},\ \delta \neq \mathrm{succ} \tag{6}$$

$$\mathrm{lc}(\ell_1, \ell_2, \delta) \leftarrow (\ell_1, m, \mathrm{succ}) \in \mathcal{E},\ (m, \ell_2, \delta) \in \mathcal{E},\ \delta \neq \mathrm{succ} \tag{7}$$

$$\mathrm{lc}(\ell_1, \ell_3, \bar{\tau}) \leftarrow (\ell_1, m, \mathrm{succ}) \in \mathcal{E},\ \ell_1 \in \mathcal{L}_I,\ \mathrm{dir}_I(\ell_1) = \tau, \quad (m, \ell_2, \bar{\tau}) \in \mathcal{E},\ (\ell_2, \ell_3, \bar{\tau}) \in \mathcal{E} \tag{8}$$

Traversal State and Reachability. The general traversal state σ (see Sect. 2.2) is instantiated for driving as $\sigma = (d, \delta, \kappa, d_\kappa, \delta_\kappa)$, where d is the accumulated distance, δ the edge type of the transition from ℓ_{prev} to ℓ, κ the lane change count, d_κ the cumulative distance at the most recent lane change, and δ_κ its direction. This yields the following predicate schema:

```
reachable(Trk, L1, L2, Step, sigma(D, Delta, K, DK, DeltaK)) :- ...
```

The step index orders lane visits but does not correspond to a fixed time interval (lanes vary in length). Lane-vehicle type compatibility is enforced via `allowed_in_lane/2`, and the recursion is bounded by $d_{\max}$ derived from the observed speed under a chosen motion model.

Start. Each vehicle is seeded at its potential start lane(s) with $s = 0$, $\kappa = 0$, $\delta_\kappa = \mathrm{none}$. Occupied lane(s) and remaining distance d_0 are determined by querying spatially nearby lanes, scoring candidates by heading alignment and containment, and applying robustness heuristics for sensor noise and low-speed ambiguity. If the vehicle is sufficiently far from the lane end, neighbouring lanes of adequate length are also admitted as start lanes.

Successor Propagation. From any state at step s with $d_{\mathrm{old}} < d_{\max}$, the vehicle advances to a successor lane ℓ', accumulating $d = d_{\mathrm{old}} + \mathrm{dist}(\ell')$ while the lane-change state is carried forward unchanged.

Lane Change Propagation. A lateral move via $\mathrm{lc}(\ell, \ell', \delta)$ is permitted provided $\kappa < \kappa_{\max}$ and ℓ' is type-compatible. Three cases govern direction and state update, all incrementing κ and recording d_{old} as the new d_κ: (i) first change ($\delta_\kappa = \mathrm{none}$): any direction permitted, δ_κ set to δ; (ii) continued direction ($\delta = \delta_\kappa$): always permitted, δ_κ unchanged; (iii) opposite direction ($\delta = \bar{\delta}_\kappa$): permitted only if a minimum recovery distance has been observed since the last lane change $d_{\mathrm{old}} - d_\kappa \geq \theta_{\mathrm{lc}}$, then δ_κ updated to δ.

Mode Selection, Ranking and Events . Applied to the driving domain, the mode selection choice rule (Sect. 2.3) takes the form:

```
{ move(Trk, L1, L2, S) : reachable(Trk, L1, L2, S, _) } 1 :- step(Trk, S).
```

In addition to the general constraints C1–C3 described in Sect. 2.3:

```
:- not move(Trk, _, _, 0), step(Trk, 0).
:- move(Trk, _, L2, S), move(Trk, L1, _, S+1), L1 != L2.
:- step(Trk, S), not move(Trk, _, _, S), move(Trk, _, _, S+1).
```

the following driving-specific constraints are enforced: (C4) minimum travel of at least the braking distance; (C5) lane change budget $\kappa_{\max}$; and (C6) minimum spacing θ_{lc} between opposite-direction changes:

```
:- move(Trk, L1, L2, S), not move(Trk, _, _, S+1), braking_distance(Trk, BD), D < BD,
   reachable(Trk, L2, _, _, _), reachable(Trk, L1, L2, S, sigma(D, _, _, _, _)).
:- #count{ S : changed_lane(Trk, S, _) } > max_lane_changes.
:- consecutive_lc(Trk, S1, S2), #sum{ D, S : move(Trk, _, L2, S),
   lane_distance(L2, D), S>=S1, S<S2}  < lc_distance_threshold.
```

braking_distance/2 is provided as a fact from the observed speed. The predicates changed_lane/3 and consecutive_lc/3 are derived helpers capturing lateral transitions and consecutive opposite-direction pairs respectively. Each move/4 is converted to at/3 representing lane occupation.

Stable models are ranked by a two-level minimisation encoding traffic norm compliance via the map's lane_mark/3 facts. At higher priority, lane changes across transitional markings (e.g., dash_solid) incur cost 1 and solid or double-solid markings incur cost 5. At lower priority, total lane change count is minimised and better start-lane heading alignment is preferred. The solver is configured with -opt-mode=optN and models=0, directing Clingo to enumerate *all* cost-optimal stable models. This ensures that every behaviourally distinct trajectory mode—not only the single highest-ranked one—is retained for downstream grouping and trajectory generation.

```
#minimize { C@2, Trk, S, Dir : changed_lane(Trk, S, Dir),
            move(Trk, L1, _, S), lc_mark_cost(L1, Dir, C) }.
#minimize { 1@1, S, Trk : changed_lane(Trk, S, _) }.
#minimize { Cost@1, Trk : in_lane(Trk, L, curr_time, D, Cost) }.
```

Blocked crossings are penalised rather than forbidden, reflecting that vehicles may cross solid markings in practice, albeit rarely. High-level events are derived as described in Sect. 2.4. Additionally, a start_lane event distinguishes modes that share the same future event sequence but start from different lanes:

```
event(start_lane(L), -1) :- at(Trk, L, 0).
event(lane_change(Trk, Dir), S) :- changed_lane(Trk, S, Dir).
event(intersection(Trk, Dir), S) :- at(Trk, L, S), intersection_lane(L, Dir).
```

Each resulting stable model constitutes a distinct trajectory mode, e.g., see the scenario of Fig. 3 that are subsequently grouped based on an event fingerprint (Sec 2.4).

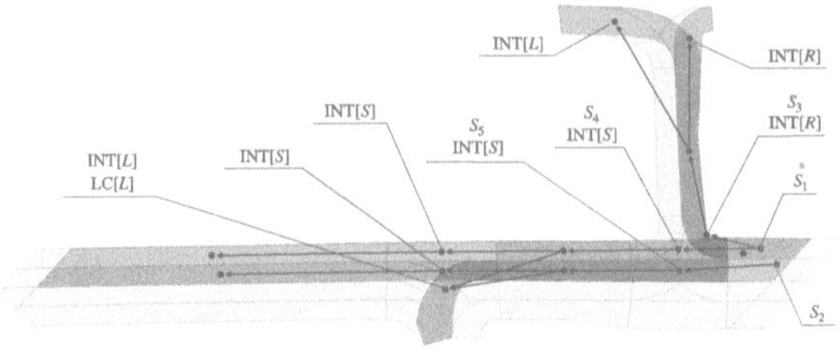

Fig. 3. Discrete Trajectory Modes. Each mode is highlighted by a path between the lane segments and their representative points •. • denotes the position of the agent. INT[S/L/R] denotes an intersection event where the agent goes *straight*, *left* or *right*, and LC[L/R] a *left* or *right* lane change.

3.2 Trajectory Generation

Following the general procedure of Sect. 2.5, each mode group G_i is converted into a continuous trajectory via *centerline construction* and *centerline following*:

Centerline Construction. Each $M_j \in G_i$ yields an ordered sequence of lane identifiers via `at/3`, from which lane centerlines are retrieved. To obtain the representative path $\mathcal{C}_i$, lane segments of each model are stitched into a continuous polyline. At junctions, a cubic Bézier bridge (a smooth cubic polynomial curve matched in position and tangent to the adjoining segments) is inserted whose longitudinal reach scales with the lateral offset, producing a smooth C^1-continuous transition reflecting natural lane-change geometry. The polylines across all $M_j \in G_i$ are then averaged via arc-length parameterisation—each resampled to a common number of points by fractional arc length and averaged element-wise—yielding $\mathcal{C}_i$ as the geometric mean of the group's paths.

Centerline Following. Assuming constant speed, the agent advances along $\mathcal{C}_i$ at its observed speed at 10 Hz. If not already within a snap threshold of $\mathcal{C}_i$, a cubic Hermite transition curve connects the current position and heading to the entry point selected by minimising Eq. (4), arriving with heading aligned to the centerline tangent. The agent then follows $\mathcal{C}_i$ for the remainder of the horizon, yielding $\text{traj}_i \in \mathbb{R}^{N\times 2}$ with $N = T/\Delta t$, $\Delta t = 0.1\,\text{s}$.

4 Empirical Evaluation with Argoverse 2

We evaluate the proposed method and its application in autonomous driving along three dimensions: **(1)** computational efficiency of the ASP solving pipeline; **(2)** geometric sufficiency of the generated lane-path modes; **(3)** trajectory forecasting accuracy against established baselines. All evaluations were conducted on an Apple MacBook Pro (M3) using 23,049 examples from the test split of Argoverse 2[3], which had a vehicle as the focal agent (as per the evaluation scheme in [19]). The following parameters were used throughout: lane change budget $\kappa_{\max} = 2$, minimum recovery distance $\theta_{\text{lc}} = 50\,\text{m}$, and a 6-second prediction horizon at 10 Hz ($N = 60$ steps).

4.1 Runtime Complexity

Figure 4 reports grounding and solving statistics. Grounding dominates, with a mean of 4.78 ms (std 2.48 ms, max 300 ms). In contrast, solving requires only 0.06 ms on average. This behaviour is consistent with the modelling strategy of deriving reachability separately from the non-deterministic mode selection, thereby shifting much of the structural computation into rule instantiation and propagation while leaving the solver with a comparatively small combinatorial search space. Additionally, the constant-speed and single-agent assumptions likely contribute to the fast solving speed. Relaxing the constant-speed assumption or extending to multi-agent settings would increase grounding cost, and characterising this scaling behaviour remains future work. The strong correlation between ground rules and total runtime ($\rho = 0.948$) confirms grounding as the primary cost driver, with the right-skewed tail attributable to dense intersection scenarios. Some outliers exhibit disproportionately high runtime relative to their grounding size, likely due to complex local connectivity, such as roundabouts, that increases the number of admissible transitions per step and thus the combinatorial search space, independent of the total lane count. Solver behaviour is lightweight (mean conflicts 3.19, choices 10.24), reflecting effective constraint pruning. On average, 5.88 stable models (std 3.28, min 2, max 28) collapse to 2.94 trajectory modes (std 1.64, min 1, max 14), confirming that event-based grouping substantially reduces the hypothesis space. Scene complexity varies widely (mean 67.10 lanes, std 31.46, max 264), reflecting the diversity of urban layouts in Argoverse 2. More generally, the admissible mode space is shaped by domain-specific constraints such as lane-change spacing and traversal bounds, introducing an explicit tradeoff between behavioural coverage, normative plausibility, and computational tractability.

[3] **Argoverse 2** [19]., www.argoverse.org. The Argoverse 2 Motion Forecasting subset is a curated collection of 250,000 scenarios for training and validation. Each scenario is 11 s long and contains the 2D, birds-eye-view centroid and heading of each tracked object sampled at 10 Hz.

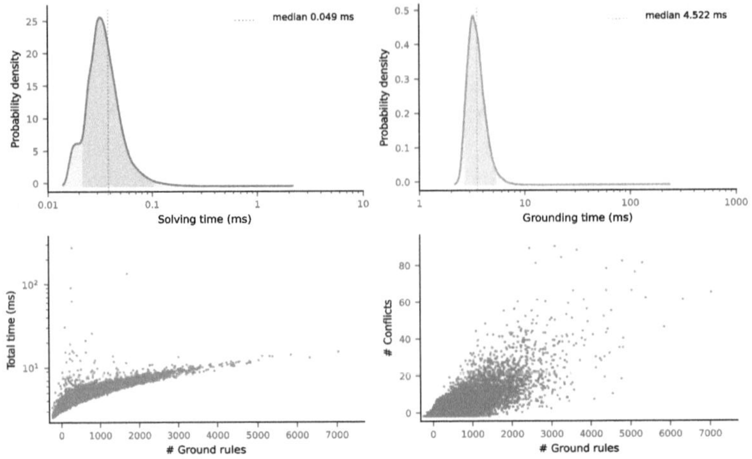

Fig. 4. ASP statistics. *Top:* distributions of solving time (left) and grounding time(right) on a log scale; dashed lines indicate medians. *Bottom:* total runtime (left) and number of conflicts (right) as a function of the number of ground rules.

Table 1. Lane path coverage. A 6-second prediction horizon.

Condition	Coverage (%) ↑
Reachable union	90.63
Oracle mode	87.78
Ranked mode	49.61

4.2 Lane Path Coverage

We evaluate geometric sufficiency by measuring the fraction of ground truth agent positions across the 6-second horizon that fall within lane polygons of the generated modes. Table 1 reports coverage under three conditions: (i) *Reachable union*: all lanes across all modes merged, giving an upper bound; (ii) *Oracle mode*: the single mode with highest coverage, measuring best-case performance; and (iii) *Ranked mode*: the mode selected by the ASP optimization.

Results. The reachable union (90.63%) and oracle mode (87.78%) confirm that the lane graph traversal generates a geometrically sufficient hypothesis space and that at least one mode closely tracks the ground truth in most scenarios. The small gap between the two (2.85 pp) indicates that the best mode rarely requires lanes outside the individually reachable set, i.e., most ground truth paths lie within a single coherent mode rather than requiring a union of several. The ranked mode drops substantially to 49.61%. This is attributable to the coarse resolution of the preference landscape. The minimisation assigns costs from a small discrete set (0, 1, or 5 per lane change, plus a count penalty), meaning that in many scenarios—particularly those where all reachable paths traverse only dashed markings and involve no lane changes—all stable models receive identical cost. Ties are broken arbitrarily, effectively reducing mode selection to random choice among equally-ranked alternatives. Closing this gap through richer preference models or learned preference weights is a natural extension of the framework. Having established that the symbolic mode space is geometrically well-founded, we evaluate continuous trajectory accuracy.

Table 2. Performance Evaluation. Results with standard trajectory metrics. Our method is compared with baseline models from [19], grouped by method type. For scenarios with less than six modes, only the available ones were used.

		top-k=1			top-k=6		
Model	**Type**	**minADE ↓**	**minFDE ↓**	**MR ↓**	**minADE ↓**	**minFDE ↓**	**MR ↓**
Constant Velocity [3]	Heuristic	7.75	17.44	0.89	–	–	–
Ours (map + const. speed)	Heuristic	6.72	16.35	0.92	4.33	10.30	0.85
Nearest Neighbor (map) [3]	Retrieval	6.45	15.51	0.84	4.30	10.08	0.78
LSTM (map) [3]	Learning	5.07	12.71	0.90	3.73	9.09	0.85
WIMP (map + social) [8]	Learning	3.09	7.71	0.84	1.47	2.90	0.42

4.3 Trajectory Evaluation

We evaluate single-agent vehicle forecasting using standard trajectory forecasting metrics. These include minimum Average Displacement Error (minADE), minimum Final Displacement Error (minFDE), and Miss Rate (FDE $> 2\,\text{m}$).

Results. Table 2 compares our results against Argoverse 2 baselines. Against the most directly comparable method—Constant Velocity, which also uses no learned components and shares the constant motion assumption—our method improves top-1 minADE (6.72 vs. 7.75), confirming that map-guided mode diversity yields meaningful gains over a single kinematic prediction. Our top-6 performance is comparable to the retrieval-based Nearest Neighbor approach despite using no training data, suggesting that explicit lane-graph reasoning recovers a similar quality of multi-modal diversity to non-parametric data-driven methods. The Miss Rate at top-1 (0.92) is slightly worse than Constant Velocity (0.89), consistent with the ranked-mode coverage gap where the conservative preference signal occasionally selects a mode that is geometrically plausible but behaviourally misaligned with the ground truth. Learning-based methods outperform ours on raw displacement metrics, as expected. WIMP [8], a graph neural network approach, additionally incorporates social context, placing it in a different class entirely.

We note that our method is not developed or positioned as a competitor or replacement of these learned approaches; rather, it constitutes an *explainable baseline* grounded in explicit reasoning over lane-structure and interaction events. Explainability is understood here as *traceability* in that each trajectory is fully traceable to its underlying stable model, event sequence, and lane-level path. This property is also illustrated in Fig. 5, which shows a few output examples. As such, the method provides a structured, interpretable foundation complementary to learned predictors, and a natural candidate for hybrid integration as a prior or constraint.

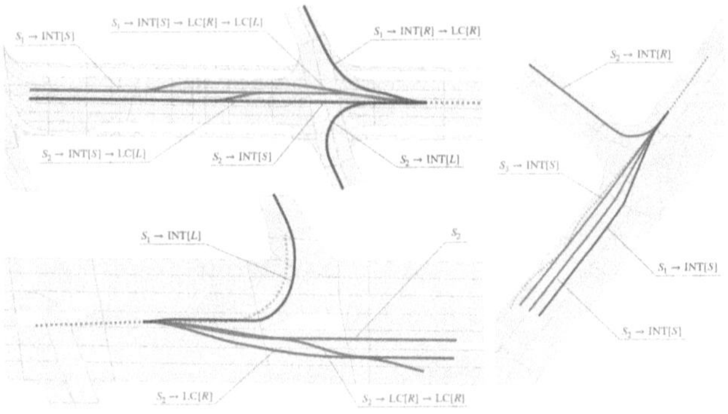

Fig. 5. Predicted Trajectories for Three Argoverse 2 Scenarios. Each coloured path corresponds to one trajectory mode, labelled by its event sequence. S_n denotes the starting node; blue dashed line indicates observation history; green dashed lines represent ground truth. Interpretations for INT[_] and LC[_] are as per Fig. 3.

5 Discussion and Related Work

Contemporary motion trajectory prediction is dominated by purely quantitative data-driven approaches that learn functional mappings from observed scene contexts to distributions over future trajectories [13]. Transformer-based architectures have emerged as the dominant paradigm [9,21,22]. For example, QCNet [22] reformulates agent–scene interaction through a query-centric representation that achieves roto-translation invariance and supports streaming scene encoding, attaining state-of-the-art performance on Argoverse 2. DeMo [21] decouples temporal and social feature extraction into separate pathways, improving efficiency and performance over end-to-end baselines while remaining within the learned latent paradigm. DONUT [9] pushes further by adopting a decoder-only autoregressive architecture inspired by language modelling, generating trajectory tokens in a single forward pass without an explicit encoder–decoder separation. While these methods achieve strong geometric accuracy on benchmarks, a structural limitation is common to all: the representations that mediate prediction—learned queries, latent modes, decoder hidden states—typically lack explicit interpretable semantics. A trajectory generated by QCNet cannot be explained in terms of which lane the vehicle was predicted to occupy, which intersection manoeuvre was anticipated, or which normative constraint was satisfied. The same geometric output could, in principle, arise from multiple qualitatively distinct behaviours without distinction. DeMo's decoupled features and DONUT's token sequence likewise provide no symbolic account of the behavioural mode selected. This opacity is not a limitation of any individual architecture but an inherent consequence of the end-to-end learning paradigm, where interpretability is not an inherent design objective, and mechanisms for systematic verification or retrospective diagnosability not directly achievable.

Goal-based and hierarchical methods [11,18,20] address the qualitative vs. quantitative gap by abstracting prediction into geometric targets or waypoints, but these targets are typically learned rather than derived from explicit commonsense reasoning over the environment structure. We take a complementary stance, closer in spirit to physics- and rule-based approaches [13]. Rather than learning to approximate the distribution of future trajectories, we enumerate qualitatively distinct behavioural hypotheses, e.g., pertaining road network geometry. Each generated trajectory is paired with a verifiable event sequence and a lane-level path, making the reasoning process fully traceable. However, the cost is geometric accuracy: a constant-speed kinematic model cannot match the displacement errors of learned predictors trained on hundreds of thousands of scenarios. On the other hand, the benefit is transparency in the sense that each output can be inspected, explained, and verified against the map and domain norms.

6 Conclusion and Outlook

We have developed a declarative method for hybrid qualitative-quantitative computation of reasonable trajectories of moving objects. The method is systematically formalised and evaluated with Argoverse 2, a state-of-the-art, community established benchmark in the domain of autonomous driving. The work is a departure from monolithic end-to-end approaches where explainability and interpretability are not design considerations per se. Our outlook is geared towards application in integrated perception and control, by combining motion trajectory commonsense about moving objects with (ASP-based) high-level visual sensemaking capabilities of *neurosymbolic vision* techniques (e.g., [12,16,17], as well as with emerging VisionâĂŞLanguage Models (VLMs; e.g., [14,15]) for low-level visual feature analysis in real-time vision tasks.

Acknowledgements. We acknowledge funding by the Swedish Research Council through the project *Counterfactual Commonsense* (Project 2022-02960_VR).

Disclosure of Interests. The authors have no competing interests to declare that are relevant to the content of this article.

References

1. Bhatt, M., Suchan, J.: Artificial visual intelligence: perceptual commonsense for human-centred cognitive technologies. In: ACAI. LNCS, vol. 13500, pp. 216–242 (2021)

2. Brewka, G., Eiter, T., Truszczyński, M.: Answer set programming at a glance. Commun. ACM **54**(12), 92–103 (2011)
3. Chang, M.F., et al.: Argoverse: 3D tracking and forecasting with rich maps. In: CVPR, pp. 8740–8749 (2019)
4. Davis, E.: Logical formalizations of commonsense reasoning: a survey. J. Artif. Intell. Res. **59**, 651–723 (2017)
5. Davis, E., Marcus, G.: Commonsense reasoning and commonsense knowledge in artificial intelligence. Commun. ACM **58**(9), 92–103 (2015)
6. European Commission: proposal for a regulation laying down harmonised rules on artificial intelligence (artificial intelligence act) (2021)
7. Gebser, M., Kaminski, R., Kaufmann, B., Schaub, T.: Clingo = ASP + control: preliminary report. CoRR **abs/1405.3694** (2014)
8. Khandelwal, S., Qi, W., Singh, J., Hartnett, A., Ramanan, D.: What-if motion prediction for autonomous driving (2020). https://arxiv.org/abs/2008.10587
9. Knoche, M., de Geus, D., Leibe, B.: DONUT: a decoder-only model for trajectory prediction. In: ICCV, pp. 28903–28912 (2025)
10. Lifschitz, V.: Answer Set Programming. Springer (2019)
11. Mangalam, K., An, Y., Girase, H., Malik, J.: From goals, waypoints & paths to long term human trajectory forecasting. In: ICCV, pp. 15213–15222 (2021)
12. Monsen, J., Suchan, J., Bhatt, M.: Probabilistic answer set programming driven ranking of dynamic space-time belief models. In: RuleML+RR, pp. 156–175 (2025)
13. Shi, J., et al.: Motion forecasting for autonomous vehicles: a survey (2025). https://arxiv.org/abs/2502.08664
14. Siméoni, O., et al.: Dinov3 (2025). https://arxiv.org/abs/2508.10104
15. Suchan, J., Baloch, S., Bhatt, M.: Towards a VLM-based foundation for generalised neurosymbolic visual commonsense. In: FoIKS, pp. 359–365 (2026)
16. Suchan, J., Bhatt, M., Monsen, J.: ASP-driven visual commonsense: a general framework for reasoning about embodied interaction in the wild. In: KR (2025)
17. Suchan, J., Bhatt, M., Varadarajan, S.: Commonsense visual sensemaking for autonomous driving: on generalised neurosymbolic online abduction integrating vision and semantics. Artif. Intell. **299**, 103522 (2021)
18. Wang, M., et al.: Ganet: goal area network for motion forecasting. In: ICRA, pp. 1609–1615 (2023)
19. Wilson, B., et al.: Argoverse 2: next generation datasets for self-driving perception and forecasting. In: NeurIPS Datasets and Benchmarks (2021)
20. Yao, Z., Li, X., Lang, B., Chuah, M.C.: Goal-lbp: goal-based local behavior guided trajectory prediction for autonomous driving. IEEE Trans. Intell. Transp. Syst. **25**(7), 6770–6779 (2024)
21. Zhang, B., Song, N., Zhang, L.: DeMo: decoupling motion forecasting into directional intentions and dynamic states. In: NeurIPS (2024)
22. Zhou, Z., Wang, J., Li, Y.H., Huang, Y.K.: Query-centric trajectory prediction. In: CVPR, pp. 17863–17873 (2023)

Flaspland: A Testbed for Routing and Scheduling in ASP

Ryan Murphy[1(✉)], Amadé Nemes[1], Javier Romero[1], and Torsten Schaub[1,2]

[1] University of Potsdam, Potsdam, Germany
{ryan.murphy, balazs.amade.nemes, javier.romero.davila, torsten.schaub}@uni-potsdam.de
[2] Potassco Solutions GmbH, Werder, Germany

Abstract. We present *flaspland*, an Answer Set Programming (ASP) testbed for tackling complex routing and scheduling problems within the Flatland railway simulation environment. To establish a solid theoretical foundation, we provide a rigorous formalization of the Flatland environment, detailing its grid-based topology and navigational dynamics. Building upon this, we propose and analyze three distinct graph-based representations to effectively encode the underlying constraints. Crucially, we introduce a twofold, path-driven ASP encoding scheme that decouples spatial routing from temporal scheduling. Our empirical results demonstrate that our approach outperforms off-the-shelf multi-agent pathfinding approaches. By establishing a testbed for real-world railway scheduling, *flaspland* facilitates the evaluation and advancement of declarative approaches to qualitative and quantitative temporal constraints.

1 Introduction

The ability of Answer Set Programming (ASP; [10]) to easily express reachability makes it a prime candidate for addressing routing problems, such as multi-agent pathfinding [5], phylogenetic inference [4], and wire routing [6]. However, this advantage is challenged once routing is combined with scheduling to enforce deadlines and durations, since fine-grained quantitative temporal reasoning cannot be feasibly represented in ASP [2].

To address this, we propose railway scheduling as a rich and scalable benchmark for exploring routing and scheduling problems in ASP. We specifically advocate for Flatland [8], a grid-based railway simulation environment developed by major European railway operators, which enables scalable experimentation with complex railway scenarios.

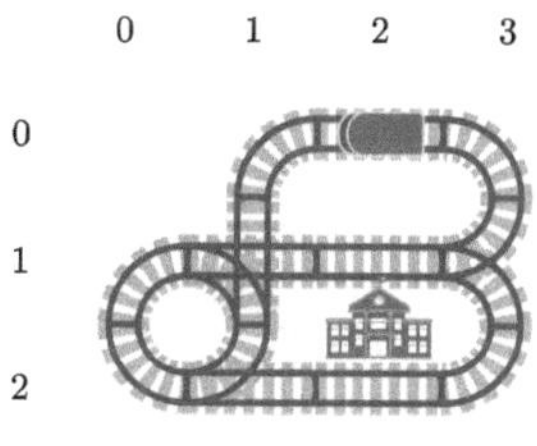

Fig. 1. Visualization of a simple Flatland scenario

The core task is to solve collision-free routing and scheduling problems, which are essentially multi-agent pathfinding problems (MAPF; [14]) augmented with quantitative constraints on train arrival and departure times, durations, energy, and speed.

W. Faber et al. (Eds.): LPNMR 2026, LNAI 16952, pp. 349–364, 2027.
https://doi.org/10.1007/978-3-032-38320-4_22

A railway network is modeled as a set of connected cells using matrix notation, as shown in Fig. 1. The traversability of cells is defined by specific track types (see Fig. 2), which dictate valid transitions. The overall objective is to navigate all trains to their destinations, respecting strict time windows and preventing collisions. Navigation is performed via discrete actions, whose executability is constrained by the train's current direction and the underlying track configuration.

Beyond quantitative scheduling constraints, such railway networks present structural challenges that differentiate this task from standard MAPF: (i) Track types strictly limit valid cell transitions, requiring precise modeling of graph connectivity. (ii) A train's ability to move depends on its current orientation, adding another layer of complexity to path planning. (iii) The network topology often features canalized passages with limited switching points, restricting navigational choices and creating bottlenecks.

In what follows, we provide a formal account of Flatland, detailing its environment, invariants, and path definitions. Although Flatland's tasks are intuitively well understood, a rigorous formalization is necessary to establish the correspondence between railway grids and their (graph-based) representations, and ultimately to ensure the correctness and completeness of ASP encodings. We then propose alternative graph-based representations of railway networks and establish their correspondence to the original grid environment. To facilitate empirical evaluation, we introduce the *flaspland* toolkit bridging ASP and the Flatland environment. Finally, we present a novel two-fold, path-driven ASP encoding scheme. Our empirical evaluation shows that our approach offers significant scalability improvements over off-the-shelf MAPF approaches.

2 Flatland Formalization

To begin with, we present some crosscutting concepts. Flatland considers a set $D = \{n, e, s, w\}$ of cardinal *directions* and a set T of *track types*. We define the following operations on directions to compute their opposite and 90-degree rotations:

1. $\overline{(\cdot)} : D \to D$ where $\overline{(\cdot)} = \{\overline{n} \mapsto s, \overline{s} \mapsto n, \overline{e} \mapsto w, \overline{w} \mapsto e\}$
2. $(\cdot)^r : D \to D$ where $(\cdot)^r = \{n^r \mapsto e,\ e^r \mapsto s,\ s^r \mapsto w,\ w^r \mapsto n\}$
3. $(\cdot)^l : D \to D$ where $(\cdot)^l = \{n^l \mapsto w,\ w^l \mapsto s,\ s^l \mapsto e,\ e^l \mapsto n\}$

Clearly, we have $\overline{\overline{d}} = d$, $d^{2r} = d^{2l} = \overline{d}$, and $d^{4r} = d^{4l} = d$ for $d \in D$.

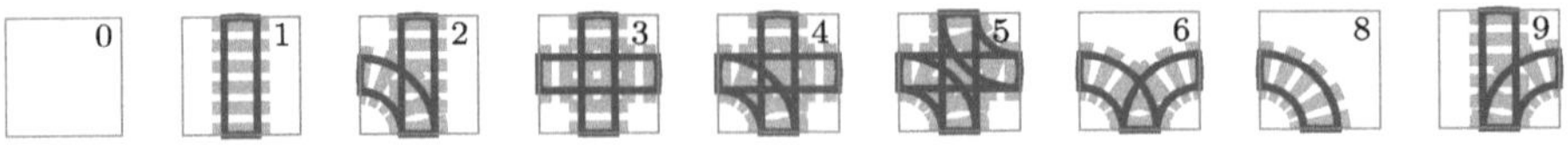

Fig. 2. Basic track types.

Flatland's general track types are shown in Fig. 2.[1] Type 0 is reserved for empty cells. Specific track types are derived by rotating these general types in 90-degree increments. For example, the simple switch at position $(2, 1)$ in Fig. 1 corresponds to Type 2

[1] We omit track type 7, the dead end, as recent versions of Flatland no longer produce environments with this type of track.

rotated by 90°, denoted as $(2, 90)$. Each track type $t \in T$ provides a set of *transitions*, captured by the relation $H_t \subseteq D \times D$ satisfying for all $d, d' \in D$:

1. $(d, d') \in H_t$ iff $(\overline{d'}, \overline{d}) \in H_t$
2. $(d, \overline{d}) \notin H_t$
3. $|\{(d, d'') \in H_t \mid d'' \in D\}| \leq 2$ and $|\{(d'', d) \in H_t \mid d'' \in D\}| \leq 2$

That is, every transition has a complementary one, no transition represents an immediate about-face, and there may be no more than two transitions for the same incoming and outgoing direction. For instance, we have $H_{(2,90)} = \{(e, e), (w, w), (e, n), (s, w)\}$.

Notation. The directions D, track types T, and transitions $(H_t)_{t \in T}$ are constant across all Flatland environments and are therefore assumed fixed in the remainder of this work.

Grids. In Flatland, a railway network is an $n \times m$ grid of cells C. We associate each *cell* $c \in C$ with a coordinate position and a track type, via the total functions:

1. $p : C \to [0, n] \times [0, m]$
2. $t : C \to T$

We require p to be a bijective function. For the cell[2] $c_{2,1}$ with the simple switch, we have $p(c_{2,1}) = (2, 1)$ and $t(c_{2,1}) = (2, 90)$. The relation $H_{t(c)}$ provides the set of transitions for a cell $c \in C$, and we call c *trivial* whenever $H_{t(c)} = \emptyset$.

The cell adjacent to cell $c \in C$ in direction $d \in D$ is defined by the partial function

1. $a : C \times D \to C$

such that

$$p(a(c, d)) = \begin{cases} (i-1, j) & \text{if } p(c) = (i, j),\ d = n, \text{ and } (i, j), (i-1, j) \in [0, n] \times [0, m] \\ (i, j+1) & \text{if } p(c) = (i, j),\ d = e, \text{ and } (i, j), (i, j+1) \in [0, n] \times [0, m] \\ (i+1, j) & \text{if } p(c) = (i, j),\ d = s, \text{ and } (i, j), (i+1, j) \in [0, n] \times [0, m] \\ (i, j-1) & \text{if } p(c) = (i, j),\ d = w, \text{ and } (i, j), (i, j-1) \in [0, n] \times [0, m] \end{cases}$$

Function a is partial because of border cells. If $a(c, d) \neq a(c, d')$ then $d \neq d'$ for all $c \in C$ and $d, d' \in D$. Moreover, we have $a(c, d) = c'$ iff $a(c', \overline{d}) = c$ for all $c, c' \in C$ and $d \in D$. For instance, we have $a(c_{2,1}, w) = c_{2,0}$ and $a(c_{2,0}, e) = c_{2,1}$, whereas $a(c_{2,1}, s)$ is undefined.

A non-trivial cell $c \in C$ is connected to another non-trivial cell $c' \in C$ in direction $d \in D$, written as $c \overset{d}{\hookrightarrow} c'$, when the following conditions hold:

1. $a(c, d) = c'$
2. $(d', d) \in H_{t(c)}$ for some $d' \in \{d, d^l, d^r\}$
3. $(d, d'') \in H_{t(c')}$ for some $d'' \in \{d, d^l, d^r\}$

---

[2] The subscript in $c_{2,1}$ is just to ease readability.

Condition 3 is equivalent to $(d'', \overline{d}) \in H_{t(c')}$. Moreover, we have $c \overset{d}{\hookrightarrow} c'$ iff $c' \overset{\overline{d}}{\hookrightarrow} c$ for all $c, c' \in C$ and $d \in D$. Continuing our example, we get $c_{2,1} \overset{w}{\hookrightarrow} c_{2,0}$ since $a(c_{2,1}, w) = c_{2,0}$, $(s, w) \in H(t(c_{2,1}))$, and $(w, n) \in H(t(c_{2,0}))$, and hence $c_{2,0} \overset{e}{\hookrightarrow} c_{2,1}$, too.

A *transit pair* (c, d) combines a non-trivial cell $c \in C$ and direction $d \in D$ such that $(d', d) \in H_{t(c)}$ for some $d' \in D$. The cell $c_{2,1}$ gives rise to three transit pairs: $(c_{2,1}, e)$, $(c_{2,1}, w)$, and $(c_{2,1}, n)$, corresponding to the three possible outgoing directions. We denote the set of all transit pairs for a grid of cells C by $\mathcal{T}(C)$. We require for each transit pair (c, d) that $c \overset{d}{\hookrightarrow} c'$ for some $c' \in C$. This condition ensures each outgoing track leads to an incoming track on the neighboring cell.

We define a *transit path* as a sequence $((c_i, d_i))_{i=0}^{n}$ of distinct transit pairs with $n > 0$ such that for all $0 \leq i < n$:

1. $c_i \overset{d_i}{\hookrightarrow} c_{i+1}$
2. $(d_i, d_{i+1}) \in H_{t(c_{i+1})}$

Transit paths are non-trivial, as they comprise at least two transit pairs. We call $((c_i, d_i))_{i=0}^{n}$ a transit path between (c_0, d_0) and (c_n, d_n). Condition 2 can be seen as an instantiation of Condition 3 in the definition of connectedness with the outgoing direction of the subsequent cell. While a cell may be revisited, each visit must be associated with a different outgoing direction. Also, all but the last direction capture transitions between cells; the final one is an arbitrary choice among all outgoing directions of the last cell.

For illustration, consider the following transit path between $c_{0,1}$ and $c_{1,2}$ in Fig. 1:

$$((c_{0,1}, s), (c_{1,1}, s), (c_{2,1}, w), (c_{2,0}, n), (c_{1,0}, e), (c_{1,1}, e), (c_{1,2}, e)) \tag{1}$$

Note that cell $c_{1,1}$ is traversed twice, once southwards and once eastwards.

In practice, Flatland environments are always strongly connected. To capture this formally, we require that for any two cells $c, c' \in C$, there is a transit path connecting some transit pairs (c, d) and (c', d') with $d, d' \in D$.

Notation. We associate a Flatland grid with its set C of cells and leave functions p, t, and a implicit.

Trains. Consider a set Z of *trains*, where each train's start and goal positions, initial orientation, earliest departure, and latest arrival are given by the functions:

1. $s : Z \to C$ and $g : Z \to C$ such that $s(z) \neq g(z)$ for all $z \in Z$
2. $o : Z \to D$ such that $(d, o(z)) \in H_{s(z)}$ for some $d \in D$ and for all $z \in Z$
3. $\delta : Z \to \mathbb{N}$ and $\alpha : Z \to \mathbb{N}$ such that $\alpha(z) > \delta(z)$ for all $z \in Z$

The provisos stipulate that the starting and goal positions differ for each train, that the initial orientation of a train is always among the outbound directions of its starting track, and that time is discrete, with the arrival time strictly exceeding the departure time.

Notation. The functions s, g, o, δ, and αassociated with the trains in Z are left implicit.

A *Flatland scenario* is a pair (C, Z), comprising a set C of cells and a set Z of trains. A train drive is a transit path that tolerates repeated transit pairs to mimic waiting, meets the train's initial orientation and its start and goal position, and respects the earliest departure time. Accordingly, we define a *train drive* for a train $z \in Z$ and some $m, n \in \mathbb{N}$ in a Flatland scenario (C, Z) as a sequence $((c_i, d_i))_{i=m}^{n}$ of transit pairs such that

1. for all $m \leq i < n$ either
   1. $c_i \overset{d_i}{\hookrightarrow} c_{i+1}$ and $(d_i, d_{i+1}) \in H_{t(c_{i+1})}$, or
   2. $(c_i, d_i) = (c_{i+1}, d_{i+1})$
2. $(c_m, d_m) = (s(z), o(z))$
3. $c_n = g(z)$ and $c_i \neq g(z)$ for all $m \leq i < n$
4. $m \geq \delta(z)$

Numbers m and n reflect the actual departure and arrival times of train z. The scheduled arrival time, $\alpha(z)$, is considered separately in delay calculations. Train drives are non-trivial since $s(z) \neq g(z)$.

Actions. Trains have four possible actions:[3] move forward (f), turn left (l), turn right (r), and wait (w). A transit pair (c, d) and one of its transitions $(d^i, d) \in H_{t(c)}$ induce the action a where:

1. $a = f$ if
   (a) $H_{t(c)} \cap (\{d^i\} \times D) = \{(d^i, d)\}$ or
   (b) $H_{t(c)} \supset \{(d, d), (d, d')\}$ for $d^i = d$ and some $d' \in \{d^l, d^r\}$
2. $a = l$ if $H_{t(c)} \supset \{(d^r, d), (d^r, d')\}$ for $d^i = d^r$ and some $d' \in \{\overline{d}, d^r\}$
3. $a = r$ if $H_{t(c)} \supset \{(d^l, d), (d^l, d')\}$ for $d^i = d^l$ and some $d' \in \{\overline{d}, d^l\}$

No navigational choice is required in (1a) since there is only one alternative when entering from direction d^i. A second analogous entry point may exist (e.g., track types 6 and 8), but the choice of action f remains unambiguous. The three other cases, (1b), (2) and (3), are analogous in that they all require choosing d as the outgoing direction from two possible alternatives, using action f, l or r, respectively. Transit pairs induce unique actions, either f, l, or r. Two identical transit pairs form a w[ait] action.

Given a train drive $((c_i, d_i))_{i=m}^{n}$ for train $z \in Z$ in a Flatland scenario (C, Z), we define a *plan* for train z in (C, Z) as a sequence $(a_i)_{i=m}^{n-1}$ of actions such that for $m \leq i < n$

1. $a_i = w$ if $(c_i, d_i) = (c_{i+1}, d_{i+1})$ and
2. a_i is induced by (c_i, d_i) otherwise.

Table 1 details a sample plan for train z traveling from $s(z) = c_{0,2}$ to $g(z) = c_{2,2}$ (in Fig. 1) given initial conditions $o(z) = w$ and $\delta(z) = 0$. The plan requires only two navigational decisions, at steps 6 and 9, with all other movements being deterministic f actions, except for the wait at step 7. The decision at step 6 is made at cell $c_{1,1}$, where the train has two possible transits: one continuing east, via (e, e), and another turning south, via (e, s), both of which are members of $H_{t(c_{1,1})}$. The choice of outbound direction e is reflected by the inclusion of $(c_{1,1}, e)$ in the train drive. Similarly, when transiting $c_{1,3}$ eastwards at step 9, the train may go north or south, since both (e, n) and (e, s) belong to $H_{t(c_{1,3})}$. The transit pair $(c_{1,3}, s)$ reflects the southbound trajectory of the train.

[3] Flatland provides a fifth action, *do nothing*, which we consider superfluous and therefore omit from this formalization.

Collisions. In Flatland, trains appear upon departure and disappear once they reach their destination. Two distinct drives $((c_i, d_i))_{i=m}^{n}$ and $((c'_i, d'_i))_{i=m'}^{n'}$ have

1. a *vertex conflict* if $c_i = c'_i$ for some $i \in [\max(m, m'), \min(n, n')]$
2. an *edge conflict* if $c_{i+1} = c'_i$ and $c_i = c'_{i+1}$ for some $i, i+1 \in [\max(m, m'), \min(n, n')]$

Solution. A *solution* to a Flatland scenario (C, Z) is a family $(\pi_z)_{z\in Z}$ of plans π_z such that all drives underlying $(\pi_z)_{z\in Z}$ are pairwisely vertex and edge conflict-free. The delay of a plan π_z for a train $z \in Z$ is defined as $delay(\pi_z) = \max(0, n - \alpha(z))$ where n is the actual arrival time of z with plan π_z. A *delay optimal* solution to (C, Z) is a solution $(\pi_z)_{z\in Z}$ to (C, Z) with a minimum value of $\sum_{z\in Z} delay(\pi_z)$

i	a_i	(c_i, d_i)
0	f	$(c_{0,2}, w)$
1	f	$(c_{0,1}, s)$
2	f	$(c_{1,1}, s)$
3	f	$(c_{2,1}, w)$
4	f	$(c_{2,0}, n)$
5	f	$(c_{1,0}, e)$
6	f	$(c_{1,1}, e)$
7	w	$(c_{1,2}, e)$
8	f	$(c_{1,2}, e)$
9	r	$(c_{1,3}, s)$
10	f	$(c_{2,3}, w)$
11		$(c_{2,2}, w)$

Table 1. A plan from $c_{0,2}$ to the station in $c_{2,2}$ in Fig. 1

3 Graph Representations

We now consider alternative graph representations for modeling railway networks in Flatland. In particular, we must account for the complex movement dynamics around switches. The adjacency of two cells is a necessary condition for a transition, but not a sufficient one. Furthermore, the incoming direction of the train determines its valid outbound movements. For instance, cell $c_{2,1}$ has three neighboring cells in Fig. 1. However, only a train facing east can transit from $c_{2,1}$ to its adjacent cells $c_{1,1}$ or $c_{2,2}$, and its neighboring cell $c_{2,0}$ can only be reached by trains facing south or west. In what follows, we translate grid environments into alternative graph structures that inherently encode these directional constraints. We establish one-to-one correspondences between transit paths in Flatland and paths within the respective graphs.

Graphs with Edge Transition Functions. Given a grid C, we define the directed graph $\mathcal{A}(C) = (V, E)$ as

1. $E = \bigcup_{c\in C, d\in D} \{(c, c') \mid c \overset{d}{\hookrightarrow} c'\}$
2. $V = \{c, c' \mid (c, c') \in E\}$

The graph $\mathcal{A}(C)$ contains no trivial cells from C. To capture transitions, we associate with each graph $\mathcal{A}(C) = (V, E)$ two partial functions on its set of edges:

1. $d : E \to D$ where $d((c, c')) = d$ if $c \overset{d}{\hookrightarrow} c'$ for $(c, c') \in E$
2. $p : E \to 2^D$ where $p((c, c')) = \{d'' \mid (d'', d) \in H_{t(c)}\}$ if $c \overset{d}{\hookrightarrow} c'$ for $(c, c') \in E$.

Function d reflects the direction of a directed edge, while p gives the necessary arriving directions when leaving a node. For illustration, consider the application of function d and p to the incoming and outgoing edges of node $c_{2,1}$ from Fig. 1.

$$d((c_{2,0}, c_{2,1})) = e \qquad p((c_{2,1}, c_{2,0})) = \{s, w\} \tag{2}$$

$$d((c_{1,1}, c_{2,1})) = s \qquad p((c_{2,1}, c_{2,2})) = \{e\} \tag{3}$$

$$d((c_{2,2}, c_{2,1})) = w \qquad p((c_{2,1}, c_{1,1})) = \{e\} \tag{4}$$

The interplay of both functions determines whether an incoming and outgoing edge form a transition over a node. This is the case for a node c, whenever $d((c', c)) \in p((c, c''))$ for some connected nodes c', c''. Four combinations of the mappings above satisfy this condition for $c_{2,1}$, which reflect the four possible transitions over $c_{2,1}$.

Given a grid C, we define a path in $\mathcal{A}(C)$ as a sequence $(c_i)_{i=0}^n$ of vertices with $n > 0$ such that

1. $(c_i, c_{i+1}) \in E$ for all $0 \leq i < n$
2. $d((c_{i-1}, c_i)) \in p((c_i, c_{i+1}))$ for all $0 < i < n$
3. if $c_i = c_j$ then $c_{i+1} \neq c_{j+1}$ for all $0 \leq i < j < n$

We call $(c_i)_{i=0}^n$ a path between c_0 and c_n in $\mathcal{A}(C)$. For example, the transit path $((c_{1,1}, s), (c_{2,1}, w), (c_{2,0}, n))$ between $c_{1,1}$ and $c_{2,0}$ in our grid C in Fig. 1 corresponds to the path $(c_{1,1}, c_{2,1}, c_{2,0})$ in $\mathcal{A}(C)$ and satisfies $d((c_{1,1}, c_{2,1})) \in p((c_{2,1}, c_{2,0}))$.

The following proposition shows that our graph representation preserves all paths in the original grid.

Proposition 1. *Let C be a grid.*

1. *If $((c_i, d_i))_{i=0}^n$ is a transit path in grid C, then $(c_i)_{i=0}^n$ is a path in the graph $\mathcal{A}(C)$.*
2. *If $(c_i)_{i=0}^n$ is a path in the graph $\mathcal{A}(C)$, then $((c_i, d_i))_{i=0}^n$ is a transit path in grid C, where $d_i = d((c_i, c_{i+1}))$ for $0 \leq i < n$ and $d_n = d((c_n, c))$ for some $c \in C$.*

Graph with Sub-nodes. Given a grid C, we define the directed graph $\mathcal{B}(C) = (V, E)$ as

1. $V = \mathcal{T}(C)$
2. $E = \{((c, d), (c', d')) \in V \times V \mid c \overset{d}{\hookrightarrow} c', (d, d') \in H_{t(c')}\}$

The graph $\mathcal{B}(C)$ connects all transit pairs of a grid. Fragmenting cells into transit pairs and relating them in terms of their connectivity allows us to account for the transitions over the various track types.

Cell $c_{2,1}$ is now decomposed into three nodes, $(c_{2,1}, e)$, $(c_{2,1}, w)$, and $(c_{2,1}, n)$, corresponding to its three transit pairs. Intuitively, the above edge transition functions are compiled into the refined graph structure. Each node (or transit pair) represents one way of exiting a node. The four possible passages over $c_{2,1}$ are reflected by the four edges entering the three nodes derived from $c_{2,1}$.

Given a grid C, we define a path in $\mathcal{B}(C)$ as a sequence $((c_i, d_i))_{i=0}^n$ of transit pairs with $n > 0$ such that

1. $((c_i, d_i), (c_{i+1}, d_{i+1})) \in E$ for all $0 \leq i < n$
2. if $(c_i, d_i) = (c_j, d_j)$, then $i = j$ for all $0 \leq i < j < n$

We call $((c_i, d_i))_{i=0}^n$ a path between (c_0, d_0) and (c_n, d_n) in $\mathcal{B}(C)$. The transit path $((c_{1,1}, s), (c_{2,1}, w), (c_{2,0}, n))$ in our grid C in Fig. 1 is also a path in $\mathcal{B}(C)$.

Proposition 2. *Let C be a grid.*

1. *If $((c_i, d_i))_{i=0}^n$ is a transit path in C, then $((c_i, d_i))_{i=0}^n$ is a path in the graph $\mathcal{B}(C)$.*
2. *If $((c_i, d_i))_{i=0}^n$ is a path in the graph $\mathcal{B}(C)$, then $((c_i, d_i))_{i=0}^n$ is a transit path in C.*

Graphs with Hyper-Edges. Given a grid C, we define the graph $\mathcal{H}(C) = (V, E)$ as

1. $E = \bigcup_{c \in C, d \in D} \{(c, c', c'') \mid c \overset{d}{\hookrightarrow} c', c' \overset{d'}{\hookrightarrow} c'', (d, d') \in H_{t(c')}\}$
2. $V = \{c, c', c'' \mid (c, c', c'') \in E\}$

The directed graph $\mathcal{H}(C)$ uses directed hyper-edges among the non-trivial cells of the original grid C. Each hyper-edge captures a valid passage over a node by connecting it to its predecessor and successor in this transition.

We get four hyper-edges centered upon node $c_{2,1}$, namely,

$$(c_{2,0}, c_{2,1}, c_{2,2}) \qquad (c_{2,0}, c_{2,1}, c_{1,1}) \tag{5}$$

$$(c_{1,1}, c_{2,1}, c_{2,0}) \qquad (c_{2,2}, c_{2,1}, c_{2,0}) \tag{6}$$

These hyper-edges correspond to the four passages over $c_{2,1}$ discussed above.

Given a grid C, we define a path in $\mathcal{H}(C)$ as a sequence $(c_i)_{i=0}^{n}$ of vertices with $n > 0$ such that

1. $(c_{i-1}, c_i, c_{i+1}) \in E$ for all $0 < i < n$
2. $(c, c_0, c_1) \in E$ and $(c_{n-1}, c_n, c') \in E$ for some $c, c' \in V$
3. if $c_i = c_j$ then $c_{i+1} \neq c_{j+1}$ for all $0 \leq i < j < n$

We call $(c_i)_{i=0}^{n}$ a path between c_0 and c_n in $\mathcal{H}(C)$. Condition 2 ensures that the constraints imposed by hyper-edges are satisfied at the endpoints of each path, and for paths of length two. For example, the transit path $((c_{1,1}, s), (c_{2,1}, w), (c_{2,0}, n))$ between $c_{1,1}$ and $c_{2,0}$ in our grid C corresponds to the path $(c_{1,1}, c_{2,1}, c_{2,0})$ in $\mathcal{H}(C) = (V, E)$ satisfying $\{(c_{0,1}, c_{1,1}, c_{2,1}), (c_{1,1}, c_{2,1}, c_{2,0}), (c_{2,1}, c_{2,0}, c_{1,0})\} \subseteq E$.

Proposition 3. *Let C be a grid.*

1. *If $((c_i, d_i))_{i=0}^{n}$ is a transit path in grid C, then $(c_i)_{i=0}^{n}$ is a path in the graph $\mathcal{H}(C)$.*
2. *If $(c_i)_{i=0}^{n}$ is a path in the graph $\mathcal{H}(C)$, then $((c_i, d_i))_{i=0}^{n}$ is a transit path in grid C, where $c_i \overset{d_i}{\hookrightarrow} c_{i+1}$ for $0 \leq i < n$ and $c_n \overset{d_n}{\hookrightarrow} c$ for some $c \in C$.*

4 *Flaspland*: Flatland to ASP and Back

Flaspland is an open-source toolkit connecting ASP with the Flatland ecosystem [8]. It converts Flatland environments into a fixed ASP fact format, and maps the resulting answer sets back to Flatland actions for execution and visualization. Flatland environments are produced as Python objects, which are then transformed into ASP facts so that they can be processed by *clingo* encodings, shown by arrow (1) in Fig. 3. By integrating directly with Flatland's native generator, *flaspland* bypasses manual instance construction and supports batch generation to streamline large-scale experiments. *Flaspland* calls user-defined encodings along with an environment to produce answer sets, shown by arrow (2) in

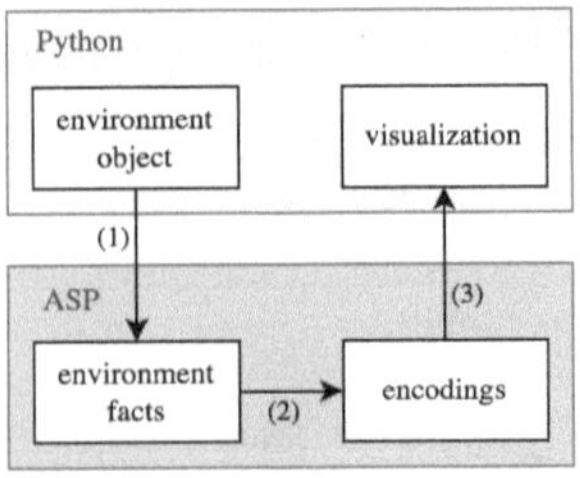

Fig. 3. *flaspland* architecture

Fig. 3. Such an architecture enables encodings to leverage alternative environment representations, such as those defined in Sect. 3, as well as encodings that handle the pathfinding logic, described in greater detail in Sect. 5. Encodings must adhere to a specific fact format to be compatible with the toolkit. *Flaspland* then translates answer sets back into Flatland actions, shown by arrow (3) in Fig. 3, allowing for immediate execution and visualization of the resulting plans. This visual feedback is crucial for debugging and validating the correctness of the ASP encodings.

Additionally, the toolkit serves as a benchmark repository for reproducible evaluation, housing all 150 environments used in the Flatland 3 competition finals. These instances vary in grid size, agent count, city distribution, train speeds, and malfunction rates. The *flaspland* toolkit is publicly available at [12].

5 Encodings

We now present the ASP encodings for addressing routing and scheduling in Flatland, starting with the representation of the environment's basic topological and navigational concepts. All encodings are available at [13].

The fact format of the basic concepts regarding directions is given in Listing 1.1.

```
     dir(n).            dir(s).          dir(w).            dir(e).
 inverse(n,s).     inverse(s,n).   inverse(w,e).     inverse(e,w).
    left(n,w).        left(s,e).      left(w,s).        left(e,n).
   right(n,e).       right(s,w).     right(w,n).       right(e,s).
  offset(n,-1,0). offset(s,1,0). offset(w,0,-1). offset(e,0,1).
```

Listing 1.1. Representation of directions (n,s,w,e)

Predicate `dir/1` gives the cardinal directions, `inverse/2` provides complementary directions, `left/2` and `right/2` capture 90-degree rotations, and `offset/3` gives a coordinate offset when moving in a certain direction.

In Flatland, each track type has a numeric identifier that is based on its possible transitions; it is represented via predicate `transition/2`. Listing 1.2 contains all facts reflecting the four transitions of the simple switch at position $(2, 1)$ in Fig. 1.[4]

```
transition(3089,(s,w))
transition(3089,(w,w))
transition(3089,(e,e))
transition(3089,(e,n))
```

Listing 1.2. Selected lines of track type representations

The original grid is represented by `cell/2` atoms, where the first argument reflects the coordinates of a cell and the second gives its track type. These coordinates serve as both the cell identifier and the value of the position function p. The available transitions for each cell are obtained by joining the `cell/2` and `transition/2` predicates.

```
start(0,(0,2),0,w).
end(0,(2,2),12).

cell((0,0),     0). cell((0,1),16386). cell((0,2),1025). cell((0,3),4608).
cell((1,0),16386). cell((1,1),38433). cell((1,2),1025). cell((1,3),6672).
```

[4] The value 3089 at $(2, 1)$ in Fig. 1 is derived from the 16-bit encoding `0000 1100 0001 0001` for $H_{t(2,1)}$. It consists of four 4-bit blocks representing incoming orientations (n,e,s,w), where each bit flags a valid outgoing direction (n,e,s,w).

```
6 cell((2,0),   72). cell((2,1), 3089). cell((2,2),1025). cell((2,3),2064).
```

Listing 1.3. The fact representation of our running example (Figure 1)

Furthermore, the instance format uses `start/4` and `end/3` atoms to define the initial and target configurations of trains. The first two arguments of these predicates identify the train z and its starting $s(z)$ or ending $g(z)$ position, respectively (e.g. Lines 1mm and 2 of Listing 1.3). The third and fourth arguments of `start/4` indicate the earliest departure time $\delta(z)$ and initial orientation $o(z)$, while the third argument of `end/3` specifies the latest arrival time $\alpha(z)$.

The adjacency function a and the connectivity relation $\hookrightarrow$ are defined in Listing 1.4, using predicates `adjacent/3` and `connected/3`, respectively.

```
adjacent((X,Y),D,(X',Y')) :-  cell((X,Y),_), cell((X',Y'),_),
    offset(D,DX,DY), X'=X+DX, Y'=Y+DY.

connected((X,Y),D,(X',Y')) :- cell((X,Y),T), cell((X',Y'),T'),
    adjacent((X,Y),D,(X',Y')),
    transition(T,(D',D)), transition(T',(D,D'')).
```

Listing 1.4. Representation of grid functions

The fact representation introduced above, generated by our *flaspland* framework from Flatland scenarios, serves as the basic input for our ASP encodings. Building upon this basis, we investigate the efficacy of the three graph-based representations defined in Sect. 3 in modeling train dynamics and interactions.

Our encoding design is driven by two main objectives. First, we aim to evaluate the computational trade-offs of the proposed topological representations, specifically regarding how the choice of structural abstraction influences ASP solving performance. Second, our encodings must robustly address the spatio-temporal complexities inherent to train scheduling. Foremost is the need to model waiting actions for collision avoidance, which inherently decouples spatial transitions from strict temporal succession. Further complexities stem from the asynchronous life-cycle of trains, such as their variable appearance, delayed departures, and disappearance upon arrival. Moreover, a train's initial orientation can typically only be verified upon its actual departure.

We address these spatio-temporal complexities by decomposing the synthesis of train drives into two distinct aspects: spatial routing and temporal scheduling. The routing component establishes the backbone of a train's journey by identifying a valid path between its start and destination. Crucially, while these paths may revisit nodes, they prohibit consecutive duplicate nodes. This abstraction of temporal waiting ensures that spatial transitions can be directly verified against the underlying track topology. The scheduling component then refines these spatial paths into fully realized train drives by inserting appropriate waiting times to enforce collision avoidance.

In the following, we present a specialized path encoding for each graph representation and subsequently integrate these encodings into a unified drive encoding. We employ the predicate `path/3` across all settings to represent paths within the respective graphs; the arguments denote the train, the node, and the node's position in the path, respectively.

Encodings Based on Directed Graphs with Edge Transition Functions. We begin by introducing encodings based on a directed graph representation augmented with edge transition functions. The encoding in Listing 1.5 maps a Flatland grid into this structure.

```
edge(C,C') :- connected(C,_,C').
node(C;C') :- edge(C,C').

d(C,C',D) :- connected(C,D,C').
p(C,C',D) :- connected(C,D',C'), cell(C,T), transition(T,(D,D')).
```

Listing 1.5. Encoding for directed graphs with edge functions.

The graph topology is captured by the predicates `node/1` and `edge/2`, while `d/3` and `p/3` encode the functions d and p, respectively.

The encoding in Listing 1.6 identifies spatial paths of length up to `h` between each train's starting and goal positions.

```
1  time(0..h).

3  path(Z,C,0; Z,C',1) :- start(Z,C,_,D), adjacent(C,D,C').
4  { path(Z,C',T+1): edge(C,C') } = 1 :-
5        path(Z,C,T), time(T+1), not eop(Z,T).

7  eop(Z,T) :- end(Z,C,_), path(Z,C,T).
8  :- start(Z,_,_,_), not eop(Z,_).

10 :- path(Z,C,T), path(Z,C',T+1), path(Z,C'',T+2),
11     d(C,C',D), not p(C',C'',D).
```

Listing 1.6. Pathfinding with edge-functions

Line 1 defines the available time steps, while Line 3 initializes each train at its designated starting position and orientation. The path is iteratively extended (Line 4–5) until the destination is reached. Termination is signaled by the `eop(Z,T)` atom (Line 7),[5] indicating that train `Z` has arrived at its destination at time step `T`. The integrity constraint in Line 8 ensures that every train eventually reaches its goal. Crucially, Line 11 enforces transition validity by applying the edge functions d and p to consecutive nodes in the path, verifying that the incoming and outgoing edge form a valid transition.

Encodings Based on Directed Graphs with Sub-nodes. We now introduce encodings that leverage the augmented node structure. The translation from the standard Flatland grid into this representation is provided in Listing 1.7.

```
node((X,Y,D)) :- cell((X,Y),T), transition(T,(_,D)).

edge((X,Y,D),(X',Y',D')) :- node((X,Y,D)), node((X',Y',D')),
    connected((X,Y),D,(X',Y')),
    cell((X',Y'),T'), transition(T',(D,D')).
```

Listing 1.7. Encoding for directed graphs with sub-nodes.

In this setting, each node corresponds to a transit pair (a cell and an outgoing direction), thereby encoding valid transitions directly into the graph's edge construction.

Listing 1.8 adapts the pathfinding logic to this refined structure.

```
time(0..h).

path'(Z,(X,Y,D),0) :- start(Z,(X,Y),_,D).
{ path'(Z,C',T+1) : edge(C,C') } = 1 :-
       path'(Z,C,T), time(T+1), not eop(Z,T).
```

[5] `eop` stands for “end of path”.

```
7  eop(Z,T) :- end(Z,(X,Y),_), path(Z,(X,Y),T).
8  :- start(Z,_,_,_), not eop(Z,_).

10 path(Z,(X,Y),T) :- path'(Z,(X,Y,D),T).
```

Listing 1.8. Pathfinding with sub-nodes

While the rules in Lines 1–8 mirror the logic of the edge-function-based encoding, they operate on transit pairs rather than simple cells. To provide a uniform interface for subsequent scheduling, the internal predicate `path'/3` is projected back onto the cell-based `path/3` in Line 10. In this representation, transition validity is guaranteed by construction and requires no explicit verification during path generation.

Encodings Based on Directed Graphs with Hyper-Edges. Lastly, we present encodings that utilize hyper-edges. Listing 1.9 provides the translation into this representation.

```
hedge(C,C',C'') :- connected(C,D,C'), connected(C',D',C''),
                   cell(C',T), transition(T,(D,D')).

node(C;C';C'') :- hedge(C,C',C'').
```

Listing 1.9. Encoding for directed graphs with hyper-edges.

While `node/1` continues to designate cell-based nodes, the valid transitions are modeled via the ternary predicate `hedge/3`. This approach naturally captures the dependencies between a node's entry and exit points.

Listing 1.10 details the corresponding pathfinding encoding.

```
1  time(0..h).

3  path(Z,C,0; Z,C',1) :- start(Z,C,_,D), adjacent(C,D,C').
4  { path(Z,C'',T+1) : hedge(C,C',C'') } = 1 :-
5        path(Z,C,T-1), path(Z,C',T), time(T+1), not eop(Z,T).

7  eop(Z,T) :- end(Z,C,_), path(Z,C,T).
8  :- start(Z,_,_,_), not eop(Z,_).
```

Listing 1.10. Pathfinding with hyper-edges

The path generation rules (Lines 1–8) leverage the hyper-edges to ensure that every step in the path is valid according to the underlying track topology. This representation is arguably the most direct, as the hyper-edges explicitly encapsulate the ternary nature of cell transitions without requiring auxiliary functions or node fragmentation.

Encodings of Train Drives. To transform spatial paths into fully realized train drives, we must account for potential waiting times at each node, which are essential for collision avoidance. Analogous to paths, train drives are represented via the `drive/3` predicate. Train waiting is modeled as a partial mapping from drive steps to path steps, captured by the `map/3` predicate, taking the train, drive step, and path step as arguments. For instance, the atoms `map(z,5,3)`, `map(z,6,3)`, `map(z,7,3)` indicate that train `z` occupies its third position in the path from time point `5` to `7`.

```
  map(Z,D-1, -1)      :- start(Z,_,D,_).
{ map(Z,D+1,P   ) } :- map(Z,D,P), not eop(Z,P), D<h.
  map(Z,D+1,P+1)      :- map(Z,D,P), not map(Z,D+1,P),
                         path(Z,_,P+1), D<h.
                      :- path(Z,_,P), not map(Z,_,P).

        drive(Z,C,D) :- path(Z,C,P), map(Z,D,P).
```

Listing 1.11. Assembling train drives from paths

The map/3 predicate is defined iteratively in Lines 1–5 of Listing 1.11. Given the earliest departure time $\delta(z)$, we initialize the mapping with drive step $\delta(z) - 1$ and path step -1. Subsequent drive steps D+1 can map to the same path step P as D (Line 2), or advance to the next path step P+1 (Lines 3-4). The integrity constraint in Line 5 ensures every path step is matched by at least one drive step. Finally, Line 7 derives the drive atoms from the path and map atoms.

Encodings of Collisions, Plans, and Delay Optimality. Beyond individual train dynamics, the feasibility of a solution hinges on the absence of inter-train interference. To this end, the vertex and edge conflict conditions established in Sect. 2 are implemented in Listing 1.12. These constraints ensure that no two trains occupy the same cell simultaneously and prevent head-on collisions by forbidding trains from traversing the same edge in opposite directions at the same time step.

```
:- 2 { drive(Z,C,T) }, cell(C,_), T=1..h.

move(C,C',T) :- connected(C,D,C'), drive(Z,C,T-1), drive(Z,C',T).
:- move(C,C',T), move(C',C,T), C < C'.
```

Listing 1.12. Vertex and edge conflicts

Finally, we address the optimization of the overall schedule. While the pathfinding component identifies valid spatial routes, the scheduling component must minimize the total deviation from the target arrival times. This is achieved by minimizing the sum of delays across all trains, effectively penalizing any dwelling time that extends a train's journey beyond its scheduled window. By combining these constraints, the resulting ASP encoding provides a complete framework for synthesizing delay-optimal solutions within the Flatland environment.

```
#minimize{ D : delay(Z,T,D), eop(Z,T) }.
```

Listing 1.13. Delay minimization

Finally, we note that the concrete sequences of actions, or plans, are implicitly defined by the underlying train drives. Within the *flaspland* framework, these plans are primarily utilized for visualization purposes and are therefore omitted here for conciseness.

Encodings Using Difference Constraints. A key advantage of our decoupled approach, separating routing from scheduling, is its inherent modularity, which facilitates the integration of alternative scheduling formalisms. Inspired by railway scheduling approaches [1], we formalize the scheduling phase using difference constraints of the form $u - v \leq d$, where u, v are integer variables and d is an integer constant. In *clingo*[DL] [7], they are represented by atoms of the form &diff{u-v}<=d (or equivalents, which can be translated back into this form). To emulate the temporal-spatial mapping within this framework, each term tuple (Z,P) is assigned an integer representing the drive step at which train Z arrives at position P on its path. For example, the three map/3 atoms discussed above are captured by assignments such as (z,3)$\mapsto$5, where (z,3) is a term and its assignment of 5 is left implicit.

```
&diff{ (Z,0  ) } >= D     :- start(Z,_,D,_).
&diff{ (Z,P-1) } < (Z,P)  :- train(Z), P=1..h.
&diff{ (Z,P  ) } <= h     :- end_of_path(Z,P).
```

```
5  { resolve((Z,P),(Z',P')) ; resolve((Z',P'),(Z,P)) } = 1 :-
6            path(Z,C,P), path(Z',C,P'), Z < Z'.

8  &diff{ (Z,P+1) } <= (Z',P') :- resolve((Z,P),(Z',P')).

10 :- resolve((Z,P),(Z',P'+1)), resolve((Z',P'),(Z,P+1)), Z < Z'.
```

Listing 1.14. Assembling train drives from paths via difference constraints

These assignments are defined in Lines 1–3. Line 1 ensures the initial path step occurs no earlier than the train's earliest departure time. Line 2 enforces chronological progression by requiring strictly increasing drive steps for all subsequent path steps. Finally, Line 3 ensures that the final path step is reached no later than the overall time horizon.

The remaining rules enforce collision avoidance. When two trains share a cell along their paths, the choice rule in Lines 5-6 resolves potential vertex conflicts by assigning traversal precedence to one of the trains. The difference constraint in Line 8 ensures that the prioritized train reaches its next path step no later than when the second train enters the contested cell. An edge conflict arises when trains `Z` and `Z'` claim mutual precedence over each other's subsequent path steps `P+1` and `P'+1`, respectively (Line 10). This cycle of mutual precedence is only possible if both trains are assigned the same drive step for their next positions, resulting in an illegal swap. The separate encoding required to derive the final `drive/3` representation is omitted for brevity.

6 Experiments

We evaluate the three proposed topological representations and their hybrid variant against a baseline encoding on 360 benchmark instances to assess performance and scalability. The baseline adapts a mature, off-the-shelf MAPF encoding [3], augmented with the necessary constraints to handle Flatland's directional dynamics. Our benchmark set is derived from the first ten environments described in Sect. 4, each a 30×30 grid populated with seven trains. To assess scalability with agent density, we varied the number of active trains while maintaining fixed track topologies. For each of the ten base environments and subset size $k \in \{2, \dots, 6\}$, we sampled seven train combinations. Including the unique full instance for $k = 7$ yields $10 \times (5 \times 7 + 1) = 360$ instances in total. For each instance, we set the maximum time horizon to the latest arrival time among its participating trains to ensure temporal feasibility. We ran all instances on a cluster with Intel Xeon E5-2650v4@2.9GHz CPUs and 64GB of RAM running Debian Linux 10. We used *clingo* 5.8 and the corresponding *clingo*[DL] version, imposing a 1500-second timeout and a 15GB memory limit per run.

Table 2 summarizes the results, comparing our four configurations EDGFUNCS, SUBNODES, HYPEDGES, and DIFCONS against the MAPF baseline across scenarios with increasing train counts ($|T|$, 2 to 7). The final row aggregates instances ($|I|$) and timeouts ($\times$), and reports weighted averages for grounding (GRD) and total (TOT) times. The MAPF baseline scales poorly. Despite fast grounding times and relatively compact groundings (e.g., 2.49M rules for 7 trains), it struggles with complex instances, exhibiting the highest average runtimes and timeout rates, and failing with as few as four trains.

Table 2. Average experimental results comparing various drive encoding strategies.

$\|T\|$	$\|I\|$	MAPF			EDGFUNCS			SUBNODES			HYPEDGES			DIFCONS		
		Grd	Tot	×	Grd	Tot	×	Grd	Tot	×	Grd	Tot	×	Grd	Tot	×
2	70	3	9	**0**	10	16	**0**	3	3	**0**	9	14	**0**	**2**	**2**	**0**
3	70	5	81	**0**	18	55	**0**	**4**	**6**	**0**	16	53	**0**	6	7	**0**
4	70	**6**	484	8	25	247	2	6	49	**0**	23	243	1	13	**14**	**0**
5	70	**8**	1069	31	33	528	14	8	165	2	29	660	19	22	**24**	**0**
6	70	**9**	1378	56	40	829	29	10	331	9	36	827	32	34	**37**	**0**
7	10	**10**	1500	10	47	951	6	11	694	4	42	1085	6	50	**52**	**0**
Tot/Avg	360	**6**	629	105	26	352	51	**6**	127	15	23	380	58	17	**18**	**0**

In contrast, our path-driven variants achieve substantially higher success rates and lower total solving times for larger train counts. Among the pure ASP variants utilizing the `map`-based encoding (Listing 1.11), SUBNODES performs best. Its superior performance correlates directly with its grounding size: SUBNODES generates compact programs (2.28M rules for 7 trains), successfully avoiding the severe computational overhead incurred with the EDGFUNCS and HYPEDGES variants (12.28M and 10.53M rules, respectively). Ultimately, the hybrid DIFCONS configuration (using SUBNODES-based path-finding) outperforms all others, maintaining low execution times with zero timeouts. Although it generates quite large programs (8.44M rules for 7 trains), *clingo*[DL] solves them exceptionally fast. This indicates that the structural encoding of the problem and the dedicated propagation of difference constraints are more critical to overall performance than raw grounding size.

7 Conclusion

While Flatland was originally conceived as a benchmark for reinforcement learning [11], the success of symbolic MAPF techniques in the 2020 Flatland competition highlighted the strengths of combinatorial approaches in this domain [9]. Building upon the successful application of ASP to real-world railway scheduling [1], we introduced *flaspland* as a dedicated testbed for tackling these challenges within a declarative framework.

This initial report provides a rigorous formalization of the Flatland environment, establishing a solid foundation for verifying the correctness of subsequent ASP encodings. We propose three distinct graph-based representations to capture the environment's topological and navigational constraints, and develop a twofold ASP scheme that effectively decouples spatial routing from temporal scheduling. Our empirical evaluation demonstrates that this path-driven representation offers significant scalability advantages over off-the-shelf MAPF encodings. Furthermore, this approach, particularly the implementation combining sub-nodes and difference constraints, illustrates the extensibility of *flaspland*, which is beneficial in pursuing further work. In fact, this implementation extends the similar combination used in [1,3] by allowing for cyclic paths. It is interesting future work to see whether such a twofold approach is beneficial in other applications. Overall, by bridging the gap between grid-based simulation and graph-based encodings, *flaspland* provides a scalable benchmark for evaluating the performance of ASP in complex, multi-agent railway scenarios.

This work acknowledges and appreciates the support of DFG grant SCHA 550/51, Germany.

References

1. Abels, D., Jordi, J., Ostrowski, M., Schaub, T., Toletti, A., Wanko, P.: Train scheduling with hybrid ASP. Theory Pract. Logic Program. **21**(3), 317–347 (2021). https://doi.org/10.1017/S1471068420000046
2. Baselice, S., Bonatti, P.A., Gelfond, M.: Towards an integration of answer set and constraint solving. In: Gabbrielli, M., Gupta, G. (eds.) ICLP 2005. LNCS, vol. 3668, pp. 52–66. Springer, Heidelberg (2005). https://doi.org/10.1007/11562931_7
3. Behrens, J., Kaminski, R., Schaub, T., Son, T., Švancara, J., Wanko, P.: Routing and scheduling in answer set programming applied to multi-agent path finding: preliminary report. CoRR abs/2403.12153 (2024). https://arxiv.org/abs/2403.12153
4. Brooks, D., Erdem, E., Erdogan, S., Minett, J., Ringe, D.: Inferring phylogenetic trees using answer set programming. J. Autom. Reason. **39**(4), 471–511 (2007)
5. Erdem, E., Kisa, D., Öztok, U., Schüller, P.: A general formal framework for pathfinding problems with multiple agents. In: desJardins, M., Littman, M. (eds.) Proceedings of the Twenty-Seventh National Conference on Artificial Intelligence (AAAI'13), pp. 290–296. AAAI Press (2013)
6. Erdem, E., Lifschitz, V., Wong, M.D.F.: Wire routing and satisfiability planning. In: Lloyd, J., et al. (eds.) CL 2000. LNCS (LNAI), vol. 1861, pp. 822–836. Springer, Heidelberg (2000). https://doi.org/10.1007/3-540-44957-4_55
7. Gebser, M., Kaminski, R., Kaufmann, B., Ostrowski, M., Schaub, T., Wanko, P.: Theory solving made easy with clingo 5. In: Carro, M., King, A., Saeedloei, N., De Vos, M. (eds.) Technical Communications of the Thirty-second International Conference on Logic Programming (ICLP'16). Open Access Series in Informatics (OASIcs), vol. 52, pp. 2:1–2:15. Schloss Dagstuhl–Leibniz-Zentrum fuer Informatik (2016)
8. Laurent, F., et al.: Flatland competition 2020: MAPF and MARL for efficient train coordination on a grid world. In: Escalante, H., Hofmann, K. (eds.) Proceedings of the NeurIPS'20 Competition and Demonstration Track. Proceedings of Machine Learning Research, vol. 133, pp. 275–301. PMLR (2021). http://proceedings.mlr.press/v133/laurent21a.html
9. Li, J., et al.: Scalable rail planning and replanning: winning the 2020 flatland challenge. In: Biundo, S., Do, M., Goldman, R., Katz, M., Yang, Q., Hankui Zhuo, H. (eds.) Proceedings of the Thirty-First International Conference on Automated Planning and Scheduling (ICAPS'21), pp. 477–485. AAAI Press (2021). https://doi.org/10.1609/icaps.v31i1.15994
10. Lifschitz, V.: Answer Set Programming. Springer (2019). https://doi.org/10.1007/978-3-030-24658-7
11. Mohanty, S., et al.: Flatland-RL: multi-agent reinforcement learning on trains. CoRR (2020). https://arxiv.org/abs/2012.05893
12. Murphy, R., Nemes, A., Romero, J., Schaub, T.: *flaspland* (2026). https://github.com/potassco/flaspland-toolkit
13. Murphy, R., Nemes, A., Romero, J., Schaub, T.: *flaspland* encodings (2026). https://github.com/potassco/flaspland-encodings
14. Stern, R., et al.: Multi-agent pathfinding: definitions, variants, and benchmarks. In: Surynek, P., Yeoh, W. (eds.) Proceedings of the Twelfth International Symposium on Combinatorial Search (SOCS'19), pp. 151–159. AAAI Press (2019)

Aspen-tree: A System for Non-ground Meta-programming in ASP

Amadé Nemes[1(✉)] and Torsten Schaub[1,2]

[1] University of Potsdam, Potsdam, Germany
{nemes,torsten.schaub}@uni-potsdam.de
[2] Potassco Solutions GmbH, Werder, Germany

Abstract. Meta-programming is a powerful technique in Answer Set Programming (ASP) for prototyping language extensions and exploring alternative semantics. While traditional approaches predominantly operate on ground logic programs, many language design tasks require the manipulation of non-ground source code prior to instantiation. We introduce *aspen-tree*, a novel system for the reification, transformation, and analysis of non-ground ASP programs. Built upon the *tree-sitter* parsing library, *aspen-tree* provides a language-independent and iterative framework for mapping source code to a reified fact base. These facts are then processed by *clingo* using meta-encodings to generate high-level transformation instructions, which are applied via a templating engine to update the source code. We demonstrate the utility of *aspen-tree* through two case studies on program analysis and transformation in ASP-Core-2.

1 Introduction

A cornerstone of the success of Answer Set Programming (ASP; [14]) is its high-performance solving engines, ranging from pioneering systems like *smodels* [17] and *dlv* [13] to the more recent *clingo* system [6]. However, while their application programming interfaces have become increasingly sophisticated, the internal architectures of these systems remain highly optimized and inherently rigid, hindering the exploration of new ASP extensions. This limitation can be overcome through meta-programming [1,4,7–10,12,18], which provides an accessible and flexible environment for prototyping alternative language designs natively within ASP. To achieve this, meta-programming relies on reification: the representation of a logic program's syntax as a set of facts. These reified facts are combined with a meta-encoding that implements the desired semantics by reinterpreting the original program's components.

Despite its benefits, existing meta-programming techniques in ASP predominantly operate on ground logic programs. However, in practice, expanding the language with novel constructs requires manipulating the non-ground source code prior to instantiation. To date, no general-purpose meta-programming framework has existed to support such pre-grounding transformations natively

W. Faber et al. (Eds.): LPNMR 2026, LNAI 16952, pp. 365–380, 2027.
https://doi.org/10.1007/978-3-032-38320-4_23

within ASP. To bridge this gap, we introduce *aspen-tree*,[1] a novel system specifically designed for the reification, transformation, and analysis of non-ground ASP programs. Demonstrating its practical viability, *aspen-tree* already serves as a core component of the *metasp* framework [10,11], where it successfully drives a preprocessing pipeline to extend *clingo* with complex new language constructs.

Aspen-tree is built upon *tree-sitter*,[2] a widely adopted parser generator library with grammars for hundreds of programming languages. Consequently, *aspen-tree* is generally language-independent; while our primary focus is on non-ground meta-programming in ASP, the system's capabilities extend seamlessly to any language with an available *tree-sitter* grammar. In particular, *tree-sitter* generates incremental parsers, allowing syntax trees to be updated efficiently in response to localized source edits. Through its integration with the *tree-sitter* API, *aspen-tree* captures these incremental changes to ensure that the reified fact base accurately reflects the source code with minimal computational overhead.

Given a specific grammar, *aspen-tree* operates through a multi-stage workflow. Initially, the source code is parsed into a syntax tree and reified into a set of ASP facts. These facts are then supplied to *clingo* alongside user-defined meta-encodings. This process yields a stable model containing high-level instructions, such as `aspen(edit(...))` for code transformations or `aspen(exception(...))` for error reporting. Finally, edits are applied to the source via a templating engine, triggering an incremental reparse to update the internal tree and fact base. This cycle can be repeated to chain multiple transformations using `aspen(next_program(...))`.

The remainder of the paper is structured as follows. Section 2 provides the necessary background on *tree-sitter* and details the reified fact representation used by *aspen-tree*. In Sect. 3, we describe the system's architecture, its workflow, and the templating mechanism used for source transformations. Section 4 illustrates the practical utility of *aspen-tree* through case studies on program analysis and transformation, specifically focusing on safety checks and syntactic shortcuts in ASP-Core-2. Finally, we discuss related work and future research directions in Sect. 5.

2 Background

While a mature *tree-sitter* grammar for *clingo* exists,[3] our examples use a minimalistic grammar[4] adhering to the ASP-Core-2 standard [3] to simplify the presentation. This underscores the generality of our approach: *aspen-tree* seamlessly supports any language with a *tree-sitter* grammar, including various ASP dialects and even languages beyond ASP. Swapping or extending grammars is effortless and requires no architectural changes.

1 https://github.com/potassco/aspen-tree.
2 https://tree-sitter.github.io/tree-sitter.
3 https://github.com/potassco/tree-sitter-clingo.
4 https://github.com/potassco/tree-sitter-aspcore2.

Our grammar for ASP-Core-2 follows the EBNF specification in [3] verbatim, except that supertype nodes such as `term` and `head` are hidden to reduce tree height. Listing 1.1 illustrates the resulting parse tree for the single-rule program "`1 <= a;b.`" as generated by *tree-sitter*. The tree nodes are listed in depth-

```
0:0  - 1:0   source_file
0:0  - 0:11    statement
0:0  - 0:11      rule
0:0  - 0:10        choice
0:0  - 0:4           lower
0:0  - 0:1             number '1'
0:2  - 0:4             relation '<='
0:5  - 0:6           "{"
0:6  - 0:9           choice_elements
0:6  - 0:7             choice_element
0:6  - 0:7               classical_atom
0:6  - 0:7                 identifier 'a'
0:7  - 0:8             ";"
0:8  - 0:9             choice_element
0:8  - 0:9               classical_atom
0:8  - 0:9                 identifier 'b'
0:9  - 0:10          "}"
0:10 - 0:11        "."
```

Listing 1.1. Parse tree of the program "`1 <= a;b`" generated by *tree-sitter*.

first order; each line represents a node, prefixed by its textual range (line and column) and indented according to its depth in the tree. Leaf nodes additionally include their source text and may be unnamed. Since grammars typically define punctuation and delimiters as unnamed nodes, their removal effectively yields an abstract syntax tree.

Listing 1.2 shows the corresponding reified ASP facts produced by *aspen-tree* for this parse tree. The reification begins with a global description: *aspen-tree* assigns each source a unique identifier (e.g., `s(0)`) and links it to its language and parse tree root node via predicates `language/2` and `source_root/2`. Node identities are established by `node/1`, while the tree structure and sibling order are captured by `child/2` and `next_sibling/2`, respectively. Finally, `type/2` and `leaf_text/2` define node categories and leaf content.

By lifting the program's syntax into this reified format, *aspen-tree* leverages the full expressive power of ASP for meta-programming. These meta-encodings allow us to reason over the reified program structure to derive predicates that drive source transformations, diagnostic reporting, and further transformation cycles.

```
language(s(0),"aspcore2"). source_root(s(0),0).
node(0). type(0,"source_file"). child(0,1).
 node(1). type(1,"statement"). child(1,2).
  node(2). type(2,"rule"). child(2,(3;4)).
   node(3). type(3,"choice"). child(3,(5;6;7;8)). next_sibling(3,4).
    node(5). type(5,"lower"). child(5,(16;17)). next_sibling(5,6).
     node(16). type(16,"number"). leaf_text(16,"1"). next_sibling(16,17).
     node(17). type(17,"relation"). leaf_text(17,"<=")
    node(6). leaf_text(6,"{"). next_sibling(6,7).
    node(7). type(7,"choice_elements"). child(7,(9;10;11)).
     node(9). type(9,"choice_element"). child(9,14). next_sibling(9,10).
      node(14). type(14,"classical_atom"). child(14,15).
       node(15). type(15,"identifier"). leaf_text(15,"a").
     node(10). leaf_text(10,";"). next_sibling(10,11).
     node(11). type(11,"choice_element"). child(11,12).
      node(12). type(12,"classical_atom"). child(12,13).
       node(13). type(13,"identifier"). leaf_text(13,"b").
    node(8). leaf_text(8,"}"). next_sibling(7,8).
  node(4). leaf_text(4,".").
```

Listing 1.2. *Aspen-tree* fact representation for parse tree of program "`1 <= a;b.`".

3 System Architecture and Workflow

Figure 1 illustrates the architecture and workflow of our *aspen-tree* system, which operates by reifying an input source and applying meta-encodings over its reified representation. To demonstrate the system's functionality, we walk through a transformation of our running example: "`1 <= a;b.`". In ASP-Core-2, the base language supports choice rules only with upper bounds, treating lower bounds as syntactic sugar. Our example transformation normalizes these rules by rewriting lower-bound constraints into their equivalent upper-bound representations.

The workflow begins in the parsing layer, where a *tree-sitter* parser for the target language generates a parse tree from the input source. Listing 1.1 shows the resulting tree for our example rule. This tree is then reified into the set of ASP facts shown in Listing 1.2 and added to the system's fact store.

Next, these facts are fed into the transformation layer alongside user-defined meta-encodings. To facilitate development, *aspen-tree* includes a library of auxiliary encodings defining common predicates derived from the core fact representation. Users can selectively include these utilities to streamline the implementation of their transformations. Finally, the reified facts and meta-encodings are passed to *clingo* to compute a stable model, which is required to be unique to provide unambiguous transformation instructions.

This stable model is scanned for instances of predicate `aspen/1`, which define operations to be executed by *aspen-tree*.

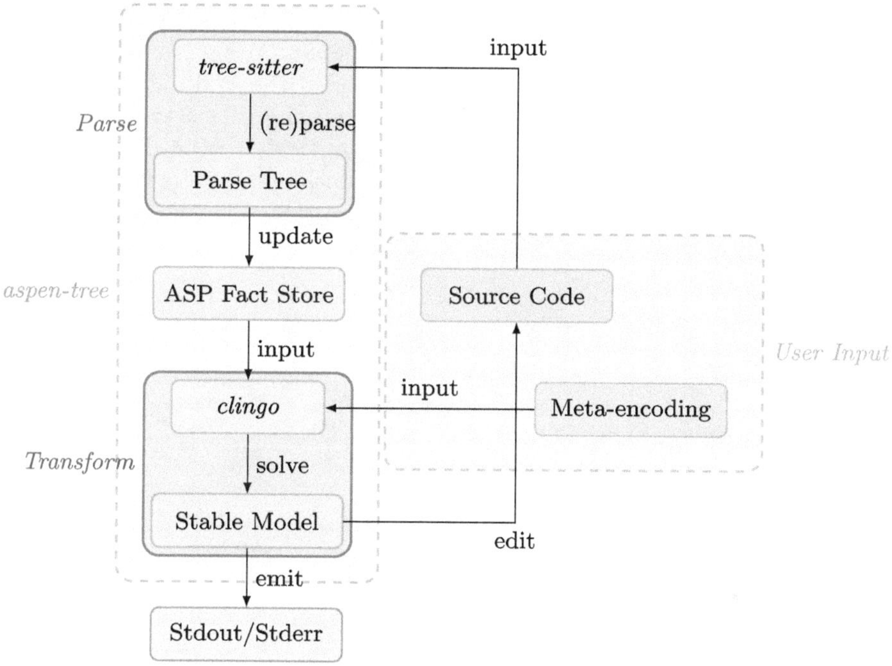

Fig. 1. System diagram of *aspen-tree*.

- The atom `aspen(replace(node(Node),Template))` describes an edit to be made to the source code. The `Template` argument may be any *clingo* symbol. This template symbol is evaluated according to a set of rules described below, and its resulting value replaces the textual span of `Node` in the source code.
- Atoms `aspen(append(node(Node),Template))` and `aspen(prepend( node(Node),Template))` behave similarly, but instead of replacing the textual span of `Node`, they append or prepend the evaluated value of the template symbol to it.
- Atoms `aspen(print(Template))`, `aspen(log(node(Node),Lvl, Template))` `aspen(exception(node(Node),Template)` print, log, and raise exception messages, respectively.
  The optional first argument `node(Node)` of `log/3` and `exception/2` may be supplied to prefix the log or exception message with the textual range (line, column) of the specified node.

The `Template` arguments of the operations above are recursively evaluated as follows:

Symbols. If a template is of the form `node(Node)`, it evaluates to the source text spanned by that node. All other basic symbols are converted directly to their string representation.

Operators. *Aspen-tree* uses nested lists of templates, which are either the empty tuple `()` or a pair `(Head, Tail)` where `Head` is a template and `Tail` is a list.

A *format symbol*, `format(FormatStr, List)`, evaluates by applying the Python `format()` method to the string `FormatStr` using the evaluated elements of `List`. This results in a string, in which the evaluated elements of `List` are inserted into the specified placeholders in `FormatStr`.
A *join symbol*, `join(Sep, List)`, evaluates by applying the Python `join()` method to the evaluated elements of `List` with the separator string `Sep`. The result is a string, in which the evaluated elements of `List` are concatenated, separated by `Sep`.

Once all edit symbols are collected and their template arguments evaluated, *aspen-tree* applies the resulting modifications to the source code.

```
1 #program choice_lower_sugar.
2 mirror("<",">"; "<=",">="; "=","="; "!=","!=").
3 mirror(B,A) :- mirror(A,B).

5 aspen(replace(node(L),"");
6       append(node(C),format(" {0} {1}",(R,(node(T),()))))) :-
7   type(C,"choice"), child(C,L), type(L,"lower"),
8   child(L,T), child(L,O), next_sibling(T,O), leaf_text(O,S),
9   mirror(S,R).
```

Listing 1.3. Meta-encoding transforming choice rules with lower bound to choice rules with upper bound.

To illustrate this process with our running example, Listing 1.3 presents the meta-encoding that implements the lower-bound rewriting transformation. Supplying the program `choice_lower_sugar` to the system triggers the grounding of this encoding over the reified fact store. Lines 2–3 define the mirror images of the relations bounding choice atoms. The rule spanning Lines 5–9 executes the actual program transformation. Its body performs pattern matching over the reified syntax tree through a sequence of joins on the `child/2` predicate. This structural query identifies choice rules restricted by lower bounds and determines the appropriate flipped bounding relation via the `mirror/2` predicate.

When grounded over the reified facts of our running example, the rule yields the following instances:

```
aspen(replace(node(5),""))
aspen(append(node(3),format(" {0} {1}",(">=",(node(16),())))))
```

The first atom instructs *aspen-tree* to delete the original lower bound by replacing the textual span of node 5 (`"1 <="`) with an empty string, temporarily reducing the program to `;b"a."`. The second atom appends a new string to the choice elements at node 3 (`;b"a"`). This string is generated by evaluating the template `format(" 0 1",(">=",(node(16),())))`. Specifically, the nested list provided as the second argument evaluates to the sequence of `">="` and `"1"`. These values are positionally inserted into the format string to yield `" >= 1"`. Appending this evaluated string to the choice atom completes the transformation, resulting in the normalized program `;b"a >= 1."`

Although our running example uses independent operations, the outcome of multiple edits generally depends on their execution order. Since a template may reference the text of a node that is itself subject to change, *aspen-tree* must explicitly manage these inter-dependencies. To ensure a consistent outcome, the system analyzes these relations to establish a topological ordering of all pending edits. If cyclical dependencies are detected, making the intended result ambiguous, the system raises an error.

After all modifications are applied, the updated source code is returned to the parsing layer, where it is efficiently reparsed by *tree-sitter*, keeping as much of the unchanged parse tree as possible. *Aspen-tree* leverages the *tree-sitter* API to identify structural differences between the updated parse tree and its prior state. Newly formed subtrees are reified and integrated into the system's fact store, linked to the preserved portions of the tree via `child/2` and `next_sibling/2` predicates. Conversely, when subtrees are deleted, *aspen-tree* isolates the corresponding facts and purges them from the fact store.

In our running example, *tree-sitter* recognizes that the subtrees representing the choice elements `;b"a"` and the terminal period `"."` remain unchanged, allowing their reified facts to be preserved. Conversely, the subtree rooted at node 5 is marked for deletion, while a new subtree spanning the text `">= 1"` is identified. Consequently, *aspen-tree* updates the fact store by removing the following atoms:

```
child(3,5). next_sibling(5,6).
node(5). type(5,"lower"). child(5,(16;17)).
node(16). type(16,"number"). leaf_text(16,"1"). next_sibling(16,17).
node(17). type(17,"relation"). leaf_text(17,"<=")
```

At the same time, the following facts are added to represent the new structure:

```
child(3,19). next_sibling(8,19).
node(19). type(19,"upper"). child(19,(20;21)).
node(20). type(20,"relation"). leaf_text(20,">="). next_sibling(20,21).
node(21). type(21,"number"). leaf_text(21,"1").
```

The integration of this new subtree into the existing parse tree is established through the new facts `child(3,19)` and `next_sibling(8,19)`.

Following these updates, the control flow typically terminates. However, if the most recent stable model includes an atom of the form `aspen(next_program(Name,Args))`, *aspen-tree* initiates a new transformation cycle. Control loops back to the transformation layer, passing the updated fact store and the activated encodings to *clingo*, which then grounds the specified program `Name` with `Args`, computes its stable model, and proceeds as before. This iterative mechanism is crucial for composing modular transformation pipelines. It allows developers to chain multiple meta-encodings and specify complex termination conditions directly within ASP. For instance, returning to our lower-bound normalization example, we can append the following fact to the encoding:

```
aspen(next_program("choice_sugar",())).
```

This instructs *aspen-tree* to follow the lower-bound elimination with the transformation detailed in Listing 1.4 below. By relying on the guarantee that choice rules now only possess upper bounds, the subsequent encoding can safely rewrite them without handling lower bounds as a special case.

4 Case Study: ASP-Core-2

To demonstrate the versatility of *aspen-tree*, we present two advanced applications of its meta-programming capabilities. First, we detail a transformation meta-encoding that compiles away choice rules. Second, we provide a diagnostic meta-encoding that verifies the safety of rules.

4.1 Rewriting Choice Rules to Disjunctive Rules

Definition of Choice Rules. The semantics of choice rules in ASP-Core-2 [3] is not defined directly, rather, it is specified as a syntactic shorthand for a set of rules. Furthermore, this translation applies exclusively to choice rules bounded solely by an (optional) upper bound. Lower bounds are treated as an independent syntactic shorthand, which is eliminated during preprocessing by the meta-encoding shown in Listing 1.3.

We briefly recall this translation, incorporating minor adaptations. Consider a choice rule of the form

$$C \prec u \leftarrow b_1, \ldots, b_n \tag{1}$$

where u is a term, each b_i is a literal, and C is a set of choice elements of the form $a : l_1, \ldots, l_k$ with atom a and literals l_j. For any atom q, let $\bar{q}$ denote the term obtained by replacing q's predicate symbol with a function symbol of the same name and arity. Furthermore, let $\hat{q} = h(\bar{q})$ and $\widehat{\neg q} = h(-\bar{q})$, where h is a fresh predicate symbol. Then, the choice rule in (1) translates to the disjunctive rules

$$a \mid \hat{a} \leftarrow b_1, \ldots, b_n, l_1, \ldots, l_k \tag{2}$$

for each choice element $(a : l_1, \ldots, l_k) \in C$, along with the constraint

$$\leftarrow b_1, \ldots, b_n, \textbf{not}\ \#\text{count}\{\bar{\hat{a}} : a, l_1, \ldots, l_k \mid (a : l_1, \ldots, l_k) \in C\} \prec u. \tag{3}$$

For instance, the following rule from [3]

$$\{p(a) : q(2); \neg p(a) : q(3)\} \leq 1 \leftarrow q(1) \tag{4}$$

is translated into the following set of rules:

$$\begin{aligned} p(a) \mid h(\bar{p}(a)) &\leftarrow q(1), q(2) \\ \neg p(a) \mid h(-\bar{p}(a)) &\leftarrow q(1), q(3) \\ &\leftarrow q(1), \textbf{not}\ \#\text{count}\{\bar{h}(\bar{p}(a)) : p(a), q(2); \\ &\qquad\qquad \bar{h}(-\bar{p}(a)) : \neg p(a), q(3)\} \leq 1. \end{aligned}$$

```
#include "aspen/generic/derived_predicates/named_child_index.lp".
#include "aspen/generic/queries/make_list.lp".
#include "aspen/aspcore2/derived_predicates/symbol_signature.lp".

#program choice_sugar.

choice(R,E) :-
  type(R,"rule"), child(R,C), type(C,"choice"),
  child(C,ES), type(ES,"choice_elements"),
  child(ES,E), type(E,"choice_element").

e_head(E,A) :- choice(R,E), child(E,A), type(A,"classical_atom").

_templ(body(R),node(B)) :- choice(R,E), child(R,B), type(B,"body").
_templ(upper(R),node(U)) :-
  choice(R,E), child(R,C), child(C,U), type(U,"upper").
_templ(cond(E),format(", {}",(nodc(LS),()))) :-
  choice(R,E), child(E,LS), type(LS,"naf_literals").

templ(I,T) :- _templ(I,T).
templ(I,"") :- default(I), not _templ(I,_).
default(body(R);upper(R);cond(E)) :- choice(R,E).

templ(hat(E),format("not_choose({0})",(node(A),()))) :- e_head(E,A).


aspen(exception(node(A),"Predicate not_choose/1 is reserved.")) :-
  type(A,"classical_atom"), symbol_signature(A,("not_choose",1)).

templ(rule(E),format("{0} | {1} :- {2}{3}.",
                     (node(A),(H,(B,(LS,())))))) :-
  choice(R,E), e_head(E,A), templ(hat(E),H),
  templ(body(R),B), templ(cond(E),LS).

templ(agg_element(E),format("{0} : {1}{2}",(H,(node(A),(LS,())))))
    :-
  choice(R,E), e_head(E,A), templ(hat(E),H), templ(cond(E),LS).

aspen(query(make_list(agg_elements(R),T,I))) :-
  choice(R,E), named_child_index(E,I), templ(agg_element(E),T).

templ(constraint(R),format(":- {0}, not #count{{ {1} }} {2}.",
                           (B,(J,(U,()))))) :-
  choice(R,E), templ(body(R),B), templ(upper(R),U),
  aspen(return(make_list(agg_elements(R)),C)), J=join("; ",C).

aspen(query(make_list(rules(R), T, I))) :-
  choice(R,E), named_child_index(E,I), templ(rule(E),T).

aspen(replace(node(R),join("\n",(T, C)))) :-
  choice(R,_), aspen(return(make_list(rules(R)), C)),
  templ(constraint(R),T).
```

Listing 1.4. Meta-encoding rewriting choice rules of form (1) into rules as in (2) and (3).

Meta-encoding. Listing 1.4 presents an *aspen-tree* meta-encoding that transforms choice rules of the form (1) into the disjunctive rules and integrity constraints defined in (2) and (3), respectively.

The initial lines (1–3) import utility encodings from *aspen-tree*, organized by language: the `generic` folder contains grammar-independent encodings, while `asp-core-2` provides those specific to the ASP-Core-2 grammar. The imported encodings define: (1) `named_child_index(Node,Idx)`, mapping a node to its index among named siblings, (2) a utility encoding for constructing lists from predicates, and (3) the ASP-Core-2 predicate `symbol_signature(Node,(Name,Arity))`, identifying the name and arity of function or atom nodes.

The core of the encoding begins in Lines 7–12 by defining predicates `choice(R, E)` and `e_head(E,A)` to link choice rules to their elements and, in turn, elements to their head atoms.

Subsequently, template symbols are defined to facilitate the creation of replacement rules. A predicate `templ(I,T)` maps each template symbol `T` to a unique identifier `I`. First, in Lines 14–18, we define template symbols for the body of a choice rule, its upper bound, and the condition of each choice element. Since these constructs are optional, Lines 20–22 set their default value to the empty string.

Next, on Line 24, for any choice element head a, we define the template symbol of $\hat{a}$, using the unary predicate symbol `not_choose` for the role of h. Note that the textual representation of q is identical to $\bar{q}$ (and that of $\neg q$ to $-\bar{q}$). Thus, for $a = q$ or $a = \neg q$, we obtain $\hat{a}$ by evaluating the template symbol. To ensure correctness, Lines 26–27 verify that `not_choose/1` is not used in the input program, emitting a located exception if it is.

With the necessary template symbols in hand, we define the template for the rules of (2) in Lines 29–32. Then, in Lines 34–35, we instantiate the template for the aggregate elements of integrity constraint (3). These aggregate elements are collected into a list using the `make_list.lp` utility encoding. This encoding takes a set of `aspen(query(make_list(ID,E,IDX)))` atoms and derives a single `aspen(return(make_list(ID),C))` atom, where `C` is the constructed list (and `ID` is an identifier shared by the atoms, and `E`, `IDX` is a desired element and its index in the list). The list is then joined with the separator ";" and used to instantiate the template for the integrity constraint (3) in Lines 40–43.

Finally, in Lines 45–50, all rules from (2) and the integrity constraint from (3) are joined, separated by newlines. *Aspen-tree* is then instructed to replace the original choice rule with the resulting template symbol.

Giving our example choice rule in (4)

```
{p(a) : q(2); -p(a) : q(3)} <= 1 :- q(1).
```

as the input program to *aspen-tree*, along with our encoding `choice_sugar` yields the following transformed program:

```
 p(a) | not_choose( p(a)) :- q(1), q(2).
-p(a) | not_choose(-p(a)) :- q(1), q(3).
:- q(1), not #count{ not_choose( p(a)) : p(a), q(2);
                     not_choose(-p(a)) : -p(a), q(3) } <= 1.
```

4.2 Safety Check in ASP-Core-2

Safety Definition. We briefly recall the definition of safety from [3], noting that this definition applies strictly to the core language, requiring choice rules to be compiled away beforehand.

Given a set of variables V and a set of atoms $B = \{b_1, \ldots, b_n\}$, a variable $v \in V$ is inductively defined as *bound* by B if v occurs outside the scope of arithmetic operators in some $b_i \in B$, and b_i is either

1. a classical atom,
2. a built-in equality atom $t = u$ or $u = t$, where the binding occurrence of v is in u, and all variables from V occurring in t are bound by $B \setminus \{b_i\}$, or
3. an aggregate atom #aggr $E = u$, where the binding occurrence of v is in u, and all variables from V occurring in E are bound by $B \setminus \{b_i\}$.

A rule (or a weak constraint) r is considered *safe* if its set of global variables V is bound by the set of non-negated body atoms in r, and, for each aggregate element in r containing a set of variables W, the subset of local variables $W \setminus V$ is bound by the non-negated atoms in the element's condition.

Consider the following example rule from [3]:

```
p(X,Y) :- q(X), #sum{S,X: r(T,X), S = (2 * T) - X} = Y.
```

The global variable `X` is bound by the body atom `q(X)`. Consequently, the global variable `Y` is bound by the aggregate atom, since the only global variable within the aggregate element is `X`, which is already bound by `q(X)`. To establish the overall safety of the rule, we must also identify bindings for the local variables within the aggregate. The local variable `T` is bound by the atom `r(T,X)`. Consequently, the built-in equality atom establishes the safety of `S`, since `T` is the only local variable appearing on the right-hand side of the equation. Having identified valid bindings for all local and global variables, we conclude that the rule is safe.

In contrast, consider the following unsafe rule, also from [3]:

```
p(X,Y) :- q(X), #sum{S,X: r(T,X), S + X = 2 * T} = Y.
```

Here, the local variable `S` is not safely bound because its occurrence in the built-in equality atom is within the scope of the `+` arithmetic operator. Hence, both the variable and the rule are unsafe.

Meta-encoding. Listing 1.5 presents an *aspen-tree* meta-encoding that verifies the safety of input programs according to this definition. If an unsafe program is detected, it raises an exception with a message detailing the unsafe rules and their associated variables.

Lines 2–4 define auxiliary predicates that provide more compact access to rule, weak constraint, and variable nodes.

The rules on Lines 6–10 use the predicate `atoms/2` to map statements to the set of atoms $b_1, \ldots, b_n$ occurring in their bodies. Using the same predicate, the rule spanning Lines 12–14 maps aggregate elements $t_1, \ldots, t_k : l_1, \ldots, l_m$ to the atoms constituting their condition. From these atom sets, the rule on Line 16 filters out those that are negated.

```
#program safety_check.
stm(S) :- type(S,("rule";"weak_constraint")).

var(V;V,N) :- type(V,"variable"), leaf_text(V,N).

atoms(S,A) :- child(S,B), type(B,"body"), child(B,NL),
  type(NL,"naf_literal"), child(NL,A), not type(A,"naf").

atoms(S,A) :- child(S,B), type(B,"body"),
                child(B,A), type(A,"aggregate").

atoms(S,A) :- type(S,"aggregate_element"), child(S,NLS),
  type(NLS,"naf_literals"), child(NLS,NL),
  type(NL,"naf_literal"), child(NL,A), not type(A,"naf").

pos_atoms(S,A) :- atoms(S,A), #false: next_sibling(N,A), type(N,"naf").

eq(A,T,U;A,U,T) :- pos_atoms(_,A), type(A,"builtin_atom"), child(A,U),
   next_sibling(U,R), leaf_text(R,"="), next_sibling(R,T).

eq(A,E,U) :- pos_atoms(_,A), type(A,"aggregate"),
  child(A,B), type(B,"upper"), child(B,R), leaf_text(R,"="),
  child(B,U), next_sibling(R,U),
  child(A,E), type(E,"aggregate_elements").

desc(S,S) :- atoms(S,_).
desc(arith,B) :- type(B,("binary_operation";"unary_operation")).
desc(T,T;U,U) :- eq(A,T,U).
desc(A,A) :- type(A,"classical_atom").
desc(A,C) :- desc(A,P), child(P,C).

scope(V,"global") :- var(V), stm(S), desc(S,V),
  not desc(S',V): atoms(S',_), desc(S,S'), S'!=S.

scope(V',"global") :- var(V,N), scope(V,"global"),
  stm(S), desc(S,V), desc(S,V'), var(V',N).

scope(V,"local") :- var(V), not scope(V,"global").

binds(S,A,V') :- binds(S,A,V), var(V,N), var(V',N), desc(S,V').

binds(S,A,V) :- pos_atoms(S,A), type(A,"classical_atom"),
  var(V), not desc(arith,V), desc(A,V).

other_binds(S,A,V) :- pos_atoms(S,A), eq(A,T,_),
  desc(T,V), var(V), binds(S,A',V), A'!=A.

binds(S,A,V) :- pos_atoms(S,A), eq(A,T,U), desc(U,V), var(V),
  scope(V,C), not desc(arith,V),
  other_binds(S,A,V'): var(V'), scope(V',C), V'!=V, desc(T,V').

aspen(exception(node(S),format("Unsafe variables in:\n{}",
                                (node(S),())));
      exception(node(V),format("Variable '{}' is unsafe.",
                                (node(V),())))) :-
  stm(S), desc(S,V), var(V), not binds(_,_,V).
```

Listing 1.5. Safety check meta-encoding.

The rules on Lines 18–24 collect built-in and aggregate equality atoms, using the predicate `eq/3` to associate them with the nodes forming the two sides of the equation. We later rely on this predicate to establish bindings for variables via the last two conditions of the safety definition.

The rules on Lines 26–30 define a descendant relation `desc/2` based on reachability via the `child/2` relation. To minimize its ground instantiation, we restrict `desc/2` to descendants of relevant nodes: atom sets, arithmetic operators, components of equality atoms, and regular atoms.

Next, Lines 32–38 establish whether a variable occurrence has global or local scope. According to Lines 32–35, a variable occurrence is global if it descends from exactly one atom set (i.e. occurs outside an aggregate element), or if another global variable occurrence in the same statement shares its name. Otherwise, the occurrence is considered local.

The remainder of the encoding defines when a variable occurrence `V` is bound by an atom `A` in an atom set `S`, representing this relation with the predicate `binds(S,A,V)`.

Line 40 specifies that an atom binding a variable occurrence within an atom set effectively binds all other occurrences of that variable within the same set. Line 42 formalizes variable binding for regular atoms, reflecting the first condition of the safety definition: a variable is bound if it occurs in an atom outside the scope of arithmetic operations.

Following that, in Lines 45–50, we define the conditions under which built-in or aggregate equality atoms bind a variable. We first unify the application of the second and third safety conditions to establish variable safety when a variable appears on the right-hand side of an equation. That is, a non-negated (built-in or aggregate) equality atom binds a local (resp. global) variable if it occurs on the right-hand side outside the scope of arithmetic operators, and all local (resp. global) variables on the left-hand side are bound by a distinct atom in the same atom set. It suffices to formalize this condition through rules using the predicate `eq(A,T,U)`. Indeed, when `A` is an aggregate atom, the variable occurrence of interest is invariably on the right-hand side, corresponding to `U`. For built-in atoms, the predicate is defined symmetrically in its last two arguments in Line 18.

To implement this, we define the predicate `other_binds(S,A,V)`, which holds if `A` is an equality atom in atom set `S`, variable `V` appears on the left-hand side of `A`, and `V` is bound by a distinct atom `A'` within the same set. Leveraging this helper predicate, the rule spanning Lines 48–50 formalizes the safety condition. That is, the conditional literal in Line 50 ensures that every variable within the same scope on the left-hand side of the equation is bound by a distinct atom in the set.

Finally, Lines 52–56 emit exception messages for all unsafe rules and variables. Each message identifies the specific rule or variable as unsafe and is prefixed with its corresponding textual range in the source code. For instance, processing the unsafe example rule with the safety meta-encoding in *aspen-tree* yields the following exception message:

```
-:1:0-53: Unsafe variables in:
p(X,Y) :- q(X), #sum{S,X: r(T,X), S + X = 2 * T} = Y.
-:1:21-22: Variable 'S' is unsafe.
-:1:34-35: Variable 'S' is unsafe.
```

This message indicates that the rule spanning the textual range in row 1, columns 0–53 is unsafe, specifically identifying the occurrences of variable S at positions 1:21–22 and 1:34–35 as the source of the violation.

5 Conclusion

We have introduced *aspen-tree*, a novel system designed to enable the reification and transformation of non-ground source code. By leveraging the *tree-sitter* parsing library, the framework provides a language-independent and iterative workflow where source code is mapped to reified facts, processed via *clingo* meta-encodings, and updated through a robust templating engine. Our case studies on choice rule normalization and variable safety verification demonstrate that *aspen-tree* effectively supports complex language extensions and diagnostic analysis within the ASP-Core-2 standard. Notably, when working with an existing *tree-sitter* grammar, a user of *aspen-tree* can engineer transformation and analysis pipelines relying only on their knowledge of the grammar's reified representation and their proficiency in ASP. Future research will focus on optimizing the transformation loop through multi-shot solving and extending the system's utility toward real-time static analysis and IDE integration.

The declarative, rule-based specification of program transformations has been investigated previously in the literature. Previous approaches primarily apply top-down rewriting strategies via ad-hoc semantics, or using term rewriting as a theoretical foundation [19]. However, the application of bottom-up logical languages such as ASP or Datalog to specify transformations and their preconditions has not been studied, and is a novelty of our approach.

In the field of static analysis, however, Datalog is a state-of-the-art approach [16]. Advantages of using Datalog include ease of declaratively modelling fixpoint calculations and reachability, as well as powerful Datalog engine implementations. Indeed, since the encodings presented in Subsect. 4.2 use only stratified negation, and does not use the clingo solver in any meaningful way, this analysis could be encoding in Datalog with minimal effort. Nonetheless, while the applications of ASP to static program analysis is largely unexplored, the usage of ASP does offer some modelling advantages, such as its powerful aggregates, and the ease of modelling inertia via strong and default negation [20]. Additionally, in recent years there have been work on integrating SMT solvers with Datalog for more advanced analyses and program repair [2,15]. Such use-cases could be tackled in ASP systems such as *clingo* using their built-in solving capabilities, and theory-solving integration [5].

This work was supported by the DFG grant SCHA 550/15, Germany.

References

1. Baral, C., Gelfond, M.: Reasoning agents in dynamic domains. In: Minker, J. (ed.) Logic-Based Artificial Intelligence, pp. 257–279. Kluwer Academic Publishers, Dordrecht (2000)
2. Bembenek, A., Greenberg, M., Chong, S.: Formulog: datalog for SMT-based static analysis. Proc. ACM Program. Lang. **4**(OOPSLA), 141:1–141:31 (2020). https://doi.org/10.1145/3428209
3. Calimeri, F., et al.: ASP-Core-2 input language format. Theory Pract. Logic Program. **20**(2), 294–309 (2020)
4. Eiter, T., Polleres, A.: Towards automated integration of guess and check programs in answer set programming: a meta-interpreter and applications. Theory Pract. Logic Program. **6**(1–2), 23–60 (2006)
5. Gebser, M., Kaminski, R., Kaufmann, B., Ostrowski, M., Schaub, T., Wanko, P.: Theory solving made easy with clingo 5. In: Carro, M., King, A., Saeedloei, N., De Vos, M. (eds.) Technical Communications of the Thirty-Second International Conference on Logic Programming (ICLP'16). Open Access Series in Informatics (OASIcs), vol. 52, pp. 2:1–2:15. Schloss Dagstuhl–Leibniz-Zentrum fuer Informatik (2016)
6. Gebser, M., Kaminski, R., Kaufmann, B., Schaub, T.: Multi-shot ASP solving with clingo. Theory Pract. Logic Program. **19**(1), 27–82 (2019). https://doi.org/10.1017/S1471068418000054
7. Gebser, M., Kaminski, R., Schaub, T.: Complex optimization in answer set programming. Theory Pract. Logic Program. **11**(4–5), 821–839 (2011)
8. Gebser, M., Pührer, J., Schaub, T., Tompits, H.: A meta-programming technique for debugging answer-set programs. In: Fox, D., Gomes, C. (eds.) Proceedings of the Twenty-Third National Conference on Artificial Intelligence (AAAI'08), pp. 448–453. AAAI Press (2008)
9. Gelfond, M., Son, T.C.: Reasoning with prioritized defaults. In: Dix, J., Pereira, L.M., Przymusinski, T.C. (eds.) LPKR 1997. LNCS, vol. 1471, pp. 164–223. Springer, Heidelberg (1998). https://doi.org/10.1007/BFb0054795
10. Hahn, S., Nemes, A., Romero, J., Schaub, T.: Meta-programming for linear-time temporal answer set programming. Submitted (2026)
11. Hahn, S., Nemes, A., Romero, J., Schaub, T.: *metasp* (2026). https://github.com/potassco/metasp
12. Kaminski, R., Romero, J., Schaub, T., Wanko, P.: How to build your own ASP-based system?! Theory Pract. Logic Program. **23**(1), 299–361 (2023). https://doi.org/10.1017/S1471068421000508
13. Leone, N., et al.: The DLV system for knowledge representation and reasoning. ACM Trans. Comput. Log. **7**(3), 499–562 (2006)
14. Lifschitz, V.: Answer Set Programming. Springer, Cham (2019). https://doi.org/10.1007/978-3-030-24658-7
15. Liu, Y., Mechtaev, S., Subotic, P., Roychoudhury, A.: Program repair guided by datalog-defined static analysis. In: Proceedings of the 31st ACM Joint European Software Engineering Conference and Symposium on the Foundations of Software Engineering (ESEC/FSE'23), pp. 1216–1228 (2023). https://doi.org/10.1145/3611643.3616363
16. Scholz, B., Jordan, H., Subotic, P., Westmann, T.: On fast large-scale program analysis in datalog. In: Proceedings of the 25th International Conference on Compiler Construction (CC'16), pp. 196–206 (2016). https://doi.org/10.1145/2892208.2892226

17. Simons, P., Niemelä, I., Soininen, T.: Extending and implementing the stable model semantics. Artif. Intell. **138**(1–2), 181–234 (2002)
18. Son, T., Baral, C., Nam, T., McIlraith, S.: Domain-dependent knowledge in answer set planning. ACM Trans. Comput. Log. **7**(4), 613–657 (2006). https://doi.org/10.1145/1183278.1183279
19. Visser, E.: A survey of rewriting strategies in program transformation systems. Electron. Notes Theor. Comput. Sci. **57**, 109–143 (2001). https://doi.org/10.1016/S1571-0661(04)00270-1
20. Yang, B., Zhang, M., Zhang, Y.: Applying answer set programming to points-to analysis of object-oriented language. In: Huang, D.-S., Gan, Y., Bevilacqua, V., Figueroa, J.C. (eds.) ICIC 2011. LNCS, vol. 6838, pp. 676–685. Springer, Heidelberg (2011). https://doi.org/10.1007/978-3-642-24728-6_91

Enumerating Stable Models of Logic Programs Using Linear Algebraic Approaches

Tuan Nguyen[1(✉)], Katsumi Inoue[2], and Chiaki Sakama[3]

[1] Hanoi University of Science and Technology, Hanoi, Vietnam
tuannq@soict.hust.edu.vn
[2] National Institute of Informatics, Tokyo, Japan
inoue@nii.ac.jp
[3] Wakayama University, Wakayama, Japan
sakama@wakayama-u.ac.jp

Abstract. Linear-algebraic methods for computing stable models of propositional logic programs have recently shown promising results. However, existing complete approaches suffer from prohibitive computational and memory costs, which limit their practical applicability, whereas incomplete approaches cannot enumerate all stable models or prove the absence of stable models. In this paper, we introduce a search-based extension of algebraic approaches to logic programming, an aspect that, to the best of our knowledge, has not been studied before. We first represent a normal logic program as a program matrix through a linear-time standardization procedure. We then reformulate fixpoint computation and the stable-model condition as sequences of linear transformations. Based on this reformulation, we propose incremental and decremental backtracking search algorithms that enumerate the stable models of a normal logic program without pre-allocating all possible initial guesses. Experiments on ground programs suggest that the proposed methods outperform previous linear-algebraic approaches and achieve performance comparable to `clingo` on certain classes of instances.

Keywords: Stable Model · Logic Programming · Linear Algebra

1 Introduction

Stable model semantics, introduced by [11], provides a formal meaning to normal logic programs and serves as a foundational semantics for Logic Programming (LP) and Answer Set Programming (ASP), which are widely used to represent knowledge and solve complex problems in Artificial Intelligence (AI).. Briefly, a normal logic program is a finite set of rules, each consisting of an atom in the head and a body containing atoms, possibly together with Negation-As-Failure (NAF) literals.

W. Faber et al. (Eds.): LPNMR 2026, LNAI 16952, pp. 381–398, 2027.
https://doi.org/10.1007/978-3-032-38320-4_24

Motivated by the growing interest in integrating symbolic and numerical reasoning, recent studies have explored linear-algebraic methods as alternatives to symbolic inference [2,24,26,30]. In this direction, Sakama et al. proposed representing logic programs as matrices, enabling the immediate consequence operator (T_P-operator) to be computed via matrix-vector multiplication [24]. This approach was later extended to disjunctive and normal logic programs [25]. Another related line of work studied the computation of 2-valued and 3-valued completion semantics of finite propositional normal logic programs in vector spaces [27].

Building on a similar representation, Aspis et al. formulated model computation in continuous vector spaces as a root-finding problem solved by Newton's method [2]. Later, Takemura and Inoue proposed a differentiable approach based on a continuous loss function whose optima correspond to supported models [30]. Representing logical formulas and constraints using matrices and tensors has since emerged as a promising direction for bridging symbolic reasoning and machine learning [12]. In this context, program matrices can also be learned through machine learning techniques. For example, Gao et al. introduced a differentiable inductive logic programming framework for learning logic programs from relational datasets [8]. Subsequently, the idea of embedding logic programs into matrix representations was extended to a differentiable first-order rule learner that demonstrated robustness to noisy data and scalability to large datasets [6]. This line of research was further expanded to support rule learning directly from raw sequential inputs [7]. More recently, Domingos proposed *Tensor Logic*, which expresses logical inference as tensor operations to unify learning and reasoning in a GPU-native framework [5].

For model computation in logic programming, these linear-algebraic approaches offer a promising way to bridge symbolic and numerical computation. Sakama et al. proposed a complete method [24], later evaluated in [20]. Their results suggest that fixpoint computation for definite programs can be significantly faster than `clingo`, a state-of-the-art ASP solver [9], by exploiting sparse representations and parallel computation. However, for normal logic programs, that method requires generating all possible initial guesses before computing fixpoints and checking stability, which becomes infeasible for large programs with more than about 20 negations. In contrast, the differentiable methods of [2] and [30] are incomplete and do not in general guarantee convergence to supported or stable models, even when they consume substantial computational resources. As a result, enumerating all stable models and proving the non-existence of stable models remain difficult, and sometimes impossible, for these methods.

This paper presents complete methods for computing stable models of normal logic programs. We introduce search into linear-algebraic approaches to logic programming, which, to the best of our knowledge, has not been previously considered. Specifically, we refine the stable-model computation of [25] by reformulating both the fixpoint and stable-model conditions as sequences of linear transformations. Based on this reformulation, we develop complete linear-algebraic search algorithms and evaluate them on ground ASP programs against

[25] and `clingo`. The results show that our methods substantially outperform previous linear-algebraic approaches and may also be advantageous over `clingo` for some classes of ground programs.

The rest of the paper is organized as follows. Section 2 reviews the background, Sect. 3 presents the matrix representation of normal programs, Sect. 4 introduces the new definition of stable model semantics, Sect. 5 describes proposed linear algebraic backtracking-based methods for computing stable models, Sect. 6 reports the experimental results, and Sects. 7 and 8 discuss related work and conclude the paper.

2 Preliminaries

We focus on propositional logic programs over a finite nonempty set of ground atoms $\mathcal{A}$. A program P is called a *normal logic program* if every rule $r \in P$ has the form:

$$h \leftarrow b_1 \wedge b_2 \wedge \ldots \wedge b_l \wedge \neg b_{l+1} \wedge \ldots \wedge \neg b_k \qquad (k \geq l \geq 0) \qquad (1)$$

where $h, b_1, \ldots, b_l, b_{l+1}, \ldots, b_k$ are atoms in $\mathcal{A}$.

For brevity, we write $head(r)$ for the head atom of a rule r, and $body(r)$ for the set of body literals of r. For a rule r, we denote by $body^+(r) = \{b_1, \ldots, b_l\}$ the atoms occurring positively in the body of r, and by $body^-(r) = \{b_{l+1}, \ldots, b_k\}$ the atoms occurring under default negation. A normal rule r is called a *fact* if $body(r) = \emptyset$, and a *constraint* if r has no head atom. A normal rule r is called a *definite rule* if $body^-(r) = \emptyset$ and $head(r)$ is an atom. A normal program P is a *definite program* if every rule in P is a definite rule.

For a logic program P, the Herbrand base $\mathscr{B}_P$ is the set of all propositional variables in P, and a Herbrand *interpretation* I is a subset of $\mathscr{B}_P$. An interpretation I is a model of P if, for every rule $r \in P$, $body^+(r) \subseteq I$ and $body^-(r) \cap I = \emptyset$ imply $head(r) \in I$. A model is minimal if none of its proper subsets is also a model. A supported model is a model I such that every $p \in I$ is derived by some rule $r \in P$ with $p = head(r)$, $body^+(r) \subseteq I$, and $body^-(r) \cap I = \emptyset$ [4,15]. Every stable model of a normal logic program is both minimal and supported [11]. Stable model semantics is defined via the program reduct $P^X = \{head(r) \leftarrow body^+(r) \mid r \in P, body^-(r) \cap X = \emptyset\}$, where X is an interpretation. Since P^X is a definite program, it has the least model.

For a definite program P, we write $LHM(P)$ for its least Herbrand model. This model is obtained as the least fixpoint of the immediate consequence operator T_P, by iteratively deriving atoms whose rule bodies are satisfied until saturation. This provides the basis for stable model semantics [11]: given a normal program P and an interpretation X, the reduct P^X is definite, and X is a stable model of P iff $X = LHM(P^X)$.

3 Logic Programs in Vector Spaces

3.1 Standardized Program

Following [19,25], we adopt the definition of *standardized program.* A logic program P is called a Singly-Defined (SD) program if $head(r_1) \neq head(r_2)$ for any two different rules r_1, r_2 in P. When P contains more than one rule with the same head $r_1, r_2, \ldots, r_n$ $(n > 1)$ such that $h = head(r_1) = head(r_2), = \cdots = head(r_n)$, replace those rules with a set of new rules: $\{h \leftarrow b_1 \vee b_2 \vee \ldots \vee b_n,\ b_1 \leftarrow body(r_1),\ b_2 \leftarrow body(r_2),\ \ldots,\ b_n \leftarrow body(r_n)\}$ $(n > 1)$, where $b_1, b_2, \ldots, b_n$ are newly introduced atoms. The resulting program Π is called a *standardized program.* It consists of *And*-rules (2) and *Or*-rules (3), and satisfies the SD condition, i.e., no two rules have the same head:

$$h \leftarrow b_1 \wedge b_2 \wedge \ldots \wedge b_l \qquad (l \geq 0) \tag{2}$$

$$h \leftarrow b_1 \vee b_2 \vee \ldots \vee b_l \qquad (l \geq 2) \tag{3}$$

For simplicity, in the standardized representation Π, we retain the notation $\neg p$ in the standardized program Π. Here, $\neg p$ is not a default-negated literal from the original program, but a fresh auxiliary variable representing not p, distinct from the atom p. It is intended to be **True** exactly when p is false. We also denote $\overline{X} = \{\neg p \mid p \in body^-(r), r \in P, p \notin X\}$ for any interpretation X of P. Example 1 presents an example of a normal program P_1 and its standardized program Π_1:

Example 1. Consider the logic program $P_1 = \{a \leftarrow b \wedge c,\ a \leftarrow f,\ a \leftarrow \neg h,\ b \leftarrow c \wedge d,\ c \leftarrow a,\ c \leftarrow \neg g,\ c \leftarrow \neg d,\ d \leftarrow e,\ e \leftarrow d,\ f \leftarrow a,\ f \leftarrow g,\ g \leftarrow a,\ g \leftarrow \neg c,\ h \leftarrow \neg a,\ \leftarrow c \wedge h,\ \leftarrow b \wedge a\}$. Its corresponding standardized program is: $\Pi_1 = \{a \leftarrow \neg h \vee f \vee x_1,\ b \leftarrow c \wedge d,\ c \leftarrow a \vee \neg d \vee \neg g,\ d \leftarrow e,\ e \leftarrow d,\ f \leftarrow a \vee g,\ g \leftarrow a \vee \neg c,\ h \leftarrow \neg a,\ x_1 \leftarrow b \wedge c,\ \leftarrow c \wedge h,\ \leftarrow b \wedge a\}$, where x_1 is introduced as the head of the rule $x_1 \leftarrow b \wedge c$.

3.2 Matrix Representation of Logic Programs

For convenience, we assume there is a way to index all literals in an LP incrementally without ambiguity so that we can easily map sets of literals to vectors.

Let $\mathscr{B}_\Pi = \{a_1, a_2, \ldots, a_n\}$ be the Herbrand base of a logic program Π under a fixed ordering. For any subset $S \subseteq \mathscr{B}_\Pi$, we define its **Herbrand base vector** as the binary vector $\mathbf{b} = (b_1, b_2, \ldots, b_n)^{\mathrm{T}} \in \{0,1\}^n$, where $n = |\mathscr{B}_\Pi|$, and for each $1 \leq i \leq n$, $b_i = 1$ if $a_i \in S$, and $b_i = 0$ otherwise. In other words, a Herbrand base vector is the characteristic vector of a subset of the Herbrand base. For example, $\mathbf{b}^{\mathrm{T}} = \overset{\begin{matrix} a & b & c & d & e & f & g & h \end{matrix}}{\begin{pmatrix} 1 & 0 & 1 & 0 & 0 & 0 & 0 & 0 \end{pmatrix}}$ is a Herbrand base vector of Π_1 in Example 1, representing the subset $\{a, c\}$ of $\mathscr{B}_{\Pi_1}$.

Let $\mathcal{A}_\Pi = \{l_1, l_2, \ldots, l_m\}$ be the set of all literals and auxiliary atoms occurring in Π, including positive atoms, negative literals, and auxiliary atoms, under a fixed ordering. We define a **reduced vector** as a binary vector

$\mathbf{y} = (y_1, y_2, \ldots, y_m)^{\mathrm{T}} \in \{0,1\}^m$, where $y_i = 1$ if l_i is included in the represented subset of $\mathcal{A}_\Pi$, and $y_i = 0$ otherwise. Here, *reduced* means that we encode only the literals and auxiliary atoms explicitly occurring in Π; positive and negative forms of an atom are both included only when they appear in the program. For example, $\mathbf{y}^{\mathrm{T}} = (\overset{a}{1}\ \overset{b}{0}\ \overset{c}{0}\ \overset{d}{1}\ \overset{e}{0}\ \overset{f}{0}\ \overset{g}{1}\ \overset{h}{0}\ \overset{x_1}{0}\ \overset{\neg a}{0}\ \overset{\neg c}{1}\ \overset{\neg d}{0}\ \overset{\neg g}{0}\ \overset{\neg h}{1})$ is a reduced vector of Π_1.

Similarly, let $\mathcal{A}_\Pi^- = \{\neg a_1, \neg a_2, \ldots, \neg a_k\}$ be the ordered set of all negative literals occurring in Π. We define a **negation-only vector** as $\mathbf{x} = (x_1, x_2, \ldots, x_k)^{\mathrm{T}} \in \{0,1\}^k$, which is a binary vector, where $x_i = 1$ if $\neg a_i$ is included in the represented subset of $\mathcal{A}_\Pi^-$, and $x_i = 0$ otherwise. In other words, a negation-only vector is the characteristic vector of a subset of the negative literals occurring in Π. For example, $\mathbf{x}^{\mathrm{T}} = (\overset{\neg a}{0}\ \overset{\neg c}{1}\ \overset{\neg d}{0}\ \overset{\neg g}{0}\ \overset{\neg h}{1})$ is a negation-only vector of Π_1, representing the subset $\{\neg c, \neg h\}$.

The negation-only vector is closely related to the full-set characterization of stable models in [22]. In particular, the support of such a vector corresponds to a candidate set of negative literals occurring in the program. Thus, the negation-only vector should not be understood as a new semantic object, but as a linear-algebraic representation of a full-set candidate. The contribution of this paper is to formulate the corresponding reduct and stable-model test through matrix-vector transformations and to exploit this formulation for incremental and decremental search.

Each of the sets $\mathscr{B}_\Pi$, $\mathcal{A}_\Pi$, and $\mathcal{A}_\Pi^-$ induces a corresponding space of binary vectors. Each vector in such a space is the characteristic vector of a subset of the associated set. Because of the one-to-one correspondence between subsets and their characteristic vectors, we use set-theoretic notation and operations interchangeably with their vector representations whenever the meaning is clear from the context. For readability, vectors are written in transposed form, and components with value 0 may be omitted when they are not relevant to the discussion.

Before constructing the program matrix, constraints are handled by a preprocessing step. Each constraint is replaced by a normal rule whose head is a fresh auxiliary atom representing a constraint violation. The matrix construction is then applied to the transformed normal program. During candidate checking, any candidate deriving such an auxiliary atom is rejected, and the final stable model is obtained by projecting the result onto the original atoms.

Our construction of the program matrix follows the approach of [25]. For a standardized logic program Π, we associate a *program matrix* $\mathbf{M}_\Pi$, which serves as the core representation for the linear algebraic fixpoint computation introduced later. Each row of $\mathbf{M}_\Pi$ corresponds to a rule in Π, and each column corresponds to a literal in $\mathcal{A}_\Pi$. For an *And*-rule with $k \geq 1$ body literals, each matrix entry corresponding to a body literal is assigned the value $1/k$. For an *Or*-rule, each such entry is assigned the value 1. Facts are represented by setting the diagonal entry of the corresponding head atom to 1. All remaining entries are set to 0. A program matrix does not encode constraints in a program. Constraint satisfaction is checked separately after computing a fixpoint. Figure 1a illustrates the program matrix $\mathbf{M}_{\Pi_1}$ for the standardized program Π_1 from Example 1. The figure also includes the *permutation matrix* $\mathbf{U}_{\Pi}$ and the *verification matrix* $\mathbf{V}_{\Pi}$ that will be defined in the following sections.

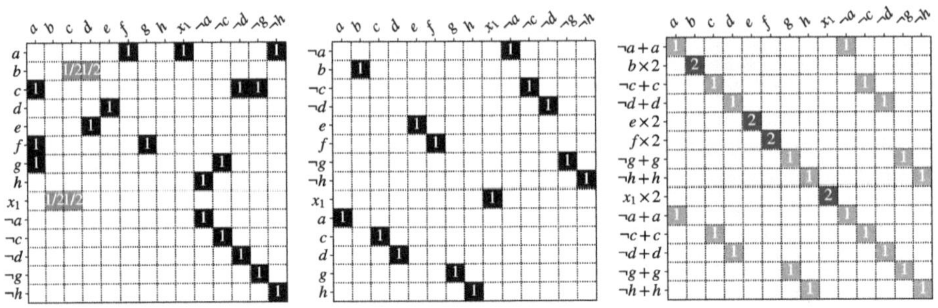

(a) $\mathbf{M}_{\Pi_1}$ (b) $\mathbf{U}_{\Pi_1}$ (c) $\mathbf{V}_{\Pi_1}$

Fig. 1. *Program matrix* $\mathbf{M}_{\Pi_1^{\wedge}}$, *permutation matrix* $\mathbf{U}_{\Pi_1}$ and *verification matrix* $\mathbf{V}_{\Pi_1}$.

4 Linear Algebraic Definition of Stable Model Semantics

This section studies stable model semantics through a sequence of linear transformations. We denote by $\mathbf{v}_{\Pi^F}$ the characteristic vector of the program facts and summarize the notation used in this section in Table 1.

For an interpretation $I \subseteq \mathscr{B}_P$, we define its core with respect to the standardized form Π of the normal program P as: $\text{core}_{\Pi}(I) = \{\neg p \in \mathcal{A}_{\Pi}^{-} \mid p \notin I\}$. Equivalently, $\text{core}_{\Pi}(I)$ is identified with its characteristic vector of the negative literals in $\mathcal{A}_{\Pi}^{-}$ that are satisfied by I. This vector is unique for each interpretation I. This representation is closely related to full-set candidates in the sense of [22]; here we use it as a linear-algebraic representation of the assumptions determining a program reduct.

Proposition 1. *Let P be a normal logic program and let Π be its standardized form. For any interpretation $X \subseteq \mathscr{B}_P$, let $\mathbf{x} = \text{core}_{\Pi}(X)$. Then the program matrix $\mathbf{M}_{\Pi}$, together with the initial vector $\mathbf{v}_{\Pi^F} + \mathbf{x}$, represents the corresponding standardized reduct determined by P^X. In particular, the fixpoint $FP(\mathbf{M}_{\Pi}, \mathbf{y}_0)$, where $\mathbf{y}_0 = \boldsymbol{expand}_{\mathcal{A}_{\Pi}}(\mathbf{v}_{\Pi^F} + \mathbf{x})$, yields the least Herbrand model of the corresponding reduct after projection onto the original atoms.*

Proof. By the definition of the Gelfond–Lifschitz reduct, a rule r of P survives in P^X iff none of the atoms occurring under default negation in r belongs to X, that is, iff $body^{-}(r) \cap X = \emptyset$. Equivalently, for every atom p occurring under default negation in r, the corresponding negative literal $\neg p$ belongs to $\text{core}_{\Pi}(X)$.

Table 1. Some notations used in this paper.

Notation	Definition/Meaning	Example
$\theta^{\Downarrow}(x)$, $\theta^{\Downarrow}(\mathbf{v})$, $\theta^{\Downarrow}(\mathbf{M})$	$\theta^{\Downarrow}(x) = \begin{cases} 1 & \text{if } x \geq 1 \\ 0 & \text{otherwise} \end{cases}$	$\theta^{\Downarrow}(0.7) = 0$, $\theta^{\Downarrow}(1.2) = 1$, $\theta^{\Downarrow}(0) = 0$
$\theta^{\Uparrow}(x)$, $\theta^{\Uparrow}(\mathbf{v})$, $\theta^{\Uparrow}(\mathbf{M})$	$\theta^{\Uparrow}(x) = \begin{cases} 1 & \text{if } x > 0 \\ 0 & \text{otherwise} \end{cases}$	$\theta^{\Uparrow}(0.7) = 1$, $\theta^{\Uparrow}(1.2) = 1$, $\theta^{\Uparrow}(0) = 0$
$\mathbf{expand}_{\mathbf{u}}(\mathbf{v})$	Expanding $\mathbf{v}$ space to $\mathbf{u}$ space (simply expanding with 0-fill).	$\mathbf{expand}_{\{a,b,\neg a,\neg b\}}(\overset{\neg a\ \ \neg b}{(0\ \ 1)}) = \overset{a\ \ b\ \ \neg a\ \ \neg b}{(0\ \ 0\ \ 0\ \ 1)}$
$\mathbf{reduce}_{\mathbf{u}}(\mathbf{v})$	Reducing $\mathbf{v}$ space to $\mathbf{u}$ space (simply extraction).	$\mathbf{reduce}_{\{a,b\}}(\overset{a\ \ b\ \ \neg a\ \ \neg b}{(0\ \ 0\ \ 0\ \ 1)}) = \overset{a\ \ b}{(0\ \ 0)}$

Therefore, the vector $\mathbf{x} = \text{core}_{\Pi}(X)$ activates exactly those negative literals whose corresponding default-negated literals are satisfied by X, and disables the rules whose negative literals are not activated. Hence, starting the matrix computation from

$$\mathbf{y}_0 = \mathbf{expand}_{\mathcal{A}_{\Pi}}(\mathbf{v}_{\Pi^F} + \mathbf{x})$$

has the same effect as constructing the reduct determined by X. After this step, the remaining program is positive, and the matrix-vector iterations compute its least fixpoint. Consequently, $FP(\mathbf{M}_{\Pi}, \mathbf{y}_0)$, after projection onto the original atoms, yields the least Herbrand model of the corresponding reduct. □

Consider the program Π_1 in Example 1, there is no fact in Π_1, so $\mathbf{v}_{\Pi^F}$ is a zero vector, to match the dimension of vector addition, we reduce it to the same space as negation-only vector $\mathbf{x}$. Note that a vector of negative literals $\mathbf{x} \subseteq \mathcal{A}_{\Pi}^{-}$ can be interpreted either as a subset of $\mathcal{A}_{\Pi_1}^{-}$ or as a subset of $\mathscr{B}_{\Pi_1}$. For example:

$$\mathbf{x} = \overset{\neg a\ \ \ \neg c\ \ \ \neg d\ \ \ \neg g\ \ \ \neg h}{\begin{pmatrix} 1 & 0 & 0 & 1 & 1 \end{pmatrix}}$$

can be interpreted as $\{\neg a, \neg g, \neg h\} \subseteq \mathcal{A}_{\Pi_1}^{-}$ or $\{c, d\} \subseteq \mathscr{B}_{\Pi_1}$. For this interpretation, the corresponding program reduct is $\Pi_1^{\{c,d\}} = \{a \leftarrow b \wedge c,\ a \leftarrow f,\ a \leftarrow,\ b \leftarrow c \wedge d,\ c \leftarrow a,\ c \leftarrow\ d \leftarrow e,\ e \leftarrow d,\ f \leftarrow a,\ f \leftarrow g,\ g \leftarrow a,\ h \leftarrow,\ \leftarrow c \wedge h,\ \leftarrow b \wedge a\}$. Computing $\mathbf{M}_{\Pi_1} \cdot (\mathbf{v}_{\Pi_1^F} + \mathbf{x})$ has the effect of disabling the rules whose negative literals are not in $\mathbf{x}$ and keeping the rules whose negative literals are in $\mathbf{x}$, which is exactly the same as computing the program reduct $\Pi_1^{\{c,d\}}$. Accordingly, Proposition 1 shows us that finding stable models can be done by finding program reducts. Thus, the problem can be reduced to finding $\mathbf{x} \in \mathcal{A}_{\Pi}^{-}$. Next, we define a sequence of linear transformations based on the vector space of $\mathbf{x}$ to realize the stable model semantics.

First, similar to Definition 13 in [25], the fixpoint computation is defined as follows:

$$\mathbf{y} = \mathbf{expand}_{\mathcal{A}_\Pi}(\mathbf{v}_{\Pi^F} + \mathbf{x}),\ \mathbf{x} \in \mathcal{A}_\Pi^-$$
$$\mathbf{y}_0 = \mathbf{y};\ \mathbf{y}_{i+1} = \theta^{\Downarrow}(\mathbf{M}_\Pi \cdot \mathbf{y}_i) \quad (i \geq 0)$$

Because of monotonicity property, at a finite deduction step $s \geq 1$, it holds that $\mathbf{y}_{s+1} = \mathbf{y}_s$ as proved in Proposition 4 in [25]. The vector $\mathbf{y}_s$ is called a *fixpoint* and is written as $\mathbf{y}_s = FP(\mathbf{M}_\Pi, \mathbf{y}_0)$. Then, as also pointed out in Theorem 1 of [25], the least Herbrand model of the corresponding program reduct is $FP(\mathbf{M}_\Pi, \mathbf{y}_0) \cap \mathscr{B}_\Pi$.

According to [24,25], from a vector $FP(\mathbf{M}_\Pi, \mathbf{y}_0)$, we can extract the least Herbrand model, by taking $FP(\mathbf{M}_\Pi, \mathbf{y}_0) \cap \mathscr{B}_\Pi$. In fact, this is corresponding to the *LHM*(P^X) of a program reduct, such that $X \cap \mathcal{A}_\Pi^- = \mathbf{x}$. By definition, X is a stable model of P iff $X =$ *LHM*(P^X). We shall define this stable model condition in vector space. Before that, let us introduce the definitions of *permutation matrix* and *verification matrix*.

Definition 1. (Permutation Matrix and Verification Matrix). *Given a standardized program Π, the permutation matrix $\mathbf{U}_\Pi$ is obtained by taking an identity matrix $\mathbf{I} \in \mathbb{R}^{n_\Pi \times n_\Pi}$ and swapping every pair of rows corresponding to each pair of positive and negative literals in Π. A verification matrix $\mathbf{V}_\Pi$ then is obtained by $\mathbf{U}_\Pi + \mathbf{I}$.*

Figure 1b and Fig. 1c show the visualization of $\mathbf{U}_{\Pi_1}$ and $\mathbf{V}_{\Pi_1}$ for Π_1. From the visualization, it is intuitive to generalize the idea behind $\mathbf{U}_\Pi$ and $\mathbf{V}_\Pi$. Given a vector $\mathbf{y} \in \mathcal{A}_\Pi$, by multiplying $\mathbf{U}_\Pi \cdot \mathbf{y}$, we obtain a vector in which all positive and negative literals are swapped. Then we compute $\mathbf{y} + \mathbf{U}_\Pi \cdot \mathbf{y} = (\mathbf{I} + \mathbf{U}_\Pi) \cdot \mathbf{y} = \mathbf{V}_\Pi \cdot \mathbf{y}$ (where $\mathbf{I}$ is an identity matrix). This performs a transformation from $\mathcal{A}_\Pi$ to an *imaginary space* where we can verify the occurrences of a pair of positive and negative literals p vs. $\neg p$ by checking that $\neg p + p = 1$. Note that writing $\neg p + p$ is just a convenient way to refer to the corresponding position of the resulting vector. If both p and $\neg p$ are present, then $\neg p + p = 2$; if none of p and $\neg p$ are present, then $\neg p + p = 0$.

By exploiting the swapping behavior of $\mathbf{U}_\Pi$, we define a *complement vector* of $\mathbf{x} \in \mathcal{A}_\Pi^-$ as follows:

$$\text{cpl}(\mathbf{x}) = \mathbf{expand}_{\mathcal{A}_\Pi}(\mathbf{x}) + \mathbf{U}_\Pi \cdot \mathbf{expand}_{\mathcal{A}_\Pi}(\mathbb{1} - \mathbf{x}) \tag{4}$$

cpl($\mathbf{x}$) is used for representing the complement of $\mathbf{x}$ in Herbrand base, but for fixpoint computation, we must start from $\mathbf{x}$ as it is an equivalent representation of a program reduct as pointed out in Proposition 1.

We are now ready to state the stable model condition:

Definition 2 (Stable Model Condition). *Given a logic program P in its standardized form Π, a vector $\mathbf{x} \in \mathcal{A}_\Pi^-$ is called a stable model core iff $\mathbf{x}$ is both initially and fixpoint consistent, and satisfies the following condition:*

$$\mathbf{reduce}_{\mathcal{A}_{\Pi}^{-}}(\mathbf{V}_{\Pi} \cdot FP(\mathbf{M}_{\Pi}, \mathbf{y}_0)) = \mathbb{1} \tag{5}$$

where $\mathbb{1}$ *is a fixed vector of 1 s.*
Then $S_{\mathbf{x}} = FP(\mathbf{M}_{\Pi}, \mathbf{y}_0) \cap \mathscr{B}_{\Pi}$ *is a stable model of* P.

For short, denote $\mathbf{reduce}_{\mathcal{A}_{\Pi}^{-}}(\mathbf{V}_{\Pi} \cdot FP(\mathbf{M}_{\Pi}, \mathbf{y}_0))$ as $\mathcal{V}_{\Pi,\mathbf{x}}$.

Theorem 1 *Any* $S_{\mathbf{x}}$ *such that* $\mathbf{x}$ *is a stable model core satisfying Definition 2 is a stable model of* P.

Proof. Given $\mathbf{x}$ is a vector together with a fixpoint vector $FP(\mathbf{M}_{\Pi}, \mathbf{y}_0)$ that satisfies Definition 2. Let $X = FP(\mathbf{M}_{\Pi}, \mathbf{y}_0) \cap \mathscr{B}_{\Pi}$ is an interpretation of P. As a consequence of Proposition 1, $\overline{X} \cap \mathcal{A}_{\Pi}^{-} = \mathbf{x}$ and $LHM(P^X) = FP(\mathbf{M}_{\Pi}, \mathbf{y}_0) \cap \mathscr{B}_{\Pi}$. Therefore, $X = LHM(P^X)$. Hence, X is a stable model of P. $S_{\mathbf{x}} = X$ and $S_{\mathbf{x}}$ is both initial and fixpoint consistent by definition, so the theorem is proved. □

Definition 2 and Theorem 1 show us that to search for stable models of P, we only need to look for the vectors $\mathbf{x} \in \mathcal{A}_{\Pi}^{-}$ that satisfy Definition 2. That is $\mathbf{x}$ is where we can get a stable model $S_{\mathbf{x}} = FP(\mathbf{M}_{\Pi}, \mathbf{y}_0) \cap \mathscr{B}_{\Pi}$. Definition 2 is equivalent to the definition in [11], but fully in vector spaces.

Figure 2 visualizes the result of the verification step for Π_1 on all 32 possible vectors $\mathbf{x} \in \mathcal{A}_{\Pi_1}^{-}$. There is only one vector $\{a, c, g\}$ satisfying (5) in Definition 2. Only one vector satisfies the stable-model condition (5); its corresponding fixpoint yields the unique stable model $\{a, c, f, g\}$ of P_1.

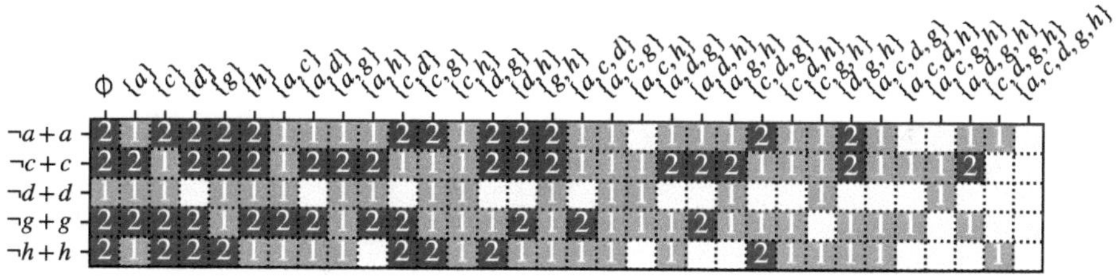

Fig. 2. Stable model verification for Π_1.

Taking a deeper look at the matrix representing all $\mathcal{V}_{\Pi_1,\mathbf{x}}$ in Fig. 2, we can observe many interesting properties that can be generalized from the stable model condition. We shall refer to $\mathbf{x}$ as an *assumption*, $FP(\mathbf{M}_{\Pi}, \mathbf{y}_0)$ as a *conclusion* from $\mathbf{x}$, and $\mathcal{V}_{\Pi,\mathbf{x}}$ as a *verified conclusion* of $\mathbf{x}$.

Proposition 2. *Under an assumption* $\mathbf{x}$ *(as a subset of* $\mathcal{A}_{\Pi}^{-}$*), if there is an index* i *such that* $\mathcal{V}_{\Pi,\mathbf{x}}[i] = 0$*, then* $cpl(\mathbf{x})$ *(as a subset of* $\mathscr{B}_{\Pi}$*) cannot be a subset of any stable model.* $\mathbf{x}$ *is referred as a* ***False*** *assumption.*

Proof. By Definition 2, $\mathbf{x}$ itself is not a stable model core. To prove the proposition, we need to prove there is no stable model core $\mathbf{x}'$ such that $\mathrm{cpl}(\mathbf{x}') \supset \mathrm{cpl}(\mathbf{x})$. Assume there is a vector $\mathbf{x}'$ such that $\mathrm{cpl}(\mathbf{x}') \supset \mathrm{cpl}(\mathbf{x})$. By definition, there must be at least an index j such that $\mathbf{x}'[j] = 0$ while $\mathbf{x}[j] = 1$ and there is no index k such that $\mathbf{x}'[j] = 1$ while $\mathbf{x}[j] = 0$ (simply means that nonzero-elements of $\mathbf{x}$ cover that of $\mathbf{x}'$). Hence, there is no way from $\mathbf{x}'$, through the defined transformations (matrix-vector multiplications and $\theta^{\Downarrow}$-thresholding), that makes $\mathcal{V}_{\Pi,\mathbf{x}'}[i]$ become 1 ($\mathcal{V}_{\Pi,\mathbf{x}'}[i]$ must be 0). Accordingly, $\mathbf{x}'$ cannot be a stable model core, therefore, the proposition is proved. □

For example, in Fig. 2, $\mathcal{V}^{\mathrm{T}}_{\Pi,\{a,h\}} = (1, 2, 1, 2, 0)$. Then, by Proposition 2, $\{a, h\}$ cannot be a part of any stable model, so that we do not need to check any superset of it.

Proposition 3. *Under an assumption* $\mathbf{x}$ *(as a subset of* $\mathcal{A}^{-}_{\Pi}$*), which is not a* ***False*** *assumption, if there is any index* i *such that* $\mathcal{V}_{\Pi,\mathbf{x}}[i] = 1$ *other than* $\mathrm{cpl}(\mathbf{x})$ *(as a subset of* $\mathscr{B}_{\Pi}$*), then to reach a stable model, the variable corresponding to that index must be* ***False*** *(must be included in* $\mathbf{x}$ *and must not be included in* $\mathrm{cpl}(\mathbf{x})$*) under assumption* $\mathbf{x}$.

Proof. Let p is a variable such that $\neg p \in \mathcal{A}^{-}_{\Pi}$, and p is corresponding to an index i in $\mathbf{x} \in \mathcal{A}^{-}_{\Pi}$. Let $FP(\mathbf{M}_{\Pi}, \mathbf{y}_0)$ be the fixpoint starting from $\mathbf{x}$. By definition, $\mathcal{V}_{\Pi,\mathbf{x}}[i] = \{0, 1, 2\}$. $\mathcal{V}_{\Pi,\mathbf{x}}[i] = 0$ only happens when $\neg p \notin \mathbf{x}$ and $p \notin FP(\mathbf{M}_{\Pi}, \mathbf{y}_0)$. On the other hand, $\mathcal{V}_{\Pi,\mathbf{x}}[i] = 2$ only happens when $\neg p \in \mathbf{x}$ and $p \in FP(\mathbf{M}_{\Pi}, \mathbf{y}_0)$. To prove the proposition, we need to prove that there is no stable model core $\mathbf{x}'$ such that $\mathrm{cpl}(\mathbf{x}') \supseteq \mathrm{cpl}(\mathbf{x}) \cup \{p\}$.
By definition, $p \notin \mathrm{cpl}(\mathbf{x})$, so $\mathbf{x}[i] = 1$. Together with $\mathcal{V}_{\Pi,\mathbf{x}}[i] = 1$, we know that $p \notin FP(\mathbf{M}_{\Pi}, \mathbf{y}_0)$ (the fixpoint starting from $\mathbf{x}$). Assume there is a vector $\mathbf{x}'$ such that $\mathrm{cpl}(\mathbf{x}') \supseteq \mathrm{cpl}(\mathbf{x}) \cup \{p\}$. By including p, $\mathbf{x}'[i] = 0$ following definition. Hence there is no way from $\mathbf{x}'$, through the defined transformations (matrix-vector multiplications and $\theta^{\Downarrow}$-thresholding), makes $\mathcal{V}_{\Pi,\mathbf{x}'}[i]$ become 1 ($\mathcal{V}_{\Pi,\mathbf{x}'}[i]$ must be 0). The proposition holds. □

For example, in Fig. 2, $\mathcal{V}^{\mathrm{T}}_{\Pi_1,\{a,c\}} = (1, 1, 1, 2, 1)$. There are indices 3 and 5 corresponding to d and h such that $\mathcal{V}_{\Pi_1,\{a,c\}}[3] = 1$, $\mathcal{V}_{\Pi_1,\{a,c\}}[5] = 1$ and $d,\ h \notin \{a, c\}$. By Proposition 3, d and h must be **False** under $\mathbf{x} = \{a, c\}$.

The idea is to construct an assumption incrementally from $\emptyset$ and test whether additional literals can be added to the current assumption. If a literal violates certain conditions, it can be excluded from all subsequent assumptions, i.e., treated as forced false. This intuition is formalized in Propositions 2 and 3, which are key to reducing the search space for stable models in the context of linear-algebraic computation.

5 In Search of Stable Models

5.1 Incremental Search

In practice, we should not compute the whole vector space shown in Fig. 2; for large search spaces, doing so is impossible. In those figures, the full input space over $\mathcal{A}^-_{\Pi_1}$ is shown only for illustration. Fortunately, Propositions 2 and 3 can be incorporated into a backtracking procedure to search for stable models incrementally. The main idea is to start from $\mathbf{x} = \emptyset$ and maintain a set $\mathcal{F}$ of literals that must be false under the current assumption $\mathbf{x}$. For simplicity, we denote $\mathcal{S}$ as the set of positive literals such that their corresponding negative literals are in $\mathcal{A}^-_{\Pi}$. This leads to *LaCIS* (**L**inear **a**lgebraic **C**omplete **I**ncremental **S**earch), shown in Algorithm 1.

Algorithm 1 Searching for stable models incrementally

LaCIS$(\mathbf{x}, \mathscr{V}_{\Pi,\mathbf{x}}, \mathscr{F}, \mathscr{S})$:

$\mathscr{F} = \mathscr{F} \cup \{p \mid \neg p \in \mathbf{x}, p$ corresponds to index i such that $\mathscr{V}_{\Pi,\mathbf{x}}[i] = 1\}$ ▷ Proposition 3
FOUND = **False**, $\mathscr{S} = \mathscr{S} \setminus \mathscr{F}$
if $|\mathscr{S}| = 0$ **then**
    return FOUND
$\mathbb{X} = init(\mathbf{x}, \mathscr{S}, \Pi^F)$
compute $\mathbb{Y} = FP(\mathbf{M}_\Pi, \mathbf{expand}_{\mathscr{A}_\Pi}(\mathbf{v}_{\Pi^F} \oplus \mathbb{X}))$
compute $\mathscr{V}_{\Pi,\mathbb{X}} = \mathbf{reduce}_{\mathscr{A}^-_\Pi}(\mathbf{V}_\Pi \cdot \mathbb{Y})$ ▷ Definition 2
if $|\{\mathscr{Y} \in \mathbb{Y} \mid \mathbf{reduce}_{\mathscr{A}^-_\Pi}(\mathbf{V}_\Pi \cdot \mathscr{Y}) = \mathbf{1}, \theta^{\Downarrow}(\mathbf{M}_{\Pi^C} \cdot \mathscr{Y}) = \mathbf{0}\}| > 0$ **then**
    output all satisfied $\mathbf{x} \cup \{s\}$ and set FOUND = **True**
$\mathscr{F} = \mathscr{F} \cup \{s \in \mathscr{S} \mid \mathscr{X} = \mathbf{x} \cup \{s\}$, there is index i such that $\mathscr{V}_{\Pi,\mathscr{X}}[i] = 0\}$ ▷ Proposition 2
$\mathscr{S} = \mathscr{S} \setminus \mathscr{F} \setminus \{s \in \mathscr{S}$ such that $\mathbf{x} \cup \{s\}$ is a stable model$\}$
for $i = 1$ to $|\mathscr{S}|$ **do**
    $s = \mathscr{S}[i]$
    if *LaCIS*$(\mathbf{x} \cup \{s\}, \mathscr{V}_{\Pi,\mathbf{x}\cup\{s\}}, \mathscr{F}, \mathscr{S}[i+1 \rightarrow])$ **then**
        FOUND = **True**
return FOUND

Overall, Algorithm 1 starts from $\mathbf{x} = \emptyset$ and gradually extends $\mathbf{x}$ by adding candidate variables. If the resulting verification vector contains a 0, we can discard that branch and all of its supersets by Proposition 2. If the vector contains some 1 s but not all 1 s, Proposition 3 lets us infer literals that must be false and prune the search further. Whenever the stable-model condition is satisfied, we output the corresponding stable model. Figure 3a illustrates the search tree of Algorithm 1 on the program Π_1 from Example 1.

5.2 Decremental Search

While *LaCIS* can be viewed as traversing the space from left to right starting at $\emptyset$ in Fig. 2, it is also possible to search in the opposite direction, that is, toward $\emptyset$. This yields a decremental strategy, *LaCDS* (**L**inear **a**lgebraic **C**omplete **D**ecremental **S**earch). Its implementation is very similar to that of *LaCIS*. Figure 3b shows the corresponding search tree.

For both incremental and decremental search methods, to avoid regenerating the same stable model, the search procedure is performed with respect to a fixed total order on atoms, say $a_1 < a_2 < \cdots < a_n$. Once an atom a_i has been selected, the subsequent search only considers atoms a_j with $j > i$. Therefore, the search enumerates subsets of atoms rather than permutations of atoms. For example,

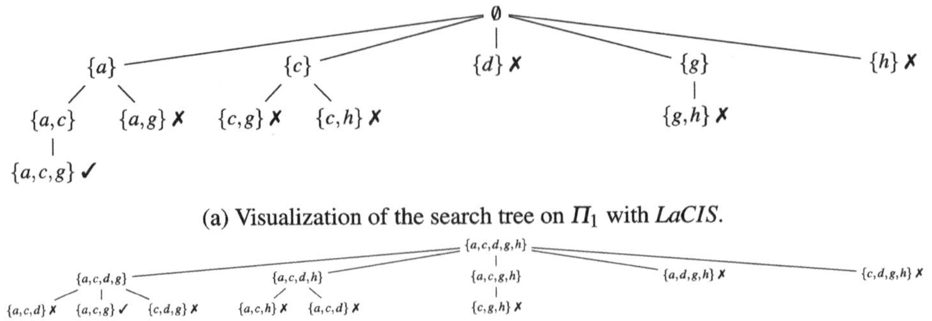

(a) Visualization of the search tree on Π_1 with *LaCIS*.

(b) Visualization of the search tree on Π_1 with *LaCDS*.

Fig. 3. Visualization of the search trees.

a stable model containing both a_1 and a_2 can be generated through the branch that selects a_1 before a_2, but the reverse order is never explored as a separate branch.

Although *LaCIS* and *LaCDS* are based on the same stable-model condition and use the same pruning principles, they differ in the direction in which the assumption space is explored. This difference affects their practical behavior, depending on where stable-model cores are located in the search space. Table 2 gives a concise comparison of the two strategies.

Table 2. Comparison between the two proposed search strategies.

Aspect	*LaCIS*	*LaCDS*
Search direction	Incremental	Decremental
Initial assumption	Starts from ∅	Starts from the full assumption
Search operation	Adds literals to the current assumption	Removes literals from the current assumption
Pruning basis	Propositions 2 and 3	Same pruning principles in the reverse direction
Suitable cases	Stable-model cores closer to ∅	Stable-model cores closer to the full assumption
Completeness	Complete enumeration	Complete enumeration
Memory usage	No pre-allocation of all assumptions	No pre-allocation of all assumptions

Remark. Although this paper focuses on complete enumeration, the stable-model condition in Equation (5) can also be reformulated as an equation-solving or optimization problem and addressed using root-finding or optimization methods. This is similar in spirit to [2,30], but our condition characterizes exactly stable models rather than possibly including supported models. Combining this condition with optimization, heuristic search, or learning-guided initialization is a promising direction for future work.

6 Experimental Results

Our goal is to improve the performance of linear-algebraic methods for stable model computation. We developed `pylalp`, an experimental pure-Python implementation using `numpy` and `scipy` for matrix operations. It implements the proposed *LaCIS* and *LaCDS* methods, as well as the previous linear-algebraic approach of [25], denoted by `pylalp`-*LA*, for comparison. Although a comparison with `clingo` [9] is not the main objective, we also report side-by-side results in several experiments. All benchmark instances are pre-grounded into propositional form, as `pylalp` currently supports only propositional logic. For `clingo`, grounding and solving times are recorded separately. For `pylalp`, we report warmup time, including standardization and matrix/vector memory allocation, and solving time. Sparse matrix formats are used by default. All experiments were conducted on a laptop running Ubuntu 20.04 LTS with an Intel Core i7-11800H CPU and 32GB RAM.

6.1 Choosing K from N Variables $\Pi_{\mathscr{C}(N,K)}$

In this experiment, we consider the problem of choosing K out of N elements, denoted by $\Pi_{\mathscr{C}(N,K)}$. For example, $\Pi_{\mathscr{C}(3,2)} = \{a_1 \leftarrow \neg a_3,\ a_1 \leftarrow \neg a_2,\ a_2 \leftarrow \neg a_3,\ a_2 \leftarrow \neg a_1,\ a_3 \leftarrow \neg a_2,\ a_3 \leftarrow \neg a_1\}$. For a given $\Pi_{\mathscr{C}(N,K)}$, there are $\mathscr{C}(N,K)$ stable models, which is already a very large number even for moderate values of N and K. We note that the same combinatorial problem can be encoded more compactly in ASP using a native cardinality rule, such as: $K\{a_1;\ldots;a_N\}K$. Such an encoding is natural for modern ASP solvers such as `clingo`. However, our matrix-based method is defined for explicit standardized representations derived from normal logic programs and cannot be applied directly to cardinality rules or aggregates. Therefore, in order to keep the comparison on the same input representation, the experiments reported here use the explicit normal-rule encoding $\Pi_{\mathscr{C}(N,K)}$ for both our methods and `clingo`. We do not include a separate experiment using `clingo`'s native cardinality-rule encoding, since it would serve only as a reference for `clingo`'s built-in aggregate handling rather than as a direct baseline for the proposed matrix-based method.

We consider two cases: (1) $\Pi_{\mathscr{C}(N,1)}$, where $K = 1$ is fixed and N varies; and (2) $\Pi_{\mathscr{C}(20,K)}$, where $N = 20$ is fixed and K varies. Case (1) is a special case of head-cycle-free disjunctive logic programs [3]. For case (1), we enumerate all N stable models; for case (2), we output up to 10 000 stable models. The results are shown in Fig. 4.

Figure 4a shows that `pylalp` - *LaCIS* performs favorably compared with `clingo` on $\Pi_{\mathscr{C}(N,1)}$. At $N = 2000$, `clingo` requires more than 6 min for grounding and almost 20 s for solving. Even if grounding time is excluded, `clingo` still remains significantly slower than `pylalp` - *LaCIS*. In contrast, `pylalp` - *LA* is limited by memory and can solve only instances with $N \leq 22$. `pylalp` - *LaCIS* finds all stable models within seconds. This behavior is expected because $\Pi_{\mathscr{C}(N,1)}$ is essentially a best-case scenario for Algorithm 1: it tests $\emptyset$ first, then all singleton

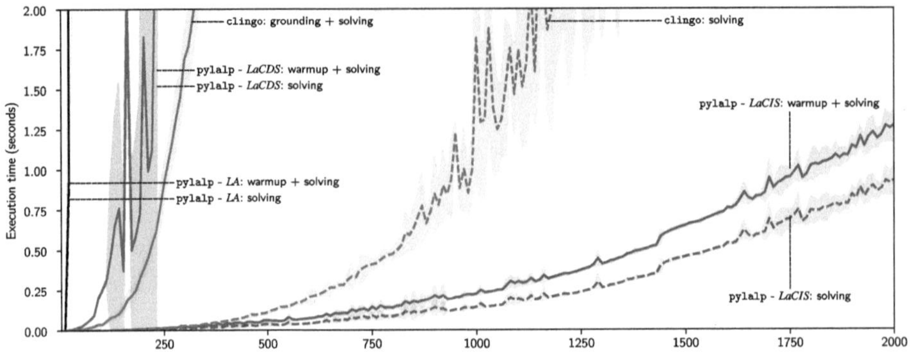

(a) $\Pi_{\mathscr{C}(N,1)}$ - find all N stable models (x-axis is N).

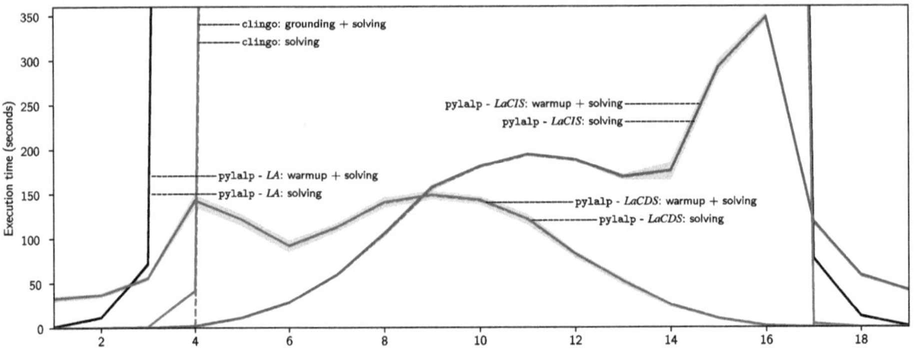

(b) $\Pi_{\mathscr{C}(20,K)}$ - find maximum 10 000 stable models (x-axis is K).

Fig. 4. Performance comparison for $\Pi_{\mathscr{C}(N,K)}$.

subsets, and stops. By contrast, `pylalp` - $LaCDS$ is less efficient here because the stable models lie closer to $\emptyset$.

The results in Fig. 4bare also notable: on our machine, `clingo` runs out of memory on instances from $\Pi_{\mathscr{C}(20,5)}$ to $\Pi_{\mathscr{C}(20,16)}$, typically after more than 3 min of execution. The same behavior can also be observed on smaller examples such as $\Pi_{\mathscr{C}(15,5)}$. In contrast, both `pylalp` - $LaCIS$ and `pylalp` - $LaCDS$ solve all cases. The runtime trend of `pylalp` - $LaCIS$ is expected because Algorithm 1 explores the search space breadth-first before going deeper. The trend for `pylalp` - $LaCDS$ is essentially the reverse of that observed for `pylalp` - $LaCIS$. The solid and dashed lines of `pylalp` - $LaCIS$ are almost identical because warmup time grows linearly and is negligible compared with solving time. Another interesting observation is that `pylalp` - LA is slower than `pylalp` - $LaCIS$ when $N \leq 3$, but faster when $17 \leq N \leq 20$. The reason is that `pylalp` - LA treats the search space uniformly by generating all possible combinations. In these particular cases, exhaustive generation and verification happen to be faster than search with pruning; in general, however, the method suffers severely from memory limitations.

6.2 Graph Coloring Problems

For the graph-coloring benchmark, we used pre-grounded normal programs in which constraints had already been normalized as described in Sect. 3. Both our implementation and `clingo` were evaluated on the same normalized programs, and models containing auxiliary violation atoms were discarded when interpreting the results. For example, a constraint forbidding adjacent vertices v_1 and v_2 from sharing the color red is represented by a rule deriving an auxiliary violation atom: $x \leftarrow col(v_1, red), col(v_2, red)$. A computed model is accepted as a valid coloring only if no such violation atom is derived; the reported coloring is then obtained by projecting the model onto the original coloring atoms.

Table 3. Results for graph coloring problems.

Graph instance ($\|N\|$ / $\|E\|$ / $\|C\|$)	*#atoms*	*#negs*	*#cons*	`pylalp` - *LA*			`pylalp` - *LaCIS*			`clingo`		
				#models	*#explored*	**Time** (s) (*mean* / *std*)	*#models*	*#explored*	**Time** (s) (*mean* / *std*)	*#models*	*#explored*	**Time** (s) (*mean* / *std*)
01_octahedral (6 / 12 / 3)	57	18	36	6 / 6	262 144	0.272 / 0.007	6 / 6	1198	0.029 / 0.000	6 / 6	13	0.010 / 0.001
02_33fan (6 / 11 / 3)	56	18	33	6 / 6	262 144	0.265 / 0.007	6 / 6	1441	0.034 / 0.000	6 / 6	13	0.006 / 0.003
03_42fan (6 / 9 / 3)	54	18	27	6 / 6	262 144	0.263 / 0.006	6 / 6	1579	0.042 / 0.001	6 / 6	13	0.011 / 0.000
04_K133 (7 / 15 / 3)	67	21	45	6 / 6	2 097 152	2.261 / 0.058	6 / 6	2923	0.078 / 0.002	6 / 6	13	0.007 / 0.006
05_43cone (7 / 16 / 3)	68	21	48	6 / 6	2 097 152	2.298 / 0.054	6 / 6	2560	0.056 / 0.001	6 / 6	13	0.011 / 0.002
06_43fan (7 / 14 / 3)	66	21	42	6 / 6	2 097 152	2.280 / 0.066	6 / 6	2948	0.083 / 0.001	6 / 6	13	0.011 / 0.001
07_52fan (7 / 11 / 3)	63	21	33	6 / 6	2 097 152	2.125 / 0.058	6 / 6	3775	0.103 / 0.002	6 / 6	13	0.011 / 0.001
08_K134 (8 / 19 / 3)	78	24	57	- / 6	-	OutOfMem	6 / 6	8157	0.207 / 0.003	6 / 6	13	0.013 / 0.000
myciel3 (11 / 20 / 4)	123	44	80	- / ?	-	OutOfMem	100 / ?	3741	0.104 / 0.002	100 / ?	205	0.016 / 0.004
myciel4 (23 / 71 / 5)	329	115	355	- / ?	-	OutOfMem	100 / ?	2750	0.133 / 0.002	100 / ?	219	0.021 / 0.004
myciel5 (47 / 236 / 6)	853	282	1416	- / ?	-	OutOfMem	100 / ?	7741	0.495 / 0.005	100 / ?	242	0.050 / 0.001
myciel6 (95 / 755 / 7)	2187	665	5285	- / ?	-	OutOfMem	100 / ?	33 019	2.416 / 0.018	100 / ?	280	0.165 / 0.010
jean (77 / 508 / 10)	2135	770	5080	- / ?	-	OutOfMem	100 / ?	30 541	2.918 / 0.023	100 / ?	276	0.178 / 0.004
huck (74 / 602 / 11)	2315	814	6622	- / ?	-	OutOfMem	100 / ?	31 374	3.684 / 0.030	100 / ?	272	0.224 / 0.004
david (87 / 812 / 11)	2824	957	8932	- / ?	-	OutOfMem	100 / ?	42 328	3.058 / 0.017	100 / ?	284	0.306 / 0.008

The current implementation of the proposed linear-algebraic approach does not include a dedicated constraint-propagation mechanism; constraints are handled only through the normalization step described above. Nevertheless, `pylalp` can still solve small graph-coloring instances. Table 3 reports the experimental results on selected graph instances[1,2]. The table records the number of *found*/*total* stable models (*#models*), the number of explored candidates (*#explored*), and the execution time, reported as mean and standard deviation (*mean*/*std*), for each algorithm.

The results show that `pylalp` - *LA* can solve only relatively small graph instances, because it explores the entire search space without pruning. In contrast, `pylalp` - *LaCIS* solves all selected instances while exploring substantially fewer candidates. In particular, `pylalp` - *LaCIS* can handle instances involving

[1] http://www.info.deis.unical.it/npdatalog/experiments/experiments.html.

[2] https://mat.tepper.cmu.edu/COLOR/instances.html.

thousands of normalized constraints, which are beyond the capability of `pylalp` - *LA*. However, `pylalp` - *LaCIS* remains slower than `clingo` in terms of execution time, since `clingo` employs highly optimized search and pruning techniques.

Discussion. The choice of $\Pi_{\mathscr{C}(N,K)}$ in 6.1 is to create a scalable problem in which stable models are located following their cardinality K in the search space growing exponentially by N. This setting requires a sophisticated search method to solve such problem instances. In summary, the proposed linear algebraic approaches are able to solve many real-world ASP problems. However, in such constraint-oriented cases like graph coloring, the algorithm has not yet achieved the same performance as `clingo` in pruning the search space. A key advantage is that the proposed methods function as enumeration algorithms, scale well, and therefore have the potential for further improvement.

7 Related Work

Stable model enumeration is one of the key computational problems in logic programming and ASP solving [1,10,23]. Algorithms for computing stable models are often based on search procedures related to DPLL and its conflict-driven extensions [16,17]. `smodels` [28], `assat(X)` [14], and `clingo` [9] are representative ASP systems following different solving paradigms. `smodels` is a DPLL-style branch-and-bound solver that follows a direct approach to stable-model computation, using propagation, lookahead, and backtracking to reduce the search space. `assat(X)` translates an ASP program into SAT via loop formulas and then uses a SAT solver `X` to find and enumerate stable models; thus, whether the resulting system is DPLL-style or CDCL-style depends on the backend solver `X`. `clingo` is based on Conflict-Driven Nogood Learning (CDNL), the ASP counterpart of CDCL, and uses the notion of *nogoods* from Constraint Satisfaction Problem (CSP) to obtain a uniform representation that supports advanced solving techniques from both CSP and SAT [10].

Search-based solvers use branching and backtracking, which are effective for pruning the search space but require specialized techniques for parallel execution. In contrast, Algorithm 1is designed to be parallelizable because it is based on linear-algebraic operations with a breadth-first search flavor. In graph theory, many breadth-first algorithms have been reformulated in linear-algebraic terms to achieve high scalability [13]. Designing a scalable linear-algebraic depth-first search remains a challenging and promising direction for future work [29].

8 Conclusion

We have presented a new linear-algebraic characterization of stable model semantics and shown its close relationship to the program reduct. Based on this stable-model condition, we proposed new algorithms for computing the stable models of normal logic programs. By introducing search into the linear-algebraic setting, we can enumerate all stable models using linear-algebraic methods, which has not been achieved before.

There are several directions for further improving the proposed method. Incorporating conflict learning and backjumping from ASP/SAT solvers is one promising direction. Another direction is to translate the stable-model condition into an optimization problem, which would allow the use of a wide range of efficient optimizers. The method could also benefit from the extension of linear-algebraic partial evaluation [18,21] to reduce the cost of fixpoint computation. Finally, the implementation can be improved further through parallelism and GPU acceleration, since linear-algebraic operations are naturally parallelizable.

Acknowledgments. This work has been supported by JST CREST Grant Number JPMJCR22D3, JSPS KAKENHI Grant Number JP25K03190 and Hanoi University of Science and Technology (HUST) under project number T2025-PC-019.

References

1. Alviano, M., Dodaro, C.: Answer set enumeration via assumption literals. In: AI* IA 2016 Advances in Artificial Intelligence: XVth International Conference of the Italian Association for Artificial Intelligence, pp. 149–163. Springer (2016)
2. Aspis, Y., Broda, K., Russo, A., Lobo, J.: Stable and supported semantics in continuous vector spaces. In: Proceedings of the 17th International Conference on Principles of Knowledge Representation and Reasoning, pp. 59–68 (2020)
3. Ben-Eliyahu, R., Dechter, R.: Propositional semantics for disjunctive logic programs. Ann. Math. Artif. Intell. **12**(1–2), 53–87 (1994)
4. Clark, K.L.: Negation as Failure. Logic and Data Bases, pp. 293–322 (1978)
5. Domingos, P.: Tensor Logic: The Language of AI. arXiv:2510.12269 arXiv preprint (2025)
6. Gao, K., Inoue, K., Cao, Y., Wang, H.: A differentiable first-order rule learner for inductive logic programming. Artif. Intell. **331**, 104108 (2024)
7. Gao, K., Inoue, K., Cao, Y., Wang, H., Yang, F.: Differentiable rule induction from raw sequence inputs. In: Proceedings of ICLR 2025 (2026)
8. Gao, K., Wang, H., Cao, Y., Inoue, K.: Learning from interpretation transition using differentiable logic programming semantics. Mach. Learn. **111**(1), 123–145 (2022)
9. Gebser, M., Kaminski, R., Kaufmann, B., Ostrowski, M., Schaub, T., Wanko, P.: Theory solving made easy with clingo 5. In: OASIcs-OpenAccess Series in Informatics, vol. 52, Schloss Dagstuhl-Leibniz-Zentrum fuer Informatik (2016)
10. Gebser, M., Kaufmann, B., Neumann, A., Schaub, T.: Conflict-driven answer set enumeration. In: Logic Programming and Nonmonotonic Reasoning: 9th International Conference, pp. 136–148. Springer (2007)
11. Gelfond, M., Lifschitz, V.: The stable model semantics for logic programming. ICLP/SLP **88**, 1070–1080 (1988)
12. Inoue, K.: Algebraic connection between logic programming and machine learning. In: Proceedings of the 17th International Symposium on Functional and Logic Programming (FLOPS 2024). LNCS, vol. 14659. Springer (2024)
13. Kepner, J., Gilbert, J.: Graph algorithms in the language of linear algebra. SIAM(2011)

14. Lin, F., Zhao, Y.: ASSAT: computing answer sets of a logic program by SAT solvers. Artif. Intell. **157**(1–2), 115–137 (2004)
15. Marek, W., Subrahmanian, V.: The relationship between stable, supported, default and autoepistemic semantics for general logic programs. Theoret. Comput. Sci. **103**(2), 365–386 (1992)
16. Marques Silva, J., Sakallah, K.: Grasp-a new search algorithm for satisfiability. In: Proceedings of International Conference on Computer Aided Design, pp. 220–227 (1996)
17. Marques Silva, J., Sakallah, K.: Grasp: a search algorithm for propositional satisfiability. IEEE Trans. Comput. **48**(5), 506–521 (1999)
18. Nguyen, H.D., Sakama, C., Sato, T., Inoue, K.: An efficient reasoning method on logic programming using partial evaluation in vector spaces. J. Log. Comput. **31**(5), 1298–1316 (2021)
19. Nguyen, T.Q., Inoue, K.: On converting logic programs into matrices. In: ICAART (2), pp. 405–415 (2023)
20. Nguyen, T.Q., Inoue, K., Sakama, C.: Enhancing linear algebraic computation of logic programs using sparse representation. N. Gener. Comput. **40**(1), 225–254 (2022)
21. Nguyen, T.Q., Inoue, K., Sakama, C.: Linear algebraic abduction with partial evaluation. In: Practical Aspects of Declarative Languages: 25th International Symposium, pp. 197–215. Springer (2023)
22. Niemelä, I.: Towards efficient default reasoning. In: IJCAI, pp. 312–318 (1995)
23. Pajunen, J., Janhunen, T.: Solution enumeration by optimality in answer set programming. Theory Pract. Logic Program. **21**(6), 750–767 (2021)
24. Sakama, C., Inoue, K., Sato, T.: Linear algebraic characterization of logic programs. In: International Conference on Knowledge Science, Engineering and Management, pp. 520–533. Springer (2017)
25. Sakama, C., Inoue, K., Sato, T.: Logic programming in tensor spaces. Ann. Math. Artif. Intell. **89**(12), 1133–1153 (2021). https://doi.org/10.1007/s10472-021-09767-x
26. Sato, T., Inoue, K., Sakama, C.: Abducing relations in continuous spaces. In: IJCAI, pp. 1956–1962 (2018)
27. Sato, T., Sakama, C., Inoue, K.: From 3-valued semantics to supported model computation for logic programs in vector spaces. In: ICAART (2), pp. 758–765 (2020)
28. Simons, P., Niemelä, I., Soininen, T.: Extending and implementing the stable model semantics. Artif. Intell. **138**(1–2), 181–234 (2002)
29. Spampinato, D.G., Sridhar, U., Low, T.M.: Linear algebraic depth-first search. In: Proceedings of the 6th ACM SIGPLAN International Workshop on Libraries, Languages and Compilers for Array Programming, pp. 93–104 (2019)
30. Takemura, A., Inoue, K.: Gradient-based supported model computation in vector spaces. In: Logic Programming and Nonmonotonic Reasoning, pp. 336–349, Springer International Publishing (2022). ISBN 978-3-031-15707-3

LLMs Find New Classes of Logic Programs

Chiaki Sakama[1,2(✉)]

[1] Wakayama University, Wakayama 640-8510, Japan
sakama@wakayama-u.ac.jp
[2] Hagoromo University of International Studies, Osaka 592-8344, Japan

Abstract. Large language models (LLMs) are often viewed as systems that reproduce existing patterns rather than generate new theoretical insights. Recent developments, however, suggest that when combined with formal verification, LLMs may assist in non-trivial theoretical exploration. In this paper, we investigate this possibility in the context of logic programming. Disjunctive logic programs (DLPs) are more expressive than normal logic programs (NLPs) but incur higher computational complexity. A classical research direction therefore seeks syntactically restricted subclasses of DLPs that can be transformed into semantically equivalent NLPs in polynomial time, such as head-cycle-free (HCF) programs via shifting. We present a case study in which LLMs are used as navigators to explore novel solutions. By challenging five state-of-the-art LLMs and rigorously verifying their outputs, we identify three previously unpublished subclasses of DLPs for which shifting preserves the stable model semantics. Beyond the specific subclasses obtained, this work demonstrates that LLM-assisted exploration, when paired with formal verification by humans, can support theoretical discovery in computer science and AI.

Keywords: Disjunctive logic programs · Head-cycle-free · Large language models

1 Introduction

Large language models (LLMs) have been viewed as probabilistic mimics, capable of summarizing existing knowledge but unable to generate genuinely novel outcomes. However, recent advances have enabled LLMs to perform complex problem solving and logical reasoning [10, 12]. When LLMs are embedded in systems that incorporate evaluation, search, and formal verification, they have been shown to contribute to mathematical discoveries [11, 14], experiment design [3, 13], and proof generation [1, 5]. These developments suggest that LLMs may serve not only as assistants, but also as generators of new scientific and mathematical knowledge.

This paper uses logic programming as a testbed for evaluating whether LLM-generated ideas can withstand formal scrutiny. In logic programming, disjunctive logic programs (DLPs) are generally more expressive than normal logic programs (NLPs), since the former resides at the second level of the polynomial hierarchy, whereas the latter resides at the first level. This complexity gap motivates the search for restricted DLP subclasses that can be reduced to equivalent NLPs in polynomial time. One such class

W. Faber et al. (Eds.): LPNMR 2026, LNAI 16952, pp. 399–414, 2027.
https://doi.org/10.1007/978-3-032-38320-4_25

is Head-Cycle-Free (HCF) DLPs such that a program has no cycle that goes through two atoms appearing in the head of a disjunctive rule [2]. For HCF DLPs, the standard shifting transformation preserves the stable model semantics [8]. Despite subsequent generalizations such as Head-Elementary-Set-Free (HEF) programs [6], it is unknown whether there are yet unidentified subclasses of DLPs that are reducible to NLPs in polynomial time.

The current study poses a challenge to five state-of-the-art LLMs, asking them to propose new subclasses of DLPs that are reducible to NLPs via shifting and to provide accompanying correctness arguments. Each proposal is rigorously analyzed, and either rejected or refined through iterative interaction and formal verification. We further analyze the relationships between the proposed subclasses and the known HEF class, establishing strict inclusions and incomparabilitics. While the practical utility of the individual subclasses may vary, the broader contribution of this work is methodological. It demonstrates that LLMs, when used as generators of candidate structures and combined with rigorous human verification, can contribute meaningfully to formal research in computational logic and artificial intelligence.

The rest of the paper is organized as follows. Section 2 reviews basic notions of logic programming and stable model semantics. Section 3 introduces the three subclasses discovered through LLM-assisted exploration and presents correctness proofs. Section 4 analyzes their relationships with the HEF class. Section 5 discusses the implications and limitations of the approach, and Sect. 6 concludes with directions for future work.

2 Preliminaries

A *disjunctive (logic) program* (DLP) considered in this paper is a finite set of *rules* of the form:

$$h_1 \vee \cdots \vee h_l \leftarrow b_1, \ldots, b_m, \, not\, b_{m+1}, \ldots, \, not\, b_n \tag{1}$$

($l \geq 0$; $n \geq m \geq 0$) where each h_i and b_j are propositional atoms and not represents default negation. A literal is either an atom or its negation. The left-hand side of $\leftarrow$ is the *head*, and the right-hand side is the *body*. For each rule r of the form (1), $H(r)$, $B^+(r)$, and $B^-(r)$ denote the sets of atoms $\{h_1, \ldots, h_l\}$, $\{b_1, \ldots, b_m\}$, and $\{b_{m+1}, \ldots, b_n\}$, respectively. Also, define $B(r) = \{b_1, \ldots, b_m, not\, b_{m+1}, \ldots, not\, b_n\}$. The rule (1) is often written as: $H(r) \leftarrow B^+(r), \mathrm{not}\, B^-(r)$ or $H(r) \leftarrow B(r)$. A rule r is called a *disjunctive rule* if $|H(r)| > 1$, and is called a *normal rule* if $|H(r)| \leq 1$. A normal rule r is a *Horn rule* if $B^-(r) = \varnothing$, and it is called a *constraint* if $H(r) = \varnothing$. A DLP P is called a *normal (logic) program* (NLP) if $|H(r)| \leq 1$ for every rule r in P. A DLP P is called a *positive program* if $B^-(r) = \varnothing$ for every rule r in P. An NLP P is called a *Horn program* if $B^-(r) = \varnothing$ for every rule r in P. We simply call P a *program* when it is unimportant to distinguish program classes.

The semantics of a DLP is defined by the *stable model semantics* [8,9]. Let $\mathrm{At}(P)$ be the set of propositional atoms occurring in a program P. An interpretation $I \subseteq \mathrm{At}(P)$ *satisfies* a rule r (written $I \models r$) if $I \models B(r)$ implies $H(r) \cap I \neq \varnothing$ where $I \models B(r)$ means $B^+(r) \subseteq I$ and $B^-(r) \cap I = \varnothing$. An interpretation I satisfying every rule in a program P is a *model* of the program (written $I \models P$). Given a positive program P, a model I of P is *minimal* if there is no model J of P such that $J \subset I$. Given a

DLP P, an interpretation I is a *stable model* of P if it coincides with a minimal model of the positive program (called a *(GL-)reduct* of P with respect to I): $P^I = \{ H(r) \leftarrow B^+(r) \mid H(r) \leftarrow B^+(r), \text{not}\, B^-(r) \in P \text{ and } B^-(r) \cap I = \varnothing \}$. Stable models coincide with minimal models in a positive program, and a stable model coincides with the least model in a Horn program. The set of stable models (resp. minimal models, least model) of P is denoted $\text{SM}(P)$ (resp. $\text{MM}(P)$, $\text{LM}(P)$).

The *(positive) dependency graph* of a program P is the directed graph $G(P) = (\text{At}(P), E)$ where $(x, y) \in E$ iff there exists a rule $r \in P$ with $x \in H(r)$ and $y \in B^+(r)$. We use standard terminology for strongly connected components (SCCs) in a graph. A directed cycle is a part of an SCC. Given a cycle $C \subseteq \text{At}(P)$, a rule $r \in P$ is *involved* in C if $H(r) \in C$. A DLP P is *Head-Cycle-Free* (HCF) if $G(P)$ contains no directed cycle that contains two different atoms from the head of a single disjunctive rule in P [2]. Let r be a rule with $H(r) = \{h_1, \ldots, h_l\}$ and $l \geq 2$:

$$h_1 \vee \cdots \vee h_l \leftarrow B(r).$$

Its *shift* (written $\text{sh}(r)$) is the collection of normal rules:

$$h_i \leftarrow B(r),\ \text{not}\big(H(r) \setminus \{h_i\}\big) \quad (i = 1, \ldots, l)$$

where $\text{not}(H(r) \setminus \{h_i\})$ abbreviates $\{not\ h_j : j \neq i\}$. Let $\text{sh}(P)$ be the program obtained from P by replacing each disjunctive rule r by its shift $\text{sh}(r)$, and keeping normal rules unchanged. Then the next result holds.

Proposition 1. ([2]) Let P be a HCF DLP. Then $\text{SM}(P) = \text{SM}(\text{sh}(P))$.

3 DLP Subclasses Found by LLM

The definitions and proofs in this section are derived from iterative interactions with LLMs and subsequently verified and refined by the (human) author. We use five LLMs: GPT-5.2 (Thinking), Gemini 2.5 Flash (thinking mode), Claude Sonnet 4.5, Grok 4, and DeepSeek-V3.2. The following prompt is given to each LLM.

> You are an expert in logic programming. Disjunctive logic programs (DLPs) are more expressive than normal logic programs (NLPs), since the former lies at the 2nd level of the polynomial hierarchy while the latter lies at the 1st level. On the other hand, a restricted class of DLPs can be transformed to semantically equivalent NLPs. One such class is the head-cycle-free DLP which has no cycle that goes through two atoms appearing in the head of a disjunctive rule. In this case, atoms in the head of a disjunctive rule are shifted to the body of the rule in their negated form, leaving one in the head. In a head-cycle-free DLP, its minimal models (or stable models) coincide with the stable models of the transformed NLP. Your task is to find a new class of DLPs that is more general than head-cycle-free DLPs. Consider only propositional cases and identify the syntax of the new program class. Add a formal proof why the shifting transformation or its variant preserves the semantics of the original program. Do not provide any one reported in the literature. Show the original result.

In the following, we provide three different classes of DLPs found by three LLMs. All definitions, theorems, proofs, and examples were generated by the LLMs and revised by the author as needed.

3.1 Negation-Separated HCF Programs (NS-HCF)

The class NS-HCF is proposed by GPT-5.2.

Definition 1 **($not_{a,b}$-Free Subprogram).**Let P be a DLP and $a, b \in \mathrm{At}(P)$. Define the *$not_{a,b}$-free subprogram*:

$$P_{a,b} = \{\, r \in P \mid a \notin B^-(r) \text{ and } b \notin B^-(r) \,\}.$$

Equivalently, $r \in P_{a,b}$ iff $B^-(r)$ contains neither $not\ a$ nor $not\ b$.

Definition 2 **(NS-HCF).** A DLP P is *Negation-Separated Head-Cycle-Free* (NS-HCF) if, for every rule $r \in P$ with $|H(r)| \geq 2$ and for every distinct pair of atoms $a, b \in H(r)$ $(a \neq b)$, a and b are *not* in the same SCC of $G(P_{a,b})$.

The key observation is that a positive dependency graph ignores default negation, even though default negation determines which rules survive the reduct under a candidate stable model. NS-HCF captures head-pair cyclicity only among rules that can survive when both head atoms are true.

Proposition 2 **(NS-HCF Extends HCF).** *Every HCF DLP is NS-HCF.*

Proof. If a DLP P is HCF, then for every distinct pair of atoms $a, b \in H(r)$ with $r \in P$, a and b are not in the same SCC of $G(P)$. Since $G(P_{a,b})$ is a subgraph of $G(P)$, the SCC-separation in P implies the SCC-separation in $P_{a,b}$. Hence, the result holds. □

The converse of Proposition 2 does not hold in general.

Example 1. (NS-HCF but not HCF) Let P be the program:

$$r_1: \ a \vee b \leftarrow,$$
$$r_2: \ a \leftarrow b, not\, a,$$
$$r_3: \ b \leftarrow a.$$

P is not HCF because there is a cycle $C = \{a, b\}$ and $H(r_1) = \{a, b\}$. For the pair (a, b), r_2 is ignored in $G(P_{a,b})$ which breaks the cycle. As a result, a and b are not in the same SCC of $G(P_{a,b})$, hence P is NS-HCF.

Thus, NS-HCF strictly generalizes HCF. Next, we show that shifting preserves stable models in NS-HCF DLPs.

Lemma 1 **(Cycle Deactivation).** *Let P be an NS-HCF DLP and M a set of atoms. If $M \in \mathrm{SM}(P)$, then for any disjunctive rule $r \in P$ such that $M \models B(r)$, no two distinct atoms $a, b \in H(r) \cap M$ belong to the same SCC in $G(P^M)$.*

Proof. Let $r \in P$ be a disjunctive rule such that $M \models B(r)$, and let $a, b \in H(r) \cap M$ ($a \neq b$) be distinct head atoms. By the definition of the GL-reduct, a rule $r \in P$ survives in P^M if and only if $B^-(r) \cap M = \varnothing$. Since $a, b \in M$, the condition $B^-(r) \cap M = \varnothing$ implies that $a \notin B^-(r)$ and $b \notin B^-(r)$. According to the definition of the $not_{a,b}$-free subprogram, any such rule r must belong to $P_{a,b}$. Consequently, the positive dependency graph of the reduct $G(P^M)$ is a subgraph of $G(P_{a,b})$. By the NS-HCF property, a and b are not in the same SCC of $G(P_{a,b})$. Since $G(P^M) \subseteq G(P_{a,b})$, a and b cannot belong to the same SCC in $G(P^M)$. □

Theorem 1 (Preservation for NS-HCF). *If a DLP P is NS-HCF, then* $\mathrm{SM}(P) = \mathrm{SM}(\mathrm{sh}(P))$.

Proof. We prove the equivalence in two directions.

(1) To show $\mathrm{SM}(P) \subseteq \mathrm{SM}(\mathrm{sh}(P))$, let $M \in \mathrm{SM}(P)$. Then M is a minimal model of the (positive) reduct P^M. We show that $M \in \mathrm{SM}(\mathrm{sh}(P))$, i.e., M is a minimal model of $\mathrm{sh}(P)^M$.

(a) First, we show $M \models \mathrm{sh}(P)^M$. Consider any rule $r \in P$. (i) If r is normal, then it is unchanged by shifting, so $M \models r$ implies $M \models \mathrm{sh}(r)$. (ii) Else if r is disjunctive and $M \not\models B(r)$, then every shifted rule obtained from r is satisfied vacuously in M. (iii) Else if r is disjunctive and $M \models B(r)$, then since $M \models r$ we have $H(r) \cap M \neq \varnothing$. Let $h \in H(r) \cap M$. The shifted rule with head h is satisfied because its head is true in M. For any other $h' \in H(r) \setminus \{h\}$, the shifted rule for h' contains not h in its body, which is false in M; hence that shifted rule is satisfied vacuously.
By (i)–(iii), $M \models \mathrm{sh}(P)$, and hence $M \models \mathrm{sh}(P)^M$.

(b) Next, we show that M is a minimal model. Assume for contradiction that there exists $N \subset M$ such that $N \models \mathrm{sh}(P)^M$. Let $S = M \setminus N \neq \varnothing$. Consider the SCC decomposition of $G(P^M)$. Choose an SCC C such that: (i) $C \cap S \neq \varnothing$, and (ii) no SCC C' with $C' \cap S \neq \varnothing$ is reachable from C (i.e., C is a sink SCC among the SCCs containing removed atoms). Let $K = M \setminus C$. Since M is a *minimal* model of P^M, K is *not* a model of P^M. Hence there exists a rule $r : H(r) \leftarrow B^+(r)$ in P^M such that $K \models B^+(r)$ and $H(r) \cap K = \varnothing$. From $H(r) \cap K = \varnothing$ and $K = M \setminus C$, we obtain $H(r) \cap M \subseteq C$. Moreover, since $M \models P^M$ and $K \models B^+(r) \subseteq M$, we have $H(r) \cap M \neq \varnothing$. Thus $H(r) \cap M$ is a nonempty subset of the SCC C.

We show $|H(r) \cap M| = 1$. If r is normal, $|H(r)| \leq 1$ and the claim is immediate. If r is disjunctive, then (as $r \in P^M$) M satisfies the corresponding body $B(r)$, and by Lemma 1 no two distinct atoms in $H(r) \cap M$ lie in the same SCC of $G(P^M)$. Since $H(r) \cap M \subseteq C$ and C is a single SCC, it follows that $|H(r) \cap M| = 1$. Let $H(r) \cap M = \{h\}$. Because $h \in C$ and $C \cap S \neq \varnothing$, we can take $h \in S$, hence $h \notin N$. Next we prove $B^+(r) \subseteq N$. Let $b \in B^+(r)$. By definition of $G(P^M)$, we have an edge (h, b), so b is reachable from h, hence the SCC containing b is reachable from C. If $b \notin N$, then that SCC would be a removed SCC reachable from C, contradicting that C is a sink SCC among removed SCCs. Therefore $b \in N$, and thus $B^+(r) \subseteq N$.

Now observe that $\mathrm{sh}(P)^M$ contains the Horn rule $h \leftarrow B^+(r)$. Indeed, if r is normal, it remains unchanged in $\mathrm{sh}(P)$ and survives into the reduct. If r is disjunctive, shifting produces the rule: $h \leftarrow B(r),\ \mathrm{not}\ (H(r) \setminus \{h\})$, and because $H(r) \cap M = \{h\}$ all other head atoms are not in M, so all negative literals are true in M and the reduct yields $h \leftarrow B^+(r)$. But $B^+(r) \subseteq N$ and $h \notin N$, so N violates this rule, contradicting $N \models \mathrm{sh}(P)^M$. Hence no such $N \subset M$ exists and M is a minimal model of $\mathrm{sh}(P)^M$. Therefore $M \in \mathrm{SM}(\mathrm{sh}(P))$, proving $\mathrm{SM}(P) \subseteq \mathrm{SM}(\mathrm{sh}(P))$.

(2) Next, to show $\mathrm{SM}(\mathrm{sh}(P)) \subseteq \mathrm{SM}(P)$, let $M \in \mathrm{SM}(\mathrm{sh}(P))$. Then M is a minimal model of $\mathrm{sh}(P)^M$. We show that $M \in \mathrm{SM}(P)$, i.e., M is a minimal model of P^M.

(a) First, we show $M \models P^M$. Consider any rule $r \in P$. If r is normal, it appears unchanged in $\mathrm{sh}(P)$, hence $M \models \mathrm{sh}(P)$ implies $M \models r$. Else if r is disjunctive and $M \models B(r)$, we show $H(r) \cap M \neq \varnothing$. Suppose otherwise that $H(r) \cap M = \varnothing$. Then for any $h \in H(r)$, the shifted rule: $h \leftarrow B(r),\ \mathrm{not}\,(H(r) \setminus \{h\})$ has its body true in M (since $B(r)$ is true and all head atoms are false, making all negative literals true), while its head is false, contradicting $M \models \mathrm{sh}(P)$. Thus $H(r) \cap M \neq \varnothing$, and so $M \models r$. Therefore $M \models P$, and hence $M \models P^M$ (every rule in P^M has its negative part satisfied by M).

(b) Next, we show that M is a minimal model. Assume for contradiction that there exists $N \subset M$ such that $N \models P^M$. We show $N \models \mathrm{sh}(P)^M$, contradicting the minimality of M for $\mathrm{sh}(P)^M$. Let $r' \in \mathrm{sh}(P)^M$. There are two cases. If r' comes from a normal rule of P, then $r' \in P^M$, so $N \models r'$. Else if r' comes from shifting a disjunctive rule $r \in P$, a shifted rule survives into the reduct $\mathrm{sh}(P)^M$ only in the Horn form $h \leftarrow B^+(r)$, and this happens only when $h \in H(r) \cap M$ and $(H(r) \setminus \{h\}) \cap M = \varnothing$, i.e., $H(r) \cap M = \{h\}$. Since $N \models P^M$, if $B^+(r) \subseteq N$ then N satisfies the reduct rule $H(r) \leftarrow B^+(r) \in P^M$, so $H(r) \cap N \neq \varnothing$. But $N \subseteq M$ and $H(r) \cap M = \{h\}$, hence necessarily $h \in N$. Therefore $N \models (h \leftarrow B^+(r)) = r'$.

Thus N satisfies every rule in $\mathrm{sh}(P)^M$, i.e., $N \models \mathrm{sh}(P)^M$. This contradicts the minimality of M as a model of $\mathrm{sh}(P)^M$. Hence no such $N \subset M$ exists, and M is a minimal model of P^M. Therefore $M \in \mathrm{SM}(P)$, proving $\mathrm{SM}(\mathrm{sh}(P)) \subseteq \mathrm{SM}(P)$. Combining (1) and (2), we obtain $\mathrm{SM}(P) = \mathrm{SM}(\mathrm{sh}(P))$, completing the proof. □

Example 2. For the program P of Example 1, it holds that $\mathrm{SM}(P) = \mathrm{SM}(\mathrm{sh}(P)) = \varnothing$.

NS-HCF is syntactic and polynomial-time checkable: for each disjunctive rule r and each pair $a \neq b \in H(r)$, build $P_{a,b}$ (or equivalently filter rules on the fly) and compute SCCs of $G(P_{a,b})$; reject if a and b fall in the same SCC. This is polynomial in $|P|$ (with a multiplicative factor in the number of head-pairs). While checking membership in NS-HCF is formally polynomial, the practical cost is far lower than a naive quadratic check of all atom pairs in $At(P)$. According to Definition 2, the SCC-separation check is restricted to distinct pairs $\{a, b\} \subseteq H(r)$ for each disjunctive rule $r \in P$. In most practical applications, the number of disjunctive rules is significantly smaller than the total number of rules, and the cardinality of $H(r)$ is typically a small constant (e.g., $|H(r)| = 2$). The overall complexity can be expressed as $O(\sum_{r \in P_{disj}} |H(r)|^2 \cdot (|V| + |E|))$, where P_{disj} is the set of disjunctive rules in P.

3.2 Trigger-Inhibited Head-Cycle Programs (TIHC)

The class TIHC is proposed by Gemini 2.5 Flash.

Definition 3 (Complement). If l is an atom a, then $\bar{l} = not\, a$; else if l is $not\, a$, then $\bar{l} = a$. We call $\bar{l}$ the *complement* of l.

Definition 4 (Inhibition). A rule r_c is *inhibited* by a rule r if the body of r_c contains a literal that is the complement of a literal in the body of r. That is,

$$B(r_c) \cap \{\bar{l} \mid l \in B(r)\} \neq \varnothing.$$

By definition, no rule is inhibited by a fact as the body of a fact is $true$. The core mechanism of TIHC is the contextual disabling of rules.

Definition 5 (TIHC). A DLP P is *Trigger-Inhibited Head-Cycle* (TIHC) if, for every rule $r \in P$ with $|H(r)| \geq 2$, the following condition holds: for every cycle C in $G(P)$ such that $|H(r) \cap C| \geq 2$, there exists at least one rule r_c involved in the cycle C such that r_c is inhibited by r.

TIHC programs generalize HCF programs by identifying cycles "guarded" by negation. Intuitively, any directed cycle between head atoms is inhibited by the rule's trigger (body). When the disjunction fires, complementary literals in the trigger logically disable the cycle's rules, preventing mutual support and ensuring stable models are preserved during shifting.

Proposition 3 (TIHC Extends HCF). *Every HCF DLP is TIHC.*

Proof. In an HCF program, no cycle C contains more than one atom from the head of any rule. Consequently, the antecedent of the TIHC condition ($|H(r) \cap C| \geq 2$) is always false, making the condition vacuously true. □

The converse of Proposition 3 does not hold in general.

Example 3. (TIHC but not HCF) Let P be the program:

$$\begin{aligned} r_1 &: \; a \vee b \leftarrow c, \\ r_2 &: \; a \leftarrow b,\; not\, c, \\ r_3 &: \; b \leftarrow a,\; not\, c, \\ r_4 &: \; c \leftarrow . \end{aligned}$$

There is a cycle $C = \{a, b\}$ in $G(P)$, so it is not HCF. For r_1 with $H(r_1) \cap C \geq 2$, r_2 is involved in the cycle C and r_2 is inhibited by r_1. Hence, P is TIHC.

Next, we show that shifting preserves stable models in TIHC DLPs.

Lemma 2 (Minimality of Shifting). *Let P be a DLP. If M is a minimal model of P^M and $|H(r) \cap M| \leq 1$ for any $r \in P$, then M is a minimal model of* $\mathrm{sh}(P)^M$.

Proof. Suppose that a disjunctive rule $r : a_1 \vee \cdots \vee a_k \leftarrow B(r)$ in P is replaced with normal rules $r_i : a_i \leftarrow B(r), not\,(H(r) \setminus \{a_i\})$ $(1 \leq i \leq k)$ in $\mathrm{sh}(P)$. Since M is a model of P, $M \not\models B(r)$ when $|H(r) \cap M| = 0$. In this case, r_i is satisfied by M. When $|H(r) \cap M| = 1$, $M \models r_i$ if $H(r) \cap M = \{a_i\}$; else if $H(r) \cap M = \{a_j\}$ $(j \neq i)$, $M \not\models not\,(H(r) \setminus \{a_i\})$. In each case, M satisfies $\mathrm{sh}(r_i)$ in $\mathrm{sh}(P)$. Hence, $M \models \mathrm{sh}(P)$, thereby a model of $\mathrm{sh}(P)^M$. Suppose that $M' \subset M$ is a model of $\mathrm{sh}(P)^M$. For each Horn rule $r : a \leftarrow B^+(r)$ in $\mathrm{sh}(P)^M$, two cases are considered. (i) the same Horn rule r is in P^M; or (ii) there is a disjunctive rule $r' : H(r') \leftarrow B^+(r')$ in P^M such that $H(r') \cap M = \{a\}$. In each case, M' satisfies the corresponding rule in P^M. Hence, M' is a model of P^M, which contradicts the fact that M is a minimal model of P^M. □

Lemma 3 (Cycle Deactivation). *Let P be a TIHC DLP and M a set of atoms. If $M \models B(r)$ for a disjunctive rule $r \in P$, then no two distinct atoms $a, b \in H(r) \cap M$ belong to the same SCC in $G(P^M)$.*

Proof. Suppose $a, b \in H(r) \cap M$ $(a \neq b)$ are in the same SCC of P^M. There must exist a cycle C in $G(P^M)$ containing both a and b. For C to exist in P^M, every rule r_c involved in the cycle must satisfy $B^-(r_c) \cap M = \varnothing$. To be $H(r_c) \cap C \subseteq M$, it must hold that $B^+(r_c) \subseteq M$. By the TIHC definition, at least one $r_c \in C$ is inhibited by r.

If the inhibiting literal $l \in B(r)$ is an atom c, then $c \in B^-(r_c)$. By $M \models B(r)$, it holds that $c \in M$, which implies $r_c \notin P^M$. Else if l is a negation *not* c, then $c \in B^+(r_c)$. By $M \models B(r)$, it holds that $c \notin M$, which implies $M \not\models B^+(r_c)$. In both cases, the cycle C is inactive or absent in P^M, contradicting the assumption that $a, b \in H(r) \cap M$ are in the same SCC of P^M. □

Theorem 2 (Preservation for TIHC). *If a DLP P is TIHC, then* $\mathrm{SM}(P) = \mathrm{SM}(\mathrm{sh}(P))$.

Proof. Let $M \in \mathrm{SM}(P)$. Then, M is a minimal model of P^M. For a disjunctive rule $r \in P$ such that $M \models B(r)$, no two distinct atoms in $H(r) \cap M$ belong to the same SCC in P^M (Lemma 3). Since no two head atoms depend on each other in $G(P^M)$, the minimality of M implies that only one atom from $H(r)$ can be true. Thus, $|H(r) \cap M| = 1$. By Lemma 2, M is a minimal model of $\mathrm{sh}(P)^M$. Thus, $M \in \mathrm{SM}(\mathrm{sh}(P))$.

Conversely, let $M \in \mathrm{SM}(\mathrm{sh}(P))$. By the construction of $\mathrm{sh}(P)$, if $M \models B(r)$ for $r \in P$, then exactly one $a_i \in H(r)$ is in M. This implies M satisfies P^M. To show that M is a minimal model of P^M, suppose there exists $M' \subset M$ that satisfies P^M. Any rule $r' \in \mathrm{sh}(P)^M$ is derived from either a normal rule in P or a disjunctive rule r where $M \models B(r)$. If $r' \in \mathrm{sh}(P)^M$ is a normal rule in P, r' is also in P^M. Since $M' \models P^M$, M' satisfies r'. Else if $r' \in \mathrm{sh}(P)^M$ is a shifted rule $a_i \leftarrow B^+(r)$ for some $r \in P$, then $M' \models B^+(r)$ implies $a_i \in M'$. Thus, M' satisfies every rule r' in $\mathrm{sh}(P)^M$. Hence, M' satisfies $\mathrm{sh}(P)^M$, which contradicts the minimality of M for $\mathrm{sh}(P)$. □

Example 4. For the program P of Example 3, it holds that $\mathrm{SM}(P) = \mathrm{SM}(\mathrm{sh}(P)) = \{\{a, c\}, \{b, c\}\}$.

The membership check for the TIHC class is performed in polynomial time without the need to explicitly enumerate cycles, despite the potentially exponential number of directed cycles in $G(P)$. The requirement that every cycle C satisfying $|H(r) \cap C| \geq 2$

must involve an inhibited rule is equivalent to ensuring that no two distinct atoms $a, b \in H(r)$ belong to the same strongly connected component (SCC) in the filtered dependency graph $G(P \setminus P_{\text{inh}(r)})$, where $P_{\text{inh}(r)}$ denotes the set of rules inhibited by rule r (Definition 4). For a program with n atoms and m rules, the verification procedure for each disjunctive rule r involves: (1) identifying $P_{\text{inh}(r)}$ in $O(m)$ time by literal comparison; (2) constructing the filtered graph and computing its SCC decomposition in $O(n+m)$ time using standard algorithms [15]. Consequently, the overall complexity of checking the TIHC property is $O(m_{disj} \cdot (n + m))$, where m_{disj} is the number of disjunctive rules. This reduction to SCC separation demonstrates that the check remains computationally feasible and avoids the intractability inherent in cycle enumeration.

3.3 Head-External Disjunctive Programs (HEDP)

The class HEDP is proposed by DeepSeek-V3.2.

Definition 6 (HEDP). A DLP P belongs to *Head-External Disjunctive Programs* (HEDP) if for every disjunctive rule $r \in P$, there is no other rule in P that has any atom from $H(r)$ in its head.

In other words, the head atoms of a disjunctive rule do not appear in the heads of other rules. This isolation makes the program's behavior much simpler to compute. By definition, deciding whether a program P is HEDP is done in linear time $O(|P|)$.

HEDP and HCF are incomparable.

Example 5. (HEDP but not HCF) Let P_1 be the program:

$$r_1 : \; a \vee b \leftarrow c,$$
$$r_2 : \; c \leftarrow a,$$
$$r_3 : \; c \leftarrow b.$$

P_1 is not HCF because there is a cycle involving a and b through the disjunctive rule r_1 and normal rules r_2 and r_3. However, P_1 is HEDP because the head atoms a and b appear only in $H(r_1)$ and not in the heads of other rules.

(HCF but not HEDP) Let P_2 be the program:

$$r_1 : \; a \vee b \leftarrow,$$
$$r_2 : \; a \leftarrow b.$$

Clearly P_2 is HCF, but it is not HEDP because $a \in H(r_1)$ is also an element in $H(r_2)$.

Next, we show that shifting preserves stable models in HEDP programs.

Lemma 4 (Exact-One Head Satisfaction). *Let P be an HEDP DLP and $I \in \text{SM}(P)$. For every disjunctive rule $r \in P$ such that $B^+(r) \subseteq I$ and $B^-(r) \cap I = \varnothing$, it holds that $|H(r) \cap I| = 1$.*

Proof. Since I is a model of P, $B^+(r) \subseteq I$ and $B^-(r) \cap I = \varnothing$ imply $H(r) \cap I \neq \varnothing$ for every $r \in P$. Suppose that two distinct atoms $a, b \in H(r)$ are in I. Consider the interpretation $J = I \setminus \{a\}$. We will show that J is a model of the reduct P^I, contradicting the minimality of I as a stable model of P. Take any rule $r' \in P^I$. We show J satisfies r'. There are two cases:

(1) r' originates from a non-disjunctive rule in P. Since a appears only in the head of the disjunctive rule r (by the HEDP property), a cannot be the head of r'. If $a \in B^+(r')$, then the body of r' is not satisfied by J (since $a \notin J$), so r' is vacuously satisfied. Otherwise, the fact that J differs from I only by the absence of a implies $J \models r'$ iff $I \models r'$.

(2) r' originates from a disjunctive rule in P. If r' originates from r itself, then in the reduct P^I it becomes $H(r) \leftarrow B^+(r)$. By $b \in J \cap H(r)$, J satisfies r'. If r' originates from a different disjunctive rule r'', then $H(r'') \cap \{a\} = \varnothing$ (again by the HEDP property). Thus, the satisfaction of r' by J follows from its satisfaction by I, as the removal of a does not affect the rule.

Therefore, J is a model of P^I. But $J \subset I$, contradicting the minimality of I for P^I. Hence, the assumption was false, and exactly one atom from $H(r)$ is in I. □

Theorem 3 (Preservation for HEDP). *If a DLP P is HEDP, then* $\mathrm{SM}(P) = \mathrm{SM}(\mathrm{sh}(P))$.

Proof. We prove both directions of the equivalence.

(1) $\mathrm{SM}(P) \subseteq \mathrm{SM}(\mathrm{sh}(P))$.
First, show $I \in \mathrm{SM}(P)$ is a model of $\mathrm{sh}(P)$. Take any rule in $\mathrm{sh}(P)$. If it originates from a non-disjunctive rule of P, satisfaction follows from I being a model of P. Else if it originates from a disjunctive rule $r \in P$, suppose $I \models B(r)$. Then, by Lemma 4, exactly one head atom of r, say a_i, is in I. The shifted rule for a_i has its body true (since the added negative literals $not\, a_j$ are true for $j \neq i$), and its head is in I. The shifted rules for other head atoms have a false negative literal $not\, a_i$ in its body and are thus satisfied. Hence, I satisfies all rules of $\mathrm{sh}(P)$.

Second, show I is the minimal model of the reduct $\mathrm{sh}(P)^I$. Assume there exists $J \subset I$ that is a model of $\mathrm{sh}(P)^I$. We show J must also be a model of P^I, contradicting the minimality of I for P^I. Take any rule $r' \in P^I$. If r' is non-disjunctive, it appears in $\mathrm{sh}(P)^I$ and is satisfied by J. Else if r' is disjunctive (i.e., $H(r') \leftarrow B^+(r')$), suppose $B^+(r') \subseteq J$. Since $J \subset I$, $B^+(r') \subseteq I$. By Lemma 4, exactly one head atom of r', say a, is in I. In $\mathrm{sh}(P)^I$, the rule $a \leftarrow B^+(r')$ exists (as all other head atoms are not in I). Since J models $\mathrm{sh}(P)^I$ and $B^+(r') \subseteq J$, we have $a \in J$. Thus, r' is satisfied by J. Therefore, J is a model of P^I, contradiction. Thus, I is the minimal (least) model of $\mathrm{sh}(P)^I$, hence a stable model of $\mathrm{sh}(P)$.

(2) $\mathrm{SM}(P) \supseteq \mathrm{SM}(\mathrm{sh}(P))$.
First, show $I \in \mathrm{SM}(\mathrm{sh}(P))$ is a model of P. Take any rule $r \in P$. If r is non-disjunctive, it is in $\mathrm{sh}(P)$ and thus satisfied by I. Else if r is disjunctive, suppose $I \models B(r)$. Consider the shifted rules in $\mathrm{sh}(P)$. If $H(r) \cap I = \varnothing$, then for each atom $a_i \in H(r)$, the corresponding shifted rule would have its body true (since all negative literals $not\, a_j$ would be true), forcing $a_i \in I$, a contradiction. Therefore, at least one head atom of r is in I, so r is satisfied.

Second, show I is a minimal model of P^I. Assume there exists $J \subset I$ that is a model of P^I. We show J must also model $\text{sh}(P)^I$, contradicting the minimality of I for $\text{sh}(P)^I$. Take any rule $r' \in \text{sh}(P)^I$. If r' originates from a non-disjunctive rule of P, then it exists in P^I and is satisfied by J. Else if r' originates from a disjunctive rule r, then r' is of the form $a \leftarrow B^+(r)$ for some head atom a, and the presence of this rule in the reduct implies that for all other head atoms a_j, $a_j \notin I$. Suppose $B(r') \subseteq J$. Then $B^+(r) \subseteq J$. Since J models P^I, some head atom of r must be in J. But the only possible head atom that could be in J (since $J \subset I$ and other $a_j \notin I$) is a. Hence, $a \in J$, and r' is satisfied. Therefore, J is a model of $\text{sh}(P)^I$, a contradiction. Thus, I is a minimal model of P^I, hence a stable model of P. □

Example 6. For the program P_1 of Example 5, it holds that $\text{SM}(P_1) = \text{SM}(\text{sh}(P_1)) = \{\varnothing\}$.

Finally, three new classes NS-HCF, TIHC and HEDP introduced in this section are incomparable with each other.

NS-HCF vs. TIHC: The NS-HCF program P in Example 1 is not TIHC because no rule in the cycle $C = \{a, b\}$ is inhibited by the fact r_1. In contrast, the TIHC program P in Example 3 is not NS-HCF. This is because for the head-pair (a, b) in r_1, the subprogram $P_{a,b}$ includes all rules r_1–r_4 and two atoms a and b remain in the same SCC of $G(P_{a,b})$, violating the condition of NS-HCF.

NS-HCF vs. HEDP: The NS-HCF program P in Example 1 is not HEDP because $H(r_1) \cap H(r_2) \neq \varnothing$. In contrast, the HEDP program P_1 in Example 5 is not NS-HCF because $P = P_{a,b}$, so a and b are in the same SCC of $P_{a,b}$.

TIHC vs. HEDP: The TIHC program P in Example 3 is not HEDP because $H(r_1) \cap H(r_2) \neq \varnothing$. In contrast, the HEDP program P_1 in Example 5 is not TIHC. This is because there is no rule r_c involved in the cycle $C = \{a, b, c\}$ such that r_c is inhibited by r_1.

NS-HCF and TIHC reduce to HCF in a positive DLP, while HEDP and HCF are incomparable even in a positive DLP (cf. Example 5).

4 Relation to HEF Programs

Gebser *et al.* ([6]) introduce the class of Head-Elementary-Set-Free (HEF) DLPs, which is strictly more general than HCF DLPs and can still be turned into NLPs in polynomial time and space by shifting the head atoms into the body. In this section, we address the relationship between HEF and the three classes of DLPs introduced in the preceding section. We first ask GPT or Gemini to investigate the relationships, and the results are verified by the author.

Definition 7 (HEF Program).[6] Let P be a DLP.

- A set Y ($\subset X$) is *outbound* in X for P if there is a rule $r \in P$ such that $H(r) \cap Y \neq \varnothing$, $B^+(r) \cap (X \setminus Y) \neq \varnothing$, $H(r) \cap (X \setminus Y) = \varnothing$, and $B^+(r) \cap Y = \varnothing$.
- A nonempty set X of atoms is *elementary* for P if all nonempty proper subsets of X are outbound in X for P.
- A DLP P is *Head-Elementary-Set-Free* (HEF) if for every rule $r \in P$, there is no elementary set Y for P such that $|H(r) \cap Y| > 1$.

4.1 NS-HCF vs. HEF

NS-HCF and HEF are incomparable in general.

Example 7. (NS-HCF but not HEF) Let P be the program:

$$r_1 : a \vee b \leftarrow,$$
$$r_2 : a \leftarrow b, not\, b,$$
$$r_3 : b \leftarrow a, not\, a.$$

For the pair (a, b) in r_1, the filtered program $P_{a,b}$ removes r_2 and r_3. Then $G(P_{a,b})$ contains no SCC, hence P is NS-HCF.

Take $X = \{a, b\}$. Its only non-empty proper subsets are $\{a\}$ and $\{b\}$.

- $Y = \{a\}$ is outbound in $X = \{a, b\}$ for P using r_2 s.t. $H(r_2) \cap Y = \{a\}$ and $B^+(r_2) \cap (X \setminus Y) = \{b\}$. $H(r_2) \cap (X \setminus Y) = \varnothing$, and $B^+(r_2) \cap Y = \varnothing$. The four outbound conditions hold.
- $Y = \{b\}$ is outbound in $X = \{a, b\}$ for P using r_3, symmetrically.

Hence, $X = \{a, b\}$ is an elementary set. But $H(r_1) \cap X = \{a, b\}$ and $|H(r_1) \cap X| = 2$, violating the condition of HEF.

(HEF but not NS-HCF) Let Q be the program:

$$r_1 : a \vee b \leftarrow,$$
$$r_2 : a \leftarrow c,$$
$$r_3 : b \leftarrow c,$$
$$r_4 : c \leftarrow a, b.$$

Q is equivalent to the HEF program Π_1 in [6]. Q is not NS-HCF because $Q_{a,b}$ equals to Q. Then, $G(Q_{a,b})$ contains an SCC involving $\{a, b\}$.

4.2 TIHC vs. HEF

TIHC and HEF are incomparable in general.

Example 8. The TIHC program P in Example 3 is not HEF. This is because $X = \{a, b\}$ is an elementary set for P as both $\{a\}$ and $\{b\}$ are outbound in X for P. On the other hand, the HEF program Q in Example 7 is not TIHC. This is because no rule in the cycle $C = \{a, b, c\}$ is inhibited by the fact r_1.

4.3 HEDP vs. HEF

HEDP is a subclass of HEF.

Proposition 4 (HEDP vs. HEF). *Every HEDP program is also an HEF program.*

Proof. Assume a program P is HEDP but not HEF. Then, there exists a rule $r \in P$ and an elementary set Y such that $|H(r) \cap Y| \geq 2$. Let a and b be two distinct atoms in $H(r) \cap Y$. By the definition of an elementary set, for the subset $Z = \{a\}$ of Y, there must exist a rule r' that provides external support: $H(r') \cap Z \neq \varnothing$ and $B^+(r') \cap (Y \setminus Z) \neq \varnothing$. The HEDP condition requires that an atom a appears in the head of only one rule—specifically, the disjunctive rule r in whose head it appears. Therefore, r' must be r itself. Consequently, $B^+(r)$ must contain an atom from $Y \setminus \{a\}$, which includes b. By a symmetric argument for atom b, $B^+(r)$ must also contain a. This creates a situation where a and b depend on each other in $G(P)$. Then the subset $\{a, b\}$ of Y is not outbound in Y for P, because $H(r) \cap Y \neq \varnothing$ implies $B^+(r) \cap Y \neq \varnothing$. This violates the definition of an elementary set. The contradiction implies that such an elementary set Y cannot exist. Therefore, the initial assumption is false, and P must be HEF. □

In Proposition 4, the inclusion is strict, i.e., there exist programs that are HEF but not HEDP.

Example 9. (HEF but not HEDP) The HEF program Q of Example 7 is not HEDP because atoms in $H(r_1)$ also appear in $H(r_2)$ and $H(r_3)$.

In Sect. 3, we have shown that HCF is a strict subclass of both NS-HCF (Proposition 2) and TIHC (Proposition 3), while HEDP and HCF are incomparable (Example 5). We have also argued that NS-HCF, TIHC and HEDP are incomparable with each other. Together with the results of this section, the relations between HCF, HEF, NS-HCF, TIHC and HEDP are summarized in Fig. 1. Note that HEDP is a strict subclass of HEF, but the HEDP condition is checked in polynomial time. In contrast, verifying the HEF property is intractable in general [7].

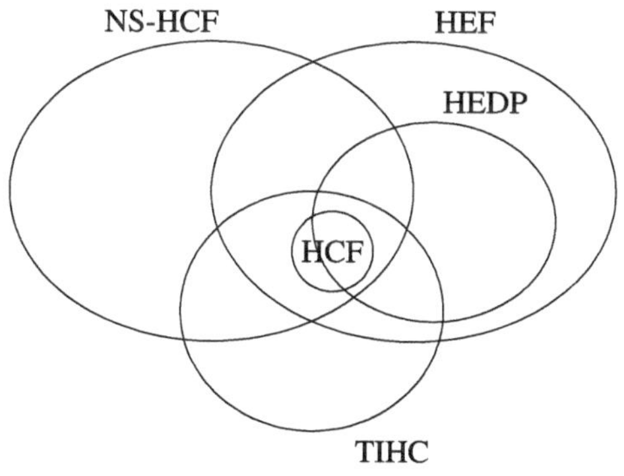

Fig. 1. Relations among HCF, HEF, NS-HCF, HEDP and TIHC

5 Discussion

In Sect. 3, three new subclasses of DLP found by ChatGPT, Gemini, and DeepSeek are presented. However, those three subclasses are obtained after iterative refinement and human verification. Given the prompt, an LLM spends a few minutes reasoning before outputting a solution. In several cases, however, generated "solutions" are incorrect and we point out the error with a counterexample. Then the LLM rethinks the problem and generates another solution. Even if a proposed solution is correct, it is sometimes trivial and uninteresting (see Appendix). The remaining two models, ClaudeSonnet and Grok, fail to generate correct solutions despite multiple attempts.

The results show that success depends on the interaction between the model's reasoning capabilities, the structure of the task, and the presence of precise feedback mechanisms. Progress is achieved through an iterative loop in which incorrect conjectures are challenged with counterexamples, prompting the model to revise its hypothesis. This workflow–LLM proposal, human critique, model revision, and formal verification–proves essential. The LLMs act as generators of structured conjectures, while correctness and significance are ultimately ensured by formal analysis by human experts.

Among the three subclasses identified, NS-HCF and TIHC refine HCF through the lens of default negation and GL-reducts. In contrast, HEDP relies on the stronger syntactic restriction. While these classes are formally correct and polynomial-time checkable, their structural constraints sometimes limit their generality and practical appeal. Nevertheless, they serve an important role in mapping the boundary of shift-based transformations and illustrating distinct mechanisms by which semantic preservation can still be achieved. Importantly, the value of this work does not rest solely on the practical usefulness of the newly identified subclasses. Rather, the results demonstrate that LLMs can assist in navigating complex theoretical design spaces, even when the target objects–here, syntactic fragments of logic programs–are constrained and sensitive to small changes. Incorrect conjectures are commonly observed during navigation, which indicates the limitation of state-of-the-art LLMs as an autonomous discovery engine. Nevertheless, they would be useful for generating hypotheses and accelerating scientific discovery together with a disciplined verification framework.

6 Conclusion

In this study, we have presented a methodological framework for LLM-assisted scientific discovery in the domain of logic programming. While the identification of three new classes of DLPs is a non-trivial outcome, the primary contribution of this research is the iterative, human-in-the-loop verification protocol that enabled these discoveries. Our study demonstrates that the value of state-of-the-art LLMs in theoretical research lies not in their ability to act as research assistants, but as generators of structured conjectures within a rigorous feedback system.

In future work, we aim to develop more autonomous discovery pipelines by enabling models to generate and test their own counterexamples during the conjecture-refinement process. Understanding the extent to which such self-critical mechanisms can reduce reliance on human verification remains an important research question. We also intend to explore the applicability of the proposed framework to other areas of formal reasoning, including first-order logic, constraint satisfaction, and computational complexity theory.

Appendix: An Example of Dialogue with ChatGPT5.2 Thinking

[prompt]: "You are an expert in logic programming ...... Show the original result."

[GPT]: *I'll propose a new syntactic class of disjunctive logic programs, strictly more general than HCF programs, and show that the standard 'shifting' transformation to a normal logic program preserves stable models for this class. ...*

New class: Cycle-Guarded Disjunctive Programs (CGD)

A program P is **cycle-guarded** *if it satisfies: For every disjunctive rule $r \in P$ and every SCC C of $G(P)$, if $|H(r) \cap C| \geq 2$, then for every distinct $p, q \in H(r) \cap C$, the program contains the constraint $\leftarrow p, q$.*

Why this strictly generalizes HCF*:*

- *If P is HCF, then for every rule r and SCC C, you never have two atoms of $H(r)$ in the same SCC. So the condition above holds vacuously.*
- *But CGD allows programs that are not HCF as long as the program explicitly forbids simultaneously choosing two of those head atoms inside that SCC.*

[prompt]: "The proposed solution is rather trivial. Consider a more sophisticated solution."

(Thinking Time: 7m 14s)

[GPT]: *Here's a genuinely structural superclass of HCF where the plain full-shift still works.*

New class: Body-Disjoint Disjunctive SCC Programs (BDD-SCC)

A program P is **BDD-SCC** *if for every SCC C of $G(P)$: $\forall r \in P : (H(r) \cap \Delta(C) \neq \varnothing) \Rightarrow (B^+(r) \cap \Delta(C) = \varnothing)$ where $\Delta(C) := \{a \in C \mid \exists r \in P : a \in H(r)$ and $|H(r) \cap C| \geq 2\}$.*

Why this strictly generalizes HCF*:*

- *If P is HCF, then for every SCC C, $|H(r) \cap C| \geq 2$ never happens, so $\Delta(C) = \varnothing$ for all C, and the condition holds trivially.*
- *BDD-SCC allows head cycles. An example (not HCF, but BDD-SCC): $\{a \vee b \leftarrow c.\ \ c \leftarrow a.\ \ c \leftarrow b\}$. Here $C = \{a, b, c\}$ is one SCC and $\Delta(C) = \{a, b\}$. Rules with the head a or b have positive body $\{c\}$, which is disjoint from $\{a, b\}$. So BDD-SCC holds, but HCF fails.*

[prompt]: "$\{\, a \vee b \leftarrow,\ \ a \leftarrow b,\ \ b \leftarrow a \,\}$ satisfies BDD-SCC but $SM(P)$ does not coincide with $SM(sh(P))$. Reconsider the problem."

(Thinking Time: 9m 13s)

[GPT]: *You're right: my earlier BDD-SCC condition was too weak, and your counterexample pinpoints exactly what went wrong—a disjunctive rule can have two head atoms that become simultaneously necessary because of a deterministic positive cycle.*

New class: Deterministically Head-Cycle-Free (dHCF)

Define the **deterministic positive dependency graph** *$G_{det}(P)$ as the directed graph on atoms with an edge $b \to a$ iff P contains a* **normal rule** *'$a \leftarrow b, \Gamma$' where $b \in B^+(r)$ and Γ is any (possibly empty) set of other body literals (positive or negative). A program P is* **deterministically head-cycle-free** *if for every disjunctive rule r and for every SCC C of $G_{det}(P)$, $|H(r) \cap S| \leq 1$.*

Why this strictly generalizes HCF*: While HCF forbids any positive cycle that contains two co-head atoms, dHCF ignores edges contributed by disjunctive rules entirely and only watches deterministic recursion. So dHCF allows genuine head cycles created via disjunctive rules and intermediate atoms (non-HCF), e.g. $\{a \vee b \leftarrow c,\ \ c \leftarrow a,\ \ c \leftarrow b\}$. Here, a, b, c are in one SCC of the usual dependency graph, so not HCF but in G_{det}, a and b are not in the same deterministic SCC, hence dHCF holds. Your counterexample: $\{a \vee b \leftarrow,\ \ a \leftarrow b,\ \ b \leftarrow a\}$ fails dHCF.*

[prompt]: "dHCF does not work for a program with constraints. Consider $\{\, p \vee q \leftarrow,\ \ p \vee r \leftarrow$

$q, \;\; q \vee s \leftarrow p, \;\; \leftarrow r, \;\; \leftarrow s\}$ which contains two constraints $\leftarrow r$ and $\leftarrow s$."

(Thinking Time: 4m 35s)

[GPT]: *You're completely right to flag that example: it shows that my 'dHCF' idea is not constraint-robust......*

References

1. Bayazit, B., Li, Y., Si, X.: A case study on the effectiveness of LLMs in verification with proof assistants. In: Proceedings of the 1st ACM SIGPLAN International Workshop on Language Models and Programming Languages (LMPL), pp. 91–105 (2025)
2. Ben-Eliyahu, R., Dechter, R.: Propositional semantics for disjunctive logic programs. Ann. Math. Artif. Intell. **12**, 53–87 (1994)
3. Boiko, D.A., MacKnight, R., Kline, B., Gomes, G.: Autonomous chemical research with large language models. Nature **624**, 570–578 (2023)
4. Eiter, T., Gottlob, G.: On the computational cost of disjunctive logic programming: propositional case. Ann. Math. Artif. Intell. **15**, 289–323 (1995)
5. First, E., Rabe, M.N., Ringer, T., Brun, Y.: Baldur: whole-proof generation and repair with large language models. In: Proceedings of the 31st ACM Joint European Software Engineering Conference and Symposium on the Foundations of Software Engineering, pp. 1229–1241 (2023)
6. Gebser, M., Lee, J., Lierler, Y.: Head-elementary-set-free logic programs. In: Baral, C., Brewka, G., Schlipf, J. (eds.) LPNMR 2007. LNCS (LNAI), vol. 4483, pp. 149–161. Springer, Heidelberg (2007). https://doi.org/10.1007/978-3-540-72200-7_14
7. Gebser, M., Lee, J., Lierler, Y.: On elementary loops of logic programs. Theory Pract. Logic Program. **11**(6), 953–988 (2011)
8. Gelfond, M., Lifschitz, V.: The stable model semantics for logic programming. In: Proceedings of the 5th International Conference and Symposium on Logic Programming, pp. 1070–1080. MIT Press (1988)
9. Gelfond, M., Lifschitz, V.: Classical negation in logic programs and disjunctive databases. N. Gener. Comput. **9**(3&4), 365–385 (1991)
10. Liu, H., et al.: Logical reasoning in large language models: a survey. arXiv (2025). https://doi.org/10.48550/arxiv.2502.09100
11. Novikov, A., et al.: AlphaEvolve: a coding agent for scientific and algorithmic discovery. arXiv:2506.13131 (2025)
12. Patil, A., Jadon, A.: Advancing reasoning in large language models: promising methods and approaches. In: Pathan, S., Pokhrel, S.R., Li, G., Barata, C. (eds.) Computational Intelligence and Soft Computing, CCIS, vol. 2852, pp. 284–298, Springer, Heidelberg (2026). https://doi.org/10.1007/978-981-95-7289-2_22
13. Qu, Y., et al.: CRISPR-GPT for agentic automation of gene-editing experiments. Nat. Biomed. Eng. (2025)
14. Romera-Paredes, B., et al.: Mathematical discoveries from program search with large language models. Nature **625**, 468–475 (2024)
15. Sharia, M.: A strong-connectivity algorithm and its applications in data flow analysis. Comput. Math. Appl. **7**(1), 67–72 (1981)

Improving Suboptimal Reduction-Based Approaches for Multi-agent Pathfinding

Torsten Schaub[1], Klaus Strauch[1(✉)], and Jiri Svancara[2]

[1] University of Potsdam, Potsdam, Germany
torsten@cs.uni-potsdam.de , kstrauch@uni-potsdam.de
[2] Charles University, Prague, Czech Republic
svancara@ktiml.mff.cuni.cz

Abstract. Multi-Agent Pathfinding (MAPF) is a fundamental problem in robotics and AI, where multiple agents must navigate a shared environment without colliding. This paper presents an approach inspired by the Rolling Horizon Collision Resolution (RHCR) algorithm, in which agent paths consider collisions only for a limited number of steps ahead, treating the remainder of each path as a single-agent problem. We reframe this approach in the context of a reduction-based solver—specifically, Answer Set Programming (ASP). This allows us to overcome a significant disadvantage of previous suboptimal reduction-based approaches: the need to ground the entire problem at once. Instead, for each agent, we ground only the steps within the current window and guide their movement via optimization statements. By significantly reducing the planning horizon, our method improves runtime over previous suboptimal reduction-based approaches on instances with large horizons, at the cost of solution quality.

1 Introduction

Multi-agent pathfinding (MAPF) involves moving multiple agents from their start positions to their designated goal positions within a shared environment. The objective is to find collision-free paths for all agents. MAPF has numerous real-world applications, such as warehousing [11], airport surface operations [12], and games [15], among others.

Naturally, MAPF has been extensively studied, having many different algorithms to solve it. For example, search-based algorithms like Conflict-based Search (CBS) [1] first compute individual paths for each agent and then resolve conflicts between them. The main advantage of this approach is that pathfinding for individual agents is a polynomial-time problem. The more challenging part is resolving path conflicts, which is handled by a separate conflict-resolution mechanism.

There are also rule-based algorithms where an agent's movement depends on its current state. For example, the priority inheritance with backtracking (PIBT) algorithm [14] uses a set of rules and priorities that determine each agent's

W. Faber et al. (Eds.): LPNMR 2026, LNAI 16952, pp. 415–429, 2027.
https://doi.org/10.1007/978-3-032-38320-4_26

movement. This results in a very fast algorithm, though it is not optimal, and is only complete for biconnected graphs, not on general graphs.

Another approach is to reduce MAPF to another formalism and leverage existing solvers. For example, the problem can be encoded as a Boolean Satisfiability (SAT) instance [18], allowing the use of any SAT solver. Hybrid approaches are also common, where part of the problem is handled via reduction and the rest through search-based techniques (e.g. [2,19]).

In this work, we focus on reduction-based approaches, and in particular on Answer Set Programming [10]. ASP is a declarative programming paradigm based on stable model semantics, which allows complex problems to be expressed compactly and intuitively.

Reduction-based approaches are commonly used to solve MAPF optimally [5,18]. However, in many applications where speed is more important than optimality, sub-optimal solutions are sufficient. Here, we focus on sub-optimal MAPF, aiming to find solutions that are close to optimal while prioritizing computational speed.

2 Background

2.1 Multi-agent Pathfinding

The *multi-agent pathfinding* problem (MAPF) [16] is a pair (G, A), where G is an undirected graph $G = (V, E)$ and A is a set of agents. Each agent $a \in A$ is associated with a start vertex $s_a \in V$ and a goal vertex $g_a \in V$.

Time is considered discrete. Between two consecutive timepoints, an agent can either move to an adjacent vertex (move action) or stay at its current vertex (wait action). The movement of an agent is captured by its path.

A *path* π_a of agent a is a list of vertices that starts at s_a and ends at g_a. Let $\pi_a(t)$ be the vertex of a at timepoint t according to π_a, then $\pi_a(0) = s_a$ and $\pi_a(|\pi_a|) = g_a$. Additionally, for all timepoints $t < |\pi_a|$, $(\pi_a(t), \pi_a(t+1)) \in E$ or $\pi_a(t) = \pi_a(t+1)$, that is, at each timepoint agent a either moves along an edge or waits at a vertex, respectively.

There is a *conflict* between paths π_a and π_b at timepoint t if $\pi_a(t) = \pi_b(t)$ (*vertex conflict*) or $\pi_a(t) = \pi_b(t+1)$ and $\pi_b(t) = \pi_a(t+1)$ (*swapping conflict*).

A *plan* Π is a set of paths, one for each agent. A *solution* is a conflict-free plan, i.e., a plan Π where no two paths of distinct agents have conflicts.

A solution is *optimal* if it has the lowest cost among all possible solutions. The cost $C(\pi_a)$ of path π_a equals the number of actions performed in π_a until the last arrival at g_a, not counting any subsequent wait actions. Formally, $C(\pi_a) = \max(\{0 < t \leq |\pi_a| \mid \pi_a(t) = g_a, \pi_a(t-1) \neq g_a\} \cup \{0\})$. Note that waiting at the goal counts towards the cost if the agent leaves the goal at any time in the future.

There are two commonly used cost functions to evaluate the quality of a plan Π:

1. *sum-of-costs* (SOC), which is the sum of costs of all paths $C_{SOC}(\Pi) = \sum_i C(\pi_i)$

2. *makespan* (MKS), which is the maximum cost among all paths $C_{MKS}(\Pi) = \max_i C(\pi_i)$.

Sum-of-costs optimal solutions are typically used in applications to minimize the usage of a resource (e.g. fuel). Makespan optimal solutions are used to minimize the time taken to complete a task.

Although the decision problem of whether a MAPF instance has any solution is polynomial [6], bounding the movement of agents turns it into an NP-complete problem [17,23]. This makes finding an optimal solution significantly harder than simply determining the existence of any solution.

In general, reduction-based approaches solve MAPF by initially searching for a solution within a given cost bound. If no solution is found, the bound is iteratively increased until one is obtained.

The current state-of-the-art reduction-based solver for sub-optimal MAPF was introduced in [21]. It builds on the optimal algorithm from [20], where a cardinality constraint is imposed on the total number of moves across all agents. If no solution is found, this bound is increased by one. The first solution found in this process is guaranteed to be optimal with respect to sum-of-costs. The sub-optimal variant relaxes this by multiplying the bound by a factor. For instance, multiplying the bound by 1.01 allows solutions that are at most one percent worse than optimal. Alternatively, the cardinality constraint can be removed altogether. This approach, however, applies specifically to sum-of-costs optimal solutions.

A simpler approach to finding sub-optimal solutions is to increase the bound by more than one in each iteration. This works for both cost functions.

2.2 Answer Set Programming

For a more detailed view of ASP, we refer to [3]. Here, we provide a brief overview.

Let $\mathcal{A}$ be a set of atoms. A rule r over $\mathcal{A}$ in ASP has the form:

$$H \text{ :- } a_1, \ldots, a_m, \mathit{not}\ a_{m+1}, \ldots, \mathit{not}\ a_n.$$

where H is the head of the rule and has the form $\{a\}$ for some atom $a \in \mathcal{A}$, which makes it a choice rule, an atom $a \in \mathcal{A}$ and it is a normal rule, or $\bot$ and it is an integrity constraint.

Intuitively, a rule states that if all atoms in the body are true, then the atom in the head is also true. Note that for choice rules, this means that we have a choice on the truth value of the head atom. For integrity constraints, the head atom is always false. Hence, we have to avoid the situation where all atoms in the body are true.

A program $\mathcal{P}$ is a set of rules. Additionally, we can define a set of optimization directives. In these directives, we specify a weight for an atom. The solver then tries to minimize the total weight of the atoms that are true in a solution. A solution of a program $\mathcal{P}$ is a set of atoms $M \subseteq \mathcal{A}$ such that all rules in $\mathcal{P}$ are satisfied by M.

2.3 ASP Encoding for MAPF

We use the ASP encoding for MAPF from [5] which can be seen in Listing 1.1. The encoding represents the graph G using atoms of the form `vertex/1` and `edge/2`. The agents are represented using atoms of the form `agent/1`. The start and goal positions of each agent are represented using atoms of the form `start/2` and `goal/2`, respectively. The position of an agent is given by the atom `at/3`, which indicates that an agent is at a specific vertex at a specific time step. The movement of agents is represented using the atom `move/4`, which indicates that an agent moves from one vertex to another at a specific time step.

Line 1 of the encoding defines the time steps for each agent based on its horizon. Line 2 initializes the position of each agent at time step 0 to its start position. Line 4 defines which moves are possible for an agent at a given time step, based on the edges of the graph and the reachability set. Line 6 updates the position of an agent based on its moves while Line 7 ensures that an agent can only move from its current position. Line 9 ensures that an agent remains at its position if it does not move. Lines 11 and 12 prevent vertex and swapping conflicts, respectively. Line 14 ensures that each agent has a defined position at each time step.

```
1  time(A,1..T) :- agent(A), horizon(A,T).
2  at(A,P,0) :- start(A,P), agent(A).
3
4  { move(A,U,V,T) : edge(U,V), reach(A,V,T), reach(A,U,T-1)
       } 1 :- time(A,T).
5
6  at(A,V,T) :- move(A,_,V,T).
7             :- move(A,U,_,T), not at(A,U,T-1).
8
9  at(A,V,T) :- at(A,V,T-1), not move(A,V,_,T), time(A,T),
       reach(A,V,T).
10
11 :- { at(A,V,T) } > 1, vertex(V), time(_,T).
12 :- move(_,U,V,T), move(_,V,U,T), U < V.
13
14 :- { at(A,V,T) } != 1, agent(A), time(A,T).
```

Listing 1.1: ASP encodings for bounded MAPF.

3 Related Work

To the best of our knowledge, the first use of a windowed approach for MAPF is in [15], where Windowed Hierarchical Cooperative A* (WHCA*) is introduced. WHCA* uses a fixed-size window to plan paths for agents using location-time A* within the window, which is a variant of A* that avoids vertices and edges used by previously planned agents. After planning the window, the planning continues to the next window until all agents reach their goals. Notably, in their setting, agents only had to reach their goal at some point in the planning. It was not required that all agents be at their goal at the same time. Additionally, agents are planned one at a time.

Later, this idea was revisited in [9], where the windowed approach is applied to lifelong MAPF, a variant in which agents receive new goals as soon as they reach their current ones. Similarly, the low-level search uses location-time A* to plan paths within a window, adapted to the lifelong setting in which an agent has a sequence of goals it must visit. In a similar manner, agents do not have to arrive at their goals at the same time, and agents are planned one at a time.

Windowed solvers were used by the winning teams of the League of Robot Runners[1] competition [4]. Since the competition required the solver to provide an action for all agents at one-second intervals, windowed solvers were a natural fit due to their fast planning time for a single window, which is sufficient to provide actions for the next couple of seconds.

A common disadvantage of windowed approaches is that they can be stuck in deadlocks. The usual approach to resolve them is to replan with a larger window size. However, this has the downside of increasing planning time significantly. In the worst case, it would devolve to planning the complete horizon at once, which is what windowed planners are trying to avoid. Recently, [22] introduced a heuristic for windowed solvers with completeness guarantees. Their approach relies on a heuristic value given to a configuration of agents, where a configuration is defined as the set of positions for each agent. The windowed solver plans the next window by choosing actions that lead to configurations with better heuristic values at the end of the window. To ensure completeness, the heuristic value of a configuration is increased whenever it is chosen. Hence, deadlocks are avoided simply because the heuristic value of a configuration worsens each time it is chosen, and eventually, all configurations will be explored. To avoid the obvious issue of the exponential number of configurations, the authors propose clustering agents into interacting groups and computing the heuristic value based on the groups and not the complete problem. The low-level solver for the configurations is a modified version of CBS that can plan for a window of size one.

All of those solvers are search-based, and they leverage some type of prioritized planning. To the best of our knowledge, our approach is the first reduction-based windowed solver for MAPF. The main difference between search-based and reduction-based solvers is that reduction-based solvers consider all agents simultaneously. Additionally, there is the benefit of easily expressing complex constraints and objectives due to the declarative nature of reduction-based approaches.

In the realm of reduction-based approaches for MAPF, most approaches focus on finding optimal solutions [5,18]. These approaches typically involve grounding the program multiple times, starting with a lower bound on the cost or horizon, depending on the cost function. If no solution is found, the bound is increased iteratively until a solution is found. This process can lead to large grounding sizes, especially for larger problem instances. Additionally, a large amount of time is spent grounding the same set of rules repeatedly.

[1] https://www.leagueofrobotrunners.org/.

Outside reduction-based approaches, Explicit Estimation CBS (EECBS) [8] is a well-known bounded-suboptimal MAPF solver. It extends the CBS algorithm by incorporating an estimation of the solution cost in the high-level search. This estimation allows EECBS to select nodes that are more likely to lead to solutions still within the sub-optimality bound. The current state-of-the-art MAPF solver is another search-based approach called LACAM [13]. It uses a similar search strategy to A*, but successor states are lazily generated using the PIBT [14] algorithm. This avoids the effort of the full expansion of all possible states, leading to significant speedups in practice. Additionally, LACAM* eventually finds optimal solutions, by expanding all possible states if given enough time.

4 Approach

Current reduction-based suboptimal approaches for Multi-Agent Pathfinding (MAPF) share a common weakness: they must ground at least to the lower bound on the number of moves. For smaller problem instances, this is not an issue, but for larger instances, it can lead to a very large number of rules.

Our approach draws inspiration from the windowed rolling horizon method [9]. The windowed rolling horizon approach plans a partial solution where collisions are considered only within a specified time window.

In our approach, we use a similar concept but do not interleave planning and execution. Instead, we perform a series of planning steps. We refer to such a step as a planning window and the amount of time steps considered is the window size. Each window begins with the agents at their last position in the previous window. The first window starts with the agents at their initial positions. Planning steps are performed iteratively until a complete solution is found.

To use this approach with ASP, we must address two key issues. First, we need a method to guide the agents toward their goals. Second, we must ensure that deadlocks are resolved.

4.1 Guiding Agents Towards Their Goals

Before presenting our methods, we define our notion of progress within a given window. Let w denote the size of the window, and let $sp(v, u)$ represent the length of the shortest path between vertices v and u. We say that an agent makes progress in a window if $sp(\pi_a(0), g(a)) > sp(\pi_a(w), g(a))$, where $\pi_a(0)$ is the agent's position at the beginning of the window, and $\pi_a(w)$ is the position at the end of the window.

We define the amount of progress as $sp(\pi_a(0), g(a)) - sp(\pi_a(w), g(a))$. Note that within each window the maximum possible progress is w.

The main idea is to encourage the solver to find solutions that maximize the overall progress of all agents within the current window. We achieve this by using optimization directives. Since progress is measured by the distance to the goal at the end of the window, we want to minimize this distance for all agents. To implement this, we perform a breadth-first search from each goal vertex. Then, for each vertex v reachable by an agent a, we add the distance to the goal $sp(v, g(a))$ as a fact with signature `dist/3`. We then use this fact in an optimization directive as follows:

```
#minimize{D@3,A : at(A,V,T), last(T), dist(A,V,D)}.
```

Here, `at(A,V,T)` indicates that agent A is at vertex V at time T, `last(T)` signifies that T is the final time step of the window, and `dist(A,V,D)` represents the distance D from vertex V to the goal of agent A. In short, this directive sums the distances of all agents to their goals at the end of the window and minimizes this sum.

If this directive is the only one we use, the solver may produce solutions where agents that have already reached their goals move away from them to make way for others, even when it is not necessary. This behavior is undesirable, as it can increase the sum-of-costs of the solution. To prevent this, we introduce an additional optimization directive with a lower priority. This directive encourages agents to remain at their goals once they reach them. We implement this using the following rule and optimization directive:

```
atgoal(A,T) :- goal(A,V), at(A,V,T), time(T).
#maximize{1@1,A,T : atgoal(A,T)}.
```

The first rule defines `atgoal/2`, indicating that agent A is at its goal vertex V at time T. The optimization directive then maximizes the total number of timesteps that agents spend at their goal vertices. This ensures that agents remain at their goals whenever possible, preventing unnecessary movements that could increase the sum-of-costs. In conjunction with the previous directive, we direct the solver to find solutions that maximize progress while keeping agents at their goals whenever possible.

4.2 Resolving Deadlocks

Consider the situation where two agents arrive at a corridor and must cross each other (Fig. 1a). In a standard setting, the solver considers the full horizon of the problem. It would then likely allow one agent to pass through the corridor while the other waits, or find alternative paths for them. In our approach, however, the agents only consider the current window. Together with the directive to maximize total progress, the solver may attempt to have both agents cross the corridor simultaneously. This results in a deadlock, as each agent waits for the other to yield.

To address this, we introduce an additional optimization directive. In the example above, the progress optimization treats two cases as equally good: (1) both agents waiting in front of each other, and (2) one agent walking back while the other proceeds through the corridor. For example, we look at Fig. 1b and 1c. At the start, when the agents meet, the sum of the distances to their goals is 70. If agent A moves back while agent B proceeds, the sum remains 70. Similarly, if agent A proceeds while agent B moves back, the sum also remains 70. No matter if the agents stay in place or one agent moves back and the other forward, the total progress is zero. We can exploit this equivalence to establish a preference between these solutions. Naturally, we prefer that one agent progresses through

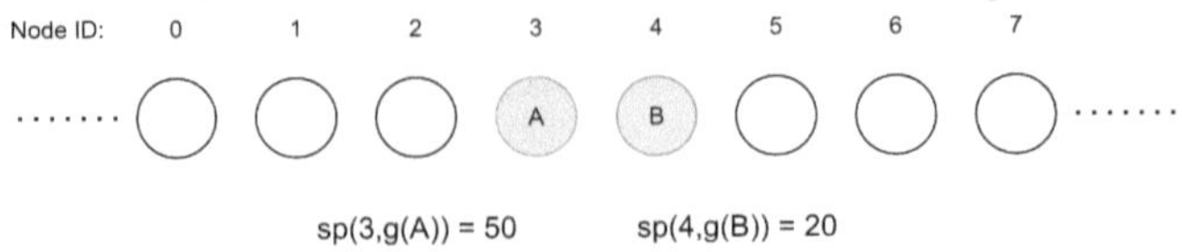

(a) Both agents waiting in front of each other.

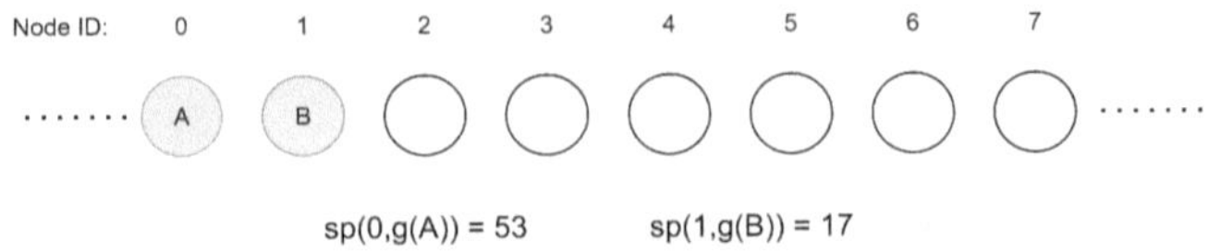

(b) Agent A moves back while Agent B proceeds.

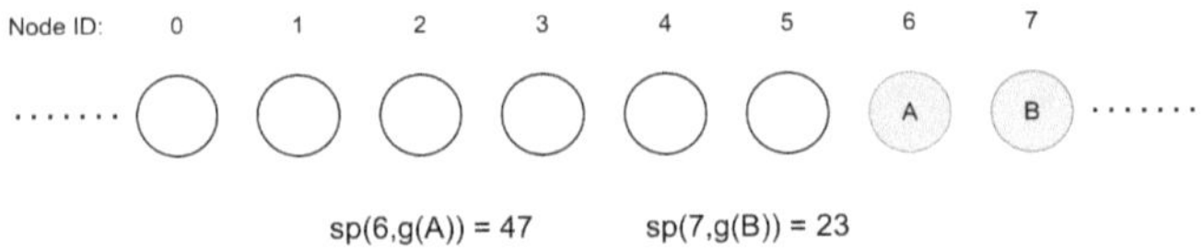

(c) Agent A proceeds while Agent B moves back.

Fig. 1: Example of a deadlock. The agents start on opposite sides of a corridor and must cross each other. All possible moves lead to the same progress of zero.

the corridor, even if the other must temporarily backtrack. To enforce this, we add a directive that minimizes the maximum remaining distance to the goal of any agent at the end of the window. This encourages the solver to prioritize the agent with the longest remaining path, effectively breaking the deadlock. We implement this using the following rules and optimization directive:

```
max(D) :- at(A,V,T), last(T), dist(A,V,D).
max(D-1) :- max(D), D > 0.
#minimize{D@2 : max(D)}.
```

Here, the first rule identifies the maximum distance D to any goal at the end of the window. The second rule generates all values from D down to zero. The optimization directive then minimizes this maximum distance. This directive has a middle priority compared to the previous ones, so that we only choose among solutions that maximize total progress, while preventing agents at their goals from exacerbating the problem. Notice that this directive resolves the deadlock only once one of the agents involved is the one with the longest remaining distance to its goal.

Unfortunately, this does not resolve all deadlocks. Consider again the situation where two agents arrive at a corridor. If both agents have similar distances to their goals, the solver is unable to break the deadlock. In this case, the identity of the agent with the longest remaining distance keeps shifting, causing the agents to move back and forth inside the corridor without making progress. This deadlock would eventually be broken if another agent joins one of the agents in the deadlock. As now two agents are going in the same direction, the minimization of the total distances will naturally prioritize the side with more agents. We note that this situation is more likely to occur in a lifelong setting than in a standard setting, as agents continually receive new goals that may require them to go through this corridor.

Another case occurs when both agents have their goals inside the corridor and must cross each other. In this situation, the agents will find a point between their goals and, as in the previous case, swing back and forth without making progress. In this case, even if many other agents push both deadlocked agents out of the corridor, we must still ensure that the deadlocked agents enter the corridor in the correct order. We note, however, that this situation would not be problematic in a lifelong version of MAPF, as an agent could simply reach its goal, receive a new one, and the deadlock would be resolved naturally.

To address both of these cases, we increase the window size until the deadlock is resolved. This approach requires detecting deadlocks effectively, making the detection strategy crucial for performance. At present, we detect deadlocks by identifying windows where no progress is made and the maximum distance to a goal does not decrease. This implies that we can only recognize a deadlock once all agents not involved have already reached their goals.

To alleviate this issue, we separate the agents into non-interacting groups, similar to [22]. Agents are considered non-interacting if they do not share any reachable vertices within the current window. This allows us to detect deadlocks within each group independently, as well as to increase the window size only for the groups involved in the deadlock. Naturally, this results in a much more efficient resolution of deadlocks, as they can be resolved much earlier. However, it is now necessary to ensure that the calculated paths of the groups are synchronized whenever a group needs to increase its window size. We ensure this by only applying the moves that occur within the original window size, and caching the rest. On subsequent windows, the next w cached moves are applied until the cache is empty.

Some optimizations that we have implemented are that singleton groups are not solved. Instead, the agent simply follows its shortest path. Additionally, if a group consists of agents that have already reached their goals, we do not solve the group, as the agents can simply stay at their goals.

Finally, we consider a version where all groups that are to be solved are merged into a single group. This version has the advantage that only a single solver call is needed per window, but the disadvantage that all agents are solved together, even if they do not interact.

Another consideration is that the window size also influences the calculation of the groups, as there are more reachable vertices that could coincide between agents. Naturally, this approach favors sparse instances with smaller window sizes.

In summary, we have 3 different approaches to grouping:

- No grouping: all agents are solved together.
- Grouping: agents are separated into non-interacting groups.

- Merged grouping: agents are separated into non-interacting groups and then groups that need solving are merged into a single group.

As an additional optimization, the caching of moves is not done for the no grouping approach, as it is not necessary.

5 Benchmarks and Experiments

We run benchmarks in the style discussed in [16]. These consist of empty, random, and warehouse maps of sizes ranging from 10×10 to 200×200 in increments of 10. Empty instances have no obstacles, while in random instances, 10–20% of the cells are randomly blocked by obstacles. Warehouse instances contain rows of shelves that are 2 cells tall and 6–10 cells long, with 1 cell wide corridors between them[2]. For each instance, we start with 5 agents and increment the number of agents by 5, up to a maximum of 400 or until a timeout occurs. Finally, we run the experiments on an Intel Xeon E5-2650v4 under Debian GNU/Linux 10, with a memory limit of 28 GB and a timeout of 5 min per instance. When a deadlock appears, the window size is increased by 1 until the deadlock is resolved. All benchmarks were run using *clingo* version 5.8.

In preliminary experiments, we found that window sizes higher than 5 resulted in significantly worse performance. Even though the solution quality is better with larger window sizes, the grounding and solving times are substantially higher, resulting in fewer solved instances. Additionally, we found that the grouping approach performed much worse than the non-grouping and merged grouping approaches. We believe this is due to the fact that the grouping approach results in many more calls to the solver, which, even when done in parallel, results in a significant overhead. Additionally, the grouping approach must resolve all deadlocks separately for each group, which can result in a larger number of solver calls with high window sizes. This is less of an issue for the merged grouping and non-grouping approaches, as they can resolve deadlocks for all agents at once. For these reasons, we show results only for the non-grouping and merged grouping approaches in the following sections, while limiting the window sizes to 2, 3, and 5.

Table 1 shows the results on all instances split by map type. Configurations starting with `FH-ASP` are our implementation of the existing approaches in ASP (Full Horizon ASP), while configurations starting with `FH-SAT` are the original SAT implementations (Full Horizon SAT) [21]. For both of these, we do not limit the cost of the solution. Configurations starting with `RH-ASP` represent our windowed approaches (Rolling Horizon ASP), followed by the window size and whether merged agent grouping is used.

It is clear that our approach solves vastly more instances regardless of the map type. Additionally, a lower window size leads to more solved instances, as the grounding and solving times are lower. This increase in solved instances comes

[2] For more details on the maps, see https://movingai.com/benchmarks/mapf/index.html.

Table 1: Results by map type. First column shows the number of solved instances. Second column shows the average difference (in percentage) to the lower bound of sum-of-costs. The second column only considers instances solved by all configurations. The best values in each column are shown in bold.

Approach	Empty		Random		Warehouse	
	Solved	SoC-%	Solved	SoC-%	Solved	SoC-%
FH-SAT	11787	1.03	7964	1.04	4018	1.07
FH-ASP	10173	**1.02**	8948	**1.03**	4567	**1.05**
RH-ASP-2	14615	1.09	**13976**	1.08	**8368**	1.41
RH-ASP-3	14533	1.09	13618	1.06	8030	1.31
RH-ASP-5	14358	1.09	13128	1.05	7989	1.18
RH-ASP-2-G	**14620**	1.10	13332	1.08	5740	1.30
RH-ASP-3-G	14523	1.10	13573	1.06	5674	1.28
RH-ASP-5-G	14329	1.09	13112	1.05	5848	1.17

at the cost of worse solution quality. As expected, a narrower window leads to higher costs as there is less lookahead. The best solution quality is achieved with a window size of 5. It still performs noticeably worse in terms of solution quality compared to the FH-ASP and FH-SAT approaches. Although not present in the table, the RH-ASP approaches also have an increased makespan compared to the FH-ASP and FH-SAT approaches, as their algorithms are naturally minimizing the makespan. However, this increase in makespan is not as pronounced as the increase in sum-of-costs.

Next, we look at the effect of grouping on the results. Surprisingly, grouping seems to have a slight negative effect on runtime. However, the quality of the solutions is improved whenever deadlocks are prominent. Since deadlocks are more likely to occur in warehouse maps due to the tight corridors, the effect of grouping on solution quality is more pronounced there. Notice that the effect of grouping on solution quality diminishes as the window size increases. This could be explained by the fact that larger window sizes allow for more lookahead, which reduces the number of deadlocks and, in turn, the effect of grouping on solution quality. Additionally, the groups found by our algorithm are larger for larger window sizes, which means that the effect of grouping is less pronounced as the number of groups is potentially smaller. If the instance is dense enough, it is possible that our algorithm finds only one group, which makes the grouping approach equivalent to the non-grouping approach.

To have a better understanding of the time and memory usage of the different approaches, we present scatter plots comparing the time and memory usage of the RH-ASP-2-G and the RH-ASP-5-G approaches against the FH-ASP and FH-SAT approaches. Figure 2 shows the scatter plots for the time. The x-axis shows the time for the RH-ASP approaches, while the y-axis shows the time for the FH-ASP and FH-SAT approaches. Each point represents an instance. If a

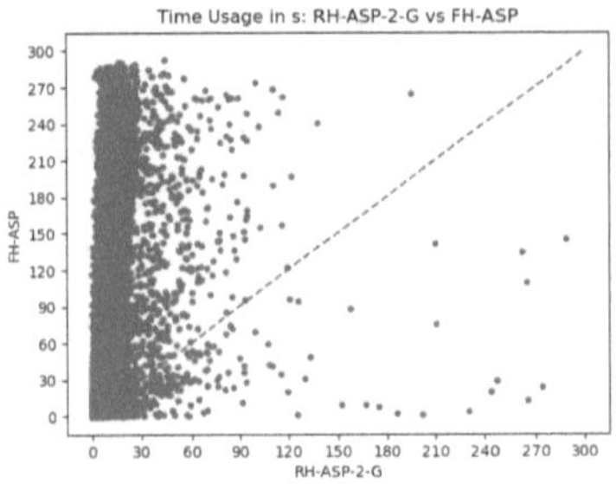

(a) Scatter plot showing the time for **RH-ASP-2-G** vs **FH-ASP**.

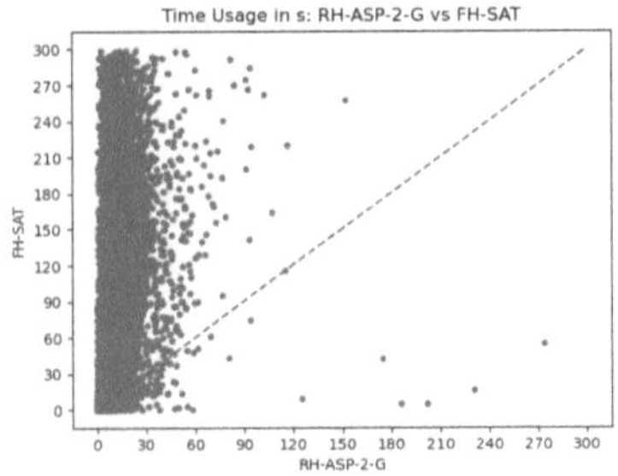

(b) Scatter plot showing the time for **RH-ASP-2-G** vs **FH-SAT**.

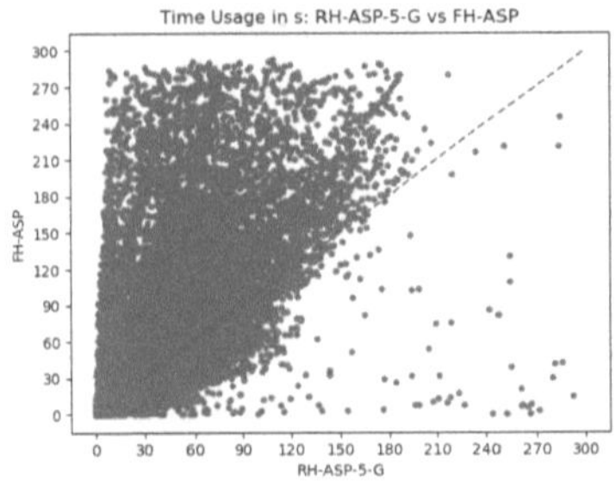

(c) Scatter plot showing the time for **RH-ASP-5-G** vs **FH-ASP**.

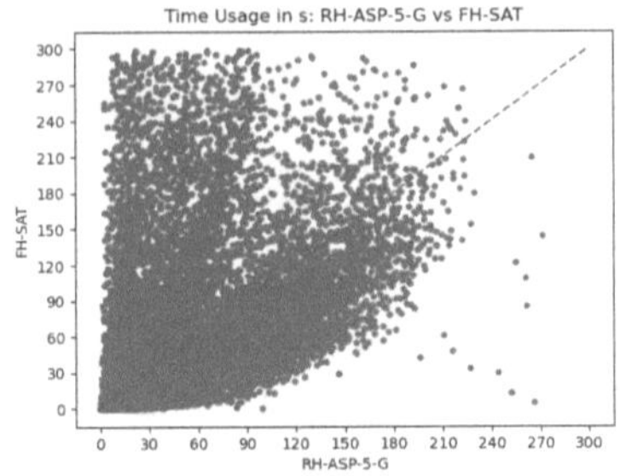

(d) Scatter plot showing the time for **RH-ASP-5-G** vs **FH-SAT**.

Fig. 2: Scatter plots showing the time for RH-ASP-2-G and RH-ASP-5-G vs FH-SAT and FH-ASP. Each point represents an instance. The x-axis shows the time for the grouping approach, while the y-axis shows the time for the FH-ASP and FH-SAT approaches.

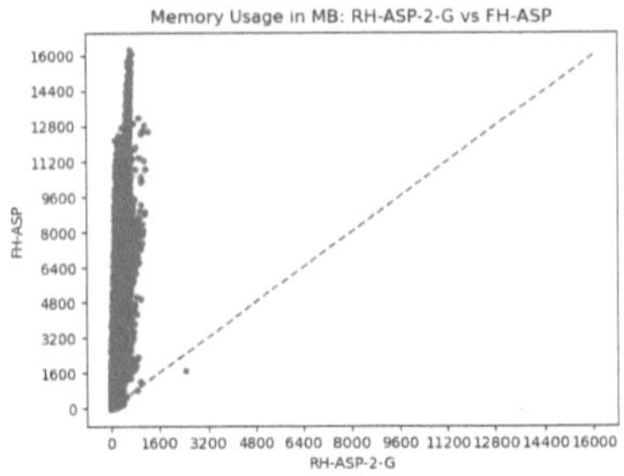

(a) Scatter plot showing the memory usage for **RH-ASP-2-G** vs **FH-ASP**.

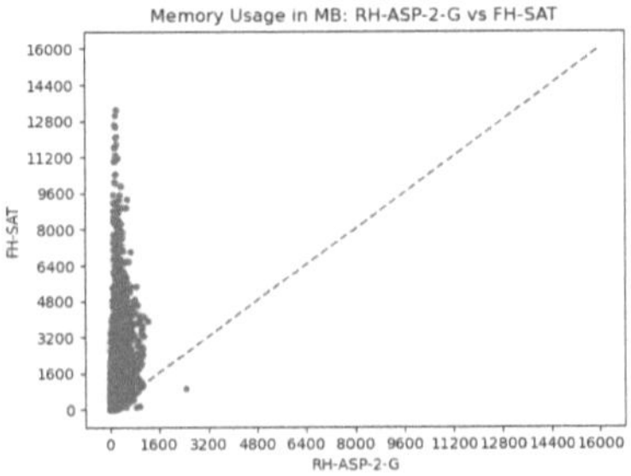

(b) Scatter plot showing the memory usage for **RH-ASP-2-G** vs **FH-SAT**.

Fig. 3: Scatter plots showing the memory usage in MB for RH-ASP-2-G vs FH-SAT and FH-ASP. Each point represents an instance. The x-axis shows the memory usage for the grouping approach, while the y-axis shows the memory usage for the FH-ASP and FH-SAT approaches.

point is above the diagonal, then the RH-ASP approaches are faster, while if a point is below the diagonal, then the FH-ASP or FH-SAT approach is faster. The plots clearly show that RH-ASP-2-G is significantly faster than the FH-ASP and FH-SAT approaches, as most points are substantially above the diagonal. If we then look at the plot for the RH-ASP-5-G approach, we can see that it is still generally faster than the FH-ASP and FH-SAT approaches. However, it is clear that the difference in time is not as pronounced as for RH-ASP-2-G. Even with the generally lower amount of solver calls and deadlocks that result from the increased window size, it leads to significantly higher grounding and solving times. The same trend is observed for grounding time.

In a similar manner, Fig. 3 shows the scatter plots for the memory usage. The x-axis shows the memory usage for the RH-ASP-2-G approach, while the y-axis shows the memory usage for the FH-ASP and FH-SAT approaches. We can clearly see that the RH-ASP-2-G approach uses significantly less memory than the FH-ASP and FH-SAT approaches. This is due to the very low horizon considered by the RH-ASP approaches. Even when the window size is increased due to deadlocks, the maximum window size in our experiments is around 20. The FH-ASP and FH-SAT approaches, on the other hand, must consider the entire horizon at once, which is frequently in the hundreds.

6 Conclusion

Current reduction-based approaches for sub-optimal MAPF rely on grounding the necessary horizon at once. This can lead to large grounding and solving times. We introduce a new solver based on the windowed rolling horizon approach to solve MAPF instances in small chunks. This leads to less expensive grounding and solving as each subproblem is many times smaller. We run benchmarks comparing our approach to existing methods and find that its runtime is improved at the cost of solution quality. Although reduction-based solvers are not the state-of-the-art for MAPF, we believe that the windowed approach can be used to improve their performance in other domains as well.

Future work includes improving the solution quality of our approach. A common idea used in the literature is to pre-calculate routes for each agent so that the paths are spread around the map. Approaches range from offline methods [25] that calculate the routes before the actual planning to online methods [24] that update the routes during planning. The routes are then used as part of a heuristic that guides the search for a solution. Integrating these ideas into an ASP-based solver is the main challenge of this approach.

Acknowledgements. This work was supported by DFG grant SCHA 550/15, Germany and by Charles University project UNCE 24/SCI/008.

References

1. Boyarski, E., et al.: ICBS: improved conflict-based search algorithm for multi-agent pathfinding. In: Yang, Q., Wooldridge, M. (eds.) Proceedings of the Twenty-fourth International Joint Conference on Artificial Intelligence (IJCAI'15), pp. 740–746. AAAI Press (2015). http://ijcai.org/proceedings/2015
2. Gange, G., Harabor, D., Stuckey, P.: Lazy CBS: implicit conflict-based search using lazy clause generation. In: Benton, J., Lipovetzky, N., Onaindia, E., Smith, D., Srivastava, S. (eds.) Proceedings of the Twenty-ninth International Conference on Automated Planning and Scheduling (ICAPS'19), pp. 155–162. AAAI Press (2019)
3. Gebser, M., Kaminski, R., Kaufmann, B., Schaub, T.: Answer Set Solving in Practice. Synthesis Lectures on Artificial Intelligence and Machine Learning, Morgan and Claypool Publishers (2012). https://doi.org/10.1007/978-3-031-01561-8
4. Jiang, H., Zhang, Y., Veerapaneni, R., Li, J.: Scaling lifelong multi-agent path finding to more realistic settings: research challenges and opportunities. In: Proceedings of the International Symposium on Combinatorial Search, vol. 17, pp. 234–242 (2024). https://doi.org/10.1609/socs.v17i1.31565
5. Kaminski, R., Schaub, T., Strauch, K., Švancara, J.: Improving the sum-of-cost methods for reduction-based multi-agent pathfinding solvers. In: Rocha, A., Steels, L., van den Herik, H. (eds.) Proceedings of the Sixteenth International Conference on Agents and Artificial Intelligence (ICAART'24), pp. 264–271. SciTePress (2024). https://doi.org/10.5220/0012353500003636. https://www.scitepress.org/ProceedingsDetails.aspx?ID=7POrHKUPtlI=
6. Kornhauser, D., Miller, G., Spirakis, P.: Coordinating pebble motion on graphs, the diameter of permutation groups, and applications. In: 25th Annual Symposium on Foundations of Computer Science, 1984, pp. 241–250 (1984). https://doi.org/10.1109/SFCS.1984.715921
7. Kraus, S. (ed.): Proceedings of the Twenty-eighth International Joint Conference on Artificial Intelligence (IJCAI'19). ijcai.org (2019)
8. Li, J., Ruml, W., Koenig, S.: EECBS: a bounded-suboptimal search for multi-agent path finding. In: Proceedings of the Thirty-fifth National Conference on Artificial Intelligence (AAAI'21), pp. 12353–12362. AAAI Press (2021)
9. Li, J., Tinka, A., Kiesel, S., Durham, J.W., Kumar, T.K.S., Koenig, S.: Lifelong multi-agent path finding in large-scale warehouses. In: Proceedings of the AAAI Conference on Artificial Intelligence, vol. 35, no. 13, pp. 11272–11281 (2021). https://doi.org/10.1609/aaai.v35i13.17344
10. Lifschitz, V.: Answer Set Programming. Springer-Verlag (2019). https://doi.org/10.1007/978-3-030-24658-7
11. Ma, H., Li, J., Kumar, T., Koenig, S.: Lifelong multi-agent path finding for online pickup and delivery tasks. In: Proceedings of the Sixteenth Conference on Autonomous Agents and MultiAgent Systems (AAMAS'17), pp. 837–845. ACM Press (2017)
12. Morris, R., et al.: Planning, scheduling and monitoring for airport surface operations. In: AAAI Workshop: Planning for Hybrid Systems (2016)
13. Okumura, K.: Engineering lacam*: towards real-time, large-scale, and near-optimal multi-agent pathfinding. ArXiv abs/2308.04292 (2023). https://api.semanticscholar.org/CorpusID:261065877
14. Okumura, K., Machida, M., Défago, X., Tamura, Y.: Priority inheritance with backtracking for iterative multi-agent path finding. In: Kraus [7], pp. 535–54. https://doi.org/10.24963/ijcai.2019/76

15. Silver, D.: Cooperative pathfinding. In: Young, R., Laird, J. (eds.) Proceedings of the First Artificial Intelligence and Interactive Digital Entertainment Conference (AIIDE'05), pp. 117–122. AAAI Press (2005)
16. Stern, R., et al.: Multi-agent pathfinding: definitions, variants, and benchmarks. In: Surynek, P., Yeoh, W. (eds.) Proceedings of the Twelfth International Symposium on Combinatorial Search (SOCS'19), pp. 151–159. AAAI Press (2019)
17. Surynek, P.: An optimization variant of multi-robot path planning is intractable. In: Fox, M., Poole, D. (eds.) Proceedings of the Twenty-fourth National Conference on Artificial Intelligence (AAAI'10), pp. 1261–1263. AAAI Press (2010). http://www.aaai.org/ocs/index.php/AAAI/AAAI10/paper/view/1768
18. Surynek, P.: Unifying search-based and compilation-based approaches to multi-agent path finding through satisfiability modulo theories. In: Kraus [7], pp. 1177–1183
19. Surynek, P.: Problem compilation for multi-agent path finding: a survey. In: De Raedt, L. (ed.) Proceedings of the Thirty-first International Joint Conference on Artificial Intelligence (IJCAI'22), pp. 5615–5622. ijcai.org (2022). https://doi.org/10.24963/ijcai.2022/783
20. Surynek, P., Felner, A., Stern, R., Boyarski, E.: Efficient SAT approach to multi-agent path finding under the sum of costs objective. In: Kaminka, G., et al., (eds.) Proceedings of the Twenty-second European Conference on Artificial Intelligence (ECAI'16), pp. 810–818. IOS Press (2016)
21. Surynek, P., Felner, A., Stern, R., Boyarski, E.: Sub-optimal sat-based approach to multi-agent path-finding problem. In: Bulitko, V., Storandt, S. (eds.) Proceedings of the Eleventh International Symposium on Combinatorial Search (SOCS'18), pp. 90–105. AAAI Press (2018)
22. Veerapaneni, R., Saleem, M.S., Li, J., Likhachev, M.: Windowed MAPF with completeness guarantees. In: Proceedings of the AAAI Conference on Artificial Intelligence, vol. 39, no. 22, pp. 23323–23332 (2025). https://doi.org/10.1609/aaai.v39i22.34499. https://ojs.aaai.org/index.php/AAAI/article/view/34499
23. Yu, J., LaValle, S.: Structure and intractability of optimal multi-robot path planning on graphs. In: desJardins, M., Littman, M. (eds.) Proceedings of the Twenty-seventh National Conference on Artificial Intelligence (AAAI'13), pp. 1443–1449. AAAI Press (2013)
24. Zang, H., et al.: Online guidance graph optimization for lifelong multi-agent path finding. In: Walsh, T., Shah, J., Kolter, Z. (eds.) Proceedings of the Thirty-eighth National Conference on Artificial Intelligence (AAAI'25), p. 10. AAAI Press (2025). https://doi.org/10.1609/aaai.v39i14.33614
25. Zhang, Y., Jiang, H., Bhatt, V., Nikolaidis, S., Li, J.: Guidance graph optimization for lifelong multi-agent path finding. In: Proceedings of the Thirty-fourth International Joint Conference on Artificial Intelligence (IJCAI'25). ijcai.org (2025). https://doi.org/10.24963/ijcai.2024/35

Adaptive Large Neighborhood Prioritized Search for Optimization in Answer Set Programming

Irumi Sugimori[1], Maki Miyashita[1], Hidetomo Nabeshima[2], Torsten Schaub[3], Takehide Soh[1], Naoyuki Tamura[4], and Mutsunori Banbara[1(✉)]

[1] Nagoya University, Nagoya, Japan
{irumi.sugimori, maki.miyashita, banbara}@nagoya-u.jp; soh@i.nagoya-u.ac.jp
[2] University of Yamanashi, Yamanashi, Japan
[3] Universität Potsdam, Potsdam, Germany
[4] Kobe University, Kobe, Japan

Abstract. We propose *Adaptive Large Neighborhood Prioritized Search* (ALNPS), a metaheuristic for solving combinatorial optimization problems. ALNPS iteratively seeks better solutions by alternately performing variability-guided destruction and prioritized search on a solution at hand. By exploiting neighborhood variability, ALNPS enables flexible and robust search while reducing the dependence on manually tuned or pre-defined parameters, especially the percentage of destruction. We present an implementation of ALNPS based on Answer Set Programming (ASP). Experimental results on course timetabling demonstrate that ALNPS significantly enhances the performance of standard ASP optimization and achieves competitive performance compared to existing ASP-based LNS methods, including ALNS and LNPS.

Keywords: Answer Set Programming · Large Neighborhood Search · Course Timetabling

1 Introduction

Hybrid search methods combining systematic and stochastic local search (SLS) have gained increasing interest for solving combinatorial optimization problems. Among these, Large Neighborhood Search (LNS; [12,14]) is one of the most studied in recent years. LNS is an SLS-based metaheuristic that starts with an initial solution and then iteratively seeks better solutions by alternately *destroy*ing and *repair*ing the current solution. Adaptive LNS (ALNS; [13]) extends LNS by incorporating multiple destroy and repair operators to improve *robustness*. Traditional LNS methods have been successfully applied to a wide range of routing

W. Faber et al. (Eds.): LPNMR 2026, LNAI 16952, pp. 430–447, 2027.
https://doi.org/10.1007/978-3-032-38320-4_27

and scheduling problems. Moreover, since the repair operators can be implemented using systematic solvers, they have been shown to be highly compatible with MaxSAT, mixed integer programming, and constraint programming.

Large Neighborhood Prioritized Search (LNPS; [16]) has recently been proposed as a method to synergistically combine the advantages of systematic and stochastic local search. The key distinction between LNPS and traditional LNS methods lies in their approach to solution reconstruction: LNPS employs *prioritized search* while LNS relies on repair strategies. Intuitively, prioritized search can be characterized as a systematic search method employing a customizable decision heuristic, such as VSIDS. LNPS can be viewed as an extension of LNS that addresses the limitations of LNS by enabling both *variability* and *optimality*. The variability of LNPS enables flexible search without heavy reliance on destroy operators, as the undestroyed part is fixed heuristically rather than rigidly and can be reassigned. As a consequence, LNPS guarantees optimal solutions.

From the perspective of Answer Set Programming (ASP; [10]), the use of LNS with ASP has been studied [7] and subsequently extended to ALNS [6]. These studies have shown that traditional LNS methods can improve the performance of ASP optimization on hard optimization problems [5]. Around the same time, LNPS was also implemented using *clingo*'s Python API for multi-shot ASP solving [9] and heuristic directives [8]. The resulting *heulingo*[LNPS] solver has demonstrated the effectiveness of LNPS compared to traditional LNS methods in both course timetabling [15] and hard optimization problems [16].

ASP-based LNS is highly sensitive to the choice of destroy operators, particularly the destruction percentage, as the preserved part of the candidate solution remains strictly fixed. To be effective, the level of destruction must strike a delicate balance: it must be large enough to ensure the resulting neighborhood contains improved solutions, yet small enough to allow the underlying ASP solver to explore the neighborhood efficiently. While LNPS reduces the reliance on precise destruction percentages by introducing neighborhood variability, and ALNS mitigates the dependence on individual operators through probabilistic selection, the a priori determination of optimal destruction levels remains a significant computational challenge. For instance, identifying optimal destruction percentages for course timetabling necessitated approximately 2,500 CPU hours [15]. This prohibitive computational overhead constitutes a major practical barrier to the application of declarative LNS methods across a wide range of optimization problems.

In this paper, we propose *Adaptive Large Neighborhood Prioritized Search* (ALNPS) and present its algorithm and implementation based on ASP. ALNPS is a metaheuristic that iteratively seeks better solutions starting from an initial solution. It alternates between performing *variability-guided destruction* and prioritized search on the current solution. The relation between ALNPS and existing LNS methods is summarized in Fig. 1.

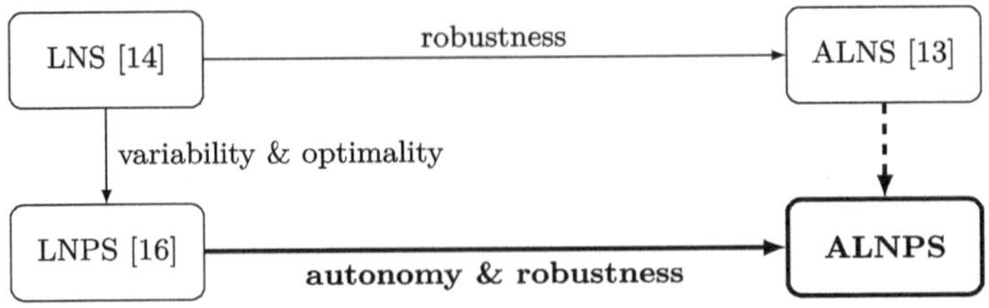

Fig. 1. The relation between ALNPS and existing LNS methods.

ALNPS extends LNPS with enhanced capabilities in *autonomy* and *robustness*. It incorporates variability-guided destruction, which automatically determines the percentage of destruction in each iteration based on the differences between consecutive solutions. ALNPS also supports multiple destroy and prioritized-search operators, enhancing robustness similarly to ALNS. We apply ALNPS to Curriculum-Based Course Timetabling (CB-CTT; [3]), a widely studied course timetabling problem. To evaluate ALNPS's effectiveness, we conduct experiments on the standard CB-CTT benchmark set [1,2,4]. We empirically evaluate the competitiveness of our ALNPS approach by comparing it with existing ASP-based LNS methods, including ALNS and LNPS.

The main results and contributions of our paper are summarized as follows:

1. We propose Adaptive Large Neighborhood Prioritized Search (ALNPS), which extends traditional ALNS by incorporating autonomy, variability, and optimality. Notably, neighborhood variability enables variability-guided destruction. This *parameter-free* destruction is challenging to achieve in traditional LNS methods due to the absence of such variability.
2. We develop an ASP-based implementation of ALNPS, resulting in the *heulingo*[ALNPS] solver. Its key advantages include a high applicability to a wide range of optimization problems due to the absence of parameter tuning for destruction and the ability to easily incorporate domain-specific heuristics in a declarative manner.
3. We develop an approach to solving Curriculum-based Course Timetabling (CB-CTT) problems based on ALNPS. Our approach relies on a high-level portfolio of multiple domain-specific ALNPS configurations that specify the behavior of the destroy and prioritized-search operators.
4. Experimental results on CB-CTT demonstrate that ALNPS can significantly enhance ASP optimization performance. *heulingo*[ALNPS] also shows that ALNPS can compete with state-of-the-art ASP-based LNS methods. Our high-level portfolio reduces the average gap to best known bounds from +467% of *clingo* to +38%. Furthermore, we find new improved bounds for 13 instances.

The proposed ALNPS constitutes a significant contribution to the state-of-the-art in ASP optimization and declarative local search methods. In particular, our approach offers a promising direction for addressing the issue of parameter tuning, a major practical limitation of local search neighborhoods.

2 Background

A Combinatorial Optimization Problem (COP) is defined as the task of finding a solution x^* such that $c(x^*) \leq c(x)$ for all $x \in X$, where X is the finite set of feasible solutions and $c : X \to \mathbb{R}$ is an objective function that maps a solution to its cost. We consider COP as a minimization problem.

Large Neighborhood Prioritized Search (LNPS; [16]) starts with an initial solution and then iteratively seeks better solutions by alternately destroying the current solution and reconstructing it using *prioritized search*, defined as a systematic search method in which the branching heuristic (e.g., VSIDS) can be configured or customized.

Algorithm 1. Large Neighborhood Prioritized Search

Input: feasible solution x, LNPS configuration γ

1: $x^* \leftarrow x$
2: **while** stop criterion is not met **do**
3: $\quad x^t \leftarrow \mathit{prioritized\text{-}search}(\mathit{destroy}(x, \gamma), \gamma)$
4: $\quad$ **if** $\mathit{accept}(x^t, x)$ **then**
5: $\qquad x \leftarrow x^t$
6: $\quad$ **end if**
7: $\quad$ **if** $c(x^t) < c(x^*)$ **then**
8: $\qquad x^* \leftarrow x^t$
9: $\quad$ **end if**
10: **end while**
11: **return** x^*

The LNPS algorithm, shown in Algorithm 1, takes as input an initial feasible solution and an LNPS configuration γ. The configuration γ specifies the behavior of the destroy and prioritized-search operators. The variable x^* represents the best solution found during the search. The variable x represents the current solution. The variable x^t represents a temporary solution which may be accepted as the current solution or discarded. The *destroy* operator randomly destroys parts of x and returns the undestroyed part. The *prioritized-search* operator reconstructs it by re-assigning values of not only variables in the destroyed part but also those in the undestroyed part.

The best solution x^* is initialized in Line 1. The loop in Lines 2–10 is repeated until a stop criterion is met. Typical choices for the stop criterion would include the optimality of x^*, a time-limit, or a limit on the number of iterations. The *destroy* and *prioritized-search* operators in Line 3 are alternately applied to find a new solution x^t. The new solution is evaluated in Line 4 to determine whether it becomes the new current solution. In Line 5, the current solution x is updated if necessary. There are several ways to implement the *accept* function. A simple strategy is to accept a new solution only if it is strictly better than the current solution. The new solution is checked in Line 7 to determine whether it is better than the best known solution. In Line 8, the current best solution x^* is updated if necessary. Finally, the best solution x^* is returned.

3 Adaptive Large Neighborhood Prioritized Search

We present Adaptive Large Neighborhood Prioritized Search (ALNPS) for solving combinatorial optimization problems. ALNPS is an extension of LNPS that enables *variability-guided destruction* and the incorporation of multiple destroy and prioritized-search operators. The key idea of ALNPS is variability-guided destruction that starts with an arbitrary percentage of destruction (0% by default) and dynamically determines the destruction percentage p for the next iteration based on the difference between the current solution x and the new solution x^t.

The use of the difference between consecutive solutions is motivated by the neighborhood variability of LNPS and ALNPS. In traditional LNS and ALNS, the undestroyed part of a solution remains fixed during repair, and thus the specified destruction percentage directly determines the amount of change introduced in each iteration. In contrast, LNPS and ALNPS employ prioritized search, where the undestroyed part is preferred heuristically rather than rigidly fixed and may therefore be modified during reconstruction. As a result, the actual amount of change introduced by a destruction-completion iteration may differ from the specified destruction percentage. The difference between the current solution and the new solution provides a simple way to observe this actual change and can therefore be used as feedback for determining the destruction percentage in subsequent iterations. Various distance measures can be used to compute this difference, such as the asymmetric set difference and the Hamming distance. For example, let x and x^t be answer sets representing the current and new solutions, respectively. The destruction percentage is computed as $p = \frac{|x - x^t|}{|x|} \times 100$ using the asymmetric set difference.

Algorithm. The ALNPS algorithm, shown in Algorithm 2, takes as input an initial feasible solution and a portfolio of ALNPS configurations Γ. In each iteration, ALNPS selects a configuration from the portfolio and applies it. In addition to x^*, x, and x^t, two new variables are introduced in the ALNPS algorithm. The variable γ represents the current configuration. The variable *stats* represents statistics, including the current solution x, the new solution x^t, their objective values, and related information.

The main differences from LNPS appear in Lines 2, 4, and 11. In Line 2, an initial configuration is selected from Γ and assigned to γ. In Line 4, the *destroy* and *prioritized-search* operators are applied according to the current configuration γ. The resulting solution and statistics are stored in x^t and *stats*, respectively. In Line 11, the current configuration γ is updated using the *updateConfig* function. The pseudo-code of the *updateConfig* function is shown in Algorithm 3. The variable γ' represents the configuration used in the next iteration. The variable p represents the destruction percentage of variability-guided destruction. First, in Line 1, γ' is selected from the portfolio of ALNPS configurations Γ by the *selectConfig* function. If γ' uses variability-guided destruction, the *computePercentage* function computes the percentage p based on the difference between x and x^t, and then the destruction percentage of γ' is updated to p. Finally, γ' is returned.

Algorithm 2. Adaptive Large Neighborhood Prioritized Search

Input: feasible solution x, portfolio of ALNPS configurations Γ

$x^* \leftarrow x$
$\gamma \leftarrow \mathit{getInitialConfig}(\Gamma)$
while stop criterion is not met **do**
  x^t, $\mathit{stats} \leftarrow \mathit{prioritized\text{-}search}(\mathit{destroy}(x, \gamma), \gamma)$
  if $\mathit{accept}(x^t, x)$ **then**
    $x \leftarrow x^t$
  end if
  if $c(x^t) < c(x^*)$ **then**
    $x^* \leftarrow x^t$
  end if
  $\gamma \leftarrow \mathit{updateConfig}(\gamma, \Gamma, \mathit{stats})$
end while
return x^*

Advantages. We discuss the major advantages of ALNPS compared with existing LNS methods. LNS strongly depends on the destroy operator, since it uses a single fixed destruction percentage that does not vary across iterations. ALNS reduces this dependence by probabilistically selecting one destroy operator from a portfolio of configurations including multiple pre-defined destruction percentages. However, determining an effective selection strategy may require additional parameter tuning. Moreover, LNS and ALNS cannot guarantee solution optimality in general. Due to the neighborhood variability, LNPS reduces dependence on the destroy operators and also guarantees solution optimality by appropriately designing a stop criterion for prioritized search. However, determining an optimal (or near-optimal) destruction percentage for each instance remains difficult. Thus, reliance on manually tuned or pre-defined destruction percentages still has inherent limitations.

In contrast, ALNPS establishes the variability-guided destruction without relying on manually tuned or pre-defined destruction percentages. Furthermore, ALNPS allows the undestroyed part to be configured via prioritized search, enabling the incorporation of domain-specific heuristics. For instance, the simplest heuristic is to preserve the current solution as much as possible. This can be easily done by setting the destruction percentage to zero (0%) and prioritizing full assignments of decision variables. Interestingly, this *zero destruction* is shown to be effective in ASP-based nurse re-scheduling [11]. Note that the zero destruction strategy is not meaningful for LNS and ALNS, as it yields the same solution.

Implementation. We extend the *heulingo*[LNPS] solver, an ASP-based LNPS implementation [16], for ALNPS by incorporating variability-guided destruction and *roulette-wheel selection strategy* [13] for configuration selection. These extensions are implemented in approximately 700 lines of Python code. We adopt the asymmetric set difference as the distance measure between consecutive solutions for variability-guided destruction, as it provides a simple and

Algorithm 3. *updateConfig* function

Input: ALNPS configuration γ, portfolio of ALNPS configurations Γ, statistics *stats*

1: $\gamma' \leftarrow selectConfig(\gamma, \Gamma, stats)$
2: **if** γ' uses variability-guided random destruction **then**
3: $p \leftarrow computePercentage(stats)$
4: $\gamma' \leftarrow updatePercentage(\gamma', p)$
5: **end if**
6: **return** γ'

efficient baseline. Alternative distance measures, such as the Hamming distance, will be investigated in future work. The resulting *heulingo*[ALNPS] accepts a COP instance in ASP fact format. These facts are then combined with ASP encodings for COP solving and for a portfolio of ALNPS configurations. The resulting ASP program is solved by our ALNPS algorithm built on ASP solvers, in our case *clingo*.

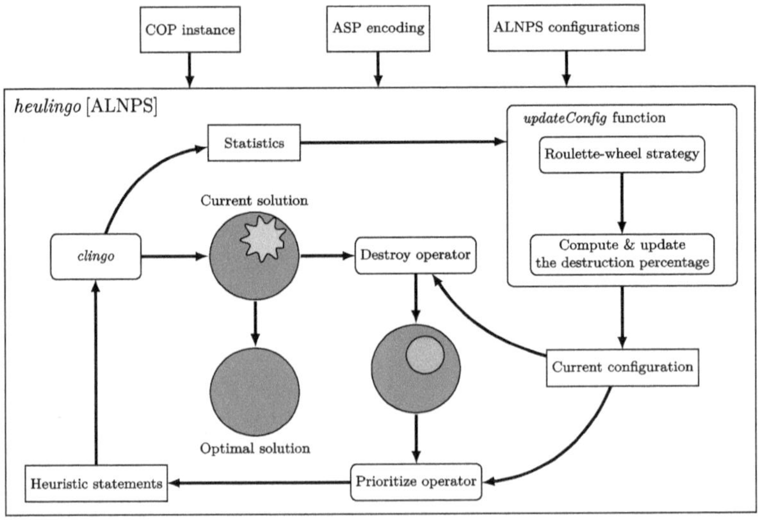

Fig. 2. The execution flow of *heulingo*[ALNPS]

The execution flow of *heulingo*[ALNPS] is illustrated in Fig. 2. First, *clingo* searches for an initial solution. The solution is then assigned to the current solution. An initial configuration is selected from a portfolio of ALNPS configurations and assigned as the current configuration. Second, in the main loop, the destroy operator destroys parts of the current solution (the red-circled part), and then the prioritize operator generates *clingo*'s `#heuristic` statements for the undestroyed part (the blue part outside the red circle), according to the current configuration. The generated `#heuristic` statements can be activated or deactivated via *external* atoms in their body later on. *clingo* then performs a heuristic search for a new solution, where the green part is reassigned. If the new solution is optimal, it is returned as the final solution.

Besides the above main loop similar to LNPS, *heulingo*[ALNPS] includes an additional loop for variability-guided destruction and the incorporation of multiple configurations. After each invocation of *clingo*, the *updateConfig* function selects a new configuration based on the statistics of the obtained solution using the roulette-wheel selection strategy. This function also computes and updates the destruction percentage based on the set difference between the current and new solutions, if the selected configuration involves a variability-guided destruction.

In addition, we introduce a *cut-off time* T to terminate *clingo*'s search in each iteration as well as in finding an initial solution. *heulingo*[ALNPS] terminates the search when T seconds have passed since *clingo* found the last solution. The cut-off time for each iteration is increased by $R\%$ when no improved solution has been found over a certain number of consecutive iterations. Instead of a cut-off time, we can also use a time-limit, solve-limit, or other criteria. However, in general, it is very difficult to estimate when *clingo* gets stuck during search. Exploring effective strategies remains future work.

heulingo[ALNPS] can be viewed as a tool for heuristically-driven answer set optimization with no parameter tuning for destruction. For *high applicability*, we present high-level portfolios of ALNPS configurations for course timetabling in Sect. 4. For *efficiency*, the question is whether *heulingo*[ALNPS] matches the performance of state-of-the-art ASP-based LNS methods. We empirically address this question in Sect. 5.

4 ALNPS Application to Course Timetabling

We present portfolios of ALNPS configurations for Curriculum-based Course Timetabling (CB-CTT; [3]). The goal of CB-CTT is to assign all lectures to timeslots and rooms so that all hard constraints are satisfied while violations of soft constraints are minimized. We use the *teaspoon* encoding [1,2] for CB-CTT. In the *teaspoon* encoding, the atom `assigned(C,R,D,P)` represents that a lecture of a course `C` is assigned to a room `R` at a period `P` on a day `D`. This atom is used to characterize a solution. The atom `assigned(C,D,P)` omits the room information.

We introduce several dedicated predicates to specify a portfolio of ALNPS configurations in a declarative way. A portfolio consists of one or more configurations together with a selection strategy. The predicate `_project/2` defines *projected atoms*, i.e., the parts of an answer set subject to ALNPS. Usually, the projected atoms characterize a solution. For example, in CB-CTT, the `assigned (C,R,D,P)` atoms characterize a solution. An ALNPS configuration can use these atoms as projected atoms, randomly destroy some of them, and prioritize the remaining atoms via domain-specific `#heuristic` directives.

Listing 1.1. The VG-Random configuration

```
1 _project((assigned,4), assigned(C,R,D,P)) :- assigned(C,R,D,P).
2 _destroy((random,auto), assigned(C,R,D,P), (C,R,D,P)) :- assigned(C,R,D
    ,P).
3 _destroy((random,auto), auto).
4 _prioritize((1,true), assigned(C,R,D,P)) :- assigned(C,R,D,P).
5 _prioritize((1,true), 1, true).
6 _config("VG-Random", (assigned,4), (random,auto), (1,true)).
7 _strategy(roulette, "VG-Random").
```

Listing 1.2. The Portfolio configuration

```
_project((assigned,4), assigned(C,R,D,P)) :- assigned(C,R,D,P).
_project((assigned,3), assigned(C,D,P)) :- assigned(C,D,P).
_destroy((random,(6;10)), assigned(C,R,D,P), (C,R,D,P)) :- assigned(C,R
    ,D,P).
_destroy((random,N), p(N)) :- N=(6;10).
_destroy((day_period,(1;2)), assigned(C,R,D,P), (D,P)) :- assigned(C,R,
    D,P).
_destroy((day_period,N), n(N)) :- N=(1;2).
_destroy((day_room,1), assigned(C,R,D,P), (D,R)) :- assigned(C,R,D,P).
_destroy((day_room,1), n(1)).
_prioritize((1,true), assigned(C,R,D,P)) :- assigned(C,R,D,P).
_prioritize((1,true), assigned(C,D,P)) :- assigned(C,D,P).
_prioritize((1,true), 1, true).
_config("Random 6%",        (assigned,4),     (random,6),       (1,true)).
_config("Day-Period",       (assigned,4),     (day_period,1),   (1,true)).
_config("Day-Room",         (assigned,4),     (day_room,1),     (1,true)).
_config("Swap-Room 10%",    (assigned,(4;3)), (random,10),      (1,true)).
_config("DP-Swap-Room 2",   (assigned,(4;3)), (day_period,2),   (1,true)).
_strategy(roulette,C) :- _config(C,_,_,_).
```

The predicates `_destroy/3` and `_destroy/2` define destroy operators, specifying which projected atoms can be destroyed and their corresponding destruction percentages (or numbers of atoms). The predicates `_prioritize/2` and `_prioritize/3` define prioritize operators, specifying which projected atoms can be prioritized and the corresponding heuristic modifiers and values for `# heuristic` directives. The predicate `_config/4` defines ALNPS configurations as combinations of projected atoms, destroy operators, and prioritize operators. The predicate `_strategy/2` defines a portfolio of configurations together with its selection strategy.

We develop three portfolios for CB-CTT solving: `VG-Random`, `Portfolio`, and `VG-Portfolio`. `VG-Random` is a distinctive ALNPS configuration that randomly destroys the current solution based on variability-guided destruction and preserves the undestroyed part as much as possible. An ASP encoding of `VG-Random` is shown in Listing 1.1. The rule in Line 1 defines a set of projected atoms named `(assigned,4)` that consists of `assigned(C,R,D,P)` atoms. The rules in Lines 2–3 define a destroy operator named `(random,auto)` that randomly selects tuples of `(C,R,D,P)` based on an automatically determined destruction percentage, and then destroys the corresponding `assigned(C,R,D,P)` atoms. The rules in Lines 4–5 define a prioritize operator named `(1,true)` that prioritizes the `assigned`

`(C,R,D,P)` atoms in the undestroyed part using `#heuristic` directives with modifier `true` and value `1` in Line 5. More precisely, these two rules generate the *clingo* directive where B is an external atom to activate or deactivate the statements in each iteration. The rule in Line 6 defines a configuration named `VG-Random` by combining the projected atoms `(assigned,4)`, the destroy operator `(random,auto)`, and the prioritize operator `(1,true)`. The rule in Line 7 defines a portfolio of `VG-Random` only, together with the roulette-wheel selection strategy (indicated by `roulette`).

The `Portfolio` portfolio includes multiple configurations: Random 6%, Day-Period, Day-Room, Swap-Room 10%, and DP-Swap-Room 2. Each single LNPS configuration with the best destruction percentages was proposed in [15]. The Random N% configuration randomly destroys N% of the current solution. The Day-Period configuration randomly selects a single day-period pair and destroys parts of the current solution including the selected pair. The Day-Room configuration is similar to Day-Period, but randomly selects a single day-room pair. The Swap-Room N% configuration randomly destroys N% of the current solution characterized by `assigned/4`, and tries to preserve not only the undestroyed part but also the atoms of `assigned/3` as much as possible. The DP-Swap-Room N configuration is similar to Swap-Room N, but randomly selects N day-period pairs and destroys all atoms containing any selected pair. An ASP encoding of `Portfolio` is shown in Listing 1.2. All five configurations are defined in Lines 12–16, which are combined in Line 17.

The `VG-Portfolio` portfolio extends `Portfolio` to variability-guided destruction, particularly for Random 6% and Swap-Room 10%. This extension can be easily done by replacing the destroy operators `(random,6)` in Line 12 and `(random,10)` in Line 15 with `(random,auto)`, as in Listing 1.1.

5 Experiments

To evaluate the effectiveness of the proposed ALNPS approach, we conduct experiments on the standard benchmark set [4] of Curriculum-Based Course Timetabling (CB-CTT). Our empirical analysis considers all 61 instances using the most difficult UD5 formulation. We use the *teaspoon* encoding [1,2] for CB-CTT solving. We compare our *heulingo*[ALNPS] solver with *clingo*, *heulingo*[LNPS], and *ALASPO*. *ALASPO* is a state-of-the-art ASP-based ALNS implementation [5,6].[1]

- We execute *clingo* version 5.8.0 for each of the two best options found in [1] for *teaspoon* encoding: model-guided optimization (bb)[2] and core-guided optimization (usc).[3]
- We run *heulingo*[LNPS] three times for each of the five configurations with the best destruction percentages found in [15]: Random 6%, Day-Period, Day-Room, Swap-Room 10%, and DP-Swap-Room 2.

---

[1] https://gitlab.tuwien.ac.at/kbs/BAI/alaspo

[2] `--opt-strategy=bb,0 --opt-heuristic=3 --restart-on-model`

[3] `--configuration=jumpy --opt-strategy=usc,11`

- We run *heulingo*[ALNPS] three times for each of three portfolios in Section 4: `VG-Random`, `Portfolio`, and `VG-Portfolio`.
- We execute *ALASPO* with the six portfolios used in [5,6], corresponding to the default portfolio combined with six selection strategies: the uniform roulette-wheel strategy, the dynamic strategy, and the self-adaptive roulette-wheel strategy with $\alpha = \{0.2, 0.4, 0.6, 0.8\}$.

We use *clingo* with usc for finding an initial solution and *clingo* with bb for each iteration, as with [15], for *heulingo*[ALNPS], *heulingo*[LNPS], and *ALASPO*. Here, an iteration refers to one invocation of neighborhood search. The time-limit is 3,600 seconds for each instance. The cut-off times of *heulingo*[ALNPS] and *heulingo*[LNPS] are set to $\frac{1}{8}$ and $\frac{1}{600}$ of the time-limit for the initial solution search and each iteration, respectively. These cut-off values were determined empirically based on our previous work [15]. All experiments are run on macOS with Intel Core i7 (6-core 3.2GHz CPU and 64GB memory).

First, we compare the results obtained with domain-independent configurations. The comparison results are shown in Table 1. The columns show, in order, the instance names, the bounds obtained by *clingo* with bb and usc, and the average, minimum, and maximum bounds obtained by *heulingo*[LNPS] with Random 6%, *heulingo*[ALNPS] with `VG-Random`, and *ALASPO* with the six portfolios. The symbol '*' indicates that the solvers guarantee the optimality. The best average of bounds in each instance is highlighted in bold. The bottom two rows show the number of best bounds and the average ratio to the bounds obtained by *clingo* with usc, respectively. The average ratio is the arithmetic mean of the per-instance ratios over all benchmark instances, i.e., $\frac{1}{|I|}\sum_{i\in I}\frac{b_i^m}{b_i^{usc}}$, where I is the set of instances, b_i^m is the bound obtained by method m for instance i, and b_i^{usc} is the bound obtained by *clingo* with usc for the same instance.

Our *heulingo*[ALNPS] solver finds the best bounds for the largest number of instances, namely 32, followed by 23 for *heulingo*[LNPS], 14 for *ALASPO*, and 8 for *clingo* with usc. Moreover, *heulingo*[ALNPS] improves the bounds of *clingo* by 50.3% on average, compared with 40.8% for *heulingo*[LNPS] and 9.8% for *ALASPO*. Although *heulingo*[ALNPS] does not require parameter tuning for destruction, it performs competitively with *heulingo*[LNPS] and *ALASPO*, which rely on manually tuned and pre-defined destruction percentages, respectively. Note that *heulingo*[ALNPS] finds six optima during the search for finding initial solutions. Although *ALASPO* cannot guarantee optimality in general, it guarantees the optimality of three instances during the search without fixed parts (i.e., 100% destruction).

A more detailed analysis shows that *heulingo*[ALNPS] with `VG-Random` improves the bounds of *heulingo*[LNPS] with Random 6% by more than 50% on the following seven instances: DDS4, DDS7, EA03, EA04, EA07, EA08, and EA10. For example, a comparison of `VG-Random` and Random 6% on DDS4 is shown in Fig. 3. The left plot shows the changes in objective values, while the right plot shows the set difference (%) between the current and improved solutions. The figure shows that Random 6% rarely improves the objective val-

Table 1. Comparison of domain-independent configurations on CB-CTT

Instance	*clingo*[ASP]		*heulingo*[LNPS] Random 6%			*heulingo*[ALNPS] VG-Random			*ALASPO*[ALNS] Portfolios		
	bb	usc	avg.	min.	max.	avg.	min.	max.	avg.	min.	max.
comp01	124	283	14.3	13	15	**11.0**	11	11	**11.0**	11	11
comp02	989	331	239.7	231	250	**233.7**	206	248	390.7	212	723
comp03	791	302	**197.0**	184	214	206.3	199	212	299.3	246	340
comp04	211	***49**	***49.0**	***49**	***49**	***49.0**	***49**	***49**	51.5	49	57
comp05	2662	1940	**928.7**	782	1029	996.3	888	1094	1643.2	1310	2064
comp06	822	1025	**209.0**	195	222	212.7	204	219	381.3	238	547
comp07	924	1149	216.0	145	312	**166.7**	139	201	856.0	315	1157
comp08	335	***55**	***55.0**	***55**	***55**	***55.0**	***55**	***55**	61.8	57	72
comp09	617	254	151.0	149	153	**149.3**	148	151	186.7	173	197
comp10	822	1229	**176.0**	149	190	239.7	190	329	541.0	223	894
comp11	287	***0**	***0.0**	***0**	***0**	***0.0**	***0**	***0**	***0.0**	***0**	***0**
comp12	2626	1246	**672.0**	668	679	693.3	670	717	1763.2	1199	2094
comp13	661	301	197.3	194	200	**196.3**	193	199	243.5	182	468
comp14	746	***67**	166.7	154	173	170.7	152	182	278.5	175	466
comp15	852	607	**224.3**	193	267	239.0	217	277	357.5	268	460
comp16	944	1090	**187.3**	178	194	351.7	206	638	544.0	196	876
comp17	979	412	**236.0**	218	247	511.0	243	650	548.2	287	792
comp18	673	471	159.7	155	166	164.7	158	168	**156.5**	141	188
comp19	890	919	199.0	196	205	**197.3**	196	198	339.2	217	471
comp20	3304	1386	656.7	555	714	**352.0**	346	359	1593.7	761	2057
comp21	893	310	**245.7**	235	256	252.0	251	253	368.7	279	529
DDS1	6536	7544	**3820.0**	3656	4031	3886.3	3848	3950	4825.0	4631	5041
DDS2	402	433	83.3	73	93	**75.3**	73	77	81.3	64	98
DDS3	**22**	391	23.3	22	24	24.7	24	26	**22.0**	22	22
DDS4	10486	3123	3177.3	3108	3237	**1273.7**	1267	1285	10234.3	9472	11629
DDS5	539	***76**	***76.0**	***76**	***76**	***76.0**	***76**	***76**	141.0	89	216
DDS6	849	964	166.3	138	188	**157.7**	135	177	774.0	251	1130
DDS7	645	1485	541.3	502	610	**113.3**	105	119	681.2	129	943
EA01	887	807	**231.7**	219	240	238.3	226	249	752.8	276	1237
EA02	1085	1215	**138.7**	124	152	160.0	146	179	151.8	130	172
EA03	8190	2555	1675.7	1612	1790	**554.3**	515	599	2732.2	2432	3230
EA04	**62**	1873	1662.0	1662	1662	257.0	245	279	578.5	18	1882
EA05	21	513	22.0	18	24	92.3	29	209	**14.0**	14	14
EA06	543	1027	214.3	193	246	**196.3**	182	206	253.3	165	420
EA07	10108	2831	2582.3	2523	2654	**713.0**	673	734	3901.8	2877	4668
EA08	356	991	893.3	846	920	79.0	72	86	**43.7**	40	56

(continued)

Table 1. (*continued*)

Instance	*clingo*[ASP]		*heulingo*[LNPS] Random 6%			*heulingo*[ALNPS] VG-Random			*ALASPO*[ALNS] Portfolios		
	bb	usc	avg.	min.	max.	avg.	min.	max.	avg.	min.	max.
EA09	**48**	865	62.0	55	70	57.0	52	64	**48.0**	48	48
EA10	1711	444	1612.3	1585	1659	**364.0**	338	393	1501.5	973	1686
EA11	211	771	45.0	41	49	46.0	40	53	**39.7**	36	41
EA12	234	518	66.3	55	80	64.7	51	81	**33.2**	27	46
erlangen2011_2	17035	17263	14877.7	14734	15029	**14379.7**	14122	14806	35374.8	33582	36934
erlangen2012_1	32541	25061	24986.7	24633	25359	**24719.0**	24601	24931	45623.5	43725	47112
erlangen2012_2	38180	34360	34769.7	34584	35084	**33663.7**	33430	33902	64823.7	62078	70509
erlangen2013_1	29459	28302	26795.0	26579	26930	**25383.7**	25199	25586	41308.3	40196	44165
erlangen2013_2	34568	29140	27818.7	27675	28026	**25796.3**	25494	26008	44059.8	43067	46610
erlangen2014_1	30249	24510	23906.3	23640	24170	**22027.7**	21872	22166	40533.3	39683	41644
test1	619	751	232.7	232	234	**232.0**	232	232	363.8	266	487
test2	24	***20**	**20.0**	20	20	20.3	20	21	***20.0**	***20**	***20**
test3	194	117	**78.0**	78	78	78.3	78	79	117.0	72	180
test4	705	260	190.0	183	203	**171.3**	164	182	358.7	258	474
toy	***0**	***0**	***0.0**	***0**	***0**	***0.0**	***0**	***0**	***0.0**	***0**	***0**
Udine1	1079	953	276.7	234	356	**271.7**	263	284	463.0	256	710
Udine2	505	402	**94.0**	92	96	100.0	97	105	183.7	137	241
Udine3	343	385	90.0	78	100	150.0	95	252	**74.7**	46	90
Udine4	400	***106**	***106.0**	***106**	***106**	***106.0**	***106**	***106**	111.2	107	118
Udine5	518	695	86.7	78	99	**85.3**	74	99	170.7	49	402
Udine6	366	628	42.0	40	43	70.7	56	81	**36.3**	36	38
Udine7	233	733	75.0	68	79	76.7	71	82	**65.8**	64	67
Udine8	606	941	**105.0**	104	106	122.3	117	126	164.5	138	200
Udine9	610	163	**78.3**	75	80	82.0	79	84	99.5	67	191
UUMCAS_A131	38929	28688	28335.7	27808	28692	**25812.0**	25661	25890	37209.2	35159	38310
#best averages	4	8	23			**32**			14		
Average ratio	1.796	1.000	0.592	0.571	0.614	**0.497**	0.462	0.532	0.902	0.680	1.173

ues. Moreover, the set differences observed when improvements are found are smaller than the specified destruction percentage of 6%. In contrast, `VG-Random` frequently improves the objective values, resulting in substantial improvements overall. In addition, the set differences are extremely small, typically less than 1%. A similar trend is observed for the other six instances. These results suggest that the manually tuned Random 6% configuration of LNPS, although effective on average over the benchmark set, is not necessarily the best destruction percentage for individual instances. In contrast, `VG-Random` automatically computes the destruction percentage for each instance, enabling it to find better solutions.

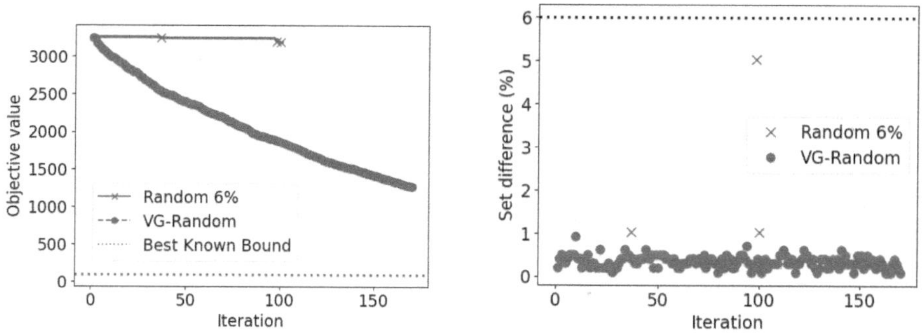

Fig. 3. Comparison of `VG-Random` and Random 6% on the DDS4 instance: objective values (left) and set differences between the current and improved solutions (right).

Second, we compare the bounds obtained with domain-specific configurations and portfolios. The results are shown in Table 2. The table is organized in the same way as Table 1. For *heulingo*[LNPS] and *heulingo*[ALNPS], the minimum bounds obtained over three runs are reported. *ALASPO* is excluded from this comparison, since it cannot handle some domain-specific configurations.

heulingo[ALNPS] with `VG-Portfolio` finds the best bounds for the largest number of instances, namely 32, followed by 28 for `Portfolio` and 19 for *heulingo*[LNPS] with DP-Swap-Room 2. The results from Tables 1–2 show that domain-specific configurations (e.g.,DP-Swap-Room 2) are more effective than domain-independent configurations (Random and `VG-Random`). They also show that portfolios combining multiple configurations are even more effective. The average usage percentages of configurations in `VG-Portfolio` over all instances are shown in Table 3. We observe that configurations with higher usage percentages tend to correspond to those with better performance in Table 2.

Finally, we compare *heulingo*[ALNPS] with the best known bounds that were obtained by state-of-the-art CB-CTT solving techniques, including simulated annealing, integer programming, SAT/MaxSAT, ASP, and many others [1,2,15]. *heulingo*[ALNPS] with `VG-Portfolio` is able to significantly reduce the average gap to +38% compared to +467% of the virtual best of *clingo*. Remarkably, *heulingo*[ALNPS] with `VG-Portfolio` matches the performance of the virtual best portfolio of all five configurations in Table 2. Moreover, *heulingo*[ALNPS] succeeds in finding improved bounds for 13 instances. The gap to the best known bound ($\sharp$) is obtained by calculating $\frac{\text{obtained bound}-\sharp}{\sharp}$. That is, 0% means that the bound matches the best known bound. +100% means that the bound is twice as large as the best known bound. For more details, please refer to our git repository: https://github.com/banbaralab/lpnmr2026/.

Table 2. Comparison of domain-specific configurations on CB-CTT

Instance	*clingo*		*heulingo*[LNPS]					*heulingo*[ALNPS]	
	bb	usc	Random 6%	Day-Period	Day-Room	Swap-Room 10%	DP-Swap-Room 2	`Portfolio`	`VG-Portfolio`
comp01	124	283	13	13	**11**	**11**	**11**	**11**	**11**
comp02	989	331	231	226	**200**	237	229	208	213
comp03	791	302	184	181	189	175	181	176	**167**
comp04	211	***49**	***49**	***49**	***49**	***49**	***49**	***49**	***49**
comp05	2662	1940	**782**	894	859	908	814	897	815
comp06	822	1025	195	165	177	142	134	106	**101**
comp07	924	1149	145	105	143	71	82	**56**	64
comp08	335	***55**	***55**	***55**	***55**	***55**	***55**	***55**	***55**
comp09	617	254	149	149	149	144	140	**138**	145
comp10	822	1229	149	148	137	105	82	**77**	78
comp11	287	***0**	***0**	***0**	***0**	***0**	***0**	***0**	***0**
comp12	2626	1246	668	655	674	618	646	**616**	643
comp13	661	301	194	178	188	161	157	**153**	**153**
comp14	746	***67**	154	159	167	110	95	94	103
comp15	852	607	**193**	201	208	201	196	**193**	199
comp16	944	1090	178	156	198	127	119	**112**	123
comp17	979	412	218	190	208	176	180	185	**165**
comp18	673	471	155	147	150	146	141	137	**131**
comp19	890	919	196	175	193	171	179	**162**	185
comp20	3304	1386	555	280	274	312	317	296	**271**
comp21	893	310	235	219	230	176	169	178	**166**
DDS1	6536	7544	3656	2893	3082	2695	2668	2742	**2609**
DDS2	402	433	73	70	70	68	68	70	**66**
DDS3	**22**	391	**22**	**22**	**22**	**22**	**22**	**22**	**22**
DDS4	10486	3123	3108	2632	1204	1129	1045	1106	**985**
DDS5	539	***76**	***76**	***76**	***76**	***76**	***76**	***76**	***76**
DDS6	849	964	138	145	187	158	163	150	**133**
DDS7	645	1485	502	86	80	55	55	52	**50**
EA01	887	807	219	228	239	204	**202**	204	206
EA02	1085	1215	124	132	132	125	122	119	**118**
EA03	8190	2555	1612	531	362	226	172	**157**	252
EA04	62	1873	1662	736	237	842	**18**	32	35
EA05	21	513	18	16	22	**14**	**14**	**14**	**14**
EA06	543	1027	193	161	150	145	147	**138**	140
EA07	10108	2831	2523	1298	705	664	546	602	**541**

(*continued*)

Table 2. (*continued*)

Instance	*clingo*		*heulingo*[LNPS]					*heulingo*[ALNPS]	
	bb	usc	Random 6%	Day-Period	Day-Room	Swap-Room 10%	DP-Swap-Room 2	`Portfolio`	`VG-Portfolio`
EA08	356	991	846	98	42	**40**	**40**	**40**	**40**
EA09	**48**	865	55	**48**	53	**48**	**48**	**48**	**48**
EA10	1711	444	1585	292	**245**	332	328	255	260
EA11	211	771	41	57	48	40	41	**36**	40
EA12	234	518	55	50	47	**27**	**27**	**27**	**27**
erlangen2011_2	17035	17263	14734	14256	**14075**	14283	14662	14397	14473
erlangen2012_1	32541	25061	24633	24088	**23592**	24133	24026	24095	24559
erlangen2012_2	38180	34360	34584	34103	**33296**	33680	33905	34293	33723
erlangen2013_1	29459	28302	26579	25324	**24297**	24675	24752	24803	24890
erlangen2013_2	34568	29140	27675	25904	**25225**	26891	26703	27084	26292
erlangen2014_1	30249	24510	23640	23057	**21739**	22595	22982	22685	22333
test1	619	751	**232**	**232**	**232**	**232**	**232**	**232**	**232**
test2	24	***20**	**20**	**20**	**20**	**20**	**20**	**20**	**20**
test3	194	117	78	78	78	74	**73**	74	74
test4	705	260	183	159	135	131	131	**115**	117
toy	***0**	***0**	***0**	***0**	***0**	***0**	***0**	***0**	***0**
Udine1	1079	953	234	231	232	211	215	**192**	216
Udine2	505	402	92	94	95	83	92	82	**79**
Udine3	343	385	78	79	91	68	67	68	**63**
Udine4	400	***106**	***106**	***106**	***106**	***106**	***106**	***106**	***106**
Udine5	518	695	78	70	71	49	49	**44**	46
Udine6	366	628	40	42	46	**36**	38	38	38
Udine7	233	733	68	68	70	**64**	**64**	66	**64**
Udine8	606	941	104	106	104	117	111	95	**85**
Udine9	610	163	75	70	81	**63**	69	65	69
UUMCAS_A131	38929	28688	27808	25165	25198	27777	**24052**	24857	24428
#best bounds	3	8	11	10	18	17	19	28	**32**
Average ratio	1.796	1.000	0.571	0.463	0.447	0.425	0.410	**0.403**	**0.403**

Table 3. The average usage percentage of each configuration in `VG-Portfolio`

	VG-Random	Day-Period	Day-Room	VG-Swap-Room	DP-Swap-Room 2
Average usage percentage (%)	16.4	17.4	19.6	24.3	22.3

6 Related Work and Conclusion

The most closely related works are Adaptive Large Neighborhood Search (ALNS) [5–7] and Large Neighborhood Prioritized Search (LNPS) [15,16], as well as the corresponding ASP-based solvers *ALASPO* and *heulingo*[LNPS], respectively.

We proposed Adaptive Large Neighborhood Prioritized Search (ALNPS) and presented an ASP-based implementation of ALNPS. The resulting *heulingo*[ALNPS] solver supports heuristically-driven answer set optimization while reducing reliance on manually tuned or pre-defined destruction percentages. All source code including *heulingo*[ALNPS] and benchmark problems is available online.[4]

Besides curriculum-based course timetabling in Sect. 5, we conducted preliminary experiments on a challenging benchmark set and ASP encodings used in [5,6,16]. We tested all *clingo* encodings with domain-independent configurations, and *clingo-dl* and *clingcon* encodings remain for future work. Compared with *clingo*, *heulingo*[ALNPS] improved on average the bounds by 35.1% for the traveling salesperson problem, 12.1% for the social golfer problem, 34.2% for sudoku puzzle generation, 6.7% for weighted strategic companies, and 1.9% for the partner units problem. *heulingo*[ALNPS] also achieved competitive performance compared with *heulingo*[LNPS] and *ALASPO*. However, it was slightly outperformed by *heulingo*[LNPS] and *ALASPO* on the shift design problem. These results suggest that the current implementation of variability-guided destruction does not always determine better destruction percentages than manually tuned or pre-defined ones. Therefore, investigating alternative distance measures for variability-guided destruction remains an important direction for future work. We will investigate these possibilities and apply our approach to solve real-world optimization problems.

Acknowledgments. This work was partially supported by JSPS KAKENHI Grant Numbers JP25K03097, JP25H01114, JP23K11047, JP26K02983, JP25K03190, and by DFG grant SCHA 550/15, Germany.

References

1. Banbara, M., et al.: teaspoon: solving the curriculum-based course timetabling problems with answer set programming. Ann. Oper. Res. **275**(1), 3–37 (2019). https://doi.org/10.1007/s10479-018-2757-7
2. Banbara, M., Soh, T., Tamura, N., Inoue, K., Schaub, T.: Answer set programming as a modeling language for course timetabling. Theory Pract. Logic Program. **13**(4–5), 783–798 (2013)
3. Bettinelli, A., Cacchiani, V., Roberti, R., Toth, P.: An overview of curriculum-based course timetabling. TOP **23**(2), 313–349 (2015). https://doi.org/10.1007/s11750-015-0366-z

[4] https://github.com/banbaralab/lpnmr2026/.

4. Bonutti, A., De Cesco, F., Di Gaspero, L., Schaerf, A.: Benchmarking curriculum-based course timetabling: formulations, data formats, instances, validation, visualization, and results. Ann. Oper. Res. **194**(1), 59–70 (2012)
5. Eiter, T., et al.: Adaptive large-neighbourhood search for optimisation in answer-set programming. Artif. Intell. **337**, 104230 (2024). https://doi.org/10.1016/J.ARTINT.2024.104230
6. Eiter, T., Geibinger, T., Higuera, N., Musliu, N., Oetsch, J., Stepanova, D.: ALASPO: an adaptive large-neighbourhood ASP optimiser. In: Kern-Isberner, G., Lakemeyer, G., Meyer, T. (eds.) Proceedings of the Nineteenth International Conference on Principles of Knowledge Representation and Reasoning (KR 2022, (2022)
7. Eiter, T., Geibinger, T., Higuera, N., Musliu, N., Oetsch, J., Stepanova, D.: Large-neighbourhood search for optimisation in answer-set solving. In: Proceedings of the Thirty-sixth AAAI Conference on Artificial Intelligence (AAAI 2022), pp. 5616–5625. AAAI Press (2022). https://doi.org/10.1609/AAAI.V36I5.20502
8. Gebser, M., Kaufmann, B., Otero, R., Romero, J., Schaub, T., Wanko, P.: Domain-specific heuristics in answer set programming. In: desJardins, M., Littman, M. (eds.) Proceedings of the Twenty-seventh National Conference on Artificial Intelligence (AAAI 2013), pp. 350–356. AAAI Press (2013)
9. Kaminski, R., Romero, J., Schaub, T., Wanko, P.: How to build your own asp-based system?! Theory Pract. Logic Program. **23**(1), 299–361 (2023). https://doi.org/10.1017/S1471068421000508
10. Lifschitz, V.: Answer Set Programming. Springer-Verlag (2019). https://doi.org/10.1007/978-3-030-24658-7
11. Nabeshima, H., Banbara, M., Schaub, T., Soh, T.: The ASP-based nurse scheduling system at the university of Yamanashi hospital. In: Proceedings of the Forty-first International Conference on Logic Programming. (ICLP 2025) (to appear)
12. Pisinger, D., Ropke, S.: Large neighborhood search. In: Gendreau, M., Potvin, J.Y. (eds.) Handbook of Metaheuristics, pp. 99–127. Springer International Publishing (2019). https://doi.org/10.1007/978-3-319-91086-4_4
13. Ropke, S., Pisinger, D.: An adaptive large neighborhood search heuristic for the pickup and delivery problem with time windows. Transp. Sci. **40**(4), 455–472 (2006). https://doi.org/10.1287/TRSC.1050.0135
14. Shaw, P.: Using constraint programming and local search methods to solve vehicle routing problems. In: Maher, M.J., Puget, J. (eds.) Proceedings of the Fourth International Conference on Principles and Practice of Constraint Programming (CP 1998). LNCS, vol. 1520, pp. 417–431. Springer (1998). https://doi.org/10.1007/3-540-49481-2_30
15. Sugimori, I., et al.: ASP-based large neighborhood prioritized search for course timetabling. In: Dodaro, C., Gupta, G., Martinez, M.V. (eds.) Proceedings of the Seventeenth International Conference on Logic Programming and Nonmonotonic Reasoning (LPNMR 2024). LNCS, vol. 15245, pp. 57–70. Springer (2024). https://doi.org/10.1007/978-3-031-74209-5_5
16. Sugimori, I., et al.: Large neighborhood prioritized search for combinatorial optimization with answer set programming. In: Marquis, P., Ortiz, M., Pagnucco, M. (eds.) Proceedings of the Twenty-first International Conference on Principles of Knowledge Representation and Reasoning (KR 2024) (2024). https://doi.org/10.24963/KR.2024/72

Efficient Grounding with Bounds using Bit Vectors

Lucas Van Laer[1,2,3,4](✉), Bart Bogaerts[1,2,4], and Joost Vennekens[4]

[1] Department of Computer Science, KU Leuven, Leuven, Belgium
bart.bogaerts@kuleuven.be
[2] Leuven.AI, KU Leuven Institute for AI, B-3000 Leuven, Belgium
[3] Flanders Make – DTAI-FET, Leuven, Belgium
[4] Vrije Universiteit Brussel, Brussel, Belgium
lucas.vanlaer@kuleuven.be, Joost.Vennekens@vub.be

Abstract. Systems for declarative problem-solving often include a "grounding" step to remove first-order variables in order to produce a purely propositional representation. Because a naive implementation of this grounding step can be highly inefficient, algorithms were created to derive new information from the problem specification which can be used to reduce the size of the grounding. In this paper, we show how to use this technique with bit vectors, thereby taking advantage of the fact that, on modern computers, logical operations on bit vectors can be executed at extreme speeds, and investigate some places where bit vectors may perform badly. We conduct an experimental analysis, which shows that bit vectors perform well on certain problems, but have limitations.

1 Introduction

Declarative problem-solving systems may handle a "high-level" problem specification by first translating it to a more "low-level" specification. This is a popular approach in areas such as Constraint Programming or Answer Set Programming, where the high-level languages use first-order variables to represent domain knowledge in a way which is independent of the size of the problem domain. In the translation to a low-level language, these first-order variables are removed by *grounding*, i.e., replacing them with domain elements in all possible ways, thereby introducing a dependency on the domain size. The resulting ground specification is typically many times larger than the high-level specification, which may make grounding challenging for large domain sizes, due to time and/or memory constraints.

Consider, for instance, the following formula in classical first-order logic (FO):

$$\forall x, y, z : edge(x, y) \land edge(y, z) \land edge(x, z) \Rightarrow p(x, y, z) \tag{1}$$

This formula expresses that p holds for all triangles in a graph. Its grounding is of size $O(n^3)$, with n the number of nodes in the graph. However, suppose the graph is already known, i.e., we are given a structure S with a domain D and

W. Faber et al. (Eds.): LPNMR 2026, LNAI 16952, pp. 448–463, 2027.
https://doi.org/10.1007/978-3-032-38320-4_28

interpretation $edge^S \subseteq D^2$ and are only interested in models S' that extend this given S with an interpretation for the predicate p. In this case, the grounding can be reduced to a conjunction $\bigwedge_{(d,e,f)\in \Delta_S} p(d,e,f)$ over the set Δ_S of all tuples $(d,e,f) \in D^3$ for which $\{(d,e),(e,f),(f,d)\} \subseteq edge^S$. Previous work introduced an efficient method for computing such reduced groundings, using bit vectors to implement the required operations [21].

Suppose now that we are interested in the task of computing a subgraph $edge/2$ of a given supergraph $super/2$, such that all triangles in this subgraph belong to p. We can reuse (1), together with the additional constraint $\forall x, y : edge(x,y) \Rightarrow super(x,y)$. However, since $edge/2$ is now no longer given, we cannot compute Δ_S, which causes the method of [21] to ground (1) over all triples in D^3.

Earlier work [26] proposed a way to avoid this. The idea of this method is to maintain for each subformula $\phi(\boldsymbol{x})$ that occurs in the theory, an approximation (L, U) of the set S of all tuples $\boldsymbol{d} \in D^n$ for which $\phi(\boldsymbol{d})$ holds, i.e., $L \subseteq S \subseteq U$. Before the grounding is actually computed, there is a propagation phase in which bounds of one (sub-)formula are used to refine bounds of other (sub-)formulas. In the case of our example, the second constraint would introduce an upper bound $edge^S \subseteq super^S$ on the interpretation of $edge$, which would then be propagated to the first constraint (1), where it would then be used to reduce the grounding to $\bigwedge_{(d,e,f)\in \Delta'_S} edge(d,e) \wedge edge(e,f) \wedge edge(f,d) \Rightarrow p(d,e,f)$, with Δ'_S the set of triangles in $super^S$. Indeed, for all other tuples, no grounding is needed since the antecedent of the implication is already guaranteed to be false.

In the practical implementation of this method, each of the bounds L and U is represented by a binary decision diagram (BDD) for FO [13], which with every operation can double in size. As such approximation methods were needed to limit the memory usage. Moreover, since equivalence checking of two (first-order)- BDDs corresponds to equivalence checking of two FO formulas, approximations and heuristics must be used to find when the propagation method has reached a fixpoint.

In this paper, we examine whether the novel bit vector method of [21] can be used to replace the BDD operations in the earlier propagation methods of [26]. On the one hand, we might expect efficiency gains from the fact that the relatively complex BDD operations are replaced by simpler bit vector operations, that can benefit from the single instruction multiple data (SIMD) parallelism of modern hardware to efficiently execute large operations. In addition, also the difficulty of checking equivalence is avoided. On the other hand, however, bit vectors excel at executing a small number of large operations, whereas an iterative propagation method may instead lead to a large number of small operations. To examine this, we also propose a new variant of the original propagation method, which imposes additional structure on the order in which propagations can be executed.

In particular, we will proceed to define an approach in which top-down and bottom-up propagations are `combined`, as done by Wittocx et al. [26], but using bit vectors instead of BDDs. We then also consider a variant in which top-down and bottom-up propagations are `separated` to impose additional structure. While this second approach greatly simplifies the propagation process, the imposed order may not always be optimal: in particular, for certain examples, this algorithm may end up essentially performing a step-by-step grounding during the propagation. We compare both of these approaches to the original methods in [26] and [21], as well as to the Answer Set Programming solver clingo [12].

2 Preliminaries

We consider classical first-order logic. A *vocabulary* Σ is a set of predicate and function symbols σ, each with an associated arity $n \geq 0$, denoted as σ/n. The symbols $\top$ and $\bot$ are used to represent true and false respectively. A *partial structure* S for a vocabulary Σ has a set of elements called its *domain* $D = domain(S)$, and assigns to each symbol $\sigma \in \Sigma$ an *interpretation* σ^S. If σ is a predicate symbol P/n, then P^S is a mapping from all tuples in D^n to $\{\mathbf{t}, \mathbf{f}, \mathbf{u}\}$ (where $\mathbf{u}$ stands for "unknown"). For a function symbol f/n, f^S is a mapping from D^{n+1} to $\{\mathbf{t}, \mathbf{f}, \mathbf{u}\}$ such that for each $\boldsymbol{d} \in D^n$, there exists at most one $e \in D$ for which $f^S(\boldsymbol{d}, e) = \mathbf{t}$. In this paper, we restrict attention to structures with a *finite* domain. Moreover, we assume that for each element $d \in domain(S)$ there exists a constant $c_d/0 \in \Sigma$ such that c_d^S is fixed to d. For convenience, we will often not distinguish between the domain element d and the constant c_d.

We call a partial structure S' an *extension* of another partial structure S if for all $\sigma \in \Sigma$ and all $\boldsymbol{d}$, if $\sigma^S(\boldsymbol{d}) \neq \mathbf{u}$, then $\sigma^{S'}(\boldsymbol{d}) = \sigma^S(\boldsymbol{d})$. A *(total) structure* is a partial structure in which all $\sigma^S(\boldsymbol{d}) \neq \mathbf{u}$ (and therefore it has no extensions except itself). In such a total structure S with domain D, the interpretation P^S of a predicate symbol P/n can be identified with a subset of D^n and the interpretation f^S of a function symbol f/n with a function $D^n \rightarrow D$, as usual.

A *term* is either a variable or a function symbol f/n applied to n terms. An *atom* is a predicate symbol P/n applied to n terms. For Φ a formula, $\boldsymbol{x}$ a tuple of variables and $\boldsymbol{t}$ a tuple of terms, $\Phi[\boldsymbol{t}/\boldsymbol{x}]$ denotes the result of replacing in Φ the free occurrences of each $x_i \in \boldsymbol{x}$ by the corresponding $t_i \in \boldsymbol{t}$. Formulas are constructed as usual by combining atoms with the logical operators $\forall, \exists, \neg, \wedge, \vee, \Rightarrow, \Leftrightarrow$. A *sentence* is a formula without free variable and a *theory* is a set of sentences.

For Φ a formula and S a partial structure, we denote by Φ^S the truth value of Φ in S under the three-valued Kleene evaluation. Note that if S is total, then $\Phi^S \neq \mathbf{u}$; in this case, we also write $S \models \Phi$ to say that $\Phi^S = \mathbf{t}$. A *model* of a theory T is a total interpretation S such that $S \models \phi$ for all $\phi \in T$. Given a partial structure S and theory T, the *model expansion problem* $MX(T, S)$ is the task of producing all models of T that extend S [18]. With a slight abuse of notation, we also write $MX(T, S)$ to denote the set of these models. We write $(T, S) \models \Phi$ to say that $S' \models \Phi$ for all $S' \in MX(T, S)$

A *grounding* of a theory T w.r.t. a partial structure S is a theory T' such that $MX(T, S) = MX(T', S)$ and T' does not contain any variables. The *naive* grounding is obtained by replacing each $\forall x : \Phi$ by $\bigwedge_{d \in domain(S)} \Phi[c_d/x]$ and each $\exists x$ by the corresponding disjunction. It is clear that the naive grounding is indeed a grounding, but in general, also other, smaller groundings exists.

3 Propagation using a combined approach

In this section, we present the first of two approaches we explore in this paper. We first give the theoretical foundations and a high-level algorithm, before discussing implementation issues.

3.1 Algorithm

When grounding T w.r.t. a partial structure S, the grounding of a formula $\Phi(\boldsymbol{x})$ for a tuple of domain elements $\boldsymbol{d}$ can be simplified to $\top$ (or $\bot$) if $\Phi(\boldsymbol{d})^S = \mathbf{t}$ (or $\mathbf{f}$, respectively). Only when $\Phi(\boldsymbol{d})^S = \mathbf{u}$, do we actually need to produce the instantiation $\Phi(\boldsymbol{d})$. To capture this idea, we introduce the following concepts.

Definition 1. *For a model expansion problem (T, S) and a formula $\Phi(\boldsymbol{x})$ with n free variables, the* certainly true set (ct-set) *of $\Phi(\boldsymbol{x})$, denoted as $\lceil \Phi(\boldsymbol{x}) \rceil_S^T$, consists of all tuples $\boldsymbol{d} \in domain(S)^n$ such that $(T, S) \models \Phi(\boldsymbol{d})$. Similarly, the* certainly false set (cf-set) *of Φ, denoted $\lfloor \Phi(\boldsymbol{x}) \rfloor_S^T$, consists of all $\boldsymbol{d}$ for which $(T, S) \models \neg\Phi(\boldsymbol{d})$. When (T, S) is clear from the context, we omit them from the notation.*

In the worst case, computing ct- and cf-sets is as difficult as solving the model expansion problem, so we will instead approximate them.

Definition 2. *In the context of a given model expansion problem (T, S), a pair (t, f) of sets of n-tuples of domain elements is called an* approximating pair *for a formula $\Phi(\boldsymbol{x})$ if $t \subseteq \lceil \Phi \rceil$ and $f \subseteq \lfloor \Phi \rfloor$. We call such a pair* total *if $t \cup f = domain(S)^n$.*

The central idea behind our approach is to associate to each subformula of T an approximating pair (such as $(\{\}, \{\})$ if no other information is available), and then iteratively refine the approximation pair associated to a formula $\Phi(\boldsymbol{x})$ by doing both bottom-up propagation of information about the approximating pairs of Φ's subformulas, and top-down propagations of information about the approximation pair of the superformula in which Φ appears. What exactly these propagations look like depends on the form of Φ. We start by considering the case of a conjunction.

Proposition 1. *For a conjunction, $\lceil \Phi_1 \wedge \Phi_2 \rceil = \lceil \Phi_1 \rceil \cap \lceil \Phi_2 \rceil$ and $\lfloor \Phi_1 \wedge \Phi_2 \rfloor = \lfloor \Phi_1 \rfloor \cup \lfloor \Phi_2 \rfloor$. If (t_1, f_1) and (t_2, f_2) are approximating pairs of Φ_1 and Φ_2, then $(t_1 \cap t_2, f_1 \cup f_2)$ is an approximating pair of $\Phi_1 \wedge \Phi_2$. If (t, f) and (t_1, f_1) are approximating pairs of $\Phi_1 \wedge \Phi_2$ and Φ_1, then $(t, f \cap t_1)$ is an approximating pair of Φ_2.*

Similarly, the case for negation is as follows:

Proposition 2. *For a negation,* $\lceil \neg\Phi \rceil = \lfloor \Phi \rfloor$ *and* $\lfloor \neg\Phi \rfloor = \lceil \Phi \rceil$. *If* (t, f) *is an approximating pair of* $\neg\Phi$, *then* (f, t) *is an approximating pair of* Φ, *and vice versa.*

Together, the propositions for conjunction and negation obviously imply a similar proposition for disjunction.

The above two propositions can be used to compute, e.g., the ct/cf-sets of $p(x, y) \wedge \neg q(x, y)$ from those of $p(x, y)$ and $q(x, y)$. However, computing the ct/cf-sets of formulas such as $p(x, y) \wedge r(x)$ or $p(x, y) \wedge q(y, x)$ is not immediately possible due to the mismatch between the number and order of the variables in the subformulas. In [21], a number of transformation were defined that can be used to eliminate such mismatches by changing the number of variables over which a ct/cf-set ranges, or the order of these variables. From now on, we will just assume that such operations are applied whenever necessary to ensure a match between the variables of different subformula.

Finally, we also need to consider the case of quantifications.

Proposition 3. *For a universal quantifier,* $\lceil \forall x : \Phi \rceil = \{(d_1, \ldots, d_n) \in domain(S)^n \mid \text{for all } d \in domain(S),\ (d, d_1, \ldots, d_n) \in \lceil \Phi \rceil\}$ *and* $\lfloor \forall x : \Phi \rfloor = \{(d_1, \ldots, d_n) \in domain(S)^n \mid \text{there exists } d \in domain(S),\ (d, d_1, \ldots, d_n) \in \lfloor \Phi \rfloor\}$. *If* (t, f) *is an approximating pair of* Φ, *then the following* (t', f') *is an approximating pair for* $\forall x : \Phi$:

- $t' = \{(d_1, \ldots, d_n) \in domain(S)^n \mid \text{for all } d \in domain(S),\ (d, d_1, \ldots, d_n) \in t\}$
- $f' = \{(d_1, \ldots, d_n) \in domain(S)^n \mid \text{there is a } d \in domain(S),\ (d, d_1, \ldots, d_n) \in f\}$

Conversely, if (t', f') *is an approximating pair of* $\forall x : \Phi$, *then the following* (t, f) *is an approximating pair for* Φ:

- $t = \{(d, \mathbf{d}) \mid d \in domain(S) \text{ and } \mathbf{d} \in t'\}$
- $f = \{\}$

The case for existential quantification can again be derived from this proposition and the one for negation.

We can use the above propositions to add additional elements to the sets t, f of an approximating pair (t, f) for a formula Φ by looking at the approximating pairs of the subformulas of Φ and of the superformula in which Φ appears.

Algorithm 1 shows how to build a concrete propagation algorithm based on this idea. As its central datastructure, the algorithm uses a mapping α of each subformula that appears anywhere in T to an approximating pair (t, f). Most of the $\alpha(\Phi)$ are initialised to $(\{\}, \{\})$, with two exceptions: for all sentences $\Phi \in T$, $\alpha(\Phi)$ that Φ must be true in all models of (T, S); for all atoms $P(\mathbf{t})$, $\alpha(\Phi)$ indicates that this atom must be true/false for all tuples $\boldsymbol{d}$ such that $P^S(\boldsymbol{d}) = \mathbf{t}/\mathbf{f}$.

To keep track of the propagation steps, a queue is used, to which a formula Φ is added whenever $\alpha(\Phi)$ changes. In each iteration of the algorithm, a formula Φ whose approximating pair has recently changed is taken from the queue, and the algorithm tries to propagate the recent changes to the subformulas and superformula of Φ. If any of those propagations actually changes some $\alpha(\Psi)$, then Ψ is requeued. A special case occurs when a propagation is made that changes $\alpha(P(\boldsymbol{t}))$ for some atom $P(\boldsymbol{t})$. In this case, the case is also recorded in the interpretation P^s of P in the structure S, and all atoms of the form $P(\boldsymbol{t}')$ must be enqueued.

Algorithm 1. Propagation algorithm

Require: A model expansion problem T, S
  $\alpha \leftarrow \{\phi \mapsto (\{\}, \{\}) \mid \phi$ is subformula appearing in $T\}$
  $queue \leftarrow []$
  for each sentence $\Phi \in T$ **do**
    $\alpha(\Phi) = (\mathbf{t}, \{\})$ and $queue.add(\Phi)$
  end for
  for each atom $P(\boldsymbol{t}) \in T$ **do**
    $\alpha(P(\boldsymbol{t})) = (\{\boldsymbol{d} \mid P^S(\boldsymbol{d}) = \mathbf{t}\}, \{\boldsymbol{d} \mid P^S(\boldsymbol{d}) = \mathbf{f}\})$ and $queue.add(P(\boldsymbol{t}))$
  end for
  while $queue$ is not empty **do**
    $\Phi \leftarrow queue.pop()$
    if Φ is an atom $P(\boldsymbol{t})$ **then**
      Extend P^S with $\alpha(P(\boldsymbol{t})) = (t, f)$, setting $P^S(\boldsymbol{d}) = \mathbf{t}/\mathbf{f}$ for each $\boldsymbol{d} \in t/f$
      Add all other atoms that contain predicate P to $queue$ and change their approximating pair in α to use P^S
    end if
    for each sub-/superformula Ψ of Φ **do**
      Propagate $\alpha(\Phi)$ to $\alpha(\Psi)$ and do $queue.add(\Psi)$ if changes made
    end for
  end while

Example 1. Consider the partial structure S with domain $\{1, 2, 3, 4, 5\}$ and p^S and q^S both mapping all elements to $\mathbf{u}$, together with the theory T consisting of the following sentences:

$$\forall x : p(x) \lor q(x). \tag{2}$$

$$\neg p(4) \Rightarrow \neg p(5). \tag{3}$$

$$p(1) \Rightarrow p(2). \tag{4}$$

$$p(1). \tag{5}$$

$$\neg p(4). \tag{6}$$

If sentence (2) is popped from the queue first, its approximating pair $(\{()\}, \emptyset)$ will be propagated to $\alpha(p(x) \lor q(x)) = (\{1, 2, 3, 4, 5\}, \emptyset)$. For (3) and (4) nothing can be propagated yet. For (5), the approximating pair $\alpha(p)$ will be changed to $(\{1\}, \emptyset)$, which triggers a change to the partial structure, i.e. $p^S(1) = \mathbf{t}$, and also causes all other atoms for p to be added to the queue. When the occurrence of $p(1)$ in (4) is selected, the approximating $\alpha(p)$ is extended to $(\{(1,2)\},\emptyset)$. From (6), it will be propagated that $\alpha(p) = (\{1,2\},\{4\})$, which will trigger a propagation in (3) that results in $\alpha(p) = (\{1,2\},\{4,5\})$. In assertion 2, the changes made to $\alpha(p)$ will trigger a propagation $\alpha(q) = (\{4,5\},\emptyset)$. After the remainder of the queue has been popped without additional propagations, the algorithm ends with a partial structure S in which:

- $p^S = \{1 \mapsto \mathbf{t}, 2 \mapsto \mathbf{t}, 3 \mapsto \mathbf{u}, 4 \mapsto \mathbf{f}, 5 \mapsto \mathbf{f}\}$
- $q^S = \{1 \mapsto \mathbf{u}, 2 \mapsto \mathbf{u}, 3 \mapsto \mathbf{u}, 4 \mapsto \mathbf{t}, 5 \mapsto \mathbf{t}\}$

The idea is now that, for any $\alpha(\Phi(\boldsymbol{x})) = (t, f)$, we can ground Φ to $\top$ for all $\boldsymbol{d} \in t$ and to $\bot$ for all $\boldsymbol{d} \in f$. For the remaining tuples $\boldsymbol{d} \notin t \cup f$, we still need to produce $\boldsymbol{d}$. To formally prove that this is correct, we first introduce the following concept.

Definition 3. *For a model expansion problem (T, S) in vocabulary Σ, let Σ^T be the vocabulary that extends T with two fresh n-ary predicate symbols P_Φ^t and P_Φ^f for each subformula Φ with n free variables that appears in T. We define the* approximative theory *T' of T as the result of recursively replacing each subformula $\Phi(\boldsymbol{x})$ in T by $\neg P_\Phi^f(\boldsymbol{x}) \wedge (\Phi(\boldsymbol{x}) \vee P_\Phi^t(\boldsymbol{x}))$.*

The idea is now just to fill in the truth values obtained in each $\alpha(\Phi) = (t, f)$ by using t as an interpretation of P_Φ^t and f as an interpretation for P_Φ^f, so that, for instance, $\neg P_\Phi^f(\boldsymbol{x}) \wedge (\Phi(\boldsymbol{x}) \vee P_\Phi^t(\boldsymbol{x}))$ reduces to $\mathbf{t}$ for each $\boldsymbol{d} \in t$. However, we must be careful here: if we just fill in $\alpha(\Phi)$ everywhere, then because for each top-level sentence $\Phi \in T$, $\alpha(\Phi) = (\{()\},\emptyset)$, we would actually reduce the entire theory to $\top$. Clearly, the resulting model expansion problem $(\top, S)$ will no longer be equivalent to the original (T, S).

The issue here is that during propagation we make the assumption that all sentences in T will be true in order to perform top-down propagations. When doing the actual grounding, however, we can no longer make this assumption because then we will have nothing to ground. Instead, we can only rely on the information that could be propagated to the interpretation of predicates/functions in S' and whatever propagations can be derived from this in a purely bottom-up manner (i.e., without assuming that all sentences will be true). The following definition formalises this idea.

Definition 4. *For a model expansion problem (T, S) in vocabulary Σ, let α be a mapping from each of the subformulas of T to an approximating pair (t, f). A function α' is called a* safe approximation mapping *of α if it maps each subformula of T to an approximating pair for the model expansion problem $(\{\}, S')$ where each $P^{S'}$ is the result of extending P^S by setting $P^{S'}(\boldsymbol{d}) = \mathbf{t}/\mathbf{f}$ for each $\boldsymbol{d} \in t/f$ with $\alpha(P) = (t, f)$.*

Now, we can prove the desired result.

Proposition 4. *Consider a model expansion problem (T, S) and a mapping α of the subformulas of T to pairs (t, f) of sets of atoms. Let α' be the safe approximation mapping of α, T' the approximative theory of T and let S' be the result of extending S with a total interpretation for each of the new predicates introduced in T' such that $(P^t_\Phi)^S = t$ and $(P^f_\Phi)^S = f$ with $\alpha(\Phi) = (t, f)$. If each $\alpha(\Phi)$ is an approximating pair of the model expansion problem $(\{\}, S)$, then $MX(T, S) = MX(T', S')$ (modulo projection of each structure onto the original vocabulary Σ).*

Putting all of this together, we can now produce a reduced grounding by recursively replacing each formula Φ by $\neg P^f_\Phi \wedge (P^t_\Phi \vee \Phi)$ and filling in the propagated truth values by assigned $(P^t_\Phi, P^f_\Phi) = \alpha(\Phi)$ for a safe approximation mapping α.

Example 1 (continued). From the partial structure S that we computed previously, we can obtain a safe approximation mapping by looking at the model expansion problem $(\{\}, S)$. Here, we find that all the sentences (3), (4), (5) and (6) have $(\mathbf{t}, \emptyset)$ as an approximation pair w.r.t. $(\{\}, S)$ and therefore do not need to be grounded. Sentence (2) only has $(\emptyset, \emptyset)$ as approximating pair, but for its immediate subformula $p(x) \vee q(x)$ we can find $(\{1, 2, 4, 5\}, \emptyset)$. We can then rewrite the theory into $\forall x : x \in \{1, 2, 4, 5\} \vee (p(x) \vee q(x))$, and eventually produce the grounding $p(3) \vee q(3)$.

We call this the `combined` approach, because whenever a formula is selected, its approximating pair is used to do both top-down and bottom-up propagation. This is essentially the same general approach as proposed by [26], but we propose a different implementation technique.

3.2 Implementation

While [26] uses Binary Decision Diagrams to represent ct-/cf sets in a syntactic way, we examine here an approach in which these sets are represented by bit vectors, similar to [21]. Essentially, the idea is that a ct/cf-set for a formula with n free variables in a structure S can be represented by a vector of $domain(S)^n$ bits, where each bit represents whether one particular n-tuple $\boldsymbol{d}$ of domain elements belongs to the set or not. Obviously, this requires some careful bookkeeping to keep track of which bit positions correspond to which tuples. Propagations between sub-/superformulas which have the same number of free variables in the same order can then be done by bitwise boolean operations, which are executed very efficiently on modern hardware.

As mentioned above, when the free variables of different subformulas do not match precisely, reordering of the bits or a change in the size of the bit vectors may be required (the detailed operations are described in [21]). However, these operations are much less efficient. As an optimisation, when computing the conjunction of two formulas whose free variables do not match precisely, we use the *sort-merge* join algorithm, to avoid the costly resizing/reordering of bit vectors.

The bit vector representation can be inefficient for sets which are either very sparse or very dense. To avoid this, we do not use normal bit vectors, but instead make use of *roaring bitmaps* [15]. These provide a compressed representation for bit vectors in which sparse segments are represented using an array of numbers and dense segments using an array of intervals. To further optimise the representation, we add to each roaring bitmap a single boolean which indicates whether the bitmap represents the actual set itself (i.e., a 1 in the bitmap indicates membership) or the complement of the set (i.e., a 0 in the bitmap indicates membership of the actual set). In this way, when propagating across negation, we avoid having to change all 1s into 0s and vice versa, and instead just flip this single bit. Lastly, we use only a single set for representing total approximating pairs, where a 1 would indicate membership in the certainly true part and 0 in the certainly false part.

4 Separating bottom-up and top-down propagations

The approach presented in the previous section mixes top-down and bottom-up propagations: whenever the approximating pair of a formula is updated, this change can be propagated to both its subformulas and to its superformula. However, one of the key strengths of the bitmap representation is that it is good for executing a small number of large operations. Therefore, it might make sense not to propagate information as soon as it becomes available, but to instead delay propagation in order to first gather multiple updates to the same approximating pair and then propagate all of these in a single big propagation step.

As we recall from the discussion of Proposition 4, information that is propagated in a top-down down way only becomes relevant once it reaches the atom level. For instance, for a theory $T = \{\forall x : \neg(p(x) \wedge q(x))\}$ and a structure S in which p and q are entirely unknown, a top-down propagation can tell us that $p(x) \wedge q(x)$ must be universally false, but this information does not help to reduce the grounding in any way. Indeed, a safe approximation mapping will have to discard this information, which will cause a full grounding to be produced any way, so the effort of doing the top-down propagation is wasted and we would like to avoid doing it.

To this end, we introduce the following concept of a *ct-target* and a *cf-target*. Intuitively, if a formula is a ct/cf-target, this means that its ct/cf-set can be updated in a top-down propagation.

Definition 5. *Let Φ be a formula and Ψ its superformula. We define ct- and cf-target by simultaneous top-down induction:*

- *If Ψ does not exist (i.e., Φ is a top-level sentence), then Φ is a ct-target*
- *If Ψ is a universal quantification or a conjunction, then if Ψ is a ct-target, so is Φ*
- *If Ψ is an existential quantification or a disjunction, then if Ψ is a cf-target, so is Φ*

- *If Ψ is a negation, then if Ψ is a ct-target (or cf-target), then Φ is a cf-target (ct-target, resp.).*

Whether a formula is ct-/cf-target depends entirely on the structure of the top-level sentence it appears in, and is easy to check. The idea is now that we only want to do top-down propagations for formulas that contain at least one atom that is a ct-/cf-target. As discussed above, none of the atoms in $\forall x : \neg(p(x) \wedge q(x))$ are ct-/cf-targets, so we will not do top-down propagation here. By contrast, for instance in $\forall x : \neg(p(x) \vee q(x))$, both atoms are cf-targets, so here we will propagate in a top-down way that both p and q must be universally false.

There are also cases in which top-down propagation to the atom-level is possible, even when the atom is not a ct-/cf-target. For instance, if we consider again $\forall x : \neg(p(x) \wedge q(x))$ but now with a structure S with domain $\{0, 1\}$ in which p is $\mathbf{t}$ for 0 and $\mathbf{f}$ for 1. In this case, top-down propagation would be able to reach the atom $q(x)$, producing $\alpha(q) = (\emptyset, \{0\})$, and the resulting safe approximation mapping would tell us that $\alpha(\neg(p(x) \wedge q(x))) = (\{0, 1\}, \emptyset)$, so the empty grounding can be produced. In general, if instead of $p(x)$ there would be a more complex formula $\Phi(x)$, bottom-up propagation might be required to figure out that this $\Phi(x)$ has a non-empty ct-set, which would allow for top-down propagation to $q(x)$.

To do this bottom-up propagation in a way that enables easy detection of ct-/cf-target, we make use of the idea of *quantification splitting* from [21]. Quantification splitting transforms a given formula Φ into a set of new formulas based on a partial structure S, or more precisely, based on which symbols have a total interpretation in S. If Φ is of the form $\forall x : \Psi$, the transformation works as follows.

Let $\gamma_1, \ldots, \gamma_m$ be the maximal subformulas of Φ that contain only symbols that have a total interpretation in S. The original formula Φ is transformed into 2^m new formulas of the form $\forall \boldsymbol{x} : (\bigwedge_{i=1}^m (\neg)\gamma_i) \Rightarrow \Psi'$, in which each γ_i appears either negated or not. Here, Ψ' is the result of replacing each subformula γ_i with $\top$ or $\bot$ depending on whether γ_i appears negated or not. The conjunction $\bigwedge_{i=1}^m (\neg)\gamma_i)$ is called the quantifier's *guard.*

The idea behind this transformation is that the ct-/cf-sets of the guards can be completely computed using bottom-up propagation, so we can equivalently view each formula $\forall \boldsymbol{x} : (\bigwedge_{i=1}^m (\neg)\gamma_i) \Rightarrow \Psi'$ as a $\forall \boldsymbol{x} \in G : \Psi'$ where G is the ct-set $\lceil \bigwedge_{i=1}^m (\neg)\gamma_i \rceil$ of the guard. In other words, the result of quantification splitting a formula Φ is essentially to remove all symbols that are fully known in S from Φ. To handle atoms $P(\boldsymbol{t})$ where the P^S is not fully known, we replace $P(\boldsymbol{t})$ with $\neg P^f(\boldsymbol{t}) \wedge (\Phi(\boldsymbol{t}) \vee P^t(\boldsymbol{t}))$ where P^t and P^f have the interpretations $\{\boldsymbol{d} \mid P^S(\boldsymbol{d}) = \mathbf{t}\}$ and $\{\boldsymbol{d} \mid P^S(\boldsymbol{d}) = \mathbf{f}\}$ respectively.

If the formula Φ is an existentially quantified $\exists \Psi$, the result of quantification splitting is a disjunction of formulas of the form $\exists \boldsymbol{x} : (\bigwedge_{i=1}^m (\neg)\gamma_i) \wedge \Psi'$. Details can be found in [21]. Lastly, to produce ct-/cf-targets for non-quantifier formulas without free variables it suffices to simplify the formulas using the interpretations in S, i.e. the formula $p() \vee t()$ can be simplified to $t()$ if $S^p = \{() \mapsto \mathbf{f}\}$.

We can combine top-down propagation to ct-/cf-targets with bottom-up quantification splitting as shown in Algorithm 2, which we refer to as the `separated` approach, because top-down and bottom-up propagation are now split into two different phases of the algorithm.

Algorithm 2. Algorithm of `separated` implementation

```
Require: S a structure over Σ, T a theory over Σ
  while fixpoint not reached do
    T ← quantification_splitting(S, T)
    for sentence Φ ∈ T do
      for atom p(t) in Φ which is a ct-target or cf-target do
        Update S with top-down propagation from Φ to p
      end for
    end for
  end while
```

Example 2. Consider the following theory T:

$$\forall x : p(x) \lor q(x). \tag{7}$$

$$p(1) \Rightarrow q(3). \tag{8}$$

and the structure S with domain $\{1, 2, 3\}$ in which q is universally unknown and $p^S = \{1 \mapsto \mathbf{t}, 2 \mapsto \mathbf{f}, 3 \mapsto \mathbf{t}\}$.

Quantification splitting will split the first formula into two:

$$\forall x \in \{1, 3\} : \top \tag{9}$$

$$\forall x \in \{2\} : q(x). \tag{10}$$

$$q(3). \tag{11}$$

Here, the first formula is trivially satisfied, so it can be removed. In the second formula, $q(x)$ is a ct-target, so it can be propagated that $q^{S'}(2) = \mathbf{t}$. Similarly, $q(3)$ is also a ct-target in the third formula, so also $q^{S'}(3) = \mathbf{t}$ is propagated.

5 The SLI system

Both the `combined` and `separated` approaches were implemented in the SLI[1] reasoning engine for the FO(·) language. We compared these two implementations with SLI, IDP3 [7] only using BDDs, and clingo [12]. The IDP3 system contains different implementations and integrations with different systems for finding solutions, in order to fairly compare the BDD approach and bit vector approach we configured IDP3 to only use the BDD-based propagations.

[1] https://gitlab.com/sli-lib/SLI

While our presentation in this paper so far has only considered first-order logic FO, the language FO(·) contains also a number of language extension, the most important being a construct for representing inductive definitions in a rule-based manner [10]. The grounding methods implemented in SLI handle this extension as well, by performing propagation on Clark's completion [5] of the rules in an inductive definition.

The SLI system uses the Z3 solver [9] as a back-end, grounding its FO(·) input to the SMT-LIB format.

6 Evaluation

We evaluated these implementations using the DIRT [22] benchmark suite, together with a new benchmark, the full benchmark results and steps to reproduce them are available online.[2] The new benchmark is called `ImplicationLadder`, it consists of two unary predicates p and q and the sentences $\forall x : p(x) \Rightarrow q(x)$, $\forall x : p(x) \Rightarrow p(x+1)$ and $p(1)$. The goal of this benchmark is to measure the performance of the worst case scenario of each propagation step only propagating a single domain element. Preliminary experiments showed that due to the treatment of nested terms in SLI, the second sentence could not be grounded efficiently and hence the effect of iterative small propagations was not tested with this benchmark. For this reason, we switched to a version where the second sentence is grounded manually.

We ran the benchmarks on a computer with an AMD EPYC 9334 and 16 GB of RAM available with a timeout of 10 minutes for each problem instance. We denote SLI_s as SLI using `separated` implementation and SLI_c using the `combined` implementation. Table 1 shows the average grounding time of all benchmarks with interesting results, for the calculation of the average grounding time a failed instance counted as 15 minutes.

For many of the `TriangleGraph` benchmarks both algorithms are competitive with both IDP3 and clingo, and occasionally outperform them. In `TriangleGraphFindAll`, the `separated` approach performs much worse than the `combined` approach. This seems to be caused by the `separated` approach extending the structure twice, once for the ct-target and once for the cf-target, while the `combined` approach is able to extend the structure using a total approximating pair represented by a single set. Both `separated` and `combined` perform better than SLI and IDP3 in `TriangleGraphSubset`, but are still substantially outperformed by clingo and dlv. The poor results of IDP3 on `TriangleGraphCheck` occurred on satisfiable instances, where early cutoff was not possible.

The results of `ImplicationLadder` show that bit vectors are not suitable for performing many small propagations.

Both clingo and dlv performed the best on `NonPartitionRemovalColoring`, while both `separated` and `combined` performed much better than SLI, and slightly better than IDP3. In `HamiltonianPath` and `Reachability` all SLI variants perform much worse than IDP3. Tthis is likely caused by the fact that SLI

[2] https://doi.org/10.48804/NW9ZE2

adds level mappings to its groundings, while IDP3 uses a solver that can handle recursive rules.

7 Related work

The main goal of this paper is to make the grounding process more efficient by exploiting information that is already present in the theory and structure. We achieved this building on previously developed techniques of grounding with bounds [26] and with bitvectors [21]. There are classes of approaches that tackle the problem of large grounding time and size (also known as the *grounding bottleneck* [1]) in different ways. The first is *lazy grounding* [4,6,8,14,19,24], a technique that, unlike the classical ground-and-solve approach, defers grounding by only grounding parts of the input problem when the solver requires it. Such lazy grounding systems typically require changes to both the solver and the grounder, and as such are more complicated to get to work than techniques such as grounding with bounds. Second, there are solvers that solve (typically in a top-down fashion), without grounding the input problem at all [16,17]. Another approach to tackle large grounding time and size is by compiling rules to propagators and making the solver use these propagators during the search process [11], allowing compiled rules to not be grounded. A different approach named body-decoupled grounding [3], decouples non-ground atoms such that the number of variables in the rule does not contribute to the overall grounding size, only the maximum predicate arity used does. All the classes of methods above could potentially be combined with the techniques presented in this paper. Indeed, lazy-grounding, solving-without-grounding and body-decoupled grounding approaches could use the bounds computed by our method for clever instantiation of variables, while compilation-based approaches could use our method to achieve more efficient propagators; investigating this possibility is a topic for future work.

8 Conclusion

In this paper, we described a theoretical method to reduce groundings using information from a theory and structure. We used this method in two concrete implementations, an implementation that followed the abstract algorithm, and one designed to propagate everything all at once using bit vectors. Experimental results of both implementations showed that they perform similarly to each other, and both have bad performance on problems where many small propagations are possible, implying that a stop criterion is likely worthwhile. Both implementations are competitive with both IDP3 using BDDs, and clingo, often outperforming IDP3 using BDDs.

This research opens up several opportunities for future work. First, it would be interesting to investigate how to deal with the issue of many small propagations and to develop methods that perform well on this kind of instances and still propagate well on more complicated problems. Second, investigating how to improve propagation for formulas with nested terms. Third, to improve trust in

Table 1. Average results of all benchmarks in seconds. The number of instances for each benchmark is shown in brackets. `NonPartitionRemovalColoring` has been shortened to `NPRC` and `PermutationPatternMatching` has been shortened to `PPM`. `TriangleGraph` has been shortened for `TG`.

	SLI	SLI_s	SLI_c	IDP3	clingo	dlv
ImplicationLadder (101)	2.21	497	498	31.6	2.41	**1.51**
TGCheck (14)	0.247	0.249	0.255	44.0	0.221	**0.148**
TGConstructAtleast (14)	0.415	0.418	**0.400**	0.885	473	709
TGConstructGraph (14)	515	**456**	**456**	475	476	710
TGContainsAll (14)	0.631	0.650	0.641	0.366	0.396	**0.261**
TGFindAll (14)	515	327	0.408	485	0.269	**0.190**
TGSubset (14)	515	389	366	489	0.329	**0.283**
NPRC (110)	104	7.09	7.23	28.6	**2.67**	2.83
CommonItem (100)	0.956	0.971	0.969	1.298	1.70	**0.936**
CompleteSets (100)	1.14	1.14	**1.13**	1.78	1.93	1.16
GraphColouring (50)	**1.26**	1.27	1.27	3.91	66.6	2.11
HamiltonianPath (20)	179	175	176	16.7	**0.170**	0.189
PPM (200)	**0.117**	0.122	0.124	242	95.7	47.0
RamseyNumbers (15)	92.1	730	594	88.8	1.70	**0.936**
Reachability (50)	526	505	506	276	0.0647	**0.0165**

combinatorial solving algorithms, there is a trend to use *certifying* algorithms in several fields, e.g., SAT solving [25], MaxSAT solving [23], and SMT solving [2]. Recently, this idea was also explored for the *grounding* phase [20]. It would be interesting to investigate how to produce certificates for the grounding methods described in this paper. An important challenge would then be how to efficiently translate the parallel reasoning steps performed using bit vectors to inherently sequential proofs that can be checked by a proof checker.

Acknowledgements. This research received funding from the Flemish Government under the "Onderzoeksprogramma Artificiële Intelligentie (AI) Vlaanderen" programme and by Flanders Innovation & Entrepreneurship (HBC.2022.0071, Tetra-project) and the European Union (ERC, CertiFOX, 101122653). Views and opinions expressed are however those of the author(s) only and do not necessarily reflect those of the European Union or the European Research Council. Neither the European Union nor the granting authority can be held responsible for them.

References

1. Balduccini, M., Lierler, Y., Schüller, P.: Prolog and ASP inference under one roof. In: LPNMR. LNCS, vol. 8148, pp. 148–160. Springer (2013). https://doi.org/10.1007/978-3-642-40564-8_15
2. Barbosa, H., et al.: Flexible proof production in an industrial-strength SMT solver. In: IJCAR. LNCS, vol. 13385, pp. 15–35. Springer (2022). https://doi.org/10.1007/978-3-031-10769-6_3
3. Besin, V., Hecher, M., Woltran, S.: Body-decoupled grounding via solving: a novel approach on the ASP bottleneck. In: Raedt, L.D. (ed.) Proceedings of the Thirty-First International Joint Conference on Artificial Intelligence, IJCAI 2022, Vienna, Austria, 23-29 July 2022, pp. 2546–2552. ijcai.org (2022)
4. Bogaerts, B., Weinzierl, A.: Exploiting justifications for lazy grounding of answer set programs. In: IJCAI, pp. 1737–1745. ijcai.org (2018)
5. Clark, K.L.: Negation as failure. In: Advances in Data Base Theory, pp. 293–322. Plemum Press, New York (1977) Logic and Data Bases
6. Dao-Tran, M., Eiter, T., Fink, M., Weidinger, G., Weinzierl, A.: Omiga: an open minded grounding on-the-fly answer set solver. JELIA. LNCS **7519**, 480–483. Springer (2012). https://doi.org/10.1007/978-3-642-33353-8_38
7. De Cat, B., Bogaerts, B., Bruynooghe, M., Janssens, G., Denecker, M.: Predicate logic as a modeling language: the IDP system. In: Declarative Logic Programming, pp. 279–323. ACM/Morgan & Claypool (2018)
8. De Cat, B., Denecker, M., Stuckey, P.J.: Lazy model expansion by incremental grounding. ICLP (Tech. Commun.). LIPIcs **17**, 201–211 (2012). Schloss Dagstuhl
9. de Moura, L.M., Bjørner, N.S.: Z3: an efficient SMT solver. In: TACAS. LNCS, vol. 4963, pp. 337–340. Springer (2008). https://doi.org/10.1007/978-3-540-78800-3_24
10. Denecker, M.: Extending classical logic with inductive definitions. In: Computational Logic. LNCS, vol. 1861, pp. 703–717. Springer (2000). https://doi.org/10.1007/3-540-44957-4_47
11. Dodaro, C., Mazzotta, G., Ricca, F.: Blending grounding and compilation for efficient ASP solving, KR (2024)
12. Gebser, M., Kaminski, R., Kaufmann, B., Schaub, T.: Multi-shot ASP solving with CLINGO. CoRR abs/1705.09811 (2017)
13. Goubault, J.: A BDD-based simplification and skolemization procedure. Log. J. IGPL **3**(6), 827–855 (1995)
14. Lefèvre, C., Nicolas, P.: The first version of a new ASP solver: ASPerix. In: LPNMR. LNCS, vol. 5753, pp. 522–527. Springer (2009). https://doi.org/10.1007/978-3-642-04238-6_52
15. Lemire, D., Kai, G.S.Y., Kaser, O.: Consistently faster and smaller compressed bitmaps with roaring. Softw. Pract. Exp. **46**(11), 1547–1569 (2016)
16. Marple, K., Gupta, G.: Galliwasp: a goal-directed answer set solver. In: LOPSTR. LNCS, vol. 7844, pp. 122–136. Springer (2012). https://doi.org/10.1007/978-3-642-38197-3_9
17. Marple, K., Salazar, E., Gupta, G.: Computing stable models of normal logic programs without grounding. CoRR abs/1709.00501 (2017)
18. Mitchell, D.G., Ternovska, E.: A framework for representing and solving NP search problems. In: AAAI, pp. 430–435. AAAI Press/The MIT Press (2005)
19. Palù, A.D., Dovier, A., Pontelli, E., Rossi, G.: GASP: answer set programming with lazy grounding. Fundam. Informaticae **96**(3), 297–322 (2009)

20. Van Caudenberg, D., Ek, A., Cantero, C., Bogaerts, B.: Towards a certifying grounder. In: Proceedings of 42nd International Conference on Logic Programming (ICLP) (2026)
21. Van Laer, L., Vandevelde, S., Vennekens, J.: Efficiently grounding FOL using bit vectors. In: Dodaro, C., Gupta, G., Martinez, M.V. (eds.) LPNMR. LNCS, vol. 15245, pp. 167–173. Springer (2024). https://doi.org/10.1007/978-3-031-74209-5_13
22. Van Laer, L., Vandevelde, S., Vennekens, J.: DIRT: a literature-based benchmark suite for grounders. In: Casini, G., Dundua, B., Kutsia, T. (eds.) LNCS, pp. 343–356. Springer (2025). https://doi.org/10.1007/978-3-032-04587-4_21
23. Vandesande, D., Coll, J., Bogaerts, B.: Certified branch-and-bound MaxSAT solving. In: AAAI, pp. 14342–14351. AAAI Press (2026)
24. Weinzierl, A., Taupe, R., Friedrich, G.: Advancing lazy-grounding ASP solving techniques - restarts, phase saving, heuristics, and more. Theory Pract. Log. Program. **20**(5), 609–624 (2020)
25. Wetzler, N., Heule, M., Hunt, W.A.: DRAT-trim: Efficient checking and trimming using expressive clausal proofs. In: Sinz, C., Egly, U. (eds.) SAT. LNCS, vol. 8561, pp. 422–429. Springer (2014). https://doi.org/10.1007/978-3-319-09284-3_31
26. Wittocx, J., Mariën, M., Denecker, M.: Grounding FO and FO(ID) with bounds. J. Artif. Intell. Res. **38**, 223–269 (2010)

Short Papers

Here-and-There with Constraints for Description Logic

Pedro Cabalar[3](✉), Stefania Costantini[2], and Alina Vozna[1,2]

[1] University of Pisa, Largo B. Pontecorvo, Pisa 56127, Italy
alina.vozna@phd.unipi.it

[2] Department of Information Engineering, Computer Science and Mathematics, University of L'Aquila, L'Aquila, Italy
stefania.costantini@univaq.it

[3] University of A Coruña, A Coruña, Spain
cabalar@udc.es

Abstract. In this short paper we introduce a theoretical framework for hybrid systems based on Answer Set Programming (ASP) modulo Description Logic (DL) theories. To this aim, we extend the formalism of Here-and-There with Constraints, mainly used before for integrating ASP with arithmetic constraints, to incorporate now theory atoms that may assert axioms or perform queries and reasoning on an external DL knowledge base. This paves the way for an alternative implementation of hybrid ASP systems interacting with large-scale existing ontologies that are treated as external theories.

Keywords: Answer Set Programming · Description Logic · Equilibrium Logic · ASP modulo theories

1 Introduction

Answer Set Programming (ASP) [8–10] and *Description Logics* (DL) [1] constitute two well-known successful formalisms for practical Knowledge Representation and Reasoning. While ASP provides a highly expressive, non-monotonic reasoning framework well-suited for modeling complex combinatorial problems and default reasoning, DL forms the logical foundation of ontologies, enabling structured representation and reasoning about domain knowledge. Several approaches have considered the implementation of hybrid systems combining ASP and DL to leverage the benefits from both approaches. Some authors, for instance, have extended the ASP semantics to incorporate DL expressions, as in `OntoDLV` [11] or have used higher-order atoms in ASP to connect to DL theories as a particular case, as done in `DLVHEX` [6]. Other approaches have focused on logical formalisations, such as the one based on First Order Equilibrium Logic [2, 12]. Another approach has consisted in defining parametrized logic programs, so other logics can be used as external theories [7].

In this paper, we consider a mixed approach, following a similar spirit to parametrized logic programs, but tackling for a logical formalisation of arbitrary formulas as in equilibrium logic. In particular, we introduce an instance of the logic of

W. Faber et al. (Eds.): LPNMR 2026, LNAI 16952, pp. 467–475, 2027.
https://doi.org/10.1007/978-3-032-38320-4_29

Here-and-There with Constraints [3], which was previously used for hybrid systems combining ASP with arithmetic constraints, and extend it with new constraint atoms to refer to DL axioms. This approach follows the same spirit as SAT modulo theories, so the reasoning tasks for the external theories are treated as a blackbox from the ASP perspective.

Unlike existing hybrid ASP–DL approaches, our proposal does not introduce new DL-specific constructs into ASP nor does it tightly couple the ASP solver with a DL reasoner. Instead, Description Logic is treated as an external constraint theory within the HT_c framework, where DL axioms and queries are represented as constraint atoms with an externally defined semantics. This provides a uniform logical characterization of ASP modulo DL theories while remaining compatible with the general HT_c framework and its existing implementations. This paves the way for a future implementation of a DL-hybrid system that exploits the already existing technology in `clingo` for other hybrid systems [4] for arithmetics such as `clingo[DL]`, `clingcon` or `clingo[LP]`.

2 Background

In this section, we recall the basic definitions of the logic of *Here-and-There with constraints* (HT_c) mostly following [3]. We define the *signature* as a triple $\langle \mathcal{X}, \mathcal{D}, \mathcal{C} \rangle$ where $\mathcal{X}$ is a set of *variables*, $\mathcal{D}$ is a set of values called the *domain* and $\mathcal{C}$ is a set of *constraint atoms*. A constraint atom represents a restriction on the relation among values of some variables, according to the semantics of some external theory. In the general case, constraints can be represented by arbitrary strings of symbols and do not need to have any structure. However, in most interesting cases, they usually have some structured form. As an example, constraint atom from *difference logic* has the general form "$x - y \leq d$" where x and y are integer variables and d is some integer constant. Although constraint atoms can be arbitrary strings, we assume that they may include, at least, occurrences of variables, like $x, y \in \mathcal{X}$ above, that act as placeholders. The set of all variables occurring in constraint atom c is denoted by $vars(c) \subseteq \mathcal{X}$. Let $\mathbf{u} \notin D$ be a distinguished symbol representing an undefined value, and let $D_{\mathbf{u}} = D \cup \{\mathbf{u}\}$ denote the extended domain. Notice that constraint atoms c with $vars(c) = \emptyset$ just amount to a truth constant $\bot$ or $\top$, and can be disregarded. We write $c[s/s']$ to represent the syntactic replacement of subexpression s by s' in constraint atom c. We also assume that $c[x/d] \in \mathcal{C}$ for any constraint atom $c[x] \in \mathcal{C}$, variable $x \in \mathcal{X}$ and $d \in \mathcal{D}_{\mathbf{u}}$. That is, the constraint that results from replacing any variable x by any element d of the extended domain is also a syntactically valid constraint atoms. In the previous example, if "$x - y \leq 5$" is a constraint then "$2 - y \leq 5$" and "$\mathbf{u} - 2 \leq 5$" must also be valid constraints, to put a pair of examples.

A *valuation* v over $\mathcal{X}, \mathcal{D}$ is a partial function from variables in $\mathcal{X}$ to domain elements in $\mathcal{D}$. The set of valuations over $\mathcal{X}$ and $\mathcal{D}$ is denoted by $\mathcal{V}^{\mathcal{X},\mathcal{D}}$, or just $\mathcal{V}$ when there is no ambiguity. Since v is a partial function, it may leave some variables $x \in \mathcal{X}$ undefined, something we will represent as $v(x) = \mathbf{u}$ where $\mathbf{u} \notin \mathcal{D}$ is a new symbol not included in the domain. Using that extended domain, a valuation can be seen as a total function of the form $v : \mathcal{X} \to \mathcal{D}_{\mathbf{u}}$. Alternatively, we may also represent v as the set of pairs $\{x \mapsto v(x) \mid x \in \mathcal{X}, v(x) \in \mathcal{D}\}$ where each x is assigned at most one domain value $v(x) \in \mathcal{D}$ (remember $\mathbf{u} \notin \mathcal{D}$). Under this set of pairs representation, we can then define the subset relation $v \subseteq v'$ between two interpretations v, v' in the standard way. It is not hard to see that $v \subseteq v'$ amounts to the condition, for all $x \in \mathcal{X}$: either $v(x) = \mathbf{u}$ or $v'(x) = v(x)$.

The *domain* of a valuation v is the set of variables that have a defined value $dom(v) \stackrel{\text{def}}{=} \{x \in \mathcal{X} \mid v(x) \neq \mathbf{u}\}$. Given a valuation $v : \mathcal{X} \to \mathcal{D}_{\mathbf{u}}$ we overload its use for the extended definition $v : \mathcal{X} \cup \mathcal{D}_{\mathbf{u}} \to \mathcal{D}_{\mathbf{u}}$ fixing $v(d) = d$ for any $d \in \mathcal{D}$ and $v(\mathbf{u}) = \mathbf{u}$.

The semantics of a constraint atom $c \in \mathcal{C}$ is defined by its *denotation* $[\![c]\!] \subseteq \mathcal{V}$ that assigns to c some set of valuations following the conditions, for all $x \in \mathcal{X}$, $v, v' \in \mathcal{V}$:

1. $v \in [\![c]\!]$ and $v \subseteq v'$ imply $v' \in [\![c]\!]$,
2. $v \in [\![c]\!]$ implies $v \in [\![c[x/v(x)]]\!]$,
3. if $v(x) = v'(x)$ for all $x \in vars(c)$ then $v \in [\![c]\!]$ iff $v' \in [\![c]\!]$.

The first condition states that for any valuation v in $[\![c]\!]$ that leaves some variables undefined we must also have all possible valuations v' in $[\![c]\!]$ with all the possible ways to complete the undefined values. For instance, if $\mathcal{X} = \{x, y\}$, $\mathcal{D}$ and $v = \{x \mapsto 3\} \in [\![c]\!]$ then $v' \in [\![c]\!]$ for all $v' = \{x \mapsto 3, y \mapsto d\}$ for $d \in \mathcal{D}$. The second condition guarantees that variables act as placeholders: for instance, if $v(x) = 5$ and $v \in [\![c]\!]$ then v must also belong to $[\![c[x/5]]\!]$. Condition 3 asserts that only the variables in $vars(c)$ are relevant for the denotation of c, while the rest of variables may freely vary.

A *formula* φ over signature $\langle \mathcal{X}, \mathcal{D}, \mathcal{C} \rangle$ is defined by the grammar:

$$\varphi ::= \bot \mid c \mid \varphi \wedge \varphi \mid \varphi \vee \varphi \mid \varphi \to \varphi \qquad \text{where } c \in \mathcal{C}.$$

We define the derived operators $\top$ as $\bot \to \bot$ and $\neg\varphi$ as $\varphi \to \bot$. Also, we define $vars(\varphi) \stackrel{\text{def}}{=} \bigcup\{vars(c) \mid c \text{ occurs in } \varphi\}$. An $\mathrm{HT}_{\mathcal{C}}$-*theory* is a set of formulas.

An *interpretation* over $\mathcal{X}, \mathcal{D}$ is a pair $\langle h, t \rangle$ of valuations over $\mathcal{X}, \mathcal{D}$ satisfying $h \subseteq t$. We say that the interpretation is *total* when $h = t$.

Definition 1 (Satisfaction of formulas). *An interpretation $\langle h, t \rangle$ satisfies a formula φ with respect to some fixed denotation $[\![\cdot]\!]$, written $\langle h, t \rangle \models \varphi$, if the following recursive conditions hold:*

1. $\langle h, t \rangle \not\models \bot$
2. $\langle h, t \rangle \models c$ *if* $h \in [\![c]\!]$
3. $\langle h, t \rangle \models \varphi \wedge \psi$ *if* $\langle h, t \rangle \models \varphi$ *and* $\langle h, t \rangle \models \psi$
4. $\langle h, t \rangle \models \varphi \vee \psi$ *if* $\langle h, t \rangle \models \varphi$ *or* $\langle h, t \rangle \models \psi$
5. $\langle h, t \rangle \models \varphi \to \psi$ *if* $\langle w, t \rangle \not\models \varphi$ *or* $\langle w, t \rangle \models \psi$ *for* $w \in \{h, t\}$

An interpretation $\langle h, t \rangle$ is a *model* of a theory Γ, written $\langle h, t \rangle \models \Gamma$, when $\langle h, t \rangle \models \varphi$ for every $\varphi \in \Gamma$. Two theories of formulas Γ, Γ' are said to be equivalent $\Gamma \equiv \Gamma'$ when they have the same models. The following proposition provides some basic, useful properties of $\mathrm{HT}_{\mathcal{C}}$.

Proposition 1. (Proposition 3 in [5]**).** *For any formula φ, we have*

1. $\langle h, t \rangle \models \varphi$ *implies* $\langle t, t \rangle \models \varphi$,
2. $\langle h, t \rangle \models \neg\varphi$ *iff* $\langle t, t \rangle \not\models \varphi$, *and*
3. *any tautology in HT is also a tautology in HT*$_c$.

Although, in general, HT$_c$ makes no assumptions about the syntactic form of constraint atoms, [4] introduced a specific case of constraint atom that is useful for proving formal results. Given some domain subset $\mathcal{D}' \subseteq \mathcal{D}$, we define an associated constraint atom $x : \mathcal{D}'$ with denotation:

$$[\![\, x : \mathcal{D}' \,]\!] \stackrel{\text{def}}{=} \{v \in \mathcal{V}^{\mathcal{X},\mathcal{D}} \mid v(x) \in \mathcal{D}'\}$$

and $vars(x : \mathcal{D}') = \{x\}$. The formula $def(x)$ stands for $x : \mathcal{D}$ and so, it holds when $v(x) \neq \mathbf{u}$.

Nonmonotonicity is achieved by selecting a kind of minimal HT$_c$ models, we call *equilibrium models* and define as follows.

Definition 2 (Equilibrium/Stable model). *A (total) interpretation* $\langle t, t \rangle$ *is an* equilibrium model *of a theory* Γ, *if* $\langle t, t \rangle \models \Gamma$ *and there is no* $h \subset t$ *such that* $\langle h, t \rangle \models \Gamma$.

If $\langle t, t \rangle$ *is an equilibrium model of* Γ, *then we say that* t *is a* stable model *of* Γ.

As explained in [5], we can capture the original logic of Here-and-There in HT$_c$ by using a signature $\langle \mathcal{X}, \mathcal{D}, \mathcal{C} \rangle$, where $\mathcal{X} = \mathcal{A}$ are the logical propositions, the domain $\mathcal{D} = \{\mathbf{t}\}$ contains a unique value (meaning "true") and the set of constraint atoms $\mathcal{C} = \mathcal{A}$ coincides with the set of propositions. In [4], a notation distinction was introduced to clarify that each logical proposition a is both a constraint atom $\mathsf{a} \in \mathcal{C}$ and a homonymous variable (using a different font) $a \in \mathcal{X}$ so that $vars(\mathsf{a}) = \{a\}$. The denotation of a regular atom is defined as:

$$[\![\, \mathsf{a} \,]\!] \stackrel{\text{def}}{=} [\![\, a : \{\mathbf{t}\} \,]\!] = \{v \in \mathcal{V}^{\mathcal{X},\mathcal{D}} \mid v(a) = \mathbf{t}\}$$

Under this representation, a regular atom can only be "true" or undefined (there is no need for an explicit value for "false"). A valuation for propositional atoms can be simply represented as a set of atoms $X = \{\mathsf{a} \mid v(a) = \mathbf{t}\}$. By doing so, it is easy to see that the definition of equilibrium and stable models in Definition 2 collapses to their standard definition for propositional theories (and so, for logic programs in ASP too).

In general, when we deal with hybrid systems, we will be interested in combining regular atoms with other types of constraint atoms. For this reason, we may assume that we deal with signatures containing at least the element $\mathbf{t} \in \mathcal{D}$, and some subset of variables $\mathcal{A} \subseteq \mathcal{X}$ including the regular atoms and satisfying the following axiom:

$$def(a) \rightarrow \mathsf{a} \tag{1}$$

for every $a \in \mathcal{A}$. This axiom states that if a has some value, it must be value $\mathbf{t}$, avoiding in this way that regular atoms may take other values from $\mathcal{D} \setminus \{\mathbf{t}\}$.

3 Description Logic HT_c

We proceed now to introduce an instance of HT_c where constraint atoms represent Description Logic axioms. In this setting, all previous definitions for HT_c are still maintained (including logical formulas and propositional atoms). We call HT_{dl} this HT_c subsystem. The HT_{dl} signature is a 4-tuple $\langle \mathcal{X}, \mathcal{D}, \mathcal{C}, \Omega \rangle$ where $\langle \mathcal{X}, \mathcal{D}, \mathcal{C} \rangle$ is a regular HT_c signature and the fourth component Ω is a (generally infinite) set of elements we call the *universe* from which multiple domains will be formed. Additionally, an HT_{dl} signature must satisfy the following conditions:

1. The set of variables $\mathcal{X} = \mathcal{A} \cup \mathcal{X}_C \cup \mathcal{X}_R \cup \mathcal{X}_O$ is partitioned into four disjoint sets: $\mathcal{A}$, the set of regular atoms; $\mathcal{X}_C$, the set of *concept names*; $\mathcal{X}_R$, the set of *role names*; and $\mathcal{X}_O$, the set of *object names*.
2. The domain $\mathcal{D} = \{\mathbf{t}\} \cup \mathcal{D}_C \cup \mathcal{D}_R$ consists again of four disjoint subsets: $\mathbf{t}$ is the element "true" for regular atoms; $\mathcal{D}_C = 2^{\Omega}$ are the possible "values" for concept variables in $\mathcal{X}_C$, being each value some set of elements; and $\mathcal{D}_R = 2^{\Omega \times \Omega}$ are the possible values for role variables in $\mathcal{X}_R$, where each value will be a set of pairs of elements from the universe. The domain for objects $\mathcal{D}_O$ is not needed as it coincides with Ω.
3. A constraint atom $c \in \mathcal{C}$ is recursively defined following the grammar:

$$c ::= o : E \mid (o_1, o_2) : R \mid E_1 \sqsubseteq E_2 \mid C \equiv E$$

where $C \in \mathcal{X}_C$, $R \in \mathcal{X}_R$ denote any concept or role variable, respectively, $o, o_1, o_2 \in \mathcal{X}_O$ are constant names and E, E_1, E_2 are *concept expressions* following, in their turn, the grammar:

$$E ::= C \mid E_1 \sqcap E_2 \mid \forall R.E \mid \exists R.E \mid {\sim} E \mid \bot$$

The connectives allowed in concept expressions above correspond to description logic $\mathcal{ALC}$, but other operators covering more expressive description logics can be easily introduced. We use the symbol $\sim$ for negation in DL, to distinguish it from $\neg$ we use for HT (or default) negation.

A valuation v in HT_{dl} is associated to a particular subset $\Delta_v \subseteq \Omega$ of the universe we call the *concept domain*. We will sometimes write Δ instead of Δ_v when clear from the context. An HT_{dl}-valuation v must satisfy, for all $x \in \mathcal{X}$ such that $v(x) \neq \mathbf{u}$:

- $v(x) = \mathbf{t}$ if $x \in \mathcal{A}$
- $v(x) \subseteq \Delta$ if $x \in \mathcal{X}_C$
- $v(x) \subseteq \Delta \times \Delta$ if $x \in \mathcal{X}_R$
- $v(x) \in \Delta$ if $x \in \mathcal{X}_O$

This means that defined regular atoms can only be assigned value $\mathbf{t}$, defined concept variables can only be assigned sets of elements from Δ and defined role variables can only be assigned sets of pairs of elements from Δ. Additionally, defined object variables can only be assigned an element value from Δ.

We extend the application of a valuation v not only to variables but also to any concept expression E (different from concept names) following the recursive conditions:

$$\begin{aligned}
v(\bot) &\stackrel{\text{def}}{=} \emptyset \\
v(E_1 \sqcap E_2) &\stackrel{\text{def}}{=} v(E_1) \cap v(E_2) \\
v(\forall R.E) &\stackrel{\text{def}}{=} \{d \in \Delta \mid \text{for all } d' \text{ s.t. } (d, d') \in v(R) : d' \in v(E)\} \\
v(\exists R.E) &\stackrel{\text{def}}{=} \{d \in \Delta \mid \text{there exists } d' \text{ s.t. } (d, d') \in v(R), d' \in v(E)\} \\
v(\sim E) &\stackrel{\text{def}}{=} \Delta \setminus v(E)
\end{aligned}$$

Definition 3. *The denotation of a HT_{dl}-constraint atom c, $[\![c]\!]$, is recursively defined as follows:*

$$\begin{aligned}
[\![o : E]\!] &\stackrel{\text{def}}{=} \{v \mid v(o) \in v(E)\} \\
[\![(o_1, o_2) : R]\!] &\stackrel{\text{def}}{=} \{v \mid (v(o_1), v(o_2)) \in v(R)\} \\
[\![E_1 \sqsubseteq E_2]\!] &\stackrel{\text{def}}{=} \{v \mid v(E_1) \subseteq v(E_2)\} \\
[\![E_1 \equiv E_2]\!] &\stackrel{\text{def}}{=} \{v \mid v(E_1) = v(E_2)\}
\end{aligned}$$

Although, in the general case in HT_{dl}, we may construct arbitrary propositional theories (formed with regular atoms and DL constraint atoms), we will be mostly interested in logic programs, that is, implications $\varphi \leftarrow \psi$ where φ is a disjunction of literals and ψ a conjunction of literals. Informally speaking, the effect produced by HT_{dl}-logic programs is that we may specify which set of axioms we wish to include in our DL theory by deriving them as constraint atoms in a logic program. Consider the following example:

Example 1. The default situation among the 192 countries in the UN is that same-sex marriage is not allowed. On the other hand, 40 countries have approved laws to allow same-sex marriages. Let $\mathcal{X}_\mathcal{C} = \{Man, Woman, Person\}$ and $\mathcal{X}_\mathcal{R} = \{married\}$, $\mathcal{X}_\mathcal{O} = \{Mary\}$. Consider the following logic program:

$$Woman \sqcap \exists married.Woman \equiv \bot \leftarrow \neg law \tag{2}$$

$$Man \sqcap \exists married.Man \equiv \bot \leftarrow \neg law \tag{3}$$

$$\exists married.\top \sqsubseteq Person \tag{4}$$

$$\forall married.\ Person \equiv \top \tag{5}$$

$$Person \equiv Man \sqcup Woman \tag{6}$$

$$Mary : Woman \tag{7}$$

$$Mary : \exists married.\top \tag{8}$$

Rules (2) and (3) forbid same-sex marriages if we cannot prove that there exists a *law* that permits them. Facts (4) and (5) state that we can only marry persons, that are defined as men or women by fact 6. Finally, (7) and (8) assert that $Mary$ is a married woman. From (2)-(8) we obtain a set of equilibrium models (they vary depending on the domain Δ) that satisfy the same set of constraint atoms and from which we can conclude $Mary : \exists married.Man$, that is, $Mary$ must have a husband. On the other hand, if we add the fact law to the same logic program, the DL constraints in the heads of (2) and (3) are no longer applicable, so we cannot derive $Mary : \exists married.Man$ any more. The effect of adding law to the program is the same as if we consider the standard DL theory formed by the facts (4)-(8).

Example 2. Consider an extended example where we do not know the gender of some new element $Chris \in \mathcal{X}_O$. Yet, we may derive that some atom $known$ holds if we know that $Chris$ is a man or we know that $Chris$ is a woman. We can represent the situation with the logic program:

$$Chris : Woman \vee Chris : Man \tag{9}$$

$$known \leftarrow Chris : Woman \tag{10}$$

$$known \leftarrow Chris : Man \tag{11}$$

From this program, we get two equilibrium models (modulo different domains Δ): one in which we derive $Chris : Woman$ and $known$, and the other one where we obtain $Chris : Man$ and $known$. This result corresponds to considering two different DL theories, depending on whether we include the DL axioms $Chris : Woman$ or $Chris : Man$, respectively. Note the difference with respect to replacing (9) with:

$$Chris : Woman \sqcup Man \tag{12}$$

In this case, we cannot derive fact $known$ any more. This is because once we state (12) instead of (9), we can no more derive the body $Chris : Man$ of rule (10) or the body $Chris : Woman$ of rule (11). As a result, atom $known$ cannot be derived either.

HT$_{dl}$ allows some limited kind of non-monotonic reasoning for DL expressions.

Example 3. Consider the classical example stating that birds that normally fly:

$$AbBird \sqsubseteq Bird \tag{13}$$

$$AbBird \sqcap Fly \equiv \bot \tag{14}$$

$$Bird \sqcap {\sim}AbBird \sqsubseteq Fly \tag{15}$$

$$Tweety : {\sim}AbBird \leftarrow Tweety : Bird \wedge \neg(Tweety : AbBird) \tag{16}$$

$$Tweety : Bird \tag{17}$$

Rules (13) and (14) state that abnormal birds are birds and that they do not fly. Rule (15) says that a normal bird can fly. Rule (16) expresses that $Tweety$ is a normal bird by default, whereas (17) tells us that $Tweety$ is a bird. From this program, we can conclude that $Tweety : {\sim}AbBird$ and so $Tweety : Fly$. However, if we add the rules:

$$Penguin \sqsubseteq AbBird$$

$$Tweety : Penguin$$

we retract those facts and eventually conclude $Tweety : {\sim}Fly$.

We may note that, in the previous example, we should have used the more general rule:

$$X : {\sim}AbBird \leftarrow X : Bird \wedge \neg(X : AbBird)$$

instead of (16). However, this rule is not propositional, as it makes use of a (logic program) variable X standing for any element in the ASP (Herbrand) domain. Note that ASP variables are quite different from constraint variables: the former can be seen as an abbreviation for all possible instantiations with domain elements in the ASP program, whereas constraint variables are entities completely external to the ASP program and interpreted through denotations, as explained before. ASP variables in HT_{dl}-logic programs introduce new issues such as safety or the difference between the ASP domain, which is usually finite and follows the unique names assumption, versus the DL domain, which is infinite and does not make any assumption on names. We leave those problems for future study.

4 Conclusions

We have introduced a logic for hybrid systems based on Answer Set Programming (ASP) modulo Description Logic (DL) theories. To do so, we extended the formalism of Here-and-There with Constraints (which was previously used for integrating ASP with arithmetic constraints) to incorporate theory atoms capable of asserting axioms and performing queries and reasoning over an external DL knowledge base. Our future work will be focused on comparing with other existing approaches, extending the current formalism to theories/programs with variables, and eventually, on the implementation of a hybrid ASP system that allows interacting with large-scale existing ontologies.

References

1. Baader, F., Horrocks, I., Lutz, C., Sattler, U.: An Introduction to Description Logic. Cambridge University Press (2017). http://www.cambridge.org/de/academic/subjects/computer-science/knowledge-management-databases-and-data-mining/introduction-description-logic?format=PB#17zVGeWD2TZUeu6s.97
2. de Bruijn, J., Pearce, D., Polleres, A., Valverde, A.: A semantical framework for hybrid knowledge bases. Knowl. Inf. Syst. **25**(1), 81–104 (2010)
3. Cabalar, P., Fandinno, J., Schaub, T., Wanko, P.: An ASP semantics for constraints involving conditional aggregates. In: Giacomo, G.D., Catalá, A., Dilkina, B., Milano, M., Barro, S., Bugarín, A., Lang, J. (eds.) ECAI 2020–24th European Conference on Artificial Intelligence, 29 August-8 September 2020, Santiago de Compostela, Spain, pp. 664–671. IOS Press, Frontiers in Artificial Intelligence and Applications (2020)
4. Cabalar, P., Fandinno, J., Schaub, T., Wanko, P.: Strong equivalence in answer set programming with constraints. CoRR abs/2502.04302 (2025). https://doi.org/10.48550/ARXIV.2502.04302
5. Cabalar, P., Kaminski, R., Ostrowski, M., Schaub, T.: An ASP semantics for default reasoning with constraints. In: Kambhampati, S. (ed.) Proceedings of the Twenty-Fifth International Joint Conference on Artificial Intelligence, IJCAI 2016, New York, NY, USA, 9-15 July 2016, pp. 1015–1021. IJCAI/AAAI Press (2016)

6. Eiter, T., Ianni, G., Schindlauer, R., Tompits, H.: DLVHEX: a prover for semantic-web reasoning under the answer-set semantics. In: Proceedings of the 2006 IEEE/WIC/ACM International Conference on Web Intelligence, pp. 1073–1074. WI 2006, IEEE Computer Society, USA (2006)
7. Gonçalves, R.: Combining rules and ontologies via parametrized logic programs. In: Papini, O., et al. (eds.) Proceedings of the Joint Ontology Workshops 2015 Episode 1: The Argentine Winter of Ontology co-located with the 24th International Joint Conference on Artificial Intelligence (IJCAI 2015), Buenos Aires, Argentina, July 25-27, 2015. CEUR Workshop Proceedings, CEUR-WS.org (2015)
8. Lifschitz, V.: Answer set planning. In: Proceedings of the ICLP-1999, pp. 23–37. MIT Press (1999)
9. Marek, V., Truszczyński, M.: Stable models and an alternative logic programming paradigm, pp. 169–181. Springer-Verlag (1999). https://doi.org/10.1007/978-3-642-60085-2_17
10. Niemelä, I.: Logic programs with stable model semantics as a constraint programming paradigm. Ann. Math. Artif. Intell. **25**(3–4), 241–273 (1999)
11. Ricca, F., Gallucci, L., Schindlauer, R., Dell'Armi, T., Grasso, G., Leone, N.: OntoDLV: an ASP-based system for enterprise ontologies. J. Log. Comput. **19**(4), 643–670 (2009)
12. Stefano, F.D., Simkus, M.: Equilibrium description logics: Results on complexity and relations to circumscription. In: Marquis, P., Ortiz, M., Pagnucco, M. (eds.) Proceedings of the 21st International Conference on Principles of Knowledge Representation and Reasoning, KR 2024, Hanoi, Vietnam. November 2-8, 2024 (2024)

Strong Equivalence of Logic Programs Relative to a User Guide

Jorge Fandinno[1](✉), Zachary Hansen[2], Yuliya Lierler[1], and Vladimir Lifschitz[3]

[1] University of Omaha Nebraska, Omaha, USA
jfandinno@unomaha.edu
[2] Boise State University, Boise, USA
[3] University of Texas at Austin, Austin, USA

Abstract. Studying strong equivalence is useful for the practice of answer set programming because of the fact that replacing a group of rules within a program by a strongly equivalent group of rules does not change the meaning of the program. But this behavior is not guaranteed when some symbols are used in the program as placeholders. We show how to remedy this issue by generalizing the definition of strong equivalence. The new definition makes this relation dependent on a user guide—a formal expression describing how programs are expected to be used.

1 Introduction

In answer set programming (ASP), two groups of rules are called strongly equivalent if replacing one by the other within any program does not affect the set of stable models. The precise meaning of this condition depends on the class of rules under consideration. Strong equivalence was defined and studied first for propositional programs [16], then for sets of propositional formulas [8], for infinitary propositional formulas [10], for programs with variables [17], for programs in the subset of the input language of the grounder GRINGO called mini-GRINGO [15] and for other languages based on the stable model semantics. The mini-GRINGO language is of particular interest because it is used by the proof assistant ANTHEM [4] to automatically verify certain types of program correspondence, such as strong equivalence.

Studying strong equivalence is useful for the practice of answer set programming because of the fact that replacing a group of rules within an ASP program by a strongly equivalent group of rules does not change the meaning of the program. If, for instance, we improved a program by replacing one of its rules by a simpler rule, and we checked that two rules are strongly equivalent, then we can conclude that the stable models of the program remained the same without even looking at the other rules.

But this behavior is not guaranteed when some symbols are used the programs as placeholders [9, Section 3.15]. Consider, for instance, the rule

$$p \leftarrow a < b. \tag{1}$$

W. Faber et al. (Eds.): LPNMR 2026, LNAI 16952, pp. 476–484, 2027.
https://doi.org/10.1007/978-3-032-38320-4_30

In the language of GRINGO, rule (1) is strongly equivalent to $p \leftarrow$ because symbolic constants are ordered lexicographically: a is less than b. But if a and b are placeholders then replacing (1) by $p \leftarrow$ does affect the meaning of the program.

In this paper we show how to generalize strong equivalence by making it dependent on a *user guide* [5, Section 3]—a formal expression describing how programs are expected to be used. A user guide can specify, in particular, that certain symbols are supposed to serve as placeholders, and tell us which combinations of values assigned to placeholders are allowed. For example, rule (1) is not strongly equivalent to $p \leftarrow$ with respect to the user guide that classifies a and b as placeholders. But these two rules will become strongly equivalent if we add to the user guide the assumptions that the value assigned to a is supposed to be a negative integer, and the value assigned to b should be positive.

After reviewing the syntax and semantics of mini-GRINGO in the next two sections, we define strong equivalence relative to a user guide in Sect. 4. In the second half of the paper we discuss the relationship between generalized strong equivalence and the logic of here-and-there.

2 Rules and Programs

Dialects of mini-GRINGO [7,14] differ by the choice of arithmetic operations included in their vocabularies. Strong equivalence relative to a user guide can be defined for an arbitrary dialect, but in this paper it is discussed in the framework of a specific dialect that includes only addition and multiplication.

We assume that three countably infinite sets of symbols are selected: *numerals*, *symbolic constants*, and *variables*. We assume that a 1-1 correspondence between numerals and integers is chosen; the numeral corresponding to an integer n is denoted by $\overline{n}$. Numerals and symbolic constants are collectively called *precomputed terms*. We assume that a total order on precomputed terms is chosen such that numerals are contiguous (that is, there are no symbolic constants between numerals), and, for any integers m and n, $\overline{m} < \overline{n}$ iff $m < n$.

Terms are formed from numerals, symbolic constants and variables using the binary function symbols $+$ and $\times$. An *atom* is an expression of the form $c(\mathbf{t})$, where c is a symbolic constant, and $\mathbf{t}$ is tuple of terms separated by commas. If $\mathbf{t}$ is empty then the parentheses can be dropped. *Literals* are expressions of the forms $c(\mathbf{t})$, *not* $c(\mathbf{t})$ and *not not* $c(\mathbf{t})$. *Comparisons* are expressions of the form $t_1 \prec t_2$ where t_1 and t_2 are terms, and $\prec$ is $=$ or one of the symbols

$$\neq \quad < \quad > \quad \leq \quad \geq \tag{2}$$

A *rule* is an expression of the form *Head* $\leftarrow$ *Body*, where *Head* is either an atom or empty, and *Body* is a conjunction of literals and comparisons, possibly empty. A *constraint* is a rule with empty head. A *choice rule* $\{c(\mathbf{t})\} \leftarrow$ *Body* is stands for

$$c(\mathbf{t}) \leftarrow \mathit{Body} \wedge \mathit{not}\ \mathit{not}\ c(\mathbf{t}).$$

A *program* is a finite set of rules.

3 Stable Models and Strong Equivalence

An atom or another syntactic expression is *ground* if it does not contain variables. A ground atom is *precomputed* if it does not contain arithmetic operations $+$, $\times$. The semantics of mini-GRINGO defines when a set of precomputed atoms is a stable model of a program Π. The definition, reviewed in this section, refers to the operator τ that transforms Π into a set of propositional formulas formed from precomputed atoms.

For a ground term t that does not contain symbolic constants in the scope of arithmetic operations, its *value* $[t]$ is the precomputed term defined as follows:

- if t is precomputed then $[t]$ is t;
- if $[t_1]$ is $\overline{m}$ and $[t_2]$ is $\overline{n}$ then $[t_1 + t_2]$ is $\overline{m+n}$, and $[t_1 \times t_2]$ is $\overline{m \times n}$.

For example, the value of $\overline{2} + \overline{3}$ is $\overline{5}$.

Rules and programs that do not contain symbolic constants in the scope of arithmetic operations are said to be in *numeric normal form (NNF)*.[1] The operator τ, which rewrites programs and expressions that may occur in them in the syntax of propositional formulas, will be defined first for ground rules in numeric normal form, and then extended to arbitrary rules and programs.

The result of applying τ to a ground atom $c(t_1, \ldots, t_k)$ that does not contain symbolic constants in the scope of arithmetic operations is defined as the precomputed atom $c([t_1], \ldots, [t_k])$. A literal *not* $c(\mathbf{t})$ is transformed by τ into $\neg\tau(c(\mathbf{t}))$, and *not not* $c(\mathbf{t})$ is transformed into $\neg\neg\tau(c(\mathbf{t}))$. A comparison $t_1 \prec t_2$ that does not contain symbolic constants in the scope of arithmetic operations is transformed into $\top$ ("true") if the relation $\prec$ holds for the pair of values $[t_1]$, $[t_2]$, and into $\bot$ ("false") otherwise. The result of applying τ to a ground NNF rule

$$c(\mathbf{t}) \leftarrow B_1 \wedge \cdots \wedge B_n \tag{3}$$

is the formula

$$\tau(B_1) \wedge \cdots \wedge \tau(B_n) \rightarrow \tau(c(\mathbf{t})).$$

A ground NNF constraint

$$\leftarrow B_1 \wedge \cdots \wedge B_n \tag{4}$$

is transformed by τ into

$$\neg(\tau(B_1) \wedge \cdots \wedge \tau(B_n)).$$

To extend the definition of τ to arbitrary rules, we define an *instance* of a rule R as a ground NNF rule that can be obtained from R by substituting precomputed terms for variables.[2] The result of applying τ to R is defined as

[1] The use of the expression "normal form" here is motivated by the fact that any rule can be rewritten as an NNF rule using additional variables [7, Section 4]. For example, the rule $q(X + a) \leftarrow p(X)$ can be rewritten as $q(X + Y) \leftarrow p(X) \wedge Y = a$.

[2] The requirement that the result of substitution be in numeric normal form is similar to the use of well-formed substitutions in the ASP-Core language [1, Section 3].

the set of formulas obtained by applying τ to instances of R. For example, instances of the rule

$$q(X, Y + \overline{1}) \leftarrow p(X, Y) \tag{5}$$

are rules of the form

$$q(t, \overline{i} + \overline{1}) \leftarrow p(t, \overline{i})$$

where t is a precomputed term, and i is an integer. The result of applying τ to R is the set of formulas of the form

$$p(t, \overline{i}) \rightarrow q(t, \overline{i+1}).$$

For any program Π, $\tau(\Pi)$ is defined as the union of the sets $\tau(R)$ over all rules R of Π. Stable models of Π are defined as stable models (answer sets) of $\tau(\Pi)$ in the sense of Ferraris [8, Section 2.1].

Sets Ω_1 and Ω_2 of propositional formulas are *strongly equivalent* if, for every set Ω of propositional formulas, $\Omega_1 \cup \Omega$ and $\Omega_2 \cup \Omega$ have the same stable models [8, Section 3]. Strong equivalence of programs Π_1, Π_2 is defined as strong equivalence of the sets $\tau(\Pi_1)$ and $\tau(\Pi_2)$. If Π_1 is strongly equivalent to Π_2 then, for any program Π, the programs $\Pi_1 \cup \Pi$ and $\Pi_2 \cup \Pi$ have the same stable models, because $\tau(\Pi_1 \cup \Pi) = \tau(\Pi_1) \cup \tau(\Pi)$ and $\tau(\Pi_2 \cup \Pi) = \tau(\Pi_2) \cup \tau(\Pi)$.

4 Valuations and User Guides

A *valuation* of a set *PH* of symbolic constants (that are meant to be used as placeholders) is a function that maps elements of *PH* to precomputed terms. For any term t and any valuation v, $v(t)$ stands for the term obtained from t by simultaneously substituting the terms $v(c)$ for all symbolic constants c that belong to the domain of v. For any rule R and any valuation v, $v(R)$ stands for the rule obtained from R by replacing, in each atom $c(t_1, \dots, t_k)$ (including those in the scope of *not*) and in each comparison $t_1 \prec t_2$, every term t_i by $v(t_i)$. For any program Π, $v(\Pi)$ stands for the set of rules $v(R)$ for all rules R of Π.

The condition on a pair of programs Π_1, Π_2 that we are interested in is strong equivalence of $v(\Pi_1)$ to $v(\Pi_2)$ for all valuations v satisfying a given user guide. To define the concept of a user guide, we need a formal language that can serve for expressing assumptions about valuations, such as "a is mapped to an integer," or "a is mapped to a negative integer." For any set *PH* of symbolic constants, let $\sigma(PH)$ be the two-sorted signature that consists of

(i) the sort *general* and its subsort *integer*,
(ii) all numerals as object constants of the sort *integer*,
(iii) symbolic constants from *PH* as object constants of the sort *general*,
(iv) the symbols $+$ and $\times$ as function constants with arguments and values of the sort *integer*,
(v) comparison symbols (2) as binary predicate constant with arguments of the sort *general*.[3]

[3] There is no need to include $=$ because equalities are considered part of every first-order language.

For any valuation v of PH, let $S(v)$ be the interpretation of $\sigma(PH)$ such that

(a) its universe of the sort *general* is the set of precomputed terms,
(b) its universe of the sort *integers* is the set of numerals,
(c) each numeral is interpreted as itself,
(d) each symbolic constant c is interpreted as $v(c)$,
(e) the function symbols $+$ and $\times$ are interpreted as usual in arithmetic, and
(f) the comparison symbols are interpreted as in the definition of mini-GRINGO (Sect. 2).

The definitions of $\sigma(PH)$ and $S(v)$ allow us to use first-order sentences to express assumptions about valuations. For instance, a valuation v maps a to a negative integer iff $S(v)$ satisfies sentence $\exists I(a = I) \wedge a < \overline{0}$, where I is an integer variable.

A *simple user guide*[4] is a pair (PH, Asm), where PH is a finite set of symbolic constants, and Asm is a finite set of sentences over $\sigma(PH)$. Elements of PH are *placeholders* of the user guide, and elements of Asm are its assumptions.

Programs Π_1 and Π_2 are *strongly equivalent* relative to a simple user guide UG if, for every valuation v of the placeholders of UG that satisfies its assumptions, $v(\Pi_1)$ is strongly equivalent to $v(\Pi_2)$. For example, $(\{a, b\}, \emptyset)$ and

$$(\{a, b\}, \{\exists I(a = I) \wedge a < \overline{0}, \exists I(b = I) \wedge b > \overline{0}\}) \tag{6}$$

are simple user guides. Rules (1) and $p \leftarrow$ are strongly equivalent relative to the latter, but they are not strongly equivalent relative to the former.

To give another example, consider the rules

$$q(X + \overline{1}) \leftarrow p(X) \wedge X < a \tag{7}$$

and

$$q(X) \leftarrow p(X - \overline{1}) \wedge X \leq a. \tag{8}$$

They are strongly equivalent relative to the user guide $(\{a\}, \emptyset)$.

5 Review: Representing Rules by First-Order Sentences

The theorem stated in the next section shows how first-order reasoning can be sometimes used for establishing strong equivalence of mini-GRINGO programs relative to a user guide. The theorem is restricted to programs in numeric normal form. Its statement refers to the translation ν [7, Section 5], which transforms NNF rules into two-sorted first-order sentences. In this section we reproduce the definition of ν for the special case of the dialect described above.

By σ we denote the two-sorted signature that consists of the sorts and symbols listed in clauses (i), (ii), (iv), (v) above and the following additional symbols:

(iii)′ all symbolic constants as object constants of the sort *general*,

[4] The word "simple" indicates that this concept is less general than user guides defined by Fandinno et al. [5].

(vi) expressions c/k, where c is a symbolic constant and k is a nonnegative integer, as k-ary predicate constants with arguments of the sort *general*.

Note that the set of terms over the signature σ and the set of mini-GRINGO terms partially overlap. On the one hand, a term over σ may include integer variables, which are not part of mini-GRINGO. In a mini-GRINGO term, on the other hand, symbolic constants and variables may occur in the scope of an arithmetic operation; this is not allowed in terms over σ, because both symbolic constants and variables are terms of the sort *general*.

Consider a rule R in numeric normal form. Applying the translation ν to R involves substituting an integer variable for each variable that occurs in R at least once in the scope of an arithmetic operation. Make the list $V_1, \ldots, V_m$ of all variables satisfying this condition, and choose m distinct integer variables $I_1, \ldots, I_m$.

Consider a term t that occurs in R. Since R is in numeric normal form, symbolic constants in t are not in the scope of arithmetic operations. It follows that the result of substituting $I_1, \ldots, I_m$ for $V_1, \ldots, V_m$ in t is a term over the signature σ. The operator that performs this transformation will be denoted by *p2f* ("programs-to-formulas"). For example, if R is rule (5) then $m = 1$, V_1 is Y, $p2f(X)$ is X, and $p2f(Y + \overline{1})$ is $I + \overline{1}$.

The result of applying ν to an atom $c(t_1, \ldots, t_k)$ occurring in R is defined as the atomic formula $(c/k)(p2f(t_1), \ldots, p2f(t_k))$. A literal *not* $c(\mathbf{t})$ that occurs in R is transformed by ν into $\neg\nu(c(\mathbf{t}))$, and *not not* $c(\mathbf{t})$ is transformed into $\neg\neg\nu(c(\mathbf{t}))$. A comparison $t_1 \prec t_2$ occurring in R is transformed into $p2f(t_1) \prec p2f(t_2)$. If R is (3) then $\nu(R)$ is defined as the universal closure of the formula

$$\nu(B_1) \wedge \cdots \wedge \nu(B_n) \rightarrow \nu(c(\mathbf{t})).$$

If R is a constraint (4) then $\nu(R)$ is the universal closure of

$$\neg(\nu(B_1) \wedge \cdots \wedge \nu(B_n)).$$

For example, the result of applying ν to rule (5) is the sentence

$$\forall X I_1((p/2)(X, I_1) \rightarrow (q/2)(X, I_1{+}1)).$$

6 Verifying Strong Equivalence

In this section, we introduce a deductive system that can be used for proving strong equivalence of NNF programs relative to a user guide. Deductive systems that allow reasoning about strong equivalence of logic programs have been developed for several classes of programs, including propositional programs [16], first-order programs [17], mini-GRINGO programs [6,12], and mini-GRINGO with counting aggregates [2,3,13]. The theorem below is a generalization of the results for mini-GRINGO to the more general case of strong equivalence relative to a user guide.

An interpretation of the signature σ is *standard* if it satisfies conditions (a)–(c), (e) and (f) above. Thus standard interpretations of σ may differ from each other by how they interpret symbols of two kinds: symbolic constants and predicate constants c/k. By *Std* we denote the set of sentences over σ that do not contain symbols of these two kinds and are satisfied by standard interpretations (by at least one, and consequently by all of them).

For any set *PH* of symbolic constants, $HT(PH)$ ("the logic of here-and-there for placeholders *PH*") is the deductive system obtained from intuitionistic predicate calculus with equality for the signature σ by adding the following axioms:

- the Hosoi axiom schema [11]: $F \vee (F \rightarrow G) \vee \neg G$,
- the static domain schema [17]: $\exists X(F \rightarrow \forall X\, F)$, where X is a general variable,
- all sentences from *Std*,
- the induction schema

$$F(\overline{0}) \wedge \forall I(I \geq \overline{0} \wedge F(I) \rightarrow F(I+\overline{1})) \rightarrow \forall I(I \geq \overline{0} \rightarrow F(I)),$$

where I is an integer variable.

Theorem. *For any NNF programs Π_1, Π_2 and any simple user guide (PH, Asm), if the formula $\nu(\Pi_1) \leftrightarrow \nu(\Pi_2)$ is derivable from Asm in the deductive system $HT(PH)$ then Π_1 is strongly equivalent to Π_2 relative to (PH, Asm).*

As an example, consider proving the strong equivalence of rules (1) and $p \leftarrow$ relative to user guide (6). According to the theorem, this can be accomplished by showing that the formula

$$(a < b \rightarrow p) \leftrightarrow (\top \rightarrow p))$$

is derivable in $HT(\{a, b\})$ from $\exists I(a = I) \wedge a < \overline{0}$ and $\exists I(b = I) \wedge b > \overline{0}$. To verify this claim, observe that $a < b$ is an intuitionistic consequence of $a < \overline{0}$, $b > \overline{0}$ and the following sentence from *Std*:

$$\forall XYZ(X < Y \wedge Z > Y \rightarrow X < Z),$$

To prove that rule (7) is strongly equivalent to rule (8) relative to the user guide $(\{a\}, \emptyset)$, we will show that the formula

$$\forall I(p(I) \wedge I < a \rightarrow q(I+\overline{1})) \leftrightarrow \forall I(p(I-\overline{1}) \wedge I \leq a \rightarrow q(I)), \tag{9}$$

where I is an integer variable, is provable in $HT(\{a\})$. Note first that the formula

$$\forall I(I - \overline{1} + \overline{1} = I) \tag{10}$$

belongs to *Std*. The formula

$$\forall IX(I - \overline{1} < X \leftrightarrow I \leq X), \tag{11}$$

where X is a general variable, belongs to *Std* as well, because numerals are contiguous (Sect. 2). From the left-hand side of (9) we derive

$$p(I - \overline{1}) \wedge I - \overline{1} < a \rightarrow q(I - \overline{1} + \overline{1}).$$

Now the right-hand side follows by (10) and (11). The other direction is similar.

Note that the theorem provides only a sufficient condition for strong equivalence relative to a user guide. Similar results for strong equivalence of mini-GRINGO programs without placeholders [6,12] only provide sufficient conditions as well. We do not know whether the condition in these theorems are also necessary, but we conjecture that it is not the case. Yet, the system can be made complete by adding deductive rules with infinitely many premises called ω-rules [6].

7 Conclusion

The generalization of strong equivalence defined in this paper can be useful in the process of developing ASP programs with placeholders. In some cases, verifying generalized strong equivalence can be accomplished by reasoning in a first-order theory based on the logic of here-and-there. In the future, we plan to relate ideas of this paper to the definition of external equivalence with respect to a user guide [5] and to incorporate a process of verifying generalized strong equivalence in a new version of the proof assistant ANTHEM [4].

Acknowledgments. We would like to thank anonymous reviewers for their valuable feedback that allowed us to improve presentation. This work was partially supported by the National Science Foundation CAREER award 2338635, USA. Any opinions, findings, and conclusions or recommendations expressed in this material are those of the authors and do not necessarily reflect the views of the National Science Foundation.

Disclosure of Interests. The authors have no competing interests to declare that are relevant to the content of this article.

References

1. Calimeri, F., et al.: ASP-Core-2 input language format. Theory Pract. Logic Program. **20**, 294–309 (2020)
2. Fandinno, J., Lifschitz, V.: Deductive systems for logic programs with counting: preliminary report. In: Dodaro, C., Gupta, G., Martinez, M. (eds.) Proceedings of the Seventeenth International Conference on Logic Programming and Nonmonotonic Reasoning (LPNMR 2024). LNAI, vol. 15245, pp. 1–14. Springer (2024). https://doi.org/10.1007/978-3-031-74209-5
3. Fandinno, J., Lifschitz, V.: Deductive systems for logic programs with counting. Theory Pract. Logic Program. **25**(5), 924–964 (2025). https://doi.org/10.1017/S1471068425100379
4. Fandinno, J., et al.: ANTHEM: answer set programming and automated theorem proving. Theory Pract. Logic Program. (2025)

5. Fandinno, J., Hansen, Z., Lierler, Y., Lifschitz, V., Temple, N.: External behavior of a logic program and verification of refactoring. Theory Pract. Logic Program. (2023)
6. Fandinno, J., Lifschitz, V.: Omega-completeness of the logic of here-and-there and strong equivalence of logic programs. In: Proceedings of International Conference on Principles of Knowledge Representation and Reasoning (2023)
7. Fandinno, J., Lifschitz, V.: A normal form for rules containing arithmetic operations. In: Proceedings of International Conference on Principles of Knowledge Representation and Reasoning (2026, to appear). https://www.cs.utexas.edu/~vl/papers/normalform_krr.pdf
8. Ferraris, P.: Answer sets for propositional theories. In: Proceedings of International Conference on Logic Programming and Nonmonotonic Reasoning (LPNMR), pp. 119–131 (2005)
9. Gebser, M., et al.: Potassco User Guide (2019). https://github.com/potassco/guide/releases/
10. Harrison, A., Lifschitz, V., Pearce, D., Valverde, A.: Infinitary equilibrium logic and strongly equivalent logic programs. Artif. Intell. **246**, 22–33 (2017)
11. Hosoi, T.: The axiomatization of the intermediate propositional systems S_n of Gödel. J. Fac. Sci. Univ. Tokyo **13**, 183–187 (1966)
12. Lifschitz, V.: Here and there with arithmetic. Theory and Practice of Logic Programming (2021)
13. Lifschitz, V.: Strong equivalence of logic programs with counting. Theory Pract. Logic Program. **22** (2022)
14. Lifschitz, V.: Generalizing the syntax of terms in mini-gringo. In: Proceedings of European Conference on Logics in Artificial Intelligence (2025)
15. Lifschitz, V., Lühne, P., Schaub, T.: Verifying strong equivalence of programs in the input language of gringo. In: Proceedings of the 15th International Conference on Logic Programming and Non-monotonic Reasoning (2019)
16. Lifschitz, V., Pearce, D., Valverde, A.: Strongly equivalent logic programs. ACM Trans. Comput. Log. **2**, 526–541 (2001)
17. Lifschitz, V., Pearce, D., Valverde, A.: A characterization of strong equivalence for logic programs with variables. In: Proceedings of International Conference on Logic Programming and Nonmonotonic Reasoning (LPNMR), pp. 188–200 (2007)

Clindocs: A System for Automatic Documentation of ASP Programs

Dominik Gerndt and Susana Hahn(✉)

Potassco Solutions GmbH, Werder, Germany
{dominik.gerndt,susana.hahn}@potassco.com

Abstract. Answer Set Programming (ASP) is widely recognized as a powerful paradigm for knowledge representation and reasoning, yet broadening its adoption beyond the core community remains a challenge. A contributing factor is the historical lack of tooling that developers take for granted in mainstream languages, such as linters, code completion, and documentation generators. This work addresses the documentation gap with *clindocs*, an automated tool that analyzes *clingo* ASP encodings and generates structured, navigable documentation from the source code and lightweight comment annotations. Built as an extension of the popular MkDocs ecosystem, it integrates seamlessly into Markdown-based documentation sites. Its main features include rendered and annotated encoding sections, predicate classification into input and output, dependency graph visualization, and a navigable glossary with per-predicate argument descriptions and file references.

1 Introduction

Answer Set Programming (ASP) [5] has seen growing adoption as its expressiveness and declarative modeling power become increasingly recognized across academic and industrial applications. Yet, reaching beyond the ASP community remains a challenge: developers accustomed to mainstream programming languages expect a mature tooling ecosystem: linting, code completion, testing frameworks, and documentation generators, that ASP has historically lacked [1]. Previous attempts to bridge this gap have proposed integrated development environments such as ASPIDE [3] and SeaLion [2]. These tools, however, focus on providing an integrated environment, driving users away from their preferred editors and workflows, and do not provide a dedicated documentation generator.

ASP encodings tend to be compact and expressive, but as they grow and predicates multiply, keeping track of their purpose, their relationships, and the overall information flow through a program becomes non-trivial even for experienced practitioners. Automatic documentation has been addressed for logic programming before: PlDoc [7] generates predicate documentation for SWI-Prolog from structured comments, but targets only Prolog and produces a standalone web

Research partially funded by DFG grant SCHA 550/15, Germany.

W. Faber et al. (Eds.): LPNMR 2026, LNAI 16952, pp. 485–493, 2027.
https://doi.org/10.1007/978-3-032-38320-4_31

interface rather than integrating into a general-purpose documentation ecosystem. Another attempt to document ASP is the *ASPDoc* system [6], a standalone CLI tool to generate static HTML pages from annotated ASP encodings. To this end, the comment-based annotation language called *LANA (Language for ANnotating Answer-set programs)* [6] is used to define explicit program blocks, atoms, types, conditions, and other elements of the encoding. However, the documentation generated by *ASPDoc*, being a standalone system, is not easily integrated into a larger documentation ecosystem, which may limit its usefulness for projects that require comprehensive documentation beyond ASP encodings. Furthermore, the LANA annotation language, while powerful, is very verbose and requires a significant learning curve, which may discourage users from adopting it for their projects.

In contrast, *clindocs* follows the same spirit while targeting ASP encodings with simpler, more intuitive annotations that lower the adoption barrier and embedding seamlessly into a modern and widely adopted documentation ecosystem. It takes as input an encoding and annotations in the form of comments, producing structured, navigable documentation directly from the source code; following the same *doc-as-code* philosophy that has proven successful in other languages. We target encodings written in *clingo* [4], one of the most widely used ASP systems, and build on a dedicated Tree-sitter grammar that covers the full *clingo* syntax including documentation annotations. The *clindocs* system is built as a handler for the `mkdocstrings` plugin, integrating natively into MkDocs[1] and the mkdocs-material theme[2], which are widely adopted tools that generate modern, searchable documentation sites from Markdown sources. This design choice means that ASP projects can adopt *clindocs* with minimal overhead and combine it freely with hand-written prose, diagrams, and examples in a single documentation site.

The main features of *clindocs* are: rendering annotated encodings with inline Markdown prose; analyzing predicates to classify them as input or output; generating a navigable glossary of predicate documentation from structured block comments; producing a compact summary table of all predicates; and visualizing inter-predicate dependencies as a graph. This paper presents the system and its features through a running Sudoku example, illustrating how *clindocs* can turn a bare ASP encoding into a fully documented, browsable reference.

2 The *clindocs* System

The system is openly available at https://potassco.org/clindocs. It was developed under the Potassco[3] umbrella, which hosts a collection of tools and libraries for ASP development. Below we describe in detail how it integrates with the MkDocs ecosystem and the documentation features it provides.

[1] https://www.mkdocs.org/.
[2] https://squidfunk.github.io/mkdocs-material/.
[3] https://potassco.org.

2.1 MkDocs Integration

MkDocs is a static site generator oriented towards project documentation, producing clean HTML sites from Markdown source files. The mkdocs-material theme extends it with a polished visual design, rich navigation, and a plug-in/extension ecosystem that is widely adopted in open-source projects. *clindocs* is implemented as a *handler* for the `mkdocstrings` plugin[4], which provides a generic mechanism for injecting auto-generated documentation into MkDocs pages. By registering the handler, *clindocs* intercepts directives in Markdown files and replaces them with rendered ASP documentation at build time. Throughout this section we use the Sudoku encoding found in Listing 1 as a running example. To include the documentation of this encoding in a Markdown page, the author adds a directive to any Markdown page using the following syntax:

```
::: sudoku.lp
    handler: asp
    options:
      encodings: true
      glossary: true
      predicate_table: true
      dependency_graph: true
```

The path to the file is resolved relative to the project root. The `handler: asp` key tells *clindocs* to process the file. The `options` block selects and configures which documentation sections are generated. The `options` block supports the following top-level keys, each controlling one generated section: `encodings`, `glossary`, `predicate_table` and `dependency_graph`. Each option is described in detail in the subsections that follow. Apart from the content that is generated from these options, *clindocs* also generates a navigation section (Fig. 1) that can be used to quickly jump to the different sections of the documentation, including the list of available predicates.

```
%# Sudoku Puzzle
% Uses the well known [puzzle](https://en.wikipedia.org/Sudoku)

#include "doc.lp".

#const dim = 3.
val(1..dim*dim).
pos(X,Y) :- val(X), val(Y).

%% Internal comment
subgrid(X,Y,(((X-1)/dim)*dim+((Y-1)/dim))) :- pos(X,Y).

% A choice rule for each cell
1 { sudoku(X,Y,V) : val(V) } 1 :- pos(X,Y).

%## Constraints
:- sudoku(X,Y,V), sudoku(X',Y,V), X != X'.
```

[4] https://mkdocstrings.github.io/.

```
:- sudoku(X,Y,V), sudoku(X,Y',V), Y != Y'.
:- sudoku(X,Y,V), sudoku(X',Y',V),
   subgrid(X,Y,S), subgrid(X',Y',S), (X,Y)!=(X',Y').

sudoku(X,Y,V) :- initial(X,Y,V).

%## Shows
#show .
#show sudoku/3.
```

Listing 1. Sudoku encoding with Markdown comments (`sudoku.lp`).

Fig. 1. Navigation menu generated for the Sudoku encoding.

2.2 Encoding Rendering

The `encodings` option instructs *clindocs* to render the ASP source file as a readable, annotated document. Inline comments written in Markdown are extracted and typeset as prose, while clingo rules and facts are preserved as formatted code blocks. This allows authors to write literate-style documentation directly inside the encoding. Single-% comments are rendered as Markdown prose, while those starting with %% are treated as non-documentation comments and ignored in the output. Two sub-options extend the section header for each file: `source: true` appends the full, unmodified source as a collapsible code block, giving readers direct access to the raw encoding; `git_link: true` adds a hyperlink to the file in the configured repository, useful for open-source projects that want to point readers to the canonical version-controlled source. For the sudoku example in Listing 1, the rendered documentation is shown in Fig. 2. The first comment is rendered in Markdown, as a header followed by the text with the link to the Wikipedia page. The comment starting with %% is ignored and not present in Fig. 2.

2.3 Predicate Analysis and Documentation

At build time, *clindocs* parses the files (including transitively included files via `#include`) and performs a lightweight static analysis of the predicate landscape.

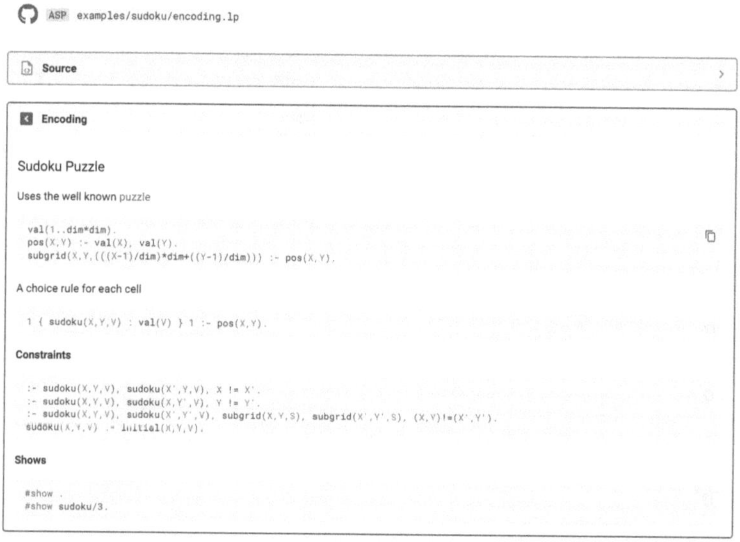

Fig. 2. Rendered encoding section for the Sudoku example.

Under the hood, this parsing is powered by *tree-sitter-clingo*[5], a robust Tree-sitter grammar that covers the entire *clingo* language, including dedicated support for the documentation strings presented in this paper. For each predicate symbol it determines: the files in which it appears, the rules in which it occurs, and its *type*: an *input* predicate is one that appears in rule bodies or as a conditional but is not defined by any rule head in the encoding; an *output* predicate is one that appears in an explicit `#show` directive. These types drive the visual styling used across all generated sections.

Authors can supply human-readable documentation for any predicate by placing a block comment with the special opening delimiter `%*!` anywhere in the included files. Because this syntax is natively supported by the underlying Tree-sitter grammar, it acts as a standardized documentation format, which will integrate smoothly with upcoming ecosystem tools like *clinsight*, a language server for ASP providing real-time editor support such as hover information, go-to-definition, and code completion. This shared foundation means the same predicate documentation will power both the generated website for the documentation and the editor experience, without any additional effort from the developer.

The comments for predicate documentation may appear in the same file as the rules or in a separate `.lp` file included via `#include`, allowing documentation to be maintained independently of the encoding logic. For our running example, the predicate docstrings are placed in `doc.lp` (Listing 2), which is referenced in Listing 1. The full content of the documentation block is ren-

[5] https://potassco.org/tree-sitter.

dered as Markdown, so authors may use any mkdocs-material feature (admonitions, tables, math, etc.). Additionally, special syntax is supported for argument documentation: starting with `Args:` followed by a Markdown list of `name: description` entries which is rendered as a table in the output.

```
%*! sudoku(X,Y,V)
Describes a sudoku board. The value of cell (X,Y) is V.

Args:
      - X: the row of the cell
      - Y: the column of the cell
      - V: the value of the cell
*%
%*! initial(X,Y,V)
Describes initial values of the sudoku board.
The value of cell (X,Y) is V.

Args:
      - X: the row of the cell
      - Y: the column of the cell
      - V: the value of the cell
*%
%*! pos(X,Y)
Describes a cell (X,Y) in the sudoku board.

Args:
      - X: the row of the cell
      - Y: the column of the cell
*%
%*! val(V)
Describes a possible value V for a cell.

Args:
      - V: the value
*%
```

Listing 2. Sudoku predicate documentation (`doc.lp`).

2.4 Dependency Graph

The `dependency_graph` option generates a graph showing how predicates depend on one another across the included encodings. An edge is drawn from predicates in the body of a rule to those in the head, if the predicate appears negated in the body the edge is shown in a dotted style. For our example, the graph generated for the Sudoku encoding is shown in Fig. 3. Input predicates are rendered in purple and shown (output) predicates in green, giving an immediate visual overview of the information flow through the encoding.

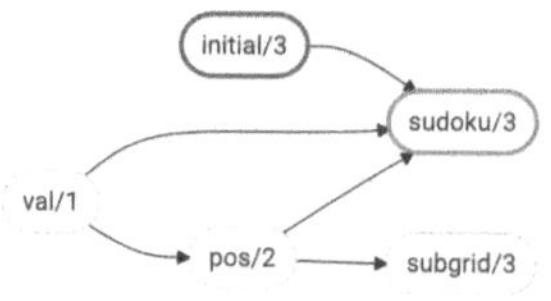

Fig. 3. Dependency graph generated for the Sudoku encoding.

2.5 Predicate Glossary

The `glossary` option generates a reference section, with one entry per predicate. Each entry renders the predicate's docstring as formatted Markdown and lists the files in which the predicate is used. Every predicate also receives a navigation entry in the page's table of contents, making large encodings easy to browse. The section supports two sub-options: `include_references` controls whether the per-file usage list is shown; `include_navigation` controls whether TOC entries are generated. Predicates without docstrings can be excluded globally via the `include_undocumented` flag. Figure 4 shows the glossary section generated for predicate `initial/3` from the comment docstring in Listing 2. The section provides the summary of the predicate, a table with the arguments and their description, and a list of the rules in which the predicate appears.

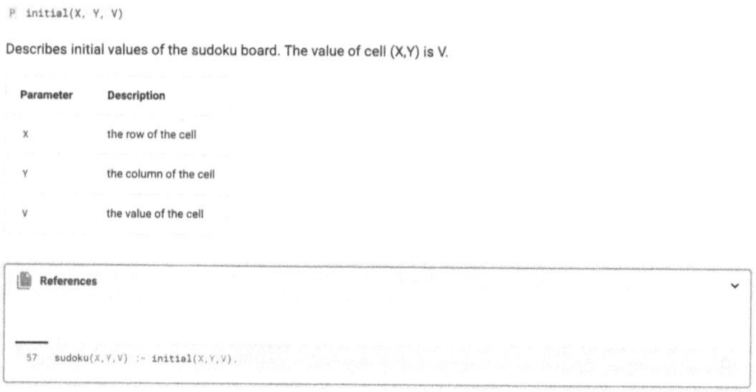

Fig. 4. Glossary section showing predicate `initial/3` with usage references.

2.6 Predicate Summary Table

The `predicate_table` option generates a compact summary table listing all predicates in the included encodings together with a short description extracted from the docstring and a type indicator. It provides readers with a quick overview before they dive into the full glossary or the encoding text. The type column uses four symbols: *Input* (indicated by a purple arrow) for predicates not defined by any rule head; *Shown explicitly* (indicated by a green eye icon) for predicates appearing in a `#show predicate/arity` directive; *Shown partially* (indicated by a green eye icon with a plus) for predicates shown via a conditional `#show` statement; and *Hidden* (indicated by an opaque crossed out eye icon) for predicates that are defined but not shown. Figure 5 shows the predicate summary table generated for the Sudoku encoding. The `initial/3` predicate is classified as an input predicate since it does not appear in any rule head, while `sudoku/3` is the only one shown explicitly, classifying it into an output predicate.

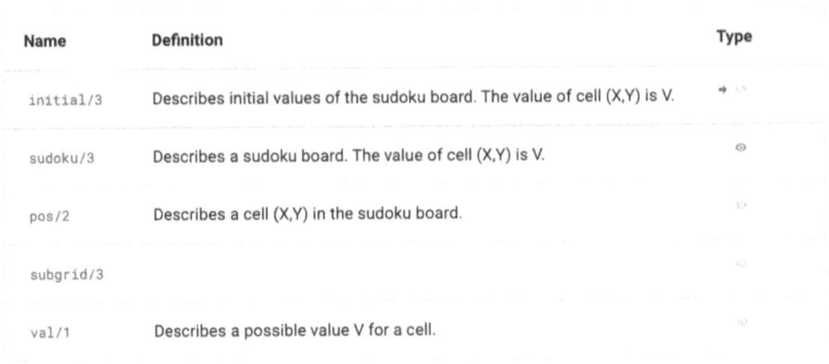

Name	Definition	Type
initial/3	Describes initial values of the sudoku board. The value of cell (X,Y) is V.	
sudoku/3	Describes a sudoku board. The value of cell (X,Y) is V.	
pos/2	Describes a cell (X,Y) in the sudoku board.	
subgrid/3		
val/1	Describes a possible value V for a cell.	

Fig. 5. Predicate summary table for the Sudoku encoding.

3 Conclusion

The quest to extend ASP with tools that simplify development is an ongoing one. With *clindocs* we have taken a step towards a more integrated ecosystem for ASP, providing a tool that automatically generates structured documentation from annotated encodings. We hope this system and its shared foundation with upcoming tools encourage the community to document and maintain their encodings. In the future, we plan to investigate an LLM-assisted documentation workflow where the system suggests documentation content based on the encoding structure, as well as tighter integration with linting and other tools to further close the gap with mainstream language ecosystems.

References

1. Brewka, G., Eiter, T., Truszczyński, M.: Answer set programming at a glance. Commun. ACM **54**(12), 92–103 (2011). https://doi.org/10.1145/2043174.2043195
2. Busoniu, P., Oetsch, J., Pührer, J., Skočovský, P., Tompits, H.: Sealion: an eclipse-based ide for answer-set programming with advanced debugging support. Theory Pract. Logic Program. **13**(4–5), 657–673 (2013)
3. Febbraro, O., Reale, K., Ricca, F.: ASPIDE: integrated development environment for answer set programming. In: Delgrande, J.P., Faber, W. (eds.) LPNMR 2011. LNCS (LNAI), vol. 6645, pp. 317–330. Springer, Heidelberg (2011). https://doi.org/10.1007/978-3-642-20895-9_37

4. Gebser, M., et al.: Potassco User Guide. University of Potsdam, 2 edn. (2015). http://potassco.org
5. Lifschitz, V.: Answer Set Programming. Springer, Cham (2019). https://doi.org/10.1007/978-3-030-24658-7
6. Vos, M.D., Kisa, D.G., Oetsch, J., Pührer, J., Tompits, H.: LANA: a language for annotating answer-set programs. In: Proceedings of the 14th International Workshop on Non-Monotonic Reasoning (NMR 2012), Rome, Italy (2012)
7. Wielemaker, J., Anjewierden, A.: Pldoc: Wiki style literate programming for prolog, arXiv preprint arXiv:0711.0618 (2007)

Model-Theoretic Characterization of Programs Under Specific Inputs

Zeynep G. Saribatur(✉), Kaan Unalan, and Stefan Woltran

Institute of Logic and Computation, TU Wien, Vienna, Austria
{zeynep.saribatur,kaan.unalan,stefan.woltran}@tuwien.ac.at

Abstract. The notion of uniform equivalence is a powerful tool for determining if two answer set programs behave identically when provided with different inputs. However, in practice, where developers are often only interested in specific problem instances, this equivalence notion might be too strict. While it is possible to use existing equivalence checkers by adding program functionality to prune non-admissible inputs, there is a lack of direct model-theoretic characterization for how programs behave under such restricted input sets. In this paper, we generalize uniform equivalence to χ-*equivalence*, where χ represents a specific set of potential input facts. We introduce χ-*models*, a novel model-theoretic characterization that tracks SE-interpretations relevant to the restricted input set. We show that deciding χ-equivalence between two programs amounts to checking whether their χ-models coincide. This approach provides a beneficial access to the semantics of the programs at hand: the number of χ-models can be significantly smaller than the total number of answer sets computed across all specific sets of facts, as we shall illustrate on some example scenarios. Finally, we also provide a first complexity analysis for the problem of deciding χ-equivalence.

Keywords: answer set programming · uniform equivalence · specific inputs

1 Introduction

Problem solving via the ASP paradigm is done by representing the problem specification, i.e., the logic of the problem, and providing the problem instance, i.e., the data, to obtain the solution to the problem. When one wants to compare the behavior of two programs under specific inputs, to check whether they provide the same answer sets, the notion of uniform equivalence [1] comes in handy. This equivalence notion decides whether the answer sets of two programs coincide under addition of any set of facts. However, in practice, it is often not necessary to guarantee equivalent outcomes for all possible inputs. Consider, for instance an encoding for a graph problem, where we expect the inputs to be facts over vertices and edges. In this case, relativized uniform equivalence [2] provides means to restrict the input to predicates representing the graph. If, in

W. Faber et al. (Eds.): LPNMR 2026, LNAI 16952, pp. 494–502, 2027.
https://doi.org/10.1007/978-3-032-38320-4_32

addition, we expect only bipartite graphs as inputs, a simple restriction of the alphabet of the facts does not help. For such scenarios, one needs to consider additional functionality in the programs that prunes out from all sets of facts those that are of interest to the problem, see e.g. [8]. This problem of verifying program behavior over specified, restricted input contexts is closely related to recent efforts in verifying refactoring in ASP, by checking a so-called external equivalence [4] which is being deployed in ASP verification tools like ANTHEM [3]. Although it is thus possible to use existing equivalence checkers [6] or verification frameworks to compare programs with respect to such restricted inputs, an alternative model-based approach would not only allow for a formally more elegant way to tackle this problem, but also might be beneficial in practice. Furthermore, having a semantic handle on a program's characteristics for a set of inputs might allow for simplification techniques to prune out parts of the program that are irrelevant for reasoning over the given inputs.

In this paper, we investigate such a model-theoretic characterization for deciding whether programs are equivalent under a set χ of inputs, generalizing concepts as (relativized) UE-models [2]. This allows to understand the semantics of the underlying behavior of program when a certain set of inputs is considered. As a toy example consider the program

$$e \leftarrow a. \qquad c \leftarrow a. \qquad g \leftarrow a. \qquad f \vee a \leftarrow e. \qquad f \vee a \leftarrow g.$$

Now let $\chi = \{\{a\}, \{e\}, \{g\}\}$ be the set of inputs that are of interest. Then the corresponding answer sets would be $\{\{aceg\}\}, \{\{aceg\}, \{ef\}\}, \{\{aceg\}, \{fg\}\}$ respectively. Observe that here $\{aecg\}$ always occurs as an answer set no matter which of the facts are added, while when adding e or f there is a difference in the second answer set. In this paper we shall define a notion of χ-models that keep track of the SE-interpretations that are of interest. In this case χ-models (as we will see later) would be $\langle ace.g., ace.g.\rangle, \langle ef, ef\rangle, \langle fg, fg\rangle$. One can see that the number of χ-models is less than the overall number of answer sets when one computes the answer sets for each specific set of facts. This might prove beneficial to decide such an equivalence-test in practice.

The main contributions of this paper are as follows: (i) We show that checking equivalence of two programs under a given collection of sets of facts, which we refer to as χ-equivalence, amounts to checking the equivalence of their χ-models. (ii) We provide a first complexity analysis for the problem of deciding χ-equivalence between two programs. (iii) We illustrate, that while a naive check of χ-equivalence would require an exhaustive enumeration of answer sets for every possible input in χ, our model-theoretic characterization allows for a much more compact representation of the programs' underlying behavior.

2 Background

We use the traditional representation of a rule r as the form

$$A_1 \vee \cdots \vee A_l \leftarrow A_{l+1}, \ldots, A_m, not\ A_{m+1}, \ldots, not\ A_n,$$

where A_i ($1 \leq i \leq n$, $0 \leq l \leq m \leq n$) are atoms from a first-order language, and *not* is default negation. We also write r as $H(r) \leftarrow B(r)$ or $H(r) \leftarrow B^+(r)$, *not* $B^-(r)$. We call $H(r) = \{A_1, \ldots, A_l\}$ the *head* of r, $B^+(r) = \{A_{l+1}, \ldots, A_m\}$ the *positive body* of r and $B^-(r) = \{A_{m+1}, \ldots, A_n\}$ the *negative body* of r. If $H(r) = \emptyset$, then r is a *constraint*. r is a (non-disjunctive) *fact* if $B(r) = \emptyset$ and $|H(r)| = 1$; for $H(r) = \emptyset$, we occasionally write $\bot$. A rule r is *normal*, if $|H(r)| \leq 1$, and *positive* if $B^-(r) = \emptyset$. A *disjunctive logic program* (DLP) is a finite set of rules. Here, we focus on propositional programs over a set of atoms from the universe $\mathcal{A}$. Programs with variables reduce to their ground versions. Unless stated otherwise the term *program* refers to a (propositional) DLP.

Let $I \subseteq \mathcal{A}$ be an intepretation. The *GL-reduct* of a program P w.r.t. I is given by $P^I = \{H(r) \leftarrow B^+(r) \mid r \in P, B^-(r) \cap I = \emptyset\}$. An interpretation I is a *model* of a program P (in symbols $I \models P$) if, for each $r \in P$, $(H(r) \cup B^-(r)) \cap I \neq \emptyset$ or $B^+(r) \not\subseteq I$; I is an *answer set*, if it is a minimal model of P^I. We denote the set of all answer sets by $AS(P)$. Two programs P_1, P_2 are *equivalent* if $AS(P_1) = AS(P_2)$, *strongly equivalent (SE)*, denoted by $P_1 \equiv P_2$, if $AS(P_1 \cup R) = AS(P_2 \cup R)$ for every R over $\mathcal{A}$, and *uniformly equivalent (UE)*, denoted by $P_1 \equiv_u P_2$ if $AS(P_1 \cup R) = AS(P_2 \cup R)$ for any set of facts R over $\mathcal{A}$.

An *SE-interpretation* is a pair $\langle X, Y \rangle$ such that $X \subseteq Y \subseteq \mathcal{A}$; it is *total* if $X = Y$ and *non-total* otherwise. An SE-interpretation $\langle X, Y \rangle$ is an *SE-model* of a program P if $Y \models P$ and $X \models P^Y$. An SE-model $\langle X, Y \rangle$ of P is called *UE-model* of P if $X = Y$ or there is no SE-model $\langle X', Y \rangle$ with $X \subset X' \subset Y$. Note that a set Y of atoms is an answer set of P if $\langle Y, Y \rangle \in SE(P)$ and no non-total $\langle X, Y \rangle \in SE(P)$ exists. Two programs P_1 and P_2 are strongly equivalent iff $SE(P_1) = SE(P_2)$ [10]; they are uniformly equivalent iff $UE(P_1) = UE(P_2)$ [1].

Relativized notions of strong/uniform equivalence consider a relaxation on the vocabulary of the added programs [2,11]. Formally, two programs P_1 and P_2 are *strongly equivalent relative to* B, denoted $P_1 \equiv^B P_2$ iff $AS(P_1 \cup R) = AS(P_2 \cup R)$ for all programs R over $B \subseteq \mathcal{A}$, and *uniformly equivalent relative to* B, denoted $P_1 \equiv^B_u P_2$, when R is restricted to set of facts over B. These naturally cover strong and uniform equivalence for $B = \mathcal{A}$. Its semantical characterization requires a generalization of SE-models as follows.

Definition 1 ([2]). *A pair of interpretations $\langle X, Y \rangle$ is a (relativized) B-SE-interpretation iff either $X = Y$ or $X \subset (Y \cap B)$. The former are called total and the latter non-total B-SE-interpretations. Moreover, a B-SE-interpretation $\langle X, Y \rangle$ is a (relativized) B-SE-model of a program P iff:*

(i) $Y \models P$;
(ii) for all $Y' \subset Y$ *with* $(Y' \cap B) = (Y \cap B)$, $Y' \not\models P^Y$; *and*
(iii) $X \subset Y$ *implies existence of a* $X' \subseteq Y$ *with* $X' \cap B = X$, *s.t.* $X' \models P^Y$ *holds.*

The set of B-SE-models of P is given by $SE^B(P)$. Programs P_1 and P_2 are strongly equivalent relative to B iff $SE^B(P_1) = SE^B(P_2)$.

Similar to relativized B-SE models, relativized B-UE-models allow to consider equivalence under the addition of facts chosen from a set B.

Definition 2 ([2]). *Let B be a set of atoms and P be a program. A pair $\langle X, Y\rangle$ is a (relativized) B-UE-model of P iff it is a B-SE-model of P and, for every B-SE-model $\langle X', Y\rangle$ of P, $X \subset X'$ implies $X' = Y$.*

The set of B-UE-models of P is given by $UE^B(P)$. Programs P_1 and P_2 are uniformly equivalent relative to B iff $UE^B(P_1) = UE^B(P_2)$.

3 Equivalence Under Specific Sets of Facts

In many practical scenarios, one is not interested in the equivalence of programs under any possible context, but rather under a specific set of relevant inputs. While relativized uniform equivalence allows for restricting the alphabet of the input facts, it does not allow for restricting the structure of the input sets themselves. In this section, we introduce the notion of χ-equivalence, where the context is restricted to a specific sets of facts χ.

We begin by formally defining χ-equivalence, which generalizes uniform equivalence by restricting the additions of facts with a predefined set χ.

Definition 3. *Given two programs P, Q over $\mathcal{A}$, a collection $\chi \subseteq 2^{\mathcal{A}}$ of set of facts, we call P and Q to be χ-equivalent if for all $X \in \chi$, $AS(P \cup X) = AS(Q \cup X)$.*

Example 1. *For $\chi = \{\{a\}, \{b\}\}$, the program $P = \{c \leftarrow b; c \leftarrow a\}$ is χ-equivalent to $Q = \{c\}$.*

The challenge lies in characterizing this equivalence without the need to iterate through every $X \in \chi$ and compute the corresponding answer sets. To this end, we propose the notion of χ-models, to filter out information irrelevant to the extensions from χ.

Definition 4. *An SE-interpretation $\langle X, Y\rangle$ is called χ-model of program P if*

(i) $Y \models P$;
(ii) there exists $X^* \in \chi$ with $X^* \subseteq Y$ such that for each X' with $X^* \subseteq X' \subset Y$, $X' \not\models P^Y$;
(iii) if $X \subset Y$, then $X \in \chi$ and
  (1) there exists X' with $X \subseteq X' \subset Y$ such that $X' \models P^Y$; and
  (2) for each such X' (with $X \subseteq X' \subset Y$ such that $X' \models P^Y$), it holds that for all X'' with $X \subset X'' \subseteq X'$, $X'' \notin \chi$.

We denote the set of all χ-models of a program P with $UE_\chi(P)$.

The conditions in Definition 4 serve to refine the space of SE-models w.r.t. χ. Condition (ii) ensures that an interpretation Y is supported as a potential answer set by at least one input $X^* \in \chi$. Meanwhile, condition (iii) handles the non-total models, identifying the maximal sub-interpretations that characterize the stability of the program under the restricted set of facts.

Below we illustrate how χ-models retain only the information necessary to determine answer sets for the specific inputs we care about.

Example 2 (Examble 1 ctd). *The SE-models of P are*

$$\langle\emptyset,\emptyset\rangle, \langle\emptyset,c\rangle, \langle c,c\rangle$$
$$\langle\emptyset,ac\rangle, \langle c,ac\rangle, \langle ac,ac\rangle, \langle\emptyset,bc\rangle, \langle c,bc\rangle, \langle bc,bc\rangle$$
$$\langle\emptyset,abc\rangle, \langle c,abc\rangle, \langle ac,abc\rangle, \langle bc,abc\rangle, \langle abc,abc\rangle$$

For $\chi = \{\{a\},\{b\}\}$, *the conditions of Definition 4 filter the SE-models of P to obtain the* χ*-models as* $\{\langle bc,bc\rangle, \langle ac,ac\rangle\}$.

Let us look at the SE-model $\langle abc,abc\rangle$. *Both of* $X_1^* = \{a\}$ *and* $X_2^* = \{b\}$ *from* χ *are subsets of* $\{a,b,c\}$. *However, the reduct* $P^{\{a,b,c\}}$ *is satisfied by* $X_1' = \{a,c\}$ *and by* $X_2' = \{b,c\}$, *where* $X_i^* \subseteq X_i' \subset \{a,b,c\}$. *As for the SE-model* $\langle c,c\rangle$, *no* $X^* \in \chi$ *exists with* $X^* \subseteq \{c\}$. *Thus condition (ii) fails for both of them.*

Now consider the SE-model $\langle ac,ac\rangle$. *Choosing* $X_1^* = \{a\}$ *satisfies condition (ii) as* $\{a\}$ *is the only interpretation between* X_1^* *and* $\{a,c\}$ *and does not model the reduct* $P^{\{a,c\}}$. *Thus, it is a valid total* χ*-model. Similar holds for* $\langle bc,bc\rangle$.

All non-total SE-models are eliminated by condition (iii), e.g., $\langle\emptyset,ac\rangle$ *is not a* χ*-model because* $X = \emptyset \notin \chi$. *For interpretations where* $X \in \chi$, *such as* $\langle a,ac\rangle$, *since no* X' *with* $\{a\} \subseteq X' \subset \{a,c\}$ *models* $P^{\{a,c\}}$, *condition (iii.1) is violated.*

Observe that, by appropriately defining the set χ, both uniform equivalence and relativized uniform equivalence become special cases.

Proposition 1. *Let P be a program and* $B \subseteq \mathcal{A}$.

(i) If $\chi = 2^{\mathcal{A}}$, *then* $UE_\chi(P) = UE(P)$.
(ii) If $\chi = 2^B$, *then* $UE_\chi(P) = UE^B(P)$.

Proof. (i) ($\subseteq$) $\langle X,Y\rangle \in UE_\chi(P)$. For $X = Y$ it is trivial. Assume $X \subset Y$. Then by item (2) of condition (iii) we get that there is no X' with some X'' such that $X \subset X'' \subseteq X'$, since $X'' \notin \chi$ cannot hold. Thus X is the maximal with $X \models P^Y$, which means $\langle X,Y\rangle \in UE(P)$.

($\supseteq$) $\langle X,Y\rangle \in UE(P)$. For $X = Y$ it is trivial, since one can set for condition (ii) $X^* = Y$. For $X \subset Y$, this X is the maximal, one picks $X' = X$ and the rest of the condition is satisfied.

(ii)($\subseteq$) $\langle X,Y\rangle \in UE_\chi(P)$. For $X = Y$, if $Y \subseteq B$ condition (ii) of Definition 1 is trivial. Otherwise from condition (ii) of Definition (4), $X^* \subseteq Y \cap B$ would hold for it to be in χ. This then satisfies condition (ii) of Definition 1. Assume $X \subset Y$. Then since $X \in \chi$ we have $X \subset Y \cap B$. Then by item (2) of condition (iii) we get that there is no X' with some X'' such that $X \subset X'' \subseteq X'$, since $X'' \notin \chi$ cannot hold. Thus X is the maximal with $X \models P^Y$, which means $\langle X,Y\rangle \in UE^B(P)$.

($\supseteq$) $\langle X,Y\rangle \in UE^B(P)$. For $X = Y$, if $Y \subseteq B$ it is trivial. Otherwise condition (ii) of Definition 1 satisfies condition (ii) of Definition (4). For $X \subset Y$, this X is the maximal, one picks $X' = X$ and the rest of the condition is satisfied.

We also see that when χ is restricted to the empty set, by Proposition 1(ii), the notion of χ-models collapses to the standard definition of an answer set.

Corollary 2. *Let P be a program and $\chi = \{\emptyset\}$. $\langle Y, Y\rangle \in UE_\chi(P)$ iff $Y \in AS(P)$.*

We now arrive at our main result, which shows that the notion of χ-equivalence can be characterized by the coincidence of χ-models.

Theorem 3. *P, Q are χ-equivalent iff χ-models of P and Q coincide.*

Proof. ($\Rightarrow$) Wlog assume $\langle X, Y\rangle$ is χ-model of P but not of Q.

Case $X = Y$. From (i)+(ii), we know that for some $X^* \in \chi$ we have $Y \in AS(P \cup X^*)$. Now if $Y \not\models Q$, we immediately reach a contradiction to P, Q being χ-equivalent. Otherwise we have from (ii) that for X^* there is some X' $X^* \subseteq X' \subset Y$, such that $X' \models Q^Y$. Thus, $Y \notin AS(Q \cup X^*)$ which contradicts P, Q being χ-equivalent.

Case $X \subset Y$. We can assume $\langle Y, Y\rangle$ is χ-model of Q - otherwise the previous case applies. By (iii.1) $Y \notin AS(P \cup X)$. If (iii.1) is violated for Q, i.e. for all X' with $X \subseteq X' \subset Y$, $X \not\models Q^Y$, we have $Y \in AS(Q \cup X)$. Hence, suppose (iii.2) is violated for Q, i.e. there exists X' with $X \subseteq X' \subset Y$ such that $X' \models Q^Y$ and an $X'' \in \chi$ with $X \subset X'' \subseteq X'$. It follows that for any $X''' \subset Y$ with $X \subseteq X'''$ and $X'' \nsubseteq X'''$, it holds that $X''' \not\models P^Y$ (otherwise, $\langle X, Y\rangle$ cannot be χ-model of P due to (iii.2) for P). We observe that $Y \notin AS(Q \cup X'')$ but $Y \in AS(P \cup X'')$.

Therefore, no such Z can model P^Y, which implies $Y \in AS(P \cup X'')$. Since $X' \models Q^Y$ and $X'' \subseteq X' \subset Y$, we simultaneously have $Y \notin AS(Q \cup X'')$, contradicting the assumption that P and Q are χ-equivalent.

($\Leftarrow$) Wlog suppose existence of Z, Y such $Y \in AS(P \cup Z)$ and $Y \notin AS(Q \cup Z)$.

We first show that $\langle Y, Y\rangle$ is a χ-model of P. Clearly, (i) $Y \models P$ holds, and for (ii) we observe that $Z \in \chi$, $Z \subseteq Y$, and for each X' with $Z \subseteq X' \subset Y$, $X' \not\models P^Y$ needs to hold.

In case $\langle Y, Y\rangle$ is not a χ-model of Q, we immediately reach a contradiction. Therefore, suppose $\langle Y, Y\rangle$ is a χ-model of Q. Hence, in order to have $Y \notin AS(Q \cup Z)$ there needs to be some X with $Z \subseteq X \subset Y$ and $X \models Q^Y$. We now construct a non-total χ-model $\langle Z', Y\rangle$ of Q by choosing Z' to be a maximal element (with respect to subset inclusion) in the set $\mathcal{C} = \{W \in \chi \mid Z \subseteq W \subseteq X \text{ and } \exists X' \text{ s.t. } W \subseteq X' \subseteq X, X' \models Q^Y\}$. Note that $\mathcal{C}$ is non-empty because $Z \in \chi$ and $Z \subseteq X$. Choosing Z' as a maximal element of $\mathcal{C}$ ensures that $Z' \in \chi$, and thus $\langle Z', Y\rangle$ is a valid χ-model of Q. On the other hand, no such $\langle Z', Y\rangle$ can be χ-model of P since otherwise there would be some X' with $Z \subseteq X' \subseteq Y$ with $X' \models P^Y$, thus violating $Y \in AS(P \cup Z)$.

4 Computational Complexity

We consider here a first result for deciding χ-equivalence, where we include χ as part of the instance.

Theorem 4. *Given two programs P, Q over $\mathcal{A}$, a collection $\chi \subseteq 2^{\mathcal{A}}$ of set of facts, deciding whether P and Q are χ-equivalent is Π_2^P-complete.*

Proof. Hardness follows from known results on special cases of χ-equivalence [2], such as uniform equivalence.

To establish membership, we first show that the problem of χ-model checking is in Δ_2^P. Given a program P, interpretations X, Y, and χ, to decide $\langle X, Y \rangle \in UE_\chi(P)$ we take care of the respective conditions in Definition 4 as follows: checking (i) is in P; checking (iii.1) is in **NP**. For (ii) and (iii.2) we make use of the fact that χ is part of the input (and thus looping over all $X \in \chi$ can be done in polynomial time with respect to the instance size) and reformulate the complementary problems. To decide (ii), loop over all $X^* \in \chi$ with $X^* \subset Y$, guess X' with $X^* \subseteq X' \subset Y$ and check $X' \models P^Y$; this yields a Δ_2^P algorithm. To decide (iii.2), guess X' with $X \subseteq X' \subset Y$, check $X' \models P^Y$ and look-up $X'' \in \chi$ with $X \subset X'' \subseteq X'$; this gives an **NP**-algorithm.

Given that χ-model checking is in Δ_2^P, it is rather straight-forward to establish Π_2^P-membership: guess $\langle X, Y \rangle$ and check that is contained in either $UE_\chi(P)$ or $UE_\chi(Q)$ but not in both.

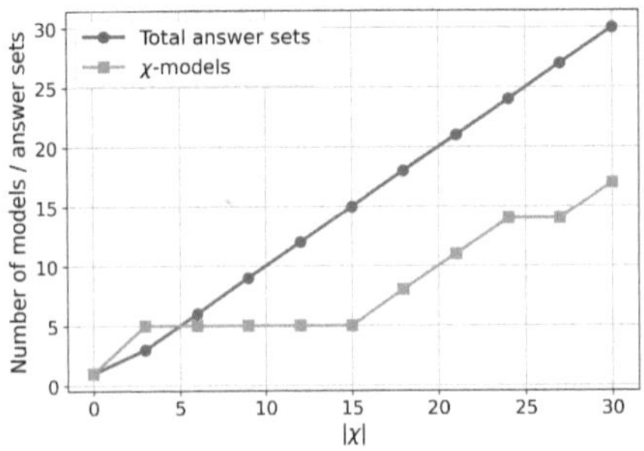

(a) Threshold-style activation

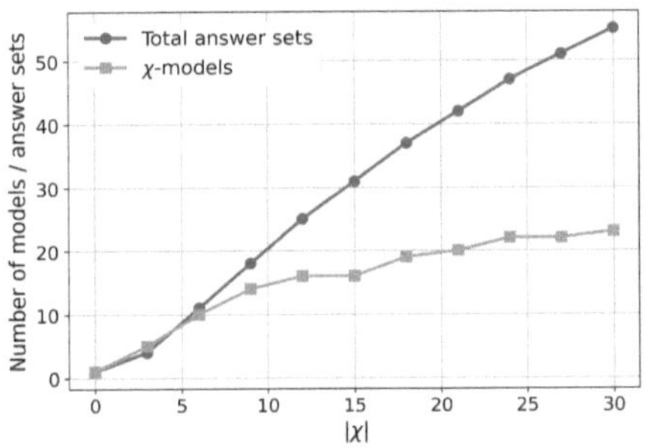

(b) Disjunctive propagation

Fig. 1. Comparison of total answer sets vs. χ-models as $|\chi|$ scales.

Thus, in this setting the complexity of χ-equivalence does not increase compared to (relativized) uniform equivalence. However, one could argue that providing χ (which might be exponentially larger than the two programs under comparisons) as input hides aspects of complexity here. For an alternative view, we move χ to the problem definition, i.e. considering different decision problems for different χ. Such an approach would require to make some assumptions, for instance that deciding whether a given set F of facts is contained in χ is feasible in polynomial time. We conjecture that viewing the problems in that way leads to a higher complexity for checking χ-equivalence resulting in Π_3^P-completeness.

5 Comparative Analysis

In this section, we analyze the representational efficiency of χ-models compared to exhaustive answer set enumeration. We demonstrate that χ-models provide a significantly more compact summary of program behavior by collapsing redundant information that standard equivalence notions would otherwise retain.

We implemented a prototype in *Python* that, given a program P and a set $\chi \subseteq 2^{\mathcal{A}}$ of fact sets, computes χ-models by filtering SE-models obtained from an external tool. For comparison, as a naive baseline, for every $X \in \chi$, we enumerated all answer sets of $P \cup X$ using `clingo`, and summed the total number.

Our evaluation focuses on two types of programs that exhibit recurring semantic behavior across many admissible inputs. One program models a pattern where many different possible fact sets exist, and once the threshold condition is satisfied, they all collapse to a single output, similar to the program $\{d \leftarrow a, b.\ ;\ d \leftarrow a, c.\ ;\ d \leftarrow b, c.\ ;\ c \leftarrow d.\ ;\ b \leftarrow d.\ ;\ a \leftarrow d.\}$. The second program is an alteration of the motivating example from Sect. 1, where every trigger activates a propagation chain at different stages while simultaneously introducing an alternative disjunctive choice. Here, different inputs generate overlapping answer sets that share large common fragments.

As shown in Figs. 1a and 1b, as the size of χ increases, the number of χ-models grows considerably slower than the total number of answer sets. Since exhaustive enumeration evaluates each input independently, its model count scales rapidly with $|\chi|$, whereas χ-models successfully filter out semantic redundancy and remain manageable even as the input space χ grows. This compact representation suggests that verifying χ-equivalence by comparing χ-models could yield significant computational advantages over checking every $X \in \chi$ individually.

6 Conclusion and Outlook

In this paper, we introduced a generalization of uniform equivalence that restricts the context of program comparison to a specific collection of sets of facts χ. By providing a model-theoretic characterization via χ-models, we showed that it is possible to capture the behavior of programs under restricted inputs in a succinct representation without resorting to exhaustive answer set enumeration. We also gave some first complexity results.

Our current investigation opens several avenues for future research. A natural next step is a performance comparison of an χ-equivalence checker with existing tools such as `lpeq` [6] and ANTHEM. For this, χ-equivalence checking would need to be reduced to ASP, using the saturation technique to compute the χ-models. Another direction is to generalize the notion of uniform abstraction [9], a uniform equivalence-like property over an abstract program Q obtained from a program P by clustering the vocabulary with a mapping m, i.e., $m(AS(P \cup F)) = AS(Q \cup m(F))$ for all $F \subseteq \mathcal{A}$. Bringing χ-equivalence to this setting will allow us to capture abstractions that can provide (abstract) answer sets which can be instantiated to any instance in χ, in the spirit of generalized planning [5,7].

Acknowledgments. This research was funded in whole or in part by the Austrian Science Fund (FWF) grants 10.55776/COE12 and 10.55776/T1315, and the Vienna Science and Technology Fund (WWTF) grant 10.47379/ICT25044.

Disclosure of Interests. The authors have no competing interests to declare that are relevant to the content of this article.

References

1. Eiter, T., Fink, M.: Uniform equivalence of logic programs under the stable model semantics. In: Palamidessi, C. (ed.) ICLP 2003. LNCS, vol. 2916, pp. 224–238. Springer, Heidelberg (2003). https://doi.org/10.1007/978-3-540-24599-5_16
2. Eiter, T., Fink, M., Woltran, S.: Semantical characterizations and complexity of equivalences in answer set programming. ACM TOCL **8**(3), 17 (2007)
3. Fandinno, J., et al.: Anthem 2.0: automated reasoning for answer set programming. Theory Pract. Logic Program. **25**(4), 668–684 (2025)
4. Fandinno, J., Hansen, Z., Lierler, Y., Lifschitz, V., Temple, N.: External behavior of a logic program and verification of refactoring. Theory Pract. Logic Program. **23**(4), 933–947 (2023)
5. Illanes, L., McIlraith, S.A.: Generalized planning via abstraction: arbitrary numbers of objects. In: Proceedings of AAAI, vol. 33, pp. 7610–7618 (2019)
6. Janhunen, T., Oikarinen, E.: LPEQ and DLPEQ — translators for automated equivalence testing of logic programs. In: Lifschitz, V., Niemelä, I. (eds.) LPNMR 2004. LNCS (LNAI), vol. 2923, pp. 336–340. Springer, Heidelberg (2003). https://doi.org/10.1007/978-3-540-24609-1_30
7. Jiménez, S., Segovia-Aguas, J., Jonsson, A.: A review of generalized planning. Knowl. Eng. Rev. **34**, e5 (2019)
8. Oetsch, J., Seidl, M., Tompits, H., Woltran, S.: Beyond uniform equivalence between answer-set programs. ACM TOCL **22**(1), 2:1–2:46 (2021)
9. Saribatur, Z.G., Knorr, M., Gonçalves, R., Leite, J.: On abstracting over the irrelevant in answer set programming. In: Proceedings of KR (2024)
10. Turner, H.: Strong equivalence for logic programs and default theories (made easy). In: Eiter, T., Faber, W., Truszczyński, M. (eds.) LPNMR 2001. LNCS (LNAI), vol. 2173, pp. 81–92. Springer, Heidelberg (2001). https://doi.org/10.1007/3-540-45402-0_6
11. Woltran, S.: Characterizations for relativized notions of equivalence in answer set programming. In: Alferes, J.J., Leite, J. (eds.) JELIA 2004. LNCS (LNAI), vol. 3229, pp. 161–173. Springer, Heidelberg (2004). https://doi.org/10.1007/978-3-540-30227-8_16

Author Index

W. Faber et al. (Eds.): LPNMR 2026, LNAI 16952, pp. 503–504, 2027.
https://doi.org/10.1007/978-3-032-38320-4

Kolibri 360 GmbH
Ferdinand-Jühlke-Straße 7
99095 Erfurt, Deutschland
produktsicherheit@kolibri360.de